Experimental Neurobiology

Experimental Neurobiology: A LABORATORY MANUAL

BY
BRUCE OAKLEY
AND
ROLLIE SCHAFER

The University of Michigan Press   Ann Arbor

Copyright © by The University of Michigan 1978
All rights reserved
ISBN 0-472-08690-1
Library of Congress Catalog Card No. 76-49153
Published in the United States of America by
The University of Michigan Press and simultaneously
in Rexdale, Canada, by John Wiley & Sons Canada, Limited
Manufactured in the United States of America

Illustrations by Ken Cassady
Design by George Lenox

*Grateful acknowledgments are made to the following
publishers, companies, and authors for permission to
adapt or reprint illustrative materials:*

Academia and Academic Press, Inc., for an illustration
from J. Bures, M. Petran, and J. Zachar, *Electrophysiological Methods in Biological Research*, 1967.
Academic Press, Inc., for illustrations from L. Packer, *Experiments in Cell Physiology*, 1967; I. Parnas and D.
Dagan, in *Advances in Insect Physiology* 8, 1971; I. Q.
Whishaw and C. H. Vanderwolf, in *Behavioral Biology*
8, 1973; R. H. Peckham and W. M. Hart, in *Experimental Eye Research* 1, 1961; D. T. Moran and J. C.
Rowley III, in the *Journal of Ultrastructure Research*
50, 1975.
Acta Physiologica Scandinavica Karolinska Institutet, for
illustrations from V. Koefoed-Johnsen and H. H. Ussing,
in *Acta Physiol. Scand.* 42, 1958; D. Ottoson, in *Acta
Physiol. Scand.* 35 (suppl., 122), 1956.
American Association for the Advancement of Science, for
an illustration from T. Hoshiko, in *Biophysics of
Physiological and Pharmacological Actions*, A. M.
Shanes, ed., AAAS publication number 69, 1961.
Copyright 1961 by the American Association for the
Advancement of Science.
American Heart Association, Inc., for an illustration from
S. Rush, J. A. Abildskov, and R. McFee, "Resistivity of
body tissues at low frequencies," in *Circulation Re-
search* 12, 1963, by permission of the American Heart
Association, Inc.
American Physiological Society, for illustrations from I.
Tasaki, in the *Journal of Neurophysiology* 17, 1954, fig. 2.
Edward Arnold Press, for an illustration from D. M. Guth-
rie and A. R. Tindall, *The Biology of the Cockroach*, 1968.
Cambridge University Press, for illustrations from R.
Granit and L. A. Riddell, in the *Journal of Physiology*
81, 1934; M. Spira, I. Parnas, and F. Bergmann, in the
Journal of Experimental Biology 50, 1969.
CIBA Pharmaceutical Company, for an adaptation of an
original painting by Frank H. Netter, M.D., in *The CIBA
Collection of Medical Illustrations*.
Grass Instrument Company, for photographs of their
equipment.
Harper & Row, Publishers, for fig. 3.11 "Anatomical terms
. . . axis of body" in *Introduction to Physiological*

Psychology by Richard F. Thompson. Copyright © by Richard F. Thompson. By permission of Harper & Row, Publishers.

William Heinemann Medical Books Ltd., for an illustration from E. Cameron, *The Cockroach*, 1961, fig. 16.

Carl D. Hopkins, for an illustration from *American Scientist* 62, 1974.

Linnean Society of London, for an illustration by S. M. Manton, in the *Journal of the Linnean Society* (zool.) 42, 1954.

J. B. Lippincott Company, for an illustration from A. W. Ham, *Histology*, 1974, p. 478.

McGraw-Hill Book Company, for illustrations from L. H. Hyman, *The Invertebrates*, vol. 1, 1940, p. 55; W. Nachtigall, *Insects in Flight*, 1974, p. 56, fig. 29.

Narco Bio-Systems, for photographs of their equipment.

Oxford University Press, for illustrations from *Doubt and Certainty in Science* by J. Z. Young, published by Oxford University Press; P. A. Meglitsch, *Invertebrate Zoology*, 1972.

Paul Parey Verlagsbuchhandlung, for an illustration from Barth, Robert H. (1970). "The Mating Behavior of *Periplaneta americana* (Linnaeus) and *Blatta orientalis* Linnaeus (Blattaria, Blattinae), with Notes on 3 Additional Species of *Periplaneta* and Interspecific Action of Female Sex Pheromones." *Z. Tierpsychol.* 27, 1970.

University of Pennsylvania Press, for an illustration from J. Erlanger and H. S. Gasser, *Electrical Signs of Nervous Activity*, 1968.

Pitman Medical Publishing, Co., for illustrations from M. A. B. Brazier, *The Electrical Activity of the Nervous System*, 1976, p. 67, fig. 6.1.

D. J. Reish, for an illustration from *Laboratory Manual for Invertebrate Zoology*, 1969.

Rockefeller University Press, for an illustration from D. T. Moran, K. M. Chapman and R. A. Ellis, in *The Journal of Cell Biology*.

The Royal Society, for illustrations from U. J. McMahan, N. C. Spitzer, and K. Peper, in *Proc. R. Soc.* B. 1972, 181, pp. 421-30; T. Weis-Fogh, in *Phil. Trans. R. Soc.* B. 1956, 239.

W. D. Russell-Hunter, for an illustration from *A Biology of Higher Invertebrates*, 1969. Macmillan Co., New York.

W. B. Saunders Company, for illustrations from J. E. Skinner, *Neuroscience: A Laboratory Manual*, 1971; C. J. Herrick and E. Crosby, *Laboratory Outline of Neurology*, 1918; A. C. Guyton, *Textbook of Medical Physiology*, 5th ed., 1976; W. Bloom and D. W. Fawcett, *A Textbook of Histology*, 1975.

Springer-Verlag, for illustrations from W. B. Kristan, Jr., G. S. Stent, and C. A. Ort, in the *Journal of Comparative Physiology* 94, 1974; U. Thurm, in *Zeitschrift für vergleichenden Physiologie* 46, 1963; W. Heiligenberg, in the *Journal of Comparative Physiology* 87, 1973.

Tektronix, Inc., for photographs of their equipment.

Virginia M. Tipton, for illustration 7.1-3*A*.

Charles Tweedle, for illustration 7.1-1.

James R. Weeks, Jr., for illustration 5.1-4.

John Wiley & Sons, Inc., for illustrations from G. von Bekesy and W. A. Rosenblith, in *Handbook of Experimental Psychology*, S. S. Stevens, ed., 1951; F. A. Cotton and G. Wilkinson, *Advanced Inorganic Chemistry*, 1972.

Williams & Wilkins Co., for an illustration from E. Eldred, in the *American Journal of Physical Medicine* 46, 1967.

The University of Wisconsin Press, for an illustration from C. N. Woolsey, in *Biological and Biochemical Bases of Behavior*, H. F. Harlow and C. N. Woolsey, eds., 1958.

The Wistar Press, for illustrations from F. A. Brown, in the *Journal of Morphology* 57, 1935; J. R. Brawer, D. K. Morest, and E. C. Kane, in the *Journal of Comparative Neurology* 155, 1974; M. Jacobson and R. Baker, in the *Journal of Comparative Neurology* 137, 1969; J. Pollack and L. Davis, in the *Journal of Comparative Neurology* 50, 1930; S. G. Nord, in the *Journal of Comparative Neurology* 130, 1967; R. Schafer and T. V. Sanchez, in the *Journal of Comparative Neurology* 149, 1973.

Gordon Wyse, for illustrations from his Ph.D. diss., University of Michigan, 1967.

Yale University Press, for illustrations from T. L. Lentz, *Primitive Nervous Systems*, 1968; A. Krogh, *The Anatomy and Physiology of Capillaries*, 1929.

To our students and teaching colleagues

Preface

This manual is intended to provide an introductory laboratory experience in neurobiology with emphasis in electrophysiological techniques. It may also be used as a source book for sequenced independent projects. Students are expected to have a background of one year in college biology, physics, and chemistry with laboratories, and a concurrent lecture in neurobiology or its equivalent. The level of sophistication (or difficulty) of the experiments is graded so that an instructor can offer the laboratory for junior and senior undergraduates, graduate students, or professional students in the biomedical sciences. The selection of experiments is diverse enough to permit choosing either a cellular or organismic approach to complement the instructor's own lecture treatment.

Each experiment was selected with three criteria in mind. An experiment ought to: (1) work in student hands; (2) utilize no highly specialized electrophysiological equipment; (3) have a balance of technical and conceptual content. Unfortunately, we had to omit some perfectly suitable experiments to limit the size of the manual. Other experiments were deleted when they turned out to be manageable only if the difficult portions were done by the instructor or other local experts. The experiments which remain are those which can be carried out by advanced undergraduates with little assistance from the instructional staff. Many instructors will, of course, want to supplement the manual with their favorite experiments and experiments in which their special expertise can be utilized.

Chapters 1 and 2 provide basic terminology, descriptions, and preliminary exercises which introduce the practical use of electrophysiological equipment. Chapter 3 gives an introductory exposure to basic mammalian brain anatomy and neuroanatomical terminology. The mammalian neuroanatomy is primarily applicable to experiments in chapter 7. Electrophysiology is applied in all of the experimental chapters (4–8). Chapter 9 is a compendium of surgical and related information to which the student is referred by some of the experiments in chapters 4 through 8. Chapter 10 is primarily for the instructor and provides construction or procurement details on equipment, supplies, electrodes, animals, solutions, and neuroactive agents.

Some laboratory experiments have obscure ancestry which denies the true originators credit for their efforts. We can at least acknowledge one important source. A decade ago the late Donald Maynard taught thirty-two students in a neurobiology laboratory at the University of Michigan in which on a given day he would preside simultaneously over eight different experiments! Some exercises in this volume reflect Maynard's influence and efforts. Since we have written many exercises of our own and substantially modified all of them based upon success and failure in the teaching laboratory, we must take full responsibility for any errors or shortcomings.

We thank the following professional neurobiologists for their encouragement and critical comments on one or more exercises: Robert Baker, William Bell, George Bittner, Theodore Bullock, Patricia Black-Cleworth, Robert Capranica, Kent Chapman, Mary Lou Cheal, Peter Coyle, Steven Easter, Charles Edwards, Milton Fingerman, Gabriel Frommer, Carl Gans, Alan Gelperin, Robert Gesteland, Daniel Green, William Jakinovich, Pamela Johns, Douglas Junge, William Kristan, John McReynolds, Nancy Milburn, Michael Mote, Timothy Neary, Samuel Nord, J. Bradley Powers, Lester Rutledge, John Schmidt, Arnold Starr, Paul Winston, Clinton Woolsey, and Gordon Wyse. We are grateful to P. Dayanandan, Ken Harper, David Ladd, Bill Lawler, Connie Mele, Tom Morrow, and Sandra Schaerer for enduring our deadlines and requests with concern and accuracy. We owe a special debt of gratitude to Sue Igras, Lee Jones, and Linda Sorkin for their many long and productive hours.

Over the years, research support from the National Institutes of Health and the National Science Foundation, NSF instructional equipment grants, and NIH training grants have contributed to the intellectual environment from which this book has emerged and have provided much of the necessary equipment for our teaching efforts. Lastly, we acknowledge gratitude to our wives who with patience and forbearance explained the nuances of the publishing trade, having earlier launched their own books.

BRUCE OAKLEY
ROLLIE SCHAFER

Contents

Introduction

To the Student:

We have done our best to develop lab experiments which work, but it should be recognized that your individual efforts are essential to success. Also recognize that most of these experiments use live animals and often entail their death ("sacrifice" is the experimenter's euphemism). This serious fact should command respect and bring forth your best efforts.

What should you expect from the laboratory? You ought to expect to obtain *data* most of the time: the more *repeatable* the data, the better. These data should be a result of your efforts, the best you can do given the limitations of time and experience. You should expect that not all records and results will be as clear and as elegant as those found in textbooks. Beyond data, it is important to obtain some hands-on experience with techniques and to develop a critical scientific attitude. Finally, do not view this laboratory as a cookbook experience—it will challenge your experimental and analytical skills and, on occasion, your patience. In the aggregate these exercises should provide a sense of independent accomplishment.

What are the practical elements of success in the laboratory? Your initial impression may be that instrumentation is the key, particularly when electrophysiological equipment is used. However, our experience has been that in most experiments it is the biological preparation, careful dissection, and subsequent gentle treatment (and in some experiments, the electrodes) which hold the key to success. Instrumentation problems generally require adjustment of a knob or connection, but injury to a biological preparation is not so readily repaired. Whether your background is in physical science, biology, or psychobiology, you should have no special difficulties carrying out the experiments, provided you have a background approximating the prerequisites indicated in the preface. We have been thorough in our explanations and figures to permit you to work more or less independently of the instructional staff.

Some of the experiments are manageable in a three-hour laboratory period provided you have read the outline in advance and begin the lab exercise without delay. In many of the experiments, however, you will have insufficient data by the end of one period. A second period will be necessary. If you work with a partner, you both should have active and complementary roles. For example, one experimenter might set up the oscilloscope, preamplifier, and nerve chamber, while the other dissects out the nerve. Reverse roles periodically.

Each experiment has several up-to-date references listed to establish the context of the experiment and the current research activity which surrounds it. In general the titles of the research and review papers will provide sufficient information to select relevant reading. Your instructor will supply information on the kinds of written records which should be kept in your laboratory notebook, the nature of the written reports to emerge, and the procedure for utilizing and cleaning up the laboratory.

To the Instructor:

In addition to surmounting the usual problems of laboratory organization, the success rate of your students can be enhanced by encouraging a division of labor between a pair of students and by arranging for prior laboratory experience with a given technique when the level of difficulty of an experiment is high. Work up to a difficult experiment and be vigilant as the students carry it out. Difficulty is rated by the number of stars assigned to each exercise, as summarized in table 10.6-1, page 350. *One star*: Students with no prior laboratory experience in neurobiology should be able to work and obtain data largely on their own. *Two stars*: Guidance is needed and some prior experience which transfers from a previous exercise is valuable (e.g., micromanipulator usage, similar dissection). *Three stars*: These are advanced experiments which require experience, efficient planning of time, and special care in dissection and in electrode and manipulator usage during recording.

Two laboratory periods will generally be required for optimal return from an experiment. Setting up and learning the procedures can often occupy most of an initial laboratory period, followed by a second period devoted to producing meaningful data. An estimate of the minimum amount of time required is listed within each experiment under the subheading "Time to complete the exercise."

At the beginning of the term students should be asked to read the material on surgical instruments and micromanipulators (pages 308–10) and electronic instrumentation (pages 2 and 10–44). This general background information is applicable to many of the experiments.

Laboratories are a notorious time sink. We have arranged to conserve preparatory and instructional time in several ways: (1) The instructions in all exercises are detailed and complete. Minimal instructional assistance is required to get to the data-taking stage. (2) Potential problems are noted in the "Pitfalls and Suggestions" and "Notes for the Instructor" sections of each experiment. (3) Each experiment has a detailed list of materials which can be used as a checklist and basis for purchases. (4) The information in chapter 10, "Laboratory Organization," will aid you to initiate a new laboratory or to reactivate it annually.

We have used frogs in several experiments because they are a hardy, easily dissected animal whose physiological responses have wide generality.[1] We urge you to stress humaneness and frugality in the use of all experimental animals. Guidelines for animal care and use have been set forth by the United States Department of Agriculture according to the Animal Welfare Act of 1970 and the Animal Welfare Act Amendments of 1976 (see U.S. Department of HEW Publication no. NIH 73-23, *Guide for the Care*

and Use of Laboratory Animals. Copies are available for $0.55 from the Superintendent of Documents, U.S. Government Printing Office, Washington, D.C. 20402.) Experimenters in countries other than the United States should consult their local regulations.

---

1. *Frog Neurobiology: A Handbook*, R. Llinas and W. Precht, eds., Springer-Verlag, New York, 1976. For laboratory instructors this is a superb reference source which contains in-depth reviews of all aspects of frog neurobiology.

1

Electrical Principles and Electrophysiological Terminology

1.1 Practical Electrophysiology

To the Student

Rationale
A working knowledge of electrophysiological instrumentation is essential to students of neurobiology because electrical methods and ideas are a vital feature of modern neurobiology.

Electrical theory
Section 1.2 is a brief, nonlaboratory review of some basic electrical terms and principles. Move right along if this is familiar to you. If electrical theory is totally foreign to you, you may want to spend a few hours with an introductory physics text or a good, practical introductory text on electricity. Students planning careers in neuroscience, biology, or medicine can extend their knowledge of bioelectronics with the aid of one of the references listed on pages 7–8.

Practical skills
In chapter 2 you will learn how to use electronic devices so that they may later be *applied* in a practical way to biological problems. We will treat such devices as oscilloscopes and preamplifiers as *operational units* which can be linked together to perform a certain job. Electronic circuitry or the components within these operational units will not be examined except when this is really pertinent to the biological application. Study chapter 1 and read over chapter 2 before going to the laboratory.

1.2   Review of Electrical Terms and Principles

Voltage

Voltage is an electrical pressure difference, that is, the electromotive force (EMF) which drives current flow in a circuit. *Potential* will be used often as a synonym for voltage, especially when referring to the voltages produced by nerve cells. Voltage or potential is measured in *volts* (V), *millivolts* (mV), or *microvolts* (μV). Volts and many of the other units of electrical measurement to follow may be prefixed with *meg-* or *mega-* ($\times 10^6$), k or *kilo-* ($\times 10^3$), *milli-* ($\times 10^{-3}$), *micro-* ($\times 10^{-6}$), *nano-* ($\times 10^{-9}$), and *pico-* ($\times 10^{-12}$).

Current

Current is the quantity of electrical charge flowing per unit time in a circuit. A current of one *ampere* is a transfer of charge of one coulomb per second. Current may be carried by *electrons*, as in a metal wire, or it may be carried by *ions*, as in biological fluids and salt solutions. Current flow is measured in *amperes* (A), *milliamperes* (mA), or *microamperes* (μA). Anodal current is positive; cathodal is negative.

Direct current vs. alternating current

Direct current (DC) is a constant flow of electricity in only one direction in a circuit. The current from a flashlight cell is a good example. *Alternating current* (AC) is an electrical flow which rapidly changes direction in a circuit. Thus, the current alternates above and below the zero level. A fluctuation of one cycle per second is a frequency of one *hertz* (Hz). The most widespread example of AC current is the 60 Hz sine wave household current used in North America (fig. 1.2-1).

Ordinarily, electrophysiologists measure *voltage*, not current. Voltage is easier to record and generally provides a good indication of the level of excitability of a nerve cell or synapse.

Resistance

Materials differ in their ability to conduct current. The lower the resistivity (specific resistance)—an intrinsic property of the material—the higher the current flow at a given voltage. If the material, such as a wire, is reduced in diameter or lengthened, it will

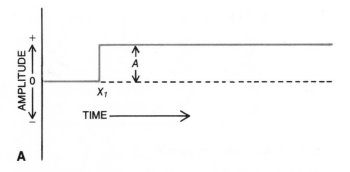

A

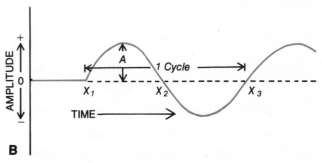

B

Fig. 1.2-1. Electrical current wave patterns. **A.** DC current; **B.** AC current. In *A*, the direct current is turned on at time X_1 and instantaneously reaches an amplitude *A*, which is maintained as long as the current is on. In *B*, an alternating current in the form of a *sine wave* begins at time X_1.

The level increases to amplitude *A*, then reverses and falls back to the zero level at time X_2 and continues to change, reaching amplitude *A* in the negative direction. In biological systems DC and AC signals are often combined into a single complex waveform.

have an increased *resistance* to current flow without a change in the material's resistivity. Ions in biological fluids conduct surprisingly well, although their resistivity is considerably higher than metals. Resistance is measured in ohms (Ω), kilohms (kΩ or k), and megohms (MΩ or M). A resistance of one ohm will pass a current of one ampere at an applied potential of one volt.

Ohm's law

Ohm's law defines the relationship between voltage, current, and resistance. The simple circuit shown in figure 1.2-2 may be used to illustrate the Ohm's law relationship. The circuit has a voltage source (battery), a switch to control the flow of current, and a resistance, *R*.

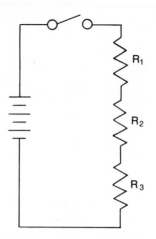

Fig. 1.2-3. Resistances in series.

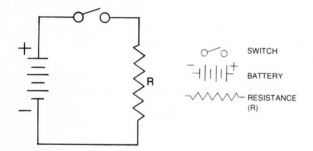

Fig. 1.2-2. Simple circuit.

The flow of current is defined by Ohm's law:

$$I = \frac{V}{R}$$

Where I = current in amperes
V (or E) = voltage in volts
R = resistance in ohms

Ohm's law is perhaps more intuitively obvious when stated in terms of the reciprocal of resistance or *conductance* (conductance = $\frac{1}{R}$ = g = mhos),

I = conductance $\times$ V. Thus, the amount of current that flows is equal to the product of the conductance and driving voltage. Conductance is expressed in mhos (mho is ohm spelled backward). You should be aware that some materials do not obey Ohm's law; their resistance does not remain constant at different voltages.

Resistances in *series* in a circuit as in figure 1.2-3 are added together to give the total resistance in the circuit:

$$R_{total} = R_1 + R_2 + R_3 + \ldots R_n$$

Resistances in *parallel* in a circuit as in figure 1.2-4 are combined in the following way:

$$R_{total} = \frac{1}{\dfrac{1}{R_1} + \dfrac{1}{R_2} + \dfrac{1}{R_3} + \ldots \dfrac{1}{R_n}}$$

Since the voltage across resistors in parallel is the same, the current must be distributed in inverse proportion to the resistances.

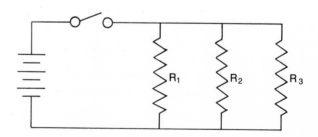

Fig. 1.2-4. Resistances in parallel.

Capacitance and time constants

Figure 1.2-5*A* illustrates a capacitor in a circuit. This device consists of two conducting layers or surfaces

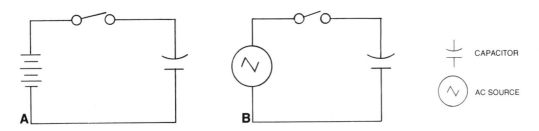

Fig. 1.2-5. Capacitors in DC and AC circuits.

which are slightly separated by a nonconducting (dielectric) material. Electrical charge from the battery builds up on each layer, positive on one, negative on the other.

The amount of charge (Q = coulomb) that the capacitor can store per volt is its *capacity* or *capacitance*; capacitance = $\frac{Q}{V}$. Capacitance is generally measured in microfarads (μF) or picofarads (pF) because the basic unit of capacitance, the farad, is too large for practical work.

It turns out that a capacitor's *time constant* is one of the most useful properties for the biologist. When a voltage is applied to the capacitor, as when the switch in figure 1.2-5A is closed, some time is required for the capacitor to charge fully. As the capacitor charges, the current flow decreases in the circuit. The time required for the capacitor to reach 63% of its full charge is the *time constant* of that capacitor. A capacitor which charges quickly (small capacitance or short time constant) will soon build up an opposing potential which fully blocks the electron flow from a DC voltage source. Only currents which alternate can pass through a capacitor (fig. 1.2-5B). In the case of alternating current, the current reverses direction before the capacitor is fully charged. The current now flows in the opposite direction and reverses the charge on the capacitor. This is repeated for each cycle of alternating current in the circuit and in this way the capacitor allows the AC current to pass.

In practical circuits, like biological preamplifiers, capacitors can be chosen to filter out unwanted signal frequencies. When connected in *series* with a source signal, a capacitor acts as a high-pass filter, i.e., it limits low frequencies in the signal more than the high frequencies. A capacitor connected in *parallel* with the source (i.e., between the source and

ground) acts as a low-pass filter which limits high frequencies more than low frequencies. Currents associated with high frequencies fail to charge the capacitor fully and are therefore shunted to ground.

The time constant in a circuit varies not only with the capacitance, but also with the amount of resistance in series with the capacitor, because current flow during the charging phase is limited by the resistance according to Ohm's law (fig. 1.2-6).

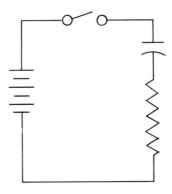

Fig. 1.2-6. Resistance and capacitance in a circuit.

The following formula gives the relationship between capacitance, circuit resistance, and the time constant:

$$T = RC$$

Where T = time constant in seconds
R = resistance in megohms (MΩ)
C = capacitance in microfarads (μF)

Capacitance and time constants are of fundamental biological importance. For example, excitable membranes display capacitance because they are composed of a nonconducting (dielectric) material which separates two conductors (the intra- and extracellular fluids). In terms of practical electrophysiology, electrode-fluid interfaces and input cables are sources of capacitance which limit high frequency responses in recording.

Biological amplifiers often have a capacitor in the input circuit or between successive stages of amplification. This kind of amplifier is described as *capacitance-coupled*, *RC-coupled*, or *AC-coupled*. Such an amplifier can only amplify AC currents (or voltages) because the capacitors in the input circuit cannot pass a steady or DC current. Amplifiers that amplify DC currents do not have input or coupling capacitors and are referred to as *DC* amplifiers. A DC amplifier can pass both AC and DC signals.

Repeating waves, no matter how complex, can be represented as a summation of different sine waves (Fourier's theorem). This helpful simplification means that amplifier characteristics can be specified in terms of the sine wave frequencies they will pass, attenuate, or eliminate. Most AC amplifiers severely attenuate frequencies below 3 Hz and thus are of limited usefulness in measuring synaptic or receptor potentials which have substantial slow wave components.

Reactance

An AC signal can flow "through" a capacitor in the sense that, as the capacitor charges and discharges, current flows in the circuit, although no electrons actually cross the gap between the plates. However, at low frequencies only a limited amount of AC current will flow in a circuit with a capacitor in series. The current-impeding property of the capacitor is called *reactance*. Capacitive reactance is given by this formula:

$$X_C = \frac{1}{2 \pi f C}$$

Where X_C = capacitive reactance in ohms
f = frequency in Hz
C = capacity in farads
π = 3.14

Impedance

Resistance and capacitive reactance are combined in the concept of *impedance*. The impedance of a circuit containing both resistance and capacitive reactance is given by this formula:

$$Z = \sqrt{R^2 + X_C^2}$$

Where Z = impedance in ohms
R = resistance in ohms
X_C = capacitive reactance in ohms

Note that impedance, resistance, and capacitive reactance are all measured in ohms. This is because each phenomenon has the same effect; each limits current flow. Inductive reactance is unimportant in physiological preparations and can therefore be ignored. Ohm's law can be applied to impedance by substituting Z for R:

$$I = \frac{V}{Z}$$

Where I = current in amperes
V = voltage in volts
Z = impedance in ohms

Impedance is important in bioelectric recording because amplifiers with high impedance inputs are generally necessary to measure the small electrical potentials generated by nerve cells. The use of a high impedance input is imperative for intracellular recording where a microelectrode is inserted into the cell through the cell membrane. A high impedance DC input ($>10^{10}\Omega$) is provided by using a preamplifier which employs a circuit called a *cathode follower*, *voltage follower*, or *emitter follower*. The main function of the preamplifier is to make the input impedance much larger than that of the microelectrode. Gain is less important; many such preamplifiers have a gain of one (unity gain).

Consider the circuit in figure 1.2-7 to understand why a high input impedance is necessary in microelectrode recording. The cell membrane is shown schematically at the left as a 90 mV potential. This potential passes through the high resistance (impedance) of the recording electrode (R_e) to point *p* where a relatively low impedance (10^6 ohms = 1 megohm) recording instrument, such as an oscilloscope (colored), has been connected. Most of the total voltage drop in the circuit will occur across the micropipette, not the oscilloscope input. The source voltage of 90 mV will be divided in the ratio of $10^7/10^6$ or 10:1 across R_e and R_o, and the oscilloscope will register only $\frac{R_o}{R_e + R_o}$ = 1/11 of the 90 mV potential.

To surmount this difficulty, one should connect a high impedance DC preamplifier to point p. If the preamplifier input impedance is relatively high, e.g., $10^{11}\Omega$, compared with the electrode resistance, most of the voltage drop will occur across the preamplifier input, i.e., the recording device now "sees" most of the potential. The preamplifier has a low impedance output to which the oscilloscope should be connected. We have thus coupled the high impedance source (membrane potential and microelectrode) to a low impedance recording instrument by using a preamplifier. An added benefit is that only a tiny current is drawn from the cell in measuring its potential.

Other concepts

The preceding qualitative description of electrical principles omits a great deal: voltage drop in series and parallel resistances; Kirchoff's laws; power; capacitors in series and parallel; inductance; inductive reactance; decibel scales; impedance matching; resonance and damping; amplifier blocking; and signal-to-noise ratio. It is hoped that this cursory review will encourage further exploration of electrical theory and bioelectronics.

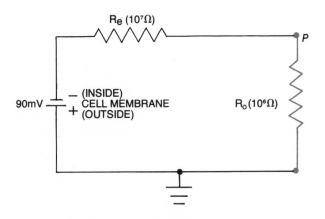

Fig. 1.2-7. Schematic circuit representing a 10 megohm micropipette (R_e) recording a 90 mV membrane potential fed directly into the vertical input of an oscilloscope (R_o, *colored*).

Selected References

BASIC ELECTRONICS
American Radio Relay League. 1976. *The radio amateur's handbook*. American Radio Relay League, Newington, Conn. This manual, intended for ham operators, contains a lucid discussion of basic electricity and electronics.
Hoenig, S. A., and Payne, F. L. 1973. *How to build and use electronic devices without frustation, panic, mountains of money, or an engineering degree*. Little, Brown, Boston. A useful, practical approach.
Malmstadt, H. V.; Enke, C. G.; and Toren, E. C., Jr. 1963. *Electronics for scientists*. W. A. Benjamin, New York. An authoritative discussion of electronic instruments, suited to the advanced student and researcher.
Offner, F. F. 1967. *Electronics for biologists*. McGraw-Hill, New York. Offner first discusses basic electronics, then covers practical application to biological problems.

BIOELECTRONICS AND ELECTROPHYSIOLOGY
Brown, P. B.; Maxfield, B. W.; and Moraff, H. 1973. *Electronics for neurobiologists*. MIT Press, Cambridge.
Bureš, J.; Petráň, M.; and Zachar, J. 1967. *Electrophysiological methods in biological research*, 3rd ed. Academic Press, New York. A comprehensive discussion of electrophysiological theory and its application in the research and teaching laboratory.
Geddes, L. A., and Baker, L. E. 1975. *Principles of applied biomedical instrumentation*, 2d ed. Wiley-Interscience, New York. A straightforward discussion of theory and its practical application.
Nastuk, W. L., ed. 1963–64. *Physical techniques in biological research: Electrophysiological methods*, vols. 5 and 6. Academic Press, New York. Advanced techniques for the research laboratory.
Strong, P. 1973. *Biophysical measurements*, no. 062–1247–00. Tektronix, Inc., Beaverton, Oreg. This is one of a series of Tektronix books on measurement and circuit concepts. It contains practical information on the biomedical application of Tektronix and other instruments not usually found in other references.
Suckling, E. E. 1961. *Bioelectricity*. McGraw-Hill, New York. This book discusses both basic electrical principles and electrobiology.
Thompson, R. F., and Patterson, M. M., eds. 1973. *Bioelectric recording techniques: Methods in physiological psychology*, vol. 1-A. Academic Press, New York. Many techniques, including unit and mass potential recording, are discussed in a practical way.
Yanof, H. M. 1972. *Biomedical electronics*. F. A. Davis Co., Philadelphia. Discusses physical principles and

theory, then illustrates application with specific, commercially available hardware.

Zucker, M. H. 1969. *Electronic circuits for the behavioral and biomedical sciences: A reference book of useful solid-state circuits*. W. H. Freeman and Co., San Francisco. A practical guide to constructing bioelectric devices.

ELECTRODES

Geddes, L. A. 1972. *Electrodes and the measurement of bioelectric events*. Wiley-Interscience, New York. A practical guide to electrodes and their use.

Lavellee, M.; Schanne, O. F.; and Hebere, N. C., eds. 1969. *Glass microelectrodes*. John Wiley and Sons, New York. A discussion of the many problems faced by researchers using glass micropipettes as electrodes.

Miller, H., and Harrison, D. C. 1974. *Biomedical electrode technology: Theory and practice*. Academic Press, New York. A book for graduate-level students or researchers, containing advanced and specialized techniques.

INTEGRATED CIRCUIT APPLICATIONS

Graeme, J. G. 1973. *Applications of operational amplifiers: Third-generation techniques*. McGraw-Hill, New York. Introduces operational amplifier use for the advanced student.

National Semiconductor Corp. 1973. *Linear applications*. Santa Clara, Calif. Frequently updated application sheets from a major manufacturer.

2

Survey of Electrophysiological Instrumentation

2.1 The Electrophysiological Setup

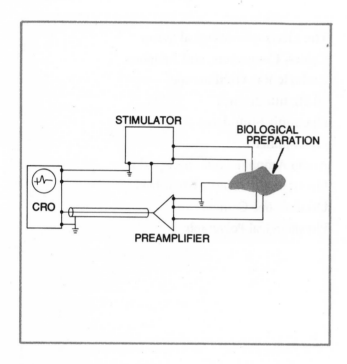

Electrophysiology is the measurement and interpretation of bioelectric signals. To measure such signals, you must first understand what equipment to use. The following is an outline of the principal components of an electrophysiological setup.

The preparation
The preparation is the animal or part of the animal whose electrical signals we want to measure. The term *preparation* is used frequently in experimental biology to designate the biological object under study.

Electrodes
Electrodes are the fine wires, plates, fluid-filled pipettes, or moist wicks used to connect the preamplifier or stimulator to the preparation. In most exercises you will use *gross electrodes*; relatively large

wires or needles made of silver, platinum, or tungsten (or cotton wicks or capillary tubes containing conducting salt solutions). A few exercises employ *microelectrodes* with tip diameters of one to several micrometers (10^{-6} meters = 1 μm).

Preamplifier
Bioelectric voltages are very small. Often they are less than a millivolt (10^{-3} V) in amplitude. If these tiny potentials are to be recorded on an oscilloscope screen or other recording device such as a polygraph or a tape recorder, they must be amplified. A separate *preamplifier* performs three functions: (1) It serves as an amplification stage before the signal is fed into the oscilloscope. (2) It serves as a high impedance interface between the preparation and its electrodes and the oscilloscope or other readout device. (3) It provides additional circuitry for other functions, such as filtering out undesirable frequencies and calibrating the size of the input signal.

Electronic stimulator
Electrical stimulation is commonly used to study excitable tissue because the magnitude, duration, frequency, etc., of an electrical pulse can be precisely controlled. Often the electronic stimulator also initiates (or "triggers") the oscilloscope sweep.

Cathode ray oscilloscope
The cathode ray oscilloscope (*CRO, oscilloscope,* or simply *scope*) is the major readout device used in electrophysiology. It receives the signal and can display it as a time-dependent function. The heart of the oscilloscope is the *cathode ray tube* (CRT), which consists of a large evacuated tube having an electron gun at one end and a screen at the other. When the beam of electrons from the gun strikes the screen, a bright spot is visible because the screen contains a thin layer of material (the *phosphor*)

which glows when hit by energetic electrons. An adjustable sweep circuit moves the beam from left to right across the screen. The beam is deflected vertically when a voltage is recorded. Thus, the vertical and horizontal movements of the beam on the screen trace a graph of voltage changes over time. In fact, the oscilloscope is simply a voltmeter with the additional dimension of time. It responds very rapidly to voltage changes because the inertia of the electron beam is infinitesimally small. A high frequency sine wave, e.g., 50,000 Hz, is easily recorded with virtually any oscilloscope. Other recording devices have to depend on slower writing mechanisms such as fine ink pens. The inertia of the pen in such devices severely limits the high frequency response, often to less than 75 Hz.

Physiological polygraph

The physiological polygraph is a multichannel recording device capable of permanently recording many kinds of physiological events. Since it is a pen-writing recorder it has a limited high-frequency response. However, this limitation is offset by the advantage of obtaining a cheap, permanent record of a number of simultaneous events. Moreover, most polygraphs are manufactured as *systems* incorporating a variety of transducing devices, so that mechanical, photic, thermal, and other energy sources, in addition to electrical voltage, can be measured.

Ancillary equipment

Other equipment is often added to an electrophysiological setup to extend its usefulness. For example, it is very useful to add an *audio amplifier* and *loudspeaker* to the system when recording nerve action potentials. The action potentials will produce audible clicks over the loudspeaker so that the experimenter is continually aware of activity in the preparation even when not looking at the oscilloscope screen. Another useful device is the *tape recorder*. A tape recorder can be used to store electrophysiological data, which can then be played back at some later time into the oscilloscope. Furthermore, the tape can be played back at a slower speed into a pen-writing recorder to get a permanent visual record of the experiment. *Cameras* are used to record oscilloscope traces. Teaching and research laboratories are usually equipped with modified Polaroid cameras. Some research laboratories additionally may use 35-mm motion picture cameras for continuous oscillographic recording on photosensitive paper or film.

2.2 Cables, Connectors, and Adapters

Introduction

In order to use electrophysiological instrumentation, connections must be made between the preparation and the various electronic instruments. The objective of this section is to make you aware of the variety of cables and connecting devices. An acquaintance with electrical hardware will save you time in later experiments.

Skim this section. Refer to it when needed in subsequent sections.

Examine the following illustrations and samples provided by the instructor to understand what is meant by:

1. *Shielded* or *coaxial* (braided covering) versus *unshielded* cables (figs. 2.2-1–2.2-3). Always use shielded cables, except for separate ground leads.
2. *BNC connectors* and *adapters* (fig. 2.2-4).
3. *UHF connectors* and *adapters* (fig. 2.2-5).
4. *Banana* and *pin* or *tip plugs* (fig. 2.2-6).
5. *Clips* and *clip leads* (fig. 2.2-7).
6. *Audio connectors* and *adapters* (fig. 2.2-8).

Note: Not all of the illustrated connectors and adapters will be available in any one laboratory. Learn the names of those which are used in the laboratory. Adapters and connectors are named for their own structure, and not for the structure of the pieces they interconnect. For example, a BNC receptacle to BNC receptacle will interconnect two BNC plugs. The "male" structure is usually referred to as plug, the "female" as a receptacle. A receptacle which accepts a banana plug is referred to as a banana jack or binding post.

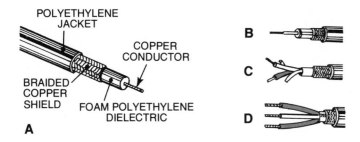

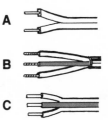

Fig. 2.2-1. Shielded (coaxial) cables. **A–B**. Single conductor shielded cable. **C–D**. Two- and three-conductor shielded cables. Each has a braided conducting shield surrounding the central conductors. This arrangement eliminates noise pickup by the central conductors.

Fig. 2.2-2. Unshielded cables. **A**. Twined; **B**. Protected with a plastic jacket.

Fig. 2.2-3. Two- and three-conductor power cables. **A**. Lamp or "zip" cord; **B**. With jacket and ground conductor (*colored*); **C**. Without jacket.

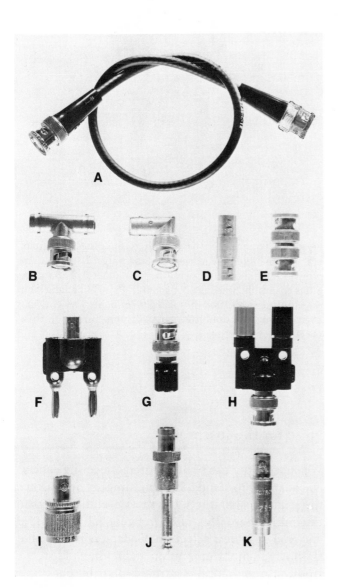

Fig. 2.2-4. BNC cable, connectors, and adapters. Most electrophysiological equipment is now equipped with BNC-type connectors. Use BNC cables and connectors when you have a choice. They are shielded and versatile. **A**. BNC connecting cable (shielded). This is the most commonly encountered cable used to interconnect electrophysiological instruments. **B**. BNC T-connector. This connector is quite useful for extension or for parallel connections, e.g., a preamplifier output connected to an oscilloscope and an audio amplifier. **C**. BNC angle adapter; **D**. BNC receptacle to BNC receptacle connector; **E**. BNC plug to BNC plug connector; **F**. Double banana plug to BNC receptacle adapter; **G**. Binding post to BNC plug adapter; **H**. BNC plug to double binding post adapter. One of the binding posts connects to the shield or ground. **I**. UHF plug to BNC receptacle adapter. This is the single most useful adapter when both BNC and UHF connectors are encountered in interconnecting instruments. **J**. Phone plug to BNC receptacle adapter; **K**. Phono plug to BNC receptacle adapter.

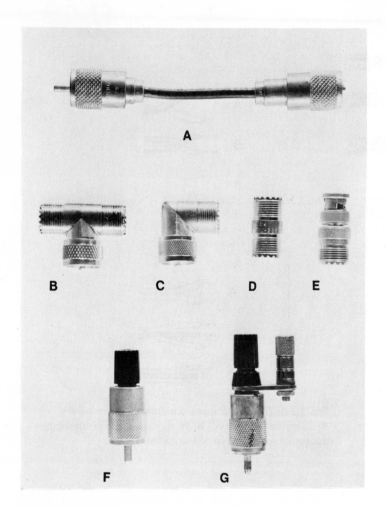

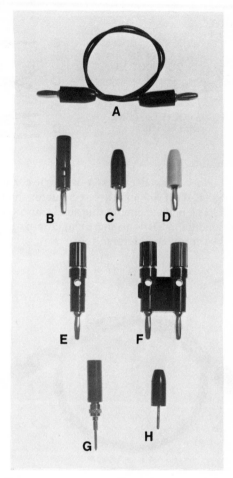

Fig. 2.2-5. UHF cable, connectors, and adapters. UHF connectors are usually encountered on older electrophysiological instruments. New instruments generally have the smaller and more easily changed BNC connectors. UHF cables and connectors are shielded. **A**. UHF connecting cable (shielded); **B**. UHF T-connector; **C**. UHF angle adapter; **D**. UHF receptacle to UHF receptacle connector; **E**. UHF receptacle to BNC plug adapter; **F**. UHF plug to binding post adapter; **G**. UHF plug to double binding post adapter. The metal binding post connects to the UHF shielding.

Fig. 2.2-6. Banana lead, banana plugs, pin plugs, and adapters. **A**. Unshielded lead with banana plugs; **B–D**. Banana plugs; **E**. Banana plug to binding post adapter; **F**. Banana plugs to double binding post adapter. Pairs of banana jacks on equipment are usually spaced 0.75 inches (1.9 cm) apart to accommodate double banana adapters similar to this. **G–H**. Pin or tip plugs.

Note for the Instructor

We suggest the use of BNC interconnecting cables and adapters to standardize and simplify operation of the student laboratory. The most useful adapters for this purpose are illustrated in figure 2.2-4 *B, F, H, I,* and *K*. The widest selection of adapters is available from Amphenol Corporation and Pomona Electronics through local electronics distributors.

Materials

Supply a representative sample of the types of cables, connectors, and adapters to be used in the laboratory during the semester.

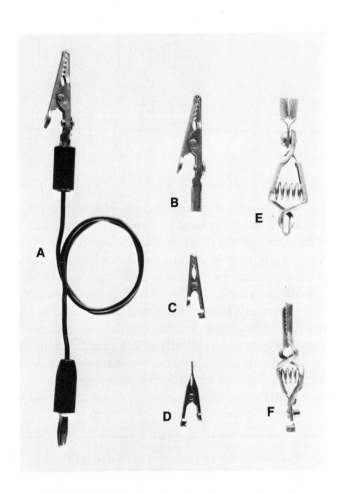

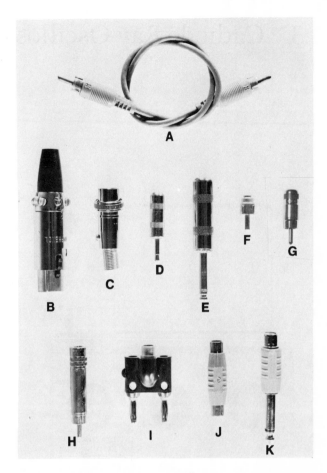

Fig. 2.2-7. Clip lead and clips. **A**. Clip lead. A clip lead may be used in a variety of ways: as a test lead, for ground connections, or for connecting instruments. **B**. Alligator clip. The back of the clip is tubular and will accept a banana plug. Thus, a cable with banana plugs can be converted to a clip lead. **C**. Minigator clip; **D**. Microgator clip. Its jaws are not serrated like other clips. **E**. Battery clip; **F**. Crocodile clip.

Fig. 2.2-8. Audio cable, plugs, connectors, and adapters. These are most often found on audio amplifiers or on older electrophysiological equipment. **A**. Audio connecting cable. This type of cable may be used to interconnect audio equipment like audio amplifiers, tape recorders, and speakers. **B**. Microphone connector (quick disconnect); **C**. Microphone connector (two contacts); **D**. Miniature phone plug; **E**. Phone plug; **F–G**. Phono plugs; **H**. Phono plug to phone jack adapter; **I**. Banana plugs to phono jack adapter; **J**. Phono jack to phono jack connector; **K**. Phone plug to phono jack adapter.

2.3 Cathode Ray Oscilloscope

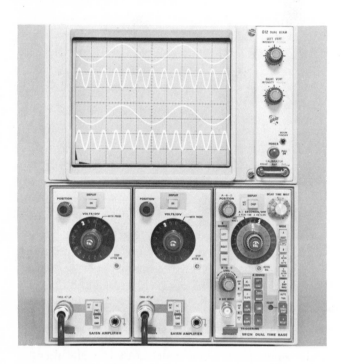

A *single-beam oscilloscope* has a single electron gun and is generally used to display one signal at a time (although there are methods of splitting a single beam to give two traces). A *dual-beam oscilloscope* has two electron guns contained in one cathode ray tube and may be used to display two different events simultaneously. Hence, a dual-beam oscilloscope is more versatile than a single-beam unit. There may be partially or completely duplicated controls for the two beams. A *storage oscilloscope* is capable of retaining the phosphorescent trace until you choose to erase it. A storage oscilloscope may be either single or dual beam.

You may wish to consult the instructor at this point for a brief explanation of the cathode ray tube if you are totally unfamiliar with the principles of its function.

Introduction

The oscilloscope is the most accurate of all the instruments in the electrophysiological laboratory. It is very expensive, but fortunately there are few ways to damage the instrument. An oscilloscope is most likely to suffer damage by: (1) using a stationary or very bright beam intense enough to damage the phosphor on the screen, or (2) plugging a high voltage source into the vertical amplifier input.

CAUTION: Do not turn the oscilloscope on until directed to do so in the following instructions.

Your oscilloscope will be one of three types: single beam, dual beam, or storage.

Laboratory Oscilloscope Turn-on Procedure

If you have a storage oscilloscope, or your equipment has not been used for some time, consult the laboratory instructor or the operating manual before turning on the power. Turn the intensity control fully counterclockwise. Turn on the power switch. (If the pilot light or dials do not light up, the unit may not be plugged into the wall receptacle.) No beam will be displayed because the intensity control is turned down.

Getting a display
Find the *time base* unit (usually at the lower right of the oscilloscope face) and turn the triggering control to *automatic* (*auto*) or to *free run*. The triggering control may be in the form of a push-button or slide switch. Turn the sweep control (labeled *sec/div*,

time/div, or *time/cm*) on the time base to 1 msec/div. Gradually, turn up the intensity control until a beam of moderate brightness appears. If no beam appears, turn the *position* control on the vertical amplifier unit back and forth until the beam appears. Turn the intensity up higher if you still do not see a beam and repeat turning the position control until a beam appears. Position the beam vertically in the center of the screen.

> Never turn the intensity control up beyond the point necessary to get a reasonably bright trace. A high intensity beam may damage the phosphor, especially if the beam is stationary.

Leave the oscilloscope on while you proceed through the following explanation. In general, turn on the oscilloscope and allow it to warm up for 30 minutes before you begin an experiment. Leave the oscilloscope and any equipment which contains vacuum tubes on continuously during the laboratory period. Turning such equipment on and off is far more wearing than leaving it on continuously. Furthermore, some instruments can produce tissue stimulating current surges when turned on or off.

Focusing the beam
Turn the sweep control to its lowest value (1–5 sec/div). Lower the intensity to produce a relatively dim spot. Note that the beam moves slowly across the oscilloscope face. Now, move the *focus control* back and forth to produce the smallest possible spot. At this setting the beam is exactly focused on the screen. If an *astigmatism control* is present, adjust it to produce the smallest possible spot. When finished, turn the sweep speed back to 1 msec/div and increase the intensity if necessary.

Operational Units

Every oscilloscope has three operational units. In many oscilloscopes these units are plug-in modules. Whether your oscilloscope has modules or is a one-piece instrument, the three operational units will be easily identifiable by their position on the front of the instrument. Examine figure 2.3-1 or your oscilloscope.

Display unit
The display unit includes the screen of the CRT and its controls. The grid lines (*graticule*) on the screen are ruled in 1 cm or ½-inch squares to aid measurement. A green filter is often present to improve trace visibility. There are knobs for controlling *intensity*, *focus*, and, generally, the *graticule* or *scale illumination*.

Dual-beam oscilloscope. (Optional explanation; omit if your oscilloscope is a single-beam model.) The display controls on a dual-beam scope are duplicated, one for each beam, and are usually arranged as concentric knobs. There may be an *intensity balance* control to vary the relative intensity of the two beams.

Storage oscilloscope. (Optional explanation; omit if you have a nonstorage scope.) A storage oscilloscope is capable of retaining a glowing trace ("storing" it) on the screen until you choose to erase it. Or, you can store a series of traces on the screen to compare them with each other. Note that the storage scope has a set of controls for the storage function: *erase*, *store*, and *brightness*. These controls will be duplicated in a *split-screen storage scope*. Split-screen storage means that traces can be stored and erased separately on the upper and lower halves of the screen.

The storage oscilloscope uses a screen with a special *bistable phosphor*. The bistable phosphor is partially excited to its first stable state by a *flood gun* which covers the whole screen with low energy electrons. In the partially excited state, the phosphor glows dimly. The CRT beam (*writing gun beam*) then produces a trace on the screen just as in a regular oscilloscope, but the trace remains luminous because the phosphor has been excited to a second stable state (stored state) which is luminous. The luminous trace is maintained by a continuing bombardment of low energy electrons from the flood gun. The flood gun electrons do not have enough energy to shift the phosphor to the stored state, but they do supply sufficient energy to keep the phosphor at the higher energy level after it has been shifted to the stored state by the writing gun beam. An *erase* control blanks the screen by actuating a circuit which first elevates the whole screen to the stored state (it flashes), then drops it back to the low energy state. The user can choose either storage or nonstorage modes with a storage oscilloscope.

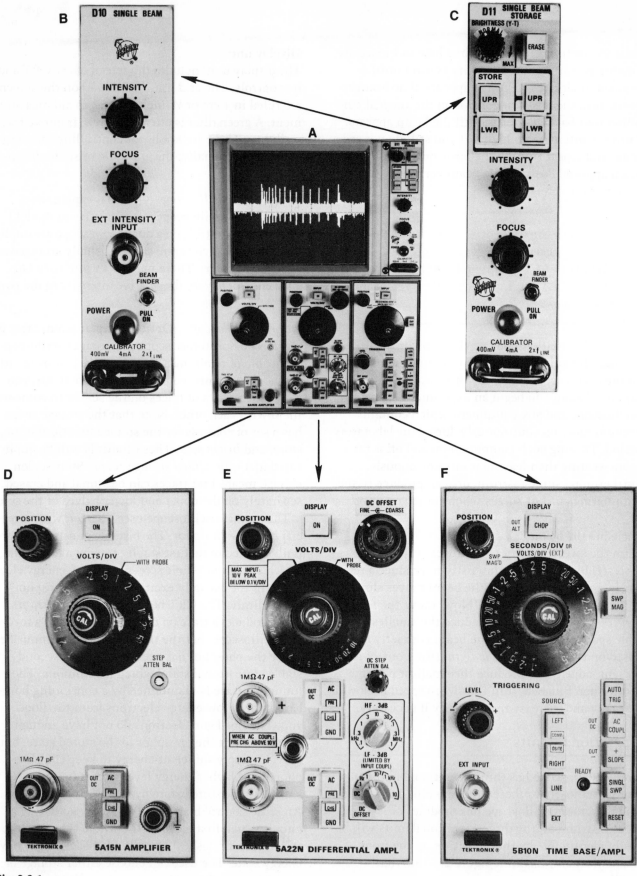

Fig. 2.3-1

Vertical amplifier

The vertical amplifier, whether a built-in or modular plug-in unit, is usually located at the lower left side of the front panel of the oscilloscope. The input of the vertical amplifier receives the external signal to be amplified. Note that the vertical amplifier has one or two input connectors which are labeled *input* or have a notation indicating the equivalent input resistance and capacitance (e.g., 1 MΩ, 47 pF). These are usually BNC or UHF receptacles with the metal core active and the casing or shell grounded. *Ground* refers to the earth outside—the third or ground prong on the oscilloscope power cord goes to the earth via the AC receptacle.

If only one input is present, the vertical amplifier is *single ended*. The input to this terminal is electrically compared with ground (zero potential) and any potential difference between it and ground is amplified.

If two inputs labeled + or *A* and − or *B* are present, the vertical amplifier is a *differential amplifier*. In a differential amplifier the two inputs are electrically compared with each other and only the difference between the two inputs is amplified. For reasons which will be discussed in section 2.6, an initial stage of differential preamplification is preferable. A differential amplifier can be converted into a single-ended amplifier by grounding one of the inputs. Some differential amplifiers have input selector switches which allow a choice of input: input *A*, input *B*, or *A minus B*. *A minus B* is the differential mode. A positive signal on input *A* will cause the beam to move upward (and a negative, downward), whereas connection to input *B* will *invert* the signal. (It is often visually useful to have a negative signal move upward.)

The vertical amplifier inputs will have switches labeled *Gnd*, *AC*, and *DC*. In the Gnd (ground) position the vertical amplifier but not the input terminal is internally connected (shorted) to ground. The AC and DC positions refer to the mode of coupling to the input (see section 1.2). In the AC mode, a capacitance is inserted in the input circuit and the amplifier cannot pass direct current. AC amplification is used when the DC part of the signal is unimportant, or when you wish to eliminate slow baseline shifts caused by extraneous DC voltages. Switch the inputs to AC for the time being. Note that there is a metal (or black plastic) binding post on the vertical

Fig. 2.3-1. A. The oscilloscope consists of the display unit (**B** and **C**), the vertical amplifiers (**D** and **E**), and the time base (**F**). This single-beam oscilloscope has spaces for two vertical amplifiers. By inserting a vertical amplifier into each space as shown, this single-beam oscilloscope converts to a dual-trace oscilloscope. The instrument produces two traces from one beam by rapidly sampling, first from one vertical amplifier, then the other, and displaying the two amplified inputs on different parts of the screen. In effect, the single beam is chopped (time shared) between the two vertical amplifiers. *B*. Display unit controls of a single-beam oscilloscope. A dual-beam oscilloscope would have dual concentric controls. *C*. Display unit controls of a storage oscilloscope which is able to store one or many traces on its screen. The trace remains luminous ("stored") on the screen until it is erased by the user. This is a split-screen storage scope because the upper and lower halves of the screen can be used to independently store and erase separate traces. *D*. Vertical amplifier. This is the unit which receives the input signal from the preamplifier or preparation. This amplifier shows the essential features of a vertical amplifier: position control, gain adjustment (V/div), and input connector (*lower left*). *E*. Vertical amplifier. This particular differential amplifier is capable of high gain (up to 10 μV/div) and is especially suited to biological recording. The amplifier also contains a bandpass filter (*lower right of unit*) and a DC offset control (*upper right*). The last two functions are explained in section 2.6. Note that it has (+) and (−) inputs and can be AC- or DC-coupled. The (+) input simply means that a positive voltage at this terminal will drive the beam upward. *F*. The time base controls the horizontal sweep of the CRT beam. It can trigger (start) the sweep by either an external electrical pulse or an internal circuit. The large dial controls the sweep speed (sec/div). All the controls below the large dial pertain to the triggering function.

amplifier section which may be labeled with the electrical symbol for ground ($\perp$). Any metal terminal connected to the chassis is a ground connection.

The main control of the vertical amplifier is the large knob labeled *volts/div* or *volts/cm*. This control varies the amplification. Note that it is calibrated over a wide range. Three terms which will be used in connection with this control are *gain*, *sensitivity*, and *amplification*. Gain is the ratio of output/input voltage of the amplifier. Hence, increasing the gain or sensitivity by turning the knob clockwise means that now a small input at a fraction of a volt will deflect the beam more. What is the maximum sensitivity? You will normally adjust this control to give enough amplification to easily observe the signal on the oscilloscope screen. Most gain controls are fitted with two concentric knobs: a small continuous control, and a large click-stop control. The continuous control should be fully rotated to the *calibrated* position. In this position the setting of the click-stop knob will accurately indicate the amplification. It is best to use the gain control in the calibrated position. Note again that the vertical amplifier has a *position* knob to control the vertical position of the sweep. Move the beam up and down and note that it is possible to make the beam disappear.

There may be a *beam-finder* button on your oscilloscope. Pushing this button will make the beam appear in either the upper or the lower half of the screen, indicating the direction from which the lost beam is returning. Some vertical amplifiers have a *DC balance* control in the form of an adjusting knob or screwdriver adjustment. Adjusting this control to prevent the beam from shifting vertically as the gain control is changed is called "balancing the amplifier." Consult your instructor or the operating manual if the trace shifts off the screen when the gain control is switched through its range. A shift of 1–2 divisions is acceptable.

Time base

The time base or horizontal plug-in unit provides the horizontal sweep of the electron beam. It has a large control knob labeled *time/div*, *sec/div*, or *sec/cm* which controls the sweep rate. It will have a pair of concentric knobs like the gain control on the vertical amplifier. The sweep control should always be in the *calibrated* position so that the setting of

the click-stop knob accurately gives the sweep rate.

The time base also has a *position* control to shift the sweeping trace right and left. Adjust the sweep rate to 1 msec/div and move the horizontal positioning knob until the beam starts at the left, flush with the first scale line on the graticule. Adjust this control similarly when experimenting.

The rest of the controls and inputs on the time base are concerned with a function called *triggering*. To trigger a sweep is to initiate one sweep of the electron beam from left to right. It is referred to as triggering because an external or internal voltage pulse is necessary to initiate or trigger the start of the sweep. The set of switches labeled *triggering*, *sweep triggering*, or *triggering mode* serves this purpose. We will now explain the various kinds of triggering.

Switch the trigger to the *automatic* position. In the automatic mode, the sweep is automatically initiated by a preset average voltage of the signal input. Or, if no input exists, the sweep will automatically trigger about 50 times each second. The setting labeled *line* provides for triggering the sweep from the 60 Hz line current. The line triggering function is useful to biologists for distinguishing 60 Hz interference from other voltages. When triggering on the line current, a 60 Hz waveform presented to the input will appear stationary on the screen and thus be readily distinguishable. The *recurrent* setting, if present, will result in triggering the beam just as soon as it returns to the starting point at the left of the screen.

The sweep can be triggered by an external voltage fed into the input marked *external input* or *external trigger* when the source or trigger input switch is set to the *external input* or *external trigger* position. It is also necessary to turn the control knob labeled *level* or *triggering level* to obtain a sweep on the external input. The level control adjusts the *sensitivity* of the triggering circuit to the amplitude of the externally applied voltage. Note the switches labeled (+) and (−) *slope* on the time base. In the (+) position the triggering circuit will start the sweep on a positive-going change in voltage on the external input, and in the (−) position the sweep will start on a negative-going voltage change. The external voltage can be either AC- or DC-coupled to the trigger circuit by switching the *AC-DC coupling* switch to the appropriate position. Use AC coupling unless you are triggering on a very slow waveform (less than 15 Hz).

Another triggering arrangement is to trigger the sweep from the input to the vertical amplifier. This is done by switching the *source* or *trigger input* switch to the *internal* position. The *level* control must then be adjusted to a sensitivity which triggers the sweep. Set the *slope* switch to whichever part of the waveform (+ or −) you wish to trigger on. In general, it is preferable to use external triggering from an electronic stimulator.

The *single-sweep* function is quite useful in photographing the trace. To get a single sweep, first depress the *reset* button. Then, trigger the sweep with an external input pulse or by depressing the *single-sweep* button.

Other functions
Most oscilloscopes have a calibration output on the front panel. For example, older Tektronix oscilloscopes have a *calibration output* which consists of a 1,000 Hz square wave whose amplitude can be varied from 0.2 mV to 100 V. Newer Tektronix equipment or that of other manufacturers have calibrators with a more limited amplitude range. The calibration output should be connected to the vertical amplifier to routinely check both the oscilloscope and the preamplifier. Be sure not to feed too high a voltage into the vertical amplifier or preamplifier input, as high voltages may damage the input transistors.

Oscilloscope Exercises

Perform the following exercises to test your understanding of oscilloscope operation.

Displaying a known output
Using an appropriate set of connecting cables, connect the calibration output to the vertical amplifier input. If adjustable, set the calibration output at 0.5 V. Adjust the vertical amplifier and time base so that the waveform is about 1 division in amplitude and 1 division in length. To obtain a stationary waveform, use *internal triggering* from the vertical amplifier input. The waveform will be a "square wave" when the vertical amplifier input is set to DC. What is its frequency? After frequency has been determined, try splitting the output from the cali-

brator in a parallel connection, e.g., via a BNC T-connector, to the vertical amplifier input and the external trigger input of the time base. Adjust the time base to trigger on this external input.

Displaying a constant voltage
Obtain a working 1.5 V flashlight cell. Hook two leads (cables) to the vertical amplifier input. Sweep the trace in automatic mode at 1 sec/div, and set the gain control on the vertical amplifier to 1 V/div. Connect the two wires together to establish a baseline (zero potential) and adjust the vertical position to coincide with one of the horizontal lines in the middle of the scale. Now, use the oscilloscope as a voltmeter to check the voltage of the flashlight cell. Touch the two leads to opposite ends of the flashlight cell and note the jump in baseline. The magnitude of the jump is the no-load voltage of the cell. Does the cell produce exactly 1.5 volts? Which way does the trace move when you reverse the leads to the battery?

Noise pickup
A continual problem in electrophysiology is noise "pickup." Spurious electrical signals are picked up from the electromagnetic and electrostatic radiations of power lines, motors, and transformers, and are amplified by the electrophysiological system. Extraneous signals are a nuisance because they often mask the small bioelectric potentials. The problem is compounded by the high impedances of biological electrodes. High impedance increases noise pickup.

Disconnect all cables from the front panel of the oscilloscope. Set the time base to trigger recurrently with a sweep speed of 5 msec/div. Set the gain control on the vertical amplifier to about 20 mV/div and, if the input is differential, ground one side to produce a single-ended input. Get a 1 m (meter) unshielded cable and plug it into the active input. Let the cable hang free or lie on the table. The signal on the screen is 60 Hz interference. The cable is acting as an antenna which picks up electromagnetic radiation from the power lines and light fixtures in the room. Move the cable around and see if the amplitude changes. Grasp the free end of the cable and note that your body is a good antenna. Now, with the other hand, touch a ground connection on the oscilloscope. (There is no danger; you are the source of the electricity, not the oscilloscope.) Note that grounding abolishes the pickup. The electrical pickup induced in the wire and your body by nearby power cables is shunted off to ground. If grounding does not entirely abolish the 60 Hz signal, wet your fingers to increase the conductivity between you and the cable and the ground.

Establish conclusively that you are really observing 60 Hz pickup. Set the time base to trigger on the line current. If there is no line trigger switch, use internal triggering. This should produce a series of standing sine waves on the screen. Adjust the gain and sweep rate to give an easily measured display. Use the sweep dial setting to determine the time in seconds and milliseconds between peaks.

Attempt to minimize the pickup from your antenna. Release the antenna and rearrange nearby power cables. Is there any equipment or table lamp nearby which might be the source of 60 Hz interference? Unplug such equipment; it is generally not sufficient merely to turn it off. Is there any change when the room lights are turned off? Is there any large metal object near the cable, the table itself for example? If so, ground the metal object with a separate cable to a ground connection on the oscilloscope. A clip lead can be used to ground the object.

After eliminating as much pickup as possible, lay the cable along the edge of the tabletop. Now, hold a grounded lead in one hand with the fingers wetted and move your body into a shielding position around (hover over) the cable. The amplitude of the interference should decrease. The electric fields in the air near the cable have been intercepted by your body and shunted off through the ground connection. This is the same phenomenon encountered when you drive a car through a metal bridge with the radio playing. The radio fades out because the bridge girders shield the radio antenna from airborne transmission signals. Now, replace the unshielded cable connected to the vertical amplifier input with a *shielded cable*. This cable is a coaxial cable which consists of a central conducting wire which is connected to the amplifier input but is surrounded by a woven shield connected to the ground. What happens to the interference? Short shielded cables should be used wherever possible.

Time measurement

Work with another student on this exercise. Obtain two 1.5 V flashlight cells and four unshielded leads

0.5–1 m long. Connect one lead to the external trigger input and one to a ground connection. Set the time base on external trigger and adjust the level control so that when the ends of the two leads are touched to the terminals of a flashlight cell, the sweep is triggered. Use DC coupling, and set the sweep rate at 0.1 sec/div.

Connect the other pair of leads to the vertical amplifier input and adjust the gain control to 0.5 V/div. The beam should jump when the free ends of the two leads are touched to the other flashlight cell terminals.

Measure your reaction time. Take the two leads connected to the vertical amplifier input, and get ready to deflect the beam when it is triggered. Your partner should trigger the beam using the leads attached to the time base. Attempt to deflect the beam vertically as soon as you see it appear. Measure the time between the appearance of the beam and its deflection. Adjust the horizontal position and sweep rate of the beam to produce as precise a measurement of your reaction time as possible. Take an average of several trials.

Optional exercise

If an audio frequency generator is available you can, by using it to produce a sine wave, investigate the meaning of triggering level and differential amplification. The audio frequency generator is an electronic oscillator which produces sine waves of varying amplitude and frequency. Inexpensive audio oscillators have a fixed frequency. Connect the output of the audio frequency generator to the input of the vertical amplifier using appropriate cables. Turn the amplitude of the audio generator to its lowest value before turning it on. Set the time base to automatic triggering and a sweep speed of 0.1 msec/div. Set the gain control on the vertical amplifier to 0.1 V/div. Turn the audio frequency generator on and adjust the amplitude so that the waveform nearly fills the screen from top to bottom. If the frequency is variable, set it to about 1,000 Hz. Now, switch the time base to internal triggering. Use AC coupling. Note that varying the triggering level control continuously changes the point of triggering on the sine wave. Does this help you to understand what the level control does? It sets the voltage height at which an incoming triggering voltage will trigger the sweep. If your oscilloscope has a differential amplifier, split the audio generator output and make a parallel connection to the two inputs (+ and −). Connect a lead between a ground terminal on the audio generator and a ground terminal on the oscilloscope. Record in single-ended mode from the (+) or *A* input. Note the waveform. Then, record in single-ended mode from the (−) or *B* input.

Finally, record in the differential mode. The sine wave disappears or diminishes greatly when recording in differential mode because signals which are common (and in phase) to *A* and *B* are rejected—*common mode rejection*.

General knob manipulation
So far you have been led through a number of manipulations. You now need to work with the oscilloscope enough to understand what you are doing. Spend some time using the controls and displaying a sine or square wave signal or the oscilloscope calibration signal. An effective way to treat the oscilloscope is by working your way through its three operational units: the display unit, the vertical amplifier, and the time base. Can you find the beam after someone else has changed the dial settings?

Materials

Materials needed at each station
Oscilloscope
Cables and connectors for connecting the calibration output to the vertical amplifier input. On newer Tektronix oscilloscopes use a clip lead attached to the calibration loop.
T-connector for splitting calibration output
4 unshielded cables with connectors appropriate to the oscilloscope, 1 m length
Shielded cable, 1 m length
2–4 clip leads
2 flashlight cells, 1.5 V
Audio frequency generator (optional)

Materials available in the laboratory
Oscilloscope operating manuals
Several different kinds of oscilloscopes, e.g., single and dual beam, and storage, if available
Extra cables, clip leads, and assorted connectors and adapters

2.4 60 Hz Interference

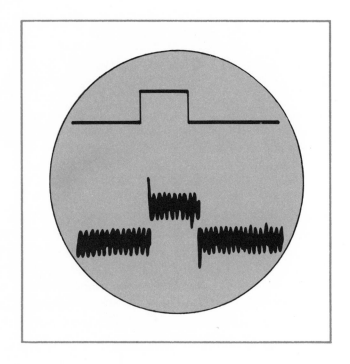

As discussed in the preceding section, 60 Hz interference is a constant nuisance in electrophysiology. The following suggestions will help you to eliminate the problem during recording.

1. *Use differential amplification* whenever possible. Any shared potentials which are in phase and common to both inputs will not be amplified. Most modern differential amplifiers have high *common mode rejection*.

2. *Use shielded cables* whenever possible. Ground leads and some input leads from high impedance electrodes are exceptions and should not be shielded. Very short leads from the preparation to a preamplifier usually need not be shielded.

3. *Make all connecting wires and cables as short as convenient.*

4. *Ground all equipment to a common point.* Your ground connections should radiate from a single point on your major readout device, i.e., the oscilloscope or polygraph.

5. *Avoid ground loops.* These are connections between different ground wires which form a continuous, looplike circuit. A ground loop acts like an antenna instead of shunting interference to ground.

6. *Work on a grounded metal plate* if possible. You may also place the preparation inside a grounded *Faraday cage*, a box made of sheet metal or wire mesh (screen). However, improvements in differential amplification have substantially lessened the need for Faraday cages.

7. *Unplug and remove any unnecessary AC-powered equipment* from the vicinity of the preparation. AC appliances or AC power cords inside a Faraday cage completely defeat its purpose. Remove AC appliances before recording, or unplug them and stow the loose cords inside the cage. Turning them off is generally insufficient.

8. *Vibrations* of the working table will produce artifacts or even destroy cells near an electrode tip. Vibration is reduced by working on a heavy metal plate resting on four 15 cm sections of rubber vacuum tubing with thick resilient walls.

9. *Start with the simplest possible hookup.* Make your connections as simple and neat as possible. Add extra ground leads only if 60 Hz AC interference is troublesome.

2.5 Electronic Stimulator

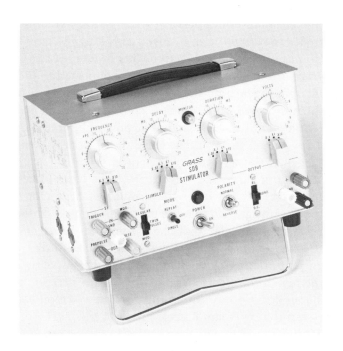

Introduction

Electrical stimulation with square waves is used extensively in electrophysiology because the amplitude, duration, and frequency can be precisely controlled. Electrical stimulation at low voltages apparently does no direct damage to tissues.

Electronic Stimulator Features

Stimulus output
The main output is labeled *stimulus output*, *stimulus*, or simply *out*. Some stimulators also have a special output connector for operating a stimulus isolation unit (SIU).

Output selector
The output selector control may have as many as three positions: *monophasic pulse*, *biphasic pulse*, or *DC*. The monophasic pulse will be used most of the time. A biphasic waveform is sometimes used to prevent electrode polarization. Monophasic waveforms can lead to an accumulation of ions at the electrodes. This is minimized by equalizing the current flow in the positive and negative directions with a biphasic waveform (fig. 2.5-1).

Output modes
Single, *twin*, and *trains* of pulses may be available (fig. 2.5-1). In the single pulse mode, only one stimulus is delivered. In the twin pulse mode, the delay control varies the time interval between two successive pulses. Stimulators capable of producing trains of pulses have extra controls for varying the duration and frequency of the train of pulses.

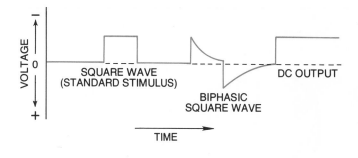

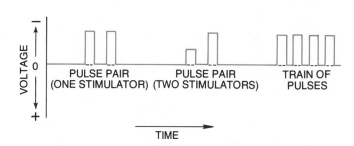

Fig. 2.5-1. Stimulus waveforms.

Polarity switch
The polarity of the square wave output can be inverted by a switch: *normal* to *reverse*, *normal* to *inverted*, or (+) to (−).

Actuating switch
A switch labeled *mode* or *stimulus mode* will be present to give either single output pulses or a *continuous* output.

Synchronous output
The *sync* or *trigger output* is the source of a pulse which can be used to trigger the oscilloscope sweep. Ordinarily, the triggering pulse starts the oscilloscope sweep at the instant the preparation is stimulated.

Delay
Some stimulators have a *delay* function in which the stimulus is sent out *after* the triggering pulse. This starts the oscilloscope sweep before the stimulus and allows the response to be centered on the display screen. That is, the *delay* control knob varies the time interval between the triggering pulse and the stimulus.

Frequency, duration, and volts controls
Knobs labeled frequency, duration, and volts control the stimulus output. Each control provides continuous variation while the selector switches below, labeled *multiply by* or *mult*, allow for variation by decades.

Stimulus Isolation Unit

(If you do not have a separate stimulus isolation unit, it may be incorporated into the stimulator.) The stimulating voltage is usually much larger than the bioelectric response. Thus, if the recording electrodes pick up a *stimulus artifact*, it may obscure the response. This problem can be alleviated by using an accessory called the *stimulus isolation unit*. Consider figure 2.5-2. The vertical column at the left represents a nerve. The nerve has five electrodes in contact with it. Electrodes 1 and 2 come from the stimulator, electrode 3 is connected to ground, and electrodes 4 and 5 are connected to the input of the preamplifier. The bioelectric response of the nerve to stimulation, i.e., compound action potential, will be amplified by the preamplifier and displayed on the oscilloscope. If the system is arranged as shown, most of the current from the stimulator enters the nerve at electrode 1 and leaves the nerve at 2. However, the stimulator is connected to the same ground that the preamplifier uses. Thus, because all the electrodes have some resistance associated with them (R_1–R_5), some of the stimulus current originating in electrode 1 is distributed to the rest of the electrodes (arrows). In order to get to electrode 5, some current must cross the region between the two recording electrodes 4 and 5. The recording electrodes pick up the voltage drop associated with this current and display it along with the bioelectric response. This is the origin of the stimulus artifact. A central ground electrode (3) has been

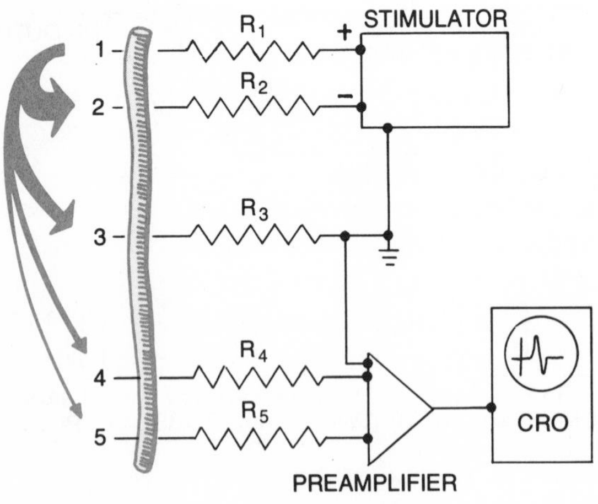

Fig. 2.5-2. Stimulating and recording from a nerve.

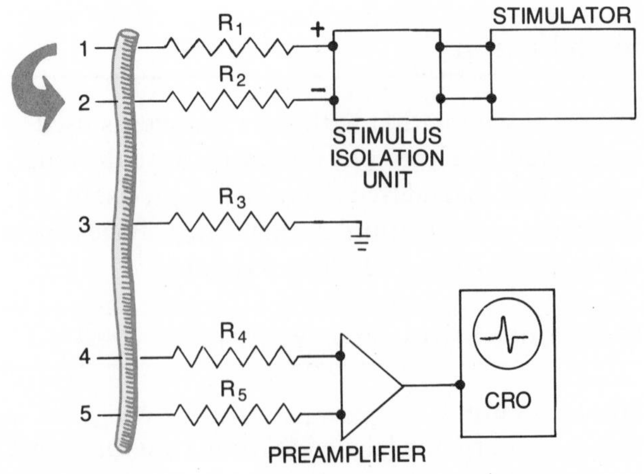

Fig. 2.5-3. Stimulating and recording using a stimulus isolation unit.

added in an effort to shunt off extraneous current, but it is not wholly effective. The stimulus artifact will often be large enough to obscure or distort the bioelectric activity, or electrically block the preamplifier.

The stimulus artifact can be minimized by using a stimulus isolation unit (SIU) inserted between the stimulator and the stimulating electrodes (fig. 2.5-3). This isolates the stimulating current from the rest of the system. Note that there is no common ground. Current which leaves by electrode 1 must return by electrode 2 (arrow). Remember that current must always complete a loop, flowing out of and back to the source by separate pathways. Since there is no pathway back to the SIU through the other electrodes (3–5), the preamplifier does not receive any of the stimulus current. In practice, there is always some leakage of current, but a small artifact is often a useful indication of stimulus onset. An SIU circuit is often built into stimulators rather than segregated in a separate unit.

Stimulator Exercises

Triggering the oscilloscope sweep with the stimulator and displaying its output

Put the stimulus mode switch in the *off* position and turn on the power to the stimulator. Connect a ground lead between ground terminals on the oscilloscope and stimulator. This will provide a return circuit for the triggering current. Connect the *trigger output* (or *sync out*) of the stimulator to the *trigger input* on the time base on the oscilloscope. Use a single, unshielded wire. Connect the *stimulus output* of the stimulator to the vertical amplifier *input* of the oscilloscope. Use a shielded cable if the connectors on the two instruments have jacks which will take coaxial cable connectors (BNC or UHF). Otherwise, use unshielded cables.

Set the oscilloscope time base to *external triggering* and a sweep rate of 5 msec/div. Use a vertical amplifier gain of 0.5 V/div. Set the stimulator as follows: *frequency* of 15 pulses/sec (pps); *delay* (if available) of 10 msec; *duration* of 10 msec; and *voltage* of 1.5 V (1.5 × 1 on the multiplier dial). Set the stimulator to give repetitive monophasic pulses. Activate the stimulus output switch and adjust the *triggering level* control on the oscilloscope until a standing wave appears on the screen. If the

wave moves across the screen, the triggering level control is probably not adjusted properly. Increase the frequency to 30 pulses/sec. Two square waves should be apparent. Double the frequency again to 60 pulses/sec. Vary the different stimulus parameters until you understand the controls. Also vary the oscilloscope controls.

Testing your understanding

Disconnect all cables and alter the settings of the controls on the stimulator and oscilloscope. Try to get a proper display of the stimulator output without consulting the step-by-step description just given. Work at this until you are able to set up without hesitation and without the need to consult the written instructions. Do not use stimulus voltages which are inappropriately high for the oscilloscope sensitivity setting.

Calibrating the stimulator

The output indicated on the stimulator controls is likely to be somewhat incorrect. For example, the voltage control might indicate an output of 10 V, yet a check with a precise voltmeter might reveal that the true output is 11.2 V. You can calibrate the stimulator output because you do have a precise voltmeter, the oscilloscope.

Calibrate the oscilloscope initially by connecting its calibration output into the vertical amplifier input. Use the screwdriver control labeled *gain* or *gain adjustment* to adjust the gain of the vertical amplifier so that an input of 1 V gives a readout of 1 V on the screen. For example, use a 1.0 V output from the calibrator with the vertical amplifier set to 0.2 V/div. The gain should be adjusted for a beam deflection of exactly five divisions on the screen. Be certain the variable sensitivity knob is clicked into the calibrated position.

Now, calibrate the stimulator's *voltage* and *duration* parameters. Tabulate the stimulator settings, e.g., 0.1 V, 0.5 V, 1 V, 5 V, 10 V, etc., and determine the true output using the oscilloscope as a voltmeter. Calibrate the stimulus duration dial with the oscilloscope time base. Write down the serial numbers of your stimulator and oscilloscope for future reference.

Stimulus isolation unit (at the instructor's option)
Connect the stimulator output to the stimulus iso-

lation unit (SIU). This may require a special connecting cable. Connect a set of leads from the SIU output to the oscilloscope input. Also connect leads for triggering the oscilloscope. Use the same stimulus and recording parameters as in the stimulator exercise. If the stimulator voltage control has an SIU position, switch to it. The voltage controls on the SIU may override and nullify the corresponding stimulator controls. Use the SIU controls and observe the waveform. Does it differ from the stimulator output previously displayed? It may be a distorted and fuzzy square wave, but it will be close enough. Note that the isolation unit has a *polarity* switch and a switch for choosing *direct* or *capacitative* coupling. Try these switches. Do enough knob turning, disconnecting, and reconnecting without written instructions to satisfy yourself that you understand how to connect and use the stimulator-SIU combination.

Never ground any of the SIU output terminals. This will negate the isolating effect of the SIU. However, maintain the stimulator-oscilloscope ground connection.

Calibrate the amplitude of the SIU output against the oscilloscope as you did for the stimulator alone. Be sure to write down the serial numbers of your equipment for future reference.

Materials

Materials needed at each station
Oscilloscope
Electronic stimulator
Stimulus isolation unit (optional)
Unshielded and shielded cables for connecting stimulator to CRO, with appropriate connectors and adapters

Materials available in the laboratory
Extra cables, connectors, and adapters
Clip leads
Screwdriver for gain calibration

2.6   Preamplifier

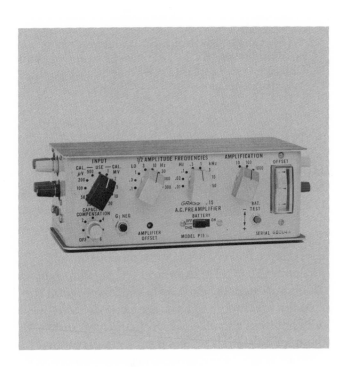

Introduction

In most cases, an amplifier separate from the oscilloscope serves as the initial input stage of an electrophysiological system. This *preamplifier* can be placed very close to the preparation to avoid the use of long input leads which might increase 60 Hz pickup and greatly increase the input capacitance. (Imagine a capacitor connecting the electrode to ground. High frequency voltages will be lost as they flow through the capacitor to ground.) The preamplifier provides an initial stage of amplification for driving the readout device (oscilloscope or polygraph). Its high input impedance also ensures that the signal voltage will not be lost across the impedance of the electrodes and the preparation.

Preamplifier Features

AC or DC input

The difference between AC and DC coupling in amplifier inputs was discussed briefly in the review of electrical principles (section 1.2). To reiterate, *AC coupling* refers to the presence of a capacitor in series with the input circuit. A capacitance will pass an alternating voltage (or alternating current), but cannot pass an unchanging voltage. A *DC* or *direct-coupled input* can pass changing voltages of very low frequencies or a standing voltage. The choice of an AC or DC preamplifier for a given application will depend on the expected range of frequencies in the signal from the biological source. Use of a DC amplifier is indicated when recording resting membrane potentials, generator potentials, receptor potentials, or synaptic potentials. Recording the slow waves of the electroencephalogram (EEG) requires an amplifier with good low frequency response, but not full DC. An AC amplifier should be used for extracellular recording of action potentials.

Differential input vs. single-ended

A *differential amplifier* (also called *push-pull*) uses two inputs. Neither input is grounded; instead the input circuit is arranged so that the voltages on the two inputs are compared with each other and only the *difference* between the two is passed. Any voltages in common will be ignored (*common mode rejection*). The differential amplifier rejects most 60 Hz and vibration-induced interference because the interfering voltage is similar on the two inputs.

Differential amplification should be used whenever possible to minimize interfering voltages. Differential amplification is also useful when recording from several pairs of electrodes simultaneously. For example, if several single-ended amplifiers were used to record the EEG at several points

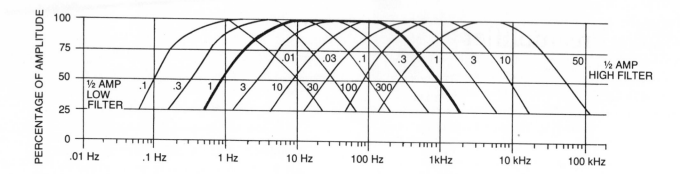

Fig. 2.6-1. Frequency response curves of the Grass P-15 preamplifier with different settings of the low and high frequency filters. The darkest curve represents the frequency response with a low frequency 1/2 amplitude setting of 1 Hz and a high frequency 1/2 amplitude setting of 1 kHz. With these settings a 2 Hz signal, for example, will be reduced to 75% of its true amplitude. (Courtesy of Grass Instrument Co.)

on the scalp, the common ground of each electrode pair would intermingle the individual signals from different areas.

A *single-ended amplifier* has a single input which is electrically compared with ground. Induced voltages from power sources and vibration are not rejected. A differential amplifier can be temporarily converted to single-ended operation by grounding one of the two active inputs. The remaining active input is thus referred to ground.

Input impedance

The input impedance of a bioelectric amplifier should be high (10^8 ohms or more). This reduces distortion of the source waveform by minimizing input reactance and matching the impedance of microelectrodes whose impedance may be very high (10^6–10^8 ohms). The high impedance also prevents distortion by limiting the current drawn from the source.

Gain

Gain is the ratio of output/input voltage. Bioelectric amplifiers have different gains. Some have a fixed gain ($\times 1$ is common on inexpensive models), but many are variable with a selector switch giving as many as three decade settings, e.g., $\times 10$, $\times 100$, and $\times 1,000$. In practice, the highest gain setting is usually the best to use since it is the least noisy. Variable gain is achieved by attenuating a high-gain circuit with different resistances.

Frequency response

Biological sources produce frequencies in the range of 0–10,000 Hz. Although neurons never discharge at rates approaching 10,000 Hz, Fourier analysis demonstrates that the waveform of a single action potential may have frequency components approaching 10,000 Hz. A typical AC preamplifier attenuates signals below 3 Hz and above 5,000 Hz.

Many preamplifiers have a selector switch (filter) which allows a choice of high frequency cutoff points. The switch selects from a group of shunt capacitors of varying capacitance. This switch may be labeled *high frequency cutoff, upper 1/2 amplitude frequency, rise time*, or *−3dB point*. One-half amplitude means that the amplitude of a sine wave of the frequency shown on the switch setting is reduced by approximately 50% (or 3 decibels [−3dB]). The cutoff is not sharp; rather it slopes off at the higher end (fig. 2.6-1).

The lower cutoff frequency may also be variable. A switch labeled *low frequency cutoff, lower 1/2 amplitude frequency, time constant*, or *−3dB point* varies the value of the capacitance *in series* with the input. Considering both filters then, the frequency response is relatively constant ("flat") in the middle range between the upper and lower cutoff points, forming the plateau on the graph in figure 2.6-1. Note that the upper and lower cutoff switches form a variable *band-pass filter* which the experimenter can adjust to fit the demands of recording. Note also that neither the upper nor the lower cutoff is sharp.

Noise

You might rightly ask, why bother with frequency filters? Why not always amplify with the widest possible frequency response? The answer is that *noise* in the preamplifier output is proportional to the width of the band of frequencies amplified. Electronic noise, as distinct from 60 Hz pickup, is an unavoidable fact of electronic circuits. For example, a simple resistance—in a wire, resistor, or electrode—will generate noise (*Johnson noise*) from the random motion of electrons or ions propelled by thermal agitation. Furthermore, you may wish to filter out some bioelectric activity which masks the response. In practice, therefore, you should limit the band pass of the preamplifier as much as possible without substantially altering the waveform of the bioelectric signal of interest.

Calibration circuit

Some preamplifiers are provided with their own calibrating source. When the *selector switch* labeled *calibration*, *calibrator*, or *cal* is in the calibration position (and set to a given value such as 10 mV), pushing the *calibration button* will result in the application of the preset DC voltage to the preamplifier input. The known voltage allows you to determine the total amplification of the preamplifier-oscilloscope system. You may *calibrate* the overall gain of your system by setting the preamplifier gain and oscilloscope gain to the desired values and testing with the calibrator to verify the total gain (see calibrator exercise, page 32). This is an excellent way to calibrate. However, note that filters may reduce the size of the calibration signal unless they are set to the widest bandwidth.

DC offset

Undesirable DC potentials may be produced at the tips of recording electrodes. On some preamplifiers, a variable control labeled *DC offset* or *input offset* can be adjusted exactly to cancel out the unwanted DC potential. For example, a -5 mV electrode potential can be cancelled by a $+5$ mV counterpotential (or bucking voltage) introduced by the preamplifier. At the correct DC offset adjustment, the *DC offset meter*, if present, will read zero and the oscilloscope trace will return to the same vertical position produced by grounding the preamplifier input.

Preamplifier power supply

Many biological preamplifiers are battery powered to avoid problems with 60 Hz pickup from a power line and to make them more portable. A battery-powered unit will have a built-in meter or external jacks for checking the battery voltage.

> Double-check at the conclusion of a laboratory period to be sure your preamplifier is turned off.

Preamplifiers with rechargeable batteries should be recharged for approximately the amount of time which they were used. Some overcharging is usually permissible.

Other functions

Some functions present in preamplifiers have not been discussed, e.g., DC balance adjustment, capacity compensation, guarded inputs, electrode resistance testing. Consult the preamplifier operating manual as required.

Preamplifier Exercises

Amplifying and displaying a known signal from the oscilloscope calibrator or electronic stimulator

Either the oscilloscope calibrator or the electronic stimulator can be used as signal sources for learning the operation of the preamplifier. The oscilloscope calibration output is less flexible but more precise.

> Keep the signal voltage low. A voltage in excess of 10–50 V will damage most preamplifiers.

Turn on the oscilloscope and preamplifier. Connect a shielded cable from the preamplifier output to the oscilloscope input. Connect a ground lead from the preamplifier to the oscilloscope if a ground connection is not made through the shielded cable or power supply. Set the oscilloscope time base to automatic triggering and a sweep rate of 5 msec/div. Use a gain of 1 V/div on the vertical amplifier and set the input to DC mode. Set the preamplifier gain to ×10 and the oscilloscope calibration output (or stimulator) to 0.1 V (100 mV). If the preamplifier has a fixed gain of

×1, increase the oscilloscope gain to 0.1 V/div. Connect a cable from the calibration output on the oscilloscope (or stimulator) to the preamplifier input. If the preamplifier has low and high frequency filters, set them to the widest possible band pass. If a stimulator is used, set the frequency at 1,000 Hz and put it in *continuous* mode.

You should get a square wave. To get a stationary display, switch the oscilloscope to internal triggering (AC coupling) and adjust the level control. The input (0.1 V) multiplied by the preamplifier gain (×10) gives 1 V. Is the square wave one division in amplitude? If it is different, either the preamplifier is not producing its rated gain, or the stimulator is not producing its stated output. (Oscilloscopes are usually accurate to within 5%.) If a stimulator is being used as the signal source, use the calibration figures for the stimulator (section 2.5) to set to a true 0.1 V. Calibrate the preamplifier for a gain of × 10. Record the calibration result and preamplifier serial number for future reference.

Reduce the calibration signal to 0.01 V (10 mV). Increase the preamplifier gain to ×100. It may be necessary to readjust the triggering level control to get a display. Is the square wave still one division in amplitude? Calibrate the preamplifier for a gain of ×100.

Set the calibration signal to 0.001 V (1 mV). Increase the preamplifier gain to ×1,000. Is the square wave one division in amplitude? Calibrate the preamplifier for a gain of ×1,000.

Calibration of preamplifier gain with the preamplifier calibrator

If your preamplifier has a built-in calibrator, switch to the calibrating position. Depress the *calibration* actuator switch (a push-button or momentary contact toggle switch). If yours is a DC preamplifier, you should get a square wave output displayed on the oscilloscope. The onset of the square wave occurs as you depress the calibration switch and it ends when the switch is released. If you have an AC amplifier, you will get two momentary deflections. The first deflection will occur as the switch is depressed, and the second will come as the switch is released. Since the capacitors in the AC amplifier input cannot pass steady (DC) current, the amplifier responds only when the voltage changes. Note that the deflections are in opposite directions. Do you understand why?

Set the calibrator to different values and determine the true gain of the preamplifier. Do the different gain settings really equal ×10, ×100, and so forth?

Calibration of total system gain

In each of the electrophysiological experiments in this manual, a suggested value for the *total system gain* will be given.

Be sure you understand what the phrase "total system gain" means.

Set the preamplifier gain to ×10 and the oscilloscope vertical amplifier gain to 10 mV/div. The total system gain is now approximately 1 mV/div. That is, 1 mV at the preamplifier input will produce a one-division deflection of the oscilloscope beam. Switch the preamplifier calibrator to 1 mV and depress the calibration button. Does the beam deflect by exactly one division? Suppose it deflects by 0.8 division rather than one full division. That means the true system gain is 0.8 mV/div.

Use different gain settings on the preamplifier and oscilloscope to familiarize yourself with the concept of total system gain. Once mastered, it will be of great benefit in your experiments. Why does ×10 (preamplification gain) multiplied by 10 mV/div (oscilloscope gain) not equal 100 mV/div? You should *divide* by 10, not multiply (10 mV/div ÷ 10 = 1 mV/div).

Effect of band-pass filters

Reconnect the oscilloscope calibration output to the preamplifier input. Adjust the gain to obtain a square wave 2 cm high. Set the oscilloscope time base to a sweep rate (1 or 2 msec/div) which displays at least one whole square wave. Now, progressively move the low frequency filter switch upward through its range of settings. What happens? This is the effect of decreasing the time constant of the input circuit; the preamplifier becomes less and less able to pass a DC current. Set the low frequency filter back to its lowest setting. Now, progressively move the high frequency filter downward through its range of settings. What is the effect? This is what happens as the rise time of the shunting capacitance is gradually increased. How would this distort a high frequency sine wave?

An audio frequency generator (sine wave generator) with variable frequency control may be available in the laboratory. It is instructive to use it as a signal source and vary the frequency to test the effect of the bandpass filters. You can treat this quantitatively by plotting the amplitude of sine waves of different frequencies with a given filter setting. A plot, such as the one shown in figure 2.6-1, can be made for your amplifier.

Materials

Materials needed at each station
Oscilloscope
Preamplifier
Electronic stimulator (optional, if oscilloscope calibration output is available)
Audio frequency generator (optional)
Shielded cables for connecting preamplifier output to oscilloscope vertical amplifier input and calibration output (stimulator or CRO) to preamplifier input, with appropriate connectors and adapters.

Materials available in the laboratory
Extra cables, connectors, and adapters
Clip leads

2.7 Audio Amplifier and Loudspeaker

Introduction

Electrophysiologists customarily include an audio amplifier and loudspeaker in the recording system when recording nerve action potentials. The experimenter then does not have to be looking at the oscilloscope screen to know that the preparation is active. Moreover, the ear can often discriminate the nature of nerve activity and changes in its rate better than the eye. The usefulness of the ear in detecting subtle changes in neuronal activity stems from the fact that the ear is more sensitive to temporal differences than the eye.

Special audio monitors for electrophysiological experimenting are available (e.g., Grass model AM-7). A simple audio amplifier and inexpensive loudspeaker used in record players or public address systems are nearly as effective (e.g., Heath model AA-18).

Audio Amplifier Exercise

The audio amplifier can be connected to the preamplifier output in parallel with the oscilloscope input, or to the vertical amplifier output (signal output) which is found at the rear of some oscilloscopes. Connection to the oscilloscope is preferable because the audio volume will automatically change when either the preamplifier or the oscilloscope gain is readjusted.

Connect the input of your audio amplifier to the signal output of the oscilloscope or to the preamplifier output in parallel with the oscilloscope input. If more than one input is available on the audio amplifier, use the jack labeled *magnetic phono input*. If the audio amplifier has a separate speaker, connect the audio amplifier output to the speaker with a pair of unshielded leads. The speaker should be marked 4, 8, or 16 ohms and should be connected to the audio amplifier terminal of the same value. Feed a signal into the preamplifier from an electronic stimulator. Set the stimulator output to 0.1 V amplitude, a duration of 1 msec, and a frequency of 100 pulses/sec. Set the gain of the preamplifier to ×10. Actuate the stimulator. Adjust the oscilloscope to give a stationary square wave display. Turn the audio amplifier on and adjust its volume to a comfortable level. The *tone* control can be set at its midpoint. The clicks heard are comparable to the sound of nerve action potentials. Experiment by altering the stimulation rate.

Materials

Materials needed at each station
Oscilloscope
Preamplifier
Electronic stimulator
Audio amplifier and loudspeaker

Shielded cables for connecting preamplifier or oscilloscope output to audio amplifier input and from stimulator output to preamplifier or oscilloscope vertical amplifier input, with appropriate connectors and adapters

Unshielded cable for connecting audio amplifier output to loudspeaker

Materials available in the laboratory

Extra cables, connectors, and adapters

Clip leads

2.8 Electrodes and Nerve Chambers

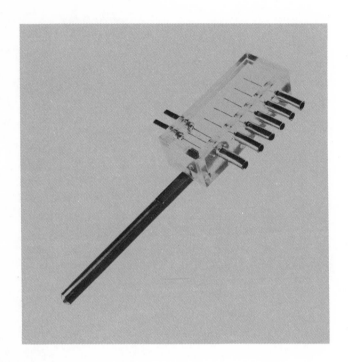

We suggest that the nerve chamber exercise be covered in the laboratory and the remainder of this section be read outside class.

How Electrodes Are Named

Recording a bioelectric signal requires the use of two or more electrodes. In single-ended recording, one electrode is the *ground* or *indifferent electrode*. The other electrode which is placed in or near the signal source is the *active electrode*. In differential recording there are usually three electrodes. A *ground electrode* is placed in electrical contact with some portion of the animal's body. The *indifferent* or *reference electrode*, connected to the negative input of the differential amplifier, is placed closer to the signal source. The *active electrode*, connected to the positive input, is placed at the signal source. In recording with nerve chambers (fig. 2.8-1) one would speak of the electrode farthest from the stimulating electrodes as the indifferent recording electrode.

Nerve Chamber Exercise

An excised nerve can be laid on a ladderlike series of wire electrodes in a nerve chamber. The nerve chamber usually consists of a Plexiglas box with a series of terminals connected to the wire electrodes (as fig. 2.8-1). The chamber can be partially filled with isotonic sodium chloride salt solution and covered to prevent the nerve from drying.

Obtain a nerve chamber and its cover. Mount it on a ringstand if it is equipped with a mounting rod. Fill the bottom of the chamber with isotonic NaCl solution (0.16 M), but keep the level of the solution several millimeters below the electrodes.

If the fluid touches the electrodes, they will short-circuit.

Thoroughly soak a 7 cm long cotton thread in a beaker of 0.16 M NaCl solution and place it in the nerve chamber so that it lies across all of the electrodes. Do not allow the ends of the thread to dangle in the fluid. Connect a set of leads to one pair of electrodes near one end of the thread (fig. 2.8-1). Connect these leads to the input of your preamplifier. Connect a second set of leads to a pair of electrodes at the opposite end of the thread. Connect these leads to the output of your stimulator. Turn on the oscilloscope and stimulator. Make appropriate connections and adjustments to trigger the oscilloscope sweep from the trigger output (sync out) of the stimulator. Set the oscilloscope sweep to 5 msec/div. Use shielded cables wherever possible.

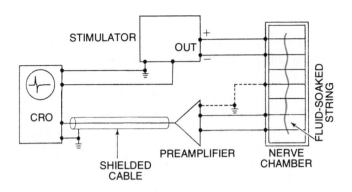

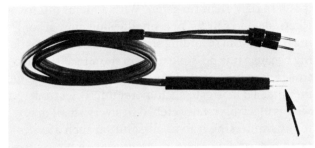

Fig. 2.8-1. Recording with a nerve chamber. Record initially without the central electrode grounded. Then, add a ground connection (*dashed line*) to observe the effect on the stimulus artifact.

Fig. 2.8-2. Electrode holder and electrodes (*arrow*).

Set the stimulator to give an output of 1 V, with a duration of 1 msec, and a frequency of 10 pulses/sec. Set the preamplifier gain to ×10 and the oscilloscope vertical amplifier gain to 0.5 V/div. Turn the preamplifier on and stimulate with pulses from the stimulator. Adjust the oscilloscope sweep and the system gain until you can discern a peaked waveform at the onset of the sweep. The peaked waveform (or double peak) which you observe results from the leakage of current through the soaked thread from the stimulating electrodes to the recording electrodes. This is called a *stimulus artifact*. A similar artifact occurs in recording from a nerve, and, if too large, will obscure the biological response. Shorten the duration of the stimulus pulse to 0.2 msec. Does the stimulus artifact disappear?

Attempt to decrease the magnitude of the artifact by connecting a ground lead to one of the electrodes between the stimulus and recording electrodes. Does it decrease? You may wish to attempt to eliminate the artifact using a stimulation isolation unit (see section 2.5). Remember this exercise when you begin using the nerve chamber, because you are likely to record similar artifacts which have no biological meaning. Small artifacts provide a useful marker on the trace, indicating the exact time of stimulus onset. Large artifacts usually obscure some of the physiological response.

Electrodes

Gross wire electrodes
Solid wires can serve in many instances as perfectly good electrodes. Figure 2.8-2 illustrates a commer-

cially available (Harvard Apparatus Co.) hand-held, bipolar stimulating electrode. An easily constructed versatile electrode holder is shown on page 336. Wires used for electrodes vary in composition. Silver is used most often, but iridium, palladium, platinum, tungsten, and stainless steel are also used. Electrodes, such as those illustrated (fig. 2.8-2), are referred to as *gross electrodes* to distinguish them from *micro*electrodes which have very fine tips. Gross electrodes can be hand held, as in stimulating muscle, or they can be mounted on a flexible lead rod or manipulator for more precise positioning.

Plate electrodes
Small circular or rectangular plates are often applied to the body surface to record potentials from deeper structures. Such electrodes are usually held in place with rubber straps, tape, or suction devices. Plate electrodes always have to be applied to hairless or shaved skin by using a layer of *electrode paste*, a conducting electrolyte-containing lotion, between the plate and the skin. Plate electrodes are commonly used to record gross potentials from the heart (electrocardiogram or ECG), brain (electroencephalogram or EEG), or skeletal muscles (electromyogram or EMG).

Metal microelectrodes
Metal *microelectrodes* are commonly used to record action potentials from single nerve cells. Such electrodes have very fine tips with diameters on the order of one to several micrometers (μm). Tungsten is the most suitable material for metal microelectrodes because the tip has the strength to penetrate tissue without bending. Steel is also used, but

it is less rigid than tungsten. With a metal micro-electrode one can make a small lesion after recording to mark the recording site. Steel is best for marking because it is possible to stain the site of the electrode tip using a technique called the Prussian blue method. To fabricate such metal microelectrodes, a wire is electrolytically etched to a very small diameter by immersing it in a salt solution such as saturated potassium nitrite (a carcinogen) or potassium chloride (KCl) and passing AC current through the electrode. The current rapidly strips metal off the tip of the wire, producing a sharp tip. The shape of the tip is controlled by the rate of dipping it in and out of the etching solution. After etching, the electrode is dipped in varnish or acrylic resin to produce an insulating coat. The tip is left uninsulated because the surface tension at the sharp tip produces a break in the liquid coating before it dries.

Metal microelectrodes are durable and easily produced, but they have a major disadvantage: they cannot be effectively used to record DC potentials, because they easily *polarize*. An electrode becomes *polarized* when it becomes surrounded by a shell of charged ions which impede the flow of electric current between the metal wire and the solution. Resistance to current flow is greatest at low frequencies, including DC. This attenuates the signal and introduces a great deal of noise and instability in the low frequency range.

Treating the surface of metal electrodes produces a *nonpolarizable* electrode which passes current more easily. For example, gross silver electrodes are often coated with silver chloride (see page 334 for construction details). Empirical tests of these *silver/silver chloride electrodes* show that their impedance is reduced to about 1/60 that of a pure silver electrode. This may result from a greatly increased electrode surface area produced by the porous coating. The silver chloride coating also acts as a source of both positive and negative ions which stabilizes the electrode-electrolyte solution interface. However, no known treatment makes metal *micro*electrodes as accurate as fluid-filled pipettes for recording low frequency or DC signals.

All electrode types produce their own DC junction potentials. An *electrode potential* is generated at the electrode-solution interface just as in a wet cell battery. This produces a problem in that the DC potential developed by the inanimate electrode is not al-ways separable from the biological potential. In addition, a large electrode potential can affect the biological tissue or the amplifier.

In practice, electrode potentials can be minimized, but not entirely eliminated, by using the same metal for both electrodes in a pair. When electrodes are composed of the same metal and are in contact with the same ionic solution, the *net* electrode potential should be zero. However, there is always a residual potential.

Fluid-filled glass electrodes

Fluid-filled glass *micropipettes* are widely employed to record bioelectric potentials and to inject dyes or chemicals into cells. The tip of the pipette is drawn out to a very small diameter by heating the middle of a capillary tube and pulling rapidly as the glass softens. An electrode pulling machine typically uses an electrically heated coil for softening the glass and a two-stage pull: first a slow pull to narrow the capillary, then a fast pull to produce a fine tip. The shape and tip size are determined by the heater temperature and the speed and timing of the pulling forces. Fragility is reduced if the micropipette has a sharp taper and a relatively short tip (fig. 2.8-3). Major difficulties with glass microelectrodes include fragility in handling, the problem of pulling an electrode with the correct shape and appropriate tip size, and difficulties in filling the fine pipette with electrolyte solution. Glass microelectrodes can now be bought from suppliers (see chapter 10), thus avoiding the problems of production.

The glass microelectrode is the most commonly used electrode for recording intracellular action po-

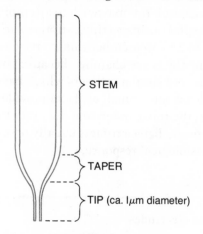

STEM

TAPER

TIP (ca. 1μm diameter)

Fig. 2.8-3. Microelectrode terminology.

tentials, resting membrane potentials, and slow potentials such as receptor and synaptic potentials. The glass microelectrode is used in both *intracellular* and *extracellular* recording. Glass electrodes pass DC potentials without the noise and attenuation characteristic of metal microelectrodes. The pipette is usually filled with 3 M KCl because a concentrated salt solution produces a lower impedance (and hence lower noise level) and KCl produces a minimal junction potential.

The impedance of the glass microelectrode is a function of the tip size. The smaller the tip, the higher the impedance, because only a small cross-sectional area of electrolyte solution is available at the electrode tip to carry current. The configuration of the tip also produces a substantial amount of capacitance. The thin glass of the electrode tip separates two conductors—the fluids inside and outside the electrode—and thus is a capacitor. If uncompensated, this capacitance limits the high frequency response of the glass electrode and distorts the high frequency components of an action potential. Thus, the capabilities of metal and glass microelectrodes are complementary. Metal microelectrodes are good for recording action potentials extracellularly and for high frequency signals, while glass microelectrodes are best for DC and low frequency signals and intracellular recording.

Materials

Materials needed at each station
Oscilloscope
Preamplifier
Electronic stimulator
Nerve chamber, its cover, and mounting stand if appropriate
Connecting cables sufficient for arrangement in figure 2.8-1, with appropriate connectors and adapters

Materials available in the laboratory
Extra cables, connectors, and adapters
Clip leads
Cotton thread
Small beakers and medicine droppers and Pasteur pipettes with bulbs
Amphibian perfusion fluid (75 ml/station)

2.9 Oscilloscope Camera

Introduction

The oscilloscope camera photographs waveforms displayed on the oscilloscope screen. In research laboratories, both still and motion picture cameras are used. A teaching laboratory is most likely to have a still camera. Most oscilloscope cameras take Polaroid pack film (type 107, 3,000-speed 8 pictures) or roll film (type 47, 3,000-speed 8 pictures). Self-developing film is more convenient and economical because the quality of the photographs can be immediately checked.

The frame of the oscilloscope screen (*bezel*) must be appropriate for mounting the particular camera to be used. With a regular (nonstorage) oscilloscope, the camera is mounted and the shutter left open during one or more sweeps of the trace. With a storage oscilloscope, the trace may be stored prior to mounting the camera. In each case, film can be conserved by putting several traces on each photograph by moving either the trace or the position of the camera back between each sweep.

Oscilloscope Camera Examination

Features of the oscilloscope camera
Method of camera mounting on the oscilloscope bezel. Some cameras will simply hang on the bezel, while others must be clamped in place with a thumbscrew or latch lever.

Lens and shutter controls. Some cameras use a single aperture, or f stop, while others have a variable diaphragm to control the lens opening. Note the shutter speed control. *T* (time) means that when the shutter button is pushed, the shutter will open and remain open until the button is pushed again. It is preferable to use the setting *B* (bulb) since the shutter will remain open only as long as the button is depressed.

Camera back or film holder. What kind of film does it take? If Polaroid, does it use roll or pack film?

Picture taking with a nonstorage oscilloscope
1. Make sure your camera will fit on the oscilloscope bezel.
2. Load the camera. Polaroid film will have loading instructions.
3. Set the oscilloscope for single trace. The waveform of interest should appear when the time base is triggered.
4. Set the intensity control to give a moderately bright trace without producing a halo.
5. Turn the graticule illuminator *off*.
6. Mount the camera. Set the aperture to f/5.6 and the shutter speed indicator to B. Lock the camera in place.
7. Look in the viewer and trigger a single sweep. Triggering is often done with the stimulator. Estimate how long it will be necessary to hold the shutter open to record the whole trace.
8. Close the viewer.
9. Remove the dark slide (blocking plate) from the camera back.
10. Open the shutter by pressing the button. Hold the button down.
11. Trigger a single sweep and allow enough time for it to traverse the screen.
12. Close the shutter by releasing the button.
13. If you want a scale on the picture, turn on the graticule illuminator to moderate brightness while watching through the viewer. Close the viewer. Open the shutter for about 1 second to photograph the illuminated scale. Note: Some newer oscilloscopes have graticules which *do not* light up. These oscilloscopes are fitted with cameras equipped with a flash mechanism to illuminate the graticule automatically when the shutter is actuated.
14. If you want additional non-overlapping traces you can move either the trace position or the film back.
15. Develop the film. Polaroid film will have developing instructions with it.
16. If the photo is good, write the important experimental conditions on the back side. If it is bad, make adjustments as indicated in the next section.

Trouble-shooting
1. *No image or totally black picture.* You may not have removed the dark slide. The shutter may not have been opened. Is the sweep triggering?
2. *Trace too dim.* Lower the f-stop setting or increase the intensity of the trace. (The lower the f-stop number, the larger the lens opening.)
3. *Trace too bright.* Decrease the intensity of the trace or increase the f-stop number. Remember, slowing the sweep speed increases the trace brightness.
4. *Light streaks or fogging.* Light may be leaking in around the bezel-camera joint or through an open viewer. General fogging with a bright graticule scale indicates that the graticule illuminator was left on when the trace was photographed. If the photo is totally fogged out, the shutter may have been opened accidentally. Look in the lens to make sure the shutter is not open when you think it is closed and vice versa.
5. *Trace or graticule scale, or both, out of focus.* Use an f-stop number larger than f-4 or focus the trace and the lens if adjustable.

Picture taking with a storage oscilloscope
1. Store the trace you wish to photograph. Use a moderately bright display, but not so bright that the trace begins to thicken and fog out.
2. Mount the camera and remove the dark slide.
3. Turn the graticule illuminator to a moderate level.
4. Open the shutter for 2–4 seconds.
5. Develop the film and inspect the results.
6. Adjust the exposure time and the graticule illuminator to achieve a proper balance of trace and scale brightness. If the oscilloscope has no graticule illuminator, you will have to flash it with the camera's graticule flasher.

2.10 Physiological Polygraph

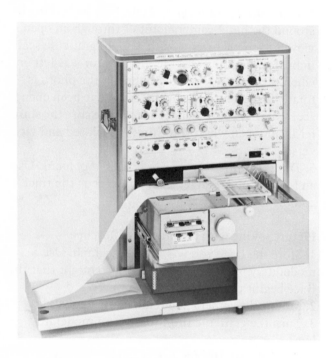

Introduction

The physiological polygraph is a multichannel recording device capable of permanently recording many kinds of physiological events. It is a versatile instrument which is best known for its use by law enforcement agencies which employ it as a lie detector.[1] The general utility of the polygraph stems from modular construction; many different kinds of physiological events can be recorded using appropriate amplifiers and transducers. Many companies manufacture polygraphs, so the unit in your laboratory might be a Narco Physiograph, a Grass Poly-

graph, a Beckman Dynograph, a Harvard Biograph, a Stoelting Econ-O-Graph, a LaFayette Datagraph, or a comparable unit.

The Polygraph

Applications

A polygraph is capable of directly recording *electrical* phenomena such as the electrocardiogram (EKG or ECG; see exercise 5.3), activity of nerves or receptor organs (exercise 6.1, 6.3), electromyogram (EMG; exercise 7.4), or electroencephalogram (EEG; exercise 7.9). With suitable transducers, other physiological activities can be recorded. For example, with a mechanoelectric transducer (force transducer, strain gauge, or myograph), an experimenter can record the *movement* of the beating heart chambers (exercise 5.3). Other transducers are available to record *temperature, heart sounds, pressure,* and *photic events*.

Limitations

The major limitation of the polygraph is its restricted high frequency response. The relatively massive writing pens have too much inertia to accurately follow frequencies in excess of about 30 Hz. Therefore, an oscilloscope should be used to record waveforms with higher frequency components, such as the nerve action potential. However, where waveform is unimportant, as in recording the *frequency* of firing in a muscle or nerve, the polygraph can often be used effectively. Sometimes fast signals are recorded on a tape recorder and played back into the polygraph at lower speed, which reduces the signal frequency relayed to the pens.

Operational units

A single channel on a polygraph consists of the *pickup device* (electrodes or a transducer), an appro-

---

1. When used as a lie detector, the polygraph records slight perturbations in a subject's physiological state during a stressful question. Minor physiological alterations result from activity in the autonomic nervous system associated with lying or evasion.

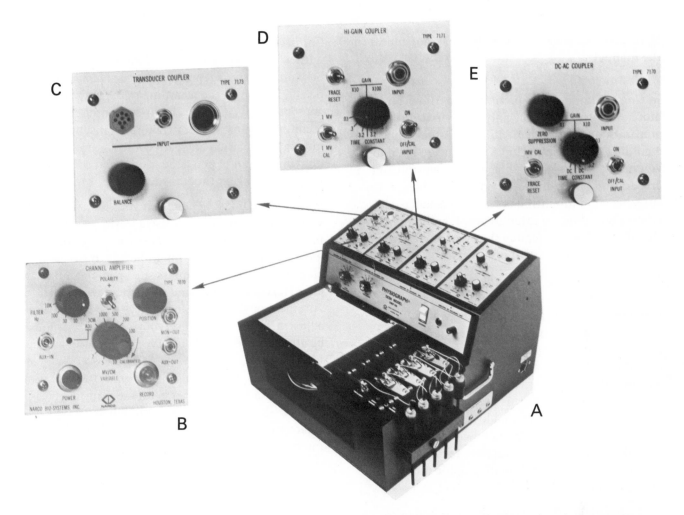

Fig. 2.10-1. Physiological polygraph and plug-in units. **A.** The polygraph system consists of a pen-writing recorder with several channels, ink supplies, and paper transport. **B.** Each channel of this unit has a *channel amplifier* (driver amplifier) which actuates the pen motor. The channel amplifier provides some amplification, a frequency filter, and a positioning control to adjust the vertical positioning of the pen on the recording paper. **C.** A *transducer coupler* connects to a force transducer or other transducer for recording nonelectrical signals such as the force of a muscle contracting or blood pressure in a large artery. **D.** A *high-gain coupler* can be used for the direct recording of either high-level electrical voltages like the ECG or low-level signals like the EEG. **E.** A *DC-AC coupler* requires high-level signals. It may be used as an interface between a high impedance preamplifier or other electrical unit and the polygraph. For each type of signal there is an appropriate coupler.

priate *channel amplifier*, *driver amplifier* or *coupler* (to magnify small electrical signals or supply current to a transducer), and a *pen-writing recorder* driven by a galvanometer or servomotor which is actuated by the amplifier output (fig. 2.10-1). Student laboratories are usually equipped with polygraphs with three or four channels plus a time and event channel, while research units may have up to twenty or thirty channels. The time and event marker provides a periodic time mark, and signals the onset of stimuli or other events for later reference when viewing the completed recording.

Operating suggestions

The variety of polygraphs available makes it impossible to give you a comprehensive set of general operating procedures. Consult your instructor or the unit's operating manual for specific instructions.

Here are some suggestions which may not appear in the manual.

Setting up and noise reduction. Sometimes fan motor vibration from the polygraph disturbs the preparation or introduces vibratory interference in a recording when using a force transducer. Therefore, you may find it useful to place the polygraph and preparation on separate, but adjacent, tables. A secure and solid mounting of force transducers also eliminates vibratory interference. Finally, use shielded cables—preferably those supplied with your unit, its amplifiers, and transducers.

Monitoring and tape recording. Since medium and high frequency signals are attenuated or lost in polygraph recording, it is often advantageous to monitor the signal using an oscilloscope and/or audio amplifier. Many polygraphs have a monitor output for each channel to accommodate such an arrangement. The monitor output can also be used for tape recording an experiment, but this may require a special tape recorder with improved low frequency response. Some manufacturers now produce multichannel integrated tape cassette recorders (e.g., Narco and Harvard) and oscillographic monitors (e.g., Narco).

Time and event. Always use the time and event channel with the time marker set to some standard rate during an experiment (1 mark/sec or 1 mark/5 sec). Then, if you forget to note or change the paper speed you will have a known time mark on your record.

Selection of force transducers. Select a force transducer with a sensitivity range suited to the preparation. For example, a relatively insensitive transducer would be appropriate for a large skeletal muscle, but a more sensitive unit would be necessary to register the force generated by the atria of an isolated frog or turtle heart. Some transducers have fixed sensitivities, while others may be adjusted as needed by the insertion of resistance springs. If necessary, you can make a transducer less sensitive by attaching it to the preparation by a spring-loaded lever, e.g., an isometric muscle lever from an old kymograph setup. Pulleys and swiveling clamps are useful to obtain the correct geometry for recording a force generated by a muscle *in vivo*.

Calibration of force transducers. When recording with a force transducer, it is always useful to know how much force is represented by a given amount of pen deflection on the recording trace. Therefore, it is appropriate to *calibrate* the force transducer before recording begins. Calibrate a force transducer by adjusting the position and gain controls to give a known amount of pen deflection when a known weight is hung on the transducer, e.g., 1 mm/g.

Ink. Use the ink supplied with your instrument. If you must substitute inks, use a fresh, sediment-free ink which is water soluble. Test your pens for proper writing before the experiment begins. If necessary, clean the pens with stainless steel pen-cleaning wire (e.g., Harvard no. 808), and rinse them with water or 70% isopropyl alcohol. In gravity-fed pens, height adjustment of the ink reservoir is crucial. Air must be allowed to enter the reservoir to replace outflowing ink.

When recording begins, first *turn down* the gain on each channel amplifier before it is turned on. Otherwise, the pen may begin to vibrate wildly, splattering ink all over you and the polygraph. If you interrupt recording for 30 minutes or more, use a sponge-rubber strip (*ink dam*) under the pen tips to prevent drying. The ink dam may also be used to prevent ink drying overnight. If the instrument is to be left for more than a week, draw water or 70% isopropyl alcohol up into the pens from a watch glass or petri dish. Use the ink dam to prevent evaporation of the alcohol during storage, and cap the ink reservoirs.

Recording paper. Check the paper supply before starting an experiment. Arrange for replacement, or you may find yourself without recording paper at a crucial point during the experiment. Always use as slow a paper speed as possible to conserve paper. Turn off the paper transport when it is not absolutely necessary during the experiment. Excessive recording speed and recording when unnecessary are a waste of expensive paper.

Shutting down. Be sure the machine is turned off. Clean pens and fill ink reservoirs with water or alcohol for extended storage. Thoroughy clean up any splattered ink and spilled salt solutions. Cover the instrument and pens appropriately. Store transducers in *protective* containers.

3   Neuroanatomy

3.1 Cellular Neuroanatomy and Histological Techniques

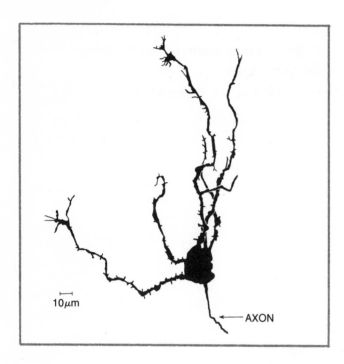

10µm

← AXON

Golgi-stained neuron is adapted from J. R. Brawer, D. K. Morest, and E. C. Kane, 1974. *J. Comp. Neurol.* 155:251–300.

Introduction

Anatomical techniques have become increasingly important in experimental neurophysiology. In fact, some electrophysiologists spend more time at the microscope than at the oscilloscope. This upsurge in the use of anatomical techniques is a result, in part, of improvements in staining and marking procedures which more accurately resolve neuronal morphology including axonal pathways and their terminations in the central nervous system.

Structure of the Nervous System

The central nervous system is composed of discrete neurons which communicate through synaptic connections; only rarely are there cytoplasmic bridges between neurons. A mammalian brain has about 10 billion neurons and 100 billion glial cells. Whereas the role of most glial cells is not yet understood, neurons have been shown to receive, process, and emit electrical and chemical signals. The neuron, as the basic structural unit, is typically depicted with a cell body, a relatively long axon, and many dendritic processes extending from the cell body (fig. 3.1-1). However, most neurons in vertebrates and invertebrates vary considerably from this pattern; note, for example, the drawing of a Golgi-stained neuron. In the vertebrate brain, neuronal cell bodies tend to be clustered in groups (*nuclei*), and axons tend to be collected into bundles (*tracts*). This facilitates neuroanatomical analysis of most brain regions, but areas such as the mammalian reticular formation and the invertebrate neuropil, where cells and axons form a seemingly disorganized and tangled feltwork, are more difficult to study with present techniques.

Two basic objectives of neuroanatomy are to determine the locations of the major nuclear groups and fiber tracts, and then to investigate the interconnections among neurons in more detail. The sheep brain dissection (exercise 3.2) will introduce you to the first approach. The wealth of material available on neurocytology (cellular neuroanatomy, including ultrastructure) will not be covered. Similarly, laboratory exercises which trace neuronal circuits by means of anatomical methods are beyond the scope of this manual.

In the exercises which explore the function of brain structures (experiments 7.5, 7.6, 7.7, 7.8, and 7.9), anatomical techniques *could* be used to determine the locus of recording or stimulating electrodes or to disclose the damage done to the brain. One would prepare stained cross sections of the brain using the following sequence of steps:

1. Perfusion of the brain via the carotid arteries with a fixative, such as formaldehyde or glutaraldehyde.
2. Removal of the brain from the skull, followed by further immersion in a fixative, and possibly embedding in a supportive medium.
3. Sectioning the brain into thin (10–50 μm) slices.
4. Staining the sections.
5. Mounting the sections on glass slides.
6. Microscopic examination.

Such procedures take days to weeks to complete, depending upon the particular methods employed. Students interested in these methods ought to take a course in neuroanatomy or histology which includes a laboratory in microtechnique. A technique for preparing brain slabs *will* be used in exercise 3.2, where brain morphology and basic nomenclature are described.

Neuroanatomical Methods

The following is a selective list of currently used neuroanatomical methods, excluding most ultrastructural methods. Each anatomical structure or objective is followed by one or more procedures. Consult figure 3.1-1 for the identification of anatomical terms.

Cell bodies
—The classic method stains the RNA of Nissl substance with basic analine dyes, such as cresyl violet or thionine

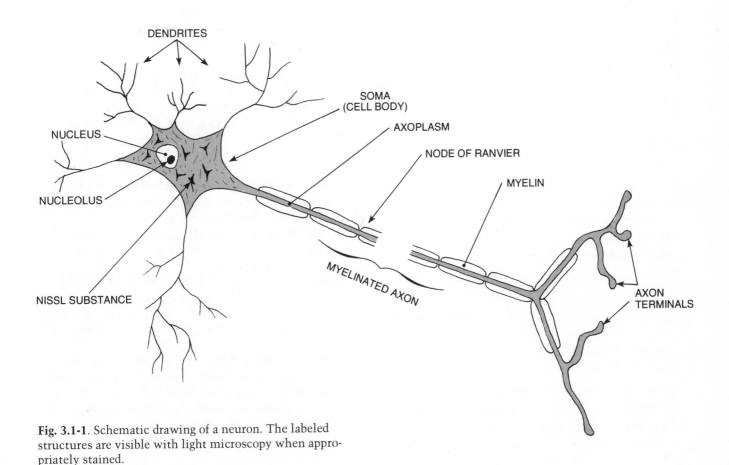

Fig. 3.1-1. Schematic drawing of a neuron. The labeled structures are visible with light microscopy when appropriately stained.

Myelinated fibers
—Modification of the Weigert method using potassium dichromate and acid fuchsin—stains the myelin sheath blue purple
—Osmium tetroxide turns the myelin sheath black

Myelinated and unmyelinated fibers
—Silver staining such as the Bodian protargol method—stains the axoplasm dark

Both cell bodies and fibers
—Methylene blue applied to living tissue as a *vital* dye
—Klüver and Barrera stain combines cell body and myelinated fiber staining procedures
—Silver stains

A few unselected neurons stained in their entirety (soma and processes with three-dimensional form)
—Golgi silver technique in many modifications

A few selected neurons stained in their entirety
—Procion dyes injected directly into a living cell through a micropipette
—Cobalt chloride taken up by diffusion or iontophoresis into cut axons or injected into the cell body
—Radioautography using radiolabeled metabolic precursors such as ^{14}C- or ^{3}H-proline injected into a cell body

Monoamine-containing neurons
—Several recent methods with formaldehyde vapors, e.g., Falck-Hillarp

Destination of axons and synaptic terminals
—Radioautography using radioactive proline or fucose injected into a ganglion, sensory organ, or brain nucleus and distributed to terminals by axoplasmic transport

Locus of the cell body of origin of exposed terminals or axons
—Horseradish peroxidase taken up by terminals and transported in the axon back to the cell body (retrograde axoplasmic transport)
—Cobalt chloride

Localization of neurotransmitter enzymes
—Tagging the enzyme with a fluorescent antibody (immunofluorescence)

Marking neurons having some special biochemical feature
—2-Deoxyglucose-^{14}C (labels neurons with high oxidative metabolism)
—6-Hydroxydopamine (selectively degenerates norepinephrine or dopamine-containing pathways)

Degenerating myelin after axons are severed from the cell body
—Marchi method using osmium tetroxide

Degenerating myelinated and unmyelinated fibers and terminals
—Fink-Heimer silver method

Dividing neurons (time of division and migration pattern in development)
—Radioautography using tritiated thymidine to label DNA.

Selected References

The references provide current sources on neuroanatomical technique. Further anatomical references can be found on pages 74 and 324.

A BRIEF INTRODUCTION TO NEUROANATOMY
Cragg, B. G. 1968. Gross, microscopical and ultramicroscopical anatomy of the adult nervous system. In *Applied neurochemistry*, ed. A. N. Davidson and J. Dobbing. Blackwell Press, London, pp. 1–47.

TECHNIQUES
Cowan, W. M. 1975. Recent advances in neuroanatomical methods. In *The nervous system*, vol. 1, ed. D. B. Tower. Raven Press, New York, pp. 59–70.
Cowan, W. M., and Cuenod, M., eds. 1975. *The use of axonal transport for studies of neuronal connectivity*. Elsevier, Amsterdam.
Heimer, L., and Lohman, A. H. M. 1975. Anatomical methods for tracing connections in the central nervous system. In *Handbook of psychobiology*, ed. M. Gazzaniga and C. Blakemore. Academic Press, New York, pp. 73–106.
Kater, S. B., and Nicholson, C., eds. 1973. *Intracellular staining in neurobiology*. Springer-Verlag, New York.
Nauta, W. J. H., and Ebbesson, S. O. E., eds. 1970. *Contemporary research methods in neuroanatomy*. Springer-Verlag, New York.

3.2   Dissection of the Sheep Brain

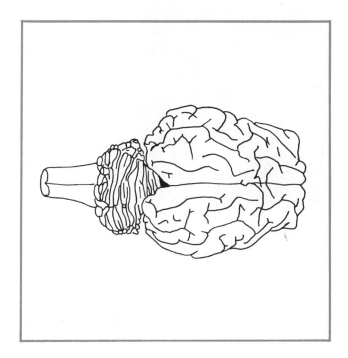

Introduction

Objectives

You will spend the equivalent of two 3-hour laboratory periods studying mammalian neuroanatomy. The sheep brain will be examined by surface morphology, gross dissection, brain slabs, and diagrams. Use of the sheep brain has a long and popular history in teaching laboratories because it is readily available, inexpensive, large, and mammalian. Our intention is to stress anatomical features for which functions are known. Two factors, however, will act to dilute this effort. First, some anatomically prominent features have poorly understood functions, e.g., hippocampus. Second, many structures with clear functions are difficult to resolve in gross dissection, e.g., cranial nerve nuclei. We will include neuroanatomical features relevant to lesioning, recording, or stimulating experiments in this manual (experiments 7.2, 7.5, 7.7, 7.8, 7.9). Beyond gaining background for future experiments, you will acquire an elementary picture of the mammalian brain.

Overview

The nervous system is composed of the central nervous system (CNS), which includes the brain and spinal cord, and the peripheral nervous system (PNS). The brain is encased in a protective skull and supported in a leathery bag (*dura mater*) which surrounds a more delicate bag (*arachnoid membrane*) which in turn contains *cerebrospinal fluid* (CSF). This arrangement provides both armor and a hydrostatic cushion (fig. 3.2-1). The spinal cord is similarly protected within the spinal canal except that the spine is jointed to bend with movements.

Input and output. The brain evolved as an enlargement at the rostral (head) end of the spinal cord and contains a flourishing development of interneurons.

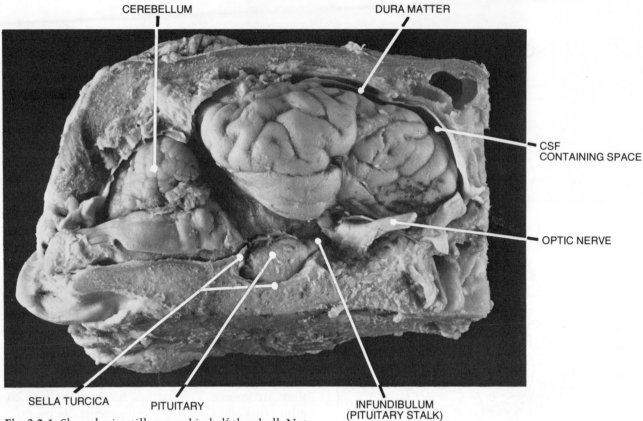

CEREBELLUM

DURA MATTER

CSF CONTAINING SPACE

OPTIC NERVE

SELLA TURCICA

PITUITARY

INFUNDIBULUM (PITUITARY STALK)

Fig. 3.2-1. Sheep brain still encased in half the skull. Note how closely the brain conforms to the cranial cavity. Figure 3.2-6 is a more fully labeled lateral view of the brain.

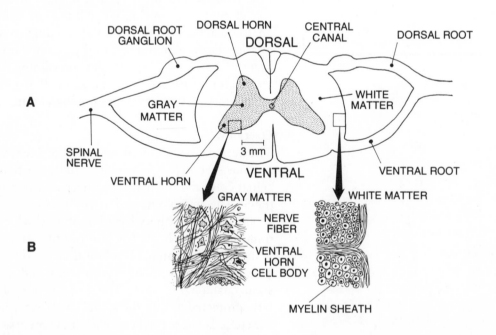

DORSAL ROOT GANGLION

DORSAL HORN

CENTRAL CANAL

DORSAL

DORSAL ROOT

A

GRAY MATTER

WHITE MATTER

3 mm

SPINAL NERVE

VENTRAL HORN

VENTRAL

VENTRAL ROOT

GRAY MATTER

WHITE MATTER

B

NERVE FIBER

VENTRAL HORN CELL BODY

MYELIN SHEATH

Fig. 3.2-2. **A**. Cross section of spinal cord showing the distribution of gray and white matter. **B**. Sections of gray matter (*left*) and white matter (*right*). Note the absence of cell bodies in white matter. The *dorsal root ganglia* contain the cell bodies of incoming sensory fibers. (Adapted from A. W. Ham, 1974. *Histology*, 7th ed., Lippincott Co., Philadelphia.)

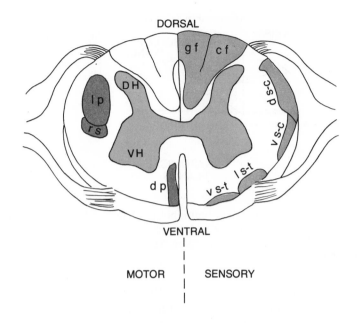

DORSAL

VENTRAL

MOTOR SENSORY

Fig. 3.2-3. Cross section through the spinal cord indicating approximate locations of some major motor pathways (*dark color on the left*) and sensory pathways (*light color on the right*). All pathways are bilaterally represented although they are not shown this way. GRAY MATTER: *DH,* dorsal horn; *VH,* ventral horn. MOTOR TRACTS: *dp,* direct pyramidal tract; *lp,* lateral pyramidal tract; *rs,* rubrospinal tract. SENSORY TRACTS: *cf,* cuneate fasciculus; *ds-c,* dorsal spinocerebellar tract; *gf,* gracile fasciculus (cf + gf = dorsal columns); *ls-t,* lateral spinothalamic tract; *vs-c,* ventral spinocerebellar tract; *vs-t,* ventral spinothalamic tract. (Adapted from an original painting by Frank H. Netter, M.D., for *The CIBA Collection of Medical Illustrations,* published by CIBA Pharmaceutical Co.)

Charles Sherrington called it "the ganglion of the distance receptors." The spinal cord receives sensory information from the body proper via axons which make up the 36 pairs of *dorsal roots* of the *spinal nerves*—1 pair for each bony vertebra—and sends out motor commands via the 36 pairs of *ventral roots* (fig. 3.2-2). The corresponding input and output for the brain are 12 pairs of *cranial nerves*. They may be sensory, motor, or mixed. In addition to the flow of information into and out of the brain and spinal cord, there is an abundant two-way communication between the brain and the spinal cord.

Spinal cord. In the spinal cord, the *white matter* (myelin of axons) is superficial and the *gray matter* (cell bodies and dendrites) is deep (fig. 3.2-2). Cell bodies of sensory neurons are located in the dorsal root ganglion. Their sensory axons enter the spinal cord and join (or innervate interneurons which join) an ascending sensory tract (either the *dorsal columns,* the *lateral* or *ventral spinothalamic tracts,* or the *spinocerebellar tracts*). Other branches of the sensory axons make *ipsilateral* (same side) or, via interneurons, *contralateral* (opposite side) reflexive connections at the same level. The spinal cord is thus composed both of axons which either ascend or descend in tracts for great distances and of local segmental circuitry (fig. 3.2-3).

Peripheral nervous system. The peripheral nervous system (PNS) includes all of those neurons or portions of neurons outside the brain or spinal cord. The autonomic nervous system (ANS) division of the PNS involves motor outflow to glands and to cardiac and smooth muscle. The anatomy of the ANS is complex. But for our purposes, we only need to mention that it is divided into outflow from the *brainstem* and *sacral* region of the spinal cord (parasympathetic), and outflow from the *thoracic* and *lumbar* (sympathetic) regions of the spinal cord (see fig. 5.2-1, page 139).

Terminology. Body Directions. Examine figure 3.2-4 in order to clarify the meaning of anatomical terms which designate *body directions*: *rostral* (head, *cephalic*) vs. *caudal* (tail); dorsal vs. ventral (*basal*); and medial vs. lateral. For primates which walk erect, anterior means ventral and posterior means dorsal. *Afferent* refers to inflow and *efferent* to outflow from a structure. If the structure is the brain or spinal cord then afferent is equivalent to sensory, and efferent to motor. *Centripetal* means toward a structure and *centrifugal* means away from a reference structure, such as the brain. *Ipsilateral* means on the same side and *contralateral* (crossed) means on the opposite side of the body, brain, or spinal cord.

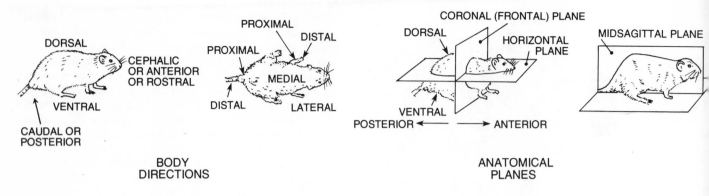

Fig. 3.2-4. Terms describing position and location in reference to the axes of the body (not the brain). A *cross section* or *transverse* section is perpendicular to the longitudinal axis of the spinal cord or brain, not the body. (Adapted from R. F. Thompson, 1975. *Introduction to Physiological Psychology*. Harper & Row, New York.)

Neuroanatomical terms. In the PNS a collection of axons which runs together in a bundle is called a *nerve*. (A single axon or fiber is not a nerve.) In the CNS a bundle of axons is usually called a *tract*, but may also be termed a *fasciculus, funiculus, column, lemniscus, peduncle,* or *brachium*! In the best of situations a specific tract is named by its origin and destination, e.g., spinothalamic tract. But, often a tract is named for the individual who found it, or by the florid imagination of a nineteenth-century neuroanatomist. A tract which crosses between the right and left sides is usually called a *commissure*, e.g., *anterior* and *posterior commissures*, a *decussation* (*pyramidal*) or *chiasm* (*optic*), but may have its own special name, e.g., *corpus callosum*. Cell bodies grouped together are called *ganglia* in the PNS and *nuclei* (and sometimes ganglia) in the CNS.

Dissecting Procedure

Brains examined in teaching laboratories are often preserved or "fixed" in 4% formaldehyde (100% formalin = 37% formaldehyde). If your hands are irritated by the preservative or you wish to retain a sensitive touch in your fingertips for the next several days following the exercise, you may elect to wear surgical gloves. A cheesecloth sack, plastic bag, or brain jar in which the labeled specimen can be kept between laboratory periods will be provided.

An orangewood manicure stick is the most valuable dissecting instrument. Do not contaminate good dissecting tools with preservatives. Even after thoroughly rinsing the tools, they might prove toxic in subsequent dissections of live material.

Some damage will inevitably occur when the brain is extracted from the skull. If your specimen has particularly well-preserved *meninges* or cranial nerves, point these out to your laboratory associates whose specimens may be less than perfect.

Make the initial dissection on the left side of the brain. The right half will be kept intact and later sectioned for examination of internal structures. Keep the specimen wet with tap water. Browning is a sign of drying which will make observation and dissection more difficult. Wet paper towels or cheesecloth should be used during the laboratory period to protect portions of the brain not being examined.

If you cannot locate a structure because of damage to your sheep brain or for some other reason, check with other students in the laboratory. Make this an *interactive* laboratory experience in which you debate and discuss the location and function of various structures.

Surface Examination

Brain membranes

Examine your specimen for brain membranes (the *meninges: dura mater, arachnoid, pia mater*), and study their structure. The dura is a tough, opaque, leathery membrane, and the pia is a thin tunic which closely adheres to the brain surface, following, for example, all of the cortical convolutions (fig. 3.2-5).

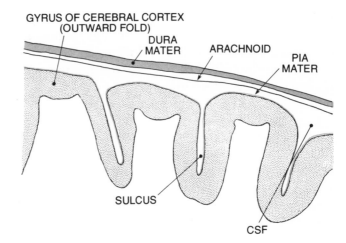

Fig. 3.2-5. A segment of convoluted cerebral cortex showing the three meningeal membranes: dura mater (*colored*), arachnoid, and pia mater (*colored*). The pia follows the cortical fissures (*sulci*). Cerebrospinal fluid (*CSF*) is found between the pia and the arachnoid layers.

Cerebrospinal fluid (CSF) and blood supply

The spinal cord has a narrow, CSF-filled central canal (fig. 3.2-2) which widens out inside the *brainstem* under the *cerebellum* to form the *IVth ventricle* (see fig. 3.2-8), narrows, then widens again in the *diencephalon* to form the *IIIrd ventricle* (see fig. 3.2-9), and spreads laterally into the *left* and *right cerebral hemispheres* to form the *Ist* and *IInd*, or *lateral ventricles*. The CSF is a clear fluid continuously exuded by specialized capillary tufts (*choroid plexus*) in the ventricles. (Plexus means network.) The internal CSF escapes from the ventricles through three small holes in the roof of the IVth ventricle and flows into the region surrounding the brain where CSF is reabsorbed by venous sinuses associated with the dura. (A *sinus* is a venous dilation, often thin-walled.) There is considerable reverse seepage from venous sinus fluid back to the CSF.

Arterial blood is supplied to the brain by several large arteries. (Sheep lack internal carotid arteries.) The *basilar artery* feeds an arterial confluence called the *circle of Willis* on the ventral surface of the brain. This collection of anastomosed vessels provides collateral circulation in the event of blockage on one side. Several veins form a brain drain into major sinuses sandwiched between layers of the dura. Examine your specimen and compare it with figure 3.2-6B to find all or part of the circle of Willis.

The *sella turcica* is part of a fibrous bony plate at the base of the brain which cradles and protects the large *pituitary* gland (*hypophysis*) (fig. 3.2-1) and hides the circle of Willis. Use a lateral approach to

remove the sella turcica if it is present on your sheep brain. Try to avoid damaging cranial nerves II–VIII (fig. 3.2-6). Bisect the pituitary and observe the difference between the anterior and posterior portions.

As a practical matter, during brain surgery on the rat in experiments in this manual, the vessels most likely to be encountered are (1) the *superior sagittal sinus* which sits astride the division between the two cerebral hemispheres and, at its caudal limit, joins (2) the left-right *transverse sinus* that lies under the anterior margin of the occipital bone, between the cerebellum and cerebrum, and (3) the numerous small vessels on the surface of the brain. Imagine that you are going to lower an electrode into the depths of the brain. You would have to cut the skin, drill a hole in the skull, and avoid sinuses near the brain as you lower the electrode. Fragile electrodes require cutting a small hole through all the meningeal membranes.

Cerebral and cerebellar cortex

Examine the upper external surface of the sheep brain. Note the *gyri* (ridges) and the *sulci* (fissures) of the cerebral cortex and the smaller convolutions of the cerebellar cortex. Identify the major structures labeled in figure 3.2-7. Defer examination of the cranial nerves. Use a scalpel to cut off a slice about 1 cm thick from the posterior pole of the left cerebral cortex and a similar slice from the left lateral border of the cerebellum. Compare the cut surfaces and observe the relation of the gray matter to the underlying white matter of the cortex.

Cranial nerves

All 12 pairs of cranial nerves pass through *foramina* (holes) at the base of the skull and all, except the Xth and XIth, are exclusively distributed to structures of the head and neck. Refer to figures 3.2-6 and 3.2-7 to identify the roots of the cranial nerves on your specimen. The cranial nerves with some of their important origins and terminations are listed next.

Olfactory nerve (Nerve I). This nerve will not be visible. The axons originate from receptors in the olfactory mucosa, make their way in bundles through holes in the cribriform plate of the skull, and enter the olfactory bulb at the base of the brain.

Optic nerve (II). Composed of axons of retinal ganglion cells. The optic nerves cross at the anterior end of the diencephalon, forming the optic chiasm. Beyond the chiasm, these fibers are referred to as the optic tracts.

Oculomotor nerve (III). This motor nerve arises from the midbrain near the midventral line. It innervates the inferior oblique muscle, and the inferior, medial, and superior rectus muscles of the eye.

Trochlear nerve (IV). This motor nerve emerges from the dorsal surface of the midbrain and then courses laterally and ventrally along the outer edge of the pons. It innervates the superior oblique muscle of the eye.

Trigeminal nerve (V). A thick mixed nerve (sensory and motor) that divides into three major trunks, the ophthalmic, maxillary, and mandibular nerves, which supply many head muscles, the teeth, and the skin of the head. The excruciating facial pains of trigeminal neuralgia may be caused by pressure on the root of the Vth nerve.

Abducens nerve (VI). This motor nerve arises from the *trapezoid body*. It innervates the lateral rectus muscle of the eye.

Facial nerve (VII). This mixed nerve arises at the junction of the pons and medulla caudal to the trigeminal nerve, and lateral to the trapezoid body. It supplies several head and facial muscles and many taste receptors of the tongue.

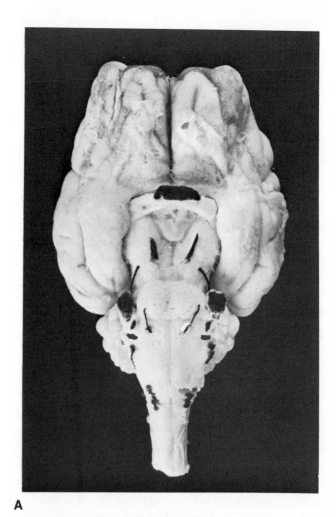

A

Fig. 3.2-6. A. Photograph of the ventral surface of the sheep brain. **B.** Line drawing of photograph. Cranial nerves II–XII *black* in *A, colored* in *B*.

54

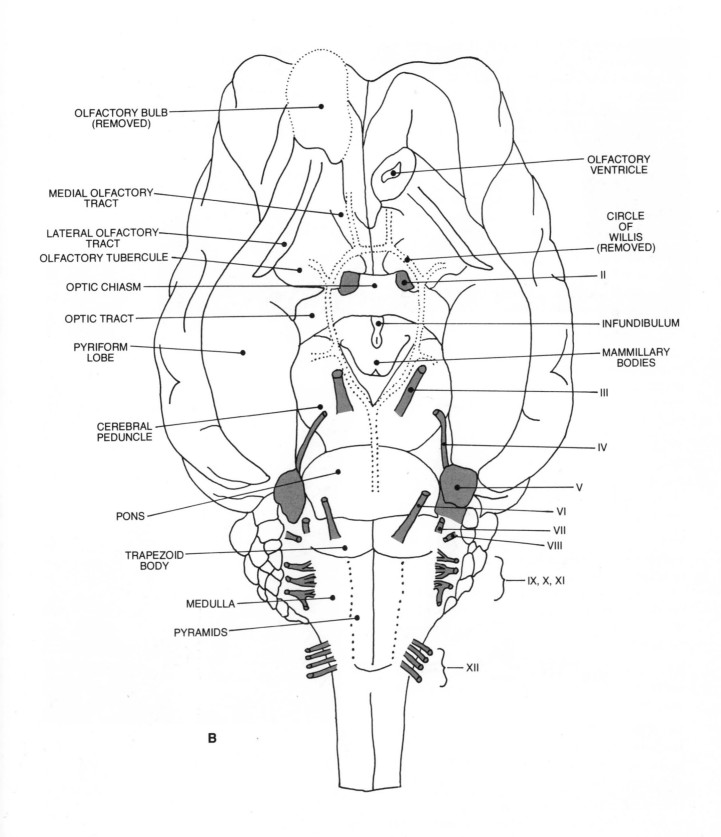

OLFACTORY BULB (REMOVED)

OLFACTORY VENTRICLE

MEDIAL OLFACTORY TRACT

CIRCLE OF WILLIS (REMOVED)

LATERAL OLFACTORY TRACT

OLFACTORY TUBERCULE

II

OPTIC CHIASM

OPTIC TRACT

INFUNDIBULUM

PYRIFORM LOBE

MAMMILLARY BODIES

III

CEREBRAL PEDUNCLE

IV

V

PONS

VI

VII

TRAPEZOID BODY

VIII

IX, X, XI

MEDULLA

PYRAMIDS

XII

B

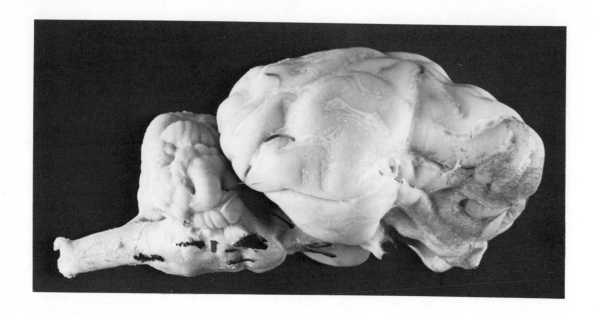

A

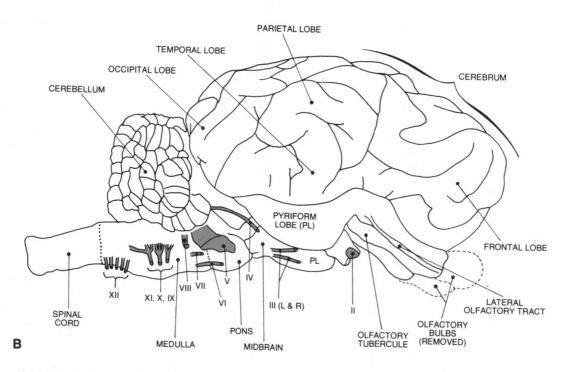

B

Fig. 3.2-7. A. Photograph and **B.** line drawing of the right side of the sheep brain. II–XII are cranial nerves. *Dotted lines* indicate divisions between spinal cord, medulla, and pons.

Statoacoustic nerve (VIII).   This sensory nerve arises just caudal to the facial nerve. It contains axons from *both* the vestibular and auditory organs of the inner ear.

Glossopharyngeal nerve (IX).   This mixed nerve arises from the medulla as a series of rootlets just behind the auditory nerve. It emerges from the jugular foramen of the skull and innervates the stylopharyngeus muscle, tongue mucosa, and taste buds.

Vagus nerve (X).   This mixed nerve also arises as a series of rootlets caudal to the origin of the IXth. It emerges through the jugular foramen and passes down to most of the thoracic and abdominal viscera. The vagus is the major parasympathetic outflow from the brain.

Spinal accessory nerve (XI).   This motor nerve arises as a series of rootlets from the side of both the medulla and the spinal cord, passing out of the skull through the jugular foramen with the IXth and Xth nerves. It innervates some muscles of the neck, shoulder, pharynx, and larynx.

Hypoglossal nerve (XII).   This motor nerve arises from the ventral surface of the medulla and innervates the muscles of the tongue.

Brainstem

The cerebellum is attached to the brainstem by three *cerebellar peduncles* (stalks or tracts) on each side. Cut through the peduncles as high up as possible, cutting into the substance of the cerebellum to avoid the structures of the medulla. Do not injure the delicate membranes beneath the cerebellum which form the roof of the IVth ventricle. Remove the cerebellar hemispheres.

Next, remove the membranous roof of the IVth ventricle to examine the dorsal surface of the medulla. Refer to figure 3.2-8A. Cranial nerves III–XII terminate or originate in *brainstem nuclei*. Some of the dorsal nuclei can be located by surface bulges in the floor of the IVth ventricle, e.g., the hypoglossal trigonum is the surface appearance of the XIIth nucleus. However, most cranial nerve nuclei lie buried within the brainstem and can only be seen in histological sections or projection drawings (fig. 3.2-8B). The anatomy of cranial nerve nuclei is complex; only the highlights are presented here. The *theory of*

nerve components may help you to organize the cranial nerve nuclei. Imagine sensory and motor "columns" projected from the spinal cord into the medulla. Motor nuclei tend to lie medial and ventral; sensory nuclei, lateral and dorsal. Sensory and motor nuclei can be subdivided into *visceral* (supplying gut and internal organs) and *somatic* (supplying skin and skeletal muscle) divisions (fig. 3.2-8C). Cranial nerve nuclei devoted to somatic function take up either an extreme medial (motor) or extreme lateral position (sensory), whereas nuclei with a visceral function have an intermediate position (both sensory and motor). Figure 3.2-8B is divided along the midline to indicate sensory nuclei on the left and motor nuclei on the right.

A simplified classification of cranial nerve components is:

Somatic motor column: III, IV, VI, XII. Note the deep *median sulcus* in the floor of the IVth ventricle. Just lateral is the slender *somatic motor column*. Superficial surface markings for the XIIth and VIth cranial nerve nuclei are visible: the *hypoglossal trigonum*, and the *facial colliculus* where the VIIth nerve passes over the nucleus of VI. The IIIrd and IVth cranial nerve nuclei in the midbrain (rostral to medulla) also belong to this column.

Visceral motor column: V, VII, X. These nuclei lie lateral to the somatic motor column and are too deep to be easily located by surface markings. The *limiting sulcus*, which can be seen laterally along the floor of the IVth ventricle, separates the medial motor columns from the lateral sensory columns.

Visceral sensory column: VII, IX, X. These nerves terminate in the *solitary nucleus* and mediate taste and other oral and pharyngeal functions.

Somatic sensory column: II, V, VIII. Many touch fibers from the skin of the trunk and limbs ascend to the brain in the *dorsal columns* (fasciculi) of the spinal cord. These first order fibers terminate (synapse) in nuclei which make visible enlargements on the dorsal surface of the medulla: the *gracile* and *cuneate nuclei*, which lie caudal to the lower end of the IVth ventricle (fig. 3.2-8A). The gracile nucleus (hindlimb touch fibers) lies most medial, and the cuneate nucleus (forelimb touch fibers) more lateral. Still more lateral is the caudal extension of the *spinal V (trigeminal) tract* and its nucleus. These three

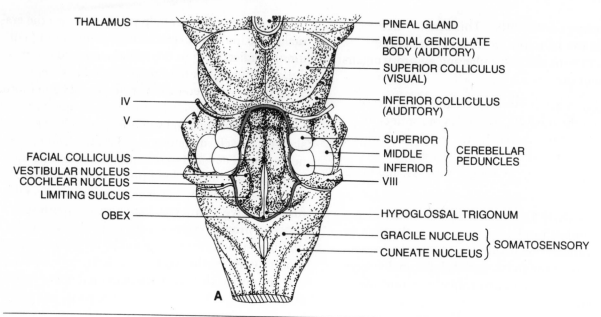

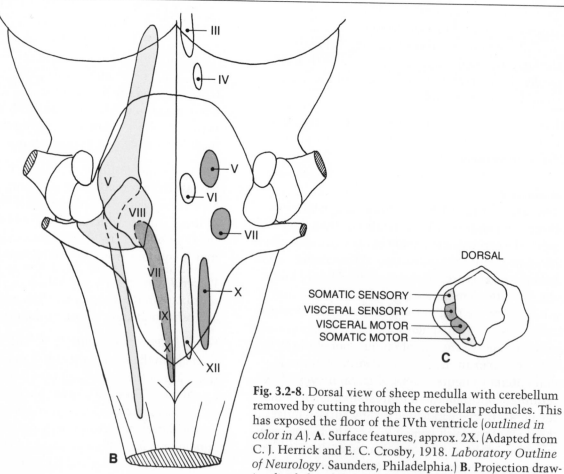

Fig. 3.2-8. Dorsal view of sheep medulla with cerebellum removed by cutting through the cerebellar peduncles. This has exposed the floor of the IVth ventricle (*outlined in color in A*). **A.** Surface features, approx. 2X. (Adapted from C. J. Herrick and E. C. Crosby, 1918. *Laboratory Outline of Neurology*. Saunders, Philadelphia.) **B.** Projection drawing divided to show major cranial nerve nuclei sensory, *on the left*, and motor *on the right*. Shading as in *C*, approx. 3X. **C.** Cross section through generalized medulla showing the mediolateral sequence of the positions of four basic classes of cranial nerve nuclei.

nuclei (cuneate, gracile, and spinal V) contain the preponderance of second order brainstem neurons (interneurons) responsive to stimulation of trunk, limb, and head skin. The *cochlear nucleus* (VIII) is a compact, crescent-shaped mass of gray matter encircling the *inferior cerebellar peduncle*, where the peduncle turns dorsally to enter the cerebellum. The *vestibular nucleus* (VIII) lies medial to the cochlear nucleus.

As you consolidate your grasp of the cranial nerve nuclei, realize that: (*a*) there are additional nuclei we have not mentioned; (*b*) there are *multiple* sensory (or motor) nuclei associated with some cranial nerves, e.g., nerve V has a *main sensory nucleus* and *spinal* and *mesencephalic nuclear extensions*; VIII has *dorsal* and *ventral cochlear nuclei*, plus vestibular nuclei with several divisions; (*c*) nerves V, VII, IX, and X have *both* sensory and motor nuclei; and (*d*) the nuclei visible as morphologically discrete clumps of cell bodies do not contain all of the sensory terminations of the primary afferents nor all of the cell bodies of the efferent fibers in cranial nerves. Techniques which trace degenerated or radio-labeled axons indicate many more terminations beyond those seen with routine staining procedures.

Midsagittal plane

Now cut out the entire brain of the sheep into right and left halves. A long, thin brain knife and cutting board are best suited to this purpose. The incision should pass through the *longitudinal fissure* between the cerebral hemispheres, downward through the *corpus callosum* in the floor of the fissure, and through the entire brainstem. *Cut smoothly and exactly in the median plane.* Cut by pulling the knife toward you with a continuous anterior-to-posterior sweep. Avoid pushing the blade straight down or sawing back and forth. The major parts of the brain are readily seen in midsagittal view: *telen*cephalon (cerebral hemispheres or *cerebrum*), *di*encephalon (thalamus and hypothalamus), *mes*encephalon (midbrain), *met*encephalon (pons and cerebellar hemispheres), and *myel*encephalon (medulla). Examine the left side of the brain to identify the median structures (fig. 3.2-9). Trace the ventricular boundaries from the IIIrd ventricle and the *interventricular foramen of Monro* (connecting canal to the lateral ventricles) to the central canal of the spinal cord (fig. 3.2-9*B*).

Note that the roof of the IIIrd ventricle is also a vascular (choroid) plexus extending from the *pineal body* to the interventricular foramen of Monro. The choroid plexus of the IIIrd ventricle continues through the interventricular foramen to become the choroid plexus of the lateral ventricles. This continuity can be seen where the *septum pellucidum* has been torn away; but do not attempt to expose it now. (The septum pellucidum is a semitransparent, membranous curtain separating the lateral ventricles. It should not be confused with the septal nuclei to be discussed later.) The choroid plexuses of the IIIrd and IVth ventricles form the true ventricular roof.

Identify the labeled structures in figure 3.2-9. Note (*a*) the regional designations: *thalamus, hypothalamus, midbrain, pons,* and *medulla*; (*b*) the commissures (fiber-tract cross connections between the two halves of the brain)—anterior, posterior, *habenular,* and corpus callosum; (*c*) *intermediate mass* of the *thalamus,* optic chiasm, *mammillary bodies, infundibulum* (= pituitary stalk); and (*d*) olfactory bulb, *cingulate gyrus, fornix.*

Tract and Internal Dissections

Association tracts

The arrangement of fibers, which comprise the white matter of the cortex, can be examined by carefully teasing the gray matter away. The dissections on the left hemisphere in this section should *not* be carried further than indicated. Use an orangewood manicure stick with a gentle stroking motion to clear gray matter from underlying white matter. Keep the brain moist while dissecting. Store the right half of the brain in moistened towels or cloth.

Intracortical association fibers. Select a region along the upper border of the median surface of the left hemisphere. Scrape away the gray matter covering two adjacent gyri to reveal the short associational (arcuate) fibers interconnecting these gyri. There are similar fibers which lie deeper in the white matter and interconnect more remote gyri. *For subsequent dissections refer to figure 3.2-10.*

Cingulum (c). The cingulum (a structure involved with emotional behavior) is a long association tract

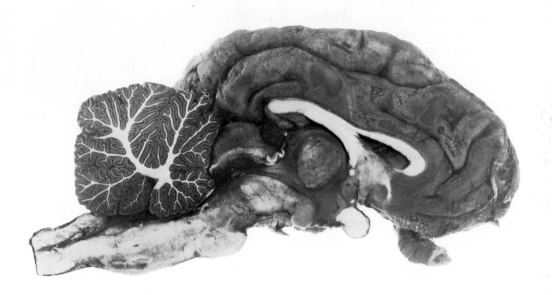

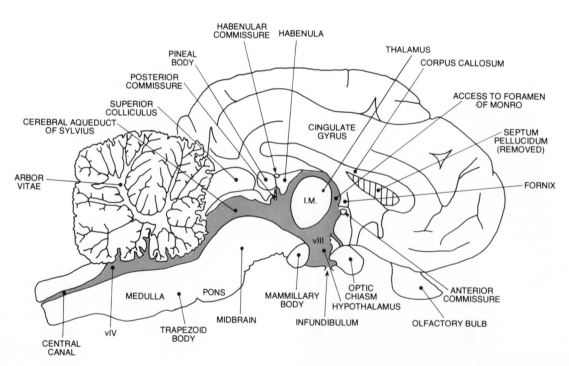

Fig. 3.2-9. Midsagittal section of the sheep brain. *I.M.* intermediate mass of the thalamus. The IIIrd ventricle (*vIII*), and the IVth ventricle (*vIV*), and cerebral aqueduct are *colored*.

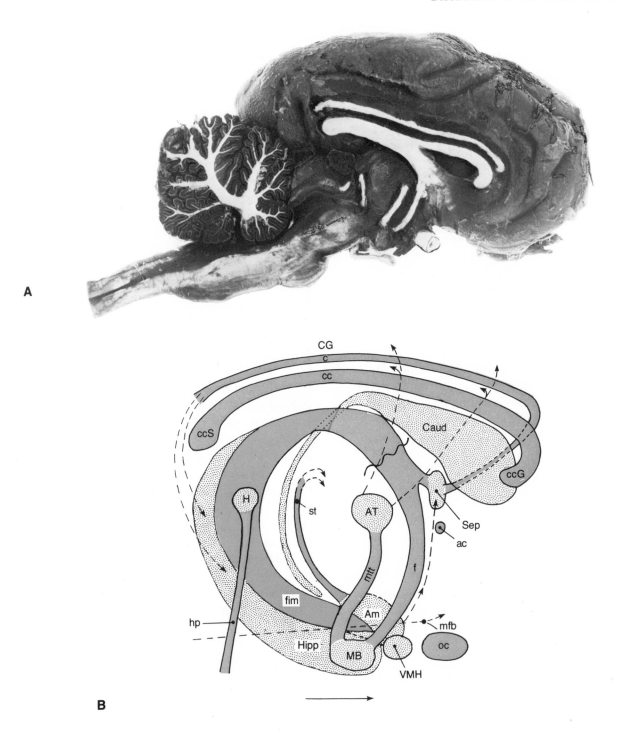

A

B

Fig. 3.2-10. A. Median surface of the brain dissected and stained to reveal portions of the following tracts: cingulum, fornix, mammillothalamic tract, and habenulo-interpeduncular tract. **B.** Expanded drawing of the tract region, including more laterally situated structures (*in gray*). All structures close to the median plane are shown *in color*. Nuclei are *stippled*; tracts are *shaded*. Diffuse tracts not evident in gross morphology are indicated by *dashed lines*. *Arrows* indicate the direction of the major projections. Fiber tracts are abbreviated with lowercase letters. *Am*, amygdala; *ac*, anterior commissure; *AT*, anterior nucleus of the thalamus; *Caud*, caudate nucleus; *c*, cingulum; *cc*, corpus callosum; *ccG*, genu of the corpus callosum; *ccS*, splenium of the corpus callosum; *CG*, cingulate gyrus; *f*, fornix; *fim*, fimbria of the hippocampus; *H*, habenula; *hp*, habenulointerpeduncular tract; *Hipp*, hippocampus; *MB*, mammillary body; *mfb*, medial forebrain bundle; *mtt*, mammillothalamic tract; *oc*, optic chiasm; *Sep*, septal nuclei; *st*, stria terminalis; *VMH*, ventromedial nucleus of the hypothalamus.

close to the median cortical surface. It lies in the cingulate gyrus (CG) and in midcourse runs parallel to the dorsal surface of the corpus callosum. Begin the dissection above the corpus callosum, and follow the cingulum in both anterior and posterior directions as in figure 3.2-10A.

Corpus callosum (cc). These fibers interconnect the folded cortex of the two hemispheres. Tease out a small portion of the callosal fibers toward their cortical terminations. These fibers run at *right angles* to those of the cingulum.

Additional tracts

Tracts are often named by hyphenated words indicating their origin (first word) and the site of termination (second word).

Mammillothalamic tract (mtt) (or tract of Vicq d'Azyr). This tract runs from the *mammillary body* (MB) forward and dorsally to the anterior nucleus of the thalamus. Expose it by scraping off the surface layer of the IIIrd ventricle starting in the vicinity of the mammillary body (fig. 3.2-10).

Fornix (f). This tract, the outflow of the *hippocampus*, should be dissected from the level of the anterior commissure ventrally to the mammillary bodies, where it terminates in the hypothalamus.

Habenulointerpeduncular tract (hp) (or *fasciculus retroflexus*). Dissection of this tract is more difficult than dissecting the mammillothalamic tract or the fornix. The habenulointerpeduncular tract runs from the habenula to the interpeduncular nucleus located near the root of nerve III (see figs. 3.2-16 and 3.2-17).

Dissection of the posterior horn of the lateral ventricle

Remove the septum pellucidum and note the large pear-shaped *caudate nucleus* (Caud) in the rostral portion of the now exposed lateral ventricle. Slice horizontally with a large scalpel to remove several thin slabs of the left cerebral hemisphere. Note the extraordinary depth of the sulci and the increase in the amount of white matter, including the vertically projecting *coronal radiations*. Continue removing slices down to the level of the corpus callosum. Make very thin slices as you near this structure, so that you do not cut deeply into the lateral ventricle.

Perhaps you can see the transverse fibers of the corpus callosum. Hold the scalpel vertically and cut through the corpus callosum from the genu to the splenium along a longitudinal path 4 mm lateral to the midline. Remove the 4 mm strip of corpus callosum.

The lateral ventricle has an *anterior* and a *posterior horn*. Look down into the recesses of the posterior horn and locate the choroid plexus lying on the surface of the fimbria of the hippocampus. The *fimbria* (fim) is a fibrous fringe of hippocampal axons which coalesce into the fornix, which is visible from the median surface.

The *hippocampus* (Hipp) and the caudate nucleus are two prominent C-shaped structures in the brain. The impact of this statement will be dramatically apparent as you work downward into the posterior horn of the lateral ventricle. The hippocampus not only extends laterally, but hooks around, heads back anteriorly, and terminates far ventrally in the pyriform lobe within 2 mm of the external brain surface. It is really a buried cortical convolution rolled into the wall of the lateral ventricle. Look down into the posterior horn and remove the cerebrum overlying the ventricle and hippocampus by cutting out wedge-shaped pieces of the cortex. Avoid cutting into the ventricle's rostral face where the tail of the caudate nucleus approaches the *amygdala* (Am). Examine the surface of the hippocampus. It is covered by a superficial layer of fibers—the *alveus* which connects medially with the fornix. Continue to remove wedges of cortex following the curvature of the posterior horn laterally and rostro-ventrally where the hippocampus and caudate nucleus terminate in the *pyriform lobe* of the cerebral cortex. Part of the amygdala (a group of nuclei) is visible as a ball-like structure protruding into the lateral ventricle deep within the pyriform lobe. The tail of the caudate nucleus ends here.

After exposing the terminal portion of the hippocampus in the pyriform lobe, cut through the fornix at the level indicated by the wavy line (~) in figure 3.2-10B. If you gently shift the loose hippocampus back and forth you can see the fimbria fitting like a cap over the protruding *pulvinar* and *lateral geniculate body* of the thalamus. Remove the hippocampus and associated structures and examine its medial surface. Note the slender *dentate gyrus* between the fimbria and the hippocampus proper.

Clean the thalamus of *choroid tela* material using forceps. The thalamus is the largest structure in the diencephalon. The lateral surface of the thalamus lies against the *internal capsule*, an enormous fiber tract uniting the cerebrum with the brainstem. The left and right thalami are oval masses of gray matter which diverge caudally and fuse anteriorly. The lateral surface of the thalamus is separated from the caudate nucleus by a groove containing the *stria terminalis*—a band of axons which course from the amygdala to the hypothalamus and other structures. Find the groove lateral to the head of the caudate and follow it a short distance ventrally. If you tease with the orangewood stick and remove a thin wedge-shaped scalpel nick from the groove area, you may be able to discover both the stria terminalis and the tail of the caudate.

Several of the structures and pathways which you have just examined are linked together to form the *Papez circuit* of the *limbic system* which plays a role in emotional behavior. Consider figure 3.2-10*B* and note the following circuit: hippocampus to fornix to mammillary bodies to mammillothalamic tract to anterior nucleus of the thalamus to cingulate gyrus to cingulum to hippocampus. (In addition to Papez's circuit there are many other interconnections and projections—a few of which are outlined here and indicated in figure 3.2-10*B*.) The fornix projects to the septal nuclei, which in turn project to the cingulum. The septal nuclei receive additional projections from the *medial forebrain bundle*. Many of these structures are involved in fight or flight reactions. Electrical stimulation of these structures is frequently positively reinforcing; that is, animals will work to receive brain stimulation.

You have now examined or considered: gross *surface features*, the 12 *cranial nerves*, the brainstem *cranial nerve nuclei* III–XII, and the *median plane*

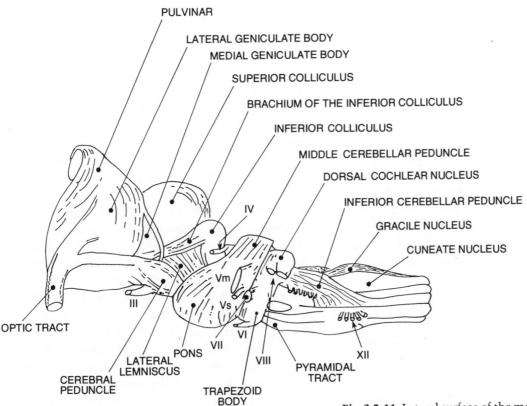

PULVINAR
LATERAL GENICULATE BODY
MEDIAL GENICULATE BODY
SUPERIOR COLLICULUS
BRACHIUM OF THE INFERIOR COLLICULUS
INFERIOR COLLICULUS
MIDDLE CEREBELLAR PEDUNCLE
DORSAL COCHLEAR NUCLEUS
INFERIOR CEREBELLAR PEDUNCLE
GRACILE NUCLEUS
CUNEATE NUCLEUS
IV
Vm
Vs
III
OPTIC TRACT
LATERAL
LEMNISCUS
CEREBRAL
PEDUNCLE
PONS
VII
VI
VIII
TRAPEZOID
BODY
PYRAMIDAL
TRACT
XII

Fig. 3.2-11. Lateral surface of the medulla, pons, midbrain, and caudal diencephalon. *Vm.* motor root of trigeminal nerve; *Vs.* sensory root of trigeminal nerve; III–XII are cranial nerves. (Adapted from C. J. Herrick and E. C. Crosby, 1918. *Laboratory Outline of Neurology*. Saunders, Philadelphia.)

including easily dissected major tracts, part of the limbic system, and the structures associated with the posterior horn of the lateral ventricle. We will now turn to the olfactory, optic, and auditory systems, and then briefly consider some remaining aspects of the brainstem.

Olfactory System

Axons of the olfactory receptors terminate in the olfactory bulb. Axons of second-order neurons leave the olfactory bulb as the medial and lateral olfactory tracts which terminate in the pyriform cortex and basal parts of the cerebral hemispheres (figs. 3.2-6 and 3.2-7).

Locate the beginning of the anterior horn of the lateral ventricle. With a scalpel slice off the overlying cerebrum and carefully follow the groove between the head of the caudate nucleus and the internal capsule forward and down into the interior of the olfactory bulb. The sheep's lateral ventricles (vI and vII) are continuous with an olfactory ventricle (vO) (see fig. 3.2-6).

Expose the brainstem and diencephalon by cutting off the remnants of the cerebrum rostral to the anterior commissure. Refer to figure 3.2-11.

Optic System

Follow the *optic tract* from the optic chiasm to the pulvinar and lateral geniculate bodies of the thalamus. (Visual fibers from the lateral geniculate body project to the occipital [visual] cortex.) Some fibers can be traced to the *superior colliculus* (the *optic tectum* of lower vertebrates). Identify the pulvinar, lateral and medial geniculate bodies, and *inferior* and superior colliculi on the lateral surface of the thalamus and midbrain (fig. 3.2-11).

Auditory System

The neuroanatomy of the *medullary* and *pontine auditory centers* is complex. Viewing the brainstem, find the *lateral lemniscus* which innervates the next higher center, the inferior colliculus (midbrain auditory reflex center). Note the *medial geniculate body* (*thalamic auditory projection*) and the interconnecting *brachium of the inferior colliculus*.

Connections with the Cerebellum

The cerebellar gray and white matter has the appearance of an *arbor vitae* ("living tree") when seen in the median plane (fig. 3.2-9). Three *cerebellar peduncles* attach the cerebellum to the brainstem. Examine the cut surfaces of the cerebellar peduncles on the dorsal medulla and separate the three peduncular bundles with the orangewood stick. Expose the *inferior peduncle* by removing the dorsal cochlear nucleus (second-order auditory neurons) (fig. 3.2-8). Tease out the fibers of the inferior peduncle downward along the dorsolateral border of the medulla as they cross the spinal V tract superficially to descend into the spinal cord where they are called the dorsal spinocerebellar tract (fig. 3.2-3). Dissect the *middle peduncle fibers* which wrap around the ventral portion of the pons. The *superior peduncle* decussates in the midbrain beneath the superior colliculus. It is more difficult to dissect; do not attempt it.

Pyramidal Tract

Locate the *pyramid* on the ventral surface just caudal to the pons and trapezoid body (fig. 3.2-6). The longitudinal pyramidal fibers run from the motor cortex to the ventral horn cells of the spinal cord. The pyramidal fibers lie just dorsal to the pontine fibers and can be revealed by stripping the fibers of the pons back slightly at the cut median surface of the brain. The fibers of the pyramidal tract and trapezoid body interdigitate. Tease apart the trapezoid body as you carefully follow the pyramidal tract spinalward as far as the pyramidal decussation. This decussation (crossover) is the anatomical explanation for the fact that the left motor cortex controls movements of the right half of the body, and vice versa. (The name pyramidal tract comes from the triangular or pyramidal appearance in cross section of the tract, not from the pyramidal neurons of the motor cortex, which contribute only a few percent of the axons in the pyramidal tract.) The pyramidal tract is the caudal extension of the *cerebral peduncle*. The cerebral peduncles contain many fibers, originating in the cortex, which project to the pons, medulla, and spinal cord. Put aside all remnants of the left half of the brain and prepare the right half of the brain for examination.

Sectioning

To complete the study of the sheep brain, you will cut the right hemisphere into six cross-sectional slabs, which can then be stained by the Prussian blue procedure. Examine the median surface (fig. 3.2-9) and relocate the anterior commissure, optic chiasm, intermediate mass of the thalamus, mammillary bodies, habenular commissure, posterior commissure, root of nerve III, splenium of the corpus callosum, superior colliculus, and pons. These structures will be used as landmarks for making cross sections. Each figure of a stained cross section (figs. 3.2-12 to 3.2-17) has two insets showing the plane of the section. Use the landmarks listed next to determine the plane of the section through the right hemisphere.

Now, use a large brain knife in the manner previously indicated to make cross sections which pass through the following locations and structures. (Hold the brain and slabs firmly in place until all cross sections are made.)

Section 1 (fig. 3.2-12) Anterior commissure and anterior portion of the optic chiasm

Section 2 (fig. 3.2-13) Posterior margin of the optic chiasm and anterior portion of the intermediate mass of the thalamus

Section 3 (fig. 3.2-14) Anterior portion of the mammillary bodies and just anterior to the habenular commissure

Section 4 (fig. 3.2-15) Posterior commissure and just posterior to the mammillary bodies

Section 5 (fig. 3.2-16) Root of cranial nerve III and just posterior to the splenium of the corpus callosum

Section 6 (fig. 3.2-17) Midsuperior colliculus and just anterior to the pons
The sections in figures 3.2-12 to 3.2-17 correspond approximately to sections S-4, 7, 8, 9, 10, and 11, respectively, of Yoshikawa (1968).

Each cut, of course, produces two faces. Because these slabs have some depth, the two faces will not appear identical in all respects. When a cut is made, the face connected to the rostral portion of the brain will be called the *posteriorly directed face*. Turn all slabs with the posteriorly directed face up. Arrange them in serial order in a tray of distilled water. Trim

the first slab to approximately the same thickness as the others. If the Prussian blue staining method is to be carried out, the instructor will now arrange to stain your sections before you examine them in detail.

Compare the brain slabs with the photographs and drawings provided and identify all named structures (figs. 3.2-12 to 3.2-17).

Your sections will not be cut in precisely the same planes as those in figures 3.2-12 to 3.2-17. However, you can capitalize on the inevitable differences between the right and left sides of the figures to make a better match to each slab. Note that there may be a difference in the anterior-posterior tilt of your slab and the corresponding figure. As you examine figures 3.2-12 to 3.2-18 and your own sections of the sheep brain, note the following regions not yet discussed which relate to sleep, wakefulness, and arousal: the *mesencephalic reticular formation*, and the *raphe nuclei* (serotonin-containing neurons). Note also several structures concerned with motor function: *globus pallidus*, *putamen* (the *corpus striatum* consists of the globus pallidus, putamen, and caudate nucleus), *red nucleus*, *medial longitudinal fasciculus*, and the *substantia nigra*. The nigrostriatal pathway (substantia nigra to corpus striatum) is a dopaminergic pathway projecting through the median forebrain bundle. Its impairment produces in the corpus striatum a dopamine deficiency which underlies Parkinson's disease.

If time permits review the salient points of the dissection guide.

Pitfalls and Suggestions

1. It is of great value to "work one's way" through a series of microscope slides of the brain from the medulla to the thalamus, preferably with some slides stained for cell bodies and others for fibers. In the absence of such slides a study of a series of plates in one or two good stereotaxic atlases can be quite informative (e.g., König and Klippel, 1963, for the rat). In this fashion you will develop a picture of the internal tract and nuclear arrangements, difficult or impossible to discern in gross dissection. Some useful references on neuroanatomy are provided on pages 48 and 74. Further references to stereotaxic atlases are located at the end of chapter 9.
2. Clean the scalpel handle and the laboratory tables

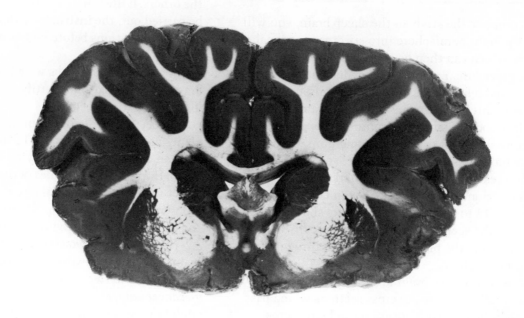

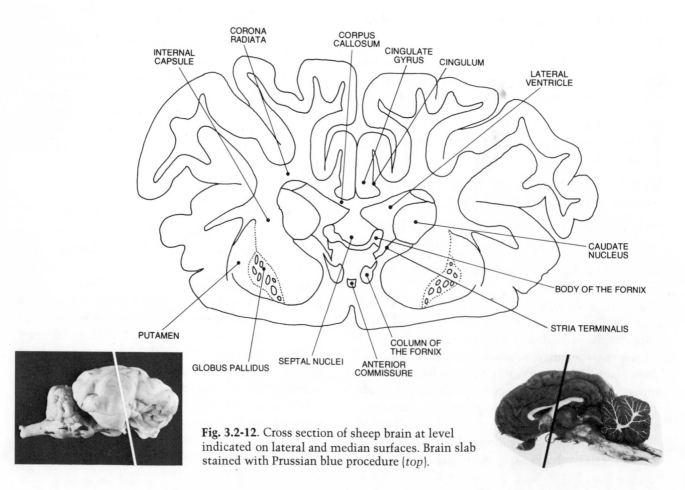

INTERNAL CAPSULE

CORONA RADIATA

CORPUS CALLOSUM

CINGULATE GYRUS

CINGULUM

LATERAL VENTRICLE

CAUDATE NUCLEUS

BODY OF THE FORNIX

STRIA TERMINALIS

PUTAMEN

GLOBUS PALLIDUS

SEPTAL NUCLEI

ANTERIOR COMMISSURE

COLUMN OF THE FORNIX

Fig. 3.2-12. Cross section of sheep brain at level indicated on lateral and median surfaces. Brain slab stained with Prussian blue procedure (*top*).

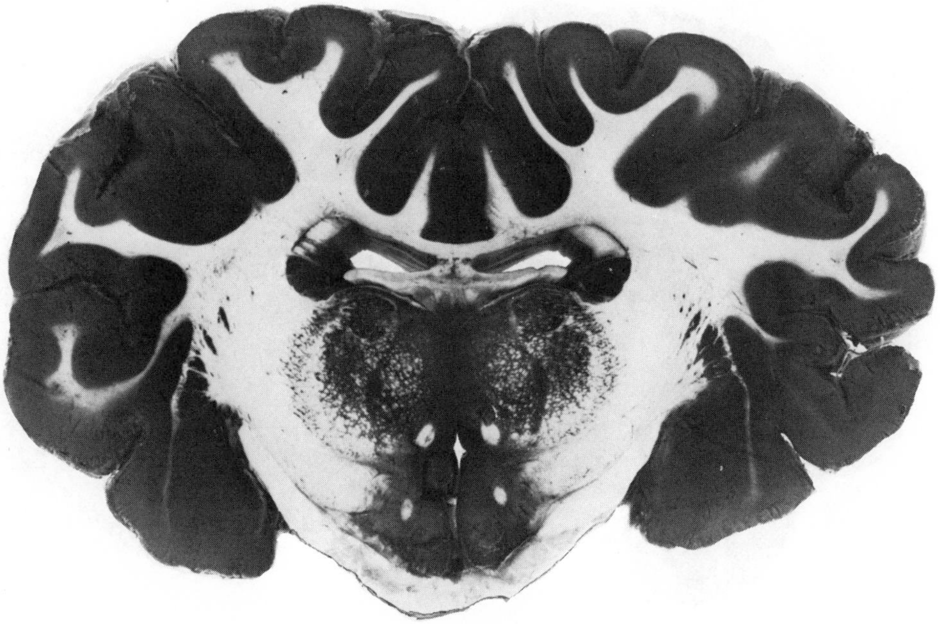

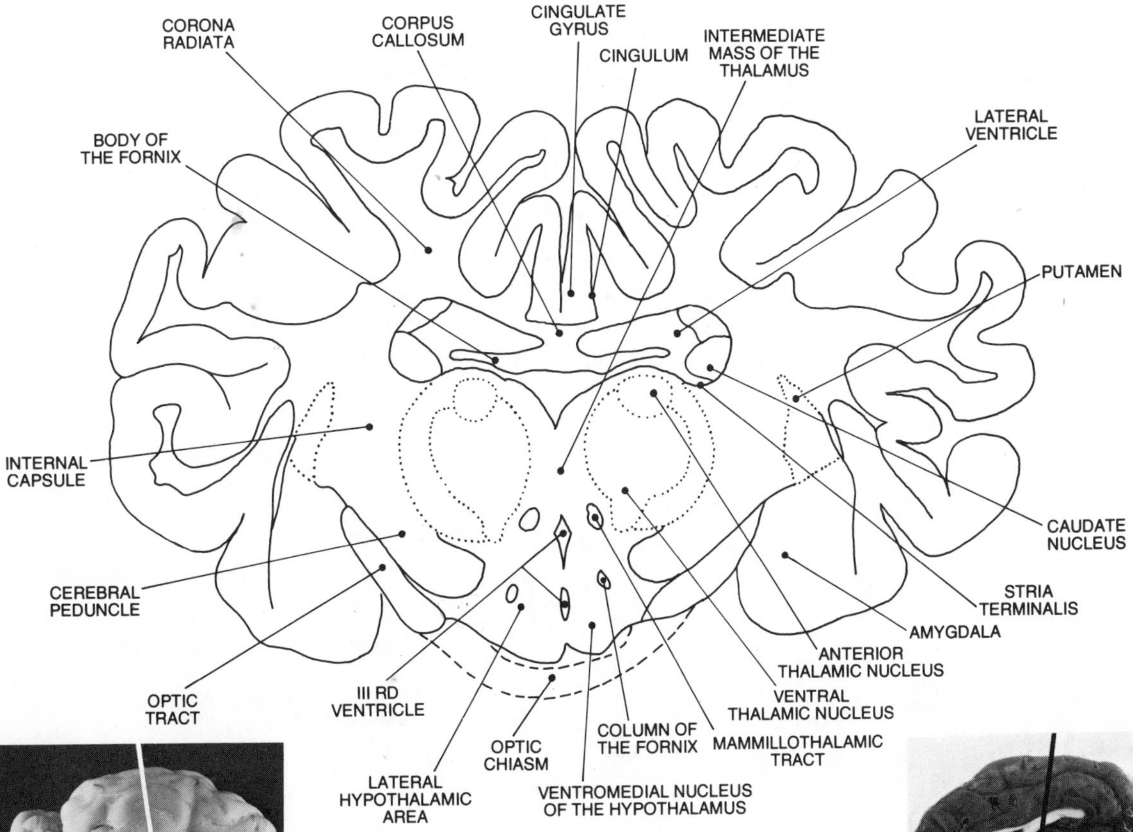
CORONA RADIATA
CORPUS CALLOSUM
CINGULATE GYRUS
CINGULUM
INTERMEDIATE MASS OF THE THALAMUS
LATERAL VENTRICLE
BODY OF THE FORNIX
PUTAMEN
INTERNAL CAPSULE
CAUDATE NUCLEUS
STRIA TERMINALIS
AMYGDALA
CEREBRAL PEDUNCLE
ANTERIOR THALAMIC NUCLEUS
VENTRAL THALAMIC NUCLEUS
OPTIC TRACT
III RD VENTRICLE
COLUMN OF THE FORNIX
MAMMILLOTHALAMIC TRACT
OPTIC CHIASM
LATERAL HYPOTHALAMIC AREA
VENTROMEDIAL NUCLEUS OF THE HYPOTHALAMUS

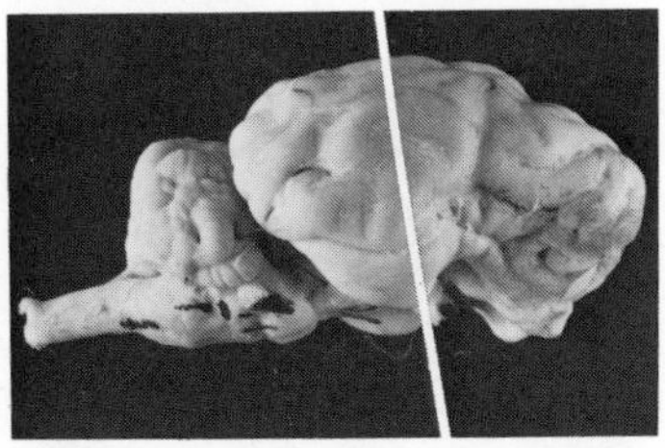

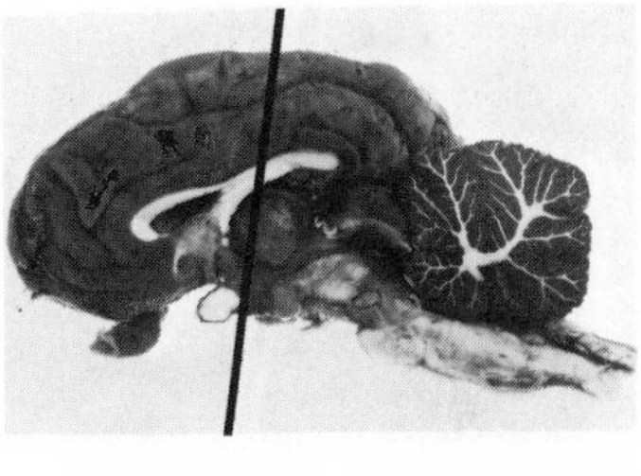

Fig. 3.2-13. Optic chiasm not in plane of section.

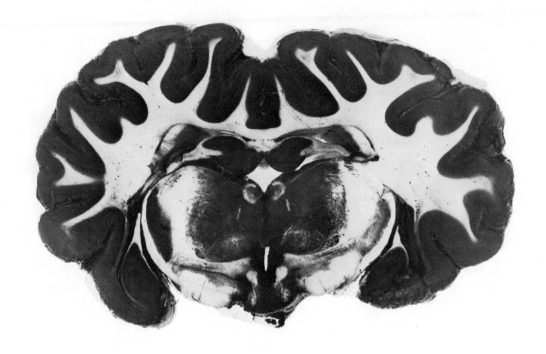

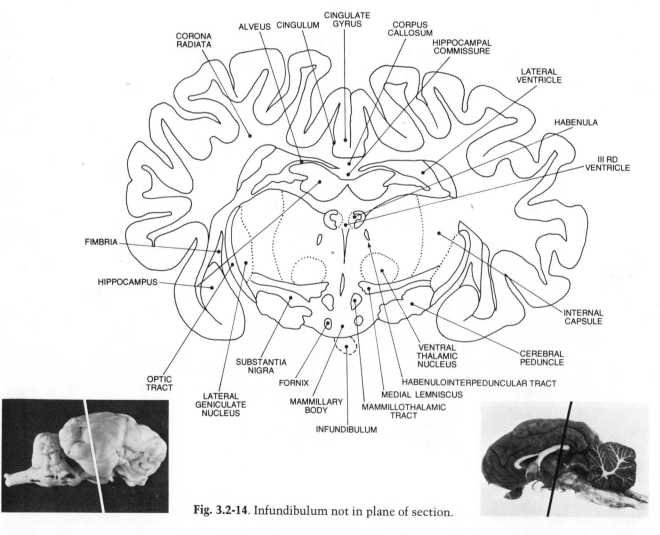

Fig. 3.2-14. Infundibulum not in plane of section.

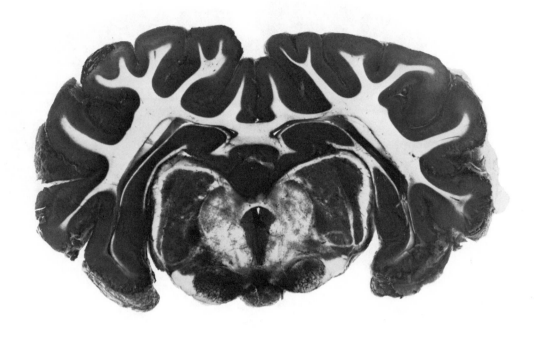

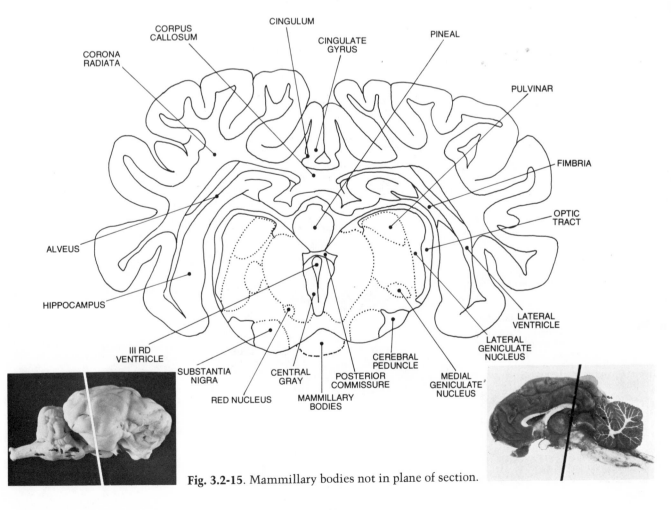

Fig. 3.2-15. Mammillary bodies not in plane of section.

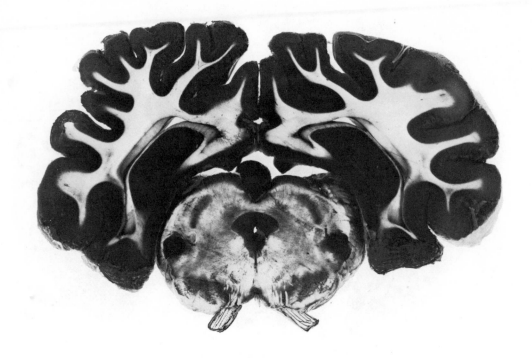

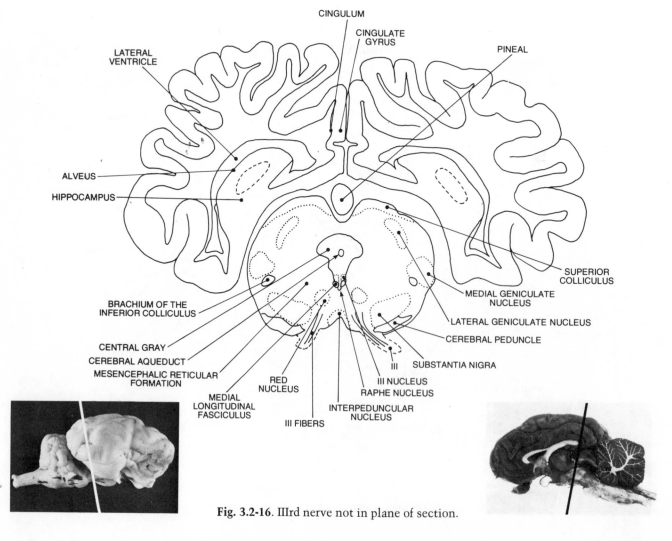

CINGULUM

CINGULATE
GYRUS

PINEAL

LATERAL
VENTRICLE

ALVEUS

HIPPOCAMPUS

SUPERIOR
COLLICULUS

MEDIAL GENICULATE
NUCLEUS

LATERAL GENICULATE NUCLEUS

CEREBRAL PEDUNCLE

BRACHIUM OF THE
INFERIOR COLLICULUS

CENTRAL GRAY

CEREBRAL AQUEDUCT

MESENCEPHALIC RETICULAR
FORMATION

MEDIAL
LONGITUDINAL
FASCICULUS

III FIBERS

RED
NUCLEUS

INTERPEDUNCULAR
NUCLEUS

III NUCLEUS

RAPHE NUCLEUS

III

SUBSTANTIA NIGRA

Fig. 3.2-16. IIIrd nerve not in plane of section.

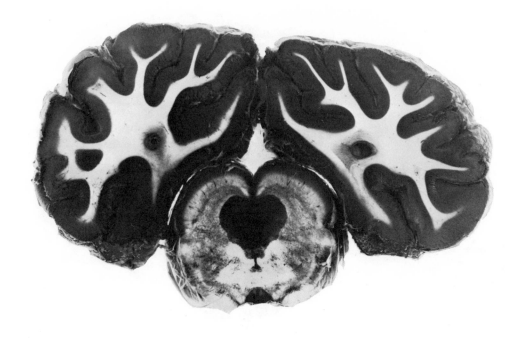

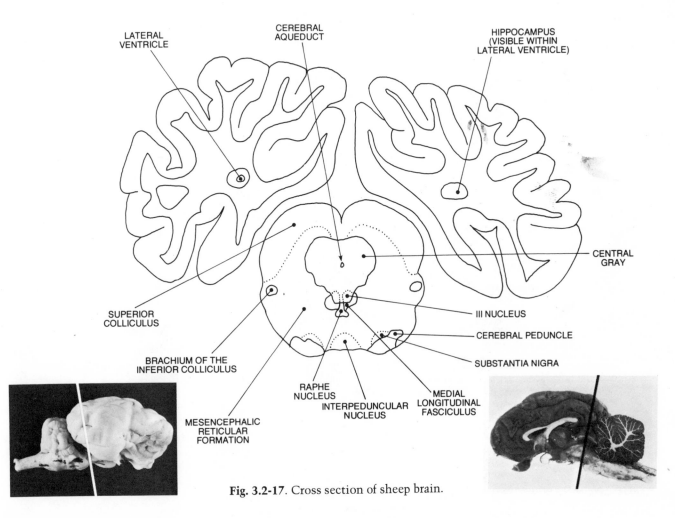

Fig. 3.2-17. Cross section of sheep brain.

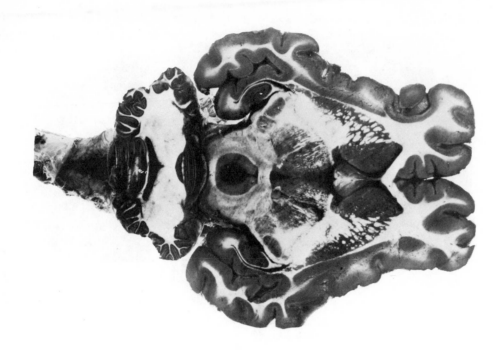

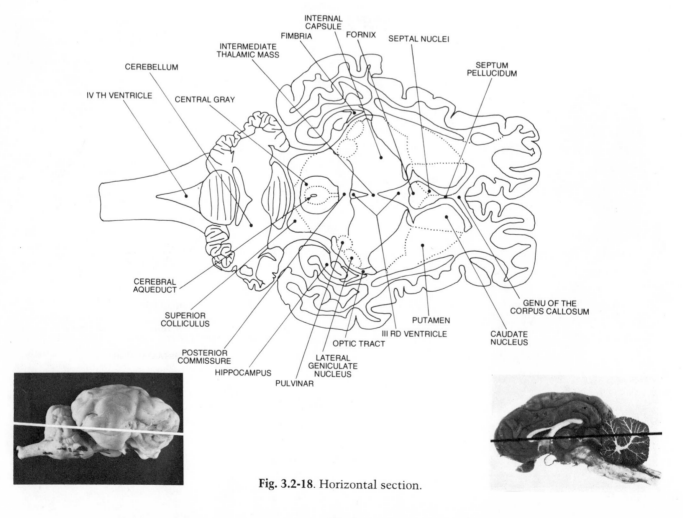

Fig. 3.2-18. Horizontal section.

of all traces of formaldehyde and preserved tissue. The physiological experiments which follow can be ruined by residual formaldehyde. Do not throw pieces and chips of brain into the sink.

3. Formaldehyde will retard healing of any cuts or sores you might have on your hands. Wash the sheep brain well in tap water before dissecting. You may protect cuts either with a waterproof adhesive or with plastic gloves.

4. The fumes from the phenol used for the Prussian blue staining reaction are irritative. If you breathe them for more than a few minutes you may develop a headache and sore throat. Use a fume hood for the phenol solution.

Materials

Materials needed for each student

No. 3 scalpel handle and no. 10 blade (or no. 4 handle and no. 22 blade)

Dissecting tray

Plastic or enamel photographic tray for holding stained cross sections (8 × 10 inch)

2 labeled widemouthed brain jars (one for the brain in 4% formaldehyde; the second for the stained brain slabs in 70% ethanol)

Old forceps

Orangewood manicure stick

Wet and dry paper towels

Plastic wrap (e.g., Saran Wrap) to cover the photographic tray

Materials needed in the laboratory

Brain knife (nick-free, 25 cm long, not serrated, slender but rigid kitchen knife; a fish fileting knife may be used)

20 × 30 cm hardwood cutting board

Scissors

Cheesecloth for wrapping pieces of the brain

String

Paper labels for cheesecloth

Masking tape to label jars

Marking pen

Extra brain jars

Sheep brains

Order at least 1.25/student

Materials for the Prussian blue staining of brain slabs

3 small Teflon-coated or nylon kitchen spatulas

2 plastic photographic trays for $FeCl_3$ and potassium ferrocyanide solutions (8 × 10 inch)

1 Pyrex tray with cover for Mulligan's solution (8 × 10 inch or smaller)

3 large plastic photographic trays (11 × 14 inch or larger) for rinsing with water

1 hot plate (60° C)

1 or 2 photographic timers with bell

Fume hood

Solutions:

70% ethanol (0.5 liters per small photographic tray containing 6 brain slabs)

1 liter each of solutions *a*, *b*, and *c* (see "Notes for the Instructor," item 3) should be sufficient to stain about 60 brain slabs. Replace $FeCl_3$ and potassium ferrocyanide when "blueing" takes longer than about 3 minutes.

Notes for the Instructor

1. Wash the sheep brains in running tap water for at least 30 minutes before the students dissect them.

2. The following display materials are helpful in orienting the student: a 20 cm length of ox spinal cord, a cross section through an ox or sheep vertebra including the spinal cord, a whole sheep brain encased in residual portions of the lateral half of the skull, a human brain specimen, a rat brain specimen, a rat head sliced through in the midsagittal plane, and Prussian blue stained sections if the students do not prepare their own.

3. The Prussian blue stain known as the Mulligan method (Northcutt et al., 1966; Hildebrand, 1968) is a superb adjunct to the laboratory. It is simple and reliable. It does require access to a fume hood to draw off the phenol fumes. Phenol selectively coats and protects the myelin from the staining reaction, which turns only the gray matter a bright blue. High contrast is achieved between white and gray (blue) matter. It is preferable to section whole brains for comparison with figures 3.2-12 to 3.2-18. A few should be made available for the class, if possible.

4. Make up the following solutions:

a. Mulligan's solution: 40 g carbolic acid (crystalline phenol); 5 g cupric sulfate ($CuSO_4$); 1.25 cc concentrated HCl; 1,000 cc distilled water

(The fumes are irritative to the mucous membranes and will also produce headaches. This solution can be stored.)
b. 1% ferric chloride (10 g $FeCl_3$ in 1,000 cc distilled water) (Make up the same day of use.)
c. 1% potassium ferrocyanide (10 g $K_4Fe(CN)_6$ in 1,000 cc distilled water) (This solution can be stored.)

The staining routine for students
1. Heat the Mulligan's solution to 60° C in a fume hood in a covered Pyrex dish or loosely capped bottle. (A room-temperature solution is somewhat less effective, but usable.)
2. Soak the brain slabs in distilled water for *10 minutes.*
3. Pour the Mulligan's solution into a Pyrex tray and gently place the slabs in the solution for *4 minutes* using a spatula (preferably Teflon-coated or nylon). Do not touch the hot phenol with your hands. Use the spatula in subsequent transfers until the slabs are blue. Avoid scratching the protective film on the surface of the brain slab. Cover the tray when not in use to prevent evaporation.
4. Transfer to a tray of cold tap water for 1 minute or less.
5. Transfer to 1% ferric chloride for 2 minutes.
6. Transfer to tap water for 3–5 minutes.
7. Transfer to 1% potassium ferrocyanide until the slabs begin to get dark blue; then remove them. The color will intensify and darken considerably during the water rinse that follows.
8. Wash for 5 minutes in gently running tap water.
9. Place in 70% ethanol for preservation.

General comments. Cover the hot phenol when not in use to retard evaporation. Students can soak their slabs of sheep brain in distilled water in their own small photographic tray, transfer the sections through the six trays required for staining and rinsing, and back into their tray containing 500 ml of 70% ethanol for examination and preservation.

If you are making stained sections for display, increase the time in step 2 from 10 minutes to 1–24 hours. In step 8 rinse for 1 hour and monitor periodically before transfering to 70% ethanol. The tap water of some communities will destain the sections in several hours.

Selected References

Barr, M. L. 1974. *The human nervous system*, 2d ed. Harper and Row, New York.

Carpenter, M. B. 1972. *Core text of neuroanatomy.* Williams and Wilkins, Baltimore.

Gardner, E. 1975. *Fundamentals of neurology*, 6th ed. W. B. Saunders, Philadelphia.

Heimer, L., and Lohman, A. H. M. 1975. Anatomical methods for tracing connections in the central nervous system. In *Handbook of psychobiology*, ed. M. S. Gazzaniga and C. Blakemore. Academic Press, New York, pp. 73–106.

Hildebrand, M. 1968. *Anatomical preparations*. University of California Press, Berkeley.

Igarashi, S., and Kamiya, J. 1972. *Atlas of the vertebrate brain: Morphologic evolution from cyclostomes to mammals*. University Park Press, Baltimore.

König, J. F. R., and Klippel, R. A. 1963. *The rat brain: A stereotaxic atlas of the forebrain and lower parts of the brain stem*. Williams and Wilkins, Baltimore.

McKenzie, J. S., and Smith, M. H. 1973. Stereotaxic methods and variability data for the brain of the Merino sheep. *J. Hirnforsch.* 14:355–66.

Nauta, W. J. H., and Ebbesson, S. O. E., eds. 1970. *Contemporary research methods in neuroanatomy*. Springer-Verlag, New York.

Netter, F. H. 1962. *Nervous system*. CIBA Collection of Medical Illustrations, vol. 1. CIBA Pharmaceutical Co.

Northcutt, R. G.; Williams, K. L.; and Barber, R. P. 1966. *Atlas of the sheep brain*, 2d ed. Stipes Publ. Co., Champaign Ill.

Romer, A. H. 1971. *The vertebrate body*, 4th ed. Saunders, Philadelphia.

Truex, R. C., and Carpenter, M. B. 1969. *Human neuroanatomy*, 6th ed. Saunders, Philadelphia.

Yoshikawa, T. 1968. *Atlas of the brains of domestic animals*. Pennsylvania State University Press, University Park.

4

Cellular Potentials and Bioelectric Activity

4.1 Active Transport of Sodium
Frog Skin

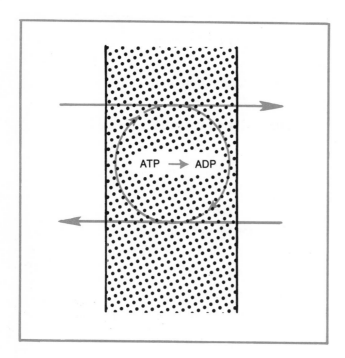

Introduction

Rationale

The plasma membranes of cells contain pumps which actively expel sodium from the cell while accumulating potassium. The result is that sodium is the most concentrated *extra*cellular cation, and potassium the major *intra*cellular cation in animals. Sodium-potassium concentration gradients across the cell membrane are the major source of electrical potentials in biological systems and provide the foundation for electrical activity in nerve cells. Figure 4.1-1 contrasts some chemical and physical properties of monovalent cations.

The sodium pump is a form of *active* transport because the process requires metabolic energy and is capable of transporting sodium up a concentration gradient. The energy is used to perform the *work* of transferring ions and is provided in animal cells by ATP. A sodium/potassium-activated ATPase enzyme has been isolated from cell membranes from many sources and is probably part of the pumping mechanism. Sodium pumps have been studied extensively in a variety of preparations including squid giant axons, toad bladders, and frog skin.

Frog skin is thin enough to permit cutaneous respiration, but has the disadvantage that water can also move into the frog by osmosis. As a result, the frog is obliged to constantly excrete excess water to maintain its osmotic balance. The kidneys, however, cannot make a completely dilute urine, so some sodium is continually excreted. This loss, added to the loss incurred by the passive outward diffusion of sodium through the skin is balanced by the active uptake of sodium through the skin. Frogs must actively extract sodium from their aquatic environment.

Sodium transport can be readily demonstrated in isolated frog skin. If a piece of frog skin is used to separate two compartments filled with equimolar salt solutions (such as amphibian perfusion solution), an electrical potential of 10–100 mV can be measured between electrodes placed in each compartment (fig. 4.1-2A). The potential across the skin is generated by active transport; positive charges (Na^+ ions) are picked up on the outside of the skin and transferred to the inside. The pump thus separates sodium ions from their anions (Cl^- ions), and the separation of charges is the measured potential. The electrical gradient set up by the sodium pump (making the skin negative outside and positive inside) draws Cl^- ions inward through the skin (fig. 4.1-2A); but since the active pumping of Na^+ ions

H																	He
Li	Be											B	C	N	O	F	Ne
Na	Mg											Al	Si	P	S	Cl	A
K	Ca	Sc	Ti	V	Cr	Mn	Fe	Co	Ni	Cu	Zn	Ga	Ge	As	Se	Br	Kr
Rb	Sr	Y	Zr	Nb	Mo	Tc	Ru	Rh	Pd	Ag	Cd	In	Sn	Sb	Te	I	Xe
Cs	Ba	–	Hf	Ta	W	Re	Os	Ir	Pt	Au	Hg	Tl	Pb	Bi	Po	At	Rn
Fr	Ra	–															

A

Element	Atomic Number	Electronic Configuration	Crystal Ionic Radius in Å	Hydrated Ionic Radius (approx.) in Å
LITHIUM	3	2,1	0.86	3.40
SODIUM	11	2,8,1	1.12	2.76
POTASSIUM	19	2,8,8,1	1.44	2.32
RUBIDIUM	37	2,8,18,8,1	1.58	2.28
CESIUM	55	2,8,18,18,8,1	1.84	2.28

B

Fig. 4.1-1. Chemistry of sodium, potassium, and lithium. **A.** Periodic table of the elements. Group I includes hydrogen and the alkali metals. **B.** Chemical properties of the alkali metals. The alkali metals (Li, Na, etc.) are grouped together in the periodic chart because they have similar chemical properties determined by the single electron in the outermost shell. The difference in hydrated ionic radius permits sodium and potassium to have very different roles in biological systems. The size of the hydrated ion decreases in the order shown because the larger the cation itself, the less it binds additional layers of water molecules beyond the primary hydration layer. (F. A. Cotton and G. Wilkinson, 1972. *Advanced Inorganic Chemistry*, 3rd ed. Wiley-Interscience, New York.)

always stays slightly ahead of the inward movement of Cl⁻ ions, the charge separation is maintained.[1]

The amount of sodium being transported can be directly measured in the following way. A second set of electrodes is connected to a battery and potentiometer, and the potential across the skin is reduced by applying a potential in the opposite direction—a "counterpotential" or "bucking voltage" (fig. 4.1-2B). The counterpotential can be gradually increased until it reduces the potential across the skin to zero. At this point the millivoltmeter will read zero. The effect of this "voltage clamp" is to stop the movement of Cl⁻ ions across the skin since there is no electrical gradient to drive them. With no concentration differences or electrical gradients across the skin, any movement of ions must necessarily be by active transport. Sodium continues to move across the skin under these conditions (see lower part of fig. 4.1-2C).

The potential across the skin can be reduced to zero because the negative electrode supplies one negatively charged electron to cancel out the charge of each Na^+ ion which is pumped through the skin. At the positive electrode, one electron is in effect removed from a Cl⁻ ion for each Na^+ which passes across the skin (fig. 4.1-2C). Thus, the battery supplies a current—the *countercurrent*—to cancel the voltage across the skin. An equal, but opposite, current is also flowing through the skin. This current is comprised of a flow of Na^+ ions propelled by the sodium pump. The *countercurrent* is a direct measure of the rate of sodium transport because the countercurrent equals the current of Na^+ ions across the skin.

You will examine mechanisms of sodium transport by measuring the countercurrent after altering the ionic makeup of the solutions used, or after applying agents such as metabolic poisons. Substitu-

---

1. Keep in mind that the isolated skin is a *model* experimental system in which some details may differ substantially from the natural condition. The outside of the skin of an intact frog in a pond is bathed in a very dilute salt solution (less than 1 mM NaCl), while the inside surface is supplied with blood and bathed in tissue fluids containing a high concentration of NaCl ($\approx$ 100 mM). In the intact frog, active chloride transport through the skin is an important mechanism of salt uptake. Experiments using more physiological conditions have also shown some active chloride transport in isolated skin (Alvarado et al., 1975).

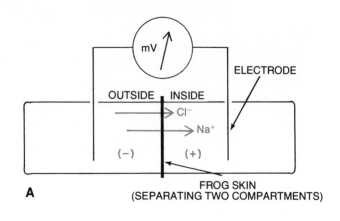

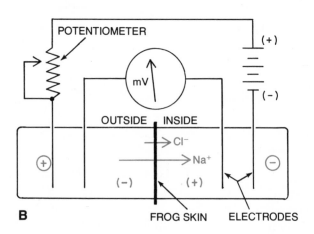

Fig. 4.1-2. Schematic drawing of apparatus for measuring the active transport of sodium in frog skin. **A** shows a piece of frog skin used to separate two compartments containing Ringer's solution. Electrodes attached to a millivoltmeter register a potential of about 50–100 mV across the skin. The potential is generated by active transport of Na^+ ions through the skin. Cl^- ions follow the electrical gradient set up by sodium pumping. **B**. A second set of electrodes attached to a battery and potentiometer is inserted on either side of the skin. The voltage across the second set of electrodes is increased gradually to balance out the potential developed by the sodium pump. Sodium continues to be pumped, but the flow of Cl^- ions decreases as the potential across the skin falls toward zero. **C**. A microammeter is added to the second circuit. A reversing switch is also added for convenience of operation (in case the skin is put in backward). The potentiometer is adjusted to exactly balance out the potential created by the skin. The reading on the millivoltmeter falls to zero. The *countercurrent* measured on the microammeter is the rate of flow of electrons which is needed to exactly cancel out the charges of the Na^+ ions moving across the skin and is a direct measure of the rate of sodium pumping.

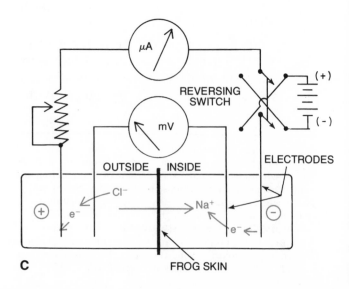

tion of various ions and experiments with ionic radioisotopes have confirmed that the net current we measure as the countercurrent is indeed the result of active sodium transport. The flux of Na⁺ ions across the frog skin has been measured in double-label experiments using the isotopes ^{24}Na and ^{22}Na on opposite sides of the skin. In general, the rate of inward movement of sodium has been found to be equal to 105% of the countercurrent, and the outward movement equal to 5% of the countercurrent. The countercurrent is, therefore, a measure of the *net* flux of sodium through the frog skin. The extra 5% moving outward and inward represents the simple *diffusion* of sodium across the skin.

Remember that you will be measuring sodium transport through a skin composed of several layers of cells, *not* through a single cell membrane. The principles of transport in the two systems are the same, so that much has been gained from the study of transport in frog skin. The site of pumping in the epithelium and a model of the pumping mechanism are shown in figures 4.1-3 and 4.1-4.

Time to complete the exercise: One 3-hour laboratory period.

Procedure

Operation of the millivoltmeter

You will use a cathode ray oscilloscope as the millivoltmeter for measuring the potential across isolated frog skin. The following are suggested settings for the oscilloscope.
Time Base
Time/division = 1 msec/div
Triggering mode = Automatic or recurrent
Vertical Amplifier
Volts/division = 20 mV/div
Position = Trace at midscale
Input selector = DC mode, differential if available
Remember: These are *suggested* settings for starting the experiment. You will benefit from readjusting the gain of the vertical amplifier to maximize the deflection produced by the potential of your frog skin. *Read out* millivoltage as a vertical displacement of the oscilloscope trace. Connect the two voltmeter inputs together to get a zero point for reference. Check the zero point after the experiment to make sure that the trace position has not drifted.

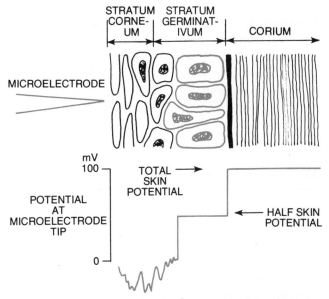

Fig. 4.1-3. Source of the potential. A microelectrode (*left*) is slowly advanced into the skin. It first encounters the epithelial layer (stratum corneum and stratum germinativum). At the outer membrane of the cells of the basal layer of the stratum germinativum the electrical potential jumps to 50 mV (*lower diagram*). As the electrode passes the inner membrane, the potential again jumps: this time to 100 mV. This experiment indicates that the cells at the base of the epithelial layer are the site of the sodium pump in frog skin. (Adapted from Hoshiko, 1961.)

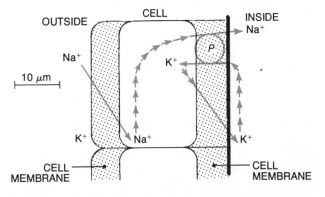

Fig. 4.1-4. Model of the epithelial cell which transports sodium in frog skin. Most animal cells are surrounded by membranes which continuously pump sodium *out* of the cell. How is it then that frog skin transports sodium inward? The paradox is explained by this model which proposes that the epithelial cell is asymmetric. The outside-facing membrane of the cell (*left side*) is considered to be permeable to Na⁺. The inside-facing membrane (*right*) is considered to be permeable to K⁺. A pump (*P*) in the inside facing membrane picks up the Na⁺ which has diffused into the cell and transports it to the inside. The pump also transports K⁺ back into the cell to maintain electrical and osmotic balance. (Adapted from Koefoed-Johnsen and Ussing, 1958.)

Operation of the frog skin transport device

The frog skin transport device has been constructed along the lines outlined schematically in figure 4.1-2C. Examine the device and check with the instructor if you cannot locate the following components: Plexiglas *skin holder*, silver/silver chloride *electrodes*, countercurrent reversing *switch*, and countercurrent *control* (potentiometer).

Measurement of Sodium Transport

After familiarization with the instrumentation, proceed to measure sodium transport across frog skin in the following steps.

1. Rinse everything with tap water, including the frog skin holders, the electrodes, and your dissecting tools. Use no soap on the apparatus. Wash your hands. Use a minimum of soap on your hands and rinse them thoroughly.

2. Switch the countercurrent switch to off.

3. Rotate the countercurrent control fully off.

4. Connect the millivoltmeter output on the transport device to the input of the oscilloscope's vertical amplifier. Use coaxial cables if possible.

5. Double pith a large frog (see page 311). Using scissors, carefully remove as large a piece of skin as possible from the ventral surface of the frog. The skin must be large enough to fit over the end of the skin holding device.

6. Slip the skin over the smaller end of one side of the skin holder so that it completely and smoothly covers the hole and the circular face of the Plexiglas holder. Slip the other part of the holder into place. Clamp the completed skin holder into the transport device *using minimum pressure on the set screw*.

7. Fill the two compartments with amphibian perfusion solution (Ringer's solution). The solutions must be the same concentration on both sides for the device to work properly. More complicated agar-filled electrodes would be required if different solutions were used.

8. Gently place the silver/silver chloride electrodes into the skin holder, connecting them to the four jacks provided. Do not place stress on the skin or mechanism when inserting electrodes. All that is necessary is for the electrodes to touch the salt solution. Therefore, simply rest the stoppers in place *without* pushing them in securely as you might in

stoppering a bottle. Force of this kind will damage both the apparatus and the frog skin.

9. Find zero potential by recording between two electrodes in the perfusion fluid on the same side of the skin. Adjust the vertical position of the beam to coincide with one of the horizontal lines in the middle of the screen.

10. Place voltage electrodes on opposite sides of the skin. Read out the voltage on the oscilloscope face by measuring the displacement of the beam from its original (zero) position. Use the oscilloscope gain control to maximize the displacement and thus make the potential easier to read. Repeat the zeroing operation if the gain is changed.

11. To measure the countercurrent:

   a. Turn the countercurrent switch on.

   b. Slowly advance the countercurrent control clockwise.

      (1) If potential reading decreases, then the countercurrent potential is in the right direction.

      (2) If potential reading increases, switch countercurrent switch to the reverse position.

   c. Continue to increase the countercurrent until the potential reads zero.

   d. Read out the countercurrent on the microammeter. *This current is an exact measure of the rate of Na^+-pumping* in the membrane. The potential *is not* a good measure of the pumping rate, although it is correlated with the pumping action.

If you are not successful in measuring the countercurrent, or have other problems with the equipment, call on the instructor for help before proceeding with the next section.

Substitution for Sodium by Potassium and Lithium

Repeat your measurements on (1) the potential and (2) the countercurrent. Has the system changed? Be sure to write down your data, noting the time for each operation which follows. If the frog skin you are using has a very low current, you may wish to obtain new skin from another frog.

Drain the perfusion fluid from both sides (without removing the skin from the holder) by removing the skin holder and inverting it over the sink until the fluid drains.

Replace the holder in the device and add perfusion fluid made up with a 75% replacement of Na^+ by K^+. Measure the potential and countercurrent after 1 minute. Replace with *normal* perfusion solution to find if the baseline ("normal" rate of pumping) has changed. Remember, you have removed the skin from its normal milieu, and it—like any other biological preparation used in a laboratory—will change over time.

Replace the normal perfusion fluid with perfusion fluid made up with a 75% replacement of Na^+ by Li^+. Measure the potential and countercurrent after 1 minute. Do not leave the Li^+ perfusion solution in the chamber for more than 1 minute. Retest the baseline with normal perfusion solution.

Repeat with normal perfusion fluid to which 2, 4-dinitrophenol (DNP) has been added to give a concentration of 1.0 mM. The DNP is a poison which uncouples oxidative phosphorylation. Periodically measure the countercurrent after a 15–20 minute period and plot the results.

Clean all the equipment carefully. It is *imperative* that you thoroughly rinse off all the DNP from both the skin holder and the electrodes.

Further experiments
If time permits, you may wish to undertake further experiments. Some additional reagents will be made available by the instructor, and they may suggest experiments to you. However, you are asked to design your own experiment. Keep in mind that *time* is an essential factor in any experiment, and that the essence of any experimental "proof" is *repeatability*. That is, the experiment should come out the same way most of the time, for you and for investigators in different laboratories.

Other reagents which may be made available are:
1. 1.0 mM *ouabain* (G-strophanthin) in perfusion fluid. (Ouabain is a cardiac glycoside similar to digitalis. It is a specific inhibitor of sodium transport. The agent is prepared from the seeds of a plant, *Strophanthus gratus*. Be careful with ouabain since it is a powerful poison and is expensive.)

2. 0.01% *ethylenediaminetetraacetate* (EDTA) in perfusion fluid. (EDTA is an agent which chelates divalent cations such as calcium and magnesium. Its use will, therefore, eliminate free divalent cations in the solution and skin.)
3. Perfusion fluid with the NaCl totally replaced by Na_2SO_4. The membranes of the cells in the frog skin are impermeable to the sulfate ion.
4. Perfusion fluid containing the normal amount of NaCl, with LiCL added in the amount of 25% of the NaCl.

Pitfalls and Suggestions

1. It is most important that the Plexiglas skin holder be treated with care. It is relatively fragile and will not withstand rough treatment.
2. Do not use alcohol of any kind in the Plexiglas skin holder. The alcohol will craze the Plexiglas, inducing tiny fractures along any lines of stress which may be present in the plastic.
3. Carefully clean your equipment *both before and after* use with any poisons.
4. Make sure that all of the solutions you use are at room temperature. If a solution has just been removed from the refrigerator, and the results of its use are compared with another solution at room temperature, your experiment will be confounded by possible temperature effects. What effects might temperature have?
5. Remember that the *current* is the most important measurement because it is a measure of the rate of sodium transport. The potential is a reflection of the active transport, but there are many other factors which help to determine the magnitude of the potential.
6. Set up your results in the form of a table showing the potential and the current for each treatment. What conclusions can you draw from these results especially as to the "proof" that Na^+ is actively transported? If you think you have shown that it is, then calculate the flux of Na^+ per unit area of skin as follows.

Using the average value of the current for several readings across the "normal" skin and the conversion factor $1 \mu A = 6.3 \times 10^{12}$ ions/sec, calculate the Na^+ flux in micromoles transported per hour. (6×10^{23} Na^+ ions is 1 mole, and 1 micromole = 10^{-6} moles.) What is the rate of transport in terms of moles of sodium transported/cm² of skin surface per hour? Determine the surface area of frog skin exposed by measuring the inside diameter of the skin holder and applying the formula $A = 0.7854d^2$, where A is the area and d the diameter.

How do the rates of transport vary under experimental conditions? Can you criticize the experimental design of the second (pages 80–81) exercise on scientific grounds? How might the experiment have been improved? How do your data compare with data produced by other groups? Is there enough data available in the class for a statistical treatment of the combined data? For example, could statistical methods be applied to class data to test the hypothesis that the magnitude of the potential observed is related to the rate of sodium transport?

Materials

Materials needed at each station

Active transport device (Figure 4.1-5 illustrates a practical active transport device which uses the circuit illustrated in figure 4.1-2C. The details of construction and dimensions may be varied to suit available materials. Use a 1.5 V mercury battery, a potentiometer, and a microammeter capable of registering 150 μA or more.)

Skin holder (Figure 4.1-6A illustrates a skin holder constructed of 1 inch [2.54 cm] O.D. Plexiglas. Three electrode ports are required for efficient operation. The edges of the device which contact the skin should be rounded with fine sandpaper to remove sharp edges. Figure 4.1-6B illustrates a simpler version constructed of 1 inch PVC tubing.)

4 silver/silver chloride electrodes (Use 24–20-gauge [0.020–0.032 inch] silver wire.) Puncture a size 00 rubber stopper with a pithing needle and force a 6–7 cm length of silver wire through the stopper. Solder a 20 cm wire fitted with a banana plug to the wire protruding from the top of the stopper. The electrodes should be chlorided before use (see page 334 for the procedure).

Oscilloscope (Almost any other type of voltmeter can be substituted for the oscilloscope. For example, a DC chart recorder or a standard electronic multimeter could be used.)

Set of leads for connecting the voltmeter output on the transport device to the oscilloscope

Solutions:
500 ml wash bottle containing normal amphibian perfusion fluid
250 ml wash bottle containing perfusion fluid made up with a 75% replacement of NaCl by KCl (potassium-substituted perfusion fluid)
250 ml wash bottle containing perfusion fluid made up with a 75% replacement of NaCl by LiCl (lithium-substituted perfusion fluid)
250 ml wash bottle containing perfusion solution made up with 1.0 mM 2,4-dinitrophenol (DNP) (DNP-containing perfusion fluid)

Materials available in the laboratory

Extra electrodes and skin holders
Voltmeter (battery tester)
Solutions:
Additional quantities of normal and modified perfusion solutions, as above
Normal perfusion solution containing 1.0 mM ouabain (G-strophanthin) (Label "Poison" with large letters.)
Normal perfusion solution containing 0.01% ethylenediaminetetraacetate (EDTA)
Perfusion solution with the NaCl totally replaced by Na_2SO_4. The Na_2SO_4 will not replace NaCl on a molar basis. Adjust the concentration of Na_2SO_4 to yield the equivalent number of Na^+ ions found in normal perfusion fluid. This will mean a reduction of anions ($SO_4^=$ ions) to one-half the concentration Cl^- ions normally found in the perfusion fluid. If you wish, sucrose may be added to the solution to increase the osmotic pressure to that of normal perfusion fluid. Sucrose is impermeable and will have no effect on the transport system.
Normal perfusion solution with LiCl added in the amount of 25% of the amount of NaCl used in making up normal perfusion solution.

Animals

Frogs (Order 1.5/station/laboratory period.) Keep the frogs in a cool place and provide them with dripping water.

Notes for the Instructor

1. Some frog skins may have low sodium currents. Obtain a fresh skin from another frog. Keep the frogs

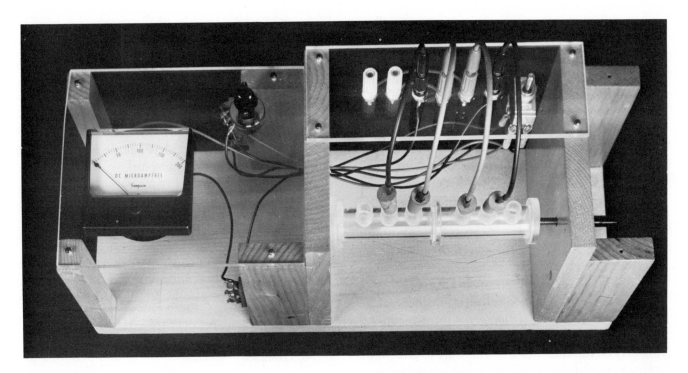

Fig. 4.1-5. Active transport device with skin holder and four electrodes in place, constructed according to the circuit shown in figure 4.1-2C. A 1/200 ampere fuse has been added to protect the microammeter in case the electrodes are accidentally shorted together. A 1.5 V mercury battery has been used with a 5 megohm potentiometer. The skin holder setscrew should be left *without* a knob to minimize the amount of pressure which can be put on the skin holder. This device has been left unlabeled for purposes of illustration, but the completed device as used in the student laboratory should be fully labeled with plastic labels (e.g., Dymo tape).

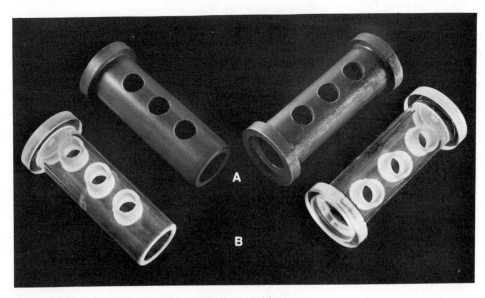

Fig. 4.1-6. Two versions of a skin holder. **A**. Holder constructed of 1 inch PVC tubing (5/32 inch walls). The total length of the holder (here about 6 inches) is the only critical measurement, since the holder must fit into the active transport device (fig. 4.1-5). **B**. Holder constructed from 1 inch Plexiglas tubing (1/8 inch walls).

at room temperature overnight before use. This seems to result in larger skin potentials.

2. In order for the system to provide a bucking current of the correct polarity with respect to the skin, the skin has to be placed in the holder with the inside and outside of the skin facing the proper directions. Label the device to show the proper orientation (e.g., "Face inside of skin left"). If students get the skin in backward, the reversing switch may be used and the two electrodes which record the potential may be crossed.

3. Stress the fragility of the Plexiglas skin holder. Students will (1) attempt to clamp it too tightly in the apparatus and (2) jam the electrodes into the electrode holes.

4. The skin is also fragile, so stress care in its handling. Free use of perfusion solution is beneficial.

5. Step-by-step procedures are given for the student to follow in the initial stages of the exercise. Since this may be the students' first exposure to electronic instrumentation, they will probably benefit from this detailed guidance. Advanced students may need more independence to profit fully from the exercise.

6. This experiment is adaptable to quantitative treatment and the use of statistics.

7. With this apparatus, using simple Ag-AgCl electrodes, the solutions on both sides of the frog skin should be the same. Agar-filled electrodes (Ussing and Zerahn, 1951) should be constructed if the use of different solutions is attempted.

8. Most of the poisons which act on this system act rather slowly and must be given time to work. However, formaldehyde is very quick acting and may be used for demonstrations. Formaldehyde is not suggested as a part of the student experiments because it tends to stick in the cracks in the Plexiglas skin holder and would poison future experiments. For a demonstration, a few drops of 10% formaldehyde can be dropped into either side of the skin holder. Be ready to measure the countercurrent, as it drops very rapidly. Rinse all equipment repeatedly after use, including the electrodes.

9. Chloride the electrodes a day or two in advance. (See page 334.) A careful plating job and equilibration will eliminate drift and spurious potentials.

10. Do not use TMS to anesthetize the frogs; it may damage the skin. (Ohr, 1976)

Selected References

You will find in the literature that transport is an area of active, ongoing research. Important recent findings concern the molecular basis of sodium, amino acid, and sugar transport; the governing relationship between transport processes and metabolism; and the interdependence of transport of different substances (cotransport).

Davson, H. 1970. *A textbook of general physiology*, vol. 2. 4th ed., J. and A. Churchill, London.

Glynn, I. M., and Karlish, S. J. D. 1975. The sodium pump. *Annu. Rev. Physiol.* 37: 13–55.

Keynes, R. D. 1969. From frog skin to sheep rumen: A survey of transport of salts and water across multicellular structures. *Q. Rev. Biophys.* 2: 177–281.

Kirschner, L. 1965. A refresher course in membrane physiology. *Am. Zool.* 10: 329–436.

Ussing, H. H.; Erlij, D.; and Lassen, U. 1974. Transport pathways in biological membranes. *Annu. Rev. Physiol.* 36: 17–49.

RESEARCH REPORTS

Alvarado, R. H.; Dietz, T. H.; and Mullen, T. L. 1975. Chloride transport across isolated skin of *Rana pipiens*. *Am. J. Physiol.* 229: 869–76.

Farquhar, M. G., and Palade, G. E. 1966. Adenosine triphosphatase localization in amphibian epidermis. *J. Cell Biol.* 30: 359–79.

Hoshiko, T. 1961. Electrogenesis in frog skin. In *Biophysics of physiological and pharmacological actions*, ed. A. M. Shanes. Am. Assoc. Adv. Sci., Washington, D.C., pp. 31–47.

Koefoed-Johnsen, V., and Ussing, H. H. 1958. The nature of the frog skin potential. *Acta Physiol. Scand.* 42: 298–308.

Ohr, E. A. 1976. Tricaine methanesulfonate II: Effects on transport of NaCl and H_2O. *Comp. Biochem. Physiol.* 54C: 19–22.

Ussing, H.H. 1949. The active ion transport through the isolated frog skin in the light of tracer studies. *Acta Physiol. Scand.* 17: 1–43.

————. 1949. The distinction by means of tracers between active transport and diffusion. *Acta Physiol. Scand.* 19: 43–56.

Ussing, H. H., and Zerahn, K. 1951. Active transport of sodium as the source of electric current in the short-circuited isolated frog skin. *Acta Physiol. Scand.* 23: 110–27.

Zerahn, K. 1955. Studies on the active transport of lithium in the isolated frog skin. *Acta Physiol. Scand.* 33: 347–58.

4.2 Compound Action Potential
Frog Sciatic Nerve

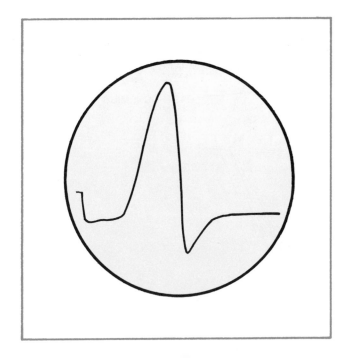

Introduction

Rationale

An action potential can be elicited simultaneously in each of thousands of axons in a peripheral nerve by electrical stimulation. The collective response is called a *compound action potential*. This may seem at first like an indiscriminate technique—recording from literally thousands of nerve fibers at once—but it is reliable and useful. With the frog sciatic nerve it is possible to explore several basic aspects of neuronal conduction, e.g., maximal firing rates, threshold phenomena, conduction velocity, and the role of axon size and myelination in conduction.

The peripheral nerves of vertebrates typically contain axons of thousands of motor and sensory neurons. Each axon conducts all-or-none, self-prop-

agating action potentials. The excitability of such axons and the conduction of action potentials over distance has been examined in great detail (see Davson, 1970, for a full treatment). The frog sciatic nerve was the classical preparation for the study of the action potential (e.g., Erlanger, Gasser, and Bishop, 1924), until it was later supplanted by intracellular recording from squid giant fibers.

Time to complete the exercise: At least one 3-hour laboratory period is necessary to complete the section on conduction velocity. A longer time period may be necessary if both dissection and electrical techniques are unfamiliar.

Procedure

Preliminary setup

It is essential to familiarize yourself with the instruments and recording system *before* beginning the dissection. The instrumentation may seem formidable, but generally it is the faltering viability of a biological preparation that ends the experiment. Therefore, any practical or conceptual problems concerning the equipment should be cleared up *before* the experimental animal is touched.

Before you proceed to the next section, read and understand the recording procedure and make preliminary adjustments based on those instructions. Also read the first item under the heading "Pitfalls and Suggestions."

Surgical procedure

Double pith a frog. Pick up a fold of skin at midabdomen with forceps and cut the skin all the way around the frog. Pull the skin down, everting it as you pull, and strip it off the legs. Tissue-gripping forceps help. See page 311 for pithing. Lay the frog dorsal side up on a clean surface and gently separate the thigh muscles with the fingers to reveal the white *sciatic nerve* and accompanying blood vessels (see fig. 4.2-1). Take care not to mistake white muscle fascia for the nerve. Separate the muscles and free the nerve from surrounding tissue in the thigh using blunt glass tools if they are available. Glass tools can be made from glass rods heated in a Bunsen burner and pulled out to produce a working tip. The tip should be fire-polished smooth to about the size of a lead pencil point which has seen some use (1 mm). Avoid motions up and down the leg; these will stretch the nerve longitudinally.

CAUTION: **Touching the nerve with the fingers, with cut muscle or other tissue, or with metal probes may damage it. Do not stretch, do not pinch, and do not dry the nerve.**

Repeated application of amphibian perfusion fluid with a medicine dropper will keep the nerve moist during the dissection.

Hold the urostyle up, and carefully cut the muscles on both sides of the bone. Now, free the caudal end of the urostyle and lift it to expose the underlying structures.

CAUTION: **Do not cut the underlying nerves when you cut the muscles around the urostyle.**

You will recognize abdominal organs. Lying dorsal to them will be the two white sciatic nerves (right and left) originating at the spinal cord and passing into each thigh. Note that each leaves the spinal cord as three roots (roots 7–9). Cut off the urostyle at its hinge. Cut the roots as close to the spinal cord as possible. Carefully ligate (tie) the roots with the end of a 10 cm length of thread. Free the nerve from the hip to the knee, lifting it with the thread as necessary.

CAUTION: **Do not stretch the nerve.**

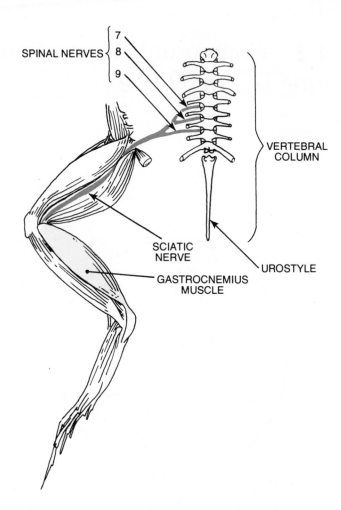

Fig. 4.2-1. Dorsal view of exposed frog right hind limb and spinal column. (Adapted from L. Packer, 1967. *Experiments in Cell Physiology*. Academic Press, New York.)

When the nerve has been totally freed, cut through the distal end with scissors. Immerse the nerve in a small beaker of frog perfusion fluid.

Arranging the nerve chamber

Fill the recording chamber with perfusion fluid to a point about 5 mm above the electrode wires. Lay the nerve lengthwise in the recording chamber so that it floats above all the electrode wires. Manipulate the nerve with glass tools if they are available. Draw off enough of the perfusion solution with a medicine dropper for the nerve to come to rest on the electrode wires which now lie above the level of the fluid. The nerve must be in physical contact with each of the electrode wires, and the level of the fluid must be well below all of the wires to prevent shorting them out. One end of the nerve may touch the perfusion fluid, but not both.

Drops of fluid which remain between the wires may short-circuit the electrodes.

Place the cover over the nerve chamber to prevent drying. Under some circumstances drying may still be a problem. If so, add a layer of mineral oil saturated with perfusion fluid atop the fluid already in the chamber. Cover the electrodes and the nerve. As oil is added it may lift the nerve off the electrodes. To prevent this, add the oil/perfusion fluid by dropping it over and on top of the nerve until the nerve is immersed. Look to see that good contact is made between the nerve and each electrode. If the nerve has floated free of some electrodes, contact can be reestablished as follows. Fill a medicine dropper with perfusion fluid. Lower the tip of the dropper beneath the oil surface and carefully squeeze out about one-half drop of fluid so that it remains attached to the dropper. Bring the drop into contact with the nerve and move it along the nerve. As the fluid encounters each electrode along the nerve, it should spread between the nerve and electrode and draw them together. Electrical contact must be established between each electrode and the nerve. Remember this technique. You may wish to use it to locally apply test solutions to nerves immersed in oil/perfusion fluid.

Recording Procedure

Arrange the electrode leads so that you stimulate and record at opposite ends of the nerve and ground the center (fig. 4.2-2). For recording, connect a pair of cables to two electrodes near the distal (thin) portion of the nerve and connect the other end of this pair of cables to the input of the preamplifier. These cables should be as short as possible to minimize the pickup of electrical interference.

Connect a third cable to one of the other electrodes about midway along the nerve and run it to a ground terminal on the preamplifier (fig. 4.2-2). Connect another pair of cables from the stimulator output to a pair of electrodes at the proximal (thick) end of the nerve. Make sure that the negative electrode is nearest the recording electrodes. The action

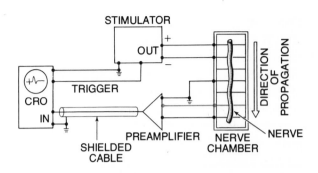

Fig. 4.2-2. Recording arrangement. An action potential is initiated at the stimulating cathode (negative-going stimulating electrode). The impulse travels down the nerve to the first recording electrode (*colored electrode*), producing a deflection of the recording trace on the oscilloscope display. The stimulus artifact (initial deflection) may be eliminated or minimized by interposing a stimulus isolation unit (SIU) between the stimulator output and stimulating electrodes.

potential is initiated at the negative electrode (cathode). The presence of the anode (positive electrode) between the cathode and recording electrodes may result in blockage of the action potential since the positive electrode hyperpolarizes the nerve.

Connect the output of the preamplifier to the input of the oscilloscope with appropriate shielded cables and connectors (fig. 4.2-2). The trigger output (synchronous output) of the stimulator should be connected to the trigger input of the oscilloscope. This arrangement synchronizes the initiation of the oscilloscope sweep with the output pulse of the stimulator. Use the following initial settings on your equipment.

Preamplifier. Input in differential mode if possible; gain of 100–1,000×; band-pass filters (if available) set at about 10 Hz (low frequency filter) and 3–5 kHz (high frequency filter).
Oscilloscope. Time base at 1 msec/div; vertical sensitivity at 0.1–0.01 V/div; trigger set on external input and the triggering level control adjusted to trigger the oscilloscope sweep when the stimulator is actuated.
Calibration. Adjust the overall system gain (preamplifier plus oscilloscope) to about 100 μV/div.

Check by using the preamplifier calibration function, if available. If you do not understand the meaning or procedure of calibration, ask your instructor. **Stimulator.**   Frequency of 7/sec; delay (if available) of about 1 msec; duration of 0.4 msec; starting voltage of 0.1 V. Activate the stimulator by placing the output mode switch in the *continuous* (multiple) position.

CAUTION: If you reach the end of the continuously variable voltage dial's excursion, turn it back down (fully counterclockwise) before you step up the voltage with the multiplier switch.

Gradually increase the stimulus voltage until a peaked waveform can be clearly seen on the screen. Try not to exceed 5–6 volts. Note that the position of the waveform on the screen and its duration are varied by the stimulation delay and duration settings, respectively. This waveform is the *stimulus artifact* and should not be confused with the actual action potential. The stimulus artifact is picked up by the recording electrodes through capacitative coupling to the stimulating electrodes. A stimulus isolator, if available, can be used to minimize the stimulus artifact. The artifact can be recorded from a thread wetted with perfusion fluid, demonstrating that the artifact has no physiological origin (see section 2.8). A large stimulus artifact may distort the waveform of the action potential. This problem can be minimized by reducing the stimulus duration as much as possible while increasing the voltage. A small stimulus artifact is often useful as a precise time marker for stimulus onset.

Eliciting the Compound Action Potential

Slowly increase the stimulus voltage from 0.1 V. Eventually, at threshold, the compound action potential should begin to appear as a deflection in the baseline of the trace at some point to the right of the stimulus artifact. As additional axons are stimulated by stronger voltages, the compound action potential will grow in amplitude. This phenomenon illustrates the differences in threshold which exist among the different sizes of fibers which make up the nerve. The more-or-less continuous growth in amplitude obscures the fact that the action potential of each individual fiber is a fixed, *all-or-none* event. If the stimulus voltage is increased slowly and smoothly, you may observe discrete jumps in the amplitude of the compound action potential as different threshold classes of nerve fibers are recruited. Notice that, as the stimulus voltage is increased, a point will be reached when the waveform of the action potential stops changing. At this point, all the fibers in the nerve are being stimulated. (To prove that the stimulus is changing smoothly and to monitor its waveform and time of occurrence, it would be valuable to also connect the stimulator output to the second channel of a dual-beam oscilloscope. Do not ground either output terminal of the stimulus isolation unit.)

The ability of the stimulus to elicit a response is dependent on the duration of the stimulus as well as its intensity. Shorten the duration of the stimulus to 0.2 msec, and reduce the stimulus *voltage* to the starting level of 0.1 V. Now, gradually increase the voltage until a response barely begins to appear. Stop increasing the voltage. Now, gradually increase the *duration* of the stimulus and note the effect. If time permits, you should determine a strength-duration curve after completing the section on refractory periods, page 92.

Distinguishing between the action potential and stimulus artifact

The following properties of the active neural response (compound action potential) distinguish it from the stimulus artifact.

1. It is not the first deflection observed.
2. Its amplitude, although initially increased by raising the stimulus intensity, is not a linear function of the stimulus strength.
3. Its duration is not a direct function of the stimulus duration.
4. It will decrease with high stimulus frequencies (500–1,000 Hz).
5. It does not have the shape of the stimulus artifact.
6. Its latency from the stimulus onset (artifact) is a direct function of the distance between the stimulating and recording electrodes. The artifact will have a fixed latency or delay from the beginning of the triggered sweep.

Analysis of the Compound Action Potential

Waveform: monophasic vs. biphasic

Decrease the stimulus voltage to the starting level of 0.1 V. Now, gradually increase the voltage until all the nerve fibers are responding and the amplitude of the compound action potential ceases to increase with increasing stimulus voltage. Increase the voltage about 10% above this point. You are now giving a so-called *supramaximal stimulus*. Reverse the polarity of the recording electrodes, if necessary, so that the initial deflection of the displayed waveform is upward. (This can generally be done at the oscilloscope.)

The shape of the waveform you observe on the oscilloscope screen depends on a number of factors. The distance between the two recording electrodes is particularly important. In addition, the waveform can be modified by changing the sweep rate (time base of the oscilloscope), changing the amplification (gain) of the preamplifier or oscilloscope, or changing the band-pass filter settings on the preamplifier or oscilloscope input.

The compound action potential recorded from an undamaged nerve should be biphasic. That is, as the action potential sweeps by the first recording electrode, it drives that electrode negative with respect to the more distant electrode. The oscilloscope trace

is deflected vertically. If you have arranged the polarity of the recording electrodes as previously called for, the initial deflection will be upward. Then, as the wave of depolarization (the action potential) arrives at the second recording electrode, making it negative, the oscilloscope trace is deflected downward because the first electrode is positive with respect to the second electrode. (Note the upper trace and its recording electrodes in figure 4.2-3.) The recording electrodes are usually not far enough apart to fully separate these two events in time, and the result is a biphasic wave which often looks something like a single sine wave. Trace or photograph it. Be sure to record the amplification and sweep rates on the back of the photographs. Also measure the distances between the stimulating and recording electrodes and record the temperature of the preparation. (In experiment 8.7 the action potentials in *Mimosa* are conducted so slowly that there is a clear separation of events at the two electrodes.)

Crush the nerve at the site of the second electrode (the electrode more distant from the stimulating electrodes) by carefully pinching with a pair of fine forceps. This should inactivate the nerve at the site of the second electrode and produce a *monophasic* recording. You may need to crush and check the nerve several times to ensure that you have a fully monophasic recording. A very tiny drop of isotonic KCl (0.16 M) applied to the crushed area will aid the development of a monophasic action potential. Use KCl if crushing is not fully effective. Do you understand the logic of its use? Trace the waveform of the monophasic action potential or use a Polaroid oscilloscope camera to photograph it. Refer to figure 4.2-3, but do not attempt to simultaneously record mono- and biphasic potentials.

Fiber groups

Within the total population of fibers there are several groups of fibers of similar diameter, and, therefore, similar threshold and conduction velocity. Connect the recording electrodes for monophasic recording. Reduce the frequency of stimulation to 5 stimulations/sec. Try to identify as many peaks of the compound action potential as possible, by slowly increasing the stimulus voltage and looking for the addition of new peaks.

It should be possible to find two of the three major peaks of the compound action potential demon-

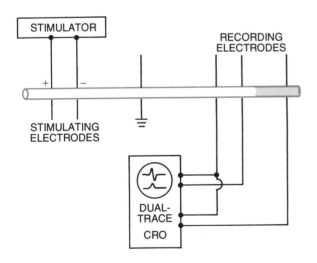

Fig. 4.2-3. Simultaneous recording of mono- and biphasic action potentials with a dual-trace oscilloscope. One end of the nerve is crushed (*colored*).

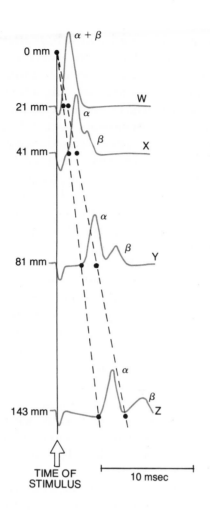

Fig. 4.2-4. Propagation of the alpha and beta waves of the compound action potential of the bullfrog. The four recordings (W–Z) were made from four different recording electrodes at distances of 21, 41, 81, and 143 mm from the site of stimulation (0 mm). As the compound action potential passes down the nerve, the alpha and beta components become separated because the velocity of propagation of the alpha and beta fibers is different. At W, near the start, the alpha and beta waves are completely merged into one wave (α and β). In records X through Z, the alpha and beta waves become separated as the running distance along the nerve increases.

The records have been arranged vertically in proportion to the distance of the respective recording electrodes from the point of stimulation (0 mm). The solid line at *left* is drawn through the point of initiation of the stimulus artifact. The *dashed lines* are drawn through the points of initiation of the alpha component and the point of initiation of the beta component. The points of initiation of the alpha and beta components are indicated by *dots* in each record. The fact that the lines are straight indicates that the velocity of propagation of the alpha and beta components along the nerve is linear. (Adapted from Erlanger and Gasser, 1968.)

strated in work by Erlanger and Gasser (1968): A (the largest), corresponding to large myelinated fibers; and C (the slowest wave), corresponding to very fine unmyelinated fibers. The other component, the B wave, is most characteristic of preganglionic autonomic fibers not present in the sciatic nerve. Within the A wave you may be able to see several subpeaks: A-alpha, A-beta, and A-delta (fig. 4.2-4). The conduction velocity of the C fibers is only about 1/100 that of the A-alpha group. Therefore, you must stimulate at a low enough rate for the C wave to appear before the next A wave occurs. The sweep rate should also be low (about 50 msec/div), and the stimulus intensity high. Determine the relative amplitudes of the various waves in your preparation. Make a tracing or photograph of the most informative recordings.

Threshold

Reduce the stimulus voltage below threshold for all the fibers. Then, gradually increase the stimulus voltage, noting the voltages at which the entire population of each wave is just fully active. Compare the thresholds you have measured with the conduction velocities of the various components of the compound action potential to be measured in the next section.

Conduction velocity

Fiber diameter is probably the most important determinant of conduction velocity, large fibers conducting faster. For bullfrog sciatic nerves the following relationship holds:

V (m/sec) = 2.5D
Where D = fiber diameter in micrometers (μm)

Determine the conduction velocities of the various fiber groups which appear as the different waves of the compound action potential. To do this, it is necessary to determine the time required for the action potential to travel a known distance. The active recording electrode can be moved in the fashion diagrammed in figure 4.2-5, the appropriate measurements made (t_1, t_2, d), and the conduction velocity calculated. Arrange the stimulating and recording electrodes so that you stimulate at the *distal* (thin) end of the nerve, and record from the proximal end. If the nerve is very short, the conduction velocity must be estimated by measuring the time interval from the beginning of the stimulus, and the distance from the stimulating cathode (negative electrode) to the recording electrode. This measure is less accurate because it includes an unknown time to initiate the impulses. The accuracy of the latter measurement is increased by using a supramaximal stimulus intensity and as *brief* a stimulus duration as is feasible.

You can read the oscilloscope display most accurately if you spread it out with a fast sweep speed. Express conduction velocity in meters per second. Use the formula given above to estimate the fiber diameters represented by the various peaks. Remember that the several waves of the compound action potential continue to become separated as they are conducted down the nerve (fig. 4.2-4). All the

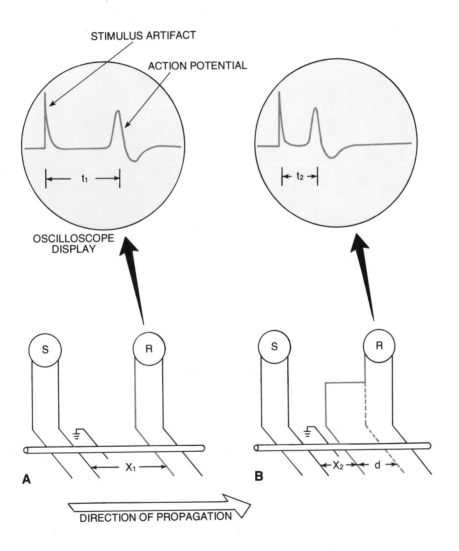

$$t_1 - t_2 = t_d$$

$$\text{Velocity (in m/sec)} = \frac{\text{distance}}{\text{time}} = \frac{d}{t_d} \quad \text{(mm/msec} = \text{m/sec)}$$

Fig. 4.2-5. Measurement of conduction velocity. The oscilloscope display indicates the time delay (t_1 and t_2) between the beginning of the stimulus artifact and the peak of the action potential. The time t_2 in *B* is shorter because one recording electrode has been moved closer to the stimulating electrode. Velocity is normally specified in meters per second which is numerically equivalent to millimeters per millisecond. The circles, *S* and *R*, refer to the *s*timulating and *r*ecording apparatus.

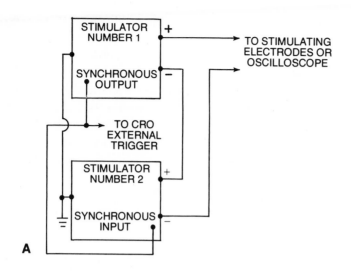

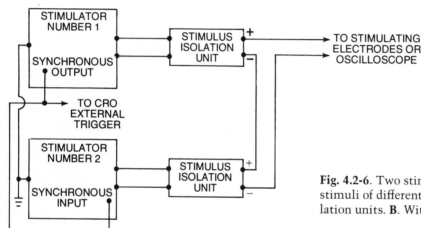

Fig. 4.2-6. Two stimulators connected to give paired stimuli of different amplitudes. **A**. Without stimulus isolation units. **B**. With stimulus isolation units.

action potentials in all of the fibers start at virtually the same time and place. Yet because they travel faster in larger fibers, the *A* wave, for example, soon leads the *C* wave. By analogy two cars may start together, but the faster will move farther and farther ahead of the slower. As you noted that the nerve conducts equally well in either direction, you may have wondered what causes the nerve under normal circumstances to conduct in only one direction. Why, for example, does the action potential not bounce back down the fiber after it reaches the end of the fiber, retracing its route in the opposite direction? The answer is that the part of the axon which has just fired an action potential momentarily has a very high threshold. It is therefore *refractory*, or resistant, to further excitation for a short period of time. To demonstrate refractoriness it is convenient to have a stimulator capable of pulse-pair stimulation.

Refractory periods

Use a pulse-pair stimulator. Set the voltage and duration of the stimulator just high enough to obtain the *A*-alpha wave clearly. Set the stimulator to give paired stimuli (7/sec) about 10 msec apart. Now, gradually decrease the time interval between the two stimuli. Note that, at some point, the amplitude of the second action potential begins to decrease. This occurs because some of the fibers are not stimulated by the second pulse. They are *relatively refractory*, meaning that the second stimulus pulse failed to overcome the raised threshold induced momentarily by the passage of the first action potential.

Investigate this *relative refractory period* by measuring response decrement as a function of the interval between the paired stimuli. Use very brief stimuli. Have the thresholds of the fibers which failed to respond to the second stimulus actually been raised by some finite amount, or are they absolutely blocked? Perhaps they would respond to a stronger second stimulus. The investigation of this problem requires the delivery of paired pulses of different amplitude. The amplitude of the second stimulus pulse has to be increased gradually (and independently of the first) until the second response equals the first. This will ordinarily require the connection of stimulators from two stations, as diagrammed in figure 4.2-6.

After you have the two stimulators connected according to the appropriate diagram, display the output of the stimulators on the oscilloscope and familiarize yourself with the various control knobs. Notice that the time interval between stimuli (*interstimulus interval* or ISI) is controlled by the delay function of the second stimulator. When you are sure of yourself, reconnect the stimulator output to the stimulating electrodes in the nerve chamber. It might prevent confusion if the control knobs on the two stimulators were temporarily labeled with masking tape labels.

To determine the absolute refractory period, adjust the first stimulator until it gives a stimulus (S_1) which is supramaximal for the *A*-alpha and *A*-beta fibers. A supramaximal stimulus in this case is a voltage twice as large as that which evokes a maximum response. Set the interstimulus interval (ISI) to 20 msec and adjust the voltage of the second stimulus (S_2) until you achieve a small, but noticeable, alpha response, about one-fourth the size of the

maximum alpha response. This is the criterion response.

Shorten the ISI and increase the S_2 voltage until the second response is at the criterion level. Repeat several times. You will eventually find some ISI after which you will be unable to evoke a response no matter how large you make S_2. This is the *absolute refractory period*.

Graph the S_2 values versus ISI and indicate the inferred absolute refractory period. Notice that this procedure measures the absolute refractory period for a group of low threshold alpha fibers. Do you understand why? If time permits, modify the experimental design to determine the absolute refractory period for the beta fibers.

Strength-duration curve
(at the instructor's option)
As mentioned earlier, the ability of the stimulus to elicit a response is dependent on the stimulus duration as well as its intensity. In other words, a response can be obtained using a strong current for a short time or a weaker current for a longer time. The relationship between strength and duration can be derived empirically for your sciatic nerve preparation.

Vary the duration and measure the threshold voltage. You may define threshold as a small, but observable, response for the purposes of this experiment. Use the appearance of this response as a criterion for concluding whether or not the stimulus is a *threshold stimulus*. If the stimulus elicits a bigger response, it is a *suprathreshold* stimulus; if it elicits a smaller response or none at all it is *subthreshold*. Start by setting the stimulus duration to 100 msec and gradually increase the stimulus intensity until a threshold response is obtained. Now, decrease the stimulus duration to 50 msec and advance the stimulus voltage until the threshold response is obtained. Continue this process for a number of different stimulus durations.

Plot a strength-duration curve on graph paper, with stimulus intensity (V) on the ordinate and duration (msec) on the abscissa. Your curve should look approximately like that in figure 4.2-7. Stimulus intensity in figure 4.2-7 is measured in terms of current (mA), but you will have to be content to measure voltage since your stimulator gives variable voltage, not current. Since the current is propor-

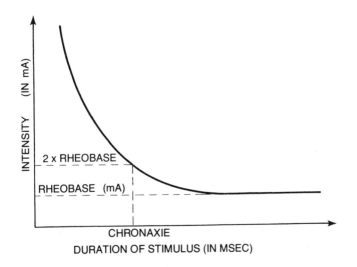

Fig. 4.2-7. A strength-duration curve.

tional to voltage (Ohm's law), the shape of the strength-duration curve will be unaffected. The minimum intensity which elicits a response at infinitely long duration is referred to as the *rheobase*. The stimulus duration required at a stimulus intensity of 2 × rheobase is defined as *chronaxie*. Chronaxie is a measure of the *excitability* of the nerve. The smaller the value of chronaxie, the more excitable the nerve. Determine rheobase (as voltage) and chronaxie for your preparation.

The concepts of rheobase and chronaxie have lost some of the theoretical importance they once had, but chronaxie is still useful to compare the excitability of different nerves or nerves and muscles. Comparison of nerve and muscle by means of determining chronaxie values has shown that muscles are less excitable than nerves. Strength-duration curves have also been used experimentally and clinically to follow the course of nerve and muscle degeneration and regeneration.

The relationship between stimulus intensity and duration in figure 4.2-7 derives from the resistance and capacitive reactance of the membrane and the intra- and extracellular fluids which retard the change in membrane potential with a stimulus. The membrane potential follows an exponential curve as it heads toward its final value, which may or may not exceed the threshold for an action potential. The *time constant* of the membrane (time required to charge to 63% of its final value) can be inferred from a strength-duration curve. We will not go through the mathematical arguments necessary to reach this conclusion, but will give you enough information to determine an approximate time constant for your preparation. Divide the rheobase intensity for your preparation by 0.63. Find the point on your curve corresponding to this intensity value and determine the corresponding time on the duration axis. This time is approximately the time constant of the axonal membranes which are stimulated when the criterion response of your preparation is elicited.

Dispersion of components of compound action potential with distance
(at the instructor's option)
You may wish to obtain data to plot your own version of figure 4.2-4. This is best done with the longest possible nerve. You might include *C* fibers. Do you think the phenomenon of "second pain" or

delayed pain could be related to the conduction velocity difference between delta and *C* pain fibers from your big toe?

Pitfalls and Suggestions

1. If you have trouble operating the oscilloscope, check for the following.

a. Nothing on the screen: Check to see that the oscilloscope is plugged in and turned on; check the intensity control; try the vertical position knob; make sure the instrument is triggering by readjusting the triggering level control and checking the triggering mode switch.
b. Nothing but vertical lines: The vertical sensitivity is probably too high (too much gain).
c. Stimulator not triggering oscilloscope sweep: Check to see that there is a ground connection between the stimulator and oscilloscope.
d. 60 Hz Interference: Double-check the ground connections. If using a Faraday cage, it should be grounded to the oscilloscope. As a last resort use aluminum foil around and under the nerve chamber to shield it, being sure to ground the aluminum foil. The foil should not touch metal electrode contacts. Use coaxial (shielded) cables if they are available. *All* cables should be as short as possible.
2. Be gentle with the nerve; do not stretch it or pinch the middle region. Do not let it dry out.
3. The nerve should make good physical contact with the recording and stimulating electrodes without being excessively wet.
4. When there is no action potential, check for the following.

a. Is the equipment set properly? If the stimulator is on, confirm that the oscilloscope and stimulator settings are in the correct ranges, that all connections are correct, and especially that the polarity of the stimulating electrodes is correct. The cathode (negative-going stimulating electrode) should be closest to the recording electrodes. If there is no stimulus artifact, check switches and connections.
b. Was the preparation injured in the dissection? Do not try to record from the extreme, mangled ends of the nerves. Shift the stimulating and/or recording electrodes closer together.
c. Has the preparation dried out? If so, there is probably little you can do except to get a new nerve.

d. Is fluid shorting out the system? If so, lower the level, or soak up with cotton any drops of perfusion solution which may be adhering to the nerve or the electrodes. Use the oil/perfusion fluid mixture to prevent this problem.

e. Equipment failures can be tracked down by substituting another SIU, preamplifier, etc. Rarely, however, is the basic equipment at fault.

Materials

Materials needed at each station
Oscilloscope
Stimulator (and isolation unit if available)
Preamplifier
Set of electrical leads and connectors
Nerve chamber and its cover
Faraday cage (if readily available; otherwise probably unnecessary with differential amplification)
2 small beakers and a medicine dropper or Pasteur pipette and bulb
2 glass tools for dissecting and manipulating nerves
Set of dissecting tools (furnished by students)

Materials available in the laboratory
Oscilloscope camera and film
Extra medicine droppers or Pasteur pipettes and bulbs
Extra glass slides
Fine cotton thread
Dissecting pans
Dissecting microscope with illuminator
Dishpan for cleanup. The oil/perfusion fluid mixture has a tendency to climb out of the chamber and deposit itself on every available surface. To facilitate cleaning the chambers, a dishpan filled with warm, soapy (Liquinox) water should be available in the laboratory. Of course, the detergent should be *thoroughly* rinsed out of the nerve chamber, or it may cause trouble for the next user.
Aluminum foil (for possible use as electrical shielding)
Plastic bag for disposal of dissected frogs
Masking tape for temporary labels
Cotton for absorbing excess fluids
Solutions:
   Amphibian perfusion solution (frog Ringer's solution) (100 ml/station)
   Mineral oil saturated with perfusion solution (100

ml/station, prepared by adding 0.5 ml Ringer's solution to 100 ml mineral oil. Shake vigorously and the oil will turn cloudy. A two-phase system remaining after persistent shaking indicates that the oil is saturated. Allow 1 hour to equilibrate. Have this prepared, ready to use if the nerve tends to dry out in the chamber. Use fresh mineral oil.)
0.16 M NaCl (20 ml/station)
0.16 M KCl (20 ml/station)

Animals
Rana pipiens (Order 1.5 frogs/station/laboratory period.) Keep the frogs in a cool place and provide them with dripping water.

Notes for the Instructor

1. This experiment is written up in more detail than most of the electrophysiological experiments which follow it. It is suggested as a reliable first experiment for the students to gain experience with electrophysiological instrumentation.
2. Do not assign this entire experiment for a single 3-hour laboratory period. The material through page 92 is about all that can be accomplished in one 3-hour period.
3. The experiment can be performed without the use of a preamplifier, as in figure 4.2-3, if the gain of the oscilloscope vertical amplifier is sufficiently high. Some Tektronix high-gain plug-in units are especially suitable for bioelectric applications since they often have frequency filters and some have external outputs suitable for driving audio amplifiers or pen-writing recorders. Students *will* have to use a preamplifier in many of the experiments in later sections.
4. Emphasize care in dissection and handling the nerve. Freeing the nerve at the point where it leaves the body cavity is the most hazardous part of the dissection and must be done with extreme care. Stress the use of glass tools wherever possible. The nerve chamber must be covered. Desiccation is the major cause of nerve conduction failure.
5. If a dual-beam oscilloscope is available, monophasic and biphasic action potentials can be recorded *simultaneously*, as indicated in the figure 4.2-3. This can be set up as a class demonstration by the instructor or one of the more advanced students.

Selected References

Davson, H. 1970. *A textbook of general physiology*, vol. 2, 4th ed., J. and A. Churchill, London.

Erlanger, J., and Gasser, H. S. 1968. *Electrical signs of nervous activity*, 2d ed. University of Pennsylvania Press, Philadelphia.

Hodgkin, A. L. 1964. *The conduction of the nervous impulse*. Charles C Thomas, Springfield, Ill.

Tasaki, I. 1968. *Nerve excitation: A macromolecular approach*. Charles C Thomas, Springfield, Ill.

RESEARCH REPORTS

Cragg, B. G., and Thomas, P. K. 1957. The relationships between conduction velocity and the diameter and internodal length of peripheral nerve fibers. *J. Physiol.* 136: 606–14.

Erlanger, J.; Gasser, H. S.; and Bishop, G. H. 1924. The compound nature of the action current of nerve as disclosed by the cathode ray oscillograph. *Am. J. Physiol.* 70: 624–66.

Erlanger, J., and Gasser, H. S. 1930. The action potential in fibers of slow conduction in spinal roots and somatic nerves. *Am. J. Physiol.* 92: 43–82.

Hill, A. V. 1936. The strength-duration relation for electric excitation of medullated nerve. *Proc. R. Soc., B.* 119: 440–53.

4.3 Compound Action Potential and Single Units
Limulus Leg Nerve

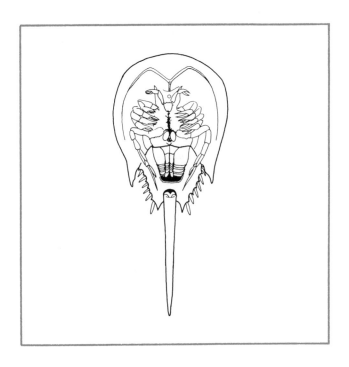

of the horseshoe crab *Limulus polyphemus*, or in the crayfish or lobster. The walking legs of *Limulus* consist of six segments. Any of the legs is a suitable source of the leg nerve. The position of the nerve within a leg is shown by the colored line in figure 4.3-1. *Limulus* walking legs have diverse and extraordinarily abundant sensory innervation (Barber, 1956; Hayes and Barber, 1967; Wyse, 1967). There are tactile receptors, chemoreceptors, warm and cold receptors, and proprioceptors for sensing joint movements. The nerve at the level of the tibia has approximately six large motor axons (27–37 μm in diameter) and about 350,000 sensory axons! All are unmyelinated. Figure 4.3-2 compares the appearance of a cross section of the *Limulus* leg nerve with a representative mammalian leg nerve and the squid giant axon. The crayfish leg nerve has 1/10 the number of axons of the *Limulus* leg nerve.

Introduction

Rationale

Arthropods have abundant sensory fibers in their peripheral nerves, but only a small fraction of the number of motor fibers present in vertebrate peripheral nerves. This small number of relatively large unmyelinated motor fibers permits recording of large extracellular action potentials from a few fibers in the arthropod nerve. Consequently, this exercise may help to bridge the conceptual gap between the compound action potential as seen in the frog sciatic nerve and the activity of single units (single axons). One or two single units can be resolved in the majority of arthropod leg nerve preparations.

In this experiment you will examine single and compound action potentials in the robust leg nerve

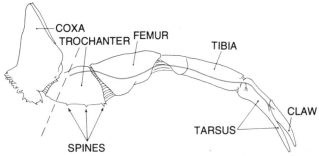

Fig. 4.3-1. Anterior view of the fourth walking leg (*left side*) of *Limulus*. The tarsus has been rotated 90° so that the claw is visible; normally the movable claw is posterior. You can readily recognize the ventral edge of the leg, even when it has been removed, by locating the stubby spines on the ventral edge of the trochanter. The position of the leg nerve as it courses through the interior of the leg is shown *colored*. The *dashed line* indicates where stout scissors should be used to cut through to remove the leg. (Adapted from Wyse, 1967.)

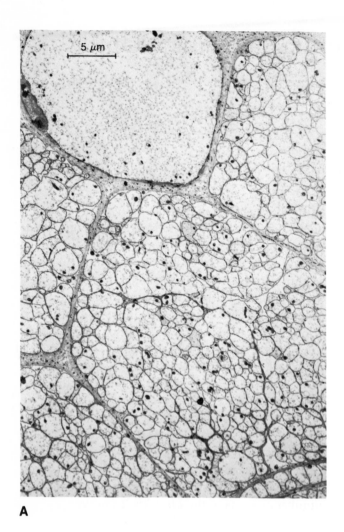

A

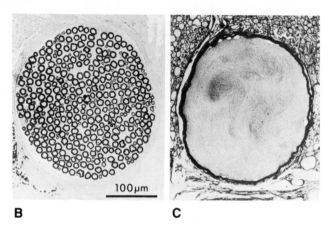

B   **C**

Fig. 4.3-2. Sizes and pattern of axons in vertebrate and invertebrate peripheral nerves. **A.** Low-power electron micrograph of a cross section of the major leg nerve of *Limulus* fixed in OsO₄ and stained with lead citrate. A large axon (containing a 5 μm scale line) and portions of four bundles (fascicles) of numerous smaller fibers are visible. (From Wyse, 1967.) **B.** Light micrograph of a cross section through a branch of the sciatic nerve in the rabbit. The thick black circles are the myelin sheaths of about 400 myelinated fibers, many of which are motor fibers. This micrograph does not demonstrate the smaller (unmyelinated) fibers. **C.** Light micrograph of a cross section through a giant nerve fiber in the squid, surrounded by smaller axons. Magnification as in *B*. (*B* and *C* from J. Z. Young, 1951. *Doubt and Certainty in Science*. Oxford University Press, London.)

Time to complete the exercise: At least one 3-hour laboratory period; two periods for a more complete and careful treatment.

Procedure

Surgical procedure
Examine a specimen of *Limulus*. Although the movable posterior tail spine and chelae (leg pincers) may appear formidable, there is no way in which the animal can inflict pain. The pincers are weak. Notice the two large faceted (compound) eyes on the rounded anterior face of the shell. It is from these eyes that we have come to understand one of the most far-reaching principles of sensory integration—*lateral inhibition*. The ventral eye on the "nose" has also been used extensively in recent studies.

Refer to figure 4.3-1 and examine a leg. Find the trochanter and feel the spines on the ventral edge. To remove a leg use stout scissors and cut through the trochanter at the position indicated by the dashed line in figure 4.3-1. The blood of *Limulus* is blue from its respiratory pigment, hemocyanin. To aid coagulation, delay a few minutes before replacing the animal in a container with sea water (it need not be completely submerged).

There are two ways to remove the nerve from the leg. Try method 1 first to gain experience.

Method 1. Slit the exoskeleton of the tibia, femur, and remaining trochanter longitudinally with stout scissors along both the dorsal and ventral ridges.

If you cut too deeply, you will injure the nerve.

Carefully spread the exoskeleton of the leg apart and look among the light yellow muscles for the whitest structure visible. This will be the leg nerve. Free the nerve wherever possible using glass tools and lateral rather than longitudinal movements. Apply sea water freely to avoid drying. When the nerve appears to be sufficiently free of attachments, cut through all the muscles, fascia, and apodemes at the most distal (tibial-tarsal) joint, leaving only the nerve bridging the gap. (Apodemes are stiff internal projections of the exoskeleton which may extend from one segment to the next to serve as leverlike attachment points for muscles.) You should use stout scissors to transect the apodeme. Slide the nerve out by slowly pulling on the tarsus. Hold the tarsus above a small beaker of sea water and snip off the nerve into the beaker. This dissection should take no more than 30 minutes.

Method 2. Once you have learned to identify the whitish appearance of the nerve, it is much faster to slip the nerve out without cutting the exoskeleton apart. This may be more useful, too, because it generally eliminates the electrically insulating nerve sheath. Cut off a leg at the site indicated in figure 4.3-1. Use good dissecting scissors and cut through the membranous tissue at the most distal joint of the detached leg. *Again, do not cut too deeply.* Carefully cut while looking for the nerve. Cut through all tissue except the nerve at the joint. Gently pull the joint apart, and the nerve should slide out of the proximal portion of the leg. Hold the tarsus above a small beaker of sea water and cut off the nerve so it falls into the beaker.

Recording Procedure

Initial arrangements

Fill the nerve chamber with sea water so that the electrodes are slightly immersed. Lay the nerve in the chamber across the electrode wires, using glass tools to situate it properly on the electrodes. Drain off enough of the sea water with a Pasteur pipette or medicine dropper to leave the nerve suspended on the electrodes. The level of sea water in the chamber must be low enough to prevent any contact between the sea water and the electrodes, but some sea water should be left in the chamber to retard drying. Place a cover over the chamber as soon as the nerve is

properly arranged. If a long recording period is anticipated, it may be necessary to use a mineral oil/sea water mixture on the nerve to retard drying. The disadvantage of the oil/sea water is that it may hinder penetration by KCl when it is later applied to the nerve for monophasic recording.

Refer to figure 4.2-2 to set up the following connections. Connect one set of cables to two electrodes near one end of the nerve. These will be the recording electrodes, and they should be plugged into the preamplifier input. Ground a central electrode with a lead to a ground connector on the preamplifier. Connect another pair of cables from the stimulator output to a pair of electrodes at the other end of the nerve. The recording electrodes should be at least 5–10 mm from the stimulating electrode. Make sure that the cathode (negative stimulating electrode) is nearest to the recording electrodes.

Connect the output of the preamplifier to the input of the oscilloscope with appropriate cables and connectors. Ground the stimulator to the oscilloscope. The trigger output (synchronous output) of the stimulator should be connected to the trigger input of the oscilloscope. Use the following initial settings on your equipment.

Preamplifier.   Input in differential mode if possible; gain of 100–1,000×; band-pass filters (if available) set at about 10 Hz (low frequency filter) and 3–5 kHz (high frequency filter).
Oscilloscope.   Time base at 5 msec/div; vertical sensitivity at 0.1–0.01 V/div; trigger set on external input and the triggering level control adjusted to trigger the oscilloscope sweep when the stimulator is actuated.
Calibration.   Adjust the overall system gain (preamplifier plus oscilloscope) to about 100 μV/div. Check by using the preamplifier calibration function, if available. If you do not understand the meaning or procedure of calibration, ask your instructor.
Stimulator.   Frequency of 7/sec; delay (if available) of about 1 msec; duration of 0.2 msec; starting voltage of 0.1 V.

Activate the stimulator by placing the output mode switch in the *continuous* position. Gradually increase the stimulus voltage until a waveform can be clearly seen on the screen. This will normally be the stimulus artifact, and is not a response of the

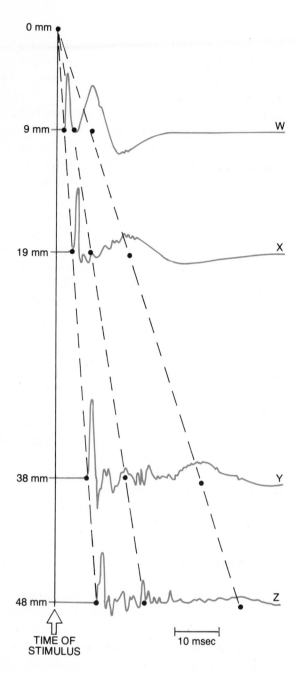

nerve. Continue to increase the stimulus strength. The amplitude of the artifact should increase linearly with the stimulus voltage. Note also that the waveform of the stimulus artifact is directly varied by changing the stimulus duration. (If you are using a dual-beam oscilloscope with differential inputs, you can simultaneously monitor the actual stimulus waveform by connecting the stimulator output to the second channel of the oscilloscope in parallel with the stimulating electrodes. Do not ground either of the stimulator output leads.)

Increase the stimulus voltage gradually. Eventually, at threshold for some of the nerve fibers, a deflection of the baseline of the trace should appear at some point to the right of the stimulus artifact. It is important to understand that this represents a time delay, called *latency*, which reflects conduction velocity. The active neural response can be distinguished because its duration and amplitude are not linear functions of the stimulus strength.

When all necessary measurements have been made, trace the waveform or use a Polaroid camera to make a permanent record. Be sure to note the sweep speed (time) and voltage calibration on the back of the tracing or photograph.

Since the number of low threshold axons, namely the larger ones, is rather small in the arthropod leg nerve, you should be able to obtain responses from one or two single fibers by manipulating the stimulus parameters. Attempt to get one or two single fibers by using stimuli of low intensity and short duration. Determine the amplitude and duration of the action potentials you record. The criteria that are commonly applied for proof that a given spike is from a single fiber are that the response has an all-or-none threshold, and that it has a fixed amplitude and waveform.

The actual waveform of a response will depend on at least four factors: (*a*) stimulus intensity and duration; (*b*) whether the recording is monophasic or biphasic; (*c*) the viability of the fibers in the nerve; and (*d*) the distance between the stimulating and recording electrodes. Figure 4.3-3 shows the change in the compound action potential waveform over distance as the impulses of slow conducting fibers lag farther and farther behind those of the larger, fast conducting axons. (A similar record for the frog sciatic nerve is explained in more detail in figure 4.2-4.)

Fig. 4.3-3. Spread in a propagated compound action potential of *Limulus* leg nerve recorded at 9, 19, 38, and 48 mm from the site of a supramaximal electrical stimulus. The compound action potential waveform spreads out as it propagates along the nerve because the slower conducted spikes (from smaller fibers) progressively lag behind the faster conducted spikes. The increasingly wider spread of the individual components is indicated by the spreading *dashed lines* connecting *dots* which show the position of individual spikes. As the compound action potential spreads out with distance, spikes of single fibers become separated and hence visible as unitary action potentials. (Adapted from Wyse, 1967.)

If necessary, turn off the stimulus and arrange the polarity of the recording electrodes so that the initial deflection of the response is upward on the oscilloscope screen. The electrode nearest the stimulating electrodes will be negative-going as the action potential passes this point. This wave of depolarization corresponds to the initial upward deflection of the displayed waveform. The downward deflection which follows is produced as the wave of depolarization sweeps by the second recording electrode. This is a *biphasic* recording of the action potential.

Nerves from some arthropods fatigue rapidly with excessively strong or prolonged stimulation. Turn off the stimulus when not making observations.

Slowly decrease the stimulating voltage until the response disappears completely. The stimulus intensity has now dropped below the threshold for even the most sensitive fibers in the nerve. Record the threshold voltage and duration. Now, increase the stimulus strength until no further change in the response pattern occurs, observing particularly the later responses. After the last fibers come in, increase the stimulus strength about 10% more. You are now applying a supramaximal stimulus at the given stimulus duration. Experiment with the stimulus duration to determine whether the response is truly maximal. For most purposes it is best to use the shortest duration which activates all the fibers since arthropod nerves, unlike the frog sciatic nerve, are prone to repetitive discharge with prolonged or excessively strong stimuli. Is it valid to assume that action potentials of the same amplitude come from repetitive discharge of the same fiber?

As you proceed, remember that you can see the response better if you adjust stimulus delay, gain, and sweep speed while observing various aspects of the response. No one setting is best for all. As already stated, the recording is probably biphasic. Shift the distal recording electrode progressively away from the stimulating electrodes, and note the changes in form and amplitude of the recorded potentials. How do you account for the observed changes? Since the compound action potential usu-

ally has a complex waveform, interpretation of biphasic recordings is difficult.

Monophasic recording
Render the recording *monophasic* by crushing the nerve at the second recording electrode with fine forceps. Apply a tiny drop of 0.16 M KCl with a pin or dissecting needle to the region of the nerve at the second recording electrode, i.e., nearest the end of the nerve.

Apply only a very small amount of KCl to the nerve. Using too much will result in its spread and the deactivation of the nerve beyond the second recording electrode.

Resume stimulating about once every 10–20 seconds. You may observe the transformation of the biphasic wave to a monophasic wave as the KCl block takes effect. The action potentials will sweep down the nerve and drive the first recording electrode negative, but will now fail to reach the second recording electrode because the membrane is no longer polarized at that site ($[K]_o \approx [K]_i$). Once the block is complete, examine and describe the components of the compound action potential. The various components have not been identified as in the frog sciatic nerve, so you can create your own classification, such as wave I, wave II, etc. If subgroups are present, these might be designated wave Ia, wave Ib, etc. Measure the approximate amplitude of the various components in millivolts. The most accurate way to measure conduction velocity is to determine the time required for the action potential to travel over a known distance. The active (colored) recording electrode can be moved in the fashion diagrammed in figure 4.2-5 and the appropriate measurements made (t_1, t_2, and d) for the conduction velocity calculation. Record the temperature. For an easier, but less accurate, measure of conduction velocity, record the intervals in milliseconds between the crests of the major components and the beginning of the stimulus artifact, and the distance between the stimulating cathode and the first recording electrode. Measurement can be aided by increasing the sweep speed to stretch the trace out.

Excitation and strength-duration curves
(at the instructor's option)
The effectiveness of a stimulus depends upon both its duration and its amplitude. The longer the stimulus, the less strength needed; and the stronger the stimulus, the shorter the duration needed. A *strength-duration* curve can be plotted by measuring the stimulus strength necessary to elicit a response at different duration settings. The minimal strength necessary at infinite duration is termed the *rheobase*; the minimal time at rheobase strength, the *utilization time*; and the time for a stimulus of twice rheobase strength, *chronaxie*. These terms no longer carry the theoretical importance they once did, but they are useful descriptive parameters. If you have never plotted a strength-duration curve before, gather the necessary data on a single fiber (if possible) and draw such a curve. See figure 4.2-7.

Try to compare this strength-duration curve with that of a second fiber (component). Should you use the stimulus strength just necessary to elicit the response of the component? Or, should you use the stimulus intensity necessary to elicit the maximum response of each component? The following recommendations are given for obtaining a strength-duration curve.

1. Use a newly dissected nerve for this portion of the experiment.
2. Begin the stimulus series with long durations and low voltages and work upward to stronger, shorter stimuli. This often tends to minimize the danger of fatigue to the nerve.
3. Square monophasic pulses must be used as stimuli.
4. If convenient, you may find it instructive to follow a series of increasing stimulus strengths immediately with a series of stimuli in decreasing order of strength.
5. Calibrate the stimulator, or better, if a dual-beam oscilloscope is available, display the stimulus voltage on the second beam by a parallel connection to the stimulator output.
6. Record the temperature.

Observe that the latency between stimulus and response for any given fiber is not constant over the entire range of effective stimuli. Thus, stimulus strength will affect determinations of conduction velocity if stimulus-response latencies rather than response-response intervals are used.

Repetitive discharges
(at the instructor's option)
Many arthropod nerve fibers tend to discharge repetitively when stimulated by long or strong stimuli. This phenomenon does not occur so readily in the peripheral axons of vertebrate nerves. Stimulate with stimulus pulses of gradually increasing duration. Observe that as the duration increases, repetitive responses appear during the prolonged stimulus pulse and often at the stimulus-off point. Reverse the polarity of the stimulating electrodes (cathode and anode) and note that many, if not all, of the repetitive responses are blocked. How many fibers are observed to discharge repetitively? What is the *frequency* of their discharge? Can the frequency be related to the strength of stimulation? Continue to increase stimulus duration. How long does the repetitive discharge continue? Can repetitively discharging fibers be stimulated by very short, but very strong stimuli?

Other electrophysiological properties
(at the instructor's option)
A number of other properties of the arthropod action potential may be profitably examined if time is available. These properties include the determination of the refractory periods of the nerve; an examination of the effects of high frequency, prolonged stimulation; or an analysis of the effects of temperature on conduction velocity, excitability, and the waveform of the action potential.

Pitfalls and Suggestions

1. The same kinds of advice given for the frog sciatic nerve experiment (4.2) hold here.
2. Be especially careful to use only a minute amount of 0.16 M KCl to produce a monophasic recording. The use of a larger amount, or a higher concentration, such as 1.0 M, may lead to the deactivation of much of the nerve.
3. The *Limulus* leg nerve is more subject to drying than the frog sciatic nerve. Be certain that the nerve chamber is completely covered over as soon as the nerve is put in place.

Materials

Materials needed at each station

Oscilloscope

Stimulator

Preamplifier

Set of electrical leads and connectors

Nerve chamber and its cover

Faraday cage (if readily available; otherwise probably
unnecessary with differential amplification)

Dissecting microscope and illuminator

Dissecting pan and insect pins

2 small beakers and 2 medicine droppers

2 glass tools to aid in freeing the nerve from surrounding tissue and in other manipulations

Set of dissecting tools (furnished by students)

Materials available in the laboratory

Oscilloscope camera and film

Wax pencil to mark beakers

Extra Pasteur pipettes or medicine droppers and
beakers

Fine cotton thread

Aluminum foil (for possible use as electrical shielding)

Extra insect pins

Extra glass slides

Microslides of arthropod peripheral nerve (optional)
(Several slides showing cross sections of arthropod
peripheral nerve may be supplemented with light
or electron micrographs and drawings in published
sources.)

Compound microscope and illuminator

Dishpan for cleanup, filled with warm, soapy
(Liquinox) water

Plastic bag for animal disposal

Solutions:

Sea water (200 ml/station)

Mineral oil saturated with sea water (100 ml/
station, prepared by the method used to make
up oil/perfusion fluid in experiment 4.2, page
95.

0.16 M KCl (100 ml)

Animals

Horseshoe crab (*Limulus polyphemus*) (Order 0.33/
station/laboratory period.) Since each *Limulus* has
a number of legs, it is not necessary to obtain very
many animals, unless different students plan to do
their experiments on different days. Horseshoe
crabs need cool, aerated sea water (see section
10.7). They can be kept for months in a simple
tank if the water is filtered and provided with air
bubblers.

Notes for the Instructor

1. The experiment is straightforward, and the only
problem may come with the dissection or drying of
the nerve. Urge the students to perform a careful
dissection.

2. Lobsters or crayfish can be substituted for
Limulus. However, their nerves are more fragile.

3. This particular experiment lacks specific instructions for certain types of data collection. For example, the questions asked in the section on repetitive
discharges (page 102) could lead to extensive data
collection. You may wish to provide more specific
guidance for the several optional exercises, depending on the type of students in your class.

Selected References

Bullock, T. H., and Horridge, G. A. 1965. *Structure and
function in the nervous systems of invertebrates*. W. H.
Freeman and Co., San Francisco.

RESEARCH REPORTS

Barber, S. B. 1956. Chemoreception and proprioreception
in *Limulus*. *J. Exp. Zool*. 131: 51–74.

Chapman, R. A. 1966. The repetitive responses of isolated
axons from the crab, *Carcinus maenas*. *J. Exp. Biol*. 45:
475–88.

Hayes, W. F. 1966. Chemoreceptor structure in *Limulus*.
J. Morphol. 119: 121–42.

Hayes, W. F., and Barber, S. B. 1967. Proprioreceptor distribution and properties in *Limulus* walking legs. *J. Exp.
Zool*. 165: 195–210.

Hodgkin, A. L. 1948. The local electric changes associated
with repetitive action in a non-medullated axon.
J. Physiol. 107: 165–81.

Patten, W., and Redenbaugh, W. A. 1900. Studies on
Limulus, vol. 2. The nervous system of *Limulus
polyphemus*, with observations upon the general anatomy. *J. Morphol*. 16: 91–200.

Wyse, G. A. 1967. Functional organization of receptors in
the claws of *Limulus polyphemus*. Ph.D. dissertation,
University of Michigan.

———. 1971. Receptor organization and function in
Limulus chelae. *Z. vergl. Physiol*. 73: 249–73.

4.4 Giant Nerve Fibers
Earthworm Nerve Cord

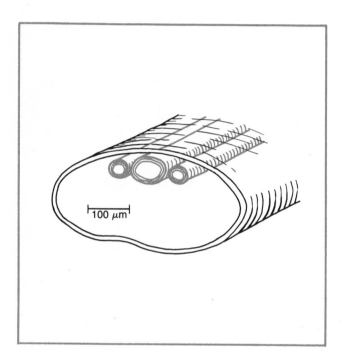

100 μm

Introduction

Rationale

Giant nerve fibers have contributed much to neurobiology because their large size makes them convenient to study. For example, one can longitudinally insert a small electrode inside some giant nerve fibers to voltage clamp the membrane. The large diameter of the axons permits stable *intra*cellular recording using relatively large capillary electrodes which are free of some of the technical problems encountered with true microelectrodes. The large electrical currents produced during an action potential also make *extra*cellular recording a relatively easy matter. The giant fibers found in squid are the source of much of our understanding about the role of the cell membrane in nerve excitation (Hodgkin and Huxley, 1952). In this experiment you will be able to record from giant fibers and measure properties of conducted action potentials.

In a great many invertebrates, fast, through-conducting pathways exist in the ventral nerve cord in the form of giant axons. The term *giant* is somewhat relative; in some species giant axons are quite small. But sometimes they attain enormous dimensions, as in the single, multicellular, syncytial giant axon of *Myxicola*, a tube-building polychaete worm. The giant fiber of *Myxicola* occupies almost the whole of the ventral nerve cord of the animal and may have a diameter of 0.5–1.0 mm.

As a rule, giant axons initiate the startle response leading to withdrawal. For example, fishermen stalking worms find themselves swearing at the organism's uncanny ability to suddenly disappear into a burrow at the slightest disturbance. It is commonly believed that the large diameter of the giant fibers is a specialization for increased conduction velocity to enhance the rapidity of escape responses.

The earthworm *Lumbricus* sp. will be used in this exercise. Its nerve cord has three giant fibers, a median giant and two lateral giants which monitor sensory input and distribute their output to the motoneurons, causing contraction of the longitudinal muscles. The median giant receives sensory input only from the anterior portion of the worm (approximately 40 segments), and the lateral giants receive sensory input only from the posterior part of the worm. Once activated, an axon will conduct impulses in both directions. You can examine reflex activity by tapping the head or tail before dissecting.

The current produced by excited giant fibers of *Lumbricus* is large enough to permit a simplified recording technique. It is sufficient to remove a ventral strip of body wall to which the nerve cord is attached and lay the strip (cord down) across the electrodes in a standard nerve chamber.

Time to complete the exercise: At least one 3-hour laboratory period is required to learn the dissection, view the waveform of the giant fiber action potentials, and determine conduction velocity. A second session is necessary to examine refractory periods and temperature effects.

Procedure

Prepared slide
Study figure 4.4-1 or a prepared slide (cross section) of the earthworm nerve cord. Note the ventral position of the cord in the body under low power. Look at the giant fibers under high power.

Surgical procedure
Place an earthworm in a small quantity of 10% ethanol until the worm is narcotized sufficiently so it will not struggle when touched (5–10 minutes). Rinse the worm with earthworm perfusion solution and immediately begin the dissection by pinning the worm down with the dorsal (dark) side up. Cut along both sides of the body (preferably with fine scissors) to produce a thin strip of ventral skin. See figure 4.4-2 for an appropriate strip width and cord location.

> The major precaution is to avoid pinching or cutting the nerve cord. If rupture of the gut occurs, quickly wash away its contents with earthworm perfusion fluid.

The final product of the operation should be a thin strip of ventral skin 4–6 cm long with the nerve cord attached and the surrounding tissue cleaned away. Remove any major portions of the gut which cover the nerve cord, using fine forceps. Small, thin remnants of the gut will not be troublesome. The nerve cord will look like a pale yellow thread; the giant fibers are embedded in the cord and will not be distinguishable. Examine with a dissecting microscope for obvious breaks or cuts in the cord. The dissection should take 20–30 minutes.

Once the strip with the nerve cord has been prepared, wash it thoroughly with earthworm perfusion fluid. Fill the nerve chamber to 1 or 2 mm below the level of the electrodes with earthworm perfusion fluid, and lay the strip on the electrode wires with

the nerve cord down. The remaining muscles may cause the preparation to contract or move about. If too much movement is encountered, it may be necessary to gently stretch and reposition the strip a few times. In general, try not to pinch the nerve cord or stretch it unnecessarily, as this can destroy the axonal membranes.

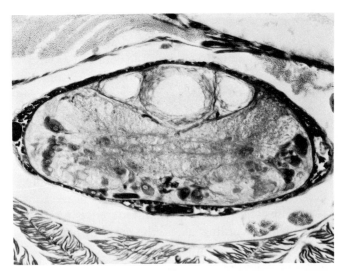

Fig. 4.4-1. Cross section of earthworm nerve cord showing three giant fibers at the top. The largest fiber (median giant) is 80 μm in diameter. Note the thick layers of glial sheathing which surround it, and, to a lesser extent, the two lateral giants. Cell bodies of neurons may be seen on the *right*, *left*, and at the *bottom*. The central area of the nerve cord, as in all invertebrates, is filled with fine nerve fibers and synaptic areas (neuropil).

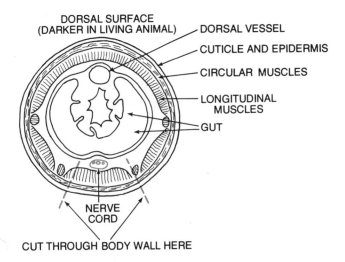

Fig. 4.4-2. Simplified cross section through the body of an earthworm. For recording from the ventral nerve cord, a strip of the ventral body wall is dissected out and laid (nerve cord down) on the nerve chamber electrodes.

When the nerve cord is properly situated on the electrodes, you may have to withdraw some of the perfusion fluid from the chamber so that the strip is fully supported by the electrodes and does not touch the fluid below. There should be no drops of fluid trapped between adjacent electrodes.

Recording Procedure

Arrange the electrode leads such that you stimulate and record at opposite ends of the cord and ground the center (fig. 4.4-3). For recording, connect one set of cables to two electrodes near one end of the nerve. Ground a central electrode with a lead to a ground connector on the preamplifier. Connect another pair of cables from the output of the stimulator to a pair of electrodes at the other end of the nerve cord. Make sure that the cathode (negative and therefore depolarizing or stimulating electrode) is nearest the recording electrodes. If 60 Hz interference is a problem during recording, shield the nerve by placing another foil sheet as a cover around the chamber. The foil *must not* touch the electrodes. Do not do this at the outset. It is preferable to start with a simple system and to check your ground leads carefully before modifying.

Connect the output of your preamplifier to the input of the oscilloscope with appropriate cables and connectors. The trigger output (synchronous output) of the stimulator should be connected to the trigger input of the oscilloscope and a ground connection made between the two instruments (fig. 4.4-3).

Use the following initial settings on your equipment.

Preamplifier.   Input in differential mode if possible; gain of 100–1,000×; band-pass filters (if available) set at about 30 Hz (low frequency filter) and 3 kHz (high frequency filter).

Oscilloscope.   Time base at 2 msec/div; vertical sensitivity at 0.1–0.01 V/div; trigger set on external input, and the triggering level control adjusted to trigger the oscilloscope sweep when the stimulator is actuated.

Calibration.   Adjust the overall system gain (preamplifier plus oscilloscope) to about 100 μV/div. Check by using the preamplifier calibration function, if available. If you do not understand the meaning or procedure of calibration, ask your instructor.

Stimulator.   Frequency of 7/sec; delay (if available) of about 1 msec; duration of 0.2 msec; starting voltage of 0.1 V.

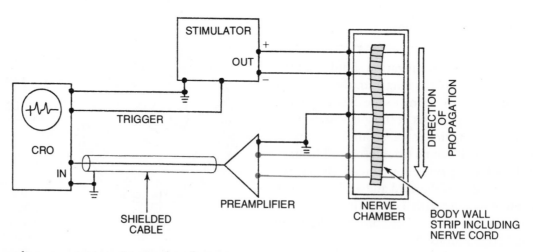

Fig. 4.4-3. Recording arrangement. A strip of earthworm body wall including the nerve cord has been placed on the recording (*colored*) and stimulating electrodes. The oscilloscope displays impulses in the median and lateral giant fibers, respectively. The first deflection of the CRO trace is the stimulus artifact.

Activate the stimulator by placing the output mode switch in the *continuous* position. Gradually increase the stimulus voltage until a waveform appears on the screen. This will normally be the stimulus artifact, and is not a response of the nerve. Continue to increase the stimulus strength. The amplitude of the artifact should increase linearly with the stimulus voltage. Also note that the duration and waveform of the stimulus artifact is continuously varied by changing the stimulus duration. Neither changing amplitude, nor changing duration is characteristic of the all-or-none action potential. (If you are using a dual-beam oscilloscope, you can simultaneously monitor the actual stimulus waveform by connecting the stimulator output to the second channel of the oscilloscope in parallel with the stimulating electrodes. However, do *not* ground either side of the stimulator output.)

Increase the stimulus voltage gradually. Eventually, at threshold, the response of one or more of the giant fibers should appear as a deflection in the baseline of the trace at some point to the right of the stimulus artifact (fig. 4.4-4). Prove to your satisfaction that the response is an all-or-none phenomenon and its amplitude unrelated to stimulus strength (unless the stimulus artifact is so large that it adds to the amplitude of the physiological response). If necessary, reverse the polarity of the recording electrodes so that the initial deflection of the displayed waveform is upward. What is the latency (in msec) to the peak of the response from the beginning of the stimulus artifact? Change the position of the recording electrodes first, then the position of the stimulating electrodes, if there is no response. Do not exceed 10–15 V. Finally, try moving the stimulating and recording electrodes closer together to find a conducting section of nerve cord.

Analysis of the Action Potential of Earthworm Giant Fibers

Median and lateral giants
Since the conduction velocity for the median giant fiber should be greater than that of the lateral giants, the median fiber's response will generally appear to the left of the summated response of the two lateral giant fibers on the oscilloscope trace. (Be sure you understand the reasoning behind this statement.) The two lateral giants tend to have the same con-

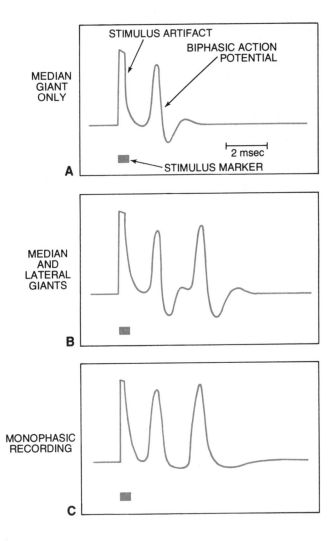

Fig. 4.4-4. Student-produced records from earthworm giant nerve fibers. In **A**, the response of the single, median giant fiber appears after the stimulus artifact. In **B**, the stimulus intensity has been increased to bring in the two lateral giant fibers, whose response is seen as a single action potential following the first (median giant) action potential. In **C**, the region around the second recording electrode has been treated with isotonic KCl to produce a pair of monophasic action potentials, the first from the median giant and the second from the two lateral giants.

duction velocity; hence their action potentials may appear as one on the oscilloscope. If only one waveform is apparent on the screen, you are recording from only one type of fiber, and the stimulus voltage will have to be increased to excite the other type of fiber. Strong electrical stimulation of the ventral nerve cord initiates action potentials in most of the fibers in the cord, but at this amplification only the action potentials produced by the three giant fibers will be visible on the oscilloscope screen. Determine the voltage threshold difference between the two types of fibers. Which type has the lower threshold? What is the difference in millivolts? Measure the size of the action potentials in mV by using the calibration circuit on your preamplifier if it has one.

The accuracy of recording the timing and duration of the action potentials can be improved by monophasic recording. The biphasic waveform you have been recording is a result of using two active electrodes. As the action potential passes down the nerve cord, it will be picked up by a recording electrode as a momentary wave of negativity corresponding to the brief period of depolarization of the fiber. In the system used so far, the wave of negativity passing the first recording electrode corresponds to the first (upward) deflection of the waveform. The second (downward) deflection of the waveform corresponds to the wave of negativity passing the second recording electrode (see fig. 4.4-4). Thus the displayed action potential is really a biphasic representation of one action potential passing two points along the nerve cord, one after the other.

Inactivate the giant fibers at the most distal recording electrode by first crushing the nerve cord at this point, and then carefully applying a very small amount of isotonic KCl (0.16 M) to the nerve cord at this site. The nerve sheath must be crushed at this point to allow the entry of the KCl.

Take care to apply only a very small amount of KCl, and this only at the appropriate site. If the KCl spreads too far along the nerve cord it could depolarize the whole preparation, and you would record no more responses.

Monitor the waveform of the action potential as the KCl block takes effect at the second recording elec-

trode. When the recording is completely monophasic, or ceases to become more monophasic, measure the duration of the action potentials of the medial and lateral giant fibers. Also, remeasure the amplitude of the action potentials and sketch or take a picture of the trace. You must calibrate the amplification of your system (oscilloscope plus preamplifier). Reading the oscilloscope sensitivity dial will not do.

Since both conduction velocity and spike amplitude (extracellular current) are greater in larger diameter fibers, why should the second impulse in your record be the larger?

Conduction velocity

To determine conduction velocity, one must know the time required for the action potential to move over a known distance. If the nerve is long enough, the active (colored) recording electrode can be moved in the fashion diagrammed in figure 4.2-5, the appropriate measurements made (t_1, t_2, d), and the conduction velocity calculated. If the nerve cord is very short, the conduction velocity may be estimated by measuring the response latency, and the distance from the stimulating cathode (negative-going stimulating electrode) to the recording electrode. Remember that the cathode ($-$) should be the stimulating electrode closest to the recording electrodes. The accuracy of the measurement is increased by using a supramaximal stimulus intensity and as brief a stimulus duration as possible. Measure the conduction velocity of both the median and the lateral giant fibers. The most accurate distance measurement is made when the strip of body wall is under slight tension.

It is interesting to correlate fiber size and conduction velocity. It is likely that the fixed sections of the earthworm and its nerve cord you examine will have suffered some shrinkage during the process of histological fixation and preparation. Measure the sizes of the median and lateral giant fibers in figure 4.4-1 if no microscopic slides are available. The diameter of the axons in fixed sections may be as little as two thirds of the living diameter. Keep in mind, too, that the sections are not necessarily from animals of the same size as those from which you have recorded. Measure the diameter of the median and lateral giant fibers in several sections with an ocular micrometer. Should you measure the diameter of the fiber alone or with its glial sheath (fig. 4.4-1)? Calibrate the ocular micrometer with a stage micrometer, if necessary. Fiber diameters are traditionally given in microns (1 mm = 1,000 μm. 1,000 μ = 1,000 μm). Are the diameters and conduction velocities proportional?

Refractory periods
(at the instructor's option)
To determine the absolute and relative refractory periods of the giant fibers, *a stimulator capable of pulse-pair stimulation is needed*. Observe the effect of changing the time interval between paired stimuli which are just above threshold intensity. What is the minimum time interval at which two responses can be obtained? Can you make the second response reappear by increasing the stimulus intensity? Attempt to determine the length of time after the first action potential when the giant fiber is totally unresponsive in spite of supramaximal stimulus intensity (i.e., the absolute refractory period). To protect the preparation, do not exceed 30 volts in this test. In these measurements, keep the first stimulus of a pair at a fixed intensity if your stimulator permits. If not, jointly vary the intensity of the pulse pair.

Also determine the duration of the relative refractory period. The relative refractory period extends from the end of the absolute refractory period to the interval at which the second stimulus at threshold intensity begins to elicit the second response. You may be able to obtain measurements for both median and lateral giant fibers.

Strength-duration curve
(at the instructor's option)
The effectiveness of a stimulus depends not only upon its voltage (strength) but also upon the length of time it lasts (duration). Determine the relationship between the duration of a stimulus and the threshold voltage. Do this for several durations. Plot the results.

Temperature effects
(at the instructor's option)
Increasing the temperature of biological systems usually increases the rate of biological processes. The ratio of increase in the rate of a given process over a Celsius span of 10° is referred to as the *temperature coefficient* or Q_{10} of that process.

$$Q_{10} = \frac{\text{rate at (temp}_1 + 10°C)}{\text{rate at temp}_1}$$

A Q_{10} value above 2 is usually attributed to a chemical process such as an enzymatic reaction. A Q_{10} value of approximately 1 is taken to indicate a physical process such as diffusion.

Determine the effect of temperature on conduction time and waveform. Prepare a fresh nerve cord and place it in a recording chamber containing a thermocouple or a small, rapidly responding thermometer. The recording chamber may then be filled with earthworm perfusion fluid/mineral oil mixture at various temperatures. Immerse the nerve cord. Take measurements 5°–10° C apart, beginning with lower temperatures and proceeding to higher temperatures. Values of 5°, 10°, 15°, 20°, and 25° would seem most appropriate. You may determine Q_{10} values for several different parameters: conduction velocity, duration of the action potential, and its magnitude. Plot your results on graph paper and determine the Q_{10} if there is a linear change with temperature.

An alternate method can also be used to measure temperature effects. Place a recording chamber containing a small thermometer and ample mineral oil/perfusion fluid in a refrigerator at 0° C or colder. Prepare a fresh nerve cord and check its viability in a chamber at room temperature. Record with the cord in contact with the mineral oil. Now you are ready for measurement of the effect of cooling. Remove the cooled chamber from the refrigerator and quickly hook it up to your apparatus. Transfer the nerve cord preparation to the cold chamber and record with the cord in contact with the mineral oil. As the temperature rises in the chamber, monitor the changing parameters of the giant fiber action potentials.

Pitfalls and Suggestions

1. Review the operation of the oscilloscope and other equipment before making the nerve cord preparation.
2. The hardest part of this exercise is the dissection. Pin the worm down and use a dissecting microscope. Avoid pinching the cord. If you are working with a partner, each of you should dissect a worm at the same time.

3. Do not allow the preparation to dry out during dissection. Use plenty of perfusion fluid. Flush digestive juices away promptly if the gut is torn.

4. Too wide and juicy a strip of body wall sometimes interferes with the recording of action potentials (refer to fig. 4.4-2).

5. Be certain that neither end of the preparation droops into the perfusion fluid. This could produce a large stimulus artifact.

6. Do not overstimulate the preparation with too frequent or excessively high stimulus intensities.

Materials

Materials needed at each station
Oscilloscope
Stimulator
Preamplifier
Electrical leads and connectors (1 set)
Nerve chamber and its cover
Faraday cage (if readily available; otherwise probably unnecessary with differential amplification)
Dissecting microscope and illuminator
Dissecting pan and insect pins
2 small beakers and 2 medicine droppers
2 glass tools to aid in dissecting and positioning the preparation without damage to the nerve cord
Dissecting tools (furnished by students)
Regulated temperature bath (optional)
Thermometer (regular mercury, or electronic if available)

Materials available in the laboratory
Oscilloscope camera and film
Extra medicine droppers and beakers
Fine cotton thread
Extra insect pins
Spare glass slides
Microslides of earthworm histology (Several slides showing gross earthworm body structure in cross section, and several slides of the earthworm nerve cord itself; may be supplemented with light or electron micrographs and drawings in published sources, e.g., Bullock and Horridge, 1965, pp. 674, 681, 703. Ann Arbor Biological Company has had some excellent earthworm cross sections available, e.g., #40390-22.)
Compound microscope and illuminator
Ocular micrometer
Stage micrometer for calibration of ocular micrometer
An illustrated dissection guide to the earthworm (e.g., Beck and Braithwaite, 1968, pp. 196–206)
Dishpan for cleanup, filled with warm, soapy (Liquinox) water
Aluminum foil (for possible use as electrical shielding)
Plastic bag for animal disposal
Solutions:
  Earthworm perfusion solution (100 ml/station)
  Isotonic KCl (0.16 M) (5 ml/station)
  Mineral oil saturated with earthworm perfusion solution (add 100 ml oil to 0.5 ml perfusion solution; shake and let settle for 1 hour)
  10% ethanol solution (50 ml/station; do not use denatured alcohol)

Animals
Lumbricus terrestris (Order at least 3 worms/station/laboratory period.) Large, healthy earthworms can be caught in suburban lawns and gardens in many areas at night, using a flashlight, stealth, and quickness. If you try it, you will be surprised at the effectiveness of the giant fiber-mediated escape response. Earthworms are not as readily available during winter in colder areas. Keep the worms cool and moist. If the worms have come from a biological supply house, leave them in the container and packing material they came in, and keep them in a refrigerator or cold room without freezing until the time of use. They can be kept in good condition in this way for several weeks.

Notes for the Instructor

1. Urge the students to make a careful and gentle, but not protracted, dissection.

2. This exercise could be conveniently divided into two separate 3-hour laboratory periods, the first for familiarization with the preparation and simple recording parameters, and the second for measurement of temperature effects.

3. Make sure that the students understand the difference between compound action potentials, as examined in the frog sciatic nerve, and the unit action potentials recorded in this exercise.

4. The introduction does not mention the fact that

the earthworm giant fibers are a chain of cells, each one segment long, juxtaposed but not fused at the septa. Conduction across the septa is probably through two-way electrical synapses.

Selected References

Bullock, T. H., and Horridge, G. A. 1965. *Structure and function in the nervous systems of invertebrates*, vol. 1. W. H. Freeman and Co., San Francisco, pp. 680–708.

Beck, D. E., and Braithwaite, L. F. 1968. *Invertebrate zoology laboratory workbook*. Burgess Publishing Co., Minneapolis, pp. 196–206.

RESEARCH REPORTS

Bullock, T. H. 1945. Functional organization of the giant nerve fiber system in *Lumbricus*. *J. Neurophysiol.* 8: 55–72.

Hodes, R. 1953. Linear relationship between fiber diameter and velocity of conduction in giant axon of squid. *J. Neurophysiol.* 16: 145–54.

Hodgkin, A. L., and Huxley, A. F. 1952. A quantitative description of membrane current and its application to conduction and excitation in nerve. *J. Physiol.* 117: 500–544.

Mulloney, B. 1970. Structure of the giant fibers of earthworms. *Science* 168: 994–96.

Rushton, W. A. H. 1946. Reflex conduction in the giant fibres of the earthworm. *Proc. R. Soc., B.* 133: 109–30.

Stough, H. B. 1926. Giant nerve fibers of the earthworm. *J. Comp. Neurol.* 40: 409–63.

Turner, R. S. 1955. Relation between temperature and conduction in nerve fibers of different sizes. *Physiol. Zool.* 28: 55–61.

4.5   The Membrane Potential
Intracellular Recording from Frog Sartorius Muscle Fibers

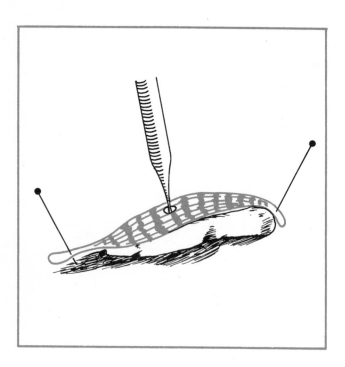

Introduction

Rationale
All living cells generate a standing voltage difference between the inside and outside of the cell. This is called the resting membrane potential (E_m). Excitable cells such as neurons and muscle cells conduct information and trigger physiological events by changes in the resting membrane potential. The membrane potential is most conveniently studied in an introductory exercise by recording the potential from the large and hardy cells of muscle.

The membrane potential of a muscle fiber (a single muscle cell) can be recorded by inserting a fine-tipped fluid-filled micropipette into the cell interior. The first membrane potentials ever recorded with intracellular micropipettes were obtained from the

preparation you will use in this exercise, the frog sartorius muscle fiber (Ling and Gerard, 1949). Micropipettes are now the universally accepted electrodes for intracellular recording from cell bodies. (The sucrose-gap technique is a useful alternative mode of recording E_m from axons too thin to penetrate with a micropipette [Julian et al., 1962].) The measurement of the membrane potential of a cell is a standard procedure in current research, as, for example, in tracking the change in potential during synaptic activation or chemical treatment. In recent years animal neurotoxins have proven particularly useful because of their selective effects on membrane function. For example, sodium conductance in the resting, but not the active, membrane is greatly increased by batrachotoxin, a toxin obtained from the skin of the Colombian arrow poison frog, *Phyllobates aurotaenia* (Narahashi et al., 1971). The melding of pharmacological and intracellular recording techniques has advanced understanding of membrane properties.

There are three technical aspects to this experiment: use of micropipettes, use of a high impedance DC preamplifier, and dissection of the sartorius muscle. The experimental objective is to measure directly the normal resting membrane potential of a muscle cell and the reduction in potential with increased external potassium concentration $[K]_o$. The techniques used in this exercise, including changing the composition of external ions, have permitted measurement of the sodium and potassium permeability ratio in resting membrane (P_{Na}/P_K) (Gorman and Marmor, 1970). Read the laboratory exercise in advance and plan your activities carefully. The sartorius muscle may be dissected out and left in a beaker of perfusion fluid until needed.

Time to complete the exercise: One 3-hour period is adequate to measure the resting potential. A second period can be devoted to the effects of varying $[K]_o$. If you are to make your own micropipettes and recording chamber, the first laboratory period will be devoted to making and filling electrodes and measuring electrode potential and electrode resistance.

Procedure

The glass micropipette

See page 38 for an introductory discussion.
You will use a micropipette filled with a conducting salt solution, e.g., 3 M KCl. The micropipette is made from a capillary tube heated in the middle and drawn out mechanically to a fine tip. Since this will be the first opportunity to use a micropipette, it is important to understand its construction and properties. Examine a partially broken pipette with a light microscope, first using 10×, then 45× objectives. A wax block on a microscope slide makes a useful micropipette holder (fig. 4.5-1). If there is an ocular micrometer (reticule) in the eyepiece, determine the tip diameter. You must calibrate the reticule with the stage micrometer unless this has been done for the microscope. Examine an unbroken (filled or unfilled) pipette and note that it is difficult to resolve the actual tip. Most of the electrode resistance (R_e) is concentrated in this fine tip, where the small cross-sectional area impedes the flow of current.

Electronic equipment

The necessity for a high impedance input. In this experiment you will use a DC preamplifier which has a high impedance input ($>10^{10}\Omega$). The circuit used in the amplifier is termed a *cathode follower, voltage follower,* or *emitter follower.* The primary function of the preamplifier is to act as an impedance-matching device between the microelectrode and the oscilloscope. Gain is less important; many such units have a gain of one (unity gain).

Consider the circuit in figure 1.2-7 on page 7 to understand why a high input impedance is necessary in microelectrode recording. The cell membrane is shown schematically at the left as a 90 mV potential. The current passes through the high resistance (impedance) of the recording electrode (R_e) to point p where we have connected a lower impedance (10^6 ohms) recording instrument such as an oscilloscope (colored). Most of the total voltage drop in the circuit

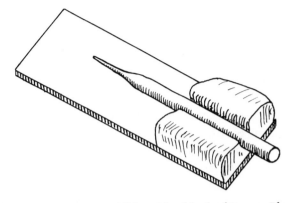

Fig. 4.5-1. Microscope slide with a block of wax or Plasticine notched to hold the micropipette for viewing with a compound microscope.

will occur across the micropipette, not the oscilloscope input. The source voltage of 90 mV will be divided in the ratio of $10^7/10^6$ or 10:1 across R_e and R_o, and the oscilloscope will register only

$$\frac{R_o}{R_e + R_o} = 1/11 \text{ of the 90 mV potential.}$$

To surmount this problem, one should connect a high impedance DC preamplifier to point p. If the preamplifier input impedance is relatively high, e.g., $10^{11}\Omega$, compared with the electrode resistance, most of the voltage drop will occur across the preamplifier input, i.e., the recording device now *sees* most of the potential. The preamplifier has a low impedance output to which the oscilloscope should be connected. We have thus matched the high impedance source (membrane potential and microelectrode) to a low impedance recording instrument using the preamplifier as a coupler. An added benefit is that only a tiny current is drawn from the cell in measuring its potential.

Initial adjustments

Turn on the oscilloscope and the DC preamplifier. Make the following initial settings.

Preamplifier. Input in differential mode if possible; band-pass filters (if available) set at DC (low frequency filter) and 10 Hz (high frequency filter).
Oscilloscope. Time base at 1 msec/div; triggering level control on automatic; input on DC; sensitivity at 1 V/div. The oscilloscope must warm up for 10 minutes before you can test the DC balance in the

next section. Do not connect the preamplifier to the oscilloscope yet.

Calibration.   Adjust the overall system gain to about 10 mV/div. Check by using the preamplifier calibration function, if available.

Checking the oscilloscope DC balance

When the oscilloscope vertical amplifier is in DC balance, you can move the sensitivity control throughout its range with no vertical shifts of the trace. Reset the vertical gain to 1 mV/div. Using the position knob, set the trace to the middle horizontal line on the screen. This is the *zero line*. If there is more than half a division of vertical movement as you reduce the gain, ask your instructor to put the oscilloscope into DC balance, unless you are familiar with the procedure. Henceforth, do not touch the oscilloscope DC balance control. Rather, use the position knob to reposition the trace vertically.

Setting the preamplifier offset to zero

DC preamplifiers have a control knob or screwdriver adjustment to apply a DC potential to their own input. We will use this to oppose (buck out, offset) the potential difference generated between the active and reference electrodes when they are both in perfusion fluid, before penetrating a cell. First, set the DC offset to zero. If there is no on-off switch for the DC offset, go through the following procedure to set the DC offset to zero. Set the system gain to 20 mV/div. Confirm that the oscilloscope vertical input is in DC mode and use its position knob to reset the trace to the zero line. With most micropipette holders it is possible to ground the active input pin. Ground it with an appropriate lead (e.g., contact pin *a* to point *b* of fig. 4.5-2*A*). Connect the preamplifier output to the appropriate vertical input of the oscilloscope. Move the trace back to the zero line with the preamplifier DC offset. Now the DC offset potential is zero.

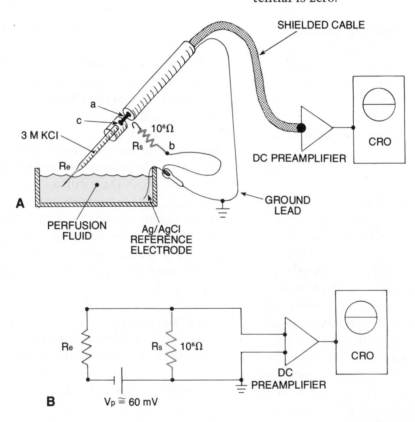

Fig. 4.5-2. R_e, electrode impedance; R_s, shunt resistance. **A.** Practical recording and electrode testing arrangement. The micropipette and Ag/AgCl reference electrode are immersed in perfusion fluid in a petri dish. The input pin *a* can be temporarily grounded to point *b* or shunted through a 1 megohm resistor (*colored*) to ground for testing the electrode impedance. During recording, the resistor R_s and its lead would lie on a piece of dry paper adjacent to the petri dish. **B.** Schematic circuit diagram of electrode testing arrangement.

Setting up the recording circuit

Examine the circuit in figure 4.5-2B. The electrode potential (V_p) passes current through the electrode resistance (R_e), the DC preamplifier, and the shunt resistor (R_s). A practical example of a recording arrangement is shown in figure 4.5-2A (W.P. Instrument Company, VF-1 voltage follower with micropipette holder). With the aid of figure 4.5-2, set up a recording circuit as follows.

Position a clean 60 mm petri dish half full of amphibian perfusion fluid under a dissecting microscope and micromanipulator. Place the chlorided silver wire reference electrode into the dish of perfusion solution. (See page 334 for the procedure for chloriding a silver wire). The chlorided silver wire leads to the ground of the DC preamplifier and to a 1 megohm shunt resistor (R_s), so that this resistor can be touched at will to the other input of the preamplifier at point a. Ground the metal base plate, and Faraday cage if present.

The pipette holder will have a chlorided silver contact (c) which couples the 3 M KCl in the micropipette to the input lead to the preamplifier. Obtain and label a small beaker containing about 25 cc of 3 M KCl. Carefully remove a micropipette from the storage container with 3 M KCl. If one with a broken tip is present, use that now. Rinse the pipette in a 500 cc beaker of distilled water placed adjacent to the micropipette storage jar. Develop a habit of rinsing all 3 M KCl from the micropipettes. Rinsing helps protect the microscope, equipment, and the sartorius muscle from the damaging effects of 3 M KCl. Keep a wet sponge at your desk and immediately wipe up any drops of spilled 3 M KCl.

---

3 M KCl leaves telltale white crystals. These should never appear on your equipment.

Examine the micropipette under the microscope and determine its tip diameter. Use a 1 cc disposable syringe to fill the micropipette and holder with 3 M KCl. Slide the micropipette without air gaps into position near the holder's chlorided silver contact. Fix the electrode holder in the micromanipulator.

Focus the dissecting microscope at low power on the perfusion fluid surface to see the tip of the micropipette touch the fluid. Illumination from the side is best. Lower the pipette until it just enters the perfusion solution. This completes the circuit in figure 4.5-2. Note: The trace may disappear when the electrodes are not in the fluid (open input).

Measuring the electrode potential

If you have carried out the instructions on page 114, the oscilloscope will be balanced and the DC offset voltage of the preamplifier will be at zero. Set the system gain to 20 mV/div. Allow the shunting resistor (R_s) and its lead to rest on a *dry* sheet of paper on the base plate or table. Make sure both electrodes are partially immersed and the preamplifier is on. Is the CRT trace about 60 mV negative with respect to the zero line? Part of this DC potential results from selective ion permeability or selective adsorption of ions by the thin glass walls at the pipette tip. This potential is called a *tip potential*. Added to this is a standing DC potential caused by the presence of the chlorided silver wires in different salt solutions, i.e., in 3 M KCl and perfusion solution. Whenever you use a new electrode, measure the total electrode potential with the micropipette in the perfusion solution. A simple way to do this with most micropipette holders is to ground the input pin (a contacting point b in fig. 4.5-2A) and compare the grounded with the ungrounded DC preamplifier input signal.

Measuring the electrode DC impedance

Touch the DC preamplifier input pin (point a in fig. 4.5-2A) with the 1 megohm resistor (R_s). This will reduce the electrode potential (V_p) from 60 mV, for example, to the shunted electrode potential (V_s). (The reduction will be small for tip diameters greater than 1 μm.) Measure V_s and calculate the electrode impedance (R_e) in megohms from the equation shown here (For derivation, see "Pitfalls and Suggestions," page 118).

$$R_e = \frac{(V_p - V_s)}{V_s}$$

Where V_p = electrode potential in mV
V_s = shunted electrode potential

For the explanation that follows, refer to figure 4.5-2. With R_s not touching the input pin, the DC preamplifier measures the voltage drop V_p across resistance R_e. When the resistance R_s is connected, it shunts the input voltage to ground. Then the DC preamplifier measures the voltage drop V_s across R_s. As current flows through the circuit in figure 4.5-2B, the electrode potential (V_p) will be dropped across R_e and R_s in proportion to their resistances. An electrode with a large, low impedance tip will result in little change on the oscilloscope screen since R_s is much greater than R_e, and most of the voltage drop is across R_s. A high impedance electrode will produce a large change in the trace position.

Figure 4.5-3 illustrates the change in CRT appearance of a 60 mV electrode potential when R_e is 2 megohms.

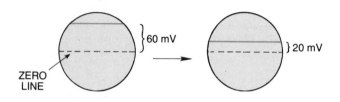

Fig. 4.5-3. Reduction in the recorded potential when the electrode potential is shunted to ground through R_s.

When you (a) develop some dexterity in handling micropipettes and the X, Y, and fine and coarse Z controls of the micromanipulator, and (b) understand the measurement of electrode potential and impedance, then select a new unbroken micropipette. Rinse it with distilled water, examine it with the microscope, record its tip diameter in your notebook, and measure the impedance. Electrodes with impedances from 3 to 50 megohms can be used in this experiment. These values indicate those electrodes with tips small enough to penetrate cells (probably $< 1 \ \mu m$). A substantial decrease in electrode potential or impedance during the course of an experiment will indicate a broken tip. An increase will indicate a plugged tip.

Checklist for measuring electrode impedance
In the future, select useable electrodes on the basis of impedance (3–50 megohms) after visually confirming that the tip is intact and free of major air bubbles. With the microfiber type of capillary (recommended for class use), small bubbles may not interrupt the electrical continuity of the salt solution inside the pipette. Check impedance as follows.

1. Immerse the tip of the pipette and reference electrodes in the perfusion fluid.
2. Ground the input pin a and position the trace on the zero line using the DC offset of the preamplifier.
3. Unground the input a and measure the deflection in mV (V_p).
4. Shunt a to ground with R_s and measure the trace deflection (V_s) from the zero line.
5. Calculate R_e (see equation on page 115).
6. Retain electrodes with impedances between 3 and 50 megohms.

Discard electrodes with impedances less than 3 megohms. If greater than 50 megohms, try to eliminate any air bubbles present by flicking the pipette with a finger with the tip down. If bubbles are not the cause of impedances greater than 50 megohms, then lower the impedance by breaking the tip in a manner recommended by the instructor, e.g., against a thin vertical strip of aluminum foil hanging from a table edge. Retest the electrode impedance after breaking.

Making the Recording Chamber

Construct the following recording chamber unless one has already been provided. Take the bottom (taller) half of a 60 mm glass petri dish and fill it one-third full with melted wax or paraffin. Beeswax or Tackiwax darkened with red wax is preferred for seeing the muscle clearly. Tilt the dish so that the wax hardens sloping down toward one edge (fig. 4.5-4). While the wax is still soft, make a depression in the lower edge and build up a small central mound about 2–3 mm high and 10 mm in diameter. The sartorius muscle will be gently stretched and pinned across this mound.

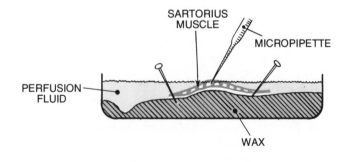

Fig. 4.5-4. Recording chamber and muscle.

Preparing the Sartorius Muscle

Double pith a small frog. Cut the skin completely around at midabdomen and pull down on the skin, everting it as you strip it completely off the legs. With stout scissors carefully split the animal's pelvis longitudinally in the exact center. Note which is belly (ventral) and back (dorsal) side, and remove each hindleg by cutting transversely just above the pelvis. Rinse the legs liberally with frog perfusion solution, because you may have released intestinal fluids. The ball at the proximal end of the femur should be visible on one leg. Place that leg in a beaker of perfusion solution for possible later use. Place the other leg ventral side up for further dissection. Consult figure 4.5-5 and use a dissecting microscope to look for the shiny white tendon of the sartorius muscle at the knee. The sartorius is a *thin* superficial muscle about 5 mm wide and 2 mm thick at the arrow. Find a favorable angle of the microscope light which will give the tendon a pearly glint.

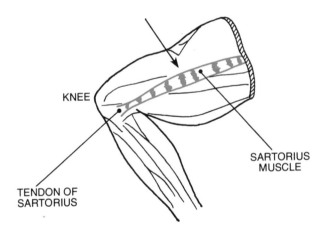

KNEE

SARTORIUS
MUSCLE

TENDON OF
SARTORIUS

Fig. 4.5-5. Medial view of frog right hindleg. The sartorius is a thin superficial muscle. *Arrow* indicates the belly of the sartorius, which is about 5 mm wide. You can locate it on the medial surface of your own thigh in the following manner. While seated in a chair, raise your leg with the knee bent so that your hip is externally rotated, i.e., knee points away from the midline, ankle points toward midline (frog position). The sartorius can be palpated where it connects to the pelvis and will be centered on the thigh.

Moisten the sartorius with perfusion solution. Remoisten every 5 minutes until the dissection is completed.

Cut the sartorius tendon at the knee and gently lift it, using your finest forceps. With a sharp scalpel or fine scissors, progressively cut the adhering connective tissue along the borders of the muscle as you *gently* peel the muscle back just as you would peel a recalcitrant banana. When the muscle is free to the hip, carefully cut the pelvic bone away from the ball of the femur and trim so that you are left with the sartorius attached to the short piece of pelvic bone. Rinse and fill the petri recording dish with perfusion solution and transfer the sartorius with the inner (deep) face upward. The deep face has less connective tissue to impede penetration by the micropipette. Gently stretch the sartorius flat and smooth over the wax hump, and pin it at both ends (fig. 4.5-4). Cover the sartorius with perfusion fluid. Raise the micropipette holder with the micromanipulator and place the petri dish under the manipulator. View the muscle with a dissecting microscope, and pin or adjust further. Note the beauty of the muscle fibers—the straight thin strands—and the bundles of axons which cross on top of these.

Measuring the resting membrane potential
Lower the micropipette into the perfusion solution and measure its impedance if you have not already done so. Then, return the trace to the zero line with the preamplifier DC offset (or the position knob of the oscilloscope). If 60 Hz interference is a problem, unplug the microscope lamp. However, do not relinquish the chance to view the muscle while recording unless it is absolutely necessary. Adjust the microscope light to maximize visibility and in particular to locate the fine micropipette in the solution. Illumination from the side is best. You should be able to see the electrode tip as it slightly dimples the surface of the muscle. If working with a partner, one person should slowly drive the electrode down with the fine Z control of the micromanipulator while observing through the microscope. The other person should concentrate exclusively on the oscilloscope display and shout some expletive when there is a

sudden 40–90 mV jump of the CRT trace. You have just penetrated a muscle fiber and are recording intracellularly. You will note that by moving the fine Z control you can pop in and out of the cell. (When you work alone, it is necessary to look at the CRT and not at the preparation.) Measure the membrane potential of this cell. After measuring, withdraw the pipette until it comes out of the muscle. (If it comes out of the fluid, the trace may disappear until the electrode is resubmerged.) Use the appropriate control on the micromanipulator to move across the muscle slightly. Lower the micropipette and penetrate another muscle cell. Measure the membrane potential of six to eight cells.

Determining the Relationship between Membrane Potential and [K]ₒ

Allow at least 1 hour for this part of the experiment. In addition to normal perfusion solution (3.0 mM KCl, 113 mM NaCl, 2.7 mM CaCl$_2$, 2.43 mM NaHCO$_3$, pH 7.2) you should use three modified perfusion solutions in which KCl has been partially substituted for NaCl (but the Ca^{++} concentration held constant). Solution **1**: 10 mM KCl, 106 mM NaCl; solution **2**: 30 mM KCl, 86 mM NaCl; solution **3**: 100 mM KCl, 16 mM NaCl. Have all four solutions available in labeled beakers. You will also need a larger waste beaker. Insert the tip of a polyethylene tube attached to a 10 cc syringe into the depression in the recording chamber and draw off all the normal perfusion solution. Completely empty this into the waste container. Use the same syringe and slowly fill the recording dish with solution 1, henceforth called *10 mM KCl perfusion solution*. After 30 seconds, totally remove this solution and replace it with fresh 10 mM KCl perfusion solution. Now wait a minimum of 10 minutes for equilibration before penetrating three to five cells to measure the membrane potential. When exchanging solution, it is important (1) to remove as much as possible, (2) to exchange twice, and (3) to wait 10 minutes. This assures the correct concentration and the exposure of deeper muscle cells. Measure membrane potentials in the same manner while the sartorius is exposed to solution 2 and to solution 3. After solution 3, test reversibility by returning to normal perfusion solution. Rinse three times with normal perfusion fluid before recording.

Data treatment

Plot the membrane potential as a function of [K]ₒ and compare with the curve predicted from the Nernst equation for the solutions used:

$$E_m = 58 \log \frac{[K]_o}{[K]_i}, \text{ where } [K]_i = 140 \text{ mM}$$

Pitfalls and Suggestions

1. It will take at least 45 minutes to measure the resting membrane potential. Plan accordingly.
2. Handling the micropipettes is the most challenging aspect of this experiment. The possibility of breakage is ever present. Slow and deliberate movements are best. Treat the micropipettes with reverence. If the tip diameter is not less than 1 μm, it is useless to proceed further.
3. Even if use of the microscope illuminator produces troublesome 60 Hz interference, be sure to look at the micropipette through the dissecting microscope as you lower it into the solution and the muscle. You will develop a feeling for your own movements and the position of the pipette and its fragility.
4. When the micropipette is being lowered into the muscle, someone must look steadily at the oscilloscope and say "stop" when the trace jumps. You can always continue after a false alarm.
5. Derivation of equation from page 115. Refer to the circuit in figure 4.5-2*A*.

Let V_e = voltage drop across the electrode, and V_s = shunted electrode potential
then $V_e + V_s = V_p$ *or* $V_e = V_p - V_s$
and $I = \dfrac{V_s}{R_s} = \dfrac{V_e}{R_e}$

substituting, $\dfrac{V_s}{R_s} = \dfrac{V_p - V_s}{R_e}$

When $R_s = 1$ megohm, then $V_s = \dfrac{V_p - V_s}{R_e}$

or $R_e = \dfrac{V_p - V_s}{V_s}$

Materials

Materials needed at each station
Oscilloscope

DC preamplifier and micropipette holder with connecting cable

Set of electrical leads and connectors

2-cm silver wire (24 gauge = 0.05 mm diameter). See page 334 for chloriding procedure.

Faraday cage (useful with high impedance electrodes)

Recording chamber (60 mm petri dish with dark-colored wax floor)

A 1 megohm resistor

4 to 6 straight pins or stout (no. 3) insect pins

Micromanipulator and stand

Dissecting microscope and movable lamp

Dissecting pan

250-ml beaker

50-ml beaker

25-ml beaker

10-cc disposable syringe with 18-gauge needle and 10 cm of PE 200 tubing

Set of dissecting tools (furnished by students)

Materials available in the laboratory

Compound microscope with 10× and 45× objectives (1/2 stations)

Micropipette holder for compound microscope use (1/2 stations)

Stage micrometer

2 micropipette storage jars (e.g., W. P. Instruments)

6–8 micropipettes/station (e.g., F. Haer Co., 1.5 mm Omega Dot capillaries, 4-inch unpulled blanks)

Plastic bag for disposal of dissected frogs

Aluminum foil

500-ml beaker of distilled water

Red wax

Tackiwax (Central Scientific)

Masking tape and felt marking pen

Solutions:

Amphibian perfusion fluid (200 ml/station) (Composition: 3.0 mM KCl, 113 mM Na Cl, 2.7 mM $CaCl_2$, 2.43 mM $NaHCO_3$, pH 7.2)

10 mM KCl perfusion solution 1 (50 ml/station) (Composition: 10 mM KCl, 106 mM NaCl, 2.7 mM $CaCl_2$, 2.43 mM $NaHCO_3$)

30 mM KCl perfusion solution 2 (50 ml/station) (Composition: 30 mM KCl, 86 mM NaCl, 2.7 mM $CaCl_2$ 2.43 mM $NaHCO_3$)

100 mM KCl perfusion solution 3 (50 ml/station) (Composition: 100 mM KCl, 16 mM NaCl, 2.7 mM $CaCl_2$, 2.43 mM $NaHCO_3$)

Animals

Frogs, *Rana pipiens* or other species (Order 1 small frog/station/laboratory period.) Keep the frogs in a cool place and provide them with dripping water.

Notes for the Instructor

1. Making microelectrodes. If you do not have ready access to a glass capillary micropipette puller, or wish to avoid the time required to make and fill pipettes conventionally, consider the following alternative. Frederick Haer and Co. has unfilled pipettes and stock tubing of Omega Dot capillary tubing (recommended: 1.5 mm diameter, 4-inch *un*-pulled blanks, cat. no. 30-32-1). A-M Systems, Inc., also have microfilament capillary glass. A 5 micron diameter solid glass rod adhering to the inner face of the capillary permits ready filling by the following method. Take a 100 ml beaker *full* of 3 M KCl, and cover snugly with Parafilm. Plunge the butt (not tip) end of a pulled micropipette through the Parafilm until immersed in the solution. Leave for 2–5 minutes. Small amounts of fluid will creep up along the microfiber and fill *only* the tip. Remove the micropipette and insert a 1½ inch 26-gauge hypodermic needle all the way to the shoulder. Slowly inject 3 M KCl as you withdraw, thereby filling the pipette. Bubbles or air gaps are not uncommon. Tap the pipette with the tip down to dislodge or break up residual bubbles. Sometimes the bubbles will disappear with time or can be driven out with a heat source such as a 75-watt incandescent bulb. Small air gaps generally do not interrupt the electrical continuity.

2. Students will need assistance on the following:

A. Filling micropipettes

B. Understanding the design of the micropipette holder and how it accommodates the pipette

C. Learning how the micropipette is electrically coupled to the preamplifier

D. Adjusting illumination to see the tip of the pipette without glare

E. Locating the sartorius tendon

3. In this experiment, most students will spend considerable time learning about (and mishandling) micropipettes. To save time we recommend not using a second micropipette as a reference electrode. The Ag/AgCl reference electrode will produce a substantial junction potential which is then used as a cali-

bration voltage instead of a separate calibrator. This potential may drift over time, but it will suffice for selecting usable electrodes.

Selected References

Hodgkin, A. L. 1964. *The conduction of the nervous impulse*. Charles C Thomas, Springfield, Ill.

Junge, D. 1976. *Nerve and muscle excitation*. Sinauer Assoc., Sunderland, Mass.

RESEARCH REPORTS

Adrian, R. H. 1956. The effect of internal and external potassium concentration on the membrane potential of frog muscle. *J. Physiol.* 133: 631–58.

Carnay, L. D., and Barry, W. H. 1969. Turbidity, birefringence and fluorescence changes in skeletal muscle coincident with the action potential. *Science* 165: 608–9.

Gorman, A. L. F., and Marmor, M. F. 1970. Temperature dependence of the sodium-potassium permeability ratio of a molluscan neurone. *J. Physiol.* 210: 919–31.

Hodgkin, A. L., and Horowicz, P. 1959. The influence of potassium and chloride ions on the membrane potential of single muscle fibres. *J. Physiol.* 148: 127–60.

Julian, F. J.; Moore, J. W.; and Goldman, D. E. 1962. Membrane potentials of the lobster giant axon obtained by use of the sucrose-gap technique. *J. Gen. Physiol.* 45: 1195–1216.

Ling, G., and Gerard, R. W. 1949. The normal membrane potential of frog sartorius fibers. *J. Cell. Comp. Physiol.* 34: 383–96.

Narahashi, T.; Albuquerque, E. X.; and Deguchi, T. 1971. Effects of batrachotoxin on membrane potential and conductance of squid giant axons. *J. Gen. Physiol.* 58: 54–70.

Nastuck, W. L., and Hodgkin, A. L. 1950. The electrical activity of single muscle fibers. *J. Cell. Comp. Physiol.* 35: 39–73.

Spyropoulos, C. S. 1972. Some observations on the electrical properties of biological membranes. In *Membranes, macroscopic systems, and models*, vol. 1, ed. G. Eisenman. Dekker, New York, pp. 267–317.

4.6 Volume Conduction
The Potential Field Generated by a Nerve Impulse

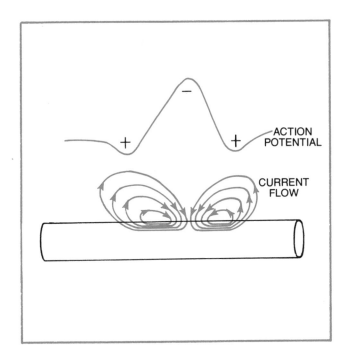

ACTION POTENTIAL

CURRENT FLOW

The diagram is adapted from M. A. B. Brazier, 1976. *The Electrical Activity of the Nervous System*. Pitman Medical Pub. Co., London.

Introduction

Rationale

Action potentials are often recorded in the laboratory from nerves suspended in air or immersed in oil. However, an intact organism or a large piece of tissue acts as a *volume conductor* in which neurons are embedded and bathed in extracellular fluid. Currents generated at one point, for instance from a nerve axon or from a cell in the brain, flow into the surrounding tissues and fluids, and may be recorded at some distance from the actual source. The geometry of the recording setup and the conducting properties of the surrounding fluids and tissues distort the magnitude, polarity, and waveform of the source potential.

Understanding potential fields produced by neurons is necessary to deduce the true nature of electrical activity at the source and to predict the effects, if any, of the current flow on neighboring tissues. This is particularly important in clinical applications. The electrocardiogram (ECG), electroencephalogram (EEG), and electromyogram (EMG) are generally recorded with external electrodes on the skin. The electrical potentials generated by a deep source, e.g., the heart, are modified considerably when they pass through the intervening tissues to the skin. Very sophisticated procedures are now available to determine the actual magnitude and source of potentials recorded at a distance in a conductive tissue medium (e.g., Freeman, 1969).

In this exercise you will accurately map the potential field generated by a known source, a compound action potential from the frog sciatic nerve. The nerve will be placed on a two-dimensional surface consisting of a flat piece of filter paper moistened with frog perfusion solution. Real tissues, of course, are three dimensional and do not conduct equally well in all directions. Table 4.6-1 shows the wide difference in conductivity (the inverse of resistance) among several different tissues. The lower the conductivity value, the greater the resistance to current flow. Perfusion fluid and blood have about the same conductivity. The conductivity of myelin, the insulating material of vertebrate nerves, is even lower than that of fat.

TABLE 4.6-1.
Tissue Conductivity

Tissue	Conductivity (avg. mhos/m)
Blood	0.67
Lung	0.05
Liver	0.14
Fat	0.04
Human trunk	0.21

(From S. Rush, J. A. Abildskov, and R. McFee, 1963. Resistivity of body tissues at low frequencies. *Circ. Res.* 12: 40–50, by permission of the American Heart Association, Inc.)

Time to complete the exercise: One 3-hour laboratory period. A second period, however, generally results in more adequate data collection.

Procedure

Recording chamber

Obtain and examine a recording chamber (fig. 4.6-1). Note that it has a well or depression cut in one end. One end of the sciatic nerve will dip into the well and rest on a pair of stimulating electrodes, while a 2 cm length at the other end will rest on the flat upper surface, surrounded by a sheet of moist filter paper.

One person may prepare the chamber surface as described here while the other prepares the sciatic nerve. Cut a piece of filter paper to cover the upper platform. From the middle of the paper carefully cut out a strip 1–2 mm wide and 3.5 cm long. The sciatic nerve will fit into this gap (fig. 4.6-1). Rule the filter paper into squares using a sharp pencil. Begin at the inner edge (nerve side) of each half and draw a grid on the filter paper with 2 mm spacings between the lines parallel to the nerve and with 5 mm spacings between the lines perpendicular to the nerve. Label one set of lines A, B, C, etc., and the other set of lines 1, 2, 3, etc. Replace the filter paper in the chamber with the ruled side uppermost.

Dissection of the sciatic nerve

Double pith a frog. Cut the skin completely around the frog at midabdomen. Hold the upper part of the frog in one hand and pull the skin off the lower abdomen and legs with the other hand, everting the skin as it is pulled off. Use a single, firm pull to remove the skin from the legs. Tissue-gripping forceps are helpful.

Lay the frog dorsal side up and refer to figure 4.2-1, page 86. Separate the muscles of the back of the upper leg from the pelvis to the knee to expose the white sciatic nerve and accompanying blood vessels. Use clean fingers and blunt probes. The nerve should not be touched at this stage.

Hold the urostyle up and carefully cut the muscles on both sides. Now, free the caudal end of the urostyle and lift it to expose the underlying structures. Lying dorsal to the abdominal organs will be the two white sciatic nerves (right and left) originating at the spinal cord and passing into each thigh. Note that each leaves the spinal column as three roots (roots 7–9). Cut off the urostyle at its hinge. Cut the roots as close to the spinal cord as possible. Cut the nerve at the most distal point near the knee and carefully

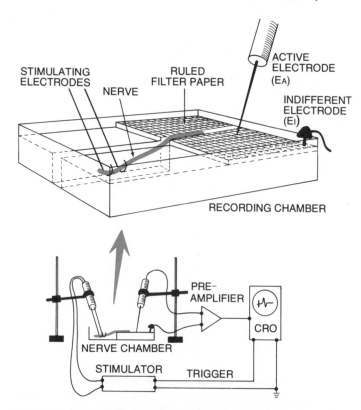

Fig. 4.6-1. Recording setup and chamber.

ligate (tie) it there with the end of a 10 cm length of thread. Completely free the nerve from the knee past the hip, lifting it with the thread as necessary.

CAUTION: Do not stretch the nerve.

It is preferable to use blunt glass tools, e.g., two glass rods drawn out and fire-polished to a blunt tip about the size of a lead pencil point which has seen some use (1 mm). When the nerve has been totally freed, immerse it in a small beaker of perfusion fluid.

Recording Procedure

Just barely saturate the filter paper in the recording chamber with perfusion fluid. Lay the sciatic nerve in the recording chamber so that a 2–3 cm length of the proximal end lies on the platform, with the distal end with the thread attached dipping into the well (fig. 4.6-1). You should trim the proximal end of the nerve so that the portion lying on the platform is a single nerve that does not include the three roots.

Keep the nerve moist with perfusion fluid throughout this process.

Obtain a pair of simulating electrodes attached to a flexible lead (Pb) rod or manipulator. Position the stimulating electrodes in the well so that the nerve is suspended on them. You may need to bend the electrodes in an upward curve to cradle the nerve properly. Now carefully adjust the position of the nerve so that it lies in a small trough formed by the inner edges of the two papers. The paper or adjacent fluid must be in contact with the nerve, but not overlapping it.

Adjust the position of the stimulating electrodes to hold the nerve aloft without touching the sides or bottom of the well. Cut the thread (and shorten the nerve if necessary) to prevent any kind of contact with the sides of the well. Now with a medicine dropper or Pasteur pipette and bulb carefully fill the well nearly full of mineral oil saturated with perfusion fluid. Dripping the oil in over the nerve on the electrodes will prevent loss of contact with the electrodes. The level of the oil should be 3–4 mm below the platform.

Do not get oil on the filter paper.

Touch the *indifferent recording electrode* (E₁) to one of the most distal corners of the filter paper. It will serve as a reference electrode. The reference electrode can be held in place with a lump of Plasticine (modeling clay) or wax on the corner of the recording chamber. The other recording electrode (Eₐ) is the *active electrode* and should be attached to a manipulator or lead rod. Touch the active electrode to the filter paper at the point where the nerve passes out of the well onto the platform.

Connect the recording electrodes to the input of the preamplifier and connect the preamplifier to the oscilloscope with appropriate cables. Connect the stimulating electrodes to the electronic stimulator by using a stimulus isolation unit (SIU) if available. The cathode (negative stimulating electrode) should be nearest the platform. Connect the trigger (synchronous) output of the stimulator to the trigger input of the oscilloscope. Ground the stimulator to the oscilloscope. Use the following initial settings on your equipment.

Preamplifier. Input in differential mode if possible; gain of 100–1,000×; band-pass filters (if available) set at about 10 Hz (low frequency filter) and 3–5 kHz (high frequency filter).

Oscilloscope. Time base at 1 msec/div; vertical sensitivity at 0.1–0.01 V/div; trigger set on external input and the triggering level control adjusted to trigger the oscilloscope sweep when the stimulator is actuated.

Calibration. Adjust the preamplifier and oscilloscope vertical gain to give a *total system gain* of approximately 100 μV/div. Verify with the preamplifier calibrator if available.

Stimulator. Frequency of 10/sec; delay (if available) of about 1 msec; duration of 0.1 msec; starting voltage of 0.1 V.

Recording

Activate the stimulator to give a continuous output. Gradually increase the stimulus voltage until the initial component of the compound action potential, the *alpha wave* of the A component, reaches a maximum amplitude with no further increase. Increase the stimulus intensity to about 110% of the level required for a maximum alpha-wave response, but below the threshold for the beta and delta waves. (Consult figure 4.2-4 if these waves are unfamiliar to you.) The beta and delta waves must not be present since their action potentials will arrive later than the alpha component and will distort the trailing edge of the potential field created by the alpha-fiber response.

Adjust the gain and sweep speed of the oscilloscope so that the compound action potential nearly fills the screen, both horizontally and vertically. Check with lower sweep speeds, though, to confirm that you have not cut off some of the later, slower potential changes in the alpha response.

Note the shape of the waveform. The waveform of the action potential of the frog sciatic nerve examined in experiment 4.2 was probably biphasic. That nerve preparation was suspended on electrodes in a nerve chamber. In the present experiment, the presence of the volume conductor will probably produce a *triphasic* waveform. Examine figure 4.6-2 to

understand why. At the site of the stimulating electrode an action potential is initiated (fig. 4.6-2A). Current flows inward through the membrane at the site of stimulation. This area is termed a current *sink*. The *source* of this current is the adjacent membrane where the current is flowing outward. (Remember, a complete circuit is necessary for current to flow.) An electrode near the nerve, but not touching it, records a negative-going potential change. When the action potential has moved down the nerve and is directly under the recording electrode (fig. 4.6-2B), the current is flowing into the nerve and the electrode records a positive-going potential change. Then, as the action potential passes the recording site (fig. 4.6-2C), the electrode records a negative-going potential because the current is again flowing outward through the membrane. Finally, as the action potential moves completely out of the region near the recording electrode, the potential returns to a still somewhat depolarized value (fig. 4.6-2D). The net result of the movement of the action potential past an electrode in the volume conductor is a triphasic wave. In a nerve passing through real tissue, with resistive and capacitative discontinuities, more complex waves may be formed.

Measuring the potential field

Survey the potential field around the nerve by moving the recording electrode to widely scattered points on the filter paper. Note that the magnitude of the action potential varies considerably depending on the distance from the nerve.

Now, measure the potential distribution systematically as follows.

1. Begin the first series of measurements by placing E_A at the intersection of the filter paper grid lines nearest the point where the nerve enters the platform. Start by selecting a set time after the beginning of the stimulus to take a measurement. For the first series of measurements, select the time at which the falling phase of the major wave of the response reaches 0 volts. Vary the delay, sweep speed, or horizontal positioning until the zero point coincides with one of the major vertical divisions of the graticule (grid) on the screen. This is the "vertical zero line." Now adjust the baseline to lie on one of the major horizontal divisions.

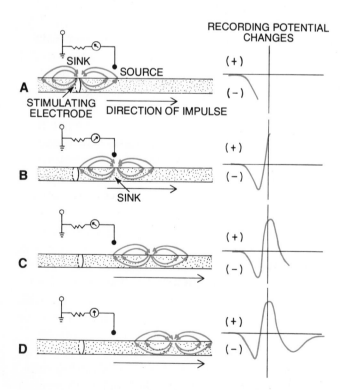

Fig. 4.6-2. Triphasic action potential produced in a volume conductor. (Adapted from Brazier, 1976.)

2. The gain and sweep speed settings just made should not be altered throughout the ensuing series of measurements.

3. Now, proceed to move the electrode in 5-mm steps along and close to the side of the nerve. For each point, measure the potential only where it crosses the vertical zero line, i.e., after the set time. At the end of the series, return the recording electrode to the starting point. The potential there should still be zero. Use this point as your control throughout all succeeding measurements, returning after each series to check that nothing has changed. (With a dual-trace oscilloscope another electrode can be permanently placed at the control point. The potential difference between it and the reference electrode can be continuously displayed on the second channel.)

4. After the first row of measurements, make a second set of measurements along a row 2 mm out from the first series. After measurements in the second row are complete, recheck the control point. Continue as rapidly as possible, moving outward from the nerve in 2-mm steps and returning to the control point at the end of each row. Continue outward as far as appropriate.

5. The other side of the nerve has not been measured, but an identical potential field distribution should be present. Check this assumption with three to four test measurements.

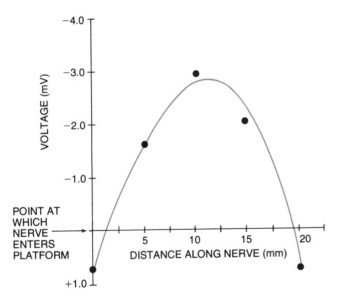

Fig. 4.6-3. Volume-conducted voltage changes. Curve drawn from measurements taken in a row 2 mm from the sciatic nerve.

6. Photograph or trace the potentials recorded along one selected row near the nerve and along a column perpendicular to the midpoint of the nerve on the platform. You can save film and obtain several exposures on a photo by moving the camera or CRT trace between each exposure. (Refer to pages 40–41 if necessary.)

Measuring the potential field at a different point in time

You can also measure the potential field at other times after the stimulus, both earlier and later. Such measurements are of value to show how the potential field surrounding the nerve changes in time as the nerve impulse passes. Do you understand that the measurements made in the previous section represent the potential distribution at a single moment in time as the action potential travels down the nerve?

Graphing the data

Electrical fields can be graphed by plotting equipotential (isopotential) lines around the electrical source, if we first treat the data in the following way.

Rule the ordinate on your graph in mV and the abscissa in mm of distance along the nerve (fig. 4.6-3). Plot each voltage measurement obtained in the first row parallel to the nerve (at 2 mm). The series of dots should describe an arc (fig. 4.6-3). Draw a smooth curve linking the dots. Graph the next row of measurements which was taken 4 mm out from the nerve and draw a smooth curve for this set of points. Continue until you have graphed all your data as in figure 4.6-4. Note that the experimenter who produced this graph (fig. 4.6-4) took measurements at even more intervals along the nerve than you did, at each 2.5 mm.

After graphing all the data to produce a family of curves you are ready to plot a series of equipotential lines. Rule a new graph with both the ordinate and abscissa in mm as in figure 4.6-5. The abscissa will still be the distance *along* the nerve but the ordinate will now be the distance *away* from the nerve. First examine figure 4.6-4. Note the horizontal line at 1.0 mV which intersects the curves at six points. For each intersection you could tabulate an X,Y coordinate value to be used to plot the 1 mV equipotential line in figure 4.6-5. X, the distance *along* the nerve, is given by the abscissa value at a point of intersec-

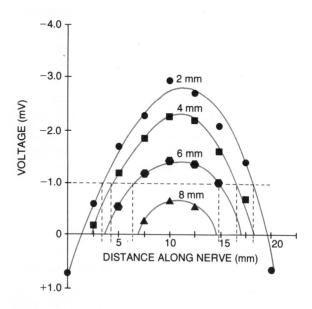

Fig. 4.6-4. Voltage along the nerve measured at several distances away from the nerve.

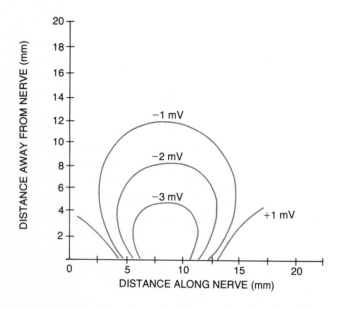

Fig. 4.6-5. Equipotential contours around a nerve.

tion, and Y, the distance *away* from the nerve, is given by the mm value of the curve intersected, e.g., first intersection point, X = 3.1, Y = 2.0 mm.

Now take your own version of figure 4.6-4 and tabulate the X,Y values of each point of intersection with a horizontal line at 1 mV. Repeat for 0.5 mV, 1.5 mV, 2.0 mV, etc. When the values have been entered on the graph, draw smooth curves for each of the voltage levels. These lines represent equipotential contours around the nerve at a given moment in time as the action potential is passing down the nerve (fig. 4.6-5).

The equipotential lines you have produced can be used to determine the length of the nerve involved in the action potential at any one time. Do you see how? What is the length of the depolarized area in your nerve? Can you also determine the lines of equal *current* from the equipotential contours (compare with fig. 4.6-2)?

Pitfalls and Suggestions

1. The nerve will tend to dry out between the well and the platform. Repeated applications of mineral oil will protect the nerve at this site.
2. Keep the oil off of the filter paper on the platform. The oil will interfere with the potential spread.
3. Read the section on graphing the data before leaving the laboratory. You may want to ask the instructor to clarify the procedure for treating the data.

Materials

Materials needed at each station
Oscilloscope (dual trace if available)
Stimulator
Preamplifier (2 if a dual-trace oscilloscope is used)
Set of electrical leads and connectors
Recording chamber (This can be constructed from
    Plexiglas according to the diagram in figure 4.6-1.
    The overall dimensions are 10 × 10 × 2 cm high.
    The dimensions are not critical and can be varied
    to suit available material. The well should be
    deep enough to accommodate filling with 7–10
    mm mineral oil/perfusion fluid. A less elegant,
    but serviceable, recording chamber can be made
    by filing a notch in one edge of a plastic petri
    dish and placing a round filter paper in the dish.

The nerve enters the dish through the notch, and the part hanging outside is stimulated.)
Micromanipulator and stand or a flexible lead (Pb) rod (for positioning the active electrode)
2 ringstands, or 2 magnetic stands and 2 right-angle clamps
2 sets of hand electrodes for stimulating and recording
3–5 cm piece of chlorided silver wire (See page 334 for chloriding instructions.)
Small beaker
Medicine dropper or Pasteur pipette for filling well
2 glass tools for dissecting and manipulating nerves
Set of dissecting tools (furnished by students)

Materials available in the laboratory
Oscilloscope camera and film
Dissecting microscope and illuminator
Extra cables and connectors
Extra medicine droppers and beakers
Fine cotton thread
Ringstands and right-angle clamps
Plasticine (modeling clay)
Plastic bag for frog disposal
Filter paper (Whatman no. 1 or equivalent)
Scissors and ruler
Solutions:
  Amphibian perfusion fluid (100 ml/station)
  Mineral oil saturated with perfusion fluid (40 ml/station; made up as in experiment 4.2)

Animals
Frogs, *Rana pipiens* or other species (Order 1 frog/station/laboratory period, 1 frog can be shared by 2 stations.) Keep the frogs in a cool place and provide them with dripping water.

Notes for the Instructor

1. Recording chambers have to be built (see "Materials").
2. This exercise can be performed in a very precise, quantitative way, and particularly appeals to students interested in biophysical methods.
3. To conserve film, obtain multiple exposures on one photograph either by shifting the CRT trace or by moving the back of the camera. Four to six traces on a photograph are reasonable.
4. Graphing the data may give the students some

problems. It is difficult to understand how equipotential contours can be generated from the measurements they have made. Be prepared to explain the method.

Selected References

Brazier, M. A. B. 1976. *The electrical activity of the nervous system*, 4th ed. Pitman Medical Pub. Co., London.
Ochs, S. 1965. *Elements of neurophysiology*. John Wiley and Sons, New York.
Plonsey, R. 1969. *Bioelectric phenomena*. McGraw-Hill, New York. (Highly mathematical.)

RESEARCH REPORTS
Freeman, J. A., and Stone, J. 1969. A technique for current density analysis of field potentials and its application to the frog cerebellum. In *Neurobiology of cerebellar evolution and development*, ed. R. Llinas. AMA, Chicago, pp. 421–30.
Geddes, L. A., and Baker, L. E. 1967. The specific resistance of biological material—A compendium of data for the biomedical engineer and physiologist. *Med. Biol. Eng.* 5: 271–93.
Lorente de No, R. 1947. *A study of nerve physiology*. Analysis of the distribution of the action currents of nerve in volume conductors. *Rockefeller Institute Studies* 132 (2): 384–482.

5

Synaptic Transmission and Effector Processes

5.1   Coelenterate Nerve Net
Luminescent Waves in the Hydroid <u>Renilla</u>

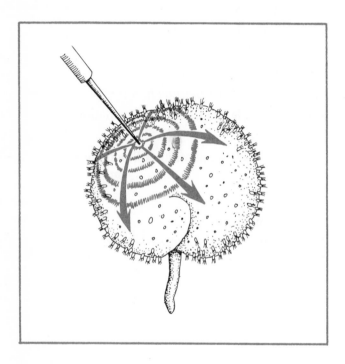

Introduction

Rationale
The nerve net of the coelenterates is the simplest true nervous system. Its study has been pursued both for its intrinsic interest and as a source of insight into the workings of higher nervous systems. The properties of a coelenterate nerve net can be demonstrated by examining the control of luminescence in the sea pansy *Renilla kollikeri*. This particular preparation is attractive because it requires no elaborate instrumentation for study. Additionally, the problem of biological luminescence is itself an intriguing phenomenon.

Nerve net function
The entire nervous system of *Renilla* consists of a *nerve net*. This name was suggested by the net-

worklike appearance of coelenterate neurons when stained with methylene blue or silver (fig. 5.1-1). In many coelenterates there are two or more functionally autonomous nerve nets which serve different purposes. Where multiple nerve nets occur, clusters of nerve cells (ganglia) coordinate the actions of the separate nets. Romanes's classical demonstration of the existence of more than one nerve net in the jellyfish *Aurelia* showed that the two nets serve different functions, conduct excitation at different rates, and are coordinated by ganglia (fig. 5.1-2). Junctions

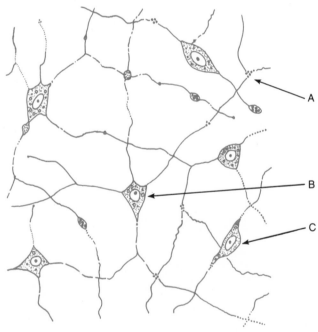

Fig. 5.1-1. The nerve net of *Hydra* drawn after vital staining with methylene blue. Synapselike connections are assumed to occur at the points of contact between fibers, *arrow* **A**. The nerve cells may take several forms, including multipolar shapes, *arrow* **B**; and bipolar shapes, *arrow* **C**. The nerve net extends throughout the body wall of the organism and into its tentacles. (Adapted from Lentz, 1968.)

analogous to synapses connect the individual nerve cells of the net to each other. Romanes's investigations (1876, 1877, 1885) were highly inventive and still seem fresh even though they were performed a century ago. His experiments demonstrate that a systematic inquisitive approach can accomplish a great deal without recourse to complex instrumentation.

Romanes used *Aurelia*, a common scyphozoan which is free-living and swims by pulsations of the bell. In figure 5.1-2*A* the bell of *Aurelia* has been inverted and spread out. The margin of the bell has a fringe of motile tentacles used in food capture. The

margin is indented at eight points where marginal ganglia occur. The marginal ganglia contain photoreceptors, chemoreceptors, and statocysts which signal orientation with respect to gravity. The mouth is found at the center of the bell and is surrounded by four gonad-containing structures.

Romanes sectioned *Aurelia* to produce the configuration in figure 5.1-2*B*. He also removed all of the marginal ganglia except the one at point *a*. Ordinarily, *Aurelia* swims by pulsations of the bell, which is induced to contract by periodic discharges from one or more of the marginal ganglia. In this configuration, discharges of the one remaining mar-

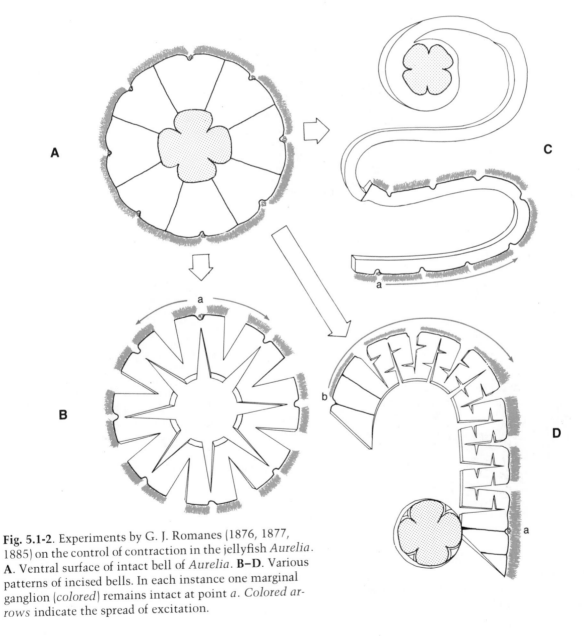

Fig. 5.1-2. Experiments by G. J. Romanes (1876, 1877, 1885) on the control of contraction in the jellyfish *Aurelia*. **A**. Ventral surface of intact bell of *Aurelia*. **B–D**. Various patterns of incised bells. In each instance one marginal ganglion (*colored*) remains intact at point *a*. *Colored arrows* indicate the spread of excitation.

ginal ganglion at *a* induced periodic waves of contraction in the bell. The contractile waves (colored arrows) traveled completely around the incised bell and collided on the opposite side.

Romanes also produced a spiral coil of the bell of *Aurelia* (fig. 5.1-2*C*). Waves of contraction (colored arrow) were able to originate at the sole remaining marginal ganglion at *a*, and pass all the way through the strip up to the mouth area. The strips of bell were as much as a meter long! Romanes assumed that the marginal ganglion induced a wave of excita-

tion in the nerve net which in turn excited the muscular cells of the bell. He concluded that the nerve cells of the nerve net were capable of exciting each other at the points of contact—synaptic connections. That is, at several points the excitation would necessarily have to be conducted from one cell to another to maintain the wave of contraction because the incisions produced a pathway too long and tortuous for an axon to follow.

In his most innovative experiment, Romanes sectioned the bell of *Aurelia* in the pattern shown in

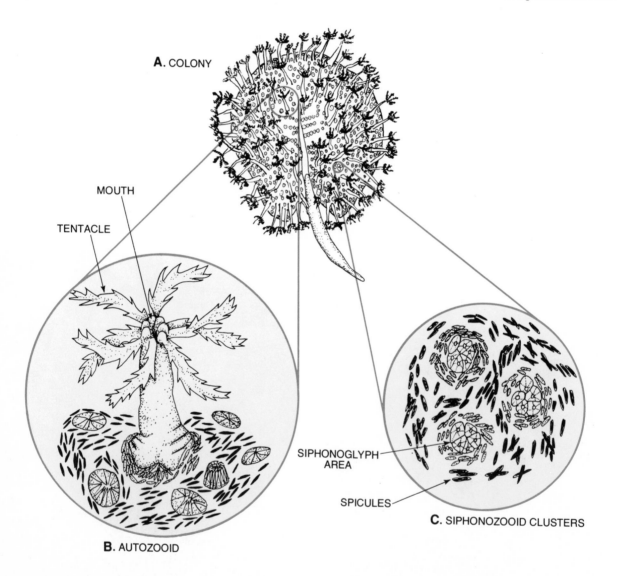

A. COLONY

MOUTH

TENTACLE

SIPHONOGLYPH
AREA

SPICULES

C. SIPHONOZOOID CLUSTERS

B. AUTOZOOID

Fig. 5.1-3. **A**. Structure of the California sea pansy, *Renilla kollikeri*, about life size. (Adapted from P. A. Meglitsch, 1967. *Invertebrate Zoology*. Oxford University Press, London.) **B**. An autozooid, magnified about 30×. **C**. Three siphonozooid clusters, magnified about 30×. (Adapted from D. J. Reish, 1969. *Laboratory Manual for Invertebrate Zoology*. Seaside Pub. Co., Long Beach, Calif.)

figure 5.1-2D. He left one marginal ganglion intact at a, but removed the others. He found that he could induce a wave of contraction in the marginal tentacles by touching point b without inducing a wave of muscular contraction in the bell. This wave of tentacular contraction (colored arrow) passed around the incisions and proceeded to the marginal ganglion at a. A wave of contraction in the bell was then reflexively initiated at a, and proceeded back toward point b. Romanes found that the wave of tentacular contraction moved at one-half the velocity of the wave of bell contraction (23 versus 46 cm/sec). He therefore concluded that *two* nerve nets are present in *Aurelia*, one to coordinate bell contraction and the other to coordinate tentacular contraction. The activity of the two nerve nets is integrated by the marginal ganglia to produce a rudimentary form of reflex action.

Behavior

Coelenterate behavior can be exceedingly complex, but the slow pace of the behavior gives a human observer the false impression of inactivity ("no behavior"). In fact, coelenterates can creep (anemones), swim (jellyfish), bend and somersault (anemones and *Hydra*), coordinate tentacle contraction (anemones and jellyfish), feed, and respond in a variety of ways to chemical and mechanical stimulation. Anemones will learn to reject pieces of filter paper soaked in fish extract after repeated attempts at digesting them. All coelenterates show habituation to repeated stimulation, and some forms seem to show position habits and retention of circadian rhythms when shifted to constant light or dark. These observations may be taken as evidence of primitive learning.

Time to complete the exercise: At least one 3-hour laboratory period; two 3-hour laboratory periods will accommodate a study of more depth and permit adjustment of specimens to more extensive surgery.

Procedure

Morphological examination of <u>Renilla</u>

Read through the following description of *Renilla*, and examine a specimen in the room light as you read. Use a dissecting microscope, if available. After

A

B

Fig. 5.1-4. **A**. Partially contracted and **B**. open tentacles and mouth of an autozooid in *Renilla kollikeri*, magnified about 80×. The action of the tentacles and mouth is coordinated by the nerve net. (Low-power scanning electron micrograph courtesy J. R. Weeks, Jr.)

20–30 minutes the room lights will be turned out and you will work in dim red light.

The California sea pansy, *Renilla kollikeri*, is a colonial anthozoan which is found in shallow subtidal waters along the California coast. The term *colonial* refers to the fact that *Renilla* is composed of several types of organisms which cooperate to form an assemblage which feeds and functions like a single animal. The colony (fig. 5.1-3) has the shape of an umbrella. The top part is called the *rachis* and the stem is the *peduncle*. The peduncle attaches the colony to the sea floor and is usually found in nature inserted in a sandy bottom.

Two kinds of secondary polyps are found on the rachis: *autozooids* (figs. 5.1-3*B* and 5.1-4) and *siphonozooids* (fig. 5.1-3*C*). The autozooids have retractile tentacles surrounding a mouth, and are capable of capturing planktonic food organisms or suspended organic matter. The siphonozooids occur in clusters. Each siphonozooid has a channel called a siphonoglyph through which water is pumped by ciliary action. Calcareous spicules, distributed over the rachis and around the siphonozooid clusters, lend structural support to the colony. The peduncle is attached to the rachis through an area called the *median dorsal track* which is devoid of polyps.

Inhalant siphonozooids on the rachis continuously pump water into the colony by ciliary action. The water circulates through the gastrovascular cavity of the rachis and passes into a canal system in the peduncle. The water finally exits through an exhalant siphonozooid at the tip of the median dorsal track. The slight internal pressure created by the pumping action serves to inflate and help support the colony.

Experimental examination of luminescent responses
You will not be able to see the conducted luminescent waves until your eyes adapt to the dark. You will probably notice in handling the *Renilla* specimen that the colony often luminesces in response to mechanical stimulation. Can you suggest a biological function(s) for this response? Is this activity related to contraction of the whole colony or retraction of individual autozooids? Luminescence is produced by an intracellular enzymatic reaction, which can be neurally triggered or directly initiated by mechanical stimulation. The waves of luminescence are neurally initiated.

Familiarize yourself with the basic luminescent responses (pinpoints and waves) and then design your own experiments to explore the form and properties of excitation and conduction in the nerve net of *Renilla*. The experiments should be carried out in a dark room, and the *Renilla* should be dark adapted for at least 1 hour before the room lights are turned out and the experiments begun. Light-adapted *Renilla* do not luminesce as readily. The organisms should be kept cool (15°–20° C) and the sea water temperature measured for each phase of your experiments.

Experiments

Here are some problems which might be explored.

1. Examine the characteristics of excitation elicited by mechanical or electrical stimulation with various strengths of stimulation. Start with electrical stimuli at one edge of the rachis (amplitude 0.1 V, duration 10 msec). Increase the amplitude if necessary. Be systematic if the stimulus parameters are varied.

2. Does *Renilla* show *facilitation* of the response with successive stimuli? In facilitation, as distinguished from summation, successive responses are larger than predicted from simple addition. For example, after several subthreshold stimulations which elicit no response, a response may suddenly appear. Therefore, facilitation is usually explored with subthreshold stimuli. Repetition rates of around one per second would be appropriate. Twin-pulse stimulation would be valuable if a suitable stimulator is available.

3. Examine refractoriness to repetitive stimulation. (How would you distinguish between local sensory adaptation or central nerve net habituation?)

4. Examine interaction between waves of activity elicited at two or more separate points on the colony. A second (or third) stimulating electrode may be connected in parallel with the first on the negative pole of the stimulator output. The use of two stimulators would permit variation in the temporal relationship of the stimuli.

5. Examine the effects of masking and light adaptation. It might be possible to separate the conduction of excitation from luminescence by light adapting a

narrow strip across the center of the rachis. For example, a central rectangle could be cut out of a paper mask used to cover the colony. The central strip could then be light adapted by exposure to a light. What questions could then be asked about the luminous waves? The converse treatment (dark adapting a central strip) could also be tried with possibly interesting results.

6. Examine the properties of the nerve net by using surgical manipulations. Inferences can be drawn concerning the distribution of fibers in the nerve net, based upon observations of the spread or blockage of activity across narrow bridges of tissue and/or around cuts through the tissue. After surgery, rinse your preparation and place it in fresh sea water. Try not to shock your preparations with large temperature changes as you rinse or change them from one container to another. Also allow sufficient recovery time after surgical operations. The classical experiments of Romanes (1876, 1877, 1885) are illustrated in figure 5.1-2, and they may suggest experiments to you. However, *Renilla* will not survive the complex surgical sections performed by Romanes. Some healing may be observed.

Pitfalls and Suggestions

1. No special suggestions are needed other than to plan out the experiments as fully as possible before beginning. Develop some *testable* hypotheses and proceed to test them. A chart for the tabulation of results is useful, especially in performing electric stimulation at different voltages and frequencies. Be systematic in data collection. Initially, explore the use of mechanical stimulation (tap or poke).

2. Voltages in excess of 10 volts should not be required. Nevertheless, as a safety precaution do not put your hand(s) in the sea water while stimulating. Strong stimulation will produce autozoid and colony retraction.

3. It may be valuable to bend the negative electrode wire and tape it to the edge of the finger bowl, so that the *Renilla* can be positioned against the exposed tip. The trembling movements of hand-held electrodes can change the current passed through the animal. At first, the luminescent response may seem unreliable; you can find ways to make it more reliable.

The room where these experiments take place must be thoroughly darkened, with windows and door cracks blacked out.

Materials

Materials needed at each station

Large cardboard box with the bottom and one side cut out (for use as a black box at each station to shield out stray light)

Black cloth to drape over the open side of the box (serves to keep the box dark when experimenting or doors to the room are opened)

Desk lamp with a red darkroom bulb (7.5 watts)

Electronic stimulator (A stimulator with pulse-pair capability is preferable.)

Set of stimulating electrodes (The stimulating electrodes must not short out too much when immersed in sea water. This requirement makes standard stimulating electrodes unsuitable since they usually have substantial areas of exposed electrode wire. Stimulating electrodes can be simply constructed by cutting the end off plastic insulated 18-gauge hookup wire *without trimming the insulation*. Connect the other end of this wire to the negative pole of the stimulator output. The tip of the free end of the wire is used as a stimulating electrode by bringing it into direct contact with the organism. Connect the other wire to the positive pole of the stimulator output and tape it to the side of the container, with the tip of the wire immersed in the sea water.)

Dissecting microscope

Standard thermometer

Stopwatch

4–5 finger bowls (for holding individual *Renilla* colonies)

Paper towels

Low power magnifying lens (optional)

Dissecting kit (furnished by students)

Materials available in the laboratory

Scissors for paper

Black paper and black cloth

Masking tape

Extra red darkroom bulbs

Extra stimulating electrodes

Stopwatches or timers
Sea water (1–2 liters/station)
Chilled sea water for use in preventing overheating
Plastic bag for animal disposal

Animals

California sea pansy, *Renilla kollikeri* (Order 3–4/
station/laboratory period.) Other species of *Renilla*
might be substituted, although this has not been
attempted by the authors. Keep *Renilla* in well-
aerated sea water. Check the salinity and temperature of the water before transferring the *Renilla* to your aquaria. Temperature should be kept
at 12°–16° C if possible, and the salinity should be
adjusted to a specific gravity of 1.025 (a salinity of
33.5°/00) by the addition of aged fresh water.
Higher temperatures will cause *Renilla* to expend
their metabolic resources at a higher rate. When
the *Renilla* arrive from the supplier, place them in
a polyethylene bag containing the water in which
they were shipped. Place the bag in your aquarium
for 30 minutes to allow the temperature to
equilibrate. Then, if time permits, gradually mix
in some of the aquarium water with the water in
the bag so that the *Renilla* are slowly acclimated
to the new water. Mix the new water into the old
in three or four steps and wait a few minutes after
each mixing. Finally, transfer the *Renilla* to the
aquarium. If the *Renilla* are to be kept more than 3
weeks, they may be fed once a week with small
brine shrimp or yeast. *Renilla* are hardy in sea
water of the proper temperature and salinity.

Notes for the Instructor

1. This exercise is purposely open ended. Since complicated techniques and equipment are not needed,
the topic lends itself well to a student-designed experiment. The students ought to be urged to do some
background reading and planning before they enter
the laboratory. This makes a good two-period experiment. The first day could be spent making initial
observations, planning the next period's experiments, and doing surgery. The students might also
be urged to prepare a list of experiments for the instructor's approval. The next period could then be
spent in quantitating results and examining the
effects of experimental surgery.
2. Arrange to have most of the *Renilla* dark adapted

for a minimum of 1 hour before the students enter
the laboratory. Some specimens should be retained
and set out separately for morphological examination at the beginning of the session.
3. The *Renilla* luminescent response has a relatively
narrow temperature range, and disappears if the
temperature is lowered very much. Therefore, it
would probably be unproductive for the students to
examine the effects of temperature on conduction.
4. It is impossible to photograph the luminescent
waves with standard photographic equipment, even
with extremely fast film speeds.
5. The students may need some explanation of
summation and *facilitation*. A study of facilitation
as well as the elements for studying spatial and temporal summation, and collision of waves are offered
under experiments 2 and 4, page 134.
6. It is assumed that the students will attempt to
measure conduction velocity, although this is not
specifically suggested. Experiment 5 (see page 134)
contains the elements for obtaining an improved
measure of conduction velocity (by using the disappearance and reappearance of the luminescent wave
as it crosses the light-adapted strip).
7. The biological function of *Renilla*'s luminescence
is unknown at present, although this should not stop
speculation. One notion is that it is a form of
aposematic (warning) coloration to discourage predation. The biological function or adaptive value of
bioluminescence is unknown for a very large
number of species.
8. Other features of the luminescent response which
might be examined are:
   a. Does the nerve net extend into the peduncle?
This could be explored surgically by splitting the
colony down the center, leaving the two halves connected only by the peduncle and stimulating one
side or the other.
   b. What are the stimuli which will elicit the after-
discharge or "frenzy" behavior?
   c. Where is the locus of facilitation? For example,
does stimulating at one point facilitate the response
at some distant point?
   d. What is the time course of light and dark adapting? This might be studied by adapting half of the
animal and using the other half as a comparison
standard.
9. Check to see that the negative wire has a bright
metallic surface flush with the insulation.

Selected References

Bullock, T. H., and Horridge, G. A. 1965. *Structure and function in the nervous systems of invertebrates*, vol 1. W. H. Freeman and Co., San Francisco, pp. 459–534.

Cormier, M. J. 1974. Flashing sea pansies and glowing midshipmen. *Natural History* 83: 26–33.

Cormier, M. J.; Lee, J.; and Wampler, J. E. 1975. Bioluminescence: Recent advances. *Annu. Rev. Biochem.* 44: 255–72.

Horridge, G. A. 1968. *Interneurons*. W. H. Freeman and Co., San Francisco, pp. 33–62.

Lentz, T. L. 1968. *Primitive nervous systems*. Yale University Press, New Haven.

Nicol, J. A. C. 1960. The regulation of light emission in animals. *Biol. Rev.* 35: 1–42.

Parker, G. H. 1919. *The elementary nervous system*. Lippincott, Philadelphia and London.

Passano, L. M., ed. 1965. Behavioral physiology of coelenterates (Symposium), *Am. Zool.* 5: 335–589.

Romanes, G. J. 1885. *Jelly-fish, star-fish, and sea-urchins, being a research on primitive nervous systems*. Kegan Paul, Trench and Co., London.

RESEARCH REPORTS

Bertsch, H. W. 1967. Effect of feeding *Armina californica* on the bioluminescence of *Renilla kollikeri*. *Veliger* 10: 440–41.

Cormier, M. J.; Hori, K.; and Karkhanis, Y. D. 1970. Studies on the bioluminescence of *Renilla reniformis* VII. Conversion of luciferin into luciferyl sulfate by luciferase sulfonkinase. *Biochem.* 9: 1184–89.

Nicol, J. A. C. 1955a. Observations on luminescence in *Renilla (Pennatulacea). J. Exp. Biol.* 32: 299–320.

———. 1955b. Nervous regulation of luminescence in the sea pansy *Renilla kollikeri. J. Exp. Biol.* 32: 619–35.

Parker, G. H. 1919. The organization of *Renilla. J. Exp. Zool.* 27: 499–507.

———. 1920a. Activities of colonial animals II. Neuromuscular movements and phosphorescence in *Renilla. J. Exp. Zool.* 31: 475–515.

———. 1920b. The phosphorescence of *Renilla. Proc. Am. Philos. Soc.* 59: 171–75.

Romanes, G. J. 1876. Preliminary observations on the locomotor system of medusae. *Philos. Trans. R. Soc. Lond.* 166: 269–313.

———. 1877. Further observations on the locomotor system of medusae. *Philos. Trans. R. Soc. Lond.* 167: 659–752.

5.2 Neuromuscular Synapse
Frog Sciatic-Gastrocnemius Junction

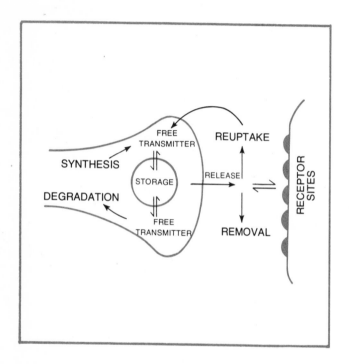

Introduction

Rationale
The neuromuscular synapse is *the* critical point of communication between the neuronal and muscular systems. Since the neuromuscular synapse of vertebrates is much more accessible than synapses within the central nervous system, it has been intensively studied as a model of general synaptic function. Consequently, the action and pharmacology of the vertebrate neuromuscular transmitter, acetylcholine (ACh), is probably the best understood among the many synaptic transmitters of the nervous system (fig. 5.2-1).

Neuromuscular organization
The axon of each vertebrate motor neuron innervates a group of muscle fibers (cells) in a specific

muscle. Ratios of 1 axon to 100–500 muscle cells are common in skeletal muscles. The motor neuron and the muscle fibers it innervates comprise the functional unit of the neuromuscular system, the *motor unit*. Each motor unit in a vertebrate behaves in an all-or-none fashion. That is, when the motor neuron fires, the muscle fibers it innervates are stimulated and contract maximally in unison. Gradation of contraction within a whole muscle is achieved primarily by varying the number of active motor units from the hundreds within the muscle.[1] Generally the different motor neurons which innervate a given muscle have different thresholds; they are not all brought into play at the same time. In practical experiments, one typically stimulates a peripheral nerve with an electrical stimulus which exceeds the threshold of all the axons in the nerve. This elicits a maximal contraction of the muscle.

Synaptic morphology
The axon of a motor nerve enters the muscle and branches profusely near the muscle fibers it innervates (see fig. 5.2-2). In many animals, including mammals, the terminal branches are unmyelinated. They expand at their ends into a series of bulbs which synapse with the muscle fiber membrane. The entire nerve terminal-muscle membrane complex is called the *motor end plate*. The muscle cell membrane is morphologically and physiologically specialized to be depolarized by acetylcholine released from the nerve terminal. The excitatory depolarization of the muscle cell membrane at the end plate initiates an action potential that spreads across

---

1. Invertebrates usually operate on a different system. Only two to six neurons innervate a single muscle. Some neurons are inhibitory. Gradation of contraction results because the contraction of muscle cells depends upon nerve impulse frequency and the relative activity of excitatory and inhibitory axons. Invertebrate muscle cells are not all-or-none.

the muscle cell membrane and ultimately triggers contraction of the muscle cell. The effect of the motor nerve fiber on the skeletal muscle cells of vertebrates is always excitatory.

Acetylcholine

The neuromuscular transmitter, *acetylcholine* (ACh), is stored in the presynaptic terminal in membrane-bound vesicles (fig. 5.2-2). Arrival of the axonal action potential at the terminal results in the expulsion of the contents of many vesicles into the 600 Å (1 angstrom = 10^{-8} cm) wide space between the nerve and muscle cell membranes. After impulse arrival, transmitter release takes about 0.3 msec, which accounts for most of the *synaptic delay*. The

acetylcholine then rapidly (0.01 msec) diffuses across the junctional cleft to the postsynaptic membrane where it exerts its effect. The acetylcholine molecules bind to specific receptor sites on the muscle cell membrane where they induce ionic permeability changes which produce a synaptic potential. The acetylcholine is rapidly hydrolyzed to choline and acetate by an enzyme, *acetylcholinesterase*, which is found in the synaptic cleft. Hydrolysis is possible because the binding of ACh to the receptor is freely reversible, and the ACh is exposed to the enzyme both before and after it binds. Enough ACh is released by the presynaptic terminal so that it will not all be hydrolyzed before it reaches the postsynaptic receptors on the muscle cell membrane. Choline is rapidly transported back into the presynaptic terminal by an efficient choline pump in

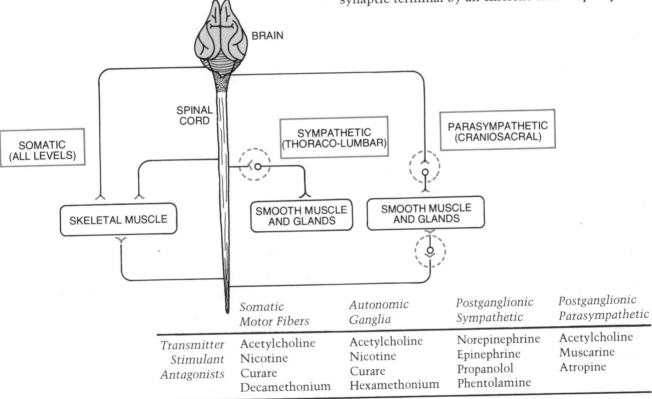

	Somatic Motor Fibers	Autonomic Ganglia	Postganglionic Sympathetic	Postganglionic Parasympathetic
Transmitter	Acetylcholine	Acetylcholine	Norepinephrine	Acetylcholine
Stimulant	Nicotine	Nicotine	Epinephrine	Muscarine
Antagonists	Curare	Curare	Propanolol	Atropine
	Decamethonium	Hexamethonium	Phentolamine	

Fig. 5.2-1. Peripheral transmitters in the vertebrate nervous system. *Anatomy.* Somatic motor fibers from all levels of the brain and spinal cord innervate skeletal muscle. Sympathetic fibers emerge only from the thoracic and lumbar divisions of the spinal cord, whereas parasympathetic fibers are craniosacral in origin. *Transmitters.* Skeletal muscle is excited by somatic motor neurons which employ acetylcholine as a transmitter. Parasympathetic fibers of the autonomic nervous system employ

acetylcholine at both the ganglionic level and at their effector sites. However, postsynaptic receptors for preganglionic and postganglionic parasympathetic fibers are somewhat different in binding properties (nicotinic versus muscarinic). Postganglionic sympathetic fibers employ norepinephrine at effector sites. *Colored* synapses are cholinergic, and the *dashed circles* represent the autonomic ganglia.

the presynaptic membrane. The choline is then acetylated by another enzyme, *choline acetyltransferase*, and the resynthesized ACh is stored anew in the presynaptic vesicles.[2]

Pharmacology

The neuromuscular junction is susceptible to many drugs which may have one of several effects.

Acetylcholinesterase inhibition. Some drugs, like physostigmine (eserine) and diisopropyl fluorophosphate (DFP), inhibit the hydrolytic enzyme. In response to the continued presence of ACh at the motor end plate, the muscle fiber first contracts but then becomes unresponsive to further stimulation (paralyzed). Injected intravenously in small quantities, a drug like DFP will induce twitching of the facial muscles and tongue. Injected in larger quantities, it will lead to death from suffocation because the breathing muscles become continuously depolarized. Similar compounds are used as nerve gases and insecticides.

Receptor blockage. Another class of drugs, including curare and its synthetic analog gallaminetriethiodide, binds to the postsynaptic receptor site and makes it unavailable to ACh binding. Curare and ACh both bind to the ACh receptor site because they have similar molecular structures; both are quaternary ammonium compounds. Curare is inhibitory because it mimics ACh without stimulating. The result of curare injection is a progressive paralysis of the skeletal musculature, starting with the muscles of the eyes and eyelids, moving to the head and neck, and finally to the limbs and breathing muscles. The effects of many drugs which block ACh receptors or inhibit acetylcholinesterase are reversible, given enough time.

Other effects. Other drugs may block neuromuscular transmission by blocking nerve action potentials (tetrodotoxin), inhibiting ACh synthesis (hemicholinium), inhibiting ACh release (procaine, botulinus toxin), mimicking ACh by depolarization

of the postsynaptic membrane (succinylcholine, decamethonium), or blocking metabolic sources of energy (cyanide).

Ions also play a role in synaptic function, and neuromuscular transmission can be affected by chang-

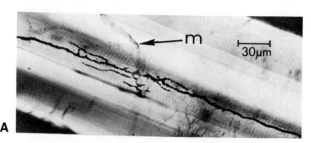

A

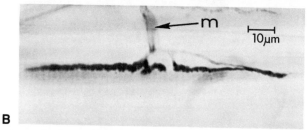

B

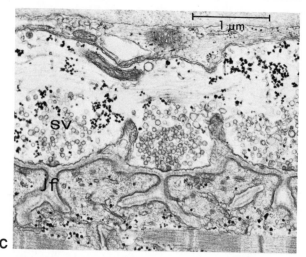

C

Fig. 5.2-2. Frog axon terminals seen with the light and electron microscopes (McMahan, Spitzer, and Peper, 1972; illustrations courtesy of U. J. McMahan). **A–B.** Axons terminating on skeletal muscle fibers. The axon terminals have been stained with zinc oxide and osmium and photographed with the light microscope (Nomarski optics). The lightly stained myelinated portion of the incoming axon (*m*) branches near the surface of the muscle fiber into terminal branches which run along the surface of the muscle fiber. **C.** Frog neuromuscular junction seen with the electron microscope. The varicosities (*dark swellings* in *B*) contain most of the synaptic vesicles (*sv*). Each axonal swelling is directly opposite a junctional fold (*jf*) in the muscle cell membrane.

---

2. ACh is inactivated by enzymatic hydrolysis, but this is not true of most other transmitters. Inactivation in synapses which use other transmitters takes place when the intact transmitter is removed by rapid re-uptake into the presynaptic terminal.

ing ionic concentrations. For example, high [K$^+$] permanently depolarizes the postsynaptic membrane, blocking the synapse.

Calcium is necessary for transmitter release from the presynaptic terminal. Low [Ca^{++}] will block ACh release in the neuromuscular synapse. High [Mg^{++}] will have the same effect because it is a divalent cation like Ca^{++} and competes for Ca^{++} binding sites in the presynaptic membrane. It may seem paradoxical, but low [Ca^{++}] in the systemic circulation (as in parathyroid gland dysfunction or the disease rickets) leads to hyperexcitability of the skeletal muscles and tetany. The explanation is that Ca^{++} is essential to membrane integrity, and prolonged Ca^{++} deficiency leads to membrane destabilization with increased permeability to N$^+$ and K$^+$. In these circumstances muscle membranes become more excitable, and spontaneous action potentials lead to muscle contraction.

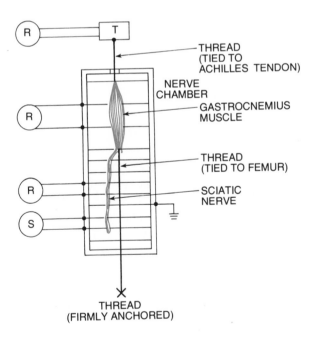

Fig. 5.2-3. Arrangement for recording from the nerve-muscle preparation using a nerve chamber. When the nerve is stimulated, the muscle contracts. The electrical activity of the nerve and muscle can be recorded simultaneously with a dual-trace oscilloscope. Muscle contraction can be recorded with a polygraph or oscilloscope fitted with an appropriate transducer and amplifier. *R.* recording device (CRO); *S.* stimulator; *T.* muscle lever or mechanoelectric transducer or post.

Time to complete the exercise: One 3-hour laboratory period. A longer time will be required for more than a cursory study of various agents which affect neuromuscular transmission.

Procedure

Surgical procedure
Double pith a frog. Cut the skin completely around the frog at midabdomen. Hold the upper part of the frog in one hand and pull the skin off the lower abdomen and legs with the other hand, everting the skin as it is pulled off. Use a single, firm pull to remove the skin from the legs. Tissue-gripping forceps are helpful. See page 311 for pithing method.

Turn the frog dorsal side up and separate the muscles of the upper leg from the pelvis to the knee to expose the sciatic nerve (fig. 4.2-1). Use clean fingers and blunt probes. The nerve should not be touched at this stage. Now, free up the nerve from its attaching connective tissue using blunt glass tools (e.g., two glass rods drawn out and fire-polished to a blunt 1 mm tip). Do not attempt to free the nerve too close to the knee joint.

CAUTION: **Do not stretch the nerve.**

Cut through the muscles and connective tissue as necessary to expose the sciatic nerve where it passes through the pelvis into the leg. Avoid touching the nerve with scissors or scalpel. Free the nerve from its attachments in the pelvic region by using the blunt glass tools. Cut the nerve roots and free the nerve all the way to the knee joint without stretching the nerve. Cut through the femur and its muscles with heavy scissors about 1 cm above (proximal to) the knee joint without severing the nerve. Tie a thread around the distal tendon (the Achilles tendon) of the gastrocnemius (calf) muscle. Now, cut the tendon free from the bone. Elevate and free the gastrocnemius muscle from the other muscles and bone and cut through the tibiofibula just below the knee joint. With minimal further dissection you should have a nerve attached to its muscle: the sciatic-gastrocnemius nerve–muscle preparation. Rinse the preparation with perfusion fluid and immerse it in a small beaker of perfusion fluid.

Recording Procedure

Mount a nerve chamber on a ringstand. Lay the nerve-muscle preparation upon the wire electrodes in the nerve chamber (fig. 5.2-3). The electrodes are used to support the preparation and to stimulate and record. In such an arrangement it is necessary to have threads tied to each end of the muscle. You should already have a thread tied to the Achilles tendon. Tie another 20 cm thread to the femur at the proximal end of the muscle. Pass the threads through holes in opposite ends of the nerve chamber. Arrange the nerve-muscle preparation as in figure 5.2-3. The nerve should be extended on the electrodes for stimulating, and the proximal end of the muscle immovably fixed with the thread so that muscle contraction does not move the nerve. The thread at the distal end of the muscle should be fixed to a muscle lever, mechanical transducer, or another ringstand so that the muscle can be stretched out across the electrodes. With the muscle just barely taut between the two stands, the chamber may be moved slightly to position the gastrocnemius-sciatic preparation optimally. Fill the bottom of the nerve chamber with perfusion fluid, but make sure that the fluid does not touch the electrodes and short them out. Cover the open top of the nerve chamber.

Hookup

Make connections to the stimulator and oscilloscope (or polygraph) as illustrated in figure 5.2-3. You can stimulate the nerve with the electronic stimulator and record the nerve action potential and the muscle action potential simultaneously if you have a dual-trace oscilloscope or a polygraph. Be sure to connect a cable from the stimulator's trigger output to the trigger input on the oscilloscope and ground any metal apparatus used to support the nerve-muscle preparation. (Optional. The polygraph can also be used to record mechanical contraction of the muscle, and, in a few laboratories, oscilloscopes with carrier amplifiers and appropriate transducers will be available for recording mechanical responses.)

Use the following initial settings on your equipment.

Preamplifier(s). Input in differential mode if possible; gain of 100–1,000×; band-pass filters (if available) set at about 10 Hz (low frequency filter) and 3 kHz (high frequency filter).

Oscilloscope. Time base at 1 msec/div; vertical sensitivity at 0.1–0.01 V/div; trigger set on external input and the triggering level control adjusted to trigger the oscilloscope sweep when the stimulator is actuated. (You may record the muscle action potential on a second channel without preamplification at a sensitivity of 2 mV/div.)

Calibration. Adjust the preamplifier and oscilloscope vertical gain to give a *total system gain* of approximately 100 μV/div. Check with the preamplifier calibrator if available.

Stimulator. Frequency of 1 pulse/5 sec; delay (if available) of about 1 msec; duration of 0.4 msec; starting voltage of 0.1 V.

When the system is set up, it will undoubtedly be necessary to make adjustments to obtain a response and optimally display it.

Initially, use only single stimuli.

Produce a single stimulus by pressing the output mode switch briefly to the *single* position. This will trigger the sweep. If the muscle does not contract, increase the stimulus voltage to 0.5 V, and stimulate again with a single pulse. Increase the stimulus voltage by steps until a maximum contraction is obtained. (Make a qualitative judgment of the point of maximum contraction by looking at the muscle while stimulating.) After this point is reached, increase the stimulus voltage by another 10% to achieve supramaximal stimulus. Do not use *continuous* (multiple) stimuli because this will needlessly fatigue the muscle.

After a consistent, maximal contraction is obtained, adjust the recording system to obtain a display of the electrical response of the nerve and/or muscle. Again, use single stimuli to avoid muscle fatigue.

Experiments

In the following experiments moisten the nerve-muscle preparation if necessary, but take care not to short out the electrodes with too much perfusion fluid.

Synaptic delay. Determine the time interval between the nerve action potential and the muscle action potential. Increase the oscilloscope sweep speed if necessary to facilitate measurement. This response-response interval is made up of three major components: (1) the conduction time along the nerve between the nerve recording site and the neuromuscular synapses, (2) the synaptic delay, and (3) the latency and conduction time of the muscle action potential to the recording electrodes. We will assume factor 3 is negligible and obtain factor 2 by subtracting factor 1 from the total response-response interval. Try to measure conduction rate in the nerve by moving the recording electrodes (consult figure 4.2-5 if you do not remember how). If you cannot determine conduction rate, use the sciatic nerve conduction velocity determined in experiment 4.2 or compute it from the latency and distance between the stimulating and first recording electrode. Calculate the nerve conduction time in msec in the nerve-muscle preparation by measuring the distance in mm between the recording electrodes on the nerve and the middle of the muscle and dividing by the conduction rate in mm/msec. Remember, m/sec ≡ mm/msec.

Subtract the nerve conduction time from the total time between the nerve action potential and the onset of the muscle action potential. The difference is a fair estimate of synaptic delay at the neuromuscular junction. How could it be made more accurate? What additional factors would be involved if the time between the nerve action potential and muscle contraction were used instead of the time between nerve and muscle action potentials? (Optional. Measure the latency between electrical activity in the muscle and the onset of contraction. What is the origin of this latency?)

Effects of frequency. You have been recording by using single stimuli. Now use repetitive stimuli at different rates to explore the following questions. Is there a temporal summation of responses to pairs or trains of stimuli? Remember, summation could refer to either muscle electrical activity or the mechanical activity of contraction. Does stimulation at high rates (greater than 80/sec) cause a reduction in muscular tension and electrical activity (Wedensky inhibition)? If there is a reduction, is this a lasting fatigue?

CAUTION: Do not attempt these tests more than a few times. The muscle will become fatigued and you will have to spend time dissecting a new preparation.

Polarity of the synapse. Rearrange the stimulating and recording electrodes so that you stimulate the muscle directly and record from the nerve. Place a ground electrode on the nerve between the muscle and the site of recording on the nerve. Is it possible to record an action potential from the nerve when the muscle is stimulated? Explain.

Centripetal activity. (Centrifugal means away from the central nervous system; centripetal, toward it.) Use the same stimulating and recording setup as in the last experiment. Stretch the muscle passively by pulling the thread attached to the Achilles tendon. Does this initiate action potentials in the nerve? What is the source of this activity? (Ground your other hand if 60 Hz pickup is a problem.)

Eserinized preparation. Rearrange the stimulating and recording electrodes to their original placement. Slowly drip eserine solution (0.01 mg/ml) on the muscle for 1 or 2 minutes. Does the eserine have any effect on the excitability and threshold? Do you recall the mechanism of action of eserine (also called physostigmine)?

Effects of drugs and other agents
(at the instructor's option)
Several agents from the following list will be supplied. You may test their effects on the nerve-muscle preparation. In general, none of the agents affects electrical transmission at the concentrations listed when applied to the muscle externally. You may begin with the original preparation, but remember that it was treated with eserine. The solutions can be slowly dripped onto the muscle, or if enough solution is available, the preparation can be soaked for 10–15 minutes in the solution of choice. Do not remove the preparation from the chamber for soaking. Plug the holes in the ends of the chamber with petroleum jelly (Vaseline) and replace the fluid in the chamber with perfusion fluid containing the

agent. Always check for reversibility, i.e., will a 15-minute soak or rinse in normal perfusion fluid restore the preparation? *It would be best to limit your tests to one aspect of neuromuscular transmission*, such as the role of acetylcholinesterase (AChE) or the effects of possible false transmitters.

Take care in handling these agents. Most are very effective poisons.

ACh esterase inhibitors
1. Eserine (0.01 mg/ml in perfusion fluid) (eserine sulfate, physostigmine sulfate)
2. Neostigmine (0.01 mg/ml in perfusion fluid) (neostigmine bromide)

Competitive inhibitors of ACh binding at post-synaptic receptor
1. Curare (0.01 mg/ml in perfusion fluid) (*d*-tubocurarine chloride)
2. Atropine (0.01 mg/ml in perfusion fluid) (atropine sulfate)

Depolarizing agents which decrease resting membrane potential
1. ACh in high concentration (0.01 mg/ml in perfusion fluid) (acetylcholine chloride)
2. Nicotine (also a competitive blocker) (0.01 mg/ml in perfusion fluid) (nicotine sulfate)
3. Tetramethylammonium (TMA) (0.01 mg/ml in perfusion fluid) (tetramethylammonium hydroxide)
4. Decamethonium (0.01 mg/ml in perfusion fluid) (decamethonium bromide)
5. Succinylcholine (0.01 mg/ml in perfusion fluid) (succinylcholine chloride)

After you are through, carefully clean all equipment to cleanse it of residual chemicals. Carefully clean the nerve chamber so that the next person's experiments are not ruined. Wash your hands.

Ionic solutions
1. High magnesium solution (50 mM $MgCl_2$ in perfusion fluid)
2. High calcium solution (50 mM $CaCl_2$ in perfusion fluid)

Design your own experiments using appropriate controls. How do you know that an observed action is on the synapse?

Effects of curare on an intact animal
(at the instructor's option)
Pith the brain of a frog. Do not pith the spinal cord. Cut the skin fully around each upper thigh. Make a similar cut around the lower part of each hindleg about two thirds of the distance to the foot. Strip the skin from the legs between the cuts. Expose the sciatic nerves in the thighs of both legs so they may be stimulated with hand-held electrodes or sleeve electrodes. Tie off the circulation (*but not the sciatic nerve*) to one of the legs with a fine thread.

Test for flexion reflexes in both legs by pinching the toes with forceps. After a short period of spinal shock produced by pithing the brain, the flexion reflexes should be easily elicited and dependable. Inject 0.2 cc of curare solution under the skin on the back. You will be injecting into an area called the *dorsal lymph sac*. Fluid from the dorsal lymph sac will shortly enter the systemic blood circulation.

Be careful with the curare-filled syringe.

Test for any diminution of flexion reflexes in each hindleg. Also, stimulate the sciatic nerve directly at intervals with a pair of hand or sleeve electrodes. Can you corroborate the suggestion that curare affects neuromuscular transmission? Is it important to also stimulate the gastrocnemious muscle directly? Do you understand why the circulation of one leg was tied off, but not the other? How does this experiment pinpoint the site of curare's effect?

Pitfalls and Suggestions

1. Be *extremely careful* with the drugs and other pharmacological agents provided. *Label all* containers of these solutions. Some are very powerful poisons. *Do not get them on your skin.* If you do get them on your skin accidentally, *wash immediately*.
2. Dissect the nerve-muscle preparation gently and keep it moist with perfusion fluid and it will work reliably.
3. Do not overstimulate the preparation. The nerve and muscle electrical activity is resistant to fatigue,

as is the neuromuscular junction to a lesser extent, but muscle contraction will decline as metabolic energy stores are used. Remember that the muscle has been separated from its oxygen and nutrient supply, the circulation.

Materials

Materials needed at each station

Oscilloscope (dual trace if available) or polygraph

Stimulator

Preamplifier (Only one is needed because the oscilloscope vertical amplifier is sufficient for the muscle action potential.)

Set of electrical leads and connectors

Nerve chamber and cover (see page 334 for construction details)

2 ringstands and 1–2 right-angle clamps

Set of hand or sleeve electrodes (e.g., Harvard no. 304, Narco no. 710–005, or see page 336) for stimulating sciatic nerve in intact preparation

Small beaker and a medicine dropper

2 glass tools for dissecting and manipulating nerves

Set of dissecting tools (furnished by students)

Materials available in the laboratory

Oscilloscope camera and film

Extra cables and connectors

Amphibian perfusion fluid (100 ml/station)

Extra medicine droppers or Pasteur pipettes with bulbs and beakers

Fine cotton thread

Dissecting microscope and dissecting pans

Plastic bag for disposal of dissected frogs

Ringstands

Right-angle clamps

Hypodermic syringes (1–5 cc, with 25–27-gauge needles)

Petroleum jelly (Vaseline)

Solutions (for dripping onto muscles, 5–10 ml/station will be needed; for soaking, 25–30 ml/station will be needed. Check the latter figure against the capacity of your nerve chambers)

a. Eserine (0.01 mg/ml in perfusion fluid) (eserine sulfate, physostigmine sulfate)

b. Neostigmine (0.01 mg/ml in perfusion fluid) (neostigmine bromide)

c. Curare (0.01 mg/ml in perfusion fluid) (*d*-tubocurarine chloride)

d. Atropine (0.01 mg/ml in perfusion fluid) (atropine sulfate)

e. ACh in high concentration (0.01 mg/ml in perfusion fluid) (acetylcholine chloride)

f. Nicotine (0.01 mg/ml in perfusion fluid) (nicotine sulfate)

g. Tetramethylammonium (TMA) (0.01 mg/ml in perfusion fluid) (tetramethylammonium hydroxide)

h. Decamethonium (0.01 mg/ml in perfusion fluid) (decamethonium bromide)

e. Succinylcholine (0.01 mg/ml in perfusion fluid) (succinylcholine chloride)

Solution (for injecting spinal animal; 0.5–1 ml/station): Curare (3.0 mg/ml) (*d*-tubocurarine chloride)

Ionic solutions for soaking or dripping onto muscles (50 ml/station)

a. High magnesium solution (50 mM $MgCl_2$ in perfusion fluid)

b. High calcium solution (50 mM $CaCl_2$ in perfusion fluid)

Animals

Frogs, *Rana pipiens* or other species (Order 1.5 frogs/station/laboratory period; or 2.5 frogs/station if the last experiment [effects of curare on an intact animal] is performed.) Keep the frogs in a cool place and provide them with dripping water.

Notes for the Instructor

1. *The instructor should carefully explain the toxicity of the agents used in this exercise and constantly monitor their use. All containers should be completely labeled. Carefully control the 1 mg/ml curare. Use a labeled syringe.*

2. Do not use DFP (diisopropyl fluorophosphate) even though it was mentioned in the "Introduction." It is far too toxic to use in the student laboratory. Cyanide is to be avoided for the same reason. Muscarine has been omitted because it is too expensive to use in the student laboratory. Tetraethylammonium (TEA) is not suggested because it is not widely available.

3. Sometimes soaking the muscle in a solution containing one of the suggested agents is not effective, or only slowly so. As a last resort, the solution can be injected into the muscle with a syringe. However,

this certainly causes tissue damage and requires the student to disrupt the recording setup.

4. Students sometimes get two twitches each time they stimulate the nerve-muscle preparation. For students who ask, this is explained as follows:

A brief stimulation of the motor nerve or the muscle directly will cause a simple muscle twitch. When the nerve is stimulated with a long square wave lasting more than a few tens of milliseconds, the muscle will twitch at both the onset and the end of the square wave. The muscle responds when the current is first applied ("make") and when it is removed ("break"), but not during the intervening period when the current is flowing. During the passage of a constant current through the nerve, the region immediately under the cathode (negative electrode) has its excitability raised because the nerve membrane is partially depolarized by the current flowing outward. The opposite happens at the anode (positive electrode) where the current flows inward. These effects are greatest at the instant the current is applied or released, but immediately subside exponentially. Thus, an action potential is produced at the cathode and no further impulses follow while the current flows. The axonal membrane behaves like a capacitor, storing some charge, so that when the current ceases to flow at "break" there is a reverse current as the capacitance is discharged. A second action potential is generated, this time at the anode, before the membrane returns to its normal resting state.

5. The classic experiment of tying off the circulation in one leg and injecting with curare dates to Claude Bernard's nineteenth-century experiments, but it is still an elegant demonstration of the locus of curare's effect. Some students should do the exercise.

Selected References

Cold Spring Harbor Laboratory. 1976. *The synapse*. Cold Spring Harb. Symp. Quant. Biol. *Biol.*, vol. 40 (40 papers).

Davson, H. 1970. *A textbook of general physiology*, vol. 2. J. A. Churchill, London.

Goodman, L. S., and Gilman, A. eds. 1975. *The pharmacological basis of therapeutics*, 5th ed. Macmillan Co., New York.

Krnjević, K. 1974. Chemical nature of synaptic transmission in vertebrates. *Physiol. Rev.* 54: 418–540.

Kuffler, S. W., and Nicholls, J. G. 1976. *From neuron to brain*. Sinauer Assoc., Sunderland, Mass.

MacIntosh, F. C. 1976. Acetylcholine. In *Basic neurochemistry*, ed. G. J. Siegel et al. Little, Brown, Boston, pp. 180–202.

RESEARCH REPORTS

Bernard, C. 1856. Physiological analysis of the properties of the muscular and nervous systems by means of curare. *C. R. Acad. Sci.* Paris. 43: 825–29.

Dale, H. H.; Feldberg, W.; and Vogt, M. 1936. Release of acetylcholine at voluntary motor nerve endings. *J. Physiol.* 86: 353–80.

Eccles, J. C.; Katz, B.; and Kuffler, S. W. 1941. Electric potential changes accompanying neuromuscular transmission. *Biol. Symp.* 3: 349–70.

Krnjević, K., and Miledi, R. 1958. Acetylcholine in mammalian neuromuscular transmission. *Nature* 182: 805–6.

Krnjević, K., and Mitchell, J. F. 1961. The release of acetylcholine in the isolated rat diaphragm. *J. Physiol.* 155: 246–52.

McMahan, U. J.; Spitzer, N. C.; and Peper, K. 1972. Visual identification of nerve terminals in living isolated skeletal muscle. *Proc. R. Soc. Lond., B.* 181: 421–30.

5.3 Cardiac Muscle and Its Neural Regulation
Turtle Heart

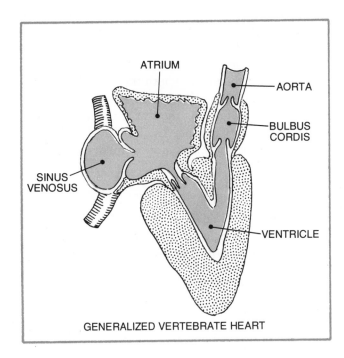

GENERALIZED VERTEBRATE HEART

Introduction

Rationale
Contraction of the vertebrate heart is inherently rhythmic (myogenic). If severed from nervous connections, removed from the body, or even cut into pieces, the cardiac muscle of a lower vertebrate such as the turtle will continue periodic contractions for some time. It is a hardy experimental preparation. In the intact animal, stroke volume (output/beat), and heart rate are adjusted by an interplay of hormonal and neural controls as well as by the heart's own intrinsic muscular responses to the filling process (Starling's law of the heart).

Normally the heart is driven by its own pacemaker: the sinus venosus of lower vertebrates or its homologue, the sinoatrial (S-A) node, in higher vertebrates. Nodal pacemaker tissue triggers the heartbeat because it has a slightly faster intrinsic rhythm than the cells of the heart chambers. Excitation is spread through low resistance junctions among muscle cells and through a specialized system of conducting fibers: the atrioventricular (A-V) node, the bundle of His, and its enlarged extension, the Purkinje fibers.

Stepwise excitation of the turtle heart takes place in the following order. The sinus venosus fires first, followed quickly by the atrial muscle which produces the *P* wave of the electrocardiogram (EKG or ECG) (fig. 5.3-1). The excitation then spreads to the A-V node where conduction is slowed considerably. The slow passage of electrical activity through the A-V node produces a pause in the ECG between the *P* and *QRS* waves called the *P-R* interval. When excitation finally leaves the A-V node and enters the ventricle's fast-conducting tissue (homologue of the bundle of His and Purkinje system of mammals), the ventricular muscle fires and the *QRS* wave appears. Repolarization of the ventricle is indicated by the *T* wave.

The heart receives dual innervation from the autonomic nervous system. Sympathetic fibers of the

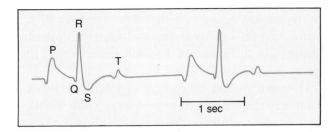

Fig. 5.3-1. Turtle electrocardiogram recorded with the recording arrangement shown in figure 5.3-2. Turtle ECG's may vary considerably depending on the placement of electrodes, but the *QRS* complex will always be easily recognized by its spikelike form.

accelerator nerve innervate the pacemaker and other nodal tissue and, to a lesser extent, the myocardial cells of the chambers. The vagus (Xth cranial nerve) provides parasympathetic innervation of the nodal tissue and atrial muscle. The right vagus principally innervates the S-A node, with some nerve fibers also going to the A-V node and atrial muscle. The left vagus mainly innervates the A-V node, with fewer fibers going to the S-A node and atria. The classic experiment of Otto Loewi demonstrated that the vagus nerves secrete a chemical substance (he called it "vagusstoff") which slows heart activity.[3] We now know that vagusstoff is the parasympathetic transmitter, acetylcholine. The sympathetic postganglionic transmitter is norepinephrine (noradrenaline), which accelerates the heart and increases the force of contraction.

Time to complete the exercise: One 3-hour laboratory period for completion of the first eight sections. More time will be required to complete the last section or to treat the earlier sections quantitatively.

Procedure

Pithing the turtle
If your turtle has not already been pithed, follow either the first or second set of directions, according to your instructor.

Pithing by brain destruction. Obtain five 40 cm lengths of stout string. Make a single half hitch (the first part of tying your shoe) at the end of a string. Place the turtle on its back and gently slip the loop over a foot as it attempts to right itself. Quickly draw the string tight and secure it with a second half hitch over the first (a square knot is best). Tie strings to the remaining legs. Finally, slip a loop of a fifth string over the head of the animal. Quickly draw the string tight at the base of the skull and complete the knot.

Obtain a pithing instrument and right the turtle. First, use the string tied to the head to pull the turtle's head forcefully out of the shell. Hold the head out with one hand by pulling the head partially downward over the edge of the plastron (lower shell), using the string. Quickly and forcefully insert the pithing instrument into the dorsal neck at the junction between the head and neck. Pass it upward into the skull through the foramen magnum and thoroughly destroy the brain with circular movements of the tip of the instrument.

Pithing with sheep castrators. Tie strings to the turtle's legs and neck as just described. Obtain a set of sheep castrators and examine their construction. Extend the head and neck from the shell by pulling forcefully on the attached string. With the sheep castrators, crush the neck in both the horizontal and vertical directions as close to the base of the skull as possible. Avoid injuring the rest of the neck or you will damage the vagus nerves. If the animal does not relax following some initial movements, repeat.

Opening the shell
Some movement of the turtle's legs will be apparent. The brain has been destroyed directly or desensitized by crushing its circulatory supply and connections to the spinal cord, so the activity observed results from spinal reflexes.

Use a hacksaw or bone saw to cut through the lateral connections between the plastron and the carapace (lower and upper shells). Cut just enough to break through the bone, but not enough to damage underlying soft tissue. Excessive bleeding indicates that you have cut too far. Sever the remaining connections between the carapace and plastron at each leg using bone-cutting pliers or wire cutters. Do not remove the plastron yet.

Securely fasten the turtle to a turtle board, using the strings tied to the legs. Gently lift one end of the plastron and use a scalpel to scrape the muscle attachments free from the plastron. Scrape, do not cut. Continue to free the plastron, minimizing damage to the underlying tissue, until the plastron can be lifted completely off.

Observation of the heart in situ
Wash away excess blood with perfusion fluid and observe the heart and internal organs. Note that the heart is enclosed in its own sac, the *pericardium*. Open the pericardium with fine scissors, being careful to avoid injury to the *frenulum*, a fine mesentery which anchors the tip (apex) of the ventricle to the

---

3. Taylor gives a particularly lively account of Loewi's discovery. (G. R. Taylor, 1963. *The Science of Life*. McGraw-Hill, New York.)

pericardium. Observe the *sinus venosus*, two *atria*, one *ventricle*, and *Remak's ganglion*. Remak's ganglion is a white transverse crescent which lies between the sinus venosus and the right atrium on the dorsal surface of the heart. It contains synapses between the pre- and postganglionic parasympathetic neurons which innervate the heart.

Observe the beating pattern. Note the point of origin of the beat and the manner of its progression across the heart.

Locating the vagus nerves
Use the scissors to cut through the skin along the midventral line of the neck. Displace the underlying muscles laterally and locate the trachea (with its white cartilaginous rings) and the carotid arteries lying along either side. It may help to trace the carotid arteries from the heart out into the neck. The right and left vagus nerves accompany the carotid arteries. Locate the vagi. They have faint cross striations, are quite white, and lie in close contact with the carotid arteries. Use drawn-out and fire-polished glass tools to manipulate the tissues.

Use extreme care in dissecting the neck and locating the vagus nerves.

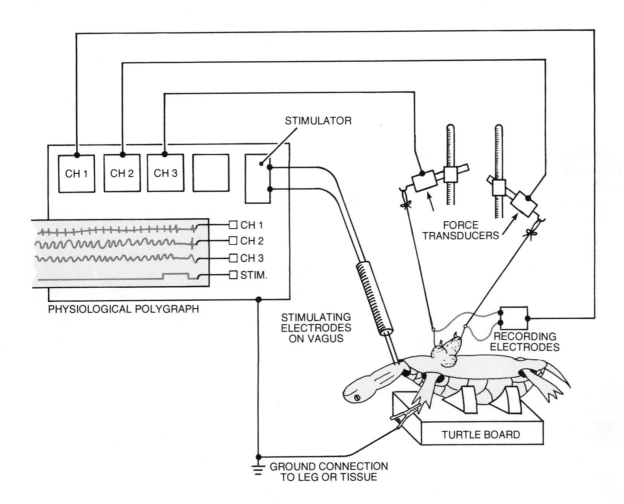

Fig. 5.3-2. Recording arrangement. Recording electrodes (*attached to colored wires*) consist of fine bent pins inserted through one of the atria and the ventricle. Strain gauges (force transducers) attached via threads to the bent pins record movements of the atria and ventricle. Stimulating electrodes on one of the vagus nerves may be used to test the effect of parasympathetic stimulation on the heart.

Carefully separate the vagi from the arteries and place a fine thread, previously soaked in perfusion fluid, underneath each nerve. *Do not ligate.* The threads will be used to elevate the nerves for stimulation. Keep this area constantly irrigated with perfusion fluid.

Recording Procedure

Arrange two strain gauges (one of medium and one of high sensitivity) on stands so that they may be positioned over the turtle. (The electrical resistance of a strain gauge changes when mechanically distorted.) Also arrange a set of stimulating electrodes on a flexible lead rod and stand so that they may be conveniently moved into position to stimulate the vagi (fig. 5.3-2). Do not attempt to position the stimulating electrodes yet. Connect the stimulating electrodes to the simulator output. Use appropriate cables and connectors to connect the strain gauges to the second and third channels of the polygraph, each of which contains a transducer amplifier (transducer coupler or carrier amplifier).

Connect a shielded input cable to the high gain amplifier of the first channel of the polygraph. (Alternately, depending on equipment at hand, the high gain amplifier may be separately positioned close to the preparation.) Connect the fine wire leads from the two recording electrodes (fine bent pins) to the input cable leading to the high gain amplifier (colored leads in fig. 5.3-2). Finally, connect a clip lead from the animal to a ground connection on either the polygraph (as shown in fig. 5.3-2) or the recording electrode cable. Ground the metal stands used to hold the transducers and stimulating electrodes if you encounter problems with 60 Hz interference. Use the following initial settings on your equipment.

High gain amplifier. Input in differential mode if possible; gain of 0.1 V/div; band-pass filters (if available) set at about 10 Hz (low frequency filter) and 3 kHz (high frequency filter).
Transducer amplifiers. Gain sufficient to cause a substantial movement of the writing pen when the transducer lever is moved slightly; band-pass filters set at about 1 Hz (low frequency filter) and 100 Hz (high frequency filter).
Stimulator. Frequency of 50/sec; duration of 1 msec; starting voltage of 0.1 V.

Tie a 30 cm length of fine thread to the head of each of the bent pin recording electrodes. Firmly tie another length of perfusion fluid-soaked thread to the frenulum at the apex of the ventricle. This thread may be used to move and hold the heart. Carefully insert one of the bent pin recording electrodes through the apex of the ventricle. Insert the other bent pin electrode through one of the atria.

Insert each pin so that it passes through muscle mass, not the lumen of the chamber. If the lumen is punctured, the heart will bleed profusely.

Tie the thread attached to the atrial electrode to the more sensitive transducer. Tie the ventricular thread to the less sensitive transducer. With the proper thread length and transducer height, the appropriate heart chamber should be only slightly elevated by tension on the thread (not as drastic as in fig. 5.3-2). Each heartbeat should move the lever on each strain gauge up and down slightly; neither lever should "bottom out" against its housing. Free movement is essential for recording the complete cardiac contraction. Once adjusted, do not disturb the spatial arrangement of the heart and transducers.

Adjust the gain, balance, and position knobs on the transducer amplifiers to begin recording the heartbeat. Adjust the sensitivity of the high gain amplifier and the position control until periodic deflections of the pen appear. Start and adjust the paper speed to a convenient, but not wasteful, rate.

Observation of the electrical and mechanical activity of the heart
First observe the two traces of mechanical activity in progress. One person should call out "A" (atria) and "V" (ventricle) while observing the heartbeat. The other person should watch the recording traces and mark them with a pencil at the points indicated by the heart observer. Stop the paper and confer on the correspondence between the recording traces and the cardiac contraction cycle. Now, restart the paper transport and observe the electrical activity. This time the polygraph operator should call out "spike" at the instant the largest deflection of the electrical trace occurs. The heart observer should note the beating heart and determine what part of

the cardiac cycle corresponds to the large spike. Stop the paper and confer, examining the simultaneous electrical and mechanical trace. What is the origin of the large spike? Repeat with the other, less prominent electrical events of the cardiac cycle.

Stimulating the vagus nerves

Position the stimulating electrodes to stimulate the *right* vagus. The electrodes should touch the nerve only. While recording, stimulate at low voltage (0.1 to 1 V) for 10 seconds. Gradually increase the voltage until an effect is achieved, or the voltage reaches a maximum of 10 volts. Can you achieve a total arrest of heartbeat by stimulating the right vagus? Stimulate continuously for 45 seconds just slightly above the lowest stimulus strength which caused complete arrest. Does the arrested heart "escape" from vagal inhibition during the application of the stimulus? What might be the explanation(s) for vagal escape?

Repeat the experiment on the *left* vagus after the electrical and mechanical activity of the heart have completely recovered. How do the results of right and left vagal stimulation compare? Can you detect changes in contractile force as well as heart rate? (A change in rate is termed a *chronotropic effect*, while a decrease in the force of contraction is called a *negative inotropic effect*.) Are the observed effects limited to the atria or ventricle? Remember that the vagi contain the parasympathetic fibers to the heart. Sympathetic stimulation intensifies heart contractions. Repeat your experiments enough times to be certain of the results.

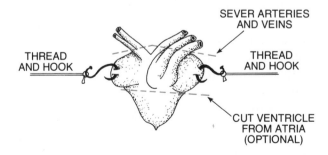

Fig. 5.3-3. Preparation of isolated atrial portion of turtle heart. One of the threads should be firmly anchored and the other attached to the force transducer. The heart will have to be immersed in perfusion fluid with the threads running vertically.

Other effects

Starling's law of the heart. Adjust the ventricular force transducer thread to exert minimum tension on the heart. Readjust the amplitude control to give a pen deflection of about 0.5 divisions with a ventricular contraction. With the paper transport engaged, increase the tension by small increments *between beats*. Look for momentary increases, then decreases, in the amplitude of contraction. You are stretching the heart muscle, and testing the physiological basis of Starling's law, in which muscle tension is proportional to the stretch produced by ventricular filling.

Refractory period. Bend the stimulating electrodes so that the tips are about 1 cm apart. Touch the tips of the electrodes to the ventricle without impeding the movement of the ventricle. Stimulate with single pulses of about 1 msec duration and 10 V amplitude. Stimulate at different times during the cardiac cycle using a high paper speed. Stop the paper transport after several stimulations. You should be able to elicit extra beats (termed *extra systoles*) at some points during diastole. Determine the earliest point when an extra beat can be stimulated. The time period between the electrical activity of the *QRS* wave and this point is the absolute refractory period of the ventricle. Are you familiar with the cellular basis of the long refractory period? What significance does the long refractory period have in heart function? Can the heart be tetanized like skeletal muscle?

Effects of acetylcholine and epinephrine on the isolated heart

(at the instructor's option)

Remove the heart from the turtle by cutting through the arteries at the anterior end and the *base* of the sinus venosus dorsally while lifting with the thread attached to the frenulum. Immediately immerse the excised heart in perfusion fluid. Remove the ventricle from the atria by cutting across the area between the atria and ventricle. Discard the ventricle. Take care not to damage the sinus area. Rinse the heart liberally with perfusion fluid and resubmerge in perfusion fluid. Insert bent pins with 30 cm threads attached through the lateral part of each atrium (fig. 5.3-3). Arrange the preparation for vertical recording (fig. 5.3-4). Use the more sensitive transducer, as the

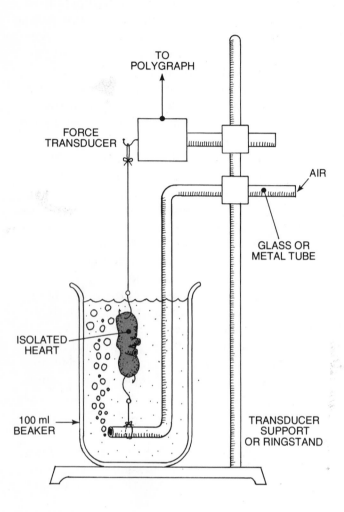

Fig. 5.3-4. Vertical recording arrangement. The isolated turtle heart is immersed in perfusion fluid which is aerated by the supporting tube.

atria are much weaker than the ventricle. Use a bit of Plasticine or Tackiwax to securely fix the attachment of the lower thread to the supporting tube. The arrangement must allow immersion of the whole preparation in a beaker of perfusion fluid. Increase the gain of the transducer amplifier and adjust the balance and position controls to get a recording of the periodic contractions of the atria. Recording and stimulating electrodes will not be used in this section.

You will be supplied with two concentrations of acetylcholine (ACh), the parasympathetic transmit-

ter, and two of epinephrine (adrenaline), the circulating hormone. The adrenal medulla releases epinephrine, whereas sympathetic postgangionic axons release the transmitter norepinephrine.

Begin recording and let the paper transport run throughout the experiment. Select a paper speed which allows you to count individual contractions and thus determine heart rate changes over the course of the experiment (e.g., 0.25 cm/sec). The strategy will be to bathe the heart preparation in perfusion fluid containing different concentrations of ACh and epinephrine. The temperature of all solutions must be the same. Note on the recording paper when treatments begin and end, the agent used, and its concentration. After establishing a basal level of activity, immerse the preparation in perfusion fluid containing 10^{-7} M epinephrine. Record until the response reaches a new basal level. Now, go back to standard perfusion fluid to test for reversibility. Try 10^{-5} M epinephrine and test for reversibility. Now, test 10^{-7} and 10^{-5} M ACh in that order. Do not omit testing for reversibility after each concentration.

Pitfalls and Suggestions

1. Attention to the geometrical relationship of turtle and recording apparatus is essential to produce meaningful and consistent results. The geometry must remain the same during each of a series of treatments for differences in the records to have meaning.
2. While you can treat heart rate and timing quantitatively, you cannot determine cardiac output with the methods described since stroke volume is not measured. Cardiac output = stroke volume × heart rate. However, the strength of ventricular contraction as indicated by the magnitude of the pen deflection is an *index* of stroke volume which may be treated semiquantitatively.
3. Use as slow a paper speed as feasible to record changes in heart rate and the overall amplitude of contraction. Conserve paper.

Materials

Materials needed at each station
Polygraph main frame
Stimulator

2 transducer amplifiers (transducer couplers or carrier amplifiers)

1 high gain amplifier (or preamplifier)

2 strain gauges (mechanical force transducers, one of high sensitivity and one of medium sensitivity)

2 stands, clamps, and connecting cables appropriate to strain gauges

1 pair recording electrodes (2 fine wires 10–15 cm long with fine pins soldered to one end and a pin plug to the other)

Input cable for high gain amplifier, capable of receiving pin plug connectors on recording electrodes

Stimulating electrodes and stand

Clip lead for use as ground electrode

Supporting tube for vertical recording (glass or metal, fig. 5.3-3)

Right-angle clamp

Turtle board

Dissecting set (furnished by students)

2 glass tools for dissecting vagi

Wash bottle for turtle perfusion fluid

5 100 ml beakers

Materials available in the laboratory

Extra polygraph paper

Pithing instrument (The dental tool called an *elevator* works very well; otherwise any strong steel probe will work, but *must* be provided with a secure handle such as that on a corkscrew. The standard wood-handle metal probe of dissection kits is too weak for the turtle.)

Alternate "pithing" instrument: sheep castrators

Hacksaw or bone saw

Bone clippers or large wire cutters

Large needle-nose pliers

Stout string

Fine cotton thread

Insect pins

Plasticene (modeling clay)

Solutions:

Turtle perfusion fluid (200 ml/station)

10^{-5}M Acetylcholine chloride in perfusion fluid (75–100 ml/station)

10^{-7}M Acetylcholine chloride in perfusion fluid (75–100 ml/station)

10^{-5}M Epinephrine (adrenaline, Adrenalin) in perfusion fluid (75–100 ml/station)

10^{-7}M Epinephrine (adrenaline, Adrenalin) in perfusion fluid (75–100 ml/station)

Animals

Turtles (*Chrysemys picta, Pseudemys* sp., or other species) (Order 1/station/laboratory period.) Keep the turtles in a cool place and provide them with dripping water.

Notes for the Instructor

1. Care in setting up and arranging the geometry of recording is essential to success. A simpler setup, using only one transducer attached to the ventricle, may be considered as an alternative.

2. The directions for stimulating the vagi are written for using standard hand electrodes attached to a flexible holder (e.g., Harvard no. 304 hand electrodes and no. 331 electrode holder). You may wish to consider cuff or sleeve electrodes as an alternative (e.g., Narco no. 710–0005). Sleeve electrodes may be slipped over each of the vagus nerves, eliminating the necessity of an extra stand and electrode holder. Sleeve electrodes must be attached carefully and students need to guard against accidently jerking on the electrode wires.

3. You may wish to have the students attempt infusing epinephrine *in vivo* rather than treating the isolated heart. In this case, it will be necessary to use a cannula inserted at the junction of the jugular veins forming the vena cavae. Use fresh 1:1,000 injectable epinephrine and do not redilute it. The problem with infusing as an experimental procedure here is that injection causes movement of the preparation and this is picked up by the force transducers.

4. The isolated heart preparation can be used as a takeoff point for testing the effects of other drugs, such as eserine (physostigmine), which potentiates the action of ACh; atropine, which blocks the action of ACh; and some of the other agents listed in exercise 5.2. Use of caffeine and other xanthine derivatives might be quite interesting to students who consume quantities of cola beverages and coffee (see L. S. Goodman and A. Gilman, eds., 1975. *The Pharmacological Basis of Therapeutics*. Macmillan, New York, pp. 367–78).

5. There is no discussion of calibration of the force transducers in this experiment, and you may wish to give oral instructions for calibration appropriate to your transducers. In general, calibration is simply a matter of adjusting the position and gain controls to give a known amount of pen deflection when a

known weight is hung on the transducer (e.g., 5 g/cm).

6. Some turtles will not extend their heads far enough out of the shell to be caught by a loop of string. If students encounter this problem, you should extract the turtle's head using a heavy pair of needle-nose pliers.

Selected References

Davson, H. 1970. *A textbook of general physiology*, vol. 2, 4th ed. J. A. Churchill, London.

Van Winkle, W. B., and Schwartz, A. 1976. Ions and inotropy. *Annu. Rev. Physiol.* 38: 247–72.

Weidmann, S. 1974. Heart: electrophysiology. *Annu. Rev. Physiol.* 36: 155–69.

RESEARCH REPORTS

Brady, A. J., and Woodbury, J. W. 1960. The sodium-potassium hypothesis as the basis of electrical action in frog ventricle. *J. Physiol.* 154: 385–407.

del Castillo, J., and Katz, B. 1955. Production of membrane potential changes in the frog's heart by inhibitory nerve impulses. *Nature* 175: 1035.

Draper, M. H., and Weidmann, S. 1951. Cardiac resting and action potentials recorded with an intracellular electrode. *J. Physiol.* 115: 74–94.

Keith, A., and Flack, M. 1907. The form and nature of the muscular connections between the primary divisions of the vertebrate heart. *J. Anat. Physiol.* 41: 172–89.

Hutter, O. F., and Trautwein, W. 1956. Vagal and sympathetic effects on the pacemaker fibres in sinus venosus of the heart. *J. Gen. Physiol.* 39: 715–33.

Loomis, A. L.; Harvey, E. N.; and MacRae, C. 1930. The intrinsic rhythm of the turtle's heart studied with a new type of chronograph, together with the effects of some drugs and hormones. *J. Gen. Physiol.* 14: 105–15.

Ringer, S. 1883. A further contribution regarding the influence of the different constituents of the blood on the contraction of the heart. *J. Physiol.* 4: 29–42. (Ionic solutions which keep a heart beating are now called Ringer's solutions.)

5.4 Smooth Muscle Regulation of Blood Flow
Microcirculation in Amphibians, Fish, and Insects

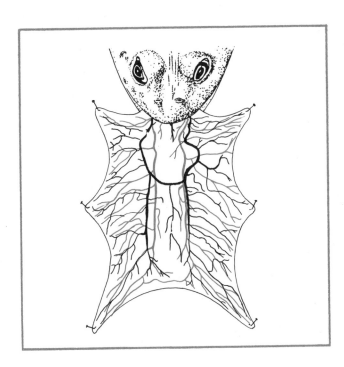

Artwork adapted from Krogh, 1929.

Introduction

Rationale

All animals, excluding the simplest invertebrates and parasites, have circulatory systems. The exact role of the circulatory system may vary considerably among.the phyla, but in most cases circulatory functions are absolutely essential to life. Smooth muscle, nerves, hormones, and local influences play a part in the control of circulation, particularly at the level of the arterioles, capillaries, and venules—the microcirculation.

The intense activity of mammalian circulation centers on gaseous and metabolic exchange between the tissues and the external environment. The human circulation is often cited for its remarkable collection of statistics: 10^9 white blood cells/body; 2.5×10^{13} red blood cells/body; 4×10^3 m² red blood cell membrane/body; 3×10^8 lung alveoli/body; 10^5 km of capillaries/body; and 15–20 metric tons of blood pumped each day. Capillary blood flow and its regulation are of particular importance because the capillaries are the site of gaseous and metabolic exchange between blood and tissues.

Capillary blood flow is regulated by adjusting the level of contraction in the smooth muscle surrounding small arteries, arterioles, venules, and the precapillary sphincters at the junctions between the terminal arterioles and capillaries. The mathematical relationship (Poiseuille's law) governing fluid flow through tubes is such that small changes in vessel radius have very large effects on blood flow. For example, doubling the radius of a vessel will multiply the rate of flow by a factor of 16. Alternately, a decrease in vessel radius by contraction of smooth muscle in the vessel walls greatly diminishes flow rate. Contraction of precapillary sphincters may block flow completely.

The arteries and larger arterioles are chiefly regulated by nerves, whereas the smaller, terminal arterioles respond to local influences (reduced oxygen, for example). Smooth muscle in veins and venules does little to control flow directly but aids the reservoir function of the venous side of the circulatory system. You will examine capillary blood flow in the frog tongue and hind foot web and experimentally alter the blood flow. Amphibian larvae, goldfish, or insects may be provided for comparative examination of the microcirculation. The control of smooth muscle is an important regulatory function of the central nervous system.

Time to complete the exercise: One 3-hour laboratory period.

155

Procedure

Observation of capillary blood flow

Obtain a 1.0 cc disposable hypodermic syringe and a 0.75-inch 23–25 gauge disposable needle. Fill it with 1.0 cc of 1.0% TMS (tricaine methanesulfonate).

Select a frog with minimal pigmentation on its feet, and weigh it. Anesthetize it by injecting 0.1 cc/10 g body weight into the dorsal lymph sac. Keep the frog in a covered dish until it no longer responds to firm, but not damaging, pinching of the *front* feet.

When the frog is fully anesthetized, place it (ventral side up) on a frog board which has been covered with fresh plastic wrapping film or aluminum foil. Use string to gently tie the frog down. Pin one of the hind feet to the board so that the web between two of the large toes is spread across the hole in the board. Spread the web gently; excessive stretch will hinder blood flow. Cover the frog with a paper towel moistened with tap water, and periodically moisten the stretched web during the exercise.

Examine the web at about 100× with a compound microscope. Look for blood corpuscles moving through the vessels. Frog red blood cells are elongated and have retained their nuclei, unlike disc-shaped mammalian red cells. Find an area with many vessels and clear microscope viewing. Can you differentiate arteries and veins? Hint: Look at flow through bifurcations of vessels.

Look for capillaries, the smallest vessels. How does the size of the red blood cells compare with the diameter of the capillaries? Note that the red blood cells pass through capillaries in single file. Can you find arterioles and venules?

Follow a single red blood cell in its journey from artery to vein. Use a stopwatch to measure the time a single cell spends in the capillary. Make 10 measurements of different cells in different capillaries and compute the average transit time. The average is approximately the amount of time a blood cell has for gaseous and metabolic exchange with the surrounding tissues.

Calibrate the ocular micrometer in your microscope using a stage micrometer supplied by the instructor. Check your calibration figures by viewing several red blood cells. Frog red cells are generally about 20 μm long with an oval cross section about 5 × 15 μm. When satisfied with your calibration,

measure the lengths of several capillaries and the average transit time for red cells in those capillaries. Are different times characteristic of different capillaries? Calculate the rate of movement of the cells through the capillaries. How does this compare with the rate of movement of individual red cells through arteries, arterioles, veins, and venules? Can you detect differences in the rate of movement of individual cells as they simultaneously pass through the same artery? This is the result of laminar flow of blood through the vessel.

Are any of the arteries or veins pulsating? Attempt to match any pulsations with the beating of the heart which can be seen through the skin on the ventral thorax. Do any of the capillaries pulsate? Finally, can you detect any fully closed capillaries or catch any in the act of closing? Do you really know how many capillaries there are in the field of view, or are some invisible?

Effect of nervous stimulation

Carefully cut through the skin around the circumference of the upper thigh. Pull the skin downward, everting it and exposing the underlying muscles of the thigh. Do not pull the skin past the knee. Locate the sciatic nerve without the use of cutting instruments. Carefully free the sciatic nerve from surrounding tissues using glass tools. When the nerve has been exposed enough for electrical stimulation, reposition the preparation under the microscope and find a suitable field in the foot webbing to examine.

Connect the leads of the stimulating electrodes to the output of the electronic stimulator. Set the stimulator to give pulses of about 0.1 V amplitude and 10 msec duration. Carefully lift the exposed portion of the sciatic nerve free of surrounding tissues, using the stimulating electrodes.

Stimulate continuously at a rate of about 1 pulse/sec, while observing the circulation. Very gradually increase the intensity to 1–2 V. This is an attempt to stimulate the vasodilator fibers in the nerve. They are best stimulated by weak, intermittent stimuli. Vasodilator fibers are far fewer in number than vasoconstrictor fibers; hence there may be some difficulty in seeing an effect. Increase the voltage (but not the rate) of stimulation as necessary to a maximum of 10 V.

Now, turn the stimulating voltage back to 0.1 V, and increase the stimulation rate to 100 pulses/sec.

Gradually increase the stimulating voltage until an effect is noted. Pick a single field to view and stay with it. Make detailed, before-and-after sketches of the field, counting the number of open capillaries rather than their percentage, as you cannot see closed capillaries. Stimulate for brief periods, and fully characterize the effects of electrical stimulation. How do you suppose different types of stimulation of the nerve elicit different responses?

Effects of noxious stimuli
Dip the tip of a dissecting needle into a solution of methyl salicylate (oil of wintergreen) and apply a very small amount to the frog web in the field of view. What is the effect and what is its time course? Does the effect involve different vessels than the effects of nerve stimulation?

Pick another unstimulated field and apply a very small amount of croton oil (a powerful irritant derived from plant seeds) to induce inflammation. Remove the oil after 3 minutes using the absorptive action of a piece of filter paper. Watch this area for about 30 minutes to note the developing inflammation. Note changes in vessel diameter, flow rate, and the movements of the larger white blood cells (leukocytes). Are these local or central nervous effects? What simple procedure would eliminate the possibility of nervous reflexes?

Observation of circulation in the tongue
Wash all chemicals off the frog's feet. Rewrap the frog board with fresh plastic film or aluminum foil. Rearrange the preparation so the tongue can be pinned out over the hole in the board as shown on page 155. Examine the circulation as in the first part of this experiment and compare it with the web circulation. Are the sizes of vessels and the rates of movement similar?

Apply the stimulating electrodes directly to the tongue, using a stimulating voltage of about 5 V and a rate of 50 pulses/sec. Adjust the voltage and frequency of stimulation as necessary to produce an effect. Allow sufficient time for a response to appear before increasing the voltage.

Effects of hormones, neurotransmitters, and drugs
Epinephrine. Apply a drop of 1:1,000 epinephrine solution (adrenaline) to the field under observation. Measure the changes as rapidly as possible and quickly wash the epinephrine away with amphibian perfusion solution. If the effect is too pronounced or too rapid for easy observation, dilute a portion of the epinephrine solution by a factor of 10 and repeat. You may also wish to repeat the experiment using norepinephrine rather than epinephrine. Epinephrine is the circulating hormone produced by the adrenal medulla, and norepinephrine is the postganglionic transmitter of the sympathetic nervous system which innervates the blood vessels.

Acetylcholine. Wash the tongue thoroughly with perfusion solution to remove all the epinephrine. Apply a drop of 10 mM acetylcholine chloride. Its effect may not be pronounced, so watch carefully. Wash the acetylcholine away after observing its effects.

Histamine. Apply a drop of 1 mM histamine. Record its effects. Histamine is released by disturbed or damaged cells and plays a role in inflammation. Kill the frog by double pithing at the end of the experiment.

Observation of circulation in goldfish tails and Xenopus tadpoles
(at the instructor's option)
You may repeat some of the observations made on the frog using a goldfish. Anesthetize the goldfish by immersion in a 1:2,000 solution of TMS. Observe the circulation in the tail fin for 10–12 minutes and return the fish to fresh water. Prolonged immersion in TMS will lead to death from respiratory failure.

The larvae of *Xenopus laevis*, the South African clawed frog, are particularly interesting. Because they are almost transparent, unlike most frog tadpoles, many of the blood vessels in the body can be seen. The nervous system is partially pigmented and is highly visible. The brain, the eyes, the olfactory placodes and nerves, etc., are all visible. Anesthetize *Xenopus* tadpoles by immersion in 1:2,000 TMS for no more than 15 minutes. When this time is up, remove the tadpole to fresh water where observations can continue for about 10 minutes before the tadpole begins to jump about.

Observation of circulation in the insect wing
(at the instructor's option)
Although insects have open circulatory systems,

they also have capillary beds in some tissues, such as the wings. In most insects, the blood serves as a transporter of nutrients, hormones, and metabolites, with the respiratory function relegated to the tracheal system. Insect blood cells (hemocytes) are concerned with protein synthesis, metabolite transport, blood clotting, and phagocytosis of disease organisms and cellular debris.

Fasten an adult cockroach (with wings) to a glass microslide using masking tape. The roach may be anesthetized with carbon dioxide to facilitate handling, but this is unnecessary. First, place a wide piece of masking tape across the antennae, head, and thorax. Then, place a thinner strip of tape along each side of the insect, firmly taping the legs to the slide. Finally, pass a thin strip of tape between the abdomen and the wings as far forward as possible, taping down the abdomen and elevating the wings slightly. The tape should be arranged so that light from the substage illuminator of the compound microscope can pass unimpeded upward through the edges of the wings.

Place the slide on the compound microscope and view the edges of the wings. Note the passage of blood cells through the "veins" of the wings. Examine the pattern of circulation and compare it with your diagrams of the vertebrate circulation. How do vessel size and rate of flow compare? In some species (*Blaberus discoidalis, Blaberus gigantea*) accessory hearts may be seen aiding circulation in the wings. Wings may also be taped or pinned in the extended (flying) position for viewing the whole pattern of circulation.

Pitfalls and Suggestions

1. Make sure you use a frog board freshly wrapped with plastic film or aluminum foil. Otherwise, the residue of methyl salicylate from previous experiments may ruin your efforts.
2. Do not overanesthetize the goldfish or tadpoles.
3. Constantly monitor your experimental subjects for revival, and reanesthetize if necessary with a reduced dose.

Materials

Materials needed at each station
Frog board (1 cm thick wooden pallet with 4.5 cm hole near one end)

Finger bowl and cover
Wash bottle filled with water and wash bottle filled with amphibian perfusion fluid
Compound microscope and a substage illuminator (or a dissecting microscope capable of 80× magnification)
Ocular micrometer in one eyepiece
Stopwatch
Electronic stimulator
Stimulating electrodes (e.g., Harvard no. 304)
Support for stimulating electrodes (e.g., ringstand, right-angle clamp, and flexible, lead rod holder like Harvard no. 331)
4 small beakers and medicine droppers or Pasteur pipettes
Glass tools for exposing nerve (2 glass rods or Pasteur pipettes pulled out to give a 1 mm fire-polished tip)
Dissecting equipment

Materials available in the laboratory
Stage micrometer (Etched stage micrometers are expensive and should be treated carefully. Inexpensive photographic replicas are available: e.g., Ann Arbor Biological Supply, no. 34999)
Plastic wrapping film (Saran Wrap) or aluminum foil
String
1.0-cc disposable hypodermic syringes and 23–25-gauge disposable needles
Extra medicine droppers or Pasteur pipettes and small beakers
Masking tape
Plain glass microslides
Filter paper
Solutions:
  TMS (tricaine methanesulfonate), 1% stock solution in amphibian perfusion fluid, for injection, 5 ml/station; or for use as an immersion anesthetic, dilute to 1:2,000 in tap water [1 ml of stock plus 19 ml water]
  Methyl salicylate (use straight from the bottle)
  Croton oil (use straight from the bottle)
  Epinephrine (adrenaline, 1:1,000 solution in water, 5 ml/station)
  Norepinephrine (noradrenaline, 1:1,000 solution, 5 ml/station)
  Acetylcholine chloride (10 mM, 5 ml/station)
  Histamine (1 mM, 5 ml/station)
  Amphibian perfusion fluid (200 ml/station)

Animals

Frogs, *Rana pipiens*, or other species (Order 1 frog/station.) Keep frogs in a cool place provided with dripping water.

Goldfish, *Carassius auratus* (optional; obtain from aquarium store; 1 goldfish/station) Keep in aerated and filtered water at room temperature.

Xenopus laevis, South African clawed frogs (optional) (Adults are obtainable from some suppliers [e.g., Mogul-Ed nos. L1275-L1277], but tadpoles are not generally available through the usual suppliers. Tadpoles or mating pairs and literature on their care and reproduction can be obtained from the Amphibian Facility, Division of Biological Sciences, Natural Science Building, University of Michigan, Ann Arbor, MI 48109. A mated pair can produce eggs every 60 days, and these raised to usable size in 4–6 weeks.) Adult *Xenopus* actively feed on chopped liver, whereas the larvae filter-feed on dry or canned pea soup. The major precaution in their care is to avoid all chlorine. They are exceptionally sensitive to chlorine and the larvae will die immediately in unaged tap water.

Cockroaches, *Periplaneta americana*, or any other winged species. (Order 1–2 cockroaches/station from Carolina Biological Supply.) Place the cockroaches in a plastic wastebasket or similar container with the upper walls smeared with petroleum jelly (Vaseline) to prevent escape. Provide them with some vertically standing pieces of cardboard to climb upon. A sponge wetted with water every few days will supply sufficient water. Feed them lab chow or dry dog food. This can be supplemented periodically with apples or other fresh fruit, although this is not necessary unless the roaches are to be kept a long time.

Notes for the Instructor

1. Anesthetizing the frog with TMS is preferable to pithing (which causes bleeding) or the use of urethane (a carcinogen). TMS solutions lose potency when left out for a few days. Injection of TMS, rather than immersion, is suggested because it is faster and acquaints the students with injection technique. Immersion in 1:2,000 TMS may be substituted for injection.

2. Using these simple preparations many other experiments are possible: effects of cold and heat, effects of topical anesthetics, effects of neurohumoral blocking agents, such as atropine and phenoxybenzamine. Lactic acid (0.5%) topically applied to the frog tongue will produce vasodilation. This has physiological interest as evidence for the effect of local metabolities.

3. The frog tongue has the most elaborate microcirculation, while *Xenopus* larvae are very good for viewing the total pattern of blood flow and the appearance of the developing nervous system.

4. Poiseuille's relationship:

Total flow (in ml/sec) =

$$F = (P_A = P_B) \cdot \left(\frac{\pi}{8}\right) \cdot \left(\frac{1}{\eta}\right) \cdot \left(\frac{R^4}{l}\right)$$

where $P_A - P_B$ is the pressure difference in dynes/cm², η the viscosity in poises, R the radius, and l the length in cm.

5. Another useful relationship for computing flow rate:

Total flow (in ml/sec) = $F = V \cdot A$

where V is the velocity in cm/sec, and
A is the cross-sectional area in cm².

6. Calibration of the ocular micrometer may need explanation.

Selected References

Charm, S. E., and Kurland, G. S. 1974. *Blood flow and microcirculation*. John Wiley, New York.

Krogh, A. 1929. *The anatomy and physiology of capillaries*, 2d ed. Yale University Press, New Haven. Reprinted 1959. Hafner Pub. Co., New York.

Maggio, E. 1965. *Microhemocirculation*. Charles C Thomas, Springfield, Ill.

Wigglesworth, V. B. 1972. *The principles of insect physiology*, 7th ed. Chapman and Hall, London.

Zweifach, B. W. 1973. Microcirculation. *Annu. Rev. Physiol.* 36: 93–123.

RESEARCH REPORTS

Altura, B. M. 1967. Evaluation of neurohumoral substances in local regulation of blood flow. *Am. J. Physiol.* 212: 1447–54.

Fulton, G. P.; Farber, E. M.; and Moreci, A. P. 1959. The mechanism of action of rubefacients. *J. Invest. Dermatol.* 33: 317–25.

Yeager, J. F., and Hendrickson, G. O. 1934. Circulation of blood in wings and wing-pads of the cockroach, *Periplaneta americana* Linn. *Ann. Ent. Soc. Am.* 27: 257–72.

5.5 Chromatophores
Neurohumoral Control in Arthropods

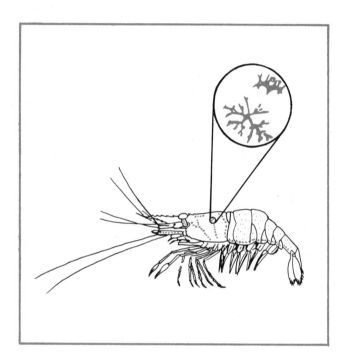

Introduction

Rationale

Chromatophores are cells which contain pigment granules whose dispersal and aggregation are under hormonal or nervous control. Chromatophores are of interest to the neurobiologist because (1) they are a special type of effector organ, and (2) they are utilized in protective roles in animal behavior. Color changes may be rapid (as in the octopus), circadian (as in the fiddler crab *Uca*), or they may take place over longer periods of time (e.g., seasonal).

Many crustaceans adapt their color and pattern of pigmentation to the background upon which they are resting. Protective coloration is of undoubted importance to these animals as a defense against predators. In species which darken on exposure to light, the chromatophores serve to shield tissues from the destructive effects of ultraviolet light. Changing to a lighter color serves to reflect thermal radiation. The ability of some animals to change color in a matter of seconds or minutes is often referred to as *physiological color change*, as distinguished from morphological color change which takes days or even months. Physiological color change is accomplished by pigment dispersion or contraction; morphological color change is accomplished by pigment synthesis or breakdown.

Chromatophores occur in several types and are usually classified according to the color of their pigment: melanophores (black), xanthophores (yellow), erythrophores (red), leukophores (white), and iridophores (iridescent or reflecting). More than one pigment may occur in a cell. If the pigment is concentrated in the center of the cell, the chromatophore appears as a small intense spot of color. Pigment dispersal reveals the full extent of the cell's branches and the maximal effect of the pigment on the overall color of the integument. Changes in dispersion of chromatophore pigments and different responses of different types of chromatophores account for the variations in color patterns that crustaceans can assume.

Time to complete the exercise: One or two laboratory periods.

Procedure

Structure and classification of chromatophores

Observe the fiddler crab, *Uca*, and/or the shrimp, *Palaemonetes*, under good illumination with the higher powers of a dissecting microscope. *Uca* may be held in the fingers, but *Palaemonetes* must be kept immersed in sea water most of the time and only briefly removed for observation. A piece of a

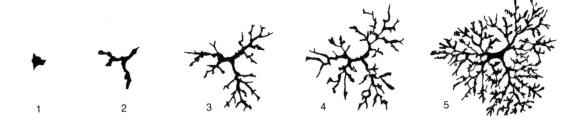

Fig. 5.5-1. Chromatophore stages. A single white reflecting chromatophore of *Palaemonetes* is shown in five different stages of pigment dispersal. (Adapted from Brown, 1935.) Healey (1954) developed the five-point classification in his studies of the minnow *Phoxinus phoxinus*: *1.* Punctate; *2.* Punctostellate; *3.* Stellate; *4.* Reticulostellate; *5.* Reticulate.

glass slide in a small petri dish may be used to keep *Palaemonetes* in the field of view under the microscope. Note the color, form, size, and distribution of chromatophores over the surface of the carapace and appendages. Notice the prominent chromatophores of *Palaemonetes* located on various internal organs. Classify the chromatophores according to color and size (fig. 5.5-1). You can observe that chromatophore shape appears variable because the limits of the cell processes are only visible if they contain pigment granules. The pigments move in and out of the cellular processes, giving the impression of contraction and expansion. Draw two or three examples of one type of chromatophore in various stages of pigment dispersal. How many stages of pigment dispersal can you distinguish?

Not all cuticular pigment is associated with the chromatophores. For example, in *Uca* some areas of the outer cuticle of the carapace may be darkly pigmented. If such is the case, and you cannot see individual chromatophore processes clearly, examine the basal segments of the legs. Be sure to observe that the various color types of chromatophores are located in specific patterns in the shrimp. Sketch these patterns for one individual. For before-and-after experiments, it is best to find an area where adjacent chromatophores are in the same state. If there is great variation, you may wish to locate a few chromatophores in the same state which you can reexamine after a treatment.

Effect of background on color change
Place three *Palaemonetes* in sea water in each of three finger bowls or large petri dishes. Surround the

sides and bottom of one container with *white* paper, and one with *black* paper. Evenly illuminate the white and black bowls from above. Place the remaining bowl in total *darkness*. Be sure to cover the bowls to prevent escape of the animals and to reduce evaporation. You may wish to mark the animals so that individuals are recognizable. Small pieces of thread can be tied to the appendages or tail.

CAUTION: Do not cook your experimental animals with the illuminating lamps. A 60-watt bulb should be at least 50 cm from the bowls.

Leave the animals in their respective environments for 2–3 hours. Then, to aid comparison of the effects of these environments on the overall body color (lightness), transfer an animal from each of the three different containers into a white container. Quantitative results can best be obtained by recording your results in tabular form. Record the condition of the majority of each type as *dispersed* (expanded), *intermediate* (stellate), or *concentrated* (punctate), or, if you wish, in accordance with the five stages illustrated in figure 5.5-1. Now transfer each of the remaining animals to the white container and score them too.

Shrimp are used in this part of the exercise because the macrurans (shrimp, lobsters, etc.) readily adapt to the color of the background. Crabs, like *Uca*, will show background responses, but not nearly as extensively. The principal chromatophore response of crabs is a diurnal variation. If macrurans are unavailable for this exercise, crabs may be observed in the daytime and at night, and the state of the chromatophores recorded as related to the light-dark cycle.

Effects of eyestalk removal

The *sinus gland* is a neurohemal organ located beside the optic ganglia in the eyestalk. It consists of a knot of swollen nerve terminals filled with neurosecretory products and it plays a major role in the control of chromatophores in decapod crustaceans. In transparent animals, such as the shrimp *Palaemonetes*, the sinus gland can be seen as a blue white mass under incident illumination.

The traditional first step in demonstrating the role of a hormone is to extirpate the tissue suspected of being the source of the hormone. Some experimenters, using careful surgical technique, have removed the sinus gland from the eyestalk. However, it is much easier, and entirely sufficient for this exercise, to remove the whole eyestalk.

Select eight new shrimp. Cut or pinch off the eyestalks at the base and save them. Place the extirpated eyestalks in a labeled container in the refrigerator to be used later as a source of the sinus gland hormone. Freeze them if they are to be used on a subsequent day. After the eyestalks have been removed, divide the eight animals equally between black and white containers as previously done with the normal, unoperated animals. Record the state of the chromatophores at the end of the laboratory period.

Cellular aspects of chromatophore control

Classically, the second step in demonstrating endocrine activity in a given organ is to observe the effect of replacing the suspected gland or an extract of it. Isolated tissue can also be used for *in vitro* assay of the action of hormones or chemical agents. This technique helps to rebut the criticism that responses observed after the injection of substances into an intact animal do not result from direct action of the hormone on the chromatophores. In crustaceans, isolated pieces of exoskeleton can be exposed to potential hormones or other agents and the effects observed. This technique will be used to examine the cellular mechanisms of chromatophore control.

Make a crude extract of 10–20 eyestalks from *Palaemonetes* or *Uca* or 6–8 eyestalks from large

crayfish. Grind eyestalks in a mortar and pestle or tissue homogenizer with 0.5 ml of sea water. You may use a pinch of clean sand in the test tube to facilitate grinding, but add sand only after the solution has been placed in the test tube. After thorough grinding, mark the initial volume on the tube, and heat the extract by immersing the test tube in a water bath at 90°–100° C for 5 minutes. This will denature the proteins, leaving the hormone. (It is assumed the hormone is nonprotein, water-soluble, and heat-stable.) Cool the mixture and replace any evaporated water. The soluble hormone may then be drawn off in the supernatant above the precipitated proteins.

Remove several pieces of the carapace from *Palaemonetes* and immerse in sea water. Under the microscope observe the chromatophores in the isolated pieces of exoskeleton periodically, and record the time course of pigment migration, by monitoring the changes in identified chromatophores.

You may now expose isolated pieces of cuticle from both normal and eyestalkless animals to different agents in order to determine their effect on the chromatophores. You might initially try the eyestalk extract. Is it reactive across species? In addition examine the effects of the following agents on *Palaemonetes* erythrophores in isolated pieces of carapace:

10 mM Acetylcholine chloride in sea water
10 mM Epinephrine in sea water
10 mM adenosine 3':5'-cyclic monophosphate (cyclic AMP) in sea water
10 mM Colchicine in sea water

It is best that you limit your investigation to one or two of these agents, rather than attempt to examine the effects of all. Arrange for appropriate controls. Some cellular effects of these agents are listed in the "Materials" section.

The most sensitive and accurate way to assay these chemicals is to place a dish with cuticle and standard volume of sea water under the microscope, observe it, add a known quantity of chemical to the dish with mixing, and note the change in the selected chromatophore(s). The idea here is to watch the changes, if any, in *specific* chromatophores. You may wish to run a series of replicates or repeat the experiment to determine the veracity of your results by demonstrating *repeatability*. Or, you may wish to repeat the experiment using different colored chromatophores, such as the leukophores. If you find a chemical which has dramatic effects, it would be appropriate to test various concentrations to produce a dose-response curve.

Pitfalls and Suggestions

1. Make a brief *outline* of your plans before proceeding with the experiment. Let your instructor know how many animals you will need.
2. Do not *cook* the experimental animals with the illuminating lamps. Eyestalkless animals may die in 1–2 days.
3. Be careful with the colchicine. It is a powerful poison. Also, cyclic AMP is expensive and should be conserved.
4. The trick in obtaining good results in the last section ("Cellular aspects of chromatophore control") is to watch changes in *specific* chromatophores. Certain chromatophores should be selected and observed *before*, *during*, and *after* chemical treatment. *Sketches* are invaluable aids to detecting changes in pigment dispersion. The changes may take several minutes.
5. Look for regions of the animal where the chromatophores are clearly visible and of similar, preferably intermediate (why?) dispersion.

Materials

Materials needed at each station
Dissecting microscope and good quality illuminator
Compound microscope and illuminator
2 desk lamps
Extra dissecting microscope illuminator (optional)
Mortar and pestle (A glass homogenizer-tissue grinder can be used, although it is expensive. It is also possible to use a test tube and thick glass rod as a grinder. One end of the glass rod should be formed into a sizeable ball in a hot flame. The use of a *very* small amount of washed and ignited sea sand facilitates the grinding action if the test tube is used. *Do not use sand in a regular tissue grinder.*)
Bunsen burner with stand or electric hotplate
Mercury thermometer
Serological pipette, 1 ml

2 250-ml beakers and 2 standard Pyrex or Kimax 15–125 mm test tubes
6 small petri dishes (for observation of isolated pieces of cuticle)
6 large petri dishes or finger bowls (for observation of whole animals)
6 covers for large petri dishes or finger bowls (to keep the animals from jumping or crawling out)

Materials available in the laboratory
Small dip net
Black and white poster paper (3 large sheets of each color/station)
Extra beakers, finger bowls, pipettes, and lamps
Sea water (a sufficient amount for the marine animals and for use as a bathing fluid for isolated pieces of cuticle from marine animals)
Solutions:
    Crayfish perfusion solution
    10 mM Acetylcholine chloride—a neuro- and neuromuscular transmitter
    10 mM Epinephrine (or norepinephrine)—a hormone (or a neuro- and neuromuscular transmitter)
    10 mM adenosine 3′:5′-cyclic monophosphate (cyclic AMP or cAMP)—this compound is the foremost "second messenger" so far discovered. Its intracellular concentration in target cells is often altered by the action of neurotransmitters or hormones on the cell membrane.
    10 mM Colchicine—Colchicine is known to disrupt the structure and function of cellular microtubules. Microtubules, in turn, are important cellular organelles which have been implicated in intracellular transport, e.g., in pigment migration.
It is a mistake to try more than two or three of these agents, as the number of observations needed and the controls required quickly mount up. It would be best to make up the solutions only after the students decide which they intend to use. The solutions should be made up in sea water or crayfish perfusion fluid, depending on which animals will be used in the experiments. It is *best to use marine species* rather than crayfish for chromatophore observation since they provide a wider selection of chromatophore types.

Animals

Shrimp (*Palaemonetes vulgaris*) (Order 16–20/station/laboratory period. *Palaemonetes vulgaris* is an Atlantic coast species; other species might be substituted, including freshwater shrimp.) The shrimp should be provided with filtered and well-aerated sea water kept at 15° C or lower, preferably with algae present. *Cover the container to keep the shrimp from jumping out.*

Fiddler Crab (*Uca pugilator*) (Order 2–3/station/laboratory period. *Uca pugilator* is an Atlantic coast species. Other species could be substituted.) Provide the fiddler crabs with a tilted container having a shallow area of sea water in which to wet their gill chambers. A dry beach area of aquarium gravel should be provided if the animals are to be kept for any length of time. Sod from a salt marsh makes a good burrowing material if the animals are to be kept several months. Both the crabs and the crayfish can be kept for periods up to a week at room temperature (20°–25° C), although it would be better to keep them cooler.

Crayfish (any species) (Order 1–2/station/laboratory period if they are to be used as the source of eyestalk extract. It is rather difficult to use them as experimental subjects because of some difficulty in seeing the chromatophores against the often dark background pigmentation.) Crayfish should be kept in fresh, well-aerated, and filtered water. Running water is best if it is available. Provide each crayfish with a hiding place in the aquarium. Clay pots of the sort used by gardeners and florists are ideal crayfish shelters. If the crayfish are to be kept for an extended period, feed them two or three times a month with cut up pieces of fish, clam, or frog. Do not overfeed. Southern crayfish seem to be more resistant to shipping death and last longer in the laboratory.

Notes for the Instructor

1. Require your students to outline their proposed experiments before they proceed. It is a good idea for each group to let you know how many animals they will need before proceeding.

2. Eyestalk removal may kill a substantial number of animals. Pooling results from several groups may be advisable. Eyestalkless fiddler crabs survive better than eyestalkless shrimp.

3. It may occur to some students that injections of eyestalk hormone into eyestalkless animals (replacement therapy) would be a valuable addition to their experiments. However, our students have had great difficulty doing this, and have killed most of the shrimp they injected. Injection, therefore, has not been suggested.

4. Observation of diurnal variations in *Uca* is possible, but has not been suggested to avoid the bother of nighttime sessions and the sometimes difficult task of following relatively small changes over a span of hours.

5. Good, short discussions of arthropod chromatophores are found in Fingerman (1969) and Wilson (1972).

Selected References

Bagnara, J. T., and Hadley, M. E. 1973. *Chromatophores and color change.* Prentice-Hall, Englewood Cliffs, N.J.

Fingerman, M. 1970. Comparative physiology: Chromatophores. *Annu. Rev. Physiol.* 32: 345–72.

Kleinholz, L. H. 1976. Crustacean neurosecretory hormones and physiological specificity. *Am. Zool.* 16: 151–66.

Parker, G. H. 1948. *Animal color changes and their neurohumors.* Cambridge University Press, Cambridge, pp. 1–22, 45–78.

Wilson, J. A. 1972. *Principles of animal physiology.* Macmillan, New York, pp. 727–40.

RESEARCH REPORTS

Brown, F. A. 1935. Color changes in *Palaemonetes*. *J. Morphol.* 57: 317–33.

Brown, F. A.; Fingerman, M.; Sandeen, M. I.; and Webb, H. M. 1954. Persistent diurnal and tidal rhythms of color change in the fiddler crab, *Uca pugnax. J. Exp. Zool.* 123: 29–60.

Ferlund, P. 1972. Crustacean color-change hormone: Amino acid sequence and chemical synthesis. *Science* 177: 173–75.

Fingerman, M. 1969. Cellular aspects of the control of physiological color changes in crustacea. *Am. Zool.* 9: 443–52.

Fujii, R., and Novales, R. R. 1969. Cellular aspects of physiological color changes in fishes. *Am. Zool.* 9: 453–63.

Healey, E. G. 1954. Color change control in *Phoxinus*. *J. Exp. Biol.* 31: 473–90.

Kleinholz, L. H. 1966. Separation and purification of eyestalk hormones. *Am. Zool.* 6: 161–67.

6

Receptor Processes

6.1 Visual Reception
Frog Electroretinogram (ERG)

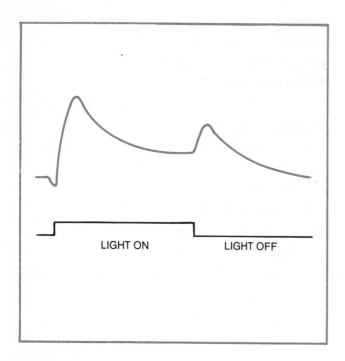

LIGHT ON   LIGHT OFF

Introduction

Rationale

Photoreception and vision are of great importance in the behavior of animals at all phylogenetic levels. Visual physiology is of particular interest to us because humans are visual animals. The eye is a complex sensory organ, but is nevertheless a good object for experimental studies because of its accessibility and because the appropriate stimulus—light—can be precisely controlled. This exercise examines a basic feature of sensory physiology, *adaptation*.

The retina of the eye, unlike most sensory organs, contains a very large number of nerve cells in addition to primary receptor cells. The axons in the optic nerve of vertebrates belong to nerve cells (called ganglion cells) that are at least third order, that is,

they are at least two synaptic connections away from the primary photoreceptors. In humans, there are about 10^6 axons of ganglion cells in each optic nerve, but about 10^8 rod cell photoreceptors and about 5×10^6 cone cell photoreceptors in the retina. Since input cells outnumber output cells, there is substantial convergence in many parts of the retina. Additional, more complex interconnections give the retina a capacity to process its own visual input extensively before the information is relayed to the brain. Consequently, when the eye responds to light, many nerve cells in the retina generate electrical potential changes. The interpretation of these electrical signals in the retina is an active area of current research.

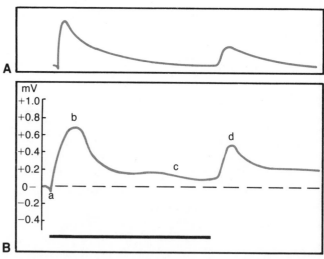

Fig. 6.1-1. Electroretinogram (ERG). **A**. Student-produced electroretinogram from a light-adapted frog eye exposed to a light beam for 2 seconds. **B**. Diagrammatic representation of the light-adapted frog ERG and its various component waves (*a, b, c, d*). The *c* wave has been accentuated for purposes of illustration; it is not normally this large. The duration of the stimulus (2 seconds) is indicated by the *black bar* in the lower part of the diagram. (Adapted from Granit and Riddell, 1934.)

166

The simplest approach to recording electrical activity of the retina is to place an "active" electrode on the cornea of the intact eye and an "indifferent" electrode on the facial skin (or any other convenient point on the body surface). When an isolated eye from a cold-blooded animal is used, the indifferent electrode is placed on the back of the eyeball. An electrical response called the *electroretinogram* (ERG) results when a flash of light is delivered to the eye (fig. 6.1-1). It is not surprising that the electroretinogram has complex origins, considering that there are at least five distinguishable types of nerve cells in the retina and at least two limiting membranes. Probably all of these and possibly some glial elements contribute to the ERG. Fortunately, it is not necessary to fully understand the origins of the ERG in order to use it as an indicator of selected visual processes. In this role the ERG has served neurophysiology well since its very early discovery by Holmgren (1865).

The ERG is a "slow" potential like the odor-initiated slow potentials of the vertebrate nose (the electro-olfactogram or EOG, experiment 6.3). The ERG consists of a predominant cornea-positive wave which has a peak amplitude of about 1 mV in the frog. This major positive wave (or *b* wave) is preceded by a quick negative deflection (the *a* wave), and is followed by a slower subtle secondary rise (the *c* wave). An off-response (or *d* wave) occurs at the end of illumination. The different waves are produced by several different types of retinal cells whose electrical activity overlaps in time. The *a* wave is generally attributed to an on-response of the receptor cells, the *b* wave to a response of the bipolar cell layer, the *c* wave to a change in the electrical state of the pigment epithelium, and the *d* wave to an off-response of the receptor cells. Separation of these various waves has been achieved experimentally using a variety of methods, including anesthesia, asphyxia, adaptation to light, and surgical and chemical means. Consult figure 6.1-1 for an illustration of the frog ERG. ERG's from other animals have different forms, depending on the types of receptors and other nerve cells present and the general arrangement of the eye. For example, the ERG of the all-cone retina of the horned toad differs considerably from the predominantly rod retina of the guinea pig. Invertebrate eyes often produce an ERG which appears inverted in comparison with the ver-

tebrate ERG. Part of the explanation for this is that the receptors of vertebrate eyes *hyper*polarize when stimulated, while those of invertebrates often *de*polarize. The frog retina, examined in this exercise, has about equal numbers of rods and cones.

The different waves of ERG stem from ongoing retinal processes that *overlap* in time. The ERG is thus a composite of several nearly simultaneous electrical changes in a retina responding to light.

The fact that the ERG waves are so large indicates that similar changes are taking place in many cells simultaneously. In the early 1930s Ragnar Granit found that small doses of ether abolished the *c* wave, while increasingly larger doses abolished first the *b* wave, then the *a* wave. This suggested that the anesthetic progressively abolished the responses of different cell types.

To the early experimenters, it seemed reasonable to attribute the different waves to different retinal cell layers. Granit developed evidence that the *b* wave is attributable to either the bipolar or ganglion cell layers. He tied off the retinal artery (which feeds the bipolar and ganglion cell layers) and found that the *b* wave gradually disappeared. The *a* wave remained strong, presumably because it originated in the receptor cell layer which is fed by the choroid artery.

When Granit disrupted the electrical activity of the ganglion cells with antidromic effects produced by stimulating the optic nerve, the *b* wave was not affected—thus suggesting that the *b* wave originates in the bipolar cell layer.

About twenty years later, W. K. Noell found that the *c* wave disappeared if the pigment layer of the retina was dissected away. Thus the pigment epithelium is probably the origin of the *c* wave. Most recently, it has been discovered that sodium aspartate prevents synaptic transmission between the receptor cells and the bipolar cell layer. When the ERG is recorded after the injection of aspartate, the *a* and *d* waves are unaffected, but the other waves are abolished. Thus, it is now possible to use the ERG to record relatively pure receptor potentials from the vertebrate eye.

Time to complete the exercise: One 3-hour laboratory period is needed to demonstrate the qualitative features of the frog ERG and to do a semiquantitative study of adaptation. A second session could be used to refine the techniques used and to produce a more quantitative study.

Procedure

Description of apparatus

Electrodes.   The electrodes used in this exercise are cotton wick electrodes. Wicks are used for their simplicity, resistance to breakage, and ability to compensate for slight movements of the subject. Consult the "Materials" section for information on constructing suitable wick electrodes.

Stimulator.   A tungsten filament (in the form of a dissecting microscope illuminator) will be used as the light source. The tungsten lamp is powered by 60 Hz line current, and, therefore, it should be kept out of the vicinity of the recording area. If a Faraday cage is used, the lamp should be placed outside the cage and, if necessary, a small hole should be cut in the side of the cage to admit the light beam. Since tungsten lamps require a considerable period of time to begin emitting light after the current is switched

on (and also remain glowing for some time after the current is switched off), a *shutter* rather than a switch will be used to control stimulus duration. Use of the power switch would also be disadvantageous because both the intensity and color change while the filament warms up and cools down. Note the complex spectral output of a tungsten filament (fig. 6.1-2B). Most of the energy of a tungsten (white) light source is actually in the longer wavelengths toward the red end of the visual spectrum.

Light Detector.   A simple photocell can be supplied for use as a light detector. The photocell should be positioned near the eye, so that it and the eye will be illuminated by the light beam. The leads from the photocell should be connected to the second vertical amplifier on your dual-trace oscilloscope or to a second channel if you are using a polygraph. The photocell output will give you a stimulus marker trace indicating the onset and cessation of light stimuli and variations in light intensity. Figure 6.1-2 indicates that the photocell is useful for measuring intensity, but not readily used in measuring the relative energy of different colored lights.

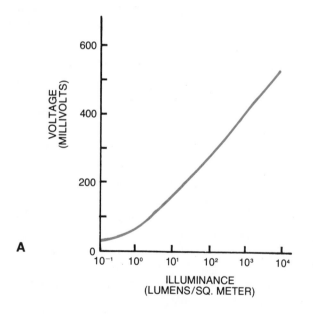

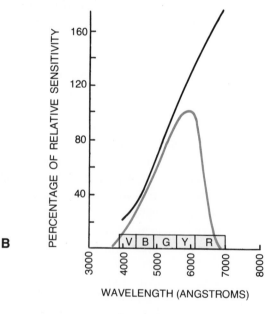

Fig. 6.1-2. Characteristics of a selenium photocell (Edmund Scientific Photocell no. 30,411). **A**. Output voltage increases nearly linearly with the intensity of illumination. **B**. The sensitivity of the photocell varies with the wavelength of the illuminating light (Edmund Scientific Co., Barrington, New Jersey). The *black curve* shows the spectral output of a tungsten filament at a temperature of 3000° K. Red (> 600 nm) wavelengths predominate. In student laboratories the filaments would be operated at a cooler temperature which would make the light even redder. The *colored bar* shows the visible wavelengths of light for the human eye (V, violet; B, blue; G, green; Y, yellow; R, red).

Controlling stimulus intensity

Neutral density filters will be available for varying the intensity of the light (fig. 6.1-3). Neutral density filters consist of suspensions of silver or carbon particles embedded in gelatin sheets or sandwiched between glass plates. The particles absorb all wavelengths about equally, hence the term *neutral*. The term *density* in this context refers to *optical density* (D) which is defined as follows. When *incident light* of intensity (I_i) passes through a filter of optical density (D), the *transmitted light* of intensity (I_t) is given by the relation:

$$I_t = (I_i)(10^{-D}) \quad Or \quad D = \log \frac{I_i}{I_t}$$

Thus, a two unit neutral density filter allows only 10^{-2} or 0.01 of the incident light to pass and absorbs 0.99 of the incident light. Neutral density filters with optical densities of 3.0, 2.0, 1.0, 0.6, and 0.3 will be supplied. In terms of *transparency*, where transparency = I_t/I_i, these filters, respectively, transmit 0.001, 0.01, 0.1, 0.25, and 0.50 of the incident light. It is useful to make up a table listing the filters available and their optical density and transparency. Such a table will help avoid confusion for those who are not used to thinking in terms of logarithmic units. In practice, filters of different optical density can also be stacked to produce light beams of intermediate intensity. For example, stacking two filters with densities of 1.0 and 0.3 would produce a combined filter with an optical density of 1.3 and a transparency of 0.05. Remember that the optical densities of stacked filters are *added* to determine the overall filtering power, but if the filtering power is figured in terms of transparency, the transparencies of stacked filters must be *multiplied* to determine the overall transparency.

Recording Procedure

Anesthesia

The frog may be immobilized either by double pithing or by injecting 0.04 cc/10 gm body weight of *d*-tubocurarine chloride (3 mg/cc) into the dorsal lymph sac. The curare will take 10–20 minutes to become fully effective. A second injection may be needed during a prolonged experiment. When the frog is paralyzed, place it on a frog board and cover it with a wet towel. Keep the frog moist during the

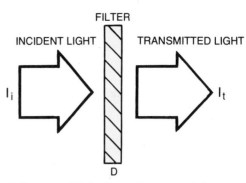

Fig. 6.1-3. Passage of light through a neutral density filter.

course of the experiment to aid cutaneous respiration. Since the frog is paralyzed, it will not be able to breathe via the lungs. Stuff enough cotton into the mouth of the frog to make the eyes protrude for ease in stimulation. Watch the animal closely for movements or other signs of revival during the experiment.

Recording arrangement

Position the frog so that the filament image from the illuminator is brought into focus near the pupil. Put a translucent piece of opal glass, white plastic, or other translucent material just in front of the pupil, so as to diffuse the light source. The diffuser should not be so close that it interferes with the recording electrode.

Prepare the active and indifferent recording electrodes according to the instructor's directions or the information in the "Materials" section. The wicks should be about 1 mm long. Wick electrodes which are too long will dry rapidly and may introduce 60 Hz interference in your recording as their resistance increases with drying.

Before positioning the active recording electrode, make a small slit in the skin about 1 cm behind the eye. Position the wick of the indifferent electrode in this slit. Place the active wick electrode on the cornea, above the pupil.

If a dual-trace oscilloscope is available, you can use a photocell to provide a stimulus marker trace. Position the small photocell so that it will be illuminated when the eye is illuminated. Connect the leads from the photocell to the input of the second channel of the dual-trace oscilloscope. Adjust the gain control on the second channel so that a substantial deflection occurs when the illuminator is actuated.

Connect the electrodes to the input of your DC preamplifier or directly into the oscilloscope input. Either method is sufficient to record the frog ERG. Use the differential mode of amplification if available. If you record using differential input, ground the body of the frog to a ground connector on the preamplifier with a clip lead attached to one of the front limbs. The ground connection will minimize 60 Hz interference. Connect the output of the preamplifier to the input of the oscilloscope. Use the following initial settings on your equipment.

Preamplifier.   Input in differential mode if possible; gain of 100–1,000×; band-pass filters (if available) set on DC (low frequency filter) and about 1 kHz (high frequency filter). If you have a DC amplifier with a DC offset position on the low frequency filter, it should be used. The DC offset control should be varied to buck out any standing voltages produced by your electrodes or the preparation. It will be necessary to readjust the DC offset periodically during the course of the experiment. If no DC preamplifier is available, connect directly to the oscilloscope vertical amplifier.

Oscilloscope.   Sweep speed at 1 div/sec; sensitivity at 0.1–0.01 V/div; high frequency filter (if available) at about 1 kHz; input in DC mode; trigger control on automatic or free run.

Calibration.   Adjust the preamplifier and oscilloscope vertical gain to give a total system gain of approximately 0.5 mV/div. Check with the preamplifier calibrator if available.

Arrange the illuminator and filter holder so that the intensity of the light can be varied by inserting neutral density filters in the light beam. A piece of cardboard can be used as a hand-held shutter between the light source and the preparation. The room should be darkened, and a dark box placed over the recording area or a black cloth cover over the Faraday cage.

Experiments

Qualitative characterization of the ERG
Actuate your recording equipment and attempt to produce a consistent ERG by modulating the illumination with the hand-held shutter. Consider the following questions.

1. What is the waveform of the ERG? How many separate peaks or troughs can you discern? What are their amplitudes, latencies, time courses, and signs (+ or −)? Draw or photograph the ERG.
2. Does the ERG depend on either stimulus intensity or duration? Insert neutral density filters to change the intensity.
3. Can you obtain a reproducible ERG with repeated stimulation at the same stimulus intensity and duration? What does the interstimulus interval need to be?

The suggestions that follow are for appropriate experiments. You are asked to complete the design of the experiments.

Quantitative relationship between amplitude and intensity
In the presence of moderate background illumination, attempt to measure the relationship between b-wave amplitude and stimulus intensity. Use the neutral density filters to vary the light intensity. Present stimuli of different intensities (1) in order of increasing intensity, and (2) as a control in order of decreasing intensity. Be sure to hold the duration of stimuli constant during the course of this experiment. If the results vary depending on the order of presentation of stimuli, what does it mean?

Check to make sure that any changes observed were not due to changes in electrode position or drying of the wick electrode. You may need to moisten the wick with perfusion solution before proceeding to the next experiment.

Adaptation
The eye is exposed daily to enormous variations in light intensity. On a bright sunny day the light flux into the eyes may be 100,000,000 times greater than it would be at night under illumination by starlight. Yet, the eye continues to detect visual contrasts and discriminate forms efficiently. This is accomplished in part through *adaptation*. Placed in dim light, the retina continuously becomes more sensitive over a period of minutes to hours (dark adaptation). Researchers often quantitatively characterize adaptation by measuring how intense a stimulus needs to be to evoke a response of an arbitrary *fixed* magnitude—the *criterion response*. If the sensitivity is increasing, it is obvious that a weaker stimulus can elicit the same criterion response. To track

170

changes in visual sensitivity in this accurate way requires that your equipment smoothly adjust the stimulus intensity to any desired value. Since this cannot be done with a few neutral density filters, we will simply measure the change in response magnitude with a fixed stimulus. It will be useful to you to know that rods and cones adapt at different rates: cones adapt in seconds and rods in minutes.

Fully light adapt the eye by training a second illuminator on the eye with near-maximum illumination for 5 minutes. Select the stimulating illumination which will give a small but measurable *b* wave in the presence of adapting illumination from the second illuminator. Show that this response is repeatable and does not change over a period of minutes under constant adapting illumination.

The time course of adaptation can be measured in the following way.

Darken the animal's chamber as completely as possible and immediately begin to track its dark adaptation by monitoring the change in *b*-wave amplitude over time with intermittent stimuli. Use short stimuli since longer stimuli may influence the time course of adaptation. Begin stimulating about 10 seconds after the adapting illuminator is turned off. Deliver stimuli at the following times after the adapting light is turned off: 10 sec, 20 sec, 50 sec, 100 sec, and thereafter at increasing intervals at 2, 4, 8, 16, 24, 36, and 48 minutes. During the latter stages of the experiment the noise level may in-

crease as the wick electrode dries out. If necessary, remoisten the wick. Be careful not to admit any light into the recording chamber. Use the DC balance function on the preamplifier or oscilloscope if it becomes necessary to reposition a drifting baseline. If the baseline is somewhat unstable toward the latter part of the experiment, try to choose a quiet period for stimulating. The first few time points are interesting; restart the experiment if you fail to get those measurements.

Effects of stimulus duration

If you progressively lengthen the stimulus duration (up to 10 seconds or more), the *d* wave may change in amplitude. Choose a suitable intensity and examine this effect.

Pitfalls and Suggestions

1. This exercise is ideally suited to a fully quantitative study. Take advantage of it.
2. DC drift is the problem most frequently encountered in this experiment. Use the position and DC balance controls on the oscilloscope to regain the trace. It may, nevertheless, be necessary to use the AC input. The kind of distortion in the slower components of the ERG obtained with AC recording is illustrated in figure 6.1-4. The practical result is a reduction in both the *b* and *d* waves.
3. When the paralytic effects of curare begin to subside, potentials from respiratory movements may cause repetitive deflections in the recording trace.
4. The frog has a photo-activated eye. That is, the control of pupillary size is intrinsic to the iris and does not involve a reflex mediated through connections to the brain as in the human eye. If the eyes of your frog have highly constricted pupils, you may have to obtain another frog. You may want to measure pupil diameter at several points during the experiment.
5. Keep your wick electrodes short and moist with amphibian perfusion fluid. If you lose the ERG trace or your recording becomes erratic, check to see that the perfusion solution in each electrode is in contact with the chlorided silver wire. A prior check of the fluid level in the capillary will prevent this problem.
6. *Do not attempt to study color vision in this exercise*, although this may seem an interesting area to investigate. It is a technically and conceptually

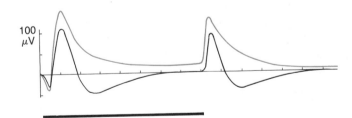

Fig. 6.1-4. AC versus DC amplification. The *colored curve* represents an idealized DC recording of a frog ERG. The *black curve* represents the result of recording the same ERG using an AC amplifier with a time constant of 1.0 second. No *c* wave is shown in either recording. The 2-second light stimulus is indicated by the *black bar*. AC amplification distorts the true DC waveform. (Adapted from Peckham and Hart, 1961.)

complex undertaking to study color vision using the ERG. However, you might think of other interesting questions to ask about the ERG. For example, what might you learn from stimulating with a flash of darkness, rather than a flash of light?

Materials

Materials needed at each station

Oscilloscope (dual trace if available, storage type if available) (A polygraph can also be used for this study.)

Preamplifier and its power supply (DC preamplification is preferred since there is a strong DC component to the ERG. See figure 6.1-4.)

Faraday cage (If available, a Faraday cage is very useful as a dark box frame.)

Electrical leads and connectors (1 set)

Dark box or black cloth cover for Faraday cage (see page 340). It is advisable to turn off the room lights, pull the window shades down, and use individual desk lamps at each station (25-watt dark red bulb).

Micromanipulator and stand

Wick-type recording electrodes. (Wick-type recording electrodes can be constructed in a variety of ways. The simplest method is to partially stuff one half of a standard capillary tube [0.9–1.1 mm I.D. × 100 mm, broken in half after nicking the center with a diamond or carbide-tipped pencil] with cotton. The cotton is left protruding at one end, and the capillary filled with amphibian perfusion fluid by capillary action. Place the opposite end [nonwick end] of the capillary tube in perfusion fluid for filling, and hold the capillary nearly horizontal while it fills. Be sure the cotton is fully saturated. Slip the butt end of the capillary over a chlorided silver wire held in a suitable holder [fig. 10.3-2]. It may be necessary to bend the wire in several places to prevent the capillary from slipping off. Silver wires for the wick electrodes may be freshly chlorided as indicated on page 334. After slipping the capillary over the chlorided silver wire, cut the wick short, so that it extends no more than 0.4 cm beyond the tip of the capillary. A long wick may dry out rapidly and pick up 60 Hz interference.

Alternate method of construction. Another method is to fill the capillaries with a 2% solution of agar in amphibian perfusion fluid. Heat 100 ml of perfusion fluid and add 2 g agar flakes or granules. Fill the capillaries with hot agar solution and allow them to cool on a horizontal surface. As before, cotton should be stuffed into one end prior to filling. The agar-filled capillaries are more resistant to drying, but they should be kept immersed in perfusion solution until used.)

Ground electrode (A clip lead will suffice.)

Photoelectric cell (An inexpensive selenium or silicon "solar cell" may be used. Solar cells can be obtained from a variety of suppliers, such as Radio Shack [Allied Radio], Lafayette Radio, or Edmund Scientific Co. Try to obtain the specifications of the cells you purchase: response decay time, spectral sensitivity, etc.)

Clamp for solar cell (The cell can be taped or glued to a small piece of wood and the wood support clamped in a standard femur clamp or other clamp.)

2–4 ringstands and 2–4 right-angle clamps

Set of neutral density filters (3.0, 2.0, 1.0, 0.6, and 0.3; obtainable from Ealing Scientific, 2225 Massachusetts Ave., Cambridge, MA 02140, and other suppliers.)

2 illuminators (Dissecting microscope illuminators which produce a focused beam of light are best.)

Light diffuser (A piece of translucent opal glass or white plastic taped to a small ringstand will work well. If this is not readily available, use a piece of thin, white paper.)

Shutter (A piece of stiff cardboard, about 6 × 12 inches in size will do nicely. Label it "ERG Shutter" so that no one will discard it.)

Materials available in the laboratory

Oscilloscope camera and film

Syringe (1 cc tuberculin with 25–27 gauge needle)

Pithing needles (Double pithing may be used as an alternative to the use of curare.)

Capillary tubes (standard size, 0.9–1.1 mm I.D. × 100 mm)

Diamond or carbide-tipped pencil (for breaking capillary tubes cleanly)

Extra silver wire (0.8–0.9 mm [20 gauge] diameter is best)

Extra illuminator bulbs

1.5 V battery or power supply for chloriding electrodes (An electronic stimulator should not be used, since you run the risk of damage through short-circuiting the output.)

Extra illuminators (for use as a source of adapting illumination)

Desk lamps with 25-watt dark red bulb (for use at individual stations when the room is darkened)

Plastic bag (for animal disposal)

Masking tape (for various fix-it jobs)

Cotton

Solutions:

Amphibian perfusion solution (50 ml/station)

Curare solution (*d*-tubocurarine chloride, 3 mg/cc, 1 cc/station). If respiratory movements occur during the course of the experiment, give an additional dose.

Animals

Frogs, *Rana pipiens* or other species (Order 1/station/ laboratory period; have 1–2 extras available in the laboratory.) Frogs should be kept in a cool place and supplied with dripping water. If so kept after an experiment, the majority will recover from the curare.

Notes for the Instructor

1. The experiment is more efficiently conducted and more rewarding when students read the instructions beforehand.

2. A single-trace oscilloscope can be used in this exercise, but then there is no stimulus marker trace to indicate intensity, latency, etc. If a polygraph is available, it may be used to produce a continuous record of the experiments. If no DC amplifier is available, it is preferable to plug the recording electrodes directly into the input of a DC oscilloscope having a gain of at least 200 μV/div.

3. The coarse DC balance may need to be adjusted to buck out the standing DC potential between the electrodes. Drift is an additional difficulty which is best eliminated by proper chloriding. Repositioning the electrodes may help.

4. Make arrangements beforehand to darken the room as much as possible. If black cloth is purchased, make sure it is really effective in blocking the light.

5. Drying and loss of perfusion solution from the wick electrode will generally be signaled by an in-

crease in the noise level, a jittery baseline, and a loss of responses to stimuli.

6. High quality optical components are available from:

a. The Ealing Corp., 2225 Massachusetts Ave., Cambridge, MA 02140. Telephone: (617) 491-5870.

b. Oriel Optics Corp., 1 Market Street, Stamford, CT 06902. Telephone: (203) 348-4247.

Selected References

The reviews cited below will give more than adequate summaries of ERG work on the frog and extensive bibliographies of the original research reports. Much of this work concerns the origins of the ERG and its variations among different animals, which is not as germane to the object of this exercise. The ERG is meant to be used as a tool in the study of adaptation in this exercise.

Brindley, G. S. 1970. *Physiology of the retina and visual pathway*. Williams and Wilkins, New York.

Brown, K. T. 1968. The electroretinogram: Its components and their origins. *Vision Res.* 8: 633–77.

Granit, R. 1947. *Sensory mechanisms of the retina*. Oxford University Press. Reprinted in 1963 by Hafner, New York.

Koopowitz, H. 1974. The electroretinogram. In *Methods in physiological psychology, vol. 1-C. Bioelectric recording techniques*, ed. R. F. Thompson and M. M. Patterson. Academic Press, New York, pp. 63–86.

Rodieck, R. W. 1973. *The vertebrate retina: Principles of structure and function*. W. H. Freeman and Co., San Francisco.

Walls, G. L. 1942. *The vertebrate eye and its adaptive radiation*. Cranbrook Inst. of Science, Bloomfield Hills. Reprinted in 1963 by Hafner, New York.

RESEARCH REPORTS

Granit, R., and Riddell, L. A. 1934. The electrical responses of light- and dark-adapted frogs' eyes to rhythmic and continuous stimuli. *J. Physiol.* 81: 1–28.

Granit, R., and Wrede, C. M. 1937. The electrical responses of light-adapted frogs' eyes to monochromatic stimuli. *J. Physiol.* 89: 239–56.

Holmgren, F. 1865–66. Method att objectivera effecten av ljusintryck på retina. *Upsala Läkaref, Förh.* 1: 177–91.

Peckham, R. H., and Hart, W. M. 1961. The geometrical analysis of the photopic corneal ERG. I. On-and-off responses. *Exp. Eye Res.* 1: 5–13.

6.2　Mechanoreception
Tactile Receptors on the Insect Leg

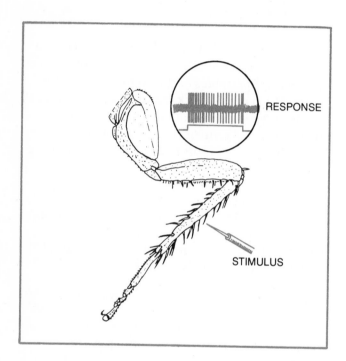

RESPONSE

STIMULUS

Introduction

Rationale

Detection of touch, substrate vibration, and airborne sound are all examples of *mechanoreception* of external stimuli. Sensory detection of changes in muscle length or tension and joint position is a class of internal mechanoreception which has been termed *proprioception*. The ability to detect external mechanical stimuli is of obvious value to the animal, but proprioception can be considered to be equally important because it is vital to central nervous control of postural adjustments and movements. One of the simplest biological preparations for the study of both touch and joint receptors is the insect leg. In arthropods, sensing of stress in the exoskeleton is another form of proprioception.

Insects are covered with cuticular sense organs called *sensilla*. Tactile sensilla in the form of hairs or bristles (sensilla chaetica) are found on all parts of the body. Clusters of fine hairs called *hair plates* occur at many articulations of the exoskeleton, such as the joints of the legs (fig. 6.2-1 *A*). When the joint is flexed the hairs are moved by contact with the adjacent surface of the attached member. The hair plates thus act as joint receptors and fit the functional definition of proprioceptors. *Proprio-* means *own*, that is, receptors stimulated by the animal's own movement.

Another type of proprioceptive cuticular sensilla is the *campaniform sensillum* (figs. 6.2-1*B* and 6.2-2). Campaniform sensilla are dome-shaped sensory organs which usually occur near joints. They are sensitive to distortion or stress of the exoskeleton, such as occurs during joint movements. Each tactile hair and campaniform sensillum has a single mechanoreceptor cell associated with it (fig. 6.2-1*B*). Tactile mechanoreceptors located on the general body surface produce phasic responses (fig. 6.2-3), while the hair plate sensilla and campaniform organs tend to be phasic-tonic. It should be noted that *within* the insect body there are proprioceptive sense organs, referred to as *chordotonal organs*, which span the joints of the insect body.

Many other types of cuticular sensilla occur on the insect body, but they are primarily chemoreceptive and will not be examined in this experiment. These include *thick-walled chemoreceptors* (or taste hairs) of the palps, antennae, and other body parts (experiment 8.4) and the *thin-walled olfactory sensilla* of the antennae (experiment 8.6).

The cockroach leg is a complex sensory-motor structure. The tibia (fig. 6.2-4*A*) is equipped with a large number of spines. The spines are not sensilla themselves, but they have campaniform sensilla at their bases. The spines act as touch receptors since the campaniform sensilla are deformed when the spine is moved (Chapman, 1965). The leg has numerous innervated hairs (setae) and a few clusters of tiny hairs called hair plates, two on the coxa and one on the trochanter (fig. 6.2-4*B*). Some groups of campaniform sensilla are associated with the joints of the leg rather than with the spines (fig. 6.2-4*B*). There are also chordotonal organs at each joint of the leg and other multiterminal sensory organs throughout the leg, although they are not visible on the external surface of the cuticle.

Time to complete the exercise: One 3-hour laboratory period.

Procedure

Examination of the cockroach leg

Remove one of the legs of an active, undamaged cockroach by cutting through the coxa with a pair of scissors. Replace the insect in its container.

Briefly examine the isolated cockroach leg under a dissecting microscope with good illumination. The major parts of the leg should be named and a brief search made for some of the sensory structures (fig. 6.2-4). The tactile setae will look like tiny hairs on the surface of the cuticle. Do not expect to see the hair plates and campaniform sensilla clearly against the dark cuticle and do not spend time looking for

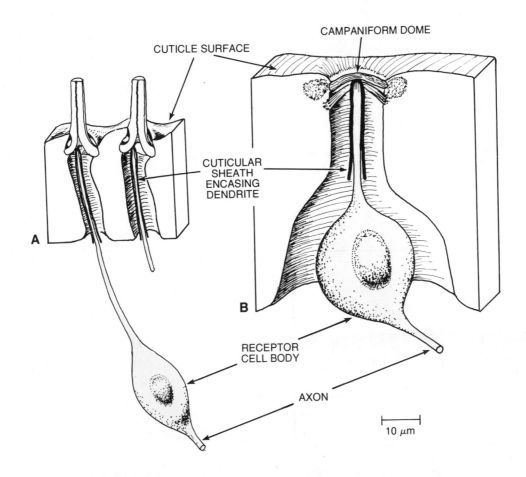

Fig. 6.2-1. Structure of mechanoreceptive sensilla. **A**. Hair plate sensillum, part of the hair plate organ as it appears with methylene blue staining. The distal nerve process of a bipolar receptor cell reaches the hair through a canal in the cuticle. (Adapted from U. Thurm, 1963. *Z. vergl. Physiol.* 46: 351–83.) **B**. Cockroach campaniform sensil-lum; the campaniform organ is a dome-shaped area on the surface of the cuticle. It, too, is innervated by a single bipolar receptor cell. (Adapted from D. T. Moran, K. M. Chapman, and R. A. Ellis, 1971. *J. Cell Biol.* 48: 155–73.)

these structures. If a white, newly molted insect is available, cut off one of its legs for observation under mineral oil on a depression slide with coverslip. Use a compound microscope in this case, and take care that no air bubbles remain trapped under the coverslip.

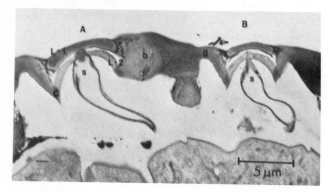

Fig. 6.2-2. Cross section through a cockroach tibia containing the caps of two campaniform sensilla. The tip of the sensory process(es) is shaped like a flat paddle; its major axis is parallel to the plane of the section in cap *A*, and perpendicular to the plane of the section in cap *B*. Note that the buttress, *b*, is much thicker than the gasket, *g*. *L-1* and *L-2* are the outer and inner layers of the cap cuticle. (From Moran and Rowley, 1975.)

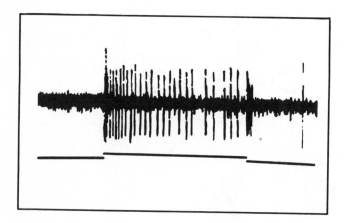

Fig. 6.2-3. Mechanoreceptor response from a tactile spine on the metathoracic leg of the cockroach *Leucophaea maderae*. The spine was deflected with an electrically driven probe at the onset of the stimulus marker (*square wave in second trace*) and released at the end of the marker. The deflection was maintained for 0.25 seconds, producing the response recorded in the upper trace.

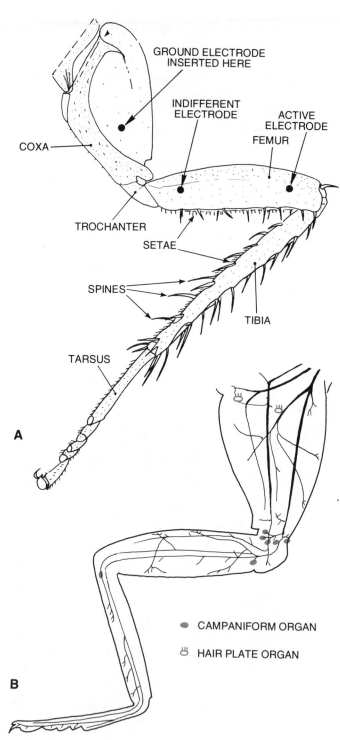

Fig. 6.2-4. **A**. Left metathoracic leg of cockroach, anterior view showing sites of electrode placement. (Adapted from Guthrie and Tindall, 1968.) **B**. Innervation of the cockroach mesothoracic leg and the sites of hair plates and campaniform organs not associated with spines. Chordotonal organs and the spine-campaniform receptor complexes are not shown. (Adapted from Guthrie and Tindall, 1968.)

Recording Procedure

Electrophysiological recording

Place the cockroach leg on a piece of Plasticine (modeling clay) which is about 3 cm thick. Form a ridge in the Plasticine and depress the coxa and femur into the Plasticine at the top of the ridge so that the tibia extends free. With this arrangement, the femorotibial joint should be freely movable and the tibial spines accessible to stimulation.

Place insect pin electrodes in the coxa and femur at the positions diagrammed in figure 6.2-4A. Insert the pins entirely through the leg into the Plasticine. This will support the pins and minimize stress on the leg. Leads should have been soldered to the pins for connection to the preamplifier input.

> Be sure to strip the lacquer or debris off the tips of the insect pins by burnishing with emery cloth or sandpaper.

Three recording electrodes should be used for best results: a ground, an "indifferent," and an "active" electrode. If the wire leads are light and flexible, the insect pin electrodes need *not* be held in an electrode holder or micromanipulator. If you have a micromanipulator, save it for mounting a stimulating probe. Plug the electrode leads into the preamplifier input and connect the preamplifier to the oscilloscope, using appropriate cables and connectors. An audio amplifier and loudspeaker should be connected to the accessory output on the oscilloscope. If no accessory output is available, split the output of the preamplifier and connect the audio amplifier and the oscilloscope in parallel. It is preferable to drive the audio amplifier with the oscilloscope accessory output if possible. Use the following initial settings on your equipment.

Preamplifier. Input in differential mode if possible; gain of 100–1,000×; band-pass filters (if available) set at about 100 Hz (low frequency filter) and 3–10 kHz (high frequency filter).
Oscilloscope. Time base at 10 msec/div; vertical sensitivity at 0.01–0.001 V/div; trigger set on automatic or free run.
Calibration. Adjust the preamplifier and oscilloscope vertical gain to give a total system gain of approximately 100 μV/div. Check with the preamplifier calibrator if available.
Audio amplifier. Volume control adjusted so that static is clearly audible, but not offensive to those around you.

Turn on all equipment and check connections. If 60 Hz noise is a problem, check the adequacy of grounding and shielding. Be prepared to readjust the gain and time base as you experiment.

Stimulation

Using a glass rod drawn to a very fine point or a sharpened dissecting needle, move individual spines on the tibia. Movements of one or more of the spines should elicit a burst of action potentials. Do all spines respond? Can you hear any neurons with "spontaneous" resting activity? Is this activity visible on the oscilloscope? Try moving the joint between the femur and tibia. Does this produce a response? Note that it is nearly impossible to keep the hand-held dissection needle from shaking when partially deflecting a tibial spine. The leg is an effective monitor of the tremor of your hand. If a micromanipulator is available, use it for precise stimulation by mounting a sharp dissecting needle on it.

Finally, it is possible to glue a stick of balsa wood or a toothpick onto the cone of a small loudspeaker. The loudspeaker can be driven by a standard electronic stimulator, providing the output is protected by a fuse.

> Check with your instructor before attempting to use an electronic stimulator to drive the loudspeaker.

The stick can be used to deflect the spines or it can be applied to the surface of the tibia to produce movement of the joint between the femur and the tibia. Alternately, you might press a bent insect pin into the balsa wood to produce a small hook for pulling upward on the spine. Cut the head of the pin off with a pair of wire cutters and press the cut end into the tip of the balsa stick. Start with a low voltage, e.g., 10 V, and observe the direction of movement of the probe before placing it on a spine. The stimulator produces a square wave output, and even inexpensive loudspeakers reproduce the waveform with fair accuracy. To reverse the direction of movement of the probe, reverse the leads attached to the loudspeaker.

Experiments

You are asked to design your own experiments. Try to be as quantitative as possible and repeat each observation several times before moving on to another test.

Here are some questions which might suggest experiments to you.

1. What is the characteristic response of the tibial spines? Does the tibial spine respond to a small angle of deflection? Does the tibial spine respond in a similar fashion when it is deflected at a large angle? Does the spine respond preferentially to movements in one direction as opposed to movements in the opposite direction? Does it make a difference if the movement of the spine is rapid or slow? Does the tibial spine keep responding when the deflection is maintained? What is the time course of adaptation?

2. Can you pick up responses when the leg joints are moved? How do the joint responses compare with the responses of the tibial spines, particularly to maintained deflection? Can you devise a way to specify angle of deflection?

3. All of the tibial spines are probably innervated. You will note that deflection of only a few spines results in clear responses. This is probably a matter of electrode placement which results in "pickup" from some neurons, but not others. Can you record from other neurons by moving the electrodes?

4. Campaniform sensilla on the leg surface (not on spines) can be stimulated with a bent insect pin applied at the dorsal head of the femur just below the knee. A yellowish stripe is sometimes present here.

Pitfalls and Suggestions

1. Clean the recording electrodes with emery cloth or fine sandpaper before inserting them in the preparation. Remember that contact with Plasticine or modeling clay may leave an oily deposit on the electrodes which might also act as insulation.

2. Make sketches of your experimental manipulations, especially those involving deflection of a spine or joint.

3. Use the dissecting scope to see exactly what and how you are stimulating.

4. Test the various spines to see if movement of one or two elicits large action potentials. Study these. With large spikes, it is possible to trigger the oscilloscope on the spike voltage, thereby beginning the trace with the onset of the response. You may wish to use this trick to observe or photograph the responses of the tibial spines. If a stimulator-driven loudspeaker is used for stimulating, the oscilloscope sweep can be triggered by the trigger output on the stimulator and the delay function used to center the response on the face of the cathode ray tube.

5. If you can record only small spikes, you should change the electrode positions or test another leg before the end of the period.

Materials

Materials needed at each station

Oscilloscope

Preamplifier

Audio amplifier and loudspeaker

Small loudspeaker (for stimulating, with a toothpick or short balsa wood stick glued to the cone) and an electronic stimulator to drive the stimulating loudspeaker (optional)

Micromanipulator (optional but quite useful)

Set of electrical leads and connectors

3 pin electrodes (constructed by soldering wire leads to the blunt ends of fine [size no. 0 or 00] insect pins which have had the lacquer removed by burnishing with fine sandpaper or emery cloth)

Faraday cage (if readily available; otherwise probably unnecessary with differential amplification)

Dissecting microscope and illuminator

4–5 extra insect pins

Sharpened dissecting needle or finely drawn glass probe

Lump of Plasticine or modeling clay

Set of dissecting tools (furnished by students)

Materials available in the laboratory

Oscilloscope camera and film

Fine thread

Extra insect pins (size no. 0 or 00)

Extra Plasticine or modeling clay

High power dissecting microscope and good illuminator (for viewing hard-to-see structures on the insect leg)

Prepared microslides of cockroach leg (These ought to come from newly molted insects so that the cuticle is semitransparent [optional; none is commercially available].)

Animals

Cockroaches of any species: *Periplaneta americana, Leucophaea maderae, Blatella* sp., *Blaberus* sp., etc. (Obtain 1 cockroach/station/laboratory period.) Place the roaches in a plastic wastebasket or other similar container with the upper walls smeared with petroleum jelly (Vaseline) to prevent their escape. Provide them with some vertically standing pieces of cardboard to climb upon. A sponge wetted with water every few days will supply sufficient water. Feed them lab chow or dry dog food. This can be supplemented periodically with apples or other fresh fruit, although it is not necessary unless the roaches are to be kept a long time.

Notes for the Instructor

1. Anesthesia is unnecessary when excising a leg from a cockroach.

2. The students may have to be encouraged to try different electrode positions if the responses they record initially are not large enough to easily see single units.

3. Be sure to check the operating manual for your electronic stimulators if they are to be used to drive a small loudspeaker for stimulating purposes. The stimulator used should have sufficient output current to drive a loudspeaker. A fuse (about 0.25 ampere) should be placed in the output if the unit does not presently have a fused output.

Selected References

Finlayson, L. H. 1968. Proprioceptors in the invertebrates. In *Invertebrate receptors*, ed. J. D. Carthy and G. E. Newell. Symp. Zool. Soc. London, no. 23. Academic Press, New York, pp. 217–49.

Guthrie, D. M., and Tindall, A. R. 1968. *The biology of the cockroach*. St. Martin's Press, New York.

Pringle, J. W. S. 1961. Proprioception in arthropods. In *The cell and the organism*, ed. J. A. Ramsay and V. B. Wigglesworth. Cambridge University Press, Cambridge, pp. 256–82.

Thurm, U. 1968. Steps in the transducer process of mechanoreceptors. In *Invertebrate receptors*, ed. J. D. Carthy and G. E. Newell. Symp. Zool. Soc. London, no. 23. Academic Press, New York, pp. 199–216.

RESEARCH REPORTS

Chapman, K. M. 1965. Campaniform sensilla on the tactile spines of the legs of the cockroach. *J. Exp. Biol.* 42: 191–203.

Chapman, K. M., and Nichols, T. R. 1969. Electrophysical demonstration that cockroach tibial tactile spines have separate sensory axons. *J. Insect Physiol.* 15: 2103–15.

Moran, D. T., and Rowley, J. C., III. 1975. High voltage and scanning electron microscopy of the site of stimulus reception of an insect mechanoreceptor. *J. Ultrastruct. Res.* 50: 38–46.

Nijenhuis, E. D., and Dresden, D. 1955. A micro-morphological study of the sensory supply of the mesothoracic leg of the American cockroach, *Periplaneta americana*. *Proc. K. ned. Akad. Wet.* 55: 300–310.

Pringle, J. W. S. 1938a. Proprioception in insects. II. The action of the campaniform sensilla on the legs. *J. Exp. Biol.* 15: 114–31.

————. 1938b. Proprioception in insects. III. The function of hair sensilla at the joints. *J. Exp. Biol.* 15: 467–73.

Pringle, J. W. S., and Wilson, V. J. 1952. The response of a sense organ to a harmonic stimulus. *J. Exp. Biol.* 29: 220–34.

Spinola, S. M., and Chapman, K. M. 1975. Proprioceptive indentation of the campaniform sensilla of cockroach legs. *J. Comp. Physiol.* 96: 257–72.

Thurm, U. 1965. An insect mechanoreceptor. Part 2. Receptor potentials. *Cold Spring Harbor Symp. Quant. Biol.* 30: 83–94.

6.3 Olfactory Reception
Frog Electro-olfactogram (EOG)

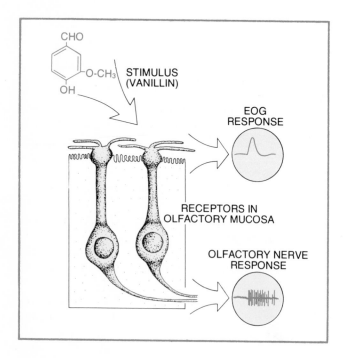

Introduction

Rationale

All receptors have slow electrical activity in the form of graded, nonpropagated potential changes. The term *receptor potential* is used to designate such potentials when they originate in a sense organ during stimulation. Some of the slow, graded potentials characteristic of the sensitive dendrites (or cell bodies) of receptor neurons are referred to as *generator potentials* because they usually lead to the generation of action potentials. The experimental analysis of receptor potentials is an important means of evaluating the transduction of stimulus energy and the coding of receptor responses into impulse frequency. The olfactory system has been chosen for study since summed olfactory receptor potentials can be recorded directly from the vertebrate olfactory mucosa without intracellular recording.

Vertebrate olfactory receptors are bipolar neurons whose cell bodies are located near the surface of the olfactory epithelium and whose axons project from the nose to the olfactory bulb of the brain. In the olfactory epithelium, the receptor dendrites extend beyond the epithelial surface where they are exposed to the fluid and air within the nasal cavity. Although the mechanism of olfactory transduction is not fully understood, the following is a widely accepted model. The dendritic membranes contain macromolecules capable of reversibly binding odorous mole-

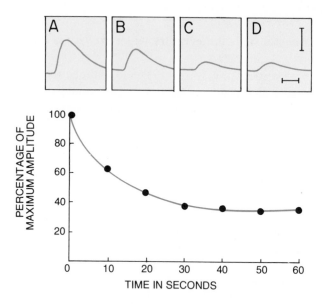

Fig. 6.3-1. Adaptation of the frog electro-olfactogram (EOG) with repeated stimulation. The *falling curve* illustrates the diminution of the EOG response during repeated stimulation with butanol at 10-second intervals. The first response is scored as 100% amplitude. The records *at the top* are the actual oscillographic recordings made during this experiment. **A**. Response to first stimulation; **B**. to second; **C**. to fourth; **D**. to seventh. The *vertical marker bar* indicates 5 mV, and the *horizontal marker* 2 seconds (Ottoson, 1956).

cules. These acceptor molecules are thought to undergo conformational changes when they interact with odorant molecules. The change of state at the acceptor sites leads to changes in the ionic permeability of the membrane and the production of a generator potential. The axons of the olfactory receptors carry action potentials whose frequency is directly proportional to the amplitude of the generator potential.

When a recording electrode is placed on the surface of the olfactory mucosa with a reference electrode in another tissue, a slow potential (surface *negative*) can be recorded when an odorous airstream is directed against the mucosa. This potential, called an *electro-olfactogram* or *EOG*, undoubtedly represents the summed activity of thousands of receptor cells (fig. 6.3-1). Studies of the EOG and other receptor potentials have indicated that substantial sensory processing of the input signal occurs at the receptor cells. The frog EOG provides an opportunity to examine some general features of sensory coding in the olfactory system. The frog is used because in many vertebrates the olfactory mucosa is a highly convoluted and inaccessible structure, but in the frog it is relatively smooth and easily exposed.

Time to complete the exercise: One 3-hour laboratory period is required for a preliminary analysis of the EOG. A second 3-hour period or longer is necessary to obtain truly quantitative data with appropriate controls included.

Procedure

Two methods of stimulation are suggested. The use of odor puffs from polyethylene wash bottles (squeeze bottles) is more likely to give large EOG's. Using a squeeze bottle pumped by a syringe (fig. 6.3-2) provides more precise control over the stimulus.

Stimulating with polyethylene wash bottles

Six polyethylene wash bottles should be obtained and the outlet tube in each adjusted so that only vapor will be expelled from the nozzle even though some liquid may remain in the bottom of the bottle. Use scrupulously clean, soap-free bottles. Before you use them, smell them to check for any extraneous odors. Select the odorants to be used, including a

control substance such as distilled water or mineral oil. Place a small piece of filter paper and no more than 0.2 ml of odorant into each labeled bottle. Use labeled, 1 cc disposable syringes with 1–1½-inch 20-gauge needles to load the squeeze bottles. The intensity of different odors can be attenuated by dilution, e.g., 1 part odorant in 9 parts inert diluent. Molar concentration series can be made up in a similar way, e.g., 1.0 M, 0.1 M, 0.01 M, 0.001 M. Use distilled water to dilute polar substances such as alcohols, and mineral oil to dilute nonpolar substances such as methyl benzoate.

Load the odorants in a different room than the one where the experiments will be carried out. Use a fume hood if available.

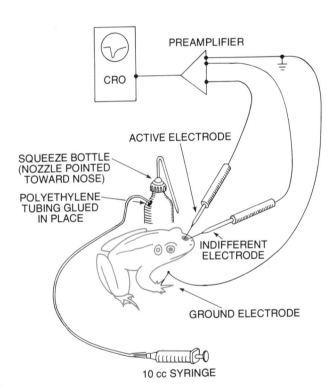

Fig. 6.3-2. Stimulating and recording arrangement. The nozzle of the odorant-containing squeeze bottle is pointed toward the frog's nose at a fixed angle and measured distance. The nose is stimulated by squeezing the bottle or depressing the plunger of the syringe. The tip of the active electrode is placed in the nasal cavity on the olfactory mucosa, while the indifferent electrode is touched to the exposed tissue at the edge of the opening.

Test the amount of odorous air expelled from each wash bottle with a moderate squeeze. Use your own nose and judgment to develop a "standard squeeze" for use in stimulating the frog nose. Select a moderate level of stimulation, not an overpowering blast of odor. For each test, the nozzle of the wash bottle should be positioned at a fixed angle and distance (4–5 cm) from the nose of the frog, and the bottle squeezed to produce a puff of odorant-containing air.

Stimulating with a syringe-squeeze bottle

The syringe-squeeze bottles should be prepared and tested beforehand by the laboratory instructor (fig. 6.3-2). Air is injected into the odorant-containing squeeze bottle from an air-filled 10 ml disposable syringe via a polyethylene tube. To prevent cross contamination and to facilitate the stimulation process, each bottle should have its own syringe.

Surgical procedure

Double pith a frog (see page 311). Place it on a dissecting tray or frog board and proceed to expose the olfactory mucosa. Use a scalpel to cut away a rectangular patch of skin between one eye and the external nare (nostril) on the same side. Refer to figure 6.3-3 for proper orientation. Then, use a scalpel (no. 15 blade) to peel off the relatively soft underlying bone and cartilage of the skull. Note the semitransparent, pigmented layer directly beneath the skull. With fine forceps carefully tear a hole in this layer which is the roof of the nasal cavity. The floor of the cavity comprises the olfactory mucosa. Enlarge the hole sufficiently so that the floor of the nasal cavity is clearly visible. Under favorable conditions it can be seen that the olfactory mucosa is pale yellow, whereas the respiratory epithelium is pink. Locate the *median (olfactory) eminence* which appears as a mound of olfactory mucosa rising from the floor of the cavity.

Cover the hole with a piece of filter paper moistened in amphibian perfusion solution while you get ready to record from the olfactory epithelium. Do not let the filter paper touch the olfactory mucosa.

Recording Procedure

The recording electrodes consist of glass micropipettes broken off to a tip diameter of about 25 μm and filled with amphibian perfusion fluid. Prepare two electrodes by slipping the butt ends of two micropipettes over the chlorided silver wires on the electrode holders. If necessary, bend the wires in several places in order to keep the micropipette from falling off. Connect the leads from the electrodes to the inputs of a DC preamplifier, or DC oscilloscope. A ground electrode consisting of a pin or clip lead may be attached to one of the legs. If shielded cables are used, connect the shielding to a ground terminal. If a preamplifier is used, connect it to the input of the oscilloscope with appropriate leads and connectors. Place the indifferent electrode on some moist exposed tissue other than the skin or olfactory epithelium, such as the exposed tissues adhering to the skull. Place the active electrode on the surface of the olfactory epithelium.

Barely touch the mucosa. Do not press or penetrate.

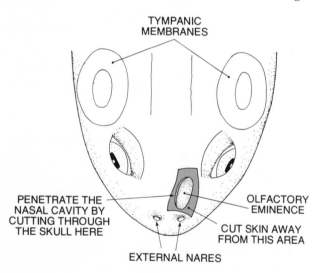

Fig. 6.3-3. Surgical entry into the nasal cavity. The skin should first be removed from a rectangular area on one side of the dorsal surface of the snout. Then, the nasal mucosa should be exposed by carefully cutting through the thin skull using a small scalpel and forceps (*oval area*). The floor of the nasal cavity is the site of the olfactory mucosa. First recordings should be attempted in the area of the olfactory eminence, a domed elevation near the middle of the nasal cavity.

Use the following initial settings on your equipment.

Preamplifier. Input in differential mode if possible; gain of 100–1,000×; band-pass filters (if available) set on DC (low frequency filter) and 5–10 Hz (high frequency filter). If a DC offset position is available on the low frequency filter it should be used and the DC offset control varied to buck out any standing voltages produced by your electrodes or the preparation. It will be necessary to readjust the DC offset periodically during the course of the experiment. AC amplification greatly distorts the EOG (fig. 6.3-4).

Oscilloscope. In DC mode; sweep speed at 1 sec/div; sensitivity at 0.5–0.05 V/div; high frequency filter (if available) at 5–10 Hz. The high frequency filters on the preamplifier and oscilloscope are set at such low values to eliminate any 60 Hz interference. If the electrodes are plugged directly into the oscilloscope, use a gain setting of 0.5 mV/div, and use the position and DC balance controls to center the trace.

Calibration. Adjust the overall system gain (preamplifier plus oscilloscope) to about 500 μV/div. Check by using the preamplifier calibration function, if available.

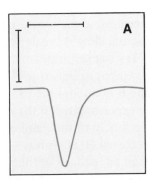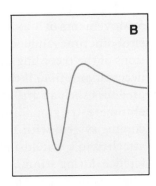

Fig. 6.3-4. Effect of AC amplification on the waveform of the EOG. **A.** DC recording of frog EOG. The nose was stimulated with a short puff of amyl acetate from a wash bottle. The trace is a monophasic negative-going (downward) wave. *Horizontal bar,* 1 second; *vertical bar,* 2 mV. Recorded with a Grass P-16 preamplifier in DC mode. **B.** AC amplification of the EOG from the same frog and recording electrode position. Calibration and stimulus identical to that in *A.* Recorded with a Grass P-15 preamplifier with the low frequency filter set on 0.1 Hz (time constant = 1 second). The monophasic wave of *A* is converted to a biphasic wave with a decreased amplitude.

Stimulating procedure
A properly arranged preparation should respond to a puff from the squeeze bottle. If you do not get a response, try again with a more vigorous puff and other odorants, then check with the instructor or move the electrode to a new position. (The median eminence is best.) Does an air puff also produce a response? If it does, move the nozzle away and reduce the vigor of the puff until there is no response to the air alone. Test the odors again with a delivery which gives little or no air flow artifact on the recording trace.

Guard against drying out the preparation during the experiment. Cover the exposed tissues during prolonged pauses in recording.

Use the syringe attached to the squeeze bottle to control more precisely the rate of application and volume of the odor puff. Refill the syringe by pulling back on the plunger. Deliver the stimulus without extraneous movement around the recording site. Are the odors equally effective?

Experiment with the system until you get consistent responses.

Do not expect to get consistent responses at stimulation rates in excess of one per minute.

Experiments

Carry out experiments 1 and 2*a* first, then design your own experiments. Some experiments which you might try follow.

1. *Change in the EOG response with repeated stimulation.* Does the EOG decrease with repeated stimulation by a single odorant? Try stimulating at 10-second intervals.

2. *Change in EOG amplitude and waveform with different pure odors.*

   a. Test three or four odorants. (Are the concentrations equal? Is molarity a measure of odor concentration, or must vapor pressure also be considered?)

   b. You might also want to try to test the similarities and differences in the EOG responses to a homologous series of odorants, such as alcohols of different chain lengths (methanol, ethanol, *n*-propanol, etc.). Or, you might want to test EOG responses to very different chemical odors, e.g., camphor versus amyl acetate. Remember that repeatability is the essence of a good scientific experiment. You should be able to demonstrate consistent responses to the same stimuli and a substantial difference between experimental and control (air only) stimulations.

Allow 50 to 100 seconds between stimuli. Do not overstimulate. Periodically use a control air puff.

---

3. *Changes in the EOG responses in a concentration series of a pure odorant.* A series might be made up of 0.001, 0.01, 0.1, and 1.0 M solutions of a water-soluble odorant, such as *n*-propanol.
4. *EOG amplitude and waveform at different sites on the olfactory mucosa.* The electrode could be relocated while keeping the odorant and time course of stimulation constant. It would be wise to include a non-olfactory area as a control.
5. *Summation of the EOG with mixtures of pure odorants.* Two odorants might be tested separately, then together, i.e., A, then B, then A + B.
6. *Cross adaptation of odorants that smell similar or have similar chemical structures.* The influence of one odorant on another's response could be tested by examining each odorant alone, then testing them in pairs with a very short time interval between stimulations, i.e., A then B at a 100-second interval; A then B at a 5-second interval; B then A at a 5-second interval.
7. *Effects of neuroactive or pharmacological agents or ionic substitution on the EOG response.* You might try to bathe the olfactory mucosa in solutions of different ionic strengths and compositions, and record the EOG response to a given odorant both before and after the treatment. Or, the effects of anesthetics on a sensory system might be examined. Would a puff of ether vapor eliminate the EOG?
8. *Change in EOG amplitude and waveform with different odorants of possible biological significance to the frog.* Experiments with pure odorants are generally done to examine the neural bases of olfaction. Another approach of interest to those with a be-

havioral or evolutionary interest is to examine responses to odorants of possible biological significance. Pheromones and sex attractants immediately come to mind. However, virtually nothing is known about the biological function of olfaction in frogs. The odors of pond water, frog urine, and putrid meat are suggested as a starting point for such an investigation.

Pitfalls and Suggestions

1. The surgical opening in the skull and associated structures must be large enough to permit one to see the tip of the electrode as it touches the tissue. If the active electrode is repositioned, it should be possible to regain the original position if you have taken care to tabulate the coordinate settings on the X, Y, and Z axes of your micromanipulator.
2. The rate of drying of the mucosa may be reduced by placing moist cotton around the wound margin to increase the relative humidity of the exposed cavity.
3. If an anesthetic drug is used rather than double pithing the frog, it may be necessary to periodically reinject the frog during the course of the experiment. Watch for movement by the frog.
4. It is important for *you* to smell the odor of each wash-bottle or syringe, including the control. This will lessen the chances of error.
5. Movements of human limbs around the recording site sometimes induce artifactual slow wave deflections of the recording trace. Try to minimize unnecessary motion. If the movement of injection produces such an artifact, and it is impossible to eliminate, try grounding the experimenter to the recording system with a clip lead held in the hand or attached to a watchband. Increased 60 Hz interference during stimulation can be reduced in the same manner. Also check the ground connections to all metal devices in the vicinity of the recording site.
6. Do not overstimulate the preparation. Repeated stimulations should be done only with an experimental purpose.
7. Perfusion fluid should be used *very sparingly* when the olfactory mucosa becomes dry looking. Be sure that the nozzle is repositioned in the same place each time. The geometry of the stimulating situation has a great deal to do with the amplitude and waveform of the EOG.
8. Be quantitative in your analysis if the data permit

it. Statistical measures of variability would be applicable with repeated trials.

9. *Limit your goals* in designing an experiment.

Materials

Materials needed at each station

DC oscilloscope or DC-coupled polygraph (A continuously recording polygraph or pen-writing recorder is useful since the polygraph provides permanent records. The amplitude of the EOG can be measured from a slowly sweeping oscilloscope trace.)

DC preamplifier (optional) (DC amplification is necessary if quantitation of the EOG is to be attempted. AC preamplifiers severely distort the EOG waveform because the EOG is a very slow potential change. If a DC preamplifier is unavailable, the recording electrodes can be plugged directly into a DC oscilloscope.)

Set of electrical leads and connectors

Faraday cage (A Faraday cage should be used if available.)

2 recording electrodes (Chloriding of silver wires is described on page 334, and an electrode holder is described on page 336. The tip of the capillary electrode should be broken off to produce a tip diameter of about 25 μm. Fill the electrode with amphibian perfusion fluid by placing the *butt end* in a beaker of Ringer's solution with the tip projecting into the air. It will fill by capillary action if the tip is not blocked. The perfusion fluid will leak out if the tip diameter is greater than 35 μm. To shorten the butt end of the capillary, nick the wall of the tube with a diamond or carbide-tipped pencil and the tube can be broken cleanly at that point.)

Ground electrode (A lead with a pin or alligator clip at one end can be used to ground one of the frog's legs.)

2 supports for the recording electrodes (It is preferable to have the electrode which will contact the olfactory mucosa attached to a micromanipulator. A dual electrode micromanipulator works best.)

Stimulation apparatus

   6 10-cc disposable syringes with 18-gauge needles

   6 40-cm lengths of 190 polyethylene tubing

   6 polyethylene wash bottles (plastic squeeze bottles)

Dissecting microscope and illuminator

Dissecting pan or frog board

Small beaker and medicine dropper

Set of dissecting tools (furnished by students)

Cotton or absorbent tissues

Materials available in the laboratory

Oscilloscope camera and film (if oscilloscopes are used)

Extra medicine droppers and beakers

Dissecting pins or insect pins

Capillary tubes (standard size, 0.9–1.1 mm I.D. × 100 mm)

Silver wire (0.8–9 mm diameter [20 gauge] is best)

Extra 1-cc disposable syringes and 25–27-gauge needles

Extra polyethylene wash bottles

Cotton and filter paper

10–12 1-ml disposable syringes with 1½–2 inch 20-gauge needles (for application of odorants)

Polyethylene tubing (190 P.E. tubing)

Amphibian perfusion solution (20 ml/station)

Odorants

Four to six compounds would be sufficient; 25–50 ml of each. The odorants with asterisks are preferable; nonpolar odorants can be diluted with mineral oil.

Methanol	Anisole
Ethanol	Geraniol
*n-Propanol	Menthol
*n-Butanol	Phenethylamine
n-Decanol	Phenyl ethyl sulfide
Pond water	(dilute if necessary
Putrid meat	in mineral oil)
*Amyl acetate	*Citronelal
n-Butyl acetate	Acetic acid
Methyl benzoate	Vanillin

Note: These odorants should be prepared for use in a room other than the one where recording is in progress. Use a fume hood if available.

Animals

Frogs (1.25/station/laboratory period) Frogs should be kept in a cool place and supplied with dripping water.

Notes for the Instructor

1. Even with a syringe-operated squeeze bottle, odor pulses from stimulation to stimulation will not be identical. The EOG's produced with this system, however, have a sharper onset, and often reach a greater amplitude than those produced with a more elaborate continuous flow system.

2. One defect in the stimulating system is that odors are not effectively removed from the recording area. The persistence of such odors results in some adaptation over time and a general decrease in responsiveness. If a vacuum line is available in the laboratory, a system can be arranged using rubber tubing and a funnel to continuously exhaust odors from the recording site. Otherwise, caution students against unnecessarily filling the room with vapors.

Selected References

Beidler, L. M., ed. 1971. *Handbook of sensory physiology, IV. Part 1: Olfaction*. Springer-Verlag, New York.

Ottoson, D. 1971. The electro-olfactogram. In *Handbook of sensory physiology, IV. Part I: Olfaction*, ed. L. M. Beidler. Springer-Verlag, New York, pp. 95–131.

———. 1974. Generator potentials. In *Transduction mechanisms in chemoreception*, ed. T. M. Poyner. Information Retrieval Ltd., London, pp. 231–40.

Phillips, D. S. 1974. Recording of bioelectric activity; the electro-olfactogram. In *Methods in physiological psychology, vol. 1-C: Bioelectric recording techniques*, ed. R. F. Thompson and M. M. Patterson. Academic Press, New York, pp. 87–95.

Takagi, S. F. 1969. EOG problems. In *Olfaction and taste III*, ed. C. Pfaffmann. Rockefeller University Press, New York, pp. 71–91.

RESEARCH REPORTS

Gesteland, R. C. 1964. Initial events of the electro-olfactogram. *Ann. N.Y. Acad. Sci.* 116: 440–47.

Gesteland, R. C.; Lettvin, J. Y.; and Pitts, W. H. 1965. Chemical transmission in the nose of the frog. *J. Physiol.* 181: 525–59.

Mozell, M. M., and Jagodowicz, M. 1974. Mechanisms underlying the analysis of odorant quality at the level of the olfactory mucosa. I. Spatiotemporal sorption patterns. *Ann. N.Y. Acad. Sci.* 237: 76–90.

Mustaparta, H. 1971. Spatial distribution of receptor-responses to stimulation with different odours. *Acta Physiol. Scand.* 82: 154–66.

Ottoson, D. 1956. Analysis of the electrical activity of the olfactory epithelium. *Acta Physiol. Scand.* 35 (suppl. 122):1–83.

6.4 Proprioception
Frog Muscle Spindle

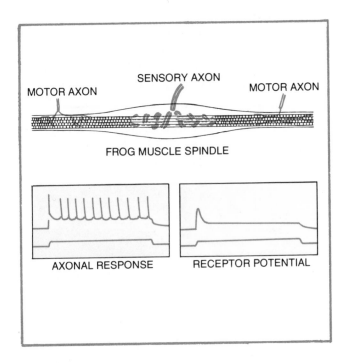

MOTOR AXON   SENSORY AXON   MOTOR AXON

FROG MUSCLE SPINDLE

AXONAL RESPONSE   RECEPTOR POTENTIAL

Introduction

Rationale

When the brain directs muscle movement, more is required beyond a set of commands for certain muscles to contract at certain times. The brain must constantly monitor the state of the muscles and joints to evaluate the results of its commands. To achieve this, all skeletal muscles, tendons, and joints are supplied with sensory receptors called *proprioceptors*. *Proprio* means *own* or *self*; hence proprioceptors are receptors for self-appraisal of the motor system. The *muscle spindle* is a *stretch receptor* found in skeletal muscles and is a classical receptor preparation. When a muscle relaxes, it lengthens and the muscle spindles respond because they are stretched. Muscle spindles also respond when a muscle is stretched by the contraction of antagonistic muscles across a joint.

Structure

Muscle spindles contain specialized muscle cells called *intrafusal fibers*. In the frog, the intrafusal fibers occur in spindle-shaped bundles of about eight fibers and generally run the entire length of the muscle. The intrafusal fibers are striated and are capable of contraction like the surrounding (*extrafusal*) muscle fibers which make up the bulk of the muscle. In the center of each intrafusal fiber is a noncontractile region innervated by sensory endings. The dendrites intertwine around the individual intrafusal fibers and then, after losing their myelin sheath, divide into fine beaded endings. (Mammalian muscle spindles have two types of innervation termed *primary* and *secondary endings*.) The axonal endings are activated when the intrafusal fibers are stretched. Stretch may be produced either by elongation of the entire muscle, or by contraction of the intrafusal fibers themselves. In frogs, the same motor axons innervate both the intra- and the extrafusal fibers. In mammals, the intrafusal muscle fibers can contract independently of muscle shortening because they are innervated by their own motor fibers, the gamma efferent system.

Function

The muscle spindles play at least three roles. They: (1) maintain tonic muscle contraction (tone); (2) initiate phasic stretch reflexes like the knee-jerk reflex; and (3) act as part of a servomechanism which indirectly activates muscles. (Experiment 7.4 discusses stretch reflexes.) The role of muscle spindles in initiating and coordinating muscle contraction is an area of active research. See a textbook of neuroscience or physiology (e.g., Guyton, 1976) for a current understanding of the reflexive control of muscle action.

    In this exercise the muscle spindle will be treated as a prototypical receptor organ, which it undoubtedly is. The frog is used because some small muscles in the frog have only one or a few muscle spindles. It is therefore possible to stretch a single muscle and record from only one receptor. If a mammalian muscle were used, it would be necessary either to dissect out a single muscle spindle or tediously subdivide the nerve to isolate a single axon. Our technique will be to isolate the tendon of one of the frog toe muscles, pull on it to stretch the muscle and its single receptor, and record from the peroneal nerve which innervates the toes.

Time to complete the exercise: One 3-hour laboratory period if the dissection is done properly the first time. The experiment may yield more data if repeated in a second 3-hour session.

Procedure

Electronic instrumentation
Mount a pair of shielded recording electrodes on a micromanipulator or flexible rod. Connect a third, ground electrode (a pin soldered to a connecting wire) to the ground terminal on the preamplifier input.

Connect the preamplifier output to the vertical amplifier input of the oscilloscope. Connect an audio amplifier and loudspeaker to the accessory output on the back of the oscilloscope, or if no accessory output is available, split the preamplifier output so that it drives both the audio amplifier and the oscilloscope. Use the following initial settings on your equipment.

Preamplifier. Input in differential mode if possible; gain of 100–1,000×; band-pass filters (if available) set at about 10 Hz (low frequency filter) and 3–5 kHz (high frequency filter).
Oscilloscope. Time base at 0.1 sec/div; vertical sensitivity at 0.01–0.001 V/div; trigger set on internal, and the triggering level control on automatic or free run.
Calibration. Adjust the preamplifier and oscilloscope vertical gain to give a total *system gain* of approximately 10 μV/div. Check with the preamplifier calibrator if available.
Audio amplifier. Set the tone control to midrange and adjust the gain until a slight hum is heard. Once recording starts, readjust the gain so that action po-

tentials are clearly audible but not offensive to those around you.

Leave all AC-powered equipment on while other arrangements are completed. Make any additional ground connections necessary to minimize 60 Hz pickup. Remove any unnecessary AC-powered equipment from the vicinity.

Tendon dissection
Double pith a frog (see page 311). Cut off one of the hindlegs at the knee with a pair of heavy scissors. Strip the skin from the leg by pulling downward and everting it. Tissue-gripping forceps will be helpful.

Once the skin has been stripped off, it is imperative that the preparation be kept moist with amphibian perfusion fluid.

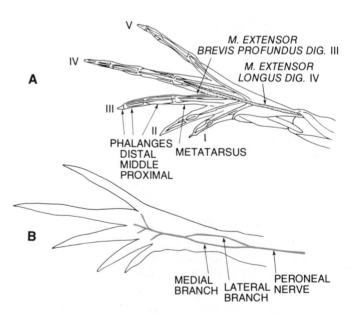

Fig. 6.4-1. Frog hind foot. **A.** Foot stripped of skin, showing the location of the muscle *extensor brevis profundus digitii III* and its tendon (*colored*). This muscle contains one or a few muscle spindles which can be stimulated by pulling the tendon. (Adapted from J. Bureš, M. Petráň, and J. Zachar, 1967. *Electrophysiological Methods in Biological Research*. Academic Press, New York.) **B.** The peroneal nerve.

Examine the ventral surface of the hind foot. Note that the white tendons to the flexor muscles of the phalanges are more robust than the tendons of the extensors on the dorsal surface. Turn the foot dorsal side up and examine the extensor tendons of digit III. First, observe the tendon which runs all the way to the final joint of the third (III) toe. It is connected to the muscle *extensor brevis profundus digitii III* (fig. 6.4-1*A*). This muscle extends the distal phalanx by pulling on its tendon. Look at the two tendons on either side of the middle phalanx of the third toe (fig. 6.4-1*A*). The tendon on the side next to the largest toe (IV) is again the tendon of the *ext. brevis profundus dig. III*; the other extends the middle phalanx. Locate the *proximal phalanx* and a third, thin tendon dorsal to the other tendons. Move the *metatarsus* and locate a fourth, a large dorsal tendon. Review this systematic progression of tendon insertions at each of the joints to confirm their identities. Use a dissecting microscope to see this more clearly.

Cut the tendon of the *ext. brevis profundus dig. III* as close to the distal phalanx as possible. Firmly tie a fine, 40–50 cm length of silk or nylon thread to the cut end of the tendon. Gently pull up on the tendon and free it from the surrounding connective tissue back to the level of the metatarsus. When the thread is gently pulled, it should move only the attached tendon and muscle but not the remainder of the toe.

Keep the preparation moist.

Nerve dissection
The sciatic nerve innervates the leg. Below the knee joint the sciatic nerve divides into two branches, the *tibial nerve* and the *peroneal nerve*. You will record from the peroneal nerve which innervates the toe muscles. (Note that the tibial nerve runs along the ventral surface of the leg and innervates the flexors, such as the gastrocnemius and the soleus muscles.)

Start on the top of the foot near the ankle and locate the peroneal nerve (fig. 6.4-1*B*). Nerves are usually associated with the black-pigmented blood vessels. Find the major vessels and spread apart the muscles to see the nerve beneath the vessel. Gently expose the peroneal nerve using fire-polished glass tools. Work toward the ankle. The peroneal nerve emerges in a dorsal position as it passes through the

ankle (tibiofibular-tarsus joint). It will be simplest to record from the whole peroneal nerve, although the sensory fiber from the muscle of interest passes through the lateral branch of the peroneal nerve (fig. 6.4-1*B*). The nerve must be freed sufficiently so the recording electrodes can be used to elevate it above the surrounding tissue. If necessary, expose the peroneal nerve to within a few millimeters of the *ext. brevis profundus dig. III*.

Use the utmost care in freeing the nerve. Do not stretch it. Keep it moist with the mineral oil/perfusion fluid mixture.

Recording Procedure

The objective will be to lift the peroneal nerve onto the electrodes for recording. The muscle (*ext. brevis profundus dig. III*) will be *gently* stretched by pulling on the thread attached to its tendon. Stretching will activate one or a few muscle spindles, and action potentials will appear in the peroneal nerve.

The recording setup requires that: (1) the string be conveniently pulled without moving the foot; (2) the recording electrodes not be shorted out by touching the underlying foot muscles; and (3) the nerve not dry out. The following arrangement is suggested.

Obtain a petri dish with a waxed cork plate and thoroughly rinse it out with tap water. Give it a final rinse with perfusion fluid. Pin the preparation to the cork with insect pins (fig. 6.4-2). Angle the pins outward so that they will not interfere with the positioning of the recording electrodes. If the foot is too large, parts of the other toes should be trimmed with scissors. Rinse the preparation with perfusion fluid after trimming.

Fix the petri dish to the recording table with soft wax on the bottom or with several strips of masking tape. If available, fix a small pulley to a ringstand and pass the thread over the pulley (fig. 6.4-2). The thread and pulley must be arranged so that later a weight can be hung on the thread to stretch the muscle. Place the pulley at a height just sufficient for the thread to clear the edge of the petri dish.

Insert the insect pin ground electrode in tissue which is remote from the nerve. Lift the peroneal nerve slightly above the underlying muscles with

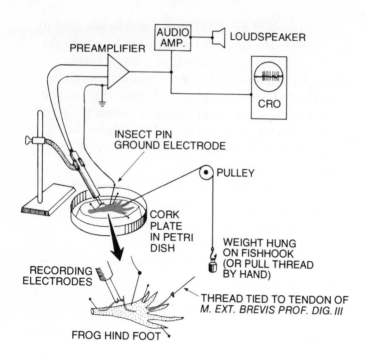

Fig. 6.4-2. Recording arrangement. The hind foot is carefully pinned to a cork plate and a thread tied to the tendon of the muscle *extensor brevis profundus digitii III*. The peroneal nerve is lifted onto the recording electrodes and the muscle spindle stimulated by pulling on the tendon.

the recording electrodes. To retard drying, coat or immerse the preparation in mineral oil saturated with perfusion fluid. An air space or oil space must intervene between the two electrodes or they will be shorted out. Adjust the system gain and the audio amplifier until action potentials are visible and audible when the tendon is gently tugged. Readjust the sweep speed if necessary. Readjust the geometry of the setup as necessary to minimize interference. You may be able to enhance the signal-to-noise ratio by recording from the lateral branch of the peroneal nerve rather than the whole nerve. You may also try to obtain fewer impulses by dissecting the tendon farther along the toe so that less tissue is stretched as the string is pulled.

Experiments

Try to vary experimental parameters under controlled conditions. The following questions may suggest problems to examine.

1. What is the characteristic response to an applied stretch? Small weights will be available so that you can stretch the muscle with a reproducible force. Tie a small fishhook to the thread. Do not hang too much weight on the hook.

2. Does the receptor adapt? Is it fast adapting? Slow adapting? Phasic-tonic? How does this compare with other receptors such as tactile receptors and joint receptors?

3. What is the relationship between the maintained frequency of firing and the intensity of a *steady* applied stretch? Can you predict the level of spontaneous activity from this relationship?

4. What is the recovery time between successive stretches?

5. What is the effect of different rates of stretch?

6. Finally, can you limit the activity to one or a few fibers by surgically cutting into the muscle a bit at a time?

Pitfalls and Suggestions

1. The dissection is the most difficult part. The nerve must not be stretched or pinched while it is being freed. If you record from too many active fibers, shift the electrodes to the lateral branch of the peroneal nerve. Remember as well, that if pulling the tendon moves the entire third toe, you will inevitably stretch several muscles and excite other stretch receptors. Free the tendon more if necessary. Do not hesitate to test the other foot.

2. The geometry of the thread and pulley arrangement is important.

3. For small increments of weight, use birdshot (nos. 7-1/2, 6, 4, 2, and BB shot). The corner may be snipped off an envelope and hung on the fishhook to hold the birdshot. Weigh the birdshot used before leaving the laboratory at the end of the period.

4. This experiment will produce quantitative data if the discharge rate can be accurately measured. A storage oscilloscope or oscilloscope camera can be used to good advantage for measuring discharge rates. Try to arrange to take a series of pictures (of increased muscle loading, for example) on the same photo by moving the camera film back or by moving the vertical placement of the beam after photographing each trace.

5. Keep the preparation moist.

Materials

Materials needed at each station

Oscilloscope
Preamplifier
Audio amplifier and loudspeaker
Set of electrical leads and connectors
Pair of recording electrodes (e.g., 24–26-gauge silver wire and the electrode holder on page 336)
Ground electrode (made from a burnished insect pin with a lead soldered to it)
Micromanipulator or flexible rod electrode holder (e.g., Harvard no. 331 electrode holder)
Dissecting microscope with illuminator
2 ringstands
2 right-angle clamps
Pulley (e.g., Harvard no. 233 light pulley)
Cork plate (made by fixing a sheet or a 5 mm section of no. 20 cork in a 60 mm petri dish with melted paraffin)
2 glass tools for dissecting and manipulating nerves
Set of dissecting tools (furnished by students)

Materials available in the laboratory

Oscilloscope camera and film
Extra cables and connectors
Extra ringstands, clamps, and pulleys
Medicine droppers and beakers
Fine silk or nylon thread
Insect pins
Masking tape and Plasticine (modeling clay)
Fishhooks (no. 14 or 16, short shank to minimize weight)

Small weights and birdshot (nos. 7-1/2, 6, 4, 2, and BB)
Envelopes (lightweight letter size)
Solutions:
    Amphibian perfusion fluid (50 ml/station)
    Mineral oil saturated with perfusion fluid (50 ml/station; made up as in experiment 4.2)

Animals

Frogs, *Rana pipiens* or other species (Order 1 frog/station/laboratory period.) Keep the frogs in a cool place and provide them with dripping water.

Notes for the Instructor

1. The experiment requires careful dissection and attention to the geometry of the setup for success. Students will require some time to find the correct tendon and the nerve. They should be encouraged to dissect both feet.

2. This experiment lends itself to the use of a spike counter for reading out impulse frequency.

3. The best possible arrangement for stimulation is to have the applied pull exactly along the normal axis of movement of the tendon. This causes minimal disturbance of the preparation. Figure 6.4-3 illustrates an alternate recording arrangement which is satisfactory in this respect.

Selected References

Granit, R. 1955. *Receptors and sensory perception*. Yale University Press, New Haven.

Gray, J. A. B. 1959. Mechanical into electrical energy in certain mechanoreceptors. *Progr. Biophys.* 9:286–324.

Guyton, A. C. 1976. *Textbook of medical physiology*. Saunders, New York.

Ottoson, D., and Shepherd, G. M. 1971. Transducer properties and integrative mechanisms in the frog's muscle spindles. In *Handbook of sensory physiology. I. Principles of receptor physiology*, ed. W. R. Lowenstein. Springer-Verlag, New York, pp. 442–99.

RESEARCH REPORTS

Gray, E. G. 1957. The spindle and extrafusal innervation of a frog muscle. *Proc. R. Soc., B.* 146: 416–30.

Katz, B. 1950. Depolarization of sensory terminals and the initiation of impulses in the muscle spindle. *J. Physiol.* 111: 261–82.

Matthews, B. H. C. 1931. The response of a single end organ. *J. Physiol.* 71: 64–110.

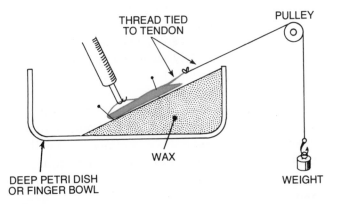

Fig. 6.4-3. Alternate recording arrangement. The pull on the tendon is more in line with its natural axis of movement.

6.5 Skin Receptive Fields
Frog Cutaneous Receptors

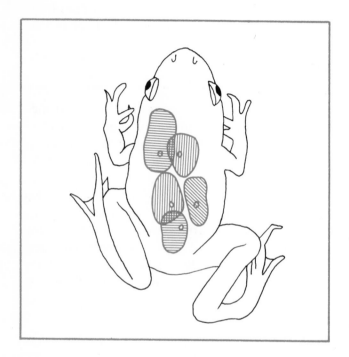

Introduction

Rationale

The immediate cause of a behavioral response is usually an environmental stimulus which is detected by *exteroceptors*. Stimuli from the viscera, muscles, and joints are detected by subsurface *enteroceptors*. In this exercise we will examine the response properties and innervation patterns of tactile receptors in frog skin.

Receptors which terminate in amphibian skin are capable of responding to touch, warmth, cold, intense stimulation, such as a pinch, and chemical irritants. Many receptors are specialized to respond to

only one of these forms of stimulation, including receptors which respond only to intense (nociceptive) stimulation. As is evident from common experience, animals are often quite adept at localizing a cutaneous stimulus. An irritating insect may be quickly removed by a swipe of a leg. Exercise 7.3 demonstrates that much of the neuronal circuitry responsible for cutaneous localization resides within the spinal cord. The receptor's role in cutaneous localization can be studied by recording from those axons which innervate the skin.

At first the problem seems elementary. The most obvious arrangement would be a wiring diagram with each point on the skin connected by its own unique axon to that location in a central "motor switchboard" which, when sufficiently activated, would initiate the correct wiping response. In the jargon of neurobiology, this would entail a *somatotopic* representation with direct reflex connections. This may be in part correct, but it is also an oversimplification which neglects important complexities. For example: (1) Axons have overlapping receptive fields (skin regions innervated by more than one axon). (2) The behavioral response threshold is lowered by stimulation elsewhere on the body. (3) Would an animal stimulated simultaneously at two widely separated points wipe halfway between? (4) In development how do the outgrowing axons find their correct terminations? As is frequently the case, what seems patently simple is actually quite sophisticated. We will not attempt to explore these issues in this experiment, but will make a beginning by examining the manner in which touch fibers respond and innervate the frog skin.

Time to complete the exercise: One 3-hour laboratory period.

Line illustration is adapted from Jacobson and Baker, 1969.

Procedure

Electronic instrumentation

Mount a pair of silver wire recording electrodes on a micromanipulator or flexible rod and connect their leads to the preamplifier input. Connect the lead of a third (ground) electrode to the ground terminal on the preamplifier input.

Connect the preamplifier output to the vertical amplifier input of the oscilloscope. Connect an audio amplifier and loudspeaker to the accessory output on the back of the oscilloscope, or if no accessory output is available, split the preamplifier output so that it drives both the audio amplifier and the oscilloscope. Use the following initial settings on your equipment.

Preamplifier. Input in differential mode if possible; gain of 100–1,000×; band-pass filters (if available) set at about 30–100 Hz (low frequency filter) and 3 kHz (high frequency filter).

Oscilloscope. Time base at 10 msec/div; vertical sensitivity at 0.1–0.01 V/div; trigger set on external input and the triggering level control on automatic or free run.

Calibration. Adjust the preamplifier and oscilloscope vertical gain to give a total *system gain* of approximately 100 μV/div. Check with the preamplifier calibrator if available.

Audio amplifier. Set the tone control to midrange and adjust the gain until a slight hum is heard. Once recording starts, readjust the gain so that action potentials are clearly audible but not offensive to those around you.

Leave all AC-powered equipment on while other arrangements are completed. Make any additional ground connections necessary to minimize 60 Hz pickup. Remove any unnecessary AC-powered equipment from the vicinity.

Operative procedure

Double pith a large frog (see page 311). With scissors cut through the skin as shown in figure 6.5-1 to produce the outline of a flap in the dorsal skin. *Do not pull the flap up yet;* simply free the skin along the cut edges. The flap should be a large one, extending from the level of the cloaca almost to the tympanic membranes. The longitudinal cut should be lateral to the dermal plica (a gold or brown longitudinal ridge of glandular accumulations on each side of the trunk).

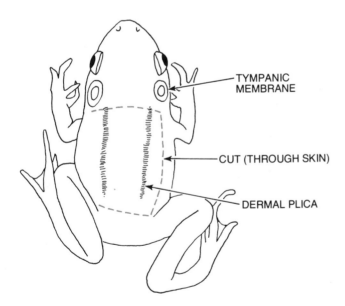

Fig. 6.5-1. Incision of the dorsal skin to expose the cutaneous nerves for recording. Cut through the skin on three sides as indicated, but *do not elevate the flap until ready to record.* (Adapted from Jacobson and Baker, 1969.)

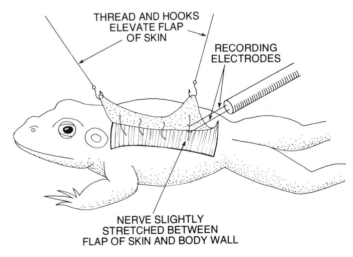

Fig. 6.5-2. Recording arrangement. The dorsal flap of skin is elevated enough to expose a cutaneous nerve. Then the recording electrodes are touched to the nerve. The nerve should be stretched only enough to accommodate electrode placement. After the first nerve is examined, it is severed and the skin flap elevated, if necessary, to allow recording from a second nerve, and so on.

Pin the animal to a frog board. Slightly elevate the skin along the longitudinal edge of the skin flap and carefully cut through the connective tissue attachments along the dermal plica. Do not lift the skin further.

Attach a bent pin or small fishhook to two 30 cm lengths of thread. Hook the free corners of the skin flap so that the thread can be used to elevate the flap (fig. 6.5-2). With Plasticine attach the free part of the threads to a horizontal bar above the frog. Now slowly pull the threads and lift the flap while watching for cutaneous nerves. The nerves pass from the body wall at the midline (along the spine) out to the dorsal skin, and look like white threads.

Do not stretch any of the nerves.

Elevate the edge of the flap with the hook and thread to expose enough of the most accessible nerve for recording. Connect the ground electrode to one of the front limbs. Record from the nerve by positioning the paired electrodes vertically against the nerve. Adjust the preamplifier to get a signal. Stimulate the external surface of the skin by touching it near the site where the nerve enters the skin. *Gently* rub the skin until action potentials are elicited by the stimulation. You should be able to discern the borders of the receptive field of the touch fibers by careful stimulation.

Keep the nerves moist with amphibian perfusion fluid or mineral oil saturated with perfusion fluid. Periodically moisten the outside of the skin with perfusion fluid.

Mapping receptive fields
By positioning the skin at different angles, and recording from different nerves you can map the receptive fields of a number of nerves. Each nerve is actually composed of many axons, not just one. Therefore, you should appreciate that these are actually *composite receptive fields* of several touch fibers firing simultaneously. Sketch an outline of the frog and its pattern of pigmentation. (A 1:1 representation is often helpful. Take measurements with a small plastic ruler.) Trace the receptive fields of the individual nerves onto your sketch. A precise map can be produced if enough care is taken with the sketch and the stimulation. Also note on your sketch the position of each nerve's exit point from the dorsal musculature and its entry point on the skin. The use of colored pencils or different symbols will minimize confusion from overlapping receptive fields.

After each nerve's receptive field has been mapped, retract the electrode and cut the nerve as close to the skin as possible. Elevate the skin a bit more and go on to the next nerve. In this way a complete map of the dorsal skin innervation can be produced. Keep the following questions in mind as you proceed. Does each nerve innervate a unique patch of skin? Can impulses be evoked by stimuli other than touching or scratching? What is the characteristic shape of cutaneous receptive fields on the frog's back? Where does the nerve contact the skin? Are any areas completely devoid of innervation? Is there bilateral symmetry between the right and left sides? Do any of the receptive fields cross the dorsal midline or are they restricted to one side? Can this pattern be related to the patterns seen in scratch reflexes (experiment 7.3)?

Consult other students and compare your results with theirs. What similarities and differences are there? If time permits you can conduct a second recording session with another frog, or perhaps with a frog or toad of a different species.

Pitfalls and Suggestions

1. Dissect carefully.
2. Pay close attention to the geometry and neatness of your setup. If you have an awkward arrangement, it may be difficult to see during stimulation or to move from one nerve to the next. Less data will be collected.
3. Drying and stretching the nerves are the major pitfalls to avoid.
4. When you stimulate with a glass probe, you may introduce 60 Hz interference. Ground your free hand to the cage or clip lead. Do not stimulate with a metal probe. It will produce artifacts.
5. Consider the significance of receptive field overlap.
6. Wiping reflexes indicate that adult frogs can accurately localize a point of irritation on the skin. Correct wiring for localization is established in de-

velopment either by cutaneous axons innervating the correct patch of skin or by chemical influence from the patch of skin which dictate appropriate central connections for its axons (Jacobson and Baker, 1969). The alternatives and mechanisms are still debated.

Materials

Materials needed at each station
Oscilloscope
Preamplifier
Audio amplifier and loudspeaker
Electrical leads and connectors (1 set)
Micromanipulator
Pair of recording electrodes (see page 336)
Ground electrode (made from a burnished insect pin with a lead soldered to it)
Frog board and pins
2 glass tools for stimulating the skin
Set of dissecting tools (furnished by students)
Ringstand with horizontal bar

Materials available in the laboratory
Oscilloscope camera and film
Dissecting microscope
Extra cables and connectors
Extra ringstands
Medicine droppers and beakers
Toothpicks for stimulating
Fine thread
Insect pins
Tackiwax or Plasticine (modeling clay)
Fishhooks (no. 14 or 16, short shank to minimize weight)
Solutions:
   Amphibian perfusion fluid (50 ml/station)
   Mineral oil saturated with perfusion fluid (50 ml/ station; 0.5 ml perfusion fluid in 100 ml mineral oil)

Animals
Frogs or toads, *Rana pipiens* or other species (Order 1 frog/station/laboratory period.) Keep the frogs in a cool place and provide them with dripping water.

Notes for the Instructor

1. The experiment requires careful attention to the geometry of the setup in recording. The students may need some suggestions on layout.
2. The experiment can be used as a takeoff point for experiments on reflex properties and cutaneous temperature receptors.
3. Do not use TMS to anesthetize the frogs; it may damage the skin.

Selected References

Iggo, A. 1974. Cutaneous receptors. In *The peripheral nervous system*, ed. J. I. Hubbard. Plenum Press, New York and London, pp. 347–404.

———. 1973. *Somatosensory system: Handbook of sensory physiology*, vol. II. Springer, Berlin.

Lynn, B. 1975. Somatosensory receptors and their CNS connections. In *Annual review of physiology*, ed. J. H. Comroe, Jr. Annual Reviews, Inc., Palo Alto, Calif., pp. 105–27.

Rose, J. E., and Mountcastle, V. B. 1959. Touch and kinesthesis. In *Handbook of physiology. I. Neurophysiology*, vol. 1, ed. J. Field. American Physiol. Soc., Washington, D.C., pp. 387–429.

RESEARCH REPORTS
Adrian, E. D.; Cattell, McK.; and Hoagland, H. 1931. Sensory discharges in single cutaneous nerve fibers. *J. Physiol.* 72: 377–91.

Baker, R. E., and Jacobson, M. 1970. Development of reflexes from skin grafts in *Rana pipiens*: Influences of size and position of the grafts. *Dev. Biol.* 22: 476–94.

Cattell, McK., and Hoagland, H. 1931. Response of tactile receptors to intermittent stimulation. *J. Physiol.* 72: 392–404.

Catton, W. T. 1958. Some properties of frog skin mechanoreceptors. *J. Physiol.* 141: 305–22.

Hogg, B. M. 1935. Slow impulses from the cutaneous nerves of the frog. *J. Physiol.* 84: 250–58.

Jacobson, M., and Baker, R. E. 1969. Development of neuronal connections with skin grafts in frogs: Behavioral and electrophysiological studies. *J. Comp. Neurol.* 137: 121–37.

Lowenstein, W. R. 1956. Excitation and changes in adaptation by stretch of mechanoreceptors. *J. Physiol.* 133: 588–602.

Silvey, G. E.; Gulley, R. L.; and Davidoff, R. A. 1974. The frog dorsal column nucleus. *Brain Res.* 73: 421–37.

Zotterman, Y. 1939. Touch, pain, and tickling: An electrophysiological investigation of cutaneous sensory nerves. *J. Physiol.* 95: 1–28.

6.6 Audition
Gerbil Cochlear Microphonics

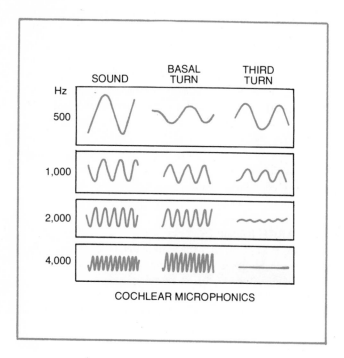

COCHLEAR MICROPHONICS

Introduction

Rationale

The sense of hearing is a special form of mechanoreception. Among the senses, hearing is probably the most refined in the ability to discriminate temporal patterns of stimulation. For example, human speech communication relies heavily on the timing of sounds, as well as pitch, location, and intensity. Echo-locating bats carry time discrimination to near perfection as they use the timing and frequency content of reflected sounds to identify objects in their environment. We will examine *cochlear microphonic potentials*, a type of *receptor potential* which follows the waveform of the stimulus with little delay or distortion.

The tympanic membrane and the bones of the middle ear communicate airborne vibrations (sound waves) to the *cochlea* (fig. 6.6-1). Vibrations set up in the cochlear fluids (perilymph) of the *scala tympani* and *scala vestibuli* are in turn communicated to *hair cells* resting on the basilar membrane (fig. 6.6-2). The hair cells are mechanoreceptors which respond to vibration by producing receptor potentials. The receptor potentials in the hair cells set up action potentials in the auditory nerve through synapses with the fibers of the auditory nerve. We will record cochlear microphonics (probable receptor potentials), not action potentials.

Wever and Bray (1930) recorded from the auditory nerve and discovered oscillating electrical potentials which followed the acoustic stimulus perfectly. Only later was it determined that this was not the nerve code (now known to be impulses) but cochlear responses volume-conducted along the auditory nerve (see exercise 4.6 on volume conduction). These oscillations are called microphonic potentials because they are generated in response to sound and

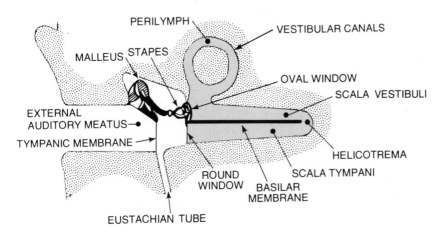

Fig. 6.6-1. A schematic drawing of the ear. The cochlea, *right*, is shown as a straight structure, but in reality it is coiled like a snail's shell. The endolymph cavity of the scala media is not shown in this drawing. (Adapted from von Bekesy and Rosenblith, 1951.)

closely follow the waveform of the acoustic stimulus. You may have encountered microphonic potentials of another kind in earlier experiments—electromechanical potentials caused by electrode vibration when you tapped the recording table. However, the microphonic potentials of the cochlea have a biological origin. They seem to be generated by shearing movements of the tectorial membrane against the cilia of the hair cells. A biological origin of cochlear potentials is implied by their disappearance shortly after interruption of the blood supply.

A standing DC potential can be recorded with a pair of glass micropipettes, one in the scala media and another in the scala tympani or vestibuli (fig. 6.6-2). This potential of 70–80 mV is thought to be generated by the stria vascularis, the membrane which lines the outer walls of the endolymphatic space (fig. 6.6-2B). When this potential is added to the resting membrane potential of the hair cells, a total potential of 140–160 mV results between the cilia of the hair cells and the fluid of the scala media. Davis (1965) has suggested that this large potential may be modulated to produce the cochlear microphonic potentials, and they, in turn, contribute to the production of action potentials in the fibers of the auditory nerve. The system has been likened to a biological resistance microphone where a large standing potential produced by the stria vascularis and hair cell membrane is modulated by vibration-induced changes in resistance (Davis, 1965).

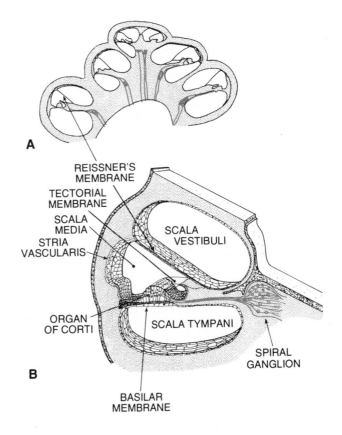

Fig. 6.6-2. A. Vertical section through the entire guinea pig cochlea. **B.** Section through a single whorl. (Adapted from W. Bloom and D. W. Fawcett, 1975. *A Textbook of Histology*, 10th ed. Saunders, Philadelphia.)

Time to complete the exercise: Two 3-hour laboratory periods: one to master anesthesia, dissection, and recording technique, and a second to collect more data. Before the laboratory period, read section 9.3.

Procedure

Electronic instrumentation
Mount a silver/silver chloride recording electrode on a micromanipulator. Connect the shielded lead of the recording electrode to the input of the preamplifier. Connect the shielded lead from a reference electrode (a pin soldered to a lead) into the second input of the preamplifier and connect the ground electrode to a ground terminal on the preamplifier. Feed the preamplifier output into the vertical amplifier input of the oscilloscope. Connect an audio amplifier to the accessory output on the back of the oscilloscope, or if no accessory output is available, split the preamplifier output so that it drives both the oscilloscope and the audio amplifier. If headphones are unavailable for use with the audio amplifier, use the oscilloscope alone.

Connect the output of the audio frequency (sine wave) generator to a small loudspeaker. Mount the loudspeaker on a small stand positioned close to the gerbil's ear. If you have a dual-trace oscilloscope, monitor the output of the audio generator (fig. 6.6-3). With the dual-trace oscilloscope you can monitor the input (the loudspeaker) to the biological system and its output (cochlear microphonics). Use the following initial settings on your equipment.

Preamplifier. Input in differential mode if possible; gain of 100–1,000×; band-pass filters (if available) set at about 100 Hz (low frequency filter) and 30 kHz (high frequency filter).
Oscilloscope. Time base at 2 msec/div; vertical sensitivity on preamplifier channel set to 0.1–0.01 V/div; vertical sensitivity on the audio frequency generator channel set to 10 V/div; trigger set on internal input to trigger from the audio frequency generator channel; and the triggering level control set to produce a stationary sine wave when the audio frequency generator is actuated.
Calibration. Adjust the preamplifier and oscilloscope vertical gain to give a total *system gain* of approximately 0.5 mV/div. Check with the preamplifier calibrator if available.
Audio Frequency Generator. Turn the amplitude control to its lowest value and set the frequency control to give a sine wave of 1,000 Hz.
Audio Amplifier. Set the tone control to midrange and adjust the gain until a slight hum is heard in the earphones. *Do not put the earphones on before turning on the equipment.* Once recording starts, readjust the gain to a comfortable level.

Leave all AC-powered equipment on while other arrangements are completed. Make any additional ground connections necessary to minimize 60 Hz pickup. Remove any unnecessary AC-powered equipment from the vicinity.

Anesthesia
Section 9.3 tells how to anesthetize a rodent. When you follow the instructions on cannulation of the trachea in section 9.3, remember that the gerbil's trachea is quite fragile. Be gentle.

Turn to section 9.3, page 313. Return to this experiment when the instructions tell you to do so.

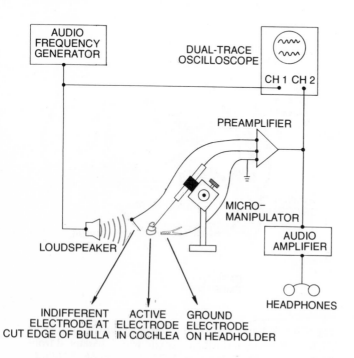

Fig. 6.6-3. Recording arrangement.

Anatomical orientation

Examine a gerbil's skull, if one is available, and locate each *tympanic bulla* on the ventral surface. The bullae are the two large bulbous structures. The cochlea is located within the cavernous bulla. If one bulla has been opened, use a stereo microscope and examine the way in which the cochlea is coiled like an old-fashioned beehive. In the living gerbil you will have to expose the cochlea, make a pinhole in it, and touch the silver electrode wire to that point. Consult figure 6.6-4.

Exposing the bulla in the anesthetized gerbil

Check to see that the external auditory meatus (ear canal) is open to sound and not full of wax. Position the gerbil ventral side up with its head to your left and the tail to your right. Expose the left bulla, i.e., the one farthest away from you. The bulla lies just behind the caudal pole of the jawbone, which you can feel with the fingers. Cut the skin above the bulla and use blunt dissection methods to move the blood vessels and salivary tissue away so that you can clean off the top of the bulla.

Avoid cutting or using sharp instruments whenever feasible. Cutting is more likely to cause bleeding than teasing and tearing with blunt instruments.

It will be necessary to remove the digastric muscle which covers the bulla's more medial aspect. Avoid the venous sinuses which are located along the anterior margin of the bulla. *Use a dissecting microscope.* With fine forceps break through the bone at the top of the bulla. Carefully chip away some of the shell-like pieces. You should immediately see a gray-looking saucer sitting on edge (fig. 6.6-4). This is the tympanic annulus, the bony support for the tympanic membrane. *It must be protected.* The cochlea lies more medial and considerably deeper. As the bone of the bulla is chipped away medially, you will probably find it necessary to reflect the soft tissues to get a better view of the interior. Readjust your microscope light. Obtain a small dulled hook attached to a 25 cm string. Insert the hook into the muscle and glandular tissue medially and pull the string over the trachea. Apply the necessary modest tension to retract the tissues, and then anchor the

end of the string with wax or Plasticine. Respiratory distress will indicate that it is compressing the trachea. Consult figure 6.6-4 to see how the cochlea extends rostrolaterally from the large bone-encased stapedial artery. The cochlea is like a beehive on its side, with the top of the beehive being the most anterior part of the cochlea. Expose the cochlea enough to allow the insertion of the recording electrode.

Inserting the recording electrode

Use a no. 1 insect pin to make a hole in each turn of the cochlea. All that is necessary is to make an entry hole large enough for the recording electrode to make fluid contact with the interior. The cochlea's bony covering is only a thin crust, most cautiously penetrated by putting the insect pin in an electrode holder and driving it down with a micromanipulator.

Insert the recording electrode into the first whorl of the cochlea. Place the indifferent pin electrode in nearby tissues, e.g., one of the neck muscles, and clip the ground electrode to the headholder.

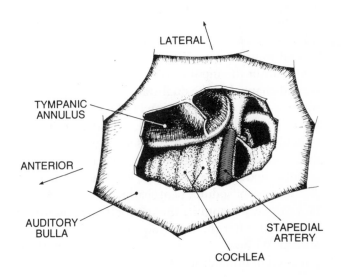

Fig. 6.6-4. Drawing of the internal structure of the left tympanic bulla of a gerbil, ventral view. The bony tympanic annulus supports the large tympanic membrane beneath it. Note the prominent stapedial artery (*colored*) at the base of the cochlea. The cochlea lies on its side with five or six visible coils.

Recording Procedure

Position the stimulating loudspeaker as near the ear as practical. Gradually increase the amplitude control of the audio frequency generator until a 1,000 Hz tone is heard. Adjust the preamplifier and oscilloscope gain to get a signal. Increase the system gain and/or the volume of the stimulating tone as necessary until a response is seen. Expect to see a sine wave much like the stimulating waveform. Once a signal appears, alter the frequency and observe the results. Listen to the signal in the headphones. How much like the stimulating tone is the cochlear microphonic potential?

Experiments

Carefully examine the form of the microphonic potential. Does it faithfully follow sound frequencies? If so, what is its range? Is there any one frequency which produces a maximal microphonic potential? What is its latency? What differences emerge when the recording electrode is moved to different whorls of the cochlea?

Can you construct a frequency-intensity curve in which you determine the intensity necessary to produce a given response amplitude at a number of frequencies?

Be aware during your experiments that there are several sources of nonlinearity in the system. You can monitor the input to the loudspeaker with the second channel of the dual-trace oscilloscope, but inexpensive loudspeakers tend to be linear only in the middle range (200–2,000 Hz). Moreover, it is difficult to measure the actual sound intensity at the ear, so we have not suggested attempting that.

At the end of the experiment, kill the animal with an overdose of sodium pentobarbital (0.3 cc). Arrange to keep recording the microphonic potentials at intervals after the injection and the death of the animal. We have not suggested the experimental application of other drugs since the cochlear microphonic potential is quite resistant to drugs.

At the end of the experiment dissect the bulla further and observe the articulations of the malleus, incus, and stapes. The stapes, which straddles the artery, is particularly interesting where it connects to the oval window. The oval window can be re-moved, and indeed it is a perfect miniature oval! Can you find the large auditory nerve?

Pitfalls and Suggestions

1. Slight or moderate reflexive response to foot pinching is expected. The animal does not feel the pinch.
2. Monitor the animal's breathing during the experiment. Be prepared to follow the recommendations in section 9.3 (see page 314) if there are difficulties with breathing.
3. The sine wave signal may sometimes be recorded by the air directly vibrating the electrode, or by electrical pickup. Check to see whether the cable leading to the loudspeaker is adjacent to or crosses over the recording cable. Separate them. Test the response with the electrode raised into the air, and also with the electrode on a dry area of bone. Repeat after the animal has been sacrificed.
4. From the velocity of sound in air, what latency would you predict between the emission of sound from the speaker and the arrival at the ear?

Materials

Materials needed at each station
Oscilloscope (dual trace if available)
Preamplifier
Audio amplifier and headphones
Audio frequency (sine wave) generator
Small loudspeaker (Extended-range high fidelity is best.)
Ringstand and clamp for loudspeaker
Micromanipulator and stand
Headholder in straight configuration (see page 315) and stand
Recording electrode (Use fine silver wire, e.g., 250 μm diameter. Chloride it according to the instructions on page 334 and mount the electrode in a holder with a shielded cable [page 336].)
Indifferent electrode (Use a pin or another chlorided silver wire of larger diameter soldered to a shielded cable.)
Ground electrode (A clip lead is sufficient.)
Dissecting microscope with boom arm and illuminator
Set of electrical leads and connectors
Set of dissecting tools (furnished by students)

Materials available in the laboratory

2 gerbil skulls (The tissue may be stripped from the skulls by simmering in hot water for several hours or by exposure to dermestid beetle larvae used by museums for this purpose.)

Oscilloscope camera and film

Extra cables and connectors

Fine thread

Insect pins (no. 1)

2 retractor hooks (Blunted no. 14 or 16 fishhooks with the barbs filed off work well.) with attached 25 cm string

1-cc disposable hypodermic syringes and disposable 23–25-gauge needles

Plasticine or Tackiwax (for holding retractor threads)

Cotton (and Gelfoam, if available)

Large rubber tubing (for artificial respiration)

Cloth towels for handling gerbils

Solutions:

Mammalian perfusion solution (100 ml/station)

Ketamine (1 cc/station/laboratory period). (Vetalar; Parke-Davis, 100 mg/cc.) See page 324, note no. 6. Alternative: sodium pentobarbital (Nembutal, 50 or 60 mg/ml), 50 cc

Animals

Mongolian gerbils, *Meriones unguiculatus* (Order 1.33 gerbils/station/laboratory period.) Keep the gerbils in clean cages supplied with nesting material (shredded paper or wood shavings). Give them ample water, rat pellets, and, once a week, guinea pig pellets. Fresh spinach or parsley will improve their condition.

Notes for the Instructor

1. Sodium pentobarbital can be used as an anesthetic (50 mg/kg bw, i.p.; followed by 80% of the initial dose 20 minutes later), but the survival rate will be lower. Unless the teaching laboratory is warm it will be a useful precaution to have a bottle of hot water or a 60-watt gooseneck lamp to keep the gerbil warm.

2. Tracheal cannulation of gerbils is a more difficult operation than with rats. Inexperienced students will need some assistance.

3. Headphones are suggested rather than a second loudspeaker which causes confusion, both for the students and for the gerbil ear.

4. Guinea pigs have large and heavy bullae, but the operation to expose them is more difficult. Furthermore, guinea pigs are more subject to sodium pentobarbital overdose. Guinea pigs are the classic experimental preparation for recording cochlear microphonic potentials.

5. Prepare two retracting hooks per station. They must be small enough and blunt enough to protect neighboring sinuses and blood vessels.

6. An insect pin with an uninsulated tip works well as a recording electrode.

7. Keep the stimulating speakers small and close to the ear to reduce room noise and boost the microphonic amplitude.

Selected References

Davis, H. 1961. Some principles of sensory receptor action. *Physiol. Rev.* 41: 391–416.

———. 1965. A model for transducer action in the cochlea. *Cold Spring Harbor Symp. Quant. Biol.* 30: 181–90.

Flock, A. 1971. Sensory transduction in hair cells. In *Handbook of sensory physiology. I. Principles of receptor physiology*, ed. W. R. Lowenstein. Springer-Verlag, New York, pp. 396–441.

Vinnikov, Ya. A. 1974. *Sensory reception: Cytology, molecular mechanisms, and evolution.* Springer-Verlag, New York.

von Bekesy, G. 1956. Current status of theories of hearing. *Science* 123: 779–83.

von Bekesy, G., and Rosenblith, W. A. 1951. The mechanical properties of the ear. In *Handbook of experimental psychology*, ed. S. S. Stevens. John Wiley and Sons, New York, pp. 1075–1115.

RESEARCH REPORTS

Brown, A. M. 1973. High frequency peaks in the cochlear microphonic response of rodents. *J. Comp. Physiol.* 83: 377–92.

Finck, A., and Sofouglu, M. 1966. Auditory sensitivity of the Mongolian gerbil. *J. Aud. Res.* 6: 313–19.

Galosy, R. A., and Lippman, L. G. 1970. Gerbil's pinnae movement as related to stimulus frequency and intensity. *Psych. Sci.* 20: 309–10.

Tasaki, I. 1954. Nerve impulses in individual auditory nerve fibers of guinea pig. *J. Neurophysiol.* 17: 97–122.

Tasaki, I.; Davis, H.; and Eldredge, D. H. 1954. Exploration of cochlear potentials in the guinea pig with a microelectrode. *J. Acoust. Soc. Am.* 26: 765–73.

Wever, E. G., and Bray, C. W. 1930. Action currents in the auditory nerve in response to acoustical stimulation. *Proc. Nat. Acad. Sci. U.S.* 16: 344–50.

7 Central Processes

7.1 Cockroach Ventral Nerve Cord
Spontaneous and Elicited Responses

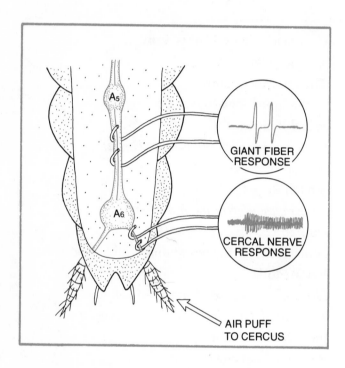

GIANT FIBER
RESPONSE

CERCAL NERVE
RESPONSE

AIR PUFF
TO CERCUS

sensitive they may be stimulated not only by direct touch, but also by vibrations of the substrate upon which the animal rests, or by air movements, including low frequency sound waves. Each of the cercal hairs has a single mechanoreceptor cell at its base. The axons of the mechanoreceptors project to the sixth (or terminal) abdominal ganglion where they make synaptic connections with two sets of giant nerve fibers, a dorsal group of fibers and a ventral group (fig. 7.1-1). The two sets of giant fibers

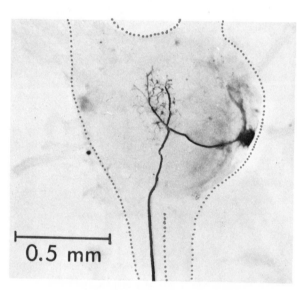

0.5 mm

Introduction

Rationale

The cockroach ventral nerve cord is a complex neuronal system. However, one example of neuronal integration can easily be explored with this preparation—the conversion of mechanosensory input from primary sensory fibers into responses of giant interneurons. The preparation is also useful to demonstrate so-called spontaneous activity in a central nervous system.

Escape responses are common among the invertebrates. In many insects, such as cockroaches and crickets, an escape response is elicited by stimulation of the *cerci*, paired mechanosensory appendages located at the tip of the abdomen. Each cercus bears a large number of long tactile hairs which are so

Fig. 7.1-1. Light micrograph of a terminal abdominal ganglion (6th) after staining *one* of the giant fibers with cobalt. The ganglion, its attached connectives, and other nerves have been outlined in *color* because the ganglion itself is not stained. The cell body of the giant fiber appears as the dark blob at the *right margin* of the ganglion. Its dendrites appear in the *middle* of the ganglion and the giant axon projects from this area into one of the connectives at the *bottom* of the micrograph. The dendrites of the giant fiber receive their excitatory input from the cercal nerves. (Photomicrograph courtesy of C. D. Tweedle.)

COCKROACH VENTRAL NERVE CORD **7.1**

project from the terminal abdominal ganglion to the thorax and head, a distance of 3–5 cm (figs. 7.1-2 and 7.1-3). The giant fibers make synaptic connections in the thoracic ganglia with interneurons involved in the evasive response. The giant fibers continue on to the subesophageal ganglia and brain. The giant fibers are important to the evasive response, but their exact role is still not clear. They may activate the coordinated leg movements which result in the insect running away. An alternate hypothesis is that the giant fibers prepare the way for coordinated evasive responses by inhibiting ongoing activity. Thus, the giant fiber responses might act as a "clear-all-stations" warning in the central nervous system prior to the escape response itself. Whatever their role, it is clear that the giant fibers communicate information on cercal stimulation to both the thoracic ganglia and brain.

Time to complete the exercise: At least one 3-hour laboratory period.

Procedure

Surgical procedure

Select a large male cockroach. Females are generally wider than males and often have egg cases (ootheca) protruding from the rear. Males can be positively identified by the presence of a pair of very fine styli protruding ventrally from the tip of the abdomen. Backlight the insect by holding it up against a bright light source and verify the presence of styli. Do not confuse the styli with the anal cerci, which are much larger, usually curved appendages. (Refer to figure 8.6-3 if uncertain.)

You may anesthetize your cockroach by placing it briefly in a beaker or jar filled with CO_2. Anesthesia is entirely optional; a firm grip on the insect is just as humane.

Do not leave the insect in the CO_2 too long.

Quickly cut off the head, legs, and wings. Pin it *ventral side down* on a small dissecting tray or a cork plate. Insert the pins so that they lean out from the body at an extreme angle and will not impede future manipulations.

Once the insect is completely pinned down, examine it under the dissecting microscope before you begin the dissection. Look at the anal cerci. The cerci are covered with 500–1,000 sense organs called *sensilla*, most of which are hairlike in structure. Notice that there is more than one type of hair. A closer examination under the compound microscope of a cleared and mounted specimen would reveal two or three types of hairs (thread hairs and bristles), and some dome-shaped sensory organs on the surface of the cuticle (campaniform sensilla). Most of the hairs and the campaniform organs are sensitive

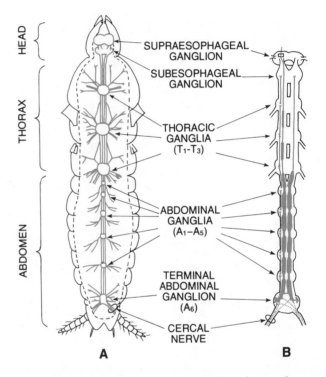

Fig. 7.1-2. Nervous system of the cockroach *Periplaneta americana*. **A**. Dissection of the nervous system (dorsal view) showing the positions and relative sizes of the ganglia. The thoracic ganglia and the terminal abdominal ganglion are the largest ganglia of the ventral nerve cord. The brain consists of the supra- and subesophageal ganglia. **B**. Schematized diagram of the cockroach nervous system showing the giant fibers and small fiber pathways in the nerve cord which are associated with the evasive response. The dorsal giant axons (*right side colored*) narrow at T3. The ventral giant axons narrow by steps (*left side colored*), but extend all the way to the supraesophageal ganglia where they activate antennal muscles (*box*). A small fiber pathway (*far left colored*) also ascends the nerve cord and is probably the pathway responsible for activating leg motor neurons. (Adapted from Cameron, 1961; and Parnas and Dagan, 1971.)

205

to mechanical stimulation. Although many of the bristles are probably chemosensitive, the primary function of the cerci is undoubtedly the reception of tactile, vibratory, and acoustic stimuli by the hairs and campaniform sensilla. The antennae at the opposite end of the organism serve a similar purpose, but are more attuned to olfactory and taste stimuli.

Begin the dissection by removing the dorsal plates (tergites) which cover the abdomen. Work slowly and carefully. After exposing the internal organs,

push the gut and other organs to one side without rupturing them. Carefully pick away the creamy white fatty tissue which occurs throughout the abdominal cavity. Note that the abdominal cavity (or hemocoel) is also filled with fine silvery tubes or *tracheae*. Work your way down to the semitransparent ventral nerve cord. Two straplike longitudinal muscles overlie the cord in the abdomen and will have to be cut away. Use fine iridectomy scissors if available. The nerve cord lies directly on top of the ventral cuticle or sternites.

The nerve cord is accompanied by some large tracheae. Carefully cut or pick away the larger tracheae. Proceed slowly: this is the crucial part of the dissection. The almost-transparent nerve cord will be hard to recognize if you have not seen it before.

Identify several abdominal ganglia and their connectives. The sixth (or terminal) abdominal ganglion is easily recognized as the largest abdominal ganglion. Identify the cercal nerves which connect at oblique angles to the posterior aspect of the terminal abdominal ganglion. Be careful not to damage them.

Take care during the dissection to keep the preparation moist with cockroach perfusion fluid, but do not use an excessive amount.

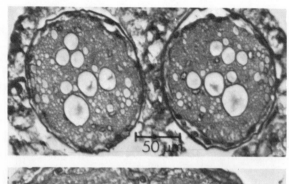

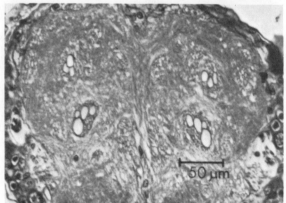

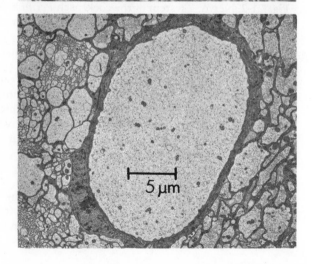

Fig. 7.1-3. Cross sections of giant fibers in the cockroach ventral nerve cord. **A.** Cross section through the connectives between the fourth and fifth abdominal ganglia (A_4–A_5), showing the separation into dorsal and ventral giant fiber groups. **B.** Cross section through abdominal ganglion A_3. The giant fibers are still recognizable as they pass through the ganglion, but the fiber diameter decreases. The cell bodies of neurons in the ganglion are recognizable, forming a rind around the periphery of the ganglion. This organization (a rind of cell bodies surrounding a core of fibers) is typical of invertebrates and is the reverse of the vertebrate spinal cord's organization. (*A* and *B* from Spira, Parnas, and Bergmann, 1969.) **C.** Electron micrograph of one of the three large ventral giant fibers in one of the abdominal connectives A_5–A_6. The giant fiber is surrounded by many smaller nerve fibers and itself is enclosed in several layers of glial sheathing (glial cell nucleus against the lower left of giant axon). (Electron micrograph courtesy of V. M. Tipton.)

Carefully free up a section of the nerve cord so you can slip your recording electrodes underneath.

Recording Procedure

Insert a ground electrode consisting of a fine silver wire into the undissected part of the thorax (see "Materials" section). Carefully insert the recording electrodes under the ventral nerve cord and lift it slightly. Using the twisted end of a Kimwipe or Kleenex, draw up excess hemolymph or cockroach perfusion solution.

> The nerve cord and the recording electrodes must be free of any adhering hemolymph or cockroach perfusion solution. These fluids will short the electrodes out and no recording will be possible. However, keep the nerve cord moist.

Connect the recording electrodes to the preamplifier input. The ground electrode should be connected to a ground terminal on the preamplifier. Connect the output of the preamplifier to the oscilloscope and set the oscilloscope to trigger automatically. Connect the audio amplifier to the vertical amplifier external output on the oscilloscope. Some vertical plug-in units on Tektronix oscilloscopes have external outputs on the front panel; other oscilloscopes have accessory outputs on the back of the instrument. If the oscilloscope has no accessory output, connect the audio amplifier and oscilloscope in parallel to the preamplifier output.

Use the following initial settings on your equipment.

Preamplifier. Input in differential mode if possible; gain of 100–1,000×; band-pass filters (if available) set at about 10 Hz (low frequency filter) and 3 kHz (high frequency filter).
Oscilloscope. Time base at 5 msec/div; vertical sensitivity at 0.1–0.01 V/div; trigger set on auto or free run, so that the beam sweeps continuously without an external triggering input.
Calibration. Adjust the overall system gain (preamplifier plus oscilloscope) to about 100 μV/div. Check by using the preamplifier calibration function, if available. If you do not understand the meaning or procedure of calibration, ask your instructor.
Audio Amplifier. Tone control at neutral settings; gain adjusted to a comfortable audio level. Noise, but not too much 60 Hz buzzing, should be quite apparent.

Recognition of nervous activity

The cockroach nerve cord displays a large amount of "spontaneous" or endogenous activity. Therefore, it will not be necessary to stimulate the preparation to record nerve impulses. Adjust and readjust the gain settings on your preamplifier and oscilloscope until nerve impulses are apparent on the oscilloscope screen and audio loudspeaker. At higher sweep rates of the oscilloscope e.g., 0.5 msec/div, the nerve impulses will look like sine waves. At lower sweep rates, the nerve impulses will look like vertical spikes of many different amplitudes. If 60 Hz noise is a problem, rearrange your leads and check all ground connections. As a last resort, attempt to shield the preparation with a makeshift cover of aluminum foil. Remember that any such shield should be fully grounded, or it will act as an antenna and induce more noise in the setup.

Experiments

Exploration of nervous activity in the ventral nerve cord

Giant Fiber Action Potentials. Obtain an empty polyethylene wash bottle. Hold the nozzle of the wash bottle near your lips and feel the intensity of the air blast produced by squeezing the bottle with different amounts of force and quickness. Choose an intensity you feel would be sufficient to vibrate the long, threadlike hairs you observed on the cerci.

Using both hands, one holding the nozzle near the cerci and the other the bottle itself, stimulate the cerci with *one* brief pulse of air. As you stimulate, observe the oscilloscope trace and attempt to observe the giant fiber spikes. There will be only one or two spikes visible per stimulation, and they may be hard to see the first time. However, they should be quite apparent on the loudspeaker. The giant fiber impulses are of greater amplitude than the endogenous activity and should be recognizable after several stimulations.

Photograph the giant fiber spikes. It would probably be best to enlist help from another student in attempting to photograph the impulses if you have been working alone. You will probably find that it is difficult to capture them on film. If a storage oscilloscope or polygraph is available you may consider using one or the other. A storage oscilloscope is preferable since the polygraph will greatly attenuate the giant fiber spikes.

Examine the giant fiber response. How many spikes are seen in each response? Does the number of spikes vary from stimulation to stimulation? Attempt to observe habituation by increasing the rate of stimulation. Rest the preparation for a few minutes. Now, use air puffs of differing intensity to stimulate. Does the form of the response change by increasing the strength of the stimulus? Try other stimuli, such as table tapping and hand clapping. Do the giant fibers respond well to sound?

Once you are satisfied with your ability to recognize the general form of the giant fiber responses, shield one of the cerci with a sturdy barrier of masking tape. Stimulate with an air puff, directing it so as to minimize the possibility of stimulating the covered cercus. Does the giant fiber response change or disappear with the elimination of half of the afferent sensory input? Now, cut the cercal nerve on the side leading to the uncovered cercus. Wait 3 or 4 minutes before stimulating. Uncover the shielded cercus and stimulate. Interpret the results.

Sensory input

Shift the recording electrodes to the remaining cercal nerve. Since the cercal fibers are considerably smaller than the giant fibers, their action potentials will be smaller in amplitude. Increase the gain of your preamplifier or oscilloscope.

Stimulate the cercus with puffs of air. The discharge in the cercal nerve will be composed of the responses of many hundreds of fibers. Pay particular attention to the duration of this mass discharge in the cercal nerve. How does the duration of the cercal nerve response compare with that of the giant fibers? Consider the large number of cercal fibers in comparison with the limited number of giant fibers. What conclusions can you make concerning the transfer function of the cercal nerve–giant fiber synapses?

Effects of neuroactive agents and insecticides

Rearrange the recording electrodes to pick up endogenous activity and giant fiber responses from the nerve cord. Stimulate the cerci to establish the presence of normal giant fiber responses. If this fails, prepare a new animal.

Note the level of spontaneous activity in the preparation. Unfortunately, it is difficult to quantify this kind of mass activity, but do your best to estimate its intensity. Apply a tiny drop of nicotine solution (1/1,000,000 w/v) to the terminal abdominal ganglion. It is not necessary to desheathe the ganglion. Note any changes which occur in the level of endogenous activity over the next few minutes. (Cigarette smoke and 0.1% ethanol are also good stimulants.) Attempt to observe any changes in the ability of the giant fibers to respond to stimulation of the anal cerci. After you have observed some definite change in the level of endogenous activity, try to reverse the process by washing the ganglion with cockroach perfusion fluid and reabsorbing the wash with a twisted Kimwipe. See the boxed cautionary note that follows. After observing the effects, if any, of washing, apply a small drop of curare solution (1/10,000 w/v) to the terminal ganglion. Does the curare reverse the process initiated by the nicotine? What is the probable cellular effect of curare? Of nicotine? Do you recall that nicotine is an old-time insecticide which was once widely used against pests like aphids?

Also observe the effects of one or more insecticides on the ventral nerve cord preparation. You may wish to use a new preparation for each agent tested. Several agents may be available, including DDT, malathion, or parathion (1/1,000,000 w/v). Try applying DDT to the *cerci*, not to the cord. What is the effect on the giant fibers of strong receptor activity? After your experiments are complete, clean all equipment carefully with soap and water.

Electrical stimulation of the cercal nerve
(at the instructor's option)
You may wish to dissect another cockroach. Arrange the recording electrodes to record giant fiber responses from the ventral nerve cord. Stimulate the cerci to establish the presence of normal giant fiber responses. Arrange a pair of stimulating electrodes in a manipulator so that the cercal nerve can be stimulated electrically. Connect the stimulating electrodes to the output of the stimulator or stimulus isolation unit. Use the following initial settings on your equipment.

Preamplifier. As before for giant fiber recording (see page 207).
Oscilloscope. Time base and vertical sensitivity as before; trigger set on external input and the triggering level control adjusted to trigger the oscilloscope sweep when the stimulator is actuated. Be sure to connect a lead between the trigger output on the stimulator and the synchronous input on the oscilloscope.
Stimulator. Use single stimuli only; delay (if available) of about 1 msec; duration of 0.4 msec; starting voltage of 0.1 V. Ground the stimulator if appropriate.
Audio Amplifier. As before (see page 207).

Stimulate with single pulses only. Start with 0.1 V and gradually increase the voltage until a giant fiber response is observed. In succeeding experiments, use a stimulus voltage about 10% above the minimum voltage necessary to elicit a maximal giant fiber response.

You are now stimulating a set of afferent sensory fibers, while recording from the giant fibers. The properties of the synapses between the cercal and giant fibers can be explored with the preparation. Synaptic adaptation or fatigue can be examined by using different stimulus frequencies or trains of stimulus pulses. The action of different drugs and

pharmacological agents on the cercal nerve–giant fiber synapses can also be examined by applying them to the terminal ganglion. If ionic substitutions (Na^+, K^+, Li^+, etc.) are to be applied, it may be useful to puncture the nerve sheath surrounding the terminal ganglion or desheathe it entirely. Design your own experiment, carefully limiting your goals and providing adequate control procedures.

Pitfalls and Suggestions

1. The crucial part of this exercise is the dissection. It is hard to recognize the nerve cord if you have not seen it before. Dissect methodically, using the microscope, taking the most care when you get near where the nerve cord ought to be found. Do not mistake the tracheae (silvery appearing) for the nerve cord (almost completely transparent).
2. Lack of a response from the nerve cord is often attributable to the electrodes shorting out from touching each other or being immersed in a conducting fluid such as hemolymph or cockroach perfusion fluid. Use of the oil/perfusion fluid mixture will help prevent this problem.
3. Try not to overstimulate the giant fibers. One stimulation per minute should be the maximum.

Materials

Materials needed at each station
Oscilloscope
Stimulator (optional)
Preamplifier
Audio amplifier and loudspeaker (The audio amplifier and loudspeaker might be considered optional, but the instructional effectiveness of the experiment is considerably lessened by omitting them.)
Set of electrical leads and connectors
Faraday cage (if readily available; otherwise probably unnecessary with differential amplification)
Pair of recording electrodes—hooked wire type (See page 336 or modify a standard Harvard hand electrode [no. 304] by replacing the standard palladium electrode wires with finer silver wires [0.25–0.5 mm diameter]. Form the electrode tips into small hooks suitable for picking up the nerve cord. Use a fine pair of needle-nose pliers, and take care not to roughen the metallic surface of the electrode wires

too much. To reduce electrical interference, it will be necessary to shield the Harvard electrode leads with a length of coaxial shielding grounded to the preamplifier input.)

Support for recording electrode (The Harvard electrode holder [no. 331] attached to a small ringstand with a right-angle clamp is suitable. As an alternative, the recording electrode can be taped to a length of rod made of lead attached to a ringstand, or the electrodes can be held in a micromanipulator.)

Ground electrode (Use a clip lead holding a piece of silver wire which can be inserted in the abdomen.)

Pair of stimulating electrodes and support (optional) (See page 336; or the Harvard hand electrode, modified as just described, and the Harvard electrode holder may be used. It is not necessary to shield the leads of the stimulating electrodes.)

Dissecting microscope and illuminator

Dissecting pan or cork plate and insect pins

Small beaker and medicine dropper or Pasteur pipette

Set of dissecting tools (furnished by students)

Materials available in the laboratory

Oscilloscope camera and film

Extra medicine droppers and beakers

Extra insect pins

Microslides of cockroach nerve cord (These may be supplemented with light or electron micrographs and drawings in published sources [e.g., Farley and Milburn, 1969; Pitman, Tweedle, and Cohen, 1973].)

Compound microscope and illuminator

An illustrated guide to cockroach anatomy (e.g., Cameron, 1961)

Dishpan for cleanup, filled with warm, soapy (Liquinox) water

Aluminum foil (for possible use as electrical shielding)

Plastic bag for animal disposal

CO_2 bottle and regulator for anesthesia (optional)

Polyethylene wash bottles for air puff stimuli

Masking tape

Solutions:

 Nicotine solution (2 ml/station; 1/1,000,000 w/v in cockroach perfusion solution)

 Cockroach perfusion solution (50 ml/station)

 Mineral oil saturated with cockroach perfusion so-

lution (50 ml/station; prepared by the method described in experiment 4.2)

Curare solution (2 ml/station; 1/10,000 w/v in cockroach perfusion solution)

Insecticide solution: DDT, malathion, or parathion (2 ml/station; 1/1,000,000 w/v in cockroach perfusion solution)

Take extreme care with these solutions. Do not get them on any of the equipment, including the electrodes. Label or tag all glassware used with these solutions and wash separately from other glassware after use.

Animals

Cockroaches (Obtain 2–3/station/laboratory period.) Any of the larger species of cockroaches will suffice. Choose males if you have a choice. *Periplaneta americana* and *Blaberus* spp. are available from a few biological supply companies. Other species are often available from entomology departments or university laboratories which conduct experiments on insects. One species, *Leucophaea maderae*, is particularly hardy in spite of surgical insult. Crickets can be used. Although they are generally smaller than cockroaches and proportionately harder to dissect, their giant fiber system is well developed. Crickets can be easily obtained from commercial cricket suppliers or local bait shops. Place the cockroaches in a plastic wastebasket or other similar container with the upper walls smeared with petroleum jelly (Vaseline) to prevent escape. Provide them with some vertically standing pieces of cardboard to climb upon. A sponge wetted with water every few days will supply sufficient water. Feed them lab chow or dry dog food. This can be periodically supplemented with apples or other fresh fruit, although it is not necessary unless the cockroaches are to be kept a long time.

Notes for the Instructor

1. Stress careful dissection. Many students will find it necessary to dissect one cockroach for practice before attempting to record. A dissected example would be a very useful demonstration.

2. Do not omit the audio amplifier and loudspeaker. The sound of nerve cells firing adds much to the exercise and, unlike the use of the oscilloscope, gives students a much better feeling for the real-time relationships of the events they are observing.

3. The instructions call for removing the head of the cockroach at the outset of the experiment. The head may be left intact until spontaneous activity is observed, and then removed to determine the effect of the cerebral ganglia on endogenous activity. However, recording from an unanesthetized preparation, even an insect, may raise questions concerning the ethical treatment of experimental animals.

4. After the students get the nerve cord onto the recording electrodes and begin recording, they often forget to keep the preparation moist. Remind them of the drying problem and if they keep forgetting, suggest the use of the mineral oil/perfusion solution mixture as a preventative. Use mineral oil only as a last resort.

5. If any of the neuroactive agents or insecticides are used, guard against their improper use and contamination of the laboratory equipment. It is best to make up only very small amounts of these solutions. This will minimize the amount of accidental spillage and will make disposal less a problem.

6. The cercal nerve–giant fiber synapses are probably cholinergic; hence the use of agents which affect acetylcholine-containing synapses.

7. If you wish to make prepared slides of the cerci, it will be necessary to clear the specimens. Obtain cerci from newly molted insects. This eliminates the need to bleach out the cuticular pigmentation. Fix the cerci for 6 hours in a modified Carnoy-Lebrun fixative (25 ml ethanol + 15 ml glacial acetic acid + 15 ml chloroform + 4.0 g mercuric chloride). Wash in 50–50 ethanol-isopropyl alcohol and dehydrate in ethanolic series (50% to 70% to 80% to 95% to 100% ethanol). Clear in xylol/phenol (3/1 + 1% ethanol), and mount in Hoyer's solution (50 g water + 30 g gum acacia [gum arabic] + 200 g chloral hydrate + 20 g glycerol). The cerci will continue to clear in this mounting medium over a period of time.

Selected References

Boistel, J. 1968. The synaptic transmission and related phenomena in insects. *Adv. Ins. Physiol.* 5: 1–57.

Bullock, T. H., and Horridge, G. A. 1965. *Structure and function in the nervous systems of invertebrates*, vol. 2. W. H. Freeman and Co., San Francisco, pp. 1133–38, 1152–53, 1198–1201.

Cameron, E. 1961. *The cockroach (Periplaneta americana L.).* William Heinemann Medical Books Ltd., London.

Parnas, I., and Dagan, D. 1971. Functional organization of giant axons in the central nervous systems of insects: New aspects. *Adv. Ins. Physiol.* 8: 96–144.

Roeder, K. D. 1967. *Nerve cells and insect behavior.* Harvard University Press, Cambridge, pp. 99–116, 141–75.

RESEARCH REPORTS

Bentley, D. 1975. Single gene cricket mutations: Effects on behavior, sensilla, sensory neurons, and identified interneurons. *Science* 187: 760–64.

Callec, J. J.; Guillet, J. C.; Pichon, Y.; and Boistel, J. 1971. Further studies on synaptic transmission in insects, II. Relations between sensory information and its synaptic integration at the level of a single giant axon in the cockroach. *J. Exp. Biol.* 55: 123–49.

Dagan, D., and Parnas, I. 1970. Giant fibre and small nerve pathways involved in the evasive response of the cockroach, *Periplaneta americana.* *J. Exp. Biol.* 52: 313–24.

Farley, R. D., and Milburn, N. S. 1969. Structure and function of the giant fibre system in the cockroach, *Periplaneta americana.* *J. Insect Physiol.* 15: 457–76.

Milburn, N. S., and Bentley, D. R. 1971. On the dendritic topology and activation of cockroach giant interneurons. *J. Insect Physiol.* 17: 607–23.

Parnas, I.; Spira, M. E.; Wernan, R.; and Bergmann, F. 1969. Nonhomogenous conduction in giant axons of the nerve cord of *Periplaneta americana.* *J. Exp. Biol.* 50: 635–49.

Pichon, Y., and Boistel, J. 1967. Microelectrode study of the resting and action potentials of the cockroach giant axon with special reference to the role played by the nerve sheath. *J. Exp. Biol.* 47: 357–73.

Pitman, R. M.; Tweedle, C. D.; and Cohen, M. J. 1973. The form of nerve cells: Determination by cobalt impregnation. In *Intracellular staining in neurobiology*, ed. S. B. Kater and C. Nicholson. Springer-Verlag, New York, pp. 83–97.

Roeder, K. D. 1948. Organization of the ascending giant fiber system in the cockroach (*Periplaneta americana*). *J. Exp. Biol.* 50: 615–27.

Spira, M.; Parnas, I.; and Bergmann, F. 1969. Organization of the giant axons of the cockroach *Periplaneta americana.* *J. Exp. Biol.* 50: 615–27.

7.2 The Rat Motor Cortex
Somatotopic Representation

SOMATOMOTOR MAP

Introduction

Rationale

To what extent are functions localized in specific regions of the cerebral cortex? Not all the answers to this important question have been discovered yet, particularly those concerning the character of the functional organization. We will approach the problem of *cortical localization* by stimulating an area known to participate in muscle control—the *motor cortex* of the cerebral hemispheres.

Cortical localization

Over the years many claims have been made for and against the localization of function within specific cortical areas. The present understanding is that specific cortical regions exist where the motor system and each major sensory system are predomi-

nately, but not exclusively, located. These areas include the *visual cortex*, the *auditory cortex*, the *somatosensory cortex* (for skin and joint sensation), and the *somatic motor cortex* (fig. 7.2-1).

In this experiment you will analyze cortical motor function by constructing a *topographic* map of the motor area based on electrical stimulation of the cortex and observation of the movements which result. In a *topographic projection* of the body, for example, the body's appearance is distorted as if one distorted a picture on a rubber sheet by stretching the face and head area; the parts stay in the same relationship to each other, but change in relative size. Such a *somatotopic* projection is characteristic of the cortex. Hughlings Jackson (1870) first postulated a somatotopic organization of the CNS motor system after observing epileptic seizures which began in the lips, spread to the face, the arms, and then to the legs—"the march of epilepsy."

Organization of the motor system

Several hundred thousand axons from neurons of the motor cortex and neighboring areas descend to the spinal cord via the *pyramidal tract* visible on the ventral surface of the brainstem. At the *pyramidal decussation* most fibers cross to the opposite side where they ultimately influence the output of interneurons and motor neurons in the spinal cord. Consequently, stimulation of the left motor cortex produces limb movements on the right side of the body and vice versa (contralateral *somatomotor* representation). However, stimulation of the facial area on the cortex can produce both contralateral and ipsilateral movements.

Experiments on the intrinsic organization of the motor cortex suggest that each muscle has its own locus of cortical representation, namely a column of cortical cells which controls contraction. Such columns are about 1 mm in diameter, are normal to the surface of the brain, and run downward through the layers of the cortex (Asanuma, 1975). A similar columnar organization is evident in the somatosensory and visual cortical areas.

An important topic of current research on the motor system is the attempt to determine the functional relationship between cortical and subcortical motor structures, like the cerebellum and corpus striatum (caudate nucleus, putamen, and globus pallidus). The emerging picture is that of cooperation among motor structures; the cerebral cortex is not unequivocally supreme in initiating or organizing body movements. Using single unit recording from chronically implanted monkeys, Evarts (1975) and others have shown that neurons of the cerebellum, globus pallidus, and motor cortex fire in advance of actual movement. It is quite possible that input from *subcortical* motor structures, with participation by *intra*cortical connections, orchestrates the contractions of individual motor columns (and thus muscles) into organized movement.

The rat is suited to cortical mapping because it has a smooth cortex. In the cat and monkey, the cortex is convoluted and some of the motor area lies hidden in sulci. Much of the rat's cortical motor area is devoted to the head and forelimbs, thereby providing an especially delicate muscular control over these areas (fig. 7.2-1). Be aware that electrical stimulation of the motor cortex produces movements which are fragmentary and sometimes jerky because electrical stimulation of the cortex does not duplicate the normal process of activation. You may find several muscles activated simultaneously and often antagonistically.

Time to complete the exercise: This is a long experiment for a 3-hour laboratory period; 4 hours is preferable. The operation will proceed more rapidly on a second rat. Before the laboratory period, read section 9.3.

Procedure

Surgical procedure
Follow the procedures for handling and anesthetizing a rat in section 9.3. Because of the time required to carry out the operation, anesthetize the rat as soon as possible. Cannulate the rat's trachea.

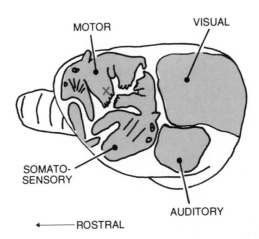

Fig. 7.2-1. Left side of the rat brain, indicating cortical representation of the motor and major sensory systems. The outlines of the rat show a distorted body surface owing to the greater neural representation of the head and forelimbs—a topographic map. Electrical stimulation at point *X* will produce movement of the right (contralateral) forelimb. (Adapted from Woolsey, 1958.)

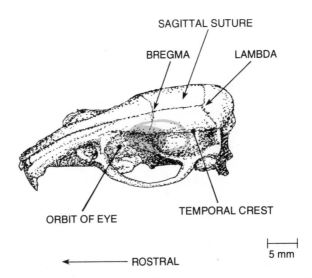

Fig. 7.2-2. View of the left side of the rat skull showing the area overlying the motor cortex (*solid color*) and the region of the skull which will be removed (*colored oval line*) when exposing the motor cortex.

Now turn to section 9.3 page 313, and return to this page only when instructed to do so on page 317.

Turn the rat over so that the top of the skull is facing upward. Check to see that the head is firmly clamped in the headholder fixed to a stand. The top and left side of the head should have been shaved. To expose the skull make a 3 cm rostro-caudal incision in the scalp halfway between the midline of the skull and the left temporal crest. You can feel this ridge with your fingers (fig. 7.2-2). Hold the scalp skin taut with the thumb and forefinger of one hand as you use the scalpel. Do not be concerned about pressing too hard; the skull will protect the brain below. Scrape the periosteum toward the sides and clean and dry the skull with cotton to reveal the suture lines on the top. (Since the periosteum is well innervated, you can expect some moderate reflexive jumping during this process. The animal is nevertheless unconscious and feels nothing. Consult your instructor regarding further anesthetic doses if the animal shows vigorous bilateral reactions.) Identify the sagittal (midline) and coronal sutures and their intersection, the bregma. From the bregma, the coronal suture extends about 6 mm to the temporal crest, at which point the skull slopes abruptly downward. You will need to remove some of the muscle attachments from this vertical surface. Refer to figure 7.2-2 and note the area in solid color representing the motor cortex beneath, and the colored oval line representing the skull area to be removed with a dental drill. Access to the skull surface is facilitated by using two or three small fishhooks, each attached to a 30 cm string. Hold the scalp opening apart with the hooks by anchoring the end of each string to a firm support with a knot or wax. Sand down the skull in the oval region indicated in figure 7.2-2, using a gentle back and forth motion of a rapidly rotating dental bur fixed in the chuck of a dental drill or Dremel Mototool. Keep the drill moving to avoid heating the cortex below. As you thin the skull you must use progressively lighter pressure until the skull is paper thin. Then use fine forceps to tease or tear off the remaining skull layer. Remove the dura mater (heavy outer meningeal membrane) with fine scissors or forceps, avoiding the midline (sagittal) sinus which bleeds profusely.

Do not penetrate into the cortex or damage the delicate surface blood vessels. Use a dissecting microscope to aid in removing the skull remnants and dura. The brain is fragile tissue.

Compare the region of cortex you have exposed with the location of the somatomotor area in figure 7.2-1. Expand the cortical exposure rostrally as necessary to include the face and forepaw area. The motor cortex extends 4–5 mm rostral to the bregma. Check the exposure with a millimeter rule.

When the exposure is completed, adjust the animal so that the top of the skull is tilted about 15 degrees away from you. Suspend the animal by taping its tail to a rod while supporting the thorax with a pad. The contralateral forelimbs and hindlimbs must hang freely where their movements will be obvious when they occur. Flexions are more common than extensions. Some movements may have a *latency* of 3–5 seconds; others may outlast the stimulus (*after discharge*) and end with jerks.

Apply several drops of *warm* mineral oil to the cortical surface. Use mineral oil throughout the experiment to make sure the cortex does not dry out.

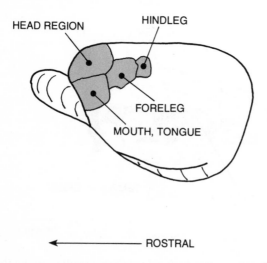

Fig. 7.2-3. View of left side of the rat brain. The motor cortex has been subdivided into four areas based upon a mapping experiment.

Preparing to map the motor cortex

Examine figure 7.2-1 again and note the extraordinary amount of cortical surface devoted to the head region. Point *X* marks a site where electrical stimulation should produce movement of the right forelimb. The somatomotor map is a pictorial way to indicate the location of various motor functions on the cortical surface. The somatomotor map of the cortex can also be plotted in a more basic, and in some ways truer, fashion (fig. 7.2-3).

Several steps are required to obtain such a map from electrical stimulation. First, insert a banana plug into the rat's anus and tape the cable leading from it to the animal's tail. Then set up the micromanipulator with the silver wire electrode such that the manipulator's Z axis is perpendicular to the cortical surface. (If you are unfamiliar with the use of a micromanipulator and vernier, consult page 308.) Do not bend the electrode once it has been arranged and positioned or you will have to readjust the coordinates for the scale drawing in your notebook.

Never hit the cortex with the electrode.
Touch it gently.

Establish a clear unambiguous reference point on the cortical surface. For example, in figure 7.2-4 the small arrow points to a bifurcation of a large blood vessel. With such a reference point, lay out an X, Y coordinate system on a gridded paper in your laboratory notebook. Let each cm in your notebook correspond to 1 mm on the cortex. The coordinates of the reference point and the general size of the exposure allow you to number the X and Y axes appropriately.

Parameters for stimulation

Begin stimulating the cortex with 50 Hz, 1 msec duration, positive square waves at 0.1 V amplitude and no delay. Use the mode switch to stimulate for 3–5 seconds (or set the stimulator for 3–5 second pulse trains). Before you start stimulating, check to see that the electrode is operational by gently placing it on the fleshy area next to the rat's ear. A muscle contraction should be easily elicited by direct stimulation at an appropriate voltage.

Test each point at intervals of 15 seconds, using 4 voltages per decade until a response occurs or the voltage reaches 15 V (e.g., 0.1 V, 0.4 V, 0.7 V, 1 V,

etc.). As you develop a feeling for the threshold voltage which will elicit movement, you can keep the stimulus voltage in that range. At high voltages the current spreads, gross body movements occur, and the map is blurred. Look for *small* movements and remember that most responses will be *contralateral* to the side stimulated. From 2V to 5V is the probable threshold range; as little as a 0.5V change may make a difference.

Mapping

Proceed rostro-caudally across the motor cortex, gently contacting and electrically stimulating every 1 mm as read from the micromanipulator vernier. Examine three or four rows of points. Begin in the foreleg area where responses should be more obvious. Plot each stimulus point on the notebook grid. Tabulate the responses observed. You may also crosshatch the appropriate region on the drawing of the rat (fig. 7.2-5) to show where the movement occurred. Trace the outline of the rat from figure 7.2-5 onto several sheets of paper to avoid confusion when areas of overlap are encountered. The same tracing can be used to indicate the results at several electrode positions on the cortical surface before you

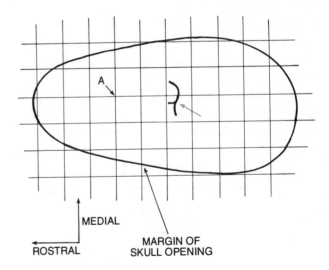

MEDIAL

ROSTRAL

MARGIN OF
SKULL OPENING

Fig. 7.2-4. Example of a scale drawing from a student's notebook showing the exposed region of the left cortex. The *colored arrow* points to a bifurcation in a prominent blood vessel. Point *A* is the site of the first stimulation point tested. Each 1 cm grid line represents 1 mm on the cortex.

begin to fill in another tracing. Blacken in the areas of the most vigorous movement. At each point determine the nature of the movement and the minimal effective voltage (threshold).

If you successfully elicit responses at a number of points, then attempt to reconstruct a composite somatomotor representation (as in figs. 7.2-1 or 7.2-2) based on response location and vigor (or threshold).

Pitfalls and Suggestions

1. Waste no time in anesthetizing the rat. Keep the rat and its cortex at 37°–39°C.
2. As you work with the dental drill, try to thin off the skull *evenly*. Try to develop a smooth back-and-forth motion. A steady light touch is necessary when the bone becomes thin. You can avoid having the drill bit grab the edge of the hole if you taper the edges as you proceed with the thinning process. The whirling drill bit will snag the skin unless you pull the skin away in advance. Use the dissecting microscope during this process. Do not plunge through when drilling.
3. Carefully protect the cortex against drying, damage to its local blood supply, damage by the dental drill, damage by the forceps, or rough use of the electrode. Any or all of these will depress the motor responses. If you are having trouble getting responses, let the cortex rest for 10 minutes and warm the rat with a 60-watt table lamp as necessary. Do not overheat or dry the cortex.
4. If the cortex is tapped with the electrode, a depression in excitability may radiate out from that point (2–3 mm/min) and inactivate the surrounding corti-

cal tissue for several minutes (spreading depression). *Very* slight dimpling is acceptable.
5. If the electrode is too close to the skin of the head, you can expect to see vigorous movements in the vicinity of the eye and ear, owing to direct muscle stimulation.
6. If you are unfamiliar with the use of a micromanipulator and vernier, read section 9.1, page 308.
7. Trauma to the cortex during the exposure is a major cause of failure to obtain a somatomotor map. Remove the dura without tearing the blood vessels which cover the cortical surface.

Materials

Materials needed at each station
Stimulator
Set of electrical leads
Silver wire electrode (0.3–0.5 mm diameter = 27–28 gauge) and holder (see page 336)
Banana plug lead, 1 m in length
Headholder in straight configuration (see page 315 and 339)
Micromanipulator with stand
Stand for rat headholder
Dissecting microscope with boom arm and illuminator
Table lamp with 60-watt bulb to warm the rat and the mineral oil (A gooseneck lamp is best.)
Small beaker with 10–15 ml of warm mineral oil, and medicine dropper
Cannula (2.5 cm length of PE 200 tubing)
Surgical needle (1/2 curved cutting edge)
20 cm surgical thread (black silk, no. 1)
2 small fishhooks, each with 30 cm thread attached

Fig. 7.2-5. Undistorted outline drawings of the right side of a rat. Use to indicate locus of movements produced during cortical stimulation.

Cotton
Set of dissecting tools (furnished by students)

Materials available in the laboratory
Triple-beam balance with pan to weigh rats
Dental drill with no. 8 cutting bur (friction grip, long shaft bur), 2 drills/3–4 stations
Rat cage (1 cage/2 stations)
2-oz rubber bulb aspirator (cutoff disposable 1 cc syringe barrel with 21-gauge blunted needle and 15 cm of PE 60 tubing)
Animal clippers
1-cc disposable hypodermic syringe and 0.75 inch 25-gauge needle
Ketamine (1 cc/station/laboratory period). Vetalar, Parke-Davis; 100 mg/cc.) See page 324, note no. 6. Alternative: sodium pentobarbital (Nembutal, 50 or 60 mg/ml), 50 cc
Tackiwax
Extra fishhooks with 30 cm thread

Animals
Rats 1.33/station/laboratory period (150–250 g females) House the rats in groups of two to eight to maintain docility. Rat pellets and water should be continuously available. Deprive the rats of food 12–24 hours before surgery to obtain more reliable induction of anesthesia with pentobarbital.

Notes for the Instructor

1. Monitor the students to see that they develop the proper technique of thinning the skull with the drill.
2. Students sometimes fail to expose the cortex sufficiently far rostrally.
3. Check to see that the cortex is *gently* contacted by the electrode, and that the electrical connection has really been made.
4. Some of the rat's movements are subtle; the vibrissae may quiver or a limb may gently bend.
5. Cannulation of the rat's trachea will generally prevent ventilation problems in rats with respiratory infections. It is also a useful technique for students to learn which may be applied in subsequent experiments.
6. If any sodium pentobarbital is used, the response will be reduced (higher threshold and less repeatable). Students may test 0.1 cc at the end of the laboratory period.

Selected References

Asanuma, H. 1975. Recent developments in the study of the columnar arrangement of neurons within the motor cortex. *Physiol. Rev.* 55: 143–56.
Evarts, E. V. 1975. Activity of cerebral neurons in relation to movement. In *The nervous system*, vol. 1, ed. D. B. Tower. Raven Press, New York, pp. 221–33.
Jackson, J. H. 1956. *Selected writings of John Hughlings Jackson*, ed. J. Taylor. Basic Books, New York.
Porter, R. 1973. Functions of the mammalian cerebral cortex in movement. In *Progress in neurobiology*, ed. G. A. Kerkut and J. W. Phillips. Pergamon, New York, pp. 1–51.
Woolsey, C. N. 1952. Patterns of localization in sensory and motor areas of the cerebral cortex. In *Biology of mental health and disease*. Paul B. Hoeber, Inc., New York, pp. 193–225.
———. 1958. Organization of somatic sensory and motor areas of the cerebral cortex. In *Biological and biochemical bases of behavior*, ed. H. F. Harlow and C. N. Woolsey. University of Wisconsin Press, Madison, pp. 63–82.

RESEARCH REPORTS
Asanuma, H., and Rosen, I. 1972. Topographical organization of cortical efferent zone projection to distal forelimb muscles in the monkey. *Exp. Brain Res.* 14: 243–56.
———. 1973. Spread of mono- and polysynaptic connections within cat's motor cortex. *Exp. Brain Res.* 16: 507–20.
Hongell, A.; Wallin, G.; and Hagbarth, K. E. 1973. Unit activity connected with movement initiation and arousal situations recorded from the ventrolateral nucleus of the human thalamus. *Acta Neurol. Scand.* 49: 681–98.
Landgren, S.; Phillips, C. G.; and Porter, R. 1962. Minimal synaptic actions of pyramidal impulses on some alpha motoneurones of the baboon's hand and forearm. *J. Physiol.* 161: 91–111.
Sakata, H., and Miyamoto, J. 1968. Topographic relationship between the receptive fields of neurons in the motor cortex and the movements elicited by focal stimulation in freely moving cats. *Japan. J. Physiol.* 18: 489–507.
Woolsey, C. N.; Settlage, P. H.; Meyer, D. R.; Sencer, W.; Hamuy, T. P.; and Travis, A. M. 1950. Patterns of localization in precentral and "supplementary" motor areas and their relationship to the concept of a premotor area. *Assc. Res. Nerv. Ment. Diseases* 30: 238–64.

7.3 Spinal Reflexes
Effects of Surgical Ablation of Higher Nervous Centers in the Frog

limb (see illustration at left). Early experimenters were particularly intrigued by the behavior of decapitated frogs which surprisingly retained the ability to right themselves, to swim, leap, and crawl. Robert Whytt (1751), working with spinal frogs (frogs with only the spinal cord portion of their CNS intact), described the essential outline of a still simpler reflex arc. Whytt showed that the incoming sensory volley initiates motor action without intervention by the brain. This line of research eventually led to Charles Sherrington's (1906) realization that reflex action is one basic form of integrative activity of the nervous system.

In this exercise, keep in mind Sherrington's caveat that the pure, unitary reflex arc is really an abstraction. Spinal reflexes involve both excitation *and* inhibition, and are subject to modification by activities at other levels in the spinal cord and by the

Introduction

Rationale

Spinal reflexes are a form of neural integration. The term *integration* means the coordination of sensory input with ongoing central nervous system (CNS) activity to produce appropriate responses. A spinal reflex, such as the knee-jerk reflex, is an almost totally automatic response controlled by segmental spinal wiring patterns laid down during development. In this experiment we will examine frog spinal reflexes.

The reflex concept has a long history. Descartes (1664) recognized that noxious stimuli were often "reflected" back upon the muscles of the offended

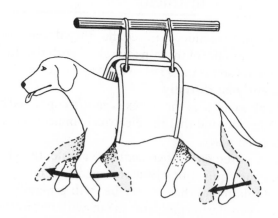

Fig. 7.3-1. Accentuated reflexes in the high spinal dog. The nerve cord was interrupted in the neck region. After several days, spinal reflexes became heightened to the extent that walking movements were elicited by patting the soles of the feet. Walking movements consist of alternated flexion and extension of the legs. Galloping sometimes occurs. (Adapted from A. C. Guyton, 1976.)

governing influences of the brain. In the mammal, in fact, spinal reflexes become "disinhibited" after the spinal cord is surgically separated from the brainstem (fig. 7.3-1), or after decerebration (fig. 7.3-2).

Time to complete the exercise: One 3-hour laboratory period. Additional time will be required if the last two sections are to be completed.

Procedure

Time and experimental animals can be conserved by reading the experiment beforehand and planning for maximum use of any one preparation.

Frogs are specialized for hopping and swimming, but their reflexes are similar to those of other vertebrates, including man. If time permits you may want to familiarize yourself with the anatomy of the hindlegs by consulting a frog dissection guide (e.g., Gilbert, 1965), or by making a brief dissection.

Limb muscles can be grouped in two classes: (1) *flexors*, which decrease the angle of a joint, drawing the limbs toward the body, and (2) *extensors*, which increase joint angle, thereby straightening a limb. Flexors and extensors are *antagonists* since they produce opposite movements of a joint. Useful limb movements occur because the muscles of one group contract together (*synergistically*) while the oppos-

Fig. 7.3-2. Hyperextension (decerebrate rigidity). Transecting the cat's midbrain between the superior and inferior colliculi results in this posture which has been described as "exaggerated standing." The antigravity reflexes which cause extensor contraction become heightened after the inhibitory influence of the cerebrum is removed. The rigidity can be eliminated by sectioning the dorsal roots of the spinal nerves, which eliminates the afferent input from muscle stretch receptors. Decerebrate rigidity thus depends on the tonic stretch reflex. (Adapted from Pollock and Davis, 1930.)

ing muscle group relaxes. This relationship between antagonist muscle groups is called *reciprocal inhibition* and is achieved by nerve connections termed *reciprocal innervation*, which are essential for orderly movement and the maintenance of posture.

Note especially that both extensors and flexors will be affected by a given reflex. Therefore, take care to identify the muscle classes involved in a given reflex and determine the role of each. Also identify the joints involved and the movements produced (flexion, extension, hyperextension, etc.). Determine if the reflex is organized as a sequence of several movements, and note the approximate durations of each stage and the total duration. In addition, for the scratch reflex, flexion reflex, and crossed extensor reflex, determine the location of the receptors involved, their adequate stimuli, and the role of stimulus strength. Take data in tabular form, one table for each section.

Experiments

Operative procedure
Reflexes should first be tested in an undamaged frog in its normal resting position. Then, two kinds of operations will be performed to evaluate the reflex role of major divisions of the central nervous system. After surgical procedures, the frog may be initially examined in the normal position. However, the postoperative frog is most easily tested while suspended in a hanging position with a bent pin inserted through the lower jaw. Test the preoperative frog gently, with minimal handling.

Decerebrate preparation. Anesthetize the frog by placing it in water containing 0.5 g/liter TMS (tricaine). Remove the frog when it no longer responds to gentle prodding. Place the frog on the table and use a sharp scalpel to section the brain. Carefully, with your forearms resting against the table edge for support, cut downward through the skull and brain in the midline at the level of the posterior edge of the eyes. Minimize the size of the wound. Do not cut any farther posteriorly, or the inner ear and its equilibrium organs will be damaged. After operating, wash the frog thoroughly in tap water, avoiding the area of the wound. Staunch any bleeding with cotton. Allow the frog to recover from the anesthetic for 20–30 minutes before testing.

This operation is analogous to a midbrain section in higher vertebrates. In the mammal, midbrain section results in rigid hyperextension of the legs (fig. 7.3-2). Do you obtain a similar result in the frog? How is the decerebrate posture of a frog different from that of a decerebrate cat? How does the normal posture of a frog differ from that of a cat?

High spinal preparation. The influence of the brain on the spinal cord can be totally removed by single pithing the frog (see page 311 for procedure). A pithing needle should be inserted anteriorly through the foramen magnum, and the brain destroyed with a side-to-side motion.

A catalog of reflexes to test
Test the following reflexes successively on normal and either decerebrate or high spinal frogs. *Make a table* of results.

Righting reflex. The righting reflex is just what the name implies. Its most striking illustration is the ability of cats to land consistently on their feet. Turn the frog on its back and observe its actions. Does the frog always turn over toward the same side?

Postural adjustments. Place the frog on a board and test its responses to right and left tipping, and to backward and forward tipping. What part of the animal maintains a constant orientation? Why?

Swimming reflex. Place the frog in an aquarium half filled with tap water and observe the swimming movements. Test in room temperature and 37° C water.

Scratch reflex. Use two kinds of stimuli to elicit the scratch reflex, (1) pricking with a pin or plastic broom bristle, and (2) touching with a small piece of paper towel moistened with 0.5% HCl. Stimulate several areas: nose; middle of the back; belly on right and left; right and left flanks adjacent to the belly; upper thigh; and right and left hind feet. First test with pin pricks, then with the HCl. Always wash off the HCl with a liberal stream of water from a wash bottle immediately after a response is elicited.

You should be impressed by the accuracy of the scratch reflex. The information produced by irritation of the skin must be processed in such a way that the appropriate muscles bring the limb to the irritated spot. The orchestration of this complicated task cannot be totally analyzed with the materials at hand, but we can explore some aspects. Is the

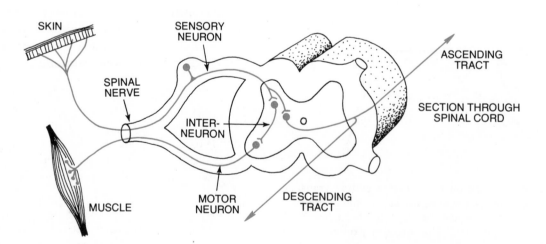

Fig. 7.3-3. Three-neuron reflex. This kind of pathway is involved in simple reflexes such as the flexion (withdrawal) reflex. Noxious stimuli to the skin are conveyed via sensory fibers to interneurons in the spinal cord which excite motor neurons. This diagram is greatly simplified. A real withdrawal reflex involves many neurons in parallel connection, many other interneurons with both excitatory and inhibitory functions, connections to the motor neurons driving synergistic and antagonistic muscles, and inputs to adjacent segments and the brain via ascending and descending tracts.

scratch reflex highly repeatable, or does it vary? Carefully note postoperative changes in the sequence and latency of any subcomponents of the response.

Flexion (withdrawal) reflex (fig. 7.3-3). Stimulate one of the toes on a hindleg of a frog with a firm pinch from a pair of forceps. Do electrical, mechanical (pin or bristle prick), and chemical (HCl) stimuli also elicit the flexion response? Are there any differences in the responses to the different stimuli? To explore the relationship between stimulus strength and response latency and magnitude, use electrical stimulation (10 msec pulses at 0.1 V). Gradually increase the voltage. You may elect to use single stimuli or repetitive stimuli of 20–30 pulses/sec. Would the use of repetitive stimuli energize a more sluggish system? Use an interval of 30–60 seconds between tests to assure recovery.

Crossed extension reflex. Place a hand under one leg of a suspended frog so that the foot is slightly lifted and the knee joint slightly flexed. Elicit the flexion reflex by pinching the other foot with forceps. Carefully feel for extension of the foot supported with your hand. Since the crossed extension reflex is somewhat difficult to observe in frogs, you may have to repeat the test several times. You may also observe the reflex in the forelimbs. What is the value of a crossed extension reflex?

Breathing reflex. Note that breathing in the normal frog involves swallowing air. Does the high spinal preparation retain the breathing reflex? Where are the respiratory centers located?

Corneal (blink) reflex. Lightly touch the cornea of the normal frog. A blink should result. The absence of this reflex is routinely used as proof of brain destruction after single pithing with a needle inserted through the foramen magnum.

Reflexogenous zones of the scratch reflex
(as time permits)
The body surface is divided into zones which are reflexly connected to the four limbs. Irritation in a given reflexogenous zone should activate one of the four limbs which can reach to the area. Use the *high spinal frog* and explore the reflexogenous zones of the four limbs (or just the two on one side if time is limited) by systematically stimulating the body surface with a needle or stiff bristle. Note which limbs respond, and mark the site of stimulation on a sketch of the frog, using a different symbol for each limb. It is probably best to explore one side of the ventral surface of the body first, being sure that test stimuli extend slightly beyond the midline toward the other side. Keep the frog moist and allow 30–60 seconds between stimuli for recovery. You should be able to produce an accurate map of each reflexogenous zone. Be sure to note any zones of overlap. Compare your map with a map produced by another student using a different frog. How similar are they?

Interaction of stimuli
(as time permits)
The interaction of reflex pathways can be demonstrated by simultaneously stimulating both legs of the *high spinal frog* with low intensity stimuli. Prepare a concentration of HCl which produces a response latency of about 3 seconds when applied to the right foot. Also arrange for repetitive electrical stimulation of the left foot at about 30 stimuli/sec and 10 msec duration. Determine the voltages just necessary for a slight response.

Use the following schedule of stimulation. Apply HCl to the right foot and determine the average latency for three to five trials. Then stimulate the left foot electrically with the previously determined suprathreshold voltage. Find the average latency for three to five trials. Retest the right foot with HCl to verify that the latency of the chemical response has not changed.

Now, stimulate both feet simultaneously, the right with HCl, and the left with a suprathreshold voltage. Record the latencies for the right and left feet in several trials. Be sure to thoroughly rinse off the HCl after each trial and to allow about 1 minute for recovery between trials. After experimenting with simultaneous stimuli, return to stimulating one foot at a time in order to confirm that there has been no latency change.

Repeat the same experiment using electrical stimuli just below threshold. Test several times; then try suprathreshold stimuli again. Finish by retesting each foot individually to confirm that there has been no change in latency for separate stimuli. Repeat or modify these experiments until a clear pattern of results emerges. Interpret the results. Attempt to draw a simple neuronal "wiring pattern" (including motor neurons, interneurons, and muscles) which would explain the results.

Tonic stretch reflex and muscle tone
(at the instructor's option)
Vertebrate skeletal muscle is equipped with stretch receptors (muscle spindles) which respond to changes in muscle length. When a muscle begins to relax, it lengthens slightly, exciting its stretch receptors. Stretch receptors also respond when the muscle is lengthened by contraction of antagonist muscles across a joint. Excitation of the stretch receptors is relayed to the motor neurons innervating the muscle, causing muscle tension to increase slightly. This serves three functions: (1) muscle *tone*, a slight amount of continuous contraction, is maintained to keep the muscle in readiness for movement; (2) feedback resistance to stretching when an antagonist muscle contracts has the effect of smoothing or damping the muscle and joint movement; and (3) finally, muscle tension acts as a servomechanism of motor control. (See Guyton, 1976, for a full discussion.)

Decerebrate a frog. Cut away a large portion of the ventral abdominal body wall and remove the intestines. Wash out the abdominal cavity with frog perfusion fluid. Locate the roots of spinal nerves VII–IX which emerge from the base of the spinal column and merge to form the sciatic nerves. Spinal nerves VIII and IX are large and will be readily apparent. Note that the sciatic nerves enter the legs.

Suspend the frog so that the legs hang freely. Feel the consistency of the muscles of the thighs. The muscles have a certain degree of tone, or firmness. Now, cut the roots of one of the sciatic nerves with a pair of fine scissors. Note the response to the stimulation of cutting and any change in leg position. After a minute or so, compare the firmness of the muscles on the right and left legs. Can you detect a difference? What is the origin of the difference? What result would you expect if only the dorsal roots of the spinal nerves were cut, rather than the whole nerves?

Thermal stimuli and adaptation to temperature
(at the instructor's option)
Obtain a new frog and single pith it (see page 311 for

procedure), producing a high spinal preparation. Suspend the frog by the lower jaw and arrange to stimulate one of its feet by dipping the foot into a beaker of water. Always dip the foot to a constant level (for example, to the "heel" of the foot) and apply the stimulus rapidly and smoothly. Record the room temperature and the temperature of the holding container in which the frog was kept.

Stimulation. Start a series of thermal stimulations with water at room temperature and stimulate the foot for 30 seconds every 3–5 minutes, increasing the water temperature 4° C at each step. *Return the foot to a beaker of water at room temperature after each stimulation.* Time the interval between stimulus and response, and note the intensity of the response. Continue to increase the temperature of the stimulating water until the response time reaches a minimal value. Now, reverse the order of the stimuli, working back downward to room temperature. After finishing, compare the two sets of data. Are they identical or have two different strength-response curves resulted? If time permits, you can repeat the experiment using the other foot.

Adaptation. Immerse one leg in 4°–6° C water and the other leg in 24°–26° C water. Allow the legs to hang in the water for 10 minutes before testing. Be sure to maintain constant water temperature for each leg.

Test the responses to a series of different temperatures by quickly raising the legs out of the two baths and dipping them both into a third bath at 15° C. Observe the response latency of each leg. After 30 seconds of stimulation, or responses by both legs, return the legs to their original adapting temperatures. Leave them for 3–5 minutes before retesting. Work upward in 4° C steps as in the previous experiment. Do not exceed 35° C. Compare the strength-response curves of the two differently adapted legs. You may also repeat the experiment, working downward rather than upward, and compare the results with those of the initial tests.

Pitfalls and Suggestions

1. Treat the frogs humanely with a careful, scientific attitude.
2. Remove the frog from the TMS as soon as it is anesthetized.

Materials

Materials needed at each station
Ringstand
Ring or shaft for suspending frogs
Electronic stimulator
Pair of stimulating electrodes
Wash bottle filled with tap water
Anesthetizing pan
Set of dissecting tools (furnished by students)

Materials available in the laboratory
Beakers, 250 and 500 ml
Masking tape
Frog boards
Wash bottles
Pins for use as suspending hooks
Ringstands
String
Stimulating pins or stiff bristles for stimulation
Paper towels
Cotton
Solutions:
  0.5% HCl (0.5–1.0 liter)
  TMS (Tricaine methanesulfonate, Metacaine [0.5
    liter of 0.5g/liter solution/station; buffered to pH
    7–8])

Animals
Frogs, *Rana pipiens* or other species (Order 2 frogs/
  station/laboratory period.) Keep the frogs in a cool
  place and provide them with dripping water.

Notes for the Instructor

1. Students may use too many frogs in this exercise.
Require an outline of proposed experiments and a
statement of the number of animals needed before
beginning.
2. Stiff bristles, if available, are usually more effective than pins in eliciting the scratch reflex. Plastic
broomstraws are very effective.

Selected References

Descartes, R. 1664. *Traite de l'homme*, 1st ed. Paris.
Gilbert, S. G. 1965. *Pictorial anatomy of the frog*, rev. ed.
  University of Washington Press, Seattle.
Guyton, A. C. 1976. *A textbook of medical physiology*,
  5th ed. Saunders, Philadelphia.
Ochs, S. 1965. *Elements of neurophysiology*. John Wiley
  and Sons, New York.
Sherrington, C. S. 1906. *The integrative action of the
  nervous system*. Yale University Press, New Haven.
  (New edition: Yale University Press, 1947.)
Whytt, R. 1751. *An essay on the vital and other involun-
  tary motions of the animal*. Hamilton, Balfour, and
  Neill, London.

RESEARCH REPORTS
Gray, J., and Lissmann, H. W. 1940. Ambulatory reflexes
  in spinal amphibians. *J. Exp. Biol.* 17: 237.
———. 1947. The co-ordination of limb movements in the
  amphibia. *J. Exp. Biol.* 23: 133.
Liddell, E. G. T., and Sherrington, C. S. 1924. Reflexes in
  response to stretch (myotatic reflexes). *Proc. R. Soc. B.*
  96: 267–83.
Pollock, J., and Davis, L. 1930. Reflex activities of a decerebrate animal. *J. Comp. Neurol.* 50: 377–411.
Sherrington, C. S. 1910. Flexion-reflex of the limb, crossed
  extension-reflex and reflex stepping and standing.
  J. Physiol. 40: 28–121.

7.4   Stretch Reflex
Myographic Recording from the Human Leg

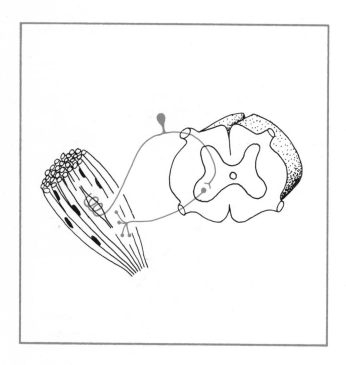

Stretch receptors, which occur in all skeletal muscles, play an especially important role in antigravity reflexes and aid in maintaining muscle tone (constant slight contraction). The importance of the stretch receptors is underscored by the fact that approximately 40% of the axons in nerves innervating skeletal muscles are sensory fibers, primarily from muscle spindles. Of the motor fibers in such nerves, about one-third are *A*-gamma axons innervating the intrafusal muscle fibers of the muscle spindles (For a more complete discussion of stretch reflex functions and muscle spindle morphology consult a physiology or neuroscience text.)

The stretch reflex (also known as the myotatic, tendon, or knee-jerk reflex) is unusual because it is monosynaptic, i.e., sensory axons from the muscle spindles synapse directly with motor neurons; there are no interneurons (fig. 7.4-1). However, this direct pathway is only part of the story. Branches of the sensory axons also spread to adjacent spinal seg-

Introduction

Rationale
Experimentation with the vertebrate stretch reflex is an excellent introduction to the subject of motor control. Consider, for example, the sequence of events which occurs when a person jumps to the floor from a low stool. The extensor muscles of the legs are stretched on landing. This also lengthens the muscle spindles, i.e., specialized stretch receptors arranged in parallel with the muscle fibers. The muscle spindle discharge is conveyed to the central nervous system via fast-conducting *A*-alpha fibers which enter the spinal cord through the dorsal roots and synapse in the anterior horn with motor neurons of the same extensor muscle. The motor neurons trigger contraction (fig. 7.4-1), thereby completing the reflex arc and opposing the force of landing.

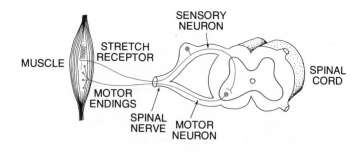

Fig. 7.4-1. A two-neuron stretch reflex. This kind of pathway is involved in the ankle-jerk and knee-jerk reflexes. Stretch of the muscle, induced experimentally by striking the tendon, results in excitation of the stretch receptor. The receptor, in turn, excites spinal motor neurons which produce muscle contraction. Although not shown here, input from stretch receptors also passes to adjacent spinal segments and ascends to the brain.

ments and to the brain. In turn, motor neurons receive facilitatory and inhibitory inputs from many sources. Motor neuron activity at any given moment in time depends on the summation of all excitatory and inhibitory inputs, including those of the muscle spindles.

In combination with other tests, stretch reflexes are employed in clinical neurology. Stretch reflexes may be accentuated, reduced, or abolished by injury or disease, but specific diagnoses can be made only after applying a number of tests. Clinicians distinguish three types of reflexes: *superficial* reflexes (such as the corneal reflex), *visceral* reflexes (such as bladder emptying), and *deep tendon reflexes* (such as the patellar and Achilles tendon reflexes which will be studied in this exercise).

Probably the most intriguing aspect of human reflexes is the progression of changes which takes place during normal development. A number of *newborn* reflexes are present at birth: grasping, sucking, rooting, etc. The newborn reflexes subside as development proceeds and the brain's inhibitory influence increases. New reflexes also appear, become modified or inhibited, and disappear. In a very real sense the developing human passes through a quadrupedal stage (with its attendant reflexes) on the way to becoming a bipedal animal. In adulthood, disease and injury may cause the reappearance of reflexes of an earlier stage of development. For example, stroking the outer margin of a newborn infant's foot will elicit a spreading of the toes and extension of the big toe. This reflex (Babinski's sign) reappears in an adult who has a damaged or diseased corticospinal system and indicates an abnormal decrease in cerebral inhibition of spinal reflex activity. The Babinski sign may also be seen during the early stages of recovery from spinal damage. We suggest that interested students examine an illustrated manual of reflex testing (e.g., Fiorentino, 1972, 1973) or a discussion of clinical analysis (e.g., Curtis, Jacobson, and Marcus, 1972) in order to appreciate better the extent and roles of reflex activity in human posture, locomotion, and development.

Time to complete the exercise: One 3-hour laboratory period. Additional time or a second period may be necessary to complete the last two optional exercises.

Procedure

Stretch reflexes can be elicited experimentally by striking the tendon of a muscle or by electrically stimulating its nerve. We will use both methods of stimulation and record the electrical response of the muscle, rather than the mechanical response, to increase the accuracy of latency measurements.

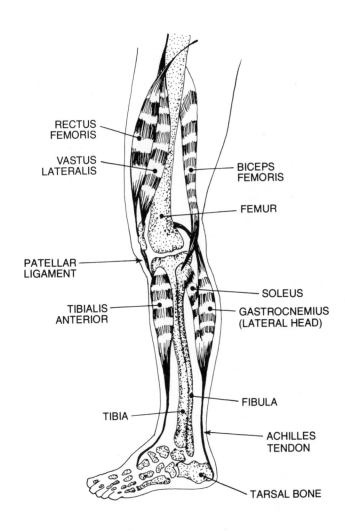

Fig. 7.4-2. Extensors and flexors of the human knee and ankle joints. Stretch reflexes are elicited by striking the patellar tendon or the Achilles tendon. The femoral nerve and spinal segments L_2–L_4 are involved in the patellar tendon reflex. The tibial nerve (a branch of the sciatic) and spinal segments L_5 and S_1, chiefly the latter, are involved in the Achilles tendon reflex. The rectus femoris and vastus lateralis are part of the quadriceps muscle.

Electromyographic recording and reflex time

Obtain a rubber percussion hammer. Seat the subject on the edge of a sturdy table so that the thighs are well supported and the legs are hanging freely. Tap the Achilles tendon with the hammer. The Achilles tendon is located above the heel and connects the gastrocnemius muscle to the tarsal bone of the foot (fig. 7.4-2). A few trials should produce a consistent reflexive contraction of the gastrocnemius. The downward movement of the foot is *plantar flexion*. The opposite, upward motion is *dorsiflexion*. Which muscles are involved in plantar flexion and dorsiflexion of the ankle joint?

Place two surface electrodes 8–10 cm apart over the belly of the gastrocnemius muscle (actually the gastrocnemius-soleus muscle complex). Place a ground electrode on the upper part of the ankle of the same leg. Use a light coating of electrically conducting electrode paste between the skin and the electrodes. Use *shielded cables* to connect the recording electrodes to the input of your oscilloscope. Use *differential input* if available; otherwise connect one of the recording leads to the ground terminal on the oscilloscope. Connect the ground electrode to the ground terminal on the oscilloscope or to the shield of the recording electrode leads (fig. 7.4-3).

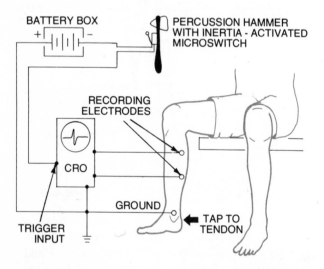

Fig. 7.4-3. Arrangement for recording from the gastrocnemius muscle. Striking the Achilles tendon with the percussion hammer elicits the stretch reflex and starts the oscilloscope sweep. The electrical activity of the muscle is displayed on the oscilloscope. It is important to use differential amplification and shielded cables.

Ask the subject to move the foot up and down, alternating plantar flexion and dorsiflexion. Set the horizontal sweep to automatic with a sweep speed of 0.5 sec/div. Switch to AC coupling on the vertical amplifier and set the band-pass filter, if present, to −3dB at 10 Hz (lower cutoff) and 3 kHz (upper cutoff). Increase the vertical gain to about 1.0 mV/div or more, until a response is seen every time the subject contracts the gastrocnemius muscle. The response is an *electromyogram* or *EMG*. The electromyogram is the summated electrical activity (action potentials) of the thousands of muscle fibers which make up the gastrocnemius. If 60 Hz pickup is a problem, rearrange the recording and ground leads to minimize it.

Use a percussion hammer with an inertia-activated switch. Connect one cable from the switch to the battery and another from the switch to the horizontal trigger input of the oscilloscope. Connect another cable from the output of the battery box to the ground terminal. Switch the trigger mode switch to external triggering. Adjust the triggering level control to trigger the oscilloscope sweep only when the hammer is lightly tapped against a solid object. Set the sweep speed to 10 msec/div.

Tap the Achilles tendon to elicit the stretch reflex while recording the electromyogram. Readjust the sweep speed to obtain the best display. Measure the *reflex time* by determining the period between the beginning of the sweep (when the hammer struck the tendon) and the onset of electrical activity in the muscle. Measure the reflex time in 10 trials, using the same tapping force. Is the reflex time constant? What is the average reflex time?

Perform additional tests, using differing amounts of force. Does the reflex time change? Why or why not? Measure the distance between the muscle belly (widest part of the muscle) and the presumed site of the sensory-motor synapse in the spinal cord. Assume that synaptic transmission takes about 0.5 msec, but remember that even though the stretch reflex is labeled a *monosynaptic* reflex, the pathway measured with this technique includes the neuromuscular synapse as well. Calculate the mean conduction rate in the nerves making up the reflex pathway. How would you design an animal experiment to measure the reflex time more precisely?

Patellar tendon (knee-jerk) reflex

Seat the subject on a sturdy table with the thighs well supported and the legs swinging freely. Place a pair of electrodes about 10 cm apart on the quadriceps muscles on the front of the thigh (fig. 7.4-2). Transfer the ground electrode to the knee. Feel the position of the patellar tendon just beneath the kneecap. Place one hand on the patella and use the other hand with the hammer to gently strike the tendon to elicit the stretch reflex. Observe the electromyogram. Measure the reflex time in 10 trials and compare this average with the average obtained for the Achilles tendon reflex. What are the possible sources of difference?

Study the effects of varying the amount of tension in the muscle by voluntary contraction on the part of the subject. Can the reflex be inhibited or enhanced in this manner? Ask the subject to lock the fingers of his two hands, one against the other, in front of his chest and pull outward at the moment the hammer strikes the patellar tendon (Jendrassik's maneuver). Is the reflex facilitated by this method? Does isometric contraction elsewhere facilitate the reflex? Speculate on the mechanism of enhancement. What synaptic inputs influence spinal motor neurons other than the excitatory input of the stretch receptors?

Electrical stimulation of the Achilles tendon reflex
(at the instructor's option)
The stretch reflex can also be elicited by direct electrical stimulation of afferent sensory fibers. In humans this is often referred to as the *H-reflex*. We will stimulate the tibial nerve through the skin at the knee, which will produce a reflexive contraction of the gastrocnemius muscle.

Recording arrangement. Place recording electrodes on the gastrocnemius muscle and a ground electrode on the foot as in figure 7.4-3. Adjust the vertical gain until a response is seen as before. Connect a triggering lead from the trigger output on the electronic stimulator to the trigger input of the oscilloscope time base. Connect a ground lead between the oscilloscope and stimulator. Set the sweep speed to 10 msec/div and switch the time base to external triggering. Reduce the stimulator voltage to its lowest possible value. Actuate the stimulator and adjust the triggering level control so that a single sweep is

triggered for each stimulus pulse. Turn the stimulator output off.

Stimulating arrangement. Tape a plate electrode just above the front of the subject's knee, using a thin film of electrode paste between the skin and the electrode. Connect this electrode to the positive output of the stimulator with an appropriate lead. Obtain a ball electrode with an insulated handle. Connect this stimulating electrode to the negative output of the stimulator, and coat the ball with a thin film of electrode paste.

Set the stimulator to give monophasic square wave stimuli at 1 pulse/sec and 0.6 msec duration. The subject should grasp the *insulated* part of the stimulating electrode and apply the ball to the hollow at the back of the knee in the midline (the popliteal fossa). The tibial nerve passes through the knee beneath this point. Stimulate at 1 pulse/sec while gradually increasing the stimulus voltage.

The subject should control both the stimulus voltage and the site of stimulation.

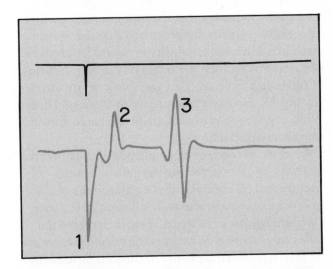

Fig. 7.4-4. Response of the gastrocnemius muscle to direct electrical stimulation of the tibial nerve. The peak in the *upper trace* is a stimulus marker which indicates the application of a 0.5 msec stimulus to the tibial nerve. The *lower trace* shows the stimulus artifact (*1*); the response of the muscle to direct stimulation of the motor neurons in the tibial nerve (*2*); and the reflexive response of the muscle elicited by stimulating the sensory fibers of the tibial nerve (*3*). Approximately 30 msec elapsed between the stimulus and the onset of the reflexive response.

Probe in different areas with the stimulating electrode while gradually increasing the voltage to 30–40 V and watching the oscilloscope screen for a reflexive response. The subject should expect to feel discomfort as the stimulating current passes through the skin. The first wave on the oscilloscope screen will be the stimulus artifact. A second wave will follow very closely or be combined with the stimulus artifact. This is the response of the muscle to direct stimulation of the *motor* fibers in the tibial nerve and is *not* a reflexive response. Look for a third wave with a latency of 25–35 msec (fig. 7.4-4). This will be the reflexive response initiated by stimulation of the sensory fibers of the tibial nerve. Readjust the gain and sweep speed to obtain the best display.

In some subjects the amplitude of the reflexive response will be larger than the response to direct stimulation. Are the magnitudes of the direct and reflexive responses linearly related to the stimulus voltage? Why might the reflexive response disappear at stimulus voltages strong enough to stimulate the motor axons?

Stimulate with increasing frequency up to 5 pulses/sec. Does the response diminish? At frequencies above 5 pulses/sec the response may decline. This indicates that the motor neurons which have reflexively discharged are in a period of inexcitability. Such inexcitability is caused by pre- and postsynaptic factors, including recurrent inhibition of the motor neurons. Can you think of any other reasons for motor neuron unresponsiveness? Hint: What happens to muscle spindle discharge during muscle contraction?

Attempt to change the amplitude of the reflexive response by (1) contracting the gastrocnemius slightly and (2) contracting the antagonists of the gastrocnemius to produce dorsiflexion of the foot. Does antagonist activity increase or decrease the reflexive response? What was the effect of synergistic activity? Illustrate your conclusions by drawing a nerve-muscle wiring diagram summarizing the probable factors at work in this system.

Reciprocal action of antagonistic muscles
(at the instructor's option)

Electromyography will be used to observe the action of two antagonistic muscles of the ankle joint—the gastrocnemius and the tibialis anterior. Contraction of the gastrocnemius produces plantar flexion of the foot, whereas contraction of the tibialis anterior results in dorsiflexion. A dual-trace oscilloscope or a polygraph will be necessary to record the electrical activity of both muscles simultaneously.

Recording arrangement. Place two recording electrodes over the belly of the gastrocnemius muscle and a ground electrode just above the ankle joint, as in figure 7.4-3. Connect these electrodes to one of the vertical amplifier inputs of one channel of a dual-trace oscilloscope using shielded cables. Use the differential mode and AC coupling.

A second pair of recording electrodes must be placed over the anterior tibialis muscle, located just lateral to the tibia in the upper part of the lower leg. Feel the subject's tibia (shinbone) at the front of the lower leg. Place your fingers 2 cm lateral to the margin of the tibia about 8–12 cm below the kneecap. Ask the subject to point the toes inward (supinating or inverting the foot) and dorsiflect the foot. You should be able to feel and see the contraction of the anterior tibialis muscle beneath the skin. Place a pair of recording electrodes over the belly of the anterior tibialis muscle and connect them to the sec-

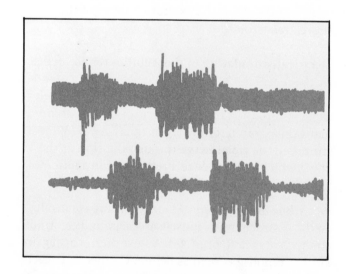

Fig. 7.4-5. Responses of the gastrocnemius muscle (*upper trace*) and the anterior tibialis muscle (*lower trace*) in a subject standing erect and rocking back and forth. Note the reciprocal firing of the two antagonistic muscles. The gastrocnemius contracts as the subject leans forward, and the tibialis anterior contracts as the subject leans backward. The upper trace is unfiltered, while the lower trace is limited to a band-pass of 0.1–10 kHz to limit noise and AC pickup.

ond channel of the dual-trace oscilloscope using shielded cables. Use differential mode and AC coupling.

Set the sweep speed of the time base to 1 sec/div and the triggering mode to automatic. Adjust the gain of both vertical amplifiers to about 1 mV/div. If frequency filters are available on the vertical amplifiers, limit the band-pass filter to lower the noise level (e.g., lower −3dB cutoff at 10 Hz and the upper −3dB cutoff at 3 kHz). If 60 Hz AC pickup is a problem, rearrange the leads, check the ground connection to the ankle, and make sure that electrode paste was used with every electrode. Ask the subject to alternate plantar flexion of the foot with dorsiflexion. Adjust the gain to get the best display of the electromyogram of each muscle.

Observation of reciprocal action. The subject should stand erect, placing more weight on the leg with the recording electrodes than on the other leg. When the subject rocks backward and forward, alternating contraction of the gastrocnemius and anterior tibialis muscles should be apparent (fig. 7.4-5). Notice that although one muscle may predominate, the other muscle may also be somewhat active. Ask the subject to stand on one foot. Co-contraction of

antagonists as observed here is necessary to stabilize joints against twisting and slipping. Joint stabilization is particularly important in leg and postural muscles which contribute to the bipedal locomotion in the human. The joints are mechanically stabilized when motionless. Stretch reflexes help to maintain balance (fig. 7.4-6). Can you detect muscle activity in a relaxed standing posture?

Within the limits of cable length and the introduction of movement artifacts you can explore the action of the ankle flexors. What happens, for example, when the subject stretches upward or squats? What other locomotory activities require the coordination of antagonists? How are such activities related to the stretch reflex studied in the first three sections of this exercise?

Multiple-joint and multiple-action muscles
(at the instructor's option)
It is easy to record from the biceps and triceps muscles of the upper arm. These antagonistic muscles are involved in a number of different movements and involve more than one joint. Explore their functions using electromyography. What is the effect of loading (increased resistance) on the electromyogram?

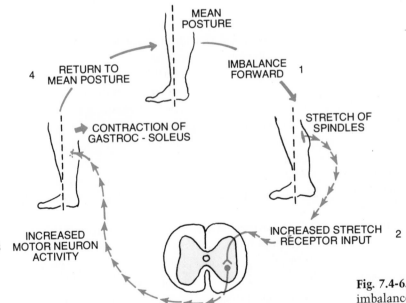

Fig. 7.4-6. Balance maintenance and the stretch reflex. An imbalance forward activates the spindles of the gastrocnemius and soleus muscles. Their activation is relayed to the motor neurons, and the muscles contract and balance is restored.

Pitfalls and Suggestions

1. In this exercise an electronic stimulator is used to stimulate a human subject. *Take care to stimulate only the leg.* If the subject touches the ball electrode with the hand, a current will pass between the hand and the other stimulating electrode on the leg, a circuit which includes the torso and the heart.

2. Prior study of the stretch reflex and reciprocal innervation in a textbook of physiology or neuroscience will make the exercise more rewarding.

3. After the experiments are completed, wash *all* electrode paste off the legs and electrodes. Electrode paste left on the skin may cause itching.

Materials

Materials needed at each station

Oscilloscope or polygraph (A dual-trace oscilloscope or polygraph is needed to perform the section on the reciprocal action of antagonistic muscles.)

Preamplifier (optional if the oscilloscope vertical amplifier sensitivity goes to 1.0 mV/div)

5 surface electrodes with attaching straps (plate electrodes, such as Harvard no. 321 or Grass no. E4).

Set of connectors and cables (Shielded coaxial cables are mandatory to suppress 60 Hz AC pickup.)

Ball-tipped stimulating electrode with insulated handle. (This is most easily made up from a phone plug. Solder a single conductor insulated lead to the tab attached to the phone plug tip, and round the tip to a ball with a file. See fig. 2.2-8E for an illustration of a phone plug.)

Percussion hammer

Percussion hammer with inertia-activated switch. (Make this up by adding a spring-loaded microswitch, e.g., Microswitch Co. series 311SM with roller lever, to the upper part of the handle. Tape the switch onto the handle after attaching a two-conductor cable to the switch. Weight the arm on the switch with a blob of solder. Arrange the switch to be activated by the inertia of the solder when the hammer is struck against a solid object.)

Battery box (Make this up by placing a 1.5 V flashlight cell in a minibox and adding binding posts and/or banana jacks. The battery is necessary to provide a triggering voltage which is actuated by the percussion hammer switch. If a battery is used without enclosing it in a minibox, solder the leads securely to the battery terminals.)

Materials available in the laboratory

Tape measure

Oscilloscope camera and film

Electrode paste

Masking tape (used to attach surface electrodes; do not use adhesive tape which is painful to pull off)

Extra cables and connectors

1 spare percussion hammer with inertia-activated switch

Notes for the Instructor

1. Safety and subject comfort should be the paramount concern of the instructor. Before the laboratory period, check all electrical equipment. Each AC-powered unit should be provided with a properly grounded three-prong power cord. Do not use equipment with any hint of malfunction. The intermittent square-wave output of the electronic stimulator is relatively innocuous, but AC line current is very dangerous, and every precaution should be taken to prevent exposure to it. Remove all unessential AC-powered equipment and metal objects. Do not use metal tables. Subjects should *not* ground themselves by touching a grounded cage or wire with their hands. Ground the leg only, as directed.

2. The stimulating electrodes will sting, especially the cathode. Discomfort can be minimized by using enough electrode paste and a smooth ball-shaped cathode. A pointed cathode will produce a high current density and attendant irritation. Current density is inversely proportional to electrode area. Long-term stimulation will lead to hyperemia at both electrodes, but more at the cathode. Bony and fatty areas should be avoided because they present more resistance and increase discomfort.

3. Time permitting, a motion picture of human reflexes is a useful adjunct.

4. We suggest that a polygraph not be used. Since high paper speeds are necessary, much wastage will occur.

5. The position suggested for the Achilles tendon reflex (legs hanging freely) is not ideal. There are two alternative positions: (1) the subject kneels on a padded table with the knee joint at a 90° angle and the feet hanging over the edge of the table; and (2) the subject reclines on his side on a padded table with one leg straight and the other leg bent at the knee and lying across the straight leg. In the second posi-

tion the tendon of the crossed leg is struck. Both positions require a padded surface and more room than may be available in many labs.

6. Your students may occasionally observe muscle action potentials (MAPS) between EMG responses. These are active, single *motor units*, not single muscle cells. The EMG is the asynchronous discharge of potentials from multiple motor units.

Selected References

Chusid, J. G., and McDonald, J. J. 1973. *Correlative neuroanatomy*, 15th ed. Lange Med. Pub., Los Altos, Calif.

Curtis, B. A.; Jacobson, S.; and Marcus, E. M. 1972. *An introduction to the neurosciences*. W. B. Saunders, Philadelphia.

Fiorentino, M. R. 1972. *Normal and abnormal development: The influence of primitive reflexes on motor development*. Charles C Thomas, Springfield, Ill. (Well-illustrated, showing normal newborn reflexes and aberrant patterns of development.)

———. 1973. *Reflex testing methods for evaluating C.N.S. development*. Charles C Thomas, Springfield, Ill. (Well-illustrated, showing reflex patterns in children.)

Ochs, S. 1965. *Elements of neurophysiology*. John Wiley and Sons, New York.

Willis, W. D., Jr., and Grossman, R. G. 1977. *Medical neurobiology: Neuroanatomical and neurophysiological principles basic to clinical neuroscience*. C. V. Mosby, St. Louis.

7.5 Somatosensory Representation in the Rat Medulla
Electrophysiological Activity in Spinal Trigeminal, Cuneate, and Gracile Nuclei

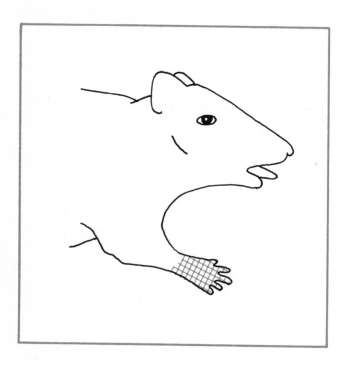

Introduction

Rationale
The processing of sensory information may be explored by electrophysiological recording from sensory relay nuclei. The receptive field and response properties of individual cells can be determined, and the topographic organization of the nucleus can be mapped.

Many cutaneous tactile sensory axons from the hindlimbs, trunk, and forelimbs travel in the dorsal columns of the spinal cord to cells of the gracile and cuneate nuclei (dorsal column nuclei) in the medulla. Trigeminal nerve innervation of the mouth area and skin of the head projects more laterally in the medulla to the spinal nucleus of the trigeminal nerve (Vth cranial nerve). Tactile information from

such cells is passed via the medial lemniscus to the thalamus and then to the somatosensory cortex of the cerebrum. Figure 7.5-1 represents a cross section of a rat's medulla on which an upside-down body with exaggerated paws and a greatly enlarged, inverted, and medially facing head is drawn. This is a simple somatotopic map showing the sites of termination of cutaneous sensory axons from different parts of the body. At other cross-sectional levels of the medulla, a similar map would be obtained.

The form of the somatotopic arrangement of the dorsal column nuclei has a straightforward explanation. At each higher segment of the spinal cord, new sensory axons are added to the *lateral* margin of the dorsal columns. Thus, at the level of the upper cord and medulla the most lateral fibers arise from the upper trunk and forelimbs. Cells of the laterally situated cuneate nucleus are responsive to tactile stimulation of the forelimbs; the more medial gracile cells are responsive to stimulation of the hindlimbs.

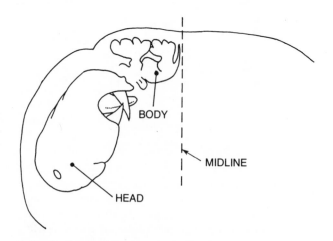

Fig. 7.5-1. Somatotopic representation of the left side of a rat's body shown in a cross section through the medulla. (Adapted from Nord, 1967.)

Figure 7.5-1 is an idealized representation of the projection of the body surface in the medulla. Figure 7.5-2, derived from a single experiment, indicates in more detail the histological features in cross section and the regions of the skin represented in four electrode tracks which penetrated into the sensory relay nuclei.

Use both figures to aid your search for the skin region which activates a cell recorded at a given electrode position. The objective will be to record extracellularly the action potentials of single somatosensory neurons with a microelectrode. The physiological properties of the neuron will be evaluated and the size and location of its receptive field marked on an appropriate diagram.

Although we simplify matters here, you should be aware that the gracile and cuneate nuclei receive input from at least two spinal pathways and from both primary and secondary afferent fibers (receptors

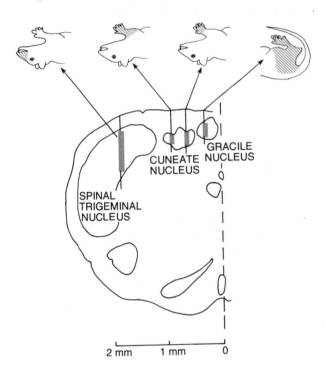

Fig. 7.5-2. Schematic drawing of the left half of a cross section through the rat medulla. The rectangular areas on each of the four electrode tracks indicate the location of cells responsive to cutaneous stimulation. The sites where stimulation was effective in eliciting a response are indicated by *shading* on the corresponding figurines *above*. Level of section: 1 mm caudal to the obex (see fig. 7.5-4). (Adapted from Nord, 1967.)

and second-order neurons). Moreover, there are descending influences on these neurons as well. The trigeminal nerve provides massive sensory input from the head region to three different nuclei in the medulla, but we will examine only the spinal nucleus (caudal portion) of the trigeminal nerve. There are no responses to nociceptive (pain) or thermal stimulation in cells of the dorsal column nuclei.

Time to complete the exercise: One laboratory period to obtain a few responses. Two periods for a more thorough analysis. Before the laboratory period, read section 9.3.

Procedure

Anesthetizing the rat
Proceed without delay to anesthetize the rat. You will have at least 15–30 minutes after the injection when you should review the section on tracheal cannulation. Turn to section 9.3 for instructions on anesthetizing and cannulating the trachea of the rat. Return to this experiment when directed to do so in section 9.3.

Turn to section 9.3, page 313.

Exposing the medulla
With the headholder attached to a rigid stand, tilt the rat's head forward so the nose is down (see fig. 7.5-3). The opening of the curved cannula should be unobstructed.

Stretch the scalp skin enough so that you have resistance to cut against. Press firmly with a scalpel to make a 3 cm midline incision in the scalp extending from the posterior part of the skull down the back of the neck. A no. 15 blade is ideal. The medulla lies somewhat unprotected between the occipital condyle and the first vertebra (atlas). Consequently, it will be necessary only to remove the overlying muscles and the flexible membranes joining the cranium with the spinal column. Figure 7.5-3 shows how to expose the medulla. Feel the occipital crest at the back of the skull at the top of the occipital bone. Remove the muscles attached to this bone. Spread the muscles laterally, two at a time, by dividing the superficial muscles along the midline with a scalpel. You must cut the muscle attachments free from the occipital bone. Repeat this process until you have diverted the three or four layers of muscle to the sides. Now use cotton to remove blood from the area. The secret of this dissection is to work up against the occipital bone. Clean it off. You should be able to dissect down to the opaque membranous tent attached to the occipital condyle—about 6 mm below the occipital crest.

Obtain your finest forceps which are sharpened to meet at the tips. Then, while looking through a microscope, seize a portion of the membrane attached to the occipital condyle. Carefully tear it back toward the vertebra. As the peeling-off process continues you will note that the last layers are transparent. Before you break through to the cerebrospinal fluid and the white medulla below, be sure that major bleeding has stopped from the surrounding tissue. This precaution will keep the medulla free of hemorrhaged blood. Refer to figure 7.5-4 for a drawing of the portion of the floor of the IVth ventricle and medulla, which should be visible. With the utmost care remove from the surface of the medulla any membranes which lie above the blood supply.

Do not damage the blood vessels.

Make careful note of the position of the obex. With an electrode you will explore the accessible region rostral to the obex and 2 mm caudal to the obex. Spend a few moments observing the pulsations of both the blood vessels and the entire medulla.

Setting up the recording equipment
Set up a micromanipulator with the electrode holder directed vertically downward, i.e., perpendicular to the surface of the medulla. If you are unfamiliar with the use of a vernier scale, consult pages 308–10.

Clip a minigator lead to the skin at the wound margin as a reference electrode. Ground the head-holder.

Connect leads from the active and reference electrodes to the input to the preamplifier. Turn on the preamplifier and the oscilloscope. Connect the output of the preamplifier to the oscilloscope input. Connect an audio amplifier and loudspeaker to the accessory output on the back of the oscilloscope, or if no accessory output is available, split the preamplifier output so that it drives both the audio amplifier and the oscilloscope. Use the following initial settings on your equipment.

Preamplifier. Input in differential mode if possible; gain of 100–1,000×; band-pass filters (if available)

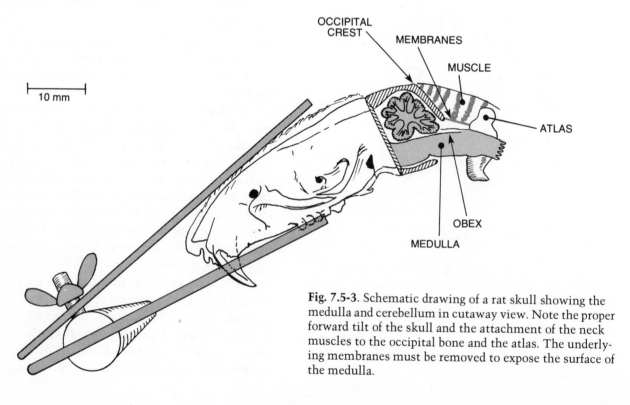

Fig. 7.5-3. Schematic drawing of a rat skull showing the medulla and cerebellum in cutaway view. Note the proper forward tilt of the skull and the attachment of the neck muscles to the occipital bone and the atlas. The underlying membranes must be removed to expose the surface of the medulla.

234

set at about 30 Hz (low frequency filter) and 3 kHz (high frequency filter).

Oscilloscope. Time base at 5 msec/div; vertical sensitivity at 0.1–0.01 V/div; trigger level control set on automatic or free run.

Calibration. Adjust the preamplifier and oscilloscope vertical gain to give a total *system gain* of approximately 100 μV/div. Check with the preamplifier calibrator, if available.

Audio Amplifier. Set the tone control to midrange and adjust the gain until a slight hum is heard. Once recording starts, readjust the gain so that action potentials are clearly audible but not offensive to those around you.

Leave all AC-powered equipment on while other arrangements are completed.

Recording Procedure

Never touch or hit the tip of the microelectrode.

Making a penetration

Place a suitable microelectrode in the electrode holder. Position the electrode over the obex and then move the electrode 1 mm caudally. Refer to figure 7.5-2, representing a section taken 1.0 mm caudal to the obex, and determine how far off the midline you would need to be to penetrate the nucleus gracilis. *The medullary somatosensory projections are all ipsilateral (same side).* Since it is probably easier for you to stimulate the side of the body nearest you, plan to explore that side of the medulla. Move the electrode accordingly.

Adjust the lighting (light from the side may help) so that you can see the electrode as you carefully lower it toward the surface of the medulla. If there are residual membranes on the surface of the medulla, it will make penetration difficult and the surface of the medulla may dimple.

Use the finest drive on the micromanipulator when you attempt to penetrate the medulla.

Penetrate the medulla. Note the scale markings or the number of millimeters per revolution, e.g., 0.25 mm, or the scale markings on the fine vertical drive to tell the approximate depth of the electrode tip.

Interpreting the electrical activity

If you find that 60 Hz interference is present, unplug or remove the microscope illuminator. (The microelectrode must be in contact with the medulla to eliminate 60 Hz.) Check or rearrange your ground connections if 60 Hz persists. These neurons are generally spontaneously active and this is an aid in locating them with the microelectrode. Many small action potentials of different sizes mean that the electrode tip is probably large, while little background activity would suggest that the tip is small. Multi-unit activity is perfectly suitable for an initial survey. Rub or stroke the appropriate skin regions to see the action potential discharge. (Actually, it is far easier to hear them over the audio monitor.) If some spikes get larger as you slowly advance the electrode, it means you are approaching one or more cells. If you get quite close to a single cell, its spikes should be larger than the others and should be of

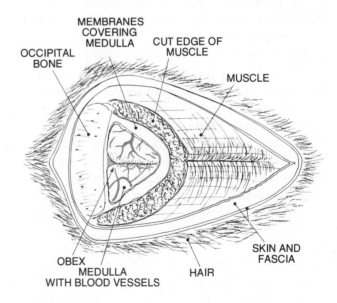

Fig. 7.5-4. View of the medulla through dissecting microscope. The obex is the tip of the "pen point" where the floor of the IVth ventricle rises to the top of the medulla. The obex will extend just barely caudal to the intact occipital bone. Any membrane remaining attached to the occipital bone may have to be reflected with forceps before the obex is seen.

uniform size. Inevitably, as you advance the electrode you will penetrate the cell membrane of some neurons or glia and a brief, screamlike crescendo of impulses will result. The electrode you use will not record intracellularly because of its relatively large size, and because the heartbeat and respiratory cycle produce movements and pulsations of the medulla which destroy neurons impaled by the electrode tip. Stop the advance of the electrode when you can clearly see action potentials. Then locate the receptive field on the body surface and test its properties.

It is important that you do not jar or bump the table or the animal. This can easily cause the electrode to move and kill cells.

Be sure to thoroughly check the forepaws. The receptive fields in the forepaws and on the head (spinal V nucleus) can be quite small and easily missed if you do not systematically touch and rub these body regions.

Mapping and defining unit responses
Locate the receptive field and record its size and position on a drawing of the animal (fig. 7.5-5). Record also the position coordinates of the microelectrode (anteroposterior, mediolateral, dorsoventral).

Determine as many physiological properties of each neuron as you can. For example, is the neuron fast or slow adapting? Does the direction of hair movement make a difference? Will it respond to steady skin displacement? (Is your hand really steady?) Is there an inhibitory "surround" which depresses the response or spontaneous activity?

Map some of the somatosensory projections. Continue to lower the electrode until you pass through the somatosensory nucleus being explored. Then, withdraw the electrode with the fine drive and lower it in a more lateral position. When you have explored the medulla at a level 1.0 mm caudal to the obex, move as close to the level of the obex as you can. Are the same body areas represented at this level?

If your microelectrode is resolving the activity of single neurons, concentrate on their properties. If you are recording multi-unit discharges, attempt to map the somatotopic representation at one level. In this case, move the electrode down into the substance of the medulla by 0.1 mm steps until the touch responses can no longer be elicited, rather than move the electrode down until one or a few single neuron discharges are evident.

At the end of the experiment, check with your instructor before sacrificing the animal with an overdose of sodium pentobarbital (0.5 cc) or an intracardiac injection of 1 cc of 3 M KCl.

Pitfalls and Suggestions

1. The membranes attached to the occipital bone are tough, but after the initial ones are peeled off they become more delicate. Adjust your movements and dissection technique accordingly. Try to prevent any bleeding onto the surface of the medulla; it makes the region much more difficult to see.
2. Recording with a microelectrode is a delicate business. You must learn to move slowly and deliberately. Microelectrodes are expensive. Maintaining their quality is the key to experimental success. Learn to use the fine control of the micromanipulator. For each new penetration you must look at the electrode to see that it is actually penetrating the medulla.

Fig. 7.5-5. Outline drawings of the rat. Copy to indicate receptive field locations.

3. You may record large spikes deep in the medulla which are spontaneously active but cannot be driven by sensory stimulation. These are probably in the reticular formation.

4. Pulsations of the medulla may make it difficult to "hold" a single neuron for more than a minute. Pulsations can be reduced somewhat by optimizing the elevation of the body and the tilt of the head before recording. Check this while looking through the microscope.

5. If you are unfamiliar with the operation of a micromanipulator and vernier, consult page 308.

Materials

Materials needed at each station
Oscilloscope
Preamplifier
Audio monitor
Set of electrical leads
Dissecting microscope with a boom arm and illuminator
Micromanipulator
Reference electrode (shielded minigator clip lead, 1 m in length)
Recording electrode holder
Microelectrode
2 stands and 2 right-angle clamps
Headholder in right-angle configuration (see pages 315 and 339)
50-cc beaker of mammalian perfusion solution
Glass (not metal) probe for stimulating skin
Cotton
Tracheal cannula (2.5 cm length of PE 200 tubing, heated into a curve)
Surgical needle (1/2 curved cutting edge)
20 cm surgical thread (black silk, no. 1)
60-watt table lamp to keep the rat warm (Gooseneck is best.)
Set of dissecting tools (furnished by students)

Materials available in the laboratory
Oscilloscope camera and film
Animal scale or triple-beam balance with a cut off plastic gallon jug to contain the animal
Work gloves
Rubber tube for artificial respiration
2-oz rubber bulb aspirator (cutoff disposable 1-cc syringe barrel with 21-gauge blunted needle and 15 cm of PE 60 tubing)
Animal clippers
1-cc disposable hypodermic syringe and 0.75-inch 25-gauge needle
Solutions:
Mammalian perfusion fluid (100 ml/station)
Sodium pentobarbital (Nembutal) (50 or 60 mg/ml) 50 cc

Animals
Rats 1.33/station/laboratory period (200–250 g females) House the rats in groups of two to eight to maintain docility. Rat pellets and water should be continuously available. Food deprive the rats 12–24 hours before the surgery to obtain more reliable induction of anesthesia.

Notes for the Instructor

1. Tungsten microelectrodes have the advantage of being easily visible (F. Haer, Co. 0.005-inch shank diameter, fine-tip profile, 25 μm exposed tip. If not special ordered, they should be cut off to a length of about 2 cm or less, the butt end scraped free of insulation and held in a suitable electrode holder [see page 336].) Glass micropipettes of 2–10 μm diameter will work, but the students have difficulty seeing them against the bright white medulla. A 50 μm enamelled nichrome or stainless steel wire is suitable for multi-unit recording. It should be short enough to remain rigid during penetration. The wire can be cut on a slant with scissors (not wire cutters), and the butt end scraped for insertion into an electrode holder. Keep the microelectrodes in a safe place until students are ready and have been provided with appropriate cautions.

2. Although single-unit responses are perhaps ideal, multi- or few-unit discharges are initially just as informative and rewarding for the student and considerably easier to obtain and maintain. The topographic representation is easier to ascertain.

3. An electromechanical tapping device, such as a toothpick glued to a small speaker cone (see experiment 6.2) is an interesting way to map out receptive fields and to determine latencies and following rates.

4. The tilt of the head may occlude the cannula opening unless the PE tubing has been curved. Heat

it in hot water, bend into a suitable arc, e.g., the arc of a 4 cm diameter circle, and cool in that position.

Selected References

Iggo, A. 1974. Cutaneous receptors. In *The peripheral nervous system*, ed. J. I. Hubbard. Plenum Press, New York and London, pp. 347–404.

———, ed. 1973. Somatosensory system. In *Handbook of sensory physiology*, vol. 2. Springer-Verlag, New York.

Lynn, B. 1975. Somatosensory receptors and their CNS connections. In *Annual review of physiology*, ed. J. H. Comroe, Jr. Annual Reviews, Inc., Palo Alto, Calif. 37: 105–27.

RESEARCH REPORTS

Johnson, J. I., Jr.; Welker, W. I.; and Pubols, B. H., Jr. 1968. Somatotopic organization of raccoon dorsal column nuclei. *J. Comp. Neurol.* 132: 1–44.

Millar, J.; Basbaum, A. I.; and Wall, P. D. 1976. Restructuring of the somatotopic map and appearance of abnormal neuronal activity in the gracile nucleus after partial deafferentation. *Exp. Neurol.* 50: 658–72.

Mosso, J. A., and Kruger, L. 1973. Receptor categories represented in spinal trigeminal nucleus caudalis. *J. Neurophysiol.* 36: 472–88.

Nord, S. G. 1967. Somatotopic organization in the spinal trigeminal nucleus, the dorsal column nuclei and related structures in the rat. *J. Comp. Neurol.* 130: 343–56.

———. 1968. Receptor field characteristics of single cells in the rat spinal trigeminal complex. *Exp. Neurol.* 21: 236–43.

Shipley, M. T. 1974. Response characteristics of single units in the rat's trigeminal nuclei to vibrissa displacements. *J. Neurophysiol.* 37: 73–90.

7.6   Frog Optic Tectum
Retinal Processing of Visual Form

Introduction

Rationale

Frogs depend on vision for the essential behavior of feeding. Their visual processes are attuned to detect the movements of small objects the size of insects and small invertebrates. When an object of suitable size enters the visual field of a hungry frog, the frog usually strikes with the mouth or tongue, but only after a noticeably long interval and sometimes after reorientation of the body. Ganglion cells in the frog retina and interneurons of the optic lobe (tectum) in the brain are highly responsive to specific features of the visual environment, e.g., dark buglike targets. This system demonstrates well the processing of sensory input.

What *are* the important features in a frog's visual field? Frogs strike only at *moving* targets of small

size. A larger moving object elicits no response or an escape reaction. If a form has no movement, it is behaviorally less meaningful. A frog may starve in the presence of freshly killed, but motionless, insects. Frogs, therefore, detect prey objects by differentiating on the basis of several criteria: movement, a certain size, contrast, and, perhaps, color since the frog has cones in the retina (Maturana, Lettvin, McCulloch, and Pitts, 1960).

Retinal processing

The retina contains photoreceptors and many interneurons. In the frog the retina carries the task of discrimination to an advanced stage. The retinal output cells are the ganglion cells whose axons project via the optic nerve to higher levels of the brain. In mammals, most of these axons go to the lateral geniculate body of the thalamus, which projects to the cerebral cortex for further processing. Many ganglion cell axons also project to the superior colliculi (tectal homologue) of the midbrain. In amphibians, most of the ganglion cells project to the optic tectum (optic lobes) located in the midbrain, but there are also other nontectal target nuclei, and among them a geniculate body. You will record responses of retinal axons in the tectum using microelectrodes. The optic nerves of the frog are almost fully crossed; that is, the visual input from the left eye goes to the right tectum, and the input of the right eye to the left tectum (fig. 7.6-1). For this reason, you must record from the tectum contralateral to (on the opposite side of) the stimulated eye.

Receptive fields

Each retinal ganglion cell reports on events within only a small area of the total visual field of the eye. This area is the *receptive field* of that ganglion cell. Ganglion cells, however, are not like small areas of film in a camera which only report light levels in that area. Instead, they can signal target size, movement, the presence and form of light-dark boundaries, etc. They are "feature detectors." The retinal ganglion cells of most vertebrates (except some amphibians, pigeons, and rabbits) have simply patterned receptive fields. Each receptive field consists of a circular center which produces either an "on response" or an "off response" to light, and a surrounding annulus ("surround") which produces a response opposite to the center. Some cells may be more complex in their requirements, needing, for example, an edge or line in the receptive field before responding.

The retinal ganglion cells of the frog are more specific in their requirements for stimulation than other vertebrates. Apparently the frog relies on earlier (more peripheral) processing of visual input. Its retina is highly specific for a few "trigger features" of the visual field, but ignores almost all others. Other vertebrates, by contrast, have ganglion cells which retain more information which is then analyzed in detail at higher levels in the central nervous system. Some differences between the frog and most other vertebrates are attributable to its insectivorous feeding habits.

At least five major classes of ganglion cells have been demonstrated in the frog. These feature detectors are:

1. *Sustained edge detectors*. These neurons have a receptive field which covers 1°–3° of the visual field. They fire a burst of impulses to movement of a light or dark edge, and continue to produce a low frequency, sustained response ("muttering") when the edge is stationary.
2. *Convex edge detectors*. These neurons respond to any small dark object moving within their field of 2°–5°. The response is maximal for spots of 1° moving across a light or patterned background.
3. *Changing contrast detectors*. These neurons have larger fields of 7°–12° and respond to a light or dark edge moving across the field.
4. *Dimming detectors*. These neurons have very large fields of up to 15°. They give a sustained response to darkening or to movement of a dark edge into their field.
5. *Dark detectors*. These neurons have large fields and produce a continuous stream of impulses whose frequency changes inversely with the light level.

Since each ganglion cell type has its own layer of terminations, the optic tectum, you may be able to record from axonal tufts with similar responses. You are unlikely to detect the more complicated responses of the intrinsic neurons of the tectum. Do not expect to record from most of the units just described. This information is presented to outline the range of possible responses you may observe, and to indicate the level of specificity single neurons possess.

Time to complete the exercise: One 3-hour laboratory period is necessary to acquaint students with the dissection and the recording setup and to obtain initial recordings. A second 3-hour period is necessary to adequately map receptive fields and response characteristics of a representative group of neurons.

Procedure

Description of electrodes and methods of stimulation

Tungsten microelectrodes with platinized exposed tips of 25 μm are recommended. Extreme care must be taken while handling the electrodes because even the slightest touch to the tip will likely bend it and make it useless for recording. Attend to your instructor's comments on microelectrodes and how to employ them.

A microscope illuminator may be used as a source of diffuse light for initial experiments with a piece of cardboard as a simple shutter. More carefully controlled stimuli will be needed for mapping the visual fields of tectal neurons. Make up a series of white cards, approximately 15 × 15 cm with one of the following figures at the center of each card: (1) a black dot 1 cm in diameter, (2) a black dot 3 cm in diameter, and (3) a black rectangle 0.5 × 5 cm. Also make up a black card with a white rectangle 0.5 × 5 cm. For stimulating, a card may be placed in the visual field of the appropriate eye and moved about to give the appearance of movement to the target at the center of the card. A penlight with the bulb taped to give a pinhole light source against a dark background can also be used as a stimulus.

Electronic instrumentation

Mount a tungsten microelectrode (insulated except at the tip) on the microelectrode holder attached to a

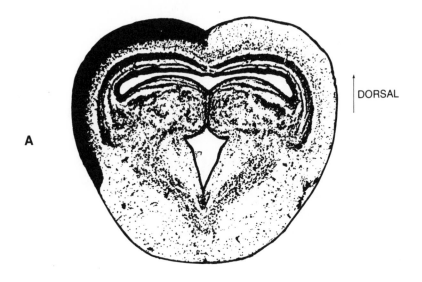

DORSAL

A

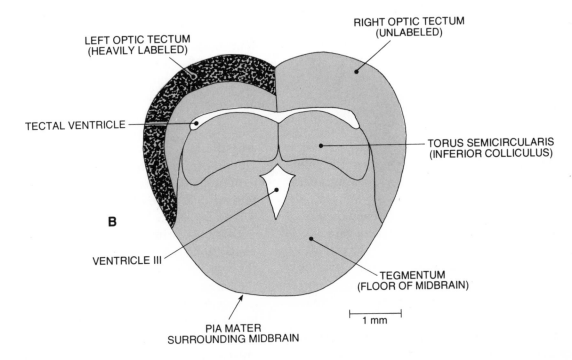

LEFT OPTIC TECTUM
(HEAVILY LABELED)

RIGHT OPTIC TECTUM
(UNLABELED)

TECTAL VENTRICLE

TORUS SEMICIRCULARIS
(INFERIOR COLLICULUS)

B

VENTRICLE III

TEGMENTUM
(FLOOR OF MIDBRAIN)

1 mm

PIA MATER
SURROUNDING MIDBRAIN

Fig. 7.6-1. Radioautograph of the toad midbrain showing heavy radioactive labeling in the left optic tectum. Tritiated proline, injected into the right eyeball, was incorporated into protein by retinal ganglion cells. Twenty-four hours later when the brain was removed, some of the protein had moved along the ganglion cell axons via axoplasmic transport to the axonal terminations in the superficial layers of the optic tectum. **A**. High contrast photograph of a Nissl-stained section through the midbrain showing a heavy coating of *black* (silver grains), indicating labeling of the left tectum. **B**. Schematic drawing illustrating the major regions of the midbrain and radioactive region of the left optic tectum. The other *dark areas* and *black spots* visible in *A* are cell nuclei, not an indication of labeling. The amphibian visual system is entirely crossed and the radiolabel injected into the right eye has appeared in the left optic tectum. (Section and photo courtesy of T. J. Neary.)

micromanipulator. Position the micromanipulator so that the electrode can be moved up and down with the fine drive (fig. 7.6-2).

Do not bend the microelectrode into a fishhook. One touch of the tip and it may be ruined.

Connect the cable from the microelectrode carrier to the input of the preamplifier. Connect the indifferent electrode (a pin soldered to a connecting wire) to the second preamplifier input. Connect a third, a ground electrode (another pin or clip lead), to the ground terminal on the preamplifier input.

Connect the preamplifier output to the vertical amplifier input of the oscilloscope. Connect an audio amplifier and loudspeaker to the accessory output on the back of the oscilloscope, or if no accessory output is available, split the preamplifier output so that it drives both the audio amplifier and the oscilloscope. Use the following initial settings on your equipment.

Preamplifier. Input in differential mode if possible; gain of 100–1,000×; band-pass filters (if available) set at about 10 Hz (low frequency filter) and 3 kHz (high frequency filter).
Oscilloscope. Time base at 20 msec/div; vertical sensitivity set at 0.1–0.01 V/div; trigger set on internal and the triggering level control set on automatic or free run.
Calibration. Adjust the preamplifier and oscilloscope vertical gain to give a total system gain of approximately 10 μV/div. Check with the preamplifier calibrator if available.
Audio Amplifier. Set the tone control to midrange and adjust the gain until a slight hum is heard. Once recording starts, readjust the gain so that action potentials are clearly audible but not offensive to those around you. The audio amplifier will be of more use than the oscilloscope in this experiment.

Leave all AC-powered equipment on while other arrangements are completed. Make any additional ground connections necessary to minimize 60 Hz pickup once the electrode is touching the brain. Remove any unnecessary AC-powered equipment from the vicinity. The microscope illuminator used as a

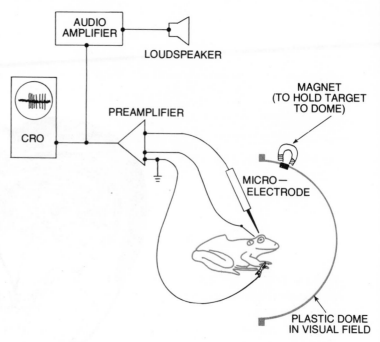

Fig. 7.6-2. Recording and stimulating arrangement. In the most elegant method, a plastic dome is placed in the frog's visual field to aid in mapping the receptive fields of tectal neurons. A magnetic target is moved about the inner surface of a white dome with an external magnet. A clear dome could also be used, and the receptive fields mapped directly onto the dome with a marking pen.

stimulator should be positioned for minimum 60 Hz interference, yet allow for good illumination.

Anesthesia

Obtain the largest frog available. Let it sit in water containing 0.5 g/liter TMS (tricaine) anesthetic. Obtain a 1.0-cc disposable hypodermic syringe and a 0.75 inch, 23–25-gauge disposable needle. Fill it with tubocurarine chloride (3 mg/cc), and inject 0.04 cc/10 gm body weight into the dorsal lymph sac of the frog.

Observe the frog every minute or so after injecting. Remove it from the TMS solution when it no longer responds to prodding or pinching from behind. The frog will be anesthetized by TMS and its muscles paralyzed by curare. During the course of the experiment, periodically observe the frog for respiratory or eye movements. During recording you should cover the frog with paper towels saturated with a weaker solution of TMS (0.05 g/liter) to ensure continued anesthesia. If the frog begins to revive (which is very unlikely) inject 0.05 cc curare solution and bathe it in 0.5 g/liter TMS solution until responses are no longer observed.

Too much TMS may weaken the tectal responses or kill the frog.

Exposing the optic tectum

The optic lobes of the frog brain are located inside the skull almost exactly between the tympanic membranes in the midline. Examine figure 7.6-3 for orientation. The objective is to cut a window in the skull (not nearly as large as that in figure 7.6-3) to expose the optic lobes. The skull is cartilaginous and can be cut or shaved through with some effort. It presents the major obstacle to a good dissection. To ensure a proper dissection obtain a *new* scalpel blade of the smallest size available (e.g., no. 12), or a new double-edged razor blade with one side protected with masking tape.

Place the frog on a frog board. Hold the upper jaw immobile with an alligator clip attached to a sturdy stand.

Remove a square patch of skin over the area between the two tympanic membranes. After the skin has been removed, carefully incise a longitudinal 0.5×1.0 cm rectangle in the skull. Gradually cut through the skull using as little force as possible.

Operate carefully and slowly. Time spent in the dissection will pay dividends later. Use your other hand to support the fingers holding the scalpel.

The brain lies in a cavity within the skull and should sink into the cranial cavity once a small amount of air is admitted. Continue the incising process until the square piece of skull can be removed without resistance. There are large blood vessels just lateral to the area being removed. Shave off the lateral margin of the opening in the skull sparingly, only enough necessary for the exposure.

When the skull has been opened, look for the optic lobes. They are pigmented and should appear very rounded and definitely lobelike (fig. 7.6-3). Blot any seepage of blood with a small swatch of cotton whorled around the tips of a pair of fine forceps. It is likely that when the piece of skull is removed, the *pineal gland* will be damaged or pulled away. It is attached to the diencephalon through a small stalk which should be visible even though the gland has been removed.

Touch the surface of one of the optic lobes to discover its consistency.

Be careful. Use a blunt probe, preferably a glass rod drawn out and fire-polished to produce a small, globular 1 mm tip.

The surface of the optic lobes, as in all vertebrate brains, is covered with a series of layers called *meninges*. There are two such layers in the frog: the *dura mater* and the *pia mater*. The outer layer, the dura mater, should be removed with fine forceps. It is clear and contains some of the black chromatophores. Remaining membranes on the surface of the optic lobes may have to be parted with watchmaker's forceps to admit the microelectrode. Defer this. Use care and operate under the dissecting microscope. Keep the preparation moist.

Recording Procedure

Place the frog in a large petri dish with some TMS (0.05 g/liter), and place a wetted towel over the body.

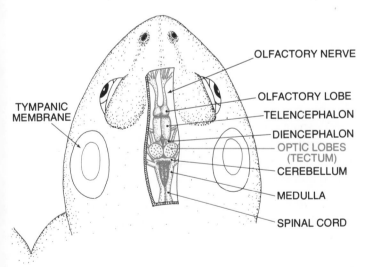

Fig. 7.6-3. Frog head and brain. A strip of skin and skull has been removed to demonstrate the location of the parts of the brain. The membrane covering the optic lobes is pigmented. The optic lobes are the target of microelectrode recording in this exercise, and *only they* should be surgically exposed for recording, not the whole brain as illustrated here.

OLFACTORY NERVE
OLFACTORY LOBE
TELENCEPHALON
DIENCEPHALON
OPTIC LOBES (TECTUM)
CEREBELLUM
MEDULLA
SPINAL CORD
TYMPANIC MEMBRANE

Do not touch or wet the tectum. Move the frog and dish to the recording site and position it so that you can stimulate the eye *contralateral* to the lobe where you intend to record. Since most of the optic nerve fibers cross over completely in the frog, it is necessary to record from the side opposite the eye being stimulated. The eye to be stimulated should have an uncluttered visual field which is easily accessible to the experimenter. Hold the head rigid.

Place a small ball of cotton in the frog's mouth to cause the eyes to bulge out and elevate the brain. Insert the indifferent electrode into tissue near the recording site. Connect the ground electrode to a front limb. Arrange the geometry of the setup so that the microelectrode can be lowered onto the surface of the optic lobe of choice. Turn on the microscope illuminator and preamplifier, and slowly lower the electrode to the surface of the optic lobe. Its angle of entry should be roughly perpendicular to the surface of the lobe at the point of contact. When the electrode contacts the surface, advance it very slowly, occasionally tapping the micromanipulator along the axis of the microelectrode until the electrode penetrates into the tectum. If the surface is substantially depressed, you should tease the surface membranes slightly with a sharp probe (avoid this unless absolutely necessary). Difficulty in inserting the electrode may indicate that the tip is blunt or bent.

After penetration, adjust the gain of the system so that noise is apparent in the oscilloscope trace (1 cm wide) and over the loudspeaker. By moving your hand all about in front of the contralateral eye at various distances from the eye, attempt to elicit a neuronal response. Even if the electrode is in the most superficial layers of the optic lobe, its tip should be near some visual neurons. Slowly advance the electrode (or withdraw if it seems you have gone too far) until responses are seen and heard. The receptive field will approximate a cone, ever expanding outward from the eye. Readjust the system for optimal display and minimal 60 Hz interference. Also test with the microscope illuminator for on and off responses by using a piece of cardboard as a shutter.

Most recordings will be *multi-unit recordings*. That is, impulses from several neurons will generally be recorded at the same time. But sometimes, one unit in particular will stand out. Probe around to get units which can be easily distinguished by larger spike height. You will undoubtedly find it easier to characterize the tectal neurons by their *sound* over the audio amplifier than the spikes seen on the oscilloscope. Create your own scale of audible burst intensity. A table is probably the best way to record data on a series of neurons.

Experiments

At this point take a moment to reflect on the nature of the receptive field of a single, visual neuron. Single neurons generally pick out very specific features of a small area in the retina's total visual field. We suggest that you arrange specific tests in a set order to discover the stimulus requirements of each neuron you encounter—the trigger feature. Consider these possible variables in the stimulus:

a. movement

b. orientation and direction of movement (e.g., movement of a line or dot laterally, vertically, and at intermediate angles)

c. rate of movement

d. size of target (e.g., 1 cm vs. 3 cm dots at the same distance)

e. shape of target (e.g., dot vs. rectangle vs. edge)

Other stimulus variables can be tested, e.g., degree of contrast, optimal size, but it is probably wisest to limit the variety of tests unless a particularly strong-responding or interesting neuron is encountered. You should also note the characteristics of each neuron's response as you test with different stimuli.

Size of receptive field. A rough estimate can be easily obtained. Does the receptive field extend only a few degrees across the retina's visual field? Across one third of the total visual field? Across all of the visual field? (It may help to know that the sun or moon subtend 0.5° of visual angle.)

Temporal pattern of excitatory response. Does the neuron produce only short bursts of impulses when the target is moved? Or, does it keep responding ("muttering") for awhile after movement stops? What is the duration of the tonic response? Does it vary?

The following are suggestions for appropriate experiments.

Characterization of different response patterns
Can you demonstrate some of the response classes

described in the "Introduction?" Do you agree with this classification? Are "on" responses to diffuse illumination present? Are "off" responses present? What is the time course of such responses? Can you demonstrate units which respond to movements of the dark targets on the white cards? What kind of orientation and motion specificity do the units display? What is the time course of their responses?

Mapping

Can you map the extent of the visual field of selected neurons? This is best done using a transparent plastic dome spanning the eye's visual field (fig. 7.6-1). If a dome is available, mark the receptive fields of a series of tectal neurons directly onto the dome with a grease pencil as you experiment. Mark each receptive field with a code number in your laboratory notebook keyed to the description of the neuron's response.

Spatial distribution of neurons in the tectum

Are there different kinds of neurons at different locations and depths within the optic lobe? Can you measure the depth of the layer which produces visual responses?

When you are through recording, sacrifice the animal by destroying its brain with a pithing needle.

Pitfalls and Suggestions

1. Take care in dissecting.
2. Treat the microelectrodes gently. They are fragile and expensive.
3. Keep the preparation moist during the experiment. A layer of mineral oil saturated with amphibian perfusion fluid spread over the surface of the brain will retard desiccation.
4. It is important to be able to look through the microscope as you lower the electrode. Drive the electrode in from an angle, if necessary.
5. Frogs with small pupils and low velocity of cells in the tectal blood vessels are not likely to give responses.

Materials

Materials needed at each station
Oscilloscope
Preamplifier

Audio amplifier and loudspeaker
Cables and connectors (1 set)
Dissecting microscope and illuminator
Micromanipulator and microelectrode carrier
Metal microelectrode (Commercial tungsten microelectrodes plated with platinum black are good [e.g., F. Haer no. B-2-10-1 or B-2-10-2]. A 25 μm exposed tip or impedances of 1 kohm to 1 megohm are appropriate.)
Indifferent electrode (an insect pin soldered to a lead)
Ground electrode (another insect pin electrode or a clip lead)
Plastic dome (optional, for mapping tectal units, obtainable from plastics or building suppliers)
Dissecting tools (furnished by students)

Materials available in the laboratory
Oscilloscope camera and film
Extra cables and connectors
White and black posterboard
Rubber cement or transparent tape
Penlights or flashlights
Masking tape
1-cc disposable hypodermic syringes and disposable 23–25-gauge needles
Cotton
Grease pencils or water-soluble marking pens
Plastic bag (for animal disposal)
Solutions:
Amphibian perfusion solution (100 ml/station)
Mineral oil saturated with amphibian perfusion solution (20 ml/station)
TMS (tricaine methanesulfonate, Metacaine [1 liter of 0.5 g/liter and 1 liter of 0.05 g/liter buffered to pH 7–8])
Curare (d-tubocurarine chloride in saline solution 3 mg [20 units]/cc; 1 cc/station)

Animals
Frogs, *Rana pipiens*, or other species (Order 1 frog/station/laboratory period.) Keep the frogs in a cool place and provide them with dripping water.

Notes for the Instructor

1. A careful dissection is essential.
2. Researchers usually employ glass pipettes filled with a low melting point alloy (Wood's metal) for this kind of procedure. Commercial tungsten mi-

croelectrodes plated with platinum black are probably easiest to use in the student laboratory. The 25 μm exposed tip and 1 k to 1 megohm impedance may vary with little effect on the results. Smaller tips and higher impedances are more likely to produce single-unit recordings, but more "silent" areas will be encountered. Multi-unit recording will be the rule. If the tungsten electrode is shortened to < 2 cm by cutting off the butt end, it will vibrate less. Electrode fragility is the bane of this experiment, since a few careless students can damage several electrodes. Dispense one electrode at a time with a stern warning about its fragility and cost. Cut and mount the terminal 2 cm of the electrode in an electrode holder (see page 336). The cut end must be scraped free of insulation.

3. A 24-inch dome intended as a transparent skylight or window can be obtained for $50–$60 from most local plastic or building suppliers. Such domes have flanges to facilitate mounting.

4. Many experimenters prefer to use goldfish for tectal recording because its skull is easier to open. It also bleeds less because the systemic blood pressure of fish is very low. The goldfish has large unpigmented optic lobes located in the head at the level of the edges of the opercular flaps. They may be easily recognized because they angle outward toward the caudal end of the brain and are separated by a striated cross-connecting tract which assumes a triangular shape with the angle of the optic lobes. The disadvantage of the goldfish is the necessity to perfuse the gills with a tube in the mouth supplying a constant stream of cool aerated water. An aerated reservoir may be placed above the goldfish for supply, and a catchment underneath to retain the water for recycling.

Anesthetize the goldfish initially by immersion in 0.2–0.5 g/liter TMS in pond water. Maintain anesthesia during recording by perfusing with 0.1–0.2 g/liter TMS in pond water. Goldfish would be well suited to an extended individual project.

Selected References

Brindley, G. S. 1970. *Physiology of the retina and visual pathway.* Williams and Wilkins, New York.

Crescitelli, F., ed. 1973. *Central processing of visual information.* A. *The visual system in education: Vertebrates. Handbook of sensory physiology,* vol. 7, part 5. Springer-Verlag, New York.

Horridge, G. A. 1968. *Interneurons.* W. H. Freeman and Co., San Francisco, pp. 244–87.

Ingle, D., and Sprague, J. M. 1975. Sensorimotor function of the midbrain tectum. *Neurosci. Res. Program Bull.* 13(2):169–288.

Jung, R., ed. 1973a. *Central processing of visual information.* A. *Integrative functions and comparative data. Handbook of sensory physiology,* vol. 7, part 3. Springer-Verlag, New York.

———., ed. 1973b. *Central processing of visual information.* B. *Visual centers in the brain. Handbook of sensory physiology,* vol. 7, part 3. Springer-Verlag, New York.

RESEARCH REPORTS

Biersner, R., and Melzak, R. 1966. Approach-avoidance responses to visual stimuli in frogs. *Exp. Neurol.* 15:418–24.

Gaze, R. M. 1958. The representation of the retina on the optic lobe of the frog. *Quart. J. Exp. Physiol.* 43:209–14.

Ingle, D. 1968. Visual releasers of prey-catching behavior in frogs and toads. *Brain Behav. Evol.* 1: 500–518.

Jacobson, M., and Gaze, R. M. 1964. Types of visual response in the optic tectum and optic nerve of the goldfish. *Quart. J. Exp. Physiol.* 49: 199–209.

Lettvin, J. Y.; Maturana, H. R.; Pitts, W. H.; and McCulloch, W. S. 1961. Two remarks on the visual system of the frog. In *Sensory communication,* ed. W. A. Rosenblith. Wiley, New York, pp. 757–76.

Maturana, H. R.; Lettvin, J. Y.; McCulloch, W. S.; and Pitts, W. H. 1960. Anatomy and physiology of vision in the frog. *J. Gen. Physiol.* 43: 129–75.

Scalia, R., and Fite, K. V. 1974. A retinotopic analysis of the central connections of the optic nerve in the frog. *J. Comp. Neurol.* 158: 455–78.

Sharma, S. C. 1972. Retinal projections in the goldfish. An experimental study. *Brain Res.* 39: 213–23.

Witpaard, J., and terKeurs, H. E. D. J. 1975. A reclassification of retinal ganglion cells in the frog, based upon tectal endings and response properties. *Vision Res.* 15: 1333–38.

7.7 Neural Regulation of Weight
Lesions in the Rat Hypothalamus

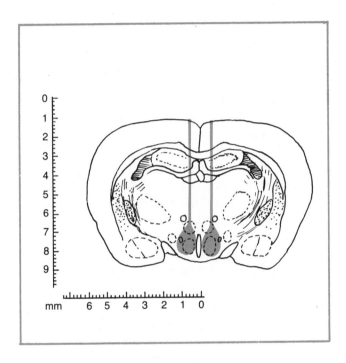

Introduction

Rationale
Making hypothalamic lesions is an excellent technical introduction to chronic stereotaxic procedures. The changes which appear after lesioning can also dramatically underscore the importance of the brain in body function. However, the precise regulatory circuitry underlying the physiological effects of hypothalamic lesions remain for future researchers to discover. You will lesion the rat hypothalamus and observe the effects on the rat's eating behavior.

The short-term control of food intake and the long-term regulation of weight are basic to an organism's survival. Not surprisingly, there is a massive flow of information to the brain from oral and gastrointestinal receptors (e.g., taste, smell, and stomach "pangs") and from receptors sensitive to molecules circulating in the bloodstream (e.g., glucose). How is this information centrally integrated in the brain? For more than 25 years it has been known that small bilateral lesions in the ventromedial hypothalamus (VMH) produce overeating and obesity in rats, whereas lesions of the lateral hypothalamic area (LHA) produce a failure to eat or drink. Consequently, the VMH came to be known as the "satiety center" and the LHA as the "feeding center." The logic of the lesion method is analogous to that used when an endocrine gland is removed. The deficit produced by destruction should be the opposite of the area's normal function. If the VMH acts to shut off eating (satiety), then its destruction should result in overeating.

This tidy picture is currently being reappraised because (1) dramatic effects on feeding can be produced by lesions elsewhere in the brain and (2) VMH and LHA lesions may be effective primarily because they destroy important axonal pathways which funnel through the hypothalamus while making synaptic connections elsewhere. Such results lessen the appropriateness of using the term *center*. Actually, it is now recognized that obesity is most effectively produced by large lesions which are ventral and lateral to the ventromedial nucleus in the region of the *ventral noradrenergic pathway*. Lesions restricted to the ventromedial nucleus proper are neither necessary (Gold, 1973) nor sufficient to produce hyperphagia and obesity (Joseph and Knigge, 1968). Similarly, lesions of the LHA destroy other pathways, such as the sensory projections from the mouth area to the thalamus. When the oral area of the sensory thalamus is destroyed, feeding deficits occur (Oakley, 1965; Zeigler and Karten, 1974). There are many widespread neural circuits which influence feeding behavior (Grossman, 1975). In the present experiment you will observe some of the consequences of disturbing the normal regulatory checks and balances on food intake.

Time to complete the exercise: One laboratory period will be required to place the lesions and oversee the animal's recovery from anesthesia. Thereafter, for 6 weeks, measurements will be taken twice a week (30 min/animal/week). Once the lesions have been placed you will make three kinds of measurements on the lesioned rats: water intake (ml/day), weight gain (g/day), and level of irritability or aggressiveness. The first laboratory period will be devoted to placing bilaterally symmetrical hypothalamic lesions. Before the laboratory period, read chapter 9.

Procedure

Testing the electrode and the lesion maker

Obtain a lesion-making device. Attach the lesioning electrode to the cathode (−) and a clip lead to the anode (+). Place the electrode and the clip in a beaker of isotonic saline solution and make sure the two do not touch. Set the rheostat to 50 kohms. This setting (the highest resistance) will produce the lowest current. The person controlling the rheostat will watch the milliammeter to determine how the current increases with rheostat dial position. The other experimenter will watch the cathode (lesioning electrode) in the beaker and note when it begins to bubble. If it bubbles only from the tip, the electrode insulation is intact. Proceed further if you have a properly insulated electrode. Reverse the polarity (electrode +) and pass about as much current as you did before.

First laboratory period

Anesthetizing the rat. Before making lesions, it is necessary to anesthetize the rat and expose the skull for the sterotaxic operation. You should turn to section 9.3 and work your way through the instructions until you are told in 9.4 to return to experiment 7.7.

Turn to section 9.3, page 313.

Making the lesion. Carefully attach the *anodal* (+) lead of the lesion maker via a minigator clip to the *lesioning electrode* with the current off. Insert the cathode (−) in the anus to complete the circuit. A banana plug works well as an anal electrode. Tape the cathodal lead to the tail so that the electrode is not pulled out accidentally.

Check to see that the circuit is complete and ready for passage of current. Lower the electrode slowly to 9.4 mm below the skull surface You will pass 1.0 mA for 45 seconds. It is useful to know that the volume of a small lesion is proportional to the amount of charge passed. Thus, 2 mA for 20 seconds is equivalent to 1 mA for 40 seconds. You may therefore adjust the amount of time upward or downward to compensate for under- or overshooting the desired current. In the circuit shown in figure 7.7-1 the rheostat should be set fully counterclockwise so that its resistance is 50 kohms. As soon as you throw the switch, turn the rheostat knob until its resistance is low enough to pass 1.0 mA as indicated by the milliammeter. At that point say "now" to the person checking the time. The person doing the timing will

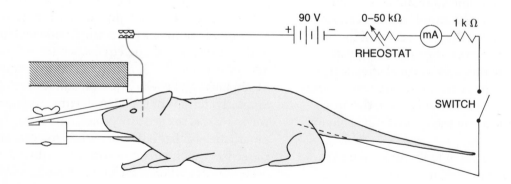

Fig. 7.7-1. Circuit diagram for producing stereotaxic lesions in the rat brain.

then say "stop" when you should switch off the current at the end of 40 seconds. Raise the electrode and repeat the procedure on the other side of the brain. You should have caused extensive bilateral destruction in the vicinity of the VMH. Move the electrode carrier entirely out of the way and suture the scalp of the rat with two or three mattress stitches, as shown in figure 9.3-3.

Recovery

Follow the instructions of section 9.4, page 323, on recovery. Your instructor will further discuss with you the care and testing arrangements. Postoperatively, each rat should be housed in a separate cage labeled with the experimenter's name.

Weight gain, water consumption, and behavioral tests

CAUTION: Handle these rats with heavy gloves. Lesioned rats may jump and bite.

Use the following routine for measurements and behavioral observations twice a week. Weigh the water bottle on the rat's cage to determine by subtraction the amount of water consumed since the previous measurement. Rinse and fill the bottle with fresh water, reweigh, and place it back on the cage.

Test the animal in its cage for irritability and aggressiveness. Devise your own standardized tests, such as touching the rat's tail with a wooden rod.

Finally remove the rat and weigh it. Replace the animal in its cage and check to see that the food supply is adequate. Record all weights and data on aggressiveness in your notebook and on a chart for class use. Include two to four normal, unoperated controls as a comparison group. (Operated controls would be preferable, except that we wish to maximize the number of hyperphagic animals available.) Chart the weight gain and water intake of the control and operated animals over the time period allotted. It will be most revealing if you plot both individual data and group data. (Note: During the first week some weight loss can be expected as a result of postoperative recovery.)

Since rats have diurnal activity rhythms (they tend to be more active at night), it is important to make all measurements at the same time of the day.

Pitfalls and Suggestions

1. The brain must be penetrated close to the sagittal sinus. Be careful of it when drilling through the skull. Tearing the dura mater may cause extensive bleeding. Seal the hole for 10 minutes with a moist compress (pledget) of cotton if this occurs.
2. Lower the electrode into the brain *slowly* when you penetrate past the dura.
3. Double-check the accuracy of the electrode position before and after you lower the electrode.
4. The current may increase exponentially while you turn the rheostat dial. Be prepared to reduce the current.
5. When you reach for a lesioned rat, it may reach for you. Wear gloves.

Materials

Materials needed at each station
Lesion-making device (Construct by using the circuit shown in figure 7.7-1. Supplies: 1 kohm resistor, 0–50 kohm rheostat; 2 45-V B batteries, toggle switch, milliammeter 0–5 mA, 22-gauge hookup wire, 2 banana jacks, and metal or plywood box large enough to accommodate the B batteries, rheostat, and meter.)
Lesion electrode (200 μm Teflon-insulated stainless steel wire; 0.5 mm bare tip at lesioning end; other end scraped for electric contact with minigator clip.)
Minigator clip lead for connecting the lesion electrode to lesioning device
Double banana lead for anal electrode
Stereotaxic apparatus (see page 339)
Cotton
Surgical needle (1/2 curved cutting edge)
20 cm surgical thread (black silk, no. 1)
2-oz rubber bulb for drying skull
100 ml beaker
70% ethanol (100 ml)
60-watt table lamp to keep rat warm (Gooseneck is best.)
Set of dissecting tools (furnished by students)

Materials available in the laboratory
2-oz rubber bulb aspirator (cutoff disposable 1-cc syringe barrel with 18-gauge blunted needle and 25 cm of PE 190 tubing)

1 pin vise with no. 52 drill bit/2 stations; for electrode holes

Animal scale or triple-beam balance with a cut off plastic gallon jug to contain the animal

Work gloves

Ear punch

Animal clippers

Extra rat cages (1 cage/3 stations)

Rat food

Rubber tube for artificial respiration

Masking tape

3 labeled 1-cc hypodermic syringes with three 0.75-inch 25-gauge needles

Animal scale

Heavy gloves

Solutions:

Mineral oil (50 ml)

Atropine sulfate (40 mg/ml) 50 cc. It must be specially prepared. Not necessary with ketamine.

Ketamine (1 cc/station/laboratory period). (Vetalar, Parke-Davis, 100 mg/cc.) See page 324, note no. 6. Alternative: sodium pentobarbital (50 mg/ml) 50 cc

Bicillin (600,000 units/ml) 5 cc

Animals

Rats. Use female albino rats weighing 200 g. (Order 1.25 rats/station/laboratory period of chronic surgery. Order an additional 2–4 rats for controls.) House the rats in individual cages with rat pellets and water ad libitum. Food deprive the rats 12–24 hours before the operation to obtain more reliable induction of anesthesia with pentobarbital.

Notes for the Instructor

1. Caution the students that the lesioned rats may be quite vicious.

2. The general precautions in sections 9.3 and 9.4 apply here.

3. It is important to arrange for twice weekly postoperative measurements. An increase in water intake may be apparent in 2 weeks and weight gain in 4 weeks. Six weeks is a minimal duration for postoperative measurement. Pairs of students can take turns carrying out measurements on all operated rats, allowing about 15 minutes per rat.

4. If time and logistics make the long-term postoperative measurements cumbersome, the instruc-

tional staff can demonstrate obesity and aggressiveness during an appropriate future laboratory session.

5. When a water bottle is inverted, some water is invariably lost. This error can be reduced by filling the bottle completely, which will more readily produce a vacuum when the bottle is inverted.

6. Atropine usually is commercially available in 4 mg/ml concentrations. The rat, which is insensitive to atropine, requires higher dosage levels. Atropine solution is made by dissolving powder in *sterile* saline or perfusion fluid. The use of Ketamine obviates the need for atropine.

Selected References

Grossman, S. P. 1975. Role of the hypothalamus in the regulation of food and water intake. *Psychol. Rev.* 82: 200–224.

Hoebel, B. G. 1971. Feeding: Neural control of intake. *Annu. Rev. Physiol.* 33: 533–68.

Novin, D.; Wyrwicka, W.; and Bray, G. A., eds. 1976. *Hunger: Basic mechanisms and clinical implications.* Raven Press, New York.

RESEARCH REPORTS

Eclancher, F., and Karli, P. 1971. Comportement d'agression interspécificque et comportement alimentaire du rat: Effets de lésions des noyaux ventro-médians de l'hypothalamus. *Brain Res.* 26: 71–79.

Gold, R. M. 1973. Hypothalamic obesity: The myth of the ventromedial nucleus. *Science* 182: 488–90.

Gold, R. M., and Proulx, D. M. 1972. Bait-shyness acquisition is impaired by VMH lesions that produce obesity. *J. Comp. Physiol. Psychol.* 79: 201–9.

Joseph, S. A., and Knigge, K. M. 1968. Effects of VMH lesions in adult and newborn guinea pigs. *Neuroendocrinology* 3: 309–31.

Millhouse, O. E. 1973. The organization of the ventromedial hypothalamic nucleus. *Brain Res.* 55: 71–87.

Oakley, B. 1965. Impaired operation behavior following lesions of the thalamic taste nucleus. *J. Comp. Physiol. Psychol.* 59: 202–10.

Powley, T. L., and Opsahl, C. A. 1974. Ventromedial hypothalamic obesity abolished by subdiaphragmatic vagotomy. *Am. J. Physiol.* 226: 25–33.

Zeigler, H. P., and Karten, H. J. 1974. Central trigeminal structures and the lateral hypothalamus syndrome in the rat. *Science* 186: 636–37.

7.8 Chronic Stimulation of the Rat Brain
Self-stimulation of the Septal Nuclei and Lateral Hypothalamic Areas

Introduction

Rationale
In the study of brain mechanisms and behavior, researchers often stimulate the brain of an unanesthetized animal through chronically implanted electrodes and observe the effects on behavior. Stimulation cannot be done under general anesthesia which alters and depresses the function of many parts of the brain, most notably areas associated with consciousness and motor behavior.

In such an experiment, one usually knows enough about the targeted brain area to anticipate the basic outcome. However, it is not uncommon to observe quite unanticipated behavior. The rewarding effects of brain stimulation (septal nuclei) were first observed in this serendipitous way: rats loitered in the region of the cage where stimulation occurred (Olds and Milner, 1954). We now know that animals will perform tasks to obtain or to terminate electrical stimulation of the brain.

In this experiment you will implant a bipolar electrode in either the septal nuclei or the lateral hypothalamic area (LHA). Electrical stimulation of both regions is positively rewarding in the sense that a rat will press a bar to "self-stimulate." In the region of the lateral hypothalamus the medial forebrain bundle is the most rewarding site for self-stimulation.

Septal nuclei. Lesion and stimulation studies of the septal region produce a variety of effects. Regional differences in the septal area undoubtedly account for some of the observed variation. Bilateral destruction of the septal area in rats can lead to hyperactivity and an easily elicited vicious rage (Brady and Nauta, 1953). But over the long term, a taming effect may emerge. A variety of other effects of lesions are known.

Lateral hypothalamic area. Bilateral lesions in the LHA produce rats which no longer eat (aphagia). Stimulation here with implanted electrodes will sometimes elicit gnawing and eating when food pellets or chewable objects are present. Such behavior is only obvious when pellets or chewable objects are present. This illustrates the fact that an experimenter may miss potential behavioral changes if the animal has no opportunity to perform the behavior.

Rats may self-stimulate with electrodes implanted in the LHA. Are we to conclude that becoming hungry is rewarding to the rat? This paradox should make the scientist leery of anthropomorphizing about the psychic state of a rat during this very *un*physiological method of activating the brain. The brain "reward areas" tend to be associated with basic biological drives, such as sexual activity, feeding, and drinking, but be aware that other considerations may enter into electrical stimulation, and a motivational explanation of behavior may be quite specious.

Time to complete the exercise: A full 3-hour laboratory period is required to implant an electrode in a rat, followed by 1 week for recovery from the effects of surgery. Two laboratory periods devoted to electrical stimulation of the brain are sufficient to attempt operant conditioning, such as bar pressing. Before the laboratory period read chapter 9. The first laboratory period will be devoted to implantation, followed by 1 week of recovery.

Procedure

Implanting the electrode
The electrode assembly which you will implant consists of two wire stimulating electrodes twisted together. A cross-sectional view of an implanted rat head is shown in figure 7.8-1. Consult with your instructor before deciding whether to implant in the lateral hypothalamic area or the septal nuclei. Then, follow the sequence of specific instructions on anesthetization, chronic surgery, stereotaxic procedures, and implantation found in sections 9.3 and 9.4. *Do not cannulate the trachea*. Return to this page when directed to do so in the instructions in 9.4.

Turn to section 9.3, page 313.

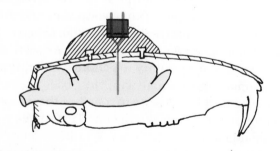

Fig. 7.8-1. Schematic drawing of a side view of the rat head showing an implanted electrode and electrical connections (*colored*) held in place by dental cement (*crosshatched*).

Behavioral testing
At least 1 week of recovery is necessary. One or two days of testing per animal will permit general observations.

Septal implants
Caution with septal implants. Lesions which might inadvertently be produced in the septal area can make very vicious and irritable animals. Excitability to touch is common after a stimulation session with these animals. Use appropriate caution.

Instrumentation for stimulation. The stimulating cable should be suspended above an aquarium or Skinner box by a 0.5–1.0 m length of rubber bands tied in a chain (fig. 7.8-2*A*). Allow the end of the cable to hang freely to within 10 cm of the center of the aquarium floor. Connect the other end of the cable to the stimulator output through a 10 kohm resistor in series or via the circuit in figure 7.8-2*B*. Use the following equipment settings.

Stimulator. Biphasic square waves; 100/sec, 0.3 msec duration; delay of zero; voltage, 3 volts initially; output switch and mode switches off.
    The 10 kohm resistor in series with the animal will maintain a reasonably constant current at any given voltage setting, even if the electrode resistance changes during stimulation. Current across the 10 kohm resistor may be calculated from Ohm's law using an oscilloscope as a voltmeter (fig. 7.8-2*B*).

Attaching the stimulating lead. Turn on the stimulator power switch with the stimulus output switch off. Check the exact location of the pins at the end of the stimulating cable. Hold the rat firmly against your side and plug the stimulating leads into its electrode assembly. Gloves may be worn if desired. Put the rat into the testing arena.

Initial stimulation. Turn on the stimulus switch and use the mode switch (or the push-button switch if the circuit in fig. 7.8-2*B* is set up) to control the presentation of the stimulus. Turn the mode switch on *continuous* and observe the rat. Watch for a head movement or the rat momentarily freezing in position as the stimulation occurs. Stimulate for about 2 seconds. Repeat at a higher voltage. Do not exceed 2 mA ($\approx$ 20 V). Does the animal react to the sound of the switch alone? Test that.

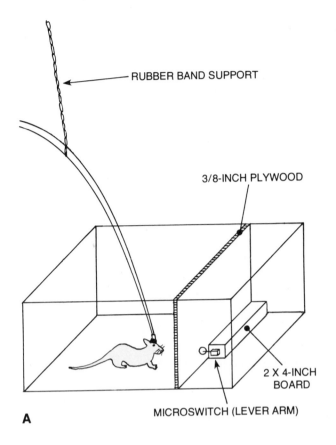

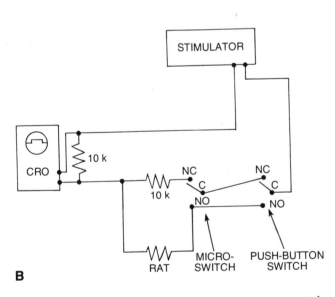

Fig. 7.8-2. A. An implanted rat approaching a microswitch connected to the stimulating electrodes. **B**. Circuitry for stimulating and monitoring. The push-button switch would directly stimulate the rat. The lever-arm micro-switch is inserted through a hole in the plywood divider for the rat to self-stimulate. Use the mode switch on the stimulator to terminate or prevent self-stimulation. *NO*. normally open; *NC*. normally closed; *C*. Common.

Shaping the animal's behavior. Shaping means training the behavior of an animal by carefully controlled timing of a reinforcing stimulus. Here the intracranial stimulation is reinforcing. If a stimulus is *positively* reinforcing you may expect the rat to repeat what it was doing at the instant stimulation occurred. Suppose you want to train the animal to go to, and stand up in, a specific corner. The method is to proceed by successive approximations, rewarding a different response (incrementing the criterion) after each performance level has been roughly achieved. Increments might be: turning toward the corner, beginning to move toward the corner, moving toward the corner, getting to the corner, putting paw on corner, standing up in corner, and standing up with one or both forepaws on the corner. A 1–2 second stimulus would be applied for each reinforcement. Attempt to shape the animal's behavior by using this method. Be patient, reinforcing only the desired movements.

If a bar or microswitch is made available to the animal, the rat may be trained to press for its own intracranial stimulation. Figure 7.8-2*A* shows a microswitch protruding through a board at one end of the arena. The rat receives a stimulus when it presses the microswitch down. The push-button microswitch is actuated by the experimenter to provide independent stimulation. In training, use continuous reinforcement, that is, a 2 second train of 0.3 msec pulses for every bar press. Training to press a bar or microswitch necessarily follows a progressive series of training steps such as: approach, close approach, touching the cage near the bar, touching the bar area with the forepaw, touching the bar with the forepaw, pressing down on the bar with the forepaw.

Attempt to train the rat to bar press; it is somewhat difficult to train the final correct movements. Do not neglect to observe and record the behavior of the rat to the stimulus prior to training. Observe the form and timing of its responses during training and the actions of the animal in the performance of fully trained responses.

LHA implants

Follow the same general procedures as in the septal implants. Initially test the influences of stimulation on the rat's behavior, then train the animal to perform a task.

In about one fourth of the animals, stimulation will produce pellet chewing and gnawing behavior as long as the stimulus is on. Furnish the test arena with some pellets and a dish of water. The test stimuli should last for 30 seconds and be adjusted to a level which arouses but does not overexcite the rat. Test self-stimulation by training the animal to press a bar. Does self-stimulation require a higher voltage?

Comparison of septal and LHA implants
How are the behaviors similar and how are they different for stimulation in these two areas? Compare the rate of decline (extinction) in bar pressing or another trained response when the stimulus has been turned off completely.

Pitfalls and Suggestions

1. If only one period is available for testing the rats, do not attempt bar-press training unless the rats have had some prior experience.
2. The wires may be tangled and twisted by the rat. Unplug the rat and straighten the wires before they stretch.
3. Septal stimulation may produce a shudder or even a seizure. Self-stimulation rates are low: 0.2/sec.
4. Automation in behavioral testing is widely employed in research, but would detract from the instructional function of this experience.

Materials

Materials needed at each station
Implantation session materials
1 premade bipolar electrode (200 μm Teflon-insulated stainless steel wire)
2 fillister head no. 72 × 1/8-inch stainless steel machine screws
Stereotaxic apparatus (see page 339)
Rat cage
Dish for dental cement
Cotton
2-oz rubber bulb for drying the skull
1 small spatula
70% alcohol (100 cc)
60-watt table lamp to keep rat warm (Gooseneck is best.)
1 set of dissecting tools (furnished by students)

Stimulation session materials
Oscilloscope
Square wave electronic stimulator
Test arena (aquarium or Skinner box)
Set of leads for stimulation (e.g., 24–26-gauge stranded, unshielded, with connector for electrode [see page 337])
2 10 kohm resistors
Chain of rubber bands 0.5–1.0 m long
3–5 rat pellets
Water in 60 mm petri dish
Plywood divider with attached microswitch for self-stimulation (or bar in Skinner box).
Push-button switch (momentary single pole double throw, silent)
Lever-arm microswitch (Unimax no. 2HBT-1)

Materials available in the laboratory
Implantation session materials (see figs. 9.1-1 and 9.4-5)
2-oz rubber bulb aspirator (cutoff disposable 1-cc syringe barrel with 18-gauge blunted needle and 25 cm of PE 190 tubing)
1 pin vise with no. 52 drill bit/2 stations for electrode and screw holes
Jeweler's screwdriver
Animal scale or triple-beam balance with a cut off plastic gallon jug to contain the animal
Work gloves
Ear punch
Animal clippers
Extra rat cages (1 cage/3 stations)
Rat food
Rubber tube for artificial respiration
Dental cement (Perm rebase and repair acrylic; Caulk NuWeld liquid and powder; or Getz Tru-Cure dental cements)
3 labeled 1-cc hypodermic syringes with three 0.75-inch 25-gauge needles
Solutions:
  Atropine sulfate (40 mg/ml) 50 cc. It must be specially prepared. Not necessary with ketamine.
  Ketamine (1 cc/station/laboratory period). (Vetalar, Parke-Davis, 100 mg/cc.) See page 324, note no. 6. Alternative: sodium pentobarbital (50 mg/ml) 50 cc
  Bicillin (600,000 units/ml) 5 cc

Stimulation session materials
1 extra stimulating lead

Animals

Rats. Use female albino rats weighing 150–200 g. Females are tamer and have less rapid weight gain. (Order 1.25 rats/station/laboratory period of chronic surgery.) House the rats in individual cages. Provide rat pellets and water ad libitum. Food deprive 12–24 hours before surgery to obtain more reliable induction of anesthesia with pentobarbital.

Notes for the Instructor

1. Details of the electrode assembly for implantation are given on page 337.
2. Atropine usually is commercially available in 4 mg/ml concentrations. The rat, which is insensitive to atropine, requires higher dosage levels. Atropine solution is made by dissolving powder in *sterile* saline or perfusion fluid. Ketamine obviates the need for atropine.
3. You will have a somewhat higher success rate with implants in the LHA. This results, in part, from the fact that the rewarding effects are stronger.
4. Make a table on the blackboard listing students' names with their assigned rats and dates of duties.
5. The instructor has three basic circuit options for brain stimulation: (*a*) brain stimulation controlled by the student with no monitoring of current—the rat is connected in series with a 10 kohm resistor directly to the stimulator; (*b*) brain stimulation by the student with current monitored (upper portion of the circuit in figure 7.8-2*B*); and (*c*) brain stimulation by either the student or the rat with current monitored (fig. 7.8-2*B*). To avoid confusion, error, and loss of time, it is valuable to "hard wire" the circuit in figure 7.8-2*B*.

Selected References

DeFrance, J., ed. In press. *The septal nuclei*. Plenum Publ. Co., New York.

Hoebel, B. G. 1971. Feeding: Neural control of intake. *Ann. Rev. Physiol.* 33: 533–68.

Valenstein, E. S. 1973. *Brain stimulation and motivation*. Scott, Foresman, Glenview, Ill.

RESEARCH REPORTS

Brady, J. V., and Nauta, W. J. H. 1953. Subcortical mechanisms in emotional behavior: Affective changes following septal forebrain lesions in the albino rat. *J. Comp. Physiol. Psychol.* 46: 339–46.

Gardner, L., and Malmo, R. B. 1969. Effects of low-level septal stimulation on escape: Significance for limbic-midbrain interactions in pain. *J. Comp. Physiol. Psychol.* 68: 65–73.

Huang, Y. H., and Routtenberg, A. 1971. Lateral hypothalamic self-stimulation pathways in *Rattus Norvegicus. Physiol. Beh.* 7: 419–32.

Miller, J. J., and Morgenson, G. J. 1971. Modulatory influences of the septum on lateral hypothalamic self stimulation. *Exp. Neurol.* 33: 671–83.

Olds, J., and Milner, P. 1954. Positive reinforcement produced by electrical stimulation of septal area and other regions of rat brain. *J. Comp. Physiol. Psychol.* 47: 419–27.

Valenstein, E. S.; Cox, V. C.; and Kakolewski, J. W. 1968. Modification of motivated behavior elicited by electrical stimulation of the hypothalamus. *Science* 159: 1119–21.

7.9 Chronic Recording from the Rat Brain
Hippocampal Theta Rhythm

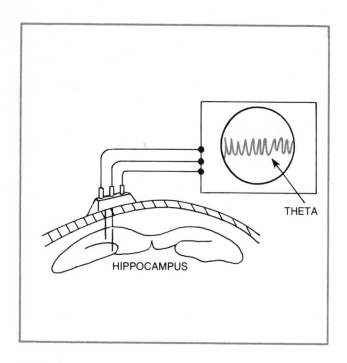

Introduction

Rationale

Brain waves are volume-conducted electrical oscillations which can be recorded from vertebrate brains. A recording of such rhythms is an *electroencephalogram* or *EEG*. Gross electrodes placed in the brain, or the surface of the brain, or even on the scalp are capable of picking up electrical oscillations. The *alpha rhythm* (8–12 Hz) is the best known brain wave. Such *slow waves* are the result of synchronized electrical activity among the dendrites and synaptic fields of millions of brain cells. Even though the EEG is a "gross" measure of brain state, it has been quite useful in brain research and is a basic tool in clinical neurology. Identifiable rhythms are often associated with specific states like sleeping, attention, or wakeful inattention; emotional changes; epileptic seizure, and so forth.

The hippocampus is among the structures of the brain which produce identifiable, easily recorded rhythms. It produces a 4–8 Hz *theta rhythm* which is associated with certain kinds of voluntary behavior. Figure 7.9-1*A* illustrates an example of hippocampal theta activity of a rat walking about in an enclosure. A few moments earlier when the rat was grooming, there was little theta activity (fig. 7.9-1*B*).

Hippocampal theta waves are easily recorded by electrodes which straddle the pyramidal cell layer of the dorsal hippocampus. Information about the cellular basis of the hippocampal theta rhythm is accumulating, but is far from complete. We know that it is correlated with the activity of an identified population of interneurons in the hippocampus (Fox and Ranck, 1975). In rats, theta activity is most pronounced (*a*) during paradoxical sleep (also called rapid eye movement or REM sleep) and (*b*) during "voluntary" as opposed to "automatic" behavioral activity (Whishaw and Vanderwolf, 1973; see table 7.9-1).

TABLE 7.9-1
Hippocampal Theta Rhythm During Behavioral Activities

Voluntary Behavior (Theta)	Automatic Behavior (No theta)
Walking	Licking
Running	Biting
Jumping	Chewing
Rearing	Shivering
Forepaw manipulations	Face washing
Digging	Scratching
Head movement	Defecating
	Urinating
	Drinking

(Adapted from Whishaw and Vanderwolf, 1973.)

Specifying the physiological meaning of the dichotomy in this table remains a challenge for the future. In the larger sense, the hippocampus epitomizes the problems associated with understanding the interior circuitry of the brain—it is in a no-man's-land which is neither sensory nor motor. This experiment is analogous to recording potentials from an integrated circuit component in the middle of a complex electronic instrument. One hopes that the potentials will be correlated with certain kinds of responses. As you progress through the experiment and examine data afterward, think about the general problem of discovering the roles of interior circuitry and strategies which might be followed. This is one of the most crucial and pervasive problems in the physiological study of the central nervous system.

Stimulation and lesion studies have indicated that the hippocampus exerts an inhibitory effect on behavior. Hippocampal stimulation with implanted electrodes decreases behavioral activity, whereas hippocampal lesions increase behavioral activity. In this experiment we will focus on the theta rhythm and its behavioral correlates. The objective will be to implant bipolar recording electrodes in the rat hippocampus and, after recovery from surgery, attempt to relate the occurrence of hippocampal theta rhythm to behavior or to stimulus conditions.

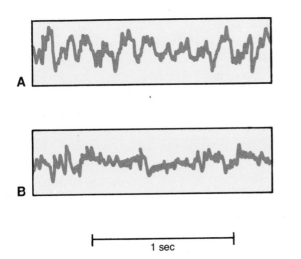

Fig. 7.9-1. A. Hippocampal theta rhythm recorded from a rat walking about in its cage. **B**. Absence of theta rhythm while the rat was licking its fur. Frequencies above 30 Hz have been filtered out in both records.

Time to complete the exercise: A full 3-hour laboratory period is required to implant an electrode, followed by 1 week for recovery from the effects of surgery. One laboratory period is sufficient for recording hippocampal theta. A second recording period would be required for a more systematic study of drug effects. Before the implantation session read chapter 9.

Procedure

Implanting the electrode

The electrode assembly which you use should have one uninsulated ground wire and two twisted insulated recording electrodes, one being 0.5 mm longer than the other. This vertical separation maximizes the recorded amplitude of the theta rhythm.

During the first laboratory period you will implant electrodes in the hippocampus of a rat. Follow in sequence the specific instructions on anesthetization, chronic surgery, stereotaxic procedures, and implantation found in sections 9.3 and 9.4. *Do not cannulate the trachea*. Return to this page when the instructions in 9.4 tell you to do so.

Turn to section 9.3, page 313.

Behavioral testing

After implantation of electrodes, the animals should be allowed to recover for about 1 week. One or two days of testing per animal will permit you to make a number of interesting observations on hippocampal theta.

Electronic instrumentation

The recording cable should be suspended above an aquarium or box by a 0.5–1.0 m length of rubber bands tied in a chain (fig. 7.9-2). The end of the cable should hang freely to within 10 cm of the center of the aquarium floor. Connect the other end of the cable to the preamplifier input. Connect the preamplifier output to the oscilloscope vertical amplifier input. Alternately, a polygraph may be fed from the accessory output of the oscilloscope or directly from the preamplifier (fig. 7.9-2). The oscilloscope can be used for monitoring, and the polygraph for taking records.

Use the following initial settings on your equipment.

Preamplifier. Input in differential mode if possible; gain of 100–1,000×; band-pass filters (if available) set at about 0.1 Hz (low frequency filter) and 0.03 kHz (high frequency filter).

Oscilloscope. Time base at 0.2 sec/div; vertical sensitivity at 0.1–0.01 V/div; triggering level control on automatic or free run.

Polygraph. If you are using a polygraph, set the paper speed at 0.2 cm/sec. Turn up the gain only while recording so that you do not inadvertently splatter ink.

Calibration. Adjust the preamplifier and oscilloscope vertical gain to give a total *system gain* of approximately 100 μV/div. Verify with the preamplifier calibrator if available. Expect theta waves of about 150 μV in amplitude.

Turn on the equipment. Check to see the exact location of the female pins at the end of the recording cable. Now, examine the protocol in your laboratory notebook to determine which of the three male pins in the rat's electrode assembly is the ground

pin. The ground pin on the end of the recording cable should be indicated. Hold the rat firmly against your side and plug the recording leads into its implant assembly with the proper orientation of ground and recording pins. You may use gloves. Put the rat into the testing arena and try to record brain wave activity. You should have no trouble with 60 Hz interference if you have set the high frequency filter low enough (30 Hz = 0.03 kHz). However, should you be unable to do this and there is 60 Hz interference, check the grounding cables carefully and remove any sources of 60 Hz which may be close to the recording area or cables. (If you have mated the recording and implant assembly improperly and grounded an active electrode pin, the theta will be diminished, but there will be no protection from 60 Hz pickup. Reverse the connection to the rat's implant assembly, if necessary.)

Recording Procedure

To conserve polygraph paper, avoid running the paper continuously. Instead, take sample records of brain waves after you have seen the activity with the oscilloscope and are ready to make permanent records.

Problems to explore

The hippocampal theta waves can be recognized by their frequency, approximately 4–8 Hz, and their regularity compared with other activity (fig. 7.9-1). Can you distinguish "movement artifacts" from the brain waves? What does wiggling the recording cable do to the record? Under what general conditions does hippocampal theta occur or not occur? Do amplitude and frequency both change or are they merely present or absent? Test the effect of several standardized stimuli such as a light, click, or odors. Is there any way in which you can reliably elicit or block theta? How does behavioral arousal or the act of "freezing" in position in response to a stimulus affect theta activity?

Try to determine whether arousal by a stimulus will produce theta with or without body movements. If the animal does not move, you must have an independent measure of arousal. Simply defining the stimulus as arousing is insufficient. Might autonomic responses provide an independent measure of the efficacy of arousal?

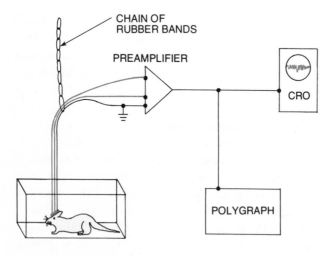

Fig. 7.9-2. Recording arrangement. The hippocampal theta activity can be recorded either on an oscilloscope or on a polygraph, or both, as illustrated. Recording leads from the electrodes implanted in the hippocampus are shown *colored*.

Drug effects

Test the effect of atropine (3 mg/kg body weight) or sodium pentobarbital (Nembutal, 5 mg/kg) on the theta rhythm. Use an intraperitoneal injection, as if you were anesthetizing the rat. Should you inject perfusion fluid or physiological saline solution (containing NaCl only) as a control to see that the injection procedure alone is not altering theta? Do you need some baseline data to see if the perfusion fluid has an effect? With these suggestions, devise a proper sequence of measurements. Using two animals (or taking 2 days) to test the effects of both atropine and sodium pentobarbital avoids any sequential or simultaneous drug interactions. If there is time, develop a dose-response curve.

Pitfalls and Suggestions

1. Proper filtering, shielded cable, and correct grounding are important in recording. If there is 60 Hz interference, a grounded sheet of aluminum foil under or around the aquarium might help.
2. With the suggested recording arrangement, the rats may over time tangle and twist the leads, especially if they circle excessively in the same direction. You may have to unplug and straighten out the recording leads once or twice during a recording session.

Materials

Materials needed at each station
Implantation session materials
1 premade bipolar electrode (200 μm Teflon-insulated stainless steel wire)
2 fillister head no. 72 × 1/8-inch stainless steel machine screws
Stereotaxic apparatus (see page 339)
Rat cage
Dish for dental cement
Cotton
2-oz rubber bulb for drying the skull
1 small spatula
70% alcohol (100 cc)
60-watt table lamp to keep rat warm (Gooseneck is best.)
Set of dissecting tools (furnished by students)

Recording session materials
Oscilloscope
Polygraph (if available)
AC preamplifier
Test arena (aquarium or Skinner box)
Set of recording leads—Microdot cable
Ground and connecting cables
Chain of rubber bands, 0.5–1.0 m long
3–5 rat pellets
Water in 60 mm petri dish

Materials available in the laboratory
Implantation session materials (see figs. 9.1-1, 9.4-4)
2-oz rubber bulb aspirator (cutoff disposable 1-cc syringe barrel with 21-gauge blunted needle and 25 cm of PE 190 tubing)
1 pin vise with no. 52 drill bit/1 station for electrode and screw holes
Jeweler's screwdriver
Animal scale or triple-beam balance with a cut off plastic gallon jug to contain the animal
Work gloves
Ear punch
Animal clippers
Extra rat cages (1 cage/3 stations)
Rat food
Rubber tube for artificial respiration
Dental cement (Perm rebase and repair acrylic; Caulk NuWeld liquid and powder; or Getz Tru-Cure dental cements)
3 labeled 1-cc hypodermic syringes with three 0.75-inch 25-gauge needles
Solutions:
Atropine sulfate (40 mg/ml) 50 cc. It must be specially prepared. Not necessary with ketamine.
Ketamine (1 cc/station/laboratory period). Vetalar, Parke-Davis, 100 mg/cc.) See page 324, note no. 6. Alternative: sodium pentobarbital (50 mg/ml) 50 cc
Bicillin (600,000 units/ml) 5 cc

Recording session materials
Oscilloscope camera and film (storage oscilloscope, if available)
Animal scales
2 1-cc labeled hypodermic syringes with two 0.75-inch 25-gauge needles
Solutions:
Atropine sulfate (4 mg/ml) 50 ml
Sodium pentobarbital (50 mg/ml) 50 cc

Animals

Rats. Use female albino rats weighing 150–200 g. Females are tamer and have less rapid weight gain. (Order 1.25 rats/station/laboratory period of chronic surgery.) House rats in individual cages. Provide food and water ad libitum. Food deprive 12–24 hours before the surgery to obtain reliable induction of anesthesia.

Notes for the Instructor

1. Details of the electrode assembly for implantation are given on page 337.
2. Atropine usually is commercially available in 4 mg/ml concentrations. The rat, which is insensitive to atropine, requires higher dosage levels. Atropine which is made up from powder must be dissolved in *sterile* saline or perfusion fluid. Ketamine obviates the need for atropine during implantation.

Selected References

Isaacson, R. L., and Pribram, K. H. 1975. *The hippocampus*, vol. 1. *Structure and development*, vol. 2. *Neurophysiology and behavior*, vol. 2. Plenum Publishing Corp., New York.

Moore, R. Y. In press. The hippocampal formation: Structure and function. *Neurosci. Res. Program Bull.*

RESEARCH REPORTS

Fox, S. E., and Ranck, J. B., Jr. 1975. Localization and anatomical identification of theta and complex spike cells in dorsal hippocampal formation of rats. *Exp. Neurol.* 49: 299–313.

Green, J. D., and Arduini, A. A. 1954. Hippocampal electrical activity arousal. *J. Neurophysiol.* 17: 533–57.

Kramis, R.; Vanderwolf, C. H.; and Bland, B. H. 1975. Two types of hippocampal rhythmical slow activity in both the rabbit and the rat: Relations to behavior and effects of atropine, diethyl ether, urethane, and pentobarbital. *Exp. Neurol.* 49: 58–85.

O'Keefe, J. 1976. Place units in the hippocampus of the freely moving rat. *Exp. Neurol.* 51: 78–109.

O'Keefe, J., and Dostrovsky, J. 1971. The hippocampus as a spatial map: Preliminary evidence from unit activity in the freely moving rat. *Brain Res.* 34: 171–75.

Whishaw, I. Q., and Vanderwolf, C. H. 1973. Hippocampal EEG and behavior: Changes in amplitude and frequency of RSA (theta rhythm) associated with spontaneous and learned movement patterns in rats and cats. *Behav. Biol.* 8: 461–84.

Winson, J. 1976. Hippocampal theta rhythm. I. Depth profiles in the curarized rat. *Brain Res.* 103: 57–70.

8   Behavior

8.1 Animal Locomotion
Descriptive Analysis of Simple Behavior

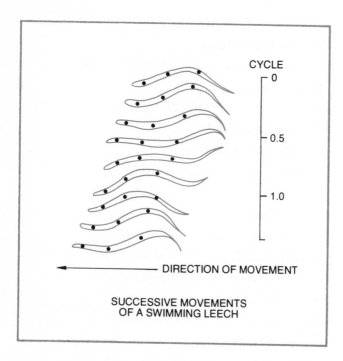

CYCLE

0

0.5

1.0

← DIRECTION OF MOVEMENT

SUCCESSIVE MOVEMENTS
OF A SWIMMING LEECH

You will find that behavioral description requires extraordinary care with words. For example, if a land animal has no legs, how does it walk or run? Does it just "locomote?" Clearly, our everyday language lacks adequately expressive words for the biologist concerned with locomotion. Therefore, be wary of loose phrases in describing locomotion of the animals provided. You will discover (1) that it is not a trivial matter to describe the sequence of movements and analyze the forces underlying locomotion, and (2) that a great deal can be accomplished without reliance on sophisticated instrumentation. It would be a mistake to undertake a physiological analysis of locomotion (or any other behavior, for that matter) without a reasonably accurate description of the movements and a grasp of the physical principles which are in operation.

Time to complete the exercise: One 2–3-hour laboratory period.

Introduction

Rationale
The initial task in the study of any behavior is accurate description. Such descriptions often involve simplification so that only specific aspects of a complex system are considered. Although sound arguments can be made for examining behavior in the field, it is often easier to examine behavior in the laboratory under controlled conditions. Locomotion has been chosen for study in this exercise because it can be effectively studied in the laboratory and is of great biological interest. The ability to swim, run, or fly rapidly and efficiently is a winning formula for evolutionary success.

Procedure

You will examine locomotion in a swimming animal (fish, tadpole, or leech), in a terrestrial animal without limbs (earthworm), or in a terrestrial animal with limbs (millipede, cockroach, or lizard). Carefully observe and describe the locomotor behavior of one species. You are allowed some experimental latitude. For example, ice can be placed in water to slow swimming movements in some animals; or the underside of the terrestrial animals can be viewed from beneath the glass floor of an aquarium. For the purposes of this exercise, however, you may not carry out experimental manipulations which permanently damage the animal.

Behavioral researchers approaching similar problems often use still and motion picture photography. However, in this exercise, gadgetry would be inap-

Line illustration is adapted from Kristan et al., 1974.

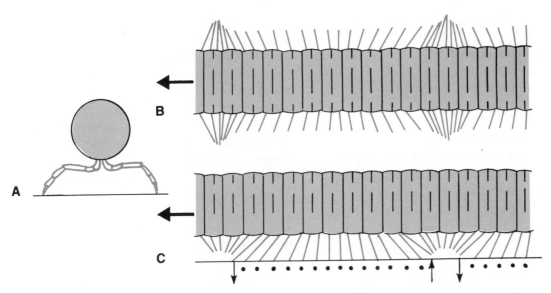

LIMB ABOUT TO BE PLACED DOWN

POINT D'APPUI (LIMB TIP ON GROUND)

LIMB NEWLY PICKED UP

Fig. 8.1-1. Locomotion in millipedes. **A.** Cross section of a millipede showing the legs. **B.** Dorsal view of part of a millipede body showing 16 segments (called diplosegments), each with two pairs of limbs. Wavelike motions of the legs pass along the body as the animal moves. The stroke of each leg is much like that of an oar on a rowboat in that the leg is lifted on the forward stroke and dropped to the surface on the power stroke. The legs undergoing the recovery stroke are bunched up and appear longer in dorsal view because they have been lifted off the ground. The arrow (*left*) indicates the direction of locomotion. **C.** Lateral view. At any one time, most of the legs contact the ground. Having many legs in the power stroke at once aids the animal in forcing its way through soil and decaying materials in its habitat. (Adapted from Manton, 1952 and 1954; and Russell-Hunter, 1969.)

propriate. Sketches, outlines, flowcharts, and vector diagrams are always useful (e.g., fig. 8.1-1). Your observations should result in a succinct, written description which would be useful to further behavioral or physiological analysis. *Work individually and independently.*

Pitfalls and Suggestions

1. Make a serious effort to treat locomotion as a physical problem. The organism can be viewed as a (biological) mass situated in or on a specified medium. Forces (vectors) of given direction and magnitude must be applied by the animal to start, turn, and stop.

2. Remember that behavior (its form, rate, duration, etc.) is often radically changed by placing animals in novel environments and subjecting them to manipulation and human observation.

3. Be forewarned that you should make objective descriptions of animal movements, not purposive statements which imply intent ("the leech tries . . .") or imply a goal or later consequences. Hinde (1970) has distinguished between description by consequence ("picking up nest material," "turning the light on," etc.) and spatiotemporal pattern descriptions ("the joint angle decreases"). Describe behavior in terms of changes in limb and body positions. You should understand these distinctions at the outset of the exercise, and if not, discuss the problem with your associates or instructor. If behavior analysis interests you, by all means examine a text in behavior or ethology (e.g., Hinde, 1970; Eibl-Eibesfeldt, 1970; Alcock, 1974). You may also want to examine the book by Gray (1953) on animal locomotion and the work by Gans (1974) on movement and muscle action, and Kandel's (1976) examination of control mechanisms at the cellular level.

Materials

Materials needed at each station
Desk lamp or microscope illuminator
Magnifying glass or dissecting microscope
Stopwatch

Materials available in the laboratory
Aquaria for the fish and to use as behavioral arenas
for the terrestrial animals (Aquaria with *clear bottoms*, if supported properly, can be used as behavioral arenas for the terrestrial animals so their
movements can be viewed from below.)

Animals
Fish (such as goldfish), or tadpoles (Order 2 fish or 2
tadpoles/every 2 stations.) Leeches *Hirudo
medicinalis*, the European medicinal leech; its
North American counterpart, *Macrobdella*;
Haemopsis, the "horse leech," and *Dina* all swim
readily. The turtle leech, *Placobdella*, does not
swim. (Order an assortment, 2/every 2 stations.)
Provide them with aged, well-aerated water at
room temperature. Aquaria are appropriate for the
fish and shallow pans are appropriate for tadpoles.
Put leeches in an aquarium with a tight top to
prevent them from crawling out at night. Be sparing in feeding the fish. Feed the tadpoles canned
spinach which has been thoroughly rinsed.
Millipedes (Order 1/every 2 stations.) Millipedes are
sometimes difficult to get in the winter. Other
myriapods (centipedes) make a good substitute,
but they move faster and are harder to analyze.
Arachnids or walking crustacea (crayfish, crabs,
etc.) can be substituted, although they tend to resemble the insect pattern. Millipedes were chosen
for the ease with which they may be viewed and
analyzed. Keep them in an aquarium with the
packing material in which they arrived. Feed
pieces of apple and laboratory chow.
Earthworms (Order 2/station.) Refrigerate until use,
without freezing, in the packing material in which
they arrived.
Cockroaches (Order 1/every station.) Slower moving
cockroaches, like *Leucophaea maderae*, *Gromphadorhina portentosa*, or *Blaberus* spp. are preferable to the fast-moving American cockroach
Periplaneta americana. Keep them in a plastic
wastepaper basket with some vertically standing

pieces of cardboard to climb upon. Smear petroleum jelly (Vaseline) around the upper walls to
prevent escape. Feed pieces of apple and laboratory
chow, and supply a sponge wetted with fresh
water every few days.
Lizards (Order 1 chameleon, *Anolis* spp.,/every 3 stations.) Turtles, salamanders, or newts can be substituted for *Anolis*, and sometimes prove to be
better subjects since they move more slowly.
However, they are more expensive. Keep them in
an aquarium with a few rocks and a shelter. Supply a 25-watt lamp at one end of the aquarium to
serve as a heat source. A fitted top or screen is
necessary to prevent escape. Feed mealworms or
other insects if the animals are to be kept for some
time. If salamanders or newts are substituted,
supply them with a cool, moist environment with
running or dripping water.

Notes for the Instructor

1. The use of more than one kind of animal by each
student is likely to invite superficial comparisons.
However, some comparisons are valuable, as between millipede and centipede locomotion.
2. Fish and tadpoles are more difficult than leeches
to analyze without the use of photographic equipment. Millipedes are easy to see, and the rate and
form of leg movement is readily apparent. Cockroaches typify the insect pattern, and lizards exemplify the reciprocal action of tetrapod limbs.
3. There may be some difficulty in getting the lizards
to move slowly enough to observe the form of leg
movement. Cooling might slow down movement,
but often results in no movement at all. Salamanders and newts are therefore a good alternative for
tetrapod locomotion.

Selected References

Alcock, J. 1974. *Animal behavior: An evolutionary approach*. Sinauer, Sunderland, Mass.
Baerends, G. P. 1971. The ethological analysis of fish behavior. In *Fish physiology. VI. Environmental relations and behavior*, ed. W. S. Hoar and D. J. Randall. Academic Press, New York, pp. 279–370.
Eibl-Eibesfeldt, I. 1970. *Ethology: The biology of behavior*. Holt, Rinehart and Winston, New York.
Gans, C. 1974. *Biomechanics: An approach to vertebrate biology*. J. B. Lippincott and Co., Philadelphia.

Gray, J. 1953. *How animals move*. Cambridge University Press, Cambridge.

Hinde, R. A. 1970. *Animal behavior: A synthesis of ethology and comparative psychology*. McGraw-Hill, New York.

Hughes, G. M. 1965. Locomotion: Terrestrial. In *The physiology of the insecta*, ed. M. Rockstein. Academic Press, New York, pp. 227–53.

Kandel, E. R. 1976. *Cellular basis of behavior: An introduction to cellular neurobiology*. W. H. Freeman and Co., San Francisco.

Nicholls, J. G., and Van Essen, D. 1974. The nervous system of the leech. *Sci. Am.* 230: 38–48.

Russell-Hunter, W. D. 1969. *A biology of higher invertebrates*. Macmillan Co., New York.

Trueman, E. R. 1975. *The locomotion of soft-bodied animals*. Edward Arnold, New York.

Wells, M. 1968. *Lower animals*. McGraw-Hill (World University Library), New York.

Wilson, D. M. 1966. Insect walking. *Annu. Rev. Entomol.* 11: 103–22.

RESEARCH REPORTS

Delcomyn, F. 1973. Motor activity during walking in the cockroach *Periplaneta americana*. II. Tethered walking. *J. Exp. Biol.* 59: 643–54.

Kristan, W. B., Jr.; Stent, G. S.; and Ort, C. A. 1974. Neuronal control of swimming in the medicinal leech. I. Dynamics of the swimming rhythm. *J. Comp. Physiol.* 94: 97–119.

Manton, S. M. 1954. The evolution of arthropodan locomotory mechanisms. Part 4: The structure, habits, and evolution of the Diplopoda. *J. Linn. Soc.* (Zool.), 42: 299–368.

———. 1958. The evolution of arthropodan locomotory mechanisms. VI. Habits and evolution of the Lysiopetaloidae (Diplopoda), some principles of leg design in Diplopoda and Chilopoda, and limb structure of Diplopoda. *J. Linn. Soc.* (Zool.) 43: 487–556.

8.2 Insect Flight
Sensory and Central Mechanisms

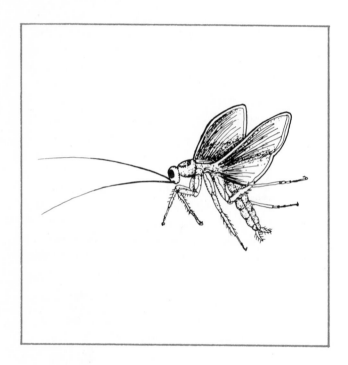

Introduction

Rationale

The ability to sustain flight has evolved in three living groups of animals: insects, birds, and bats. Flight is the most complex form of locomotion and requires an advanced neuromuscular system for coordination. The evolutionary success of flying animals comes largely from exploiting the aerial environment.

Insects are particularly favored in the evolution of flight. Their small size leads to a large ratio of surface area to mass. The power-to-weight ratio in insects is enhanced by the air tubes or trachea which go directly to the tissues and thus eliminate the need for a complex and heavy circulatory system. The exoskeleton provides a strong and light structural

material, and the skeletal veins, air-filled tubes which support the membranous wings, would be only slightly stronger even if they were made of a light metal like titanium. Finally, streamlining of the body is unimportant to most flying insects since they are light and fly at low speed. Birds in general have had to evolve streamlined shapes, but insects have been free to develop other morphological adaptations without the overriding necessity to streamline the body.

Cockroaches, the subject of this exercise, represent a group of relatively unspecialized fliers. In fact, immature cockroaches (nymphs or larvae) do not have wings, and in some species the adults are wingless, or only the male adults have wings. Cockroaches have changed little since they evolved during the Carboniferous period, before the appearance of flowering plants. The specialized fliers, bees, flies, and moths, evolved later during the Mesozoic period. Bee flight muscles, for example, are highly specialized with dense arrays of contractile proteins and numerous mitochondria, whereas in cockroaches the flight muscles are not too different from leg muscles (fig. 8.2-1). We will use cockroaches because they are large, hardy, and easily obtained and will maintain a regular and sustained flight.

Time to complete the exercise: One 3-hour laboratory period.

Procedure

Obtain an adult male cockroach (see experiment 8.6 for sexing cockroaches). Attach a wooden applicator stick to the pronotum (the shieldlike area behind the head) using melted wax. Hold the insect still while the wax solidifies. After the wax hardens, carefully separate the cockroach from its grip on your hand without breaking the wax bond. Suspend the mounted cockroach in air by attaching the applicator stick to a horizontal rod fixed to a ringstand. Give the cockroach a small styrofoam ball to grip with the feet while it hangs in the air. Similarly prepare three or four more males.

Normal flight

Suspend a cockroach in front of a small fan which is plugged into an autotransformer. Use a swivel clamp for mounting so that the flying attitude may be varied. The fan will act as a simple wind tunnel. Adjust a stroboscopic lamp to shine on the cockroach, but do not turn it on yet.

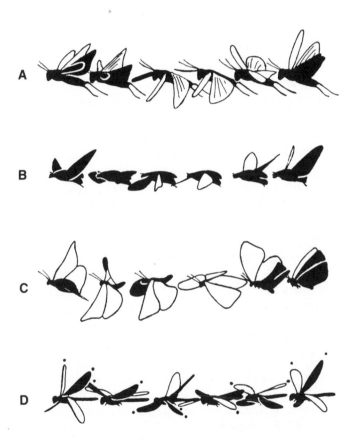

Fig. 8.2-1. Wing movements in insect flight. These are sketches of wing movements taken from high-speed cine photographs. The progression of wing movements reads from right to left. The upper surface of the wing is *white* and the lower surface *black*. **A.** The locust beats its fore- and hindwings slightly out of phase. **B.** Beetle. **C.** The butterfly beats its fore- and hindwings exactly in phase. **D.** The dragonfly beats the fore- and hindwings exactly out of phase to neutralize torque. The wing tips of the forewings are marked with *black dots*. (Adapted from Nachtigall, 1974.)

The flashing of a stroboscope will trigger epileptic seizures in some people. If you feel "odd," ill at ease, or dizzy during the course of the experiment, leave the vicinity of the flashing light.

Turn the fan on and adjust the autotransformer to subject the insect to a low velocity breeze (1–2 m/sec ≈ 2–4 mph, if you can estimate it). Now, remove the styrofoam ball from the cockroach's grip, using care to avoid pulling the insect off the applicator stick. At this point the insect may begin to fly. If not, give it from 30 seconds to 1 minute before doing anything more.

After a period of time with no flight, attempt to trigger flying with a slight increase in wind velocity and by touching or lightly pinching the tip of the abdomen. Let it grip one end of a glass rod, which you then withdraw. If this does not initiate flight, discard the animal and get another.

When flying is obtained, turn the room lights off and the stroboscope on. Adjust the stroboscope frequency in the range of 20–40 flashes/sec until the wing motion appears nearly stopped.

CAUTION: The fan blades may appear to be still or only slowly moving. This is an illusion! They are rapidly moving and are dangerous!

Determine the frequency of wing beat of the forewings by finding the fastest flashing rate which produces the appearance of completely stopped motion. (If the strobe light is not calibrated, you will not be able to measure the frequency unless you drive the strobe with a stimulator.)

Observe the movements of the fore- and hindwings by adjusting the stroboscope to make it appear that they are flapping very slowly. Do they beat together or out of phase? If out of phase, how far out of phase? (See fig. 8.2-2.) How steady is the rate of beating? Do you suppose the rate of beating would change if the wings were lightened by clipping them shorter? Do not test this now.

Does the angle of incidence (angle of attack) of the wings change during their reciprocating motion?

Some insects, such as the bee, change the angle of incidence to achieve lift on the upstroke as well as the downstroke. Is this true of the cockroach? Can you detect changes in posture and wing attitude when the insect corrects for the roll, yaw, and pitch that you induce by turning the insect (fig. 8.2-3)? After observing, give the styrofoam ball back to the cockroach to terminate the flight and rest the insect. Turn the strobe light off.

Experiments

As evident from the questions just asked, there are many aspects to winged flight. Take a few minutes to read over the following and plan a set of experiments. Three main areas of investigation are available with the tools you have at hand.

Aerodynamics

The questions in "Normal flight" dealt primarily with the mechanical aspects of flying, and may have suggested experiments to do. It ought to be possible

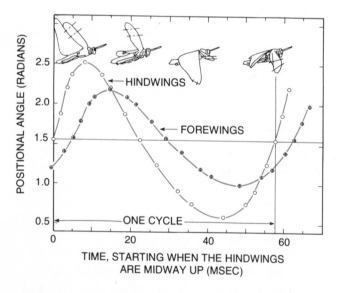

Fig. 8.2-2. Standard wing stroke of the locust *Schistocerca gregaria.* The typical wing positions shown above the curves were drawn from photographs. The *dotted lines* on the forewings are thin filaments glued there to indicate the twisting of the wing plane. The wing tips are marked by *black dots.* The two sine waves represent the up-and-down strokes of the fore- and hindwings. (Adapted from Weis-Fogh, 1956b.)

to analyze the flight response into subcomponents: movements of the fore- and hindwings; position of the body, legs, and antennae; action of a single wing; or the effects of changes in the body position and direction of the wind stream. If you have read discussions of animal aerodynamics, such as those by Pringle (1957), Pennycuick (1972), or Nachtigall (1974), you may be able to ask more informed questions. This preparation is strongly encouraged if more than one laboratory period is available.

Sensory mechanisms

Insects apparently depend on the simultaneous activation of several kinds of sensory receptors to initiate and maintain flight. The most complete analyses of the sensory mechanisms of insect flight have come from the locust and bee. With modifications, these observations also apply to cockroaches.

Flight is induced in a number of insects by the removal of support. Receptors on the legs thus contribute to the initiation of flight. You may observe the effects of support and lack thereof by repeatedly removing the styrofoam ball from the grasp of the cockroach. Is this sufficient to sustain flight in the absence of wind? How may seconds is flight sustained without wind? What is the effect of repeated trials? What is the influence of changing the time interval between trials? How many legs must be touching a surface to inhibit flight? You may consider amputating legs or parts of legs to eliminate sensory input, but remember that the acute trauma may confound the results of your experiments. Despite this, amputation experiments often work well in insects and other arthropods.

Receptors on the head and antennae may also play a role in flight. For example, stimulation of groups of tactile hairs on the head of the locust will result in sustained flight if support is simultaneously removed. Examine the head of a cockroach with a magnifying glass or dissecting microscope. Are hairs visible which might serve a similar purpose? The receptors on the head can be selectively stimulated by a fine jet of air from a Pasteur pipette connected via rubber tubing to an air line. Alternatively, sensory input from tactile hairs can be eliminated by covering them with grease, e.g., silicone stopcock grease, or extra-fast drying modeling cement.

The influence of the antennae on flight is more difficult to test. Amputation of the antennae of

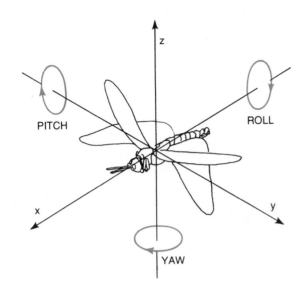

z

PITCH   ROLL

x   y

YAW

Fig. 8.2-3. Roll, yaw, and pitch in a flying locust. (Adapted from Weis-Fogh, 1956b.)

cockroaches usually leads to a general depression of activity; hence it is probably a relatively poor experimental approach. On the other hand, since many of the proprioceptors of the antennae are located in the first three basal segments, it would be possible to inactivate them by immobilizing the bases of the antennae with cement. This will not, however, eliminate tactile input from the antennae because tactile hairs are found on every segment.

Tactile receptors and proprioceptors are also found on the wings. In the locust, the stimulation of air moving across the wings is sufficient to maintain flight once it has begun, but it is an insufficient stimulus to initiate flight. Does a similar mechanism operate in the cockroach? You may want to use the fine jet of air to explore this problem. You may also consider amputation of the wings and observation of other components of the flight posture. Use of larvae (nymphs) without wings may be useful to observe postural responses in cockroaches without wings.

Finally, the possible influence of the caudal cerci located at the tip of the abdomen can be evaluated. They are an important mechanoreceptive input (see experiment 7.1). The cerci can be stimulated with an air jet or they can be amputated.

Central mechanisms

Complete reflexive pathways for walking are often present in the thoracic ganglia of insects like cockroaches. For example, a male praying mantis which has been beheaded will continue circular walking movements for days. This particular example is extreme and related to the sexual behavior of the mantis, but it illustrates the degree of autonomy possible in individual ganglia. You may want to ask whether the three thoracic ganglia of the cockroach contain a complete set of neural circuits for flying.

Tests of the question of autonomy will have to rely on ablation (surgical destruction) of the two major areas of the cockroach brain: the supra- and the subesophageal ganglia (see fig. 7.1-2, page 205). The objective will be to remove any influence they might have on the thoracic ganglia. The supraesophageal ganglion can be destroyed by inserting a hot needle into the head capsule between the compound eyes and antennae. Use a blunt needle (about 1 mm diameter) which is nearly red hot.

Although preliminary observations are possible, one or more hours may be required for a stable recovery state. Plan your experiments accordingly. You should prepare several insects since some ablations may be faulty.

The supra- and subesophageal ganglia may be totally removed simply by beheading the insect. Less recovery time will be needed after beheading. If excessive bleeding takes place, *lightly* cauterize the wound with a hot needle.

The abdominal ganglia also influence the activity of the thoracic ganglia. Therefore, you may want to sever the nerve cord between the abdomen and thorax in a few insects. This can be done by cutting a small, transverse slit in the ventral abdomen at the first or second segment (sternite) behind the thorax. After making the slit, insert the opened tips of a fine pair of scissors into the opening and snip. Since the nerve cord is adjacent to the sternite, you will cut through it. Do not insert the scissors too far or you will also cut the gut. Cutting the nerve cord at this site will eliminate all afferent input from the abdomen, including the sensory input from the cerci.

Pitfalls and Suggestions

1. Turn the strobe lamp off when it is not in use. Flashing strobe lamps may trigger epileptiform sei-

zures in some people, as noted previously, and long-term exposure will make most persons develop a headache. Do not look directly into the lamp at any time.

2. Be ready to make observations and take data when the insect begins flying. Terminate flight by replacing the styrofoam ball whenever you are not making observations. Avoid fatiguing the insect as this will affect your results.

3. The wax is more likely to hold the animal if the wax is curved around the lateral edges of the tergum.

Materials

Materials needed at each station
2 ringstands
5 short rods, about 0.32 × 20 cm (1/4 × 8 inches)
5 right-angle clamps
Swivel clamp
Fan (A small, plastic-blade fan is safest, e.g., Rotron Muffin Fan available from electronics suppliers.)
Autotransformer (AC rheostat for controlling fan speed; low amperage capacity is sufficient.)
Stroboscopic lamp (A photic stimulator can be used; e.g., Grass Instrument Co. PS22 or PS33.)
5 styrofoam balls, about 2–3 cm in diameter
Bunsen burner or soldering iron for melting wax
Glass rod with fire-polished ends
Pithing needle and 1 pair of fine scissors (furnished by students)

Materials available in the laboratory
Applicator sticks
Wax (e.g., in order of preference, S. S. White Crown Sticky Wax, Surgident Periphery Wax, Cenco Universal Red Wax)
Extra right-angle clamps, swivel clamps, ringstands, and rods
Extra styrofoam balls
Beakers or other containers for melting wax
Pasteur pipettes or glass tubing pulled out to 1–2 mm tips
Rubber tubing, approximately 7 mm (1/4 inch) inside diameter
Silicone stopcock grease (a viscous grease, such as Dow Corning silicone stopcock grease) or fast-drying modeling cement (e.g., Testors extra-fast drying cement for wood models available from hobby shops)

Fine camel hair paintbrushes or bristles from a larger paintbrush, for stimulating the anal cerci
Magnifying glass
Dissecting microscope and illuminator

Animals
Periplaneta americana are available commercially from Carolina Biological Supply. (Order 7–8 cockroaches/station.) Other species, such as *Leucophaea maderae*, may also be used as long as the adults have wings. In some parts of the country, wild cockroaches can be trapped. Trapping may be advantageous because wild cockroaches are often more vigorous fliers than laboratory-reared cockroaches. Flying grasshoppers or beetles can be used if they are available. Place the roaches in a plastic wastebasket or a similar container with the upper walls smeared with petroleum jelly (Vaseline) to prevent escape. Provide the roaches with vertically standing pieces of cardboard to climb upon. A sponge wetted with water every few days will supply sufficient water. Feed lab chow or dry dog food. Supplement with apples or oranges periodically if the roaches are kept for a long period.

Notes for the Instructor

1. The most difficulty will be encountered in fixing the insects to applicator sticks with wax. The bond between the cockroach and the stick is usually broken by students who hastily try to pull the insect's grip loose by pulling on the stick. Pull gently, freeing one leg at a time.

2. Caution the students not to look directly in the light. Also caution them to avoid the fan blades, which may appear slowly moving or stationary in the flashing light. Do not use the strobe light in the presence of an epileptic.

3. Check the instruction manual for the strobe lamp to determine if there is any suggested limitation on continuous operation. Some units require periodic resting.

Selected References

Nachtigall, W. 1974. *Insects in flight: A glimpse behind the scenes in biophysical research*. McGraw-Hill, New York.

Pennycuick, C. 1972. *Animal flight*. The Institute of Biology's Studies in Biology, no. 33. Edward Arnold Pub. Ltd., London.

Pringle, J. W. S. 1957. *Insect flight*. Cambridge University Press, Cambridge.

———. 1968. Comparative physiology of the flight motor. *Adv. Insect Physiol.* 5: 163–227.

Rainey, R. C. 1976. *Insect flight*. Symp. Royal Entomol. Soc. 7. Halsted (Wiley), New York.

Wells, M. 1968. *Lower animals*. McGraw-Hill, New York.

Weis-Fogh, T. 1956a. The flight of locusts. *Sci. Am.* 194: 116–24.

Wilson, D. M. 1968a. The flight control system of the locust. *Sci. Am.* 218: 83–90.

———. 1968b. The nervous control of insect flight and related behavior. *Adv. Insect. Physiol.* 5: 289–338.

RESEARCH REPORTS

Altman, J. S. 1974. Changes in the flight motor pattern during the development of the Australian plague locust, *Chortoicetes terminifera. J. Comp. Physiol.* 97: 127–42.

Camhi, J. M. 1970. Sensory control of abdomen posture in flying locusts. *J. Exp. Biol.* 52: 533–38.

Gettrup, E. 1965. Sensory mechanisms in locomotion: The campaniform sensilla of the insect wing and their function during flight. *Cold Spring Harbor Symp. Quant. Biol.* 30: 615–22.

Jensen, M. 1956. Biology and physics of locust flight. III. The aerodynamics of locust flight. *Philos. Trans. B.* 239: 511–52.

Kutsch, W. 1974. The influence of the wing sense organs on the flight motor pattern in maturing adult locusts. *J. Comp. Physiol.* 88: 413–24.

Weis-Fogh, T. 1956b. Biology and physics of locust flight. II. Flight performance of the desert locust. *Phil. Trans. B.* 239: 459–510.

———. 1956c. Biology and physics of locust flight. IV. Notes on sensory mechanisms in locust flight. *Phil. Trans. B.* 239: 553–84.

Weis-Fogh, T., and Jensen, M. 1956. Biology and physics of locust flight. I. Basic principles in insect flight. A Critical review. *Phil. Trans. B.* 239: 415–58.

Wendler, G. 1974. The influence of proprioceptive feedback on locust flight co-ordination. *J. Comp. Physiol.* 88: 173–200.

Wilson, D. M. 1961. The central nervous control of flight in a locust. *J. Exp. Biol.* 38: 471–90.

Wilson, D. M., and Weis-Fogh, T. 1962. Patterned activity of co-ordinated motor units, studied in flying locusts. *J. Exp. Biol.* 39: 643–67.

8.3   Electrolocation and Electrocommunication
Electrical Signals and Behavior of Weakly Electric Fish

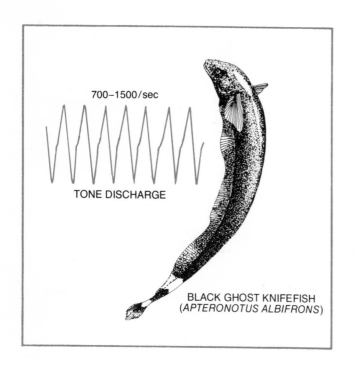

700–1500/sec

TONE DISCHARGE

BLACK GHOST KNIFEFISH
(*APTERONOTUS ALBIFRONS*)

Introduction

Rationale
Communication among animals often involves visual displays and sounds. Communication, however, can also be mediated by other stimuli such as odors (pheromones), vibrations (the spider's web is an example), and in some species of fish by weak electric currents. Weakly electric fish provide insight into the evolution of communications systems and behavior. Moreover, the anatomy and physiology of the electric organ discharge is of interest in its own right as a physiological mechanism.

Electric discharges from fish were used by Roman and Egyptian physicians as a primitive form of electrotherapy for headaches and other ills. Nineteenth-century physiologists used electric fish in the study of animal electricity. The frontispiece in Du Bois-Reymond's classic work on bioelectricity (*Untersuchungen über thierische Elektricität*, 1848) displayed the electric fish *Torpedo*, an electric eel, and a frog's leg, all of which contributed to early understanding of animal electricity. In 1844, Matteucci pressed a *Torpedo* between two conducting metal plates and recorded the resulting discharge as a spark between two brass balls attached to two discharging rods; a biological variant of the static machines of the period (fig. 8.3-1). Matteucci thus demonstrated the electrical nature of the *Torpedo's* ability to stun in an experiment analogous to Benjamin Franklin's demonstration of the electrical origin of lightning a century earlier. Electric fish have continued to be of interest, and quite recently have proven to be an ideal source of material for isolation and chemical characterization of the acetylcholine receptor proteins of synaptic junctions.

Based on the strength of the discharge, electric fish fall into two groups. Some, such as the eels and rays, produce powerful discharges that stun prey and ward off predators. A second group uses very weak discharges in communication and sensory evaluation (probing) of their surroundings (fig. 8.3-2). The probing function is only loosely analogous to sonar, for it operates through the detection of distortions in an electric field in the watery environment, not by detecting echos or reflections (fig. 8.3-3). Two major groups of freshwater fish have independently evolved the ability to communicate electrically and to use weak electric currents to probe their surroundings: the gymnotids in South America and the mormyrids in Africa. A species which often occurs in commercial aquarium stores is the glass knife fish, *Eigenmannia virescens*, a South American gymnotid.

Fish electric organs have two developmental origins. Most electric organs consist of long columns of

272

multinucleated cells called electrocytes. The electrocytes are concentrated toward the tail region of the fish (fig. 8.3-2*A*). The electrocytes are cells which have been derived developmentally from muscular tissue and, like vertebrate skeletal muscle, are controlled by cholinergic motor neurons. Such muscle-derived electric organs are found in most of the gymnotids and mormyrids and in the marine elasmobranchs (Bennett, 1971). Neurally derived electric organs are only found in one family of the gymnotids. These electric organs consist of a large bundle of myelinated axons running down each side of the fish into the tail. Regardless of their derivation, the electric organs of weakly electric fish, such as *Eigenmannia*, produce no more than a few tenths of a volt even at peak discharge, and are used solely for probing and communication. The electric organs of stunning fish have great numbers of electrocytes arranged in series. The batterylike arrangement enables them to sum many small potentials into a high voltage. The current output is augmented by columns of electrocytes connected in parallel. The 2,000 electrocyte columns of *Torpedo nobiliana*, an Atlantic ray, can briefly deliver the staggering current of 50 amperes at 55 volts.

Weakly electric fish emit continuous electric signals while detecting their own electric field and those produced by other fish. Electroreception, or the *detection* of electric currents by fish, is accomplished by specialized electroreceptor organs derived from the lateral line organs. There are two

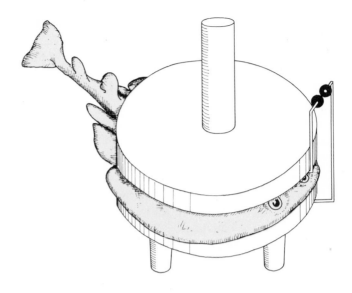

Fig. 8.3-1. *Torpedo* compressed between two plates. When the electric organ discharges, a spark jumps the gap between the two brass balls at the end of the discharging rods. (Adapted from Matteucci, C., 1848. *Lectures on the Physical Phenomena of Living Beings*. Trans. J. Periera, Lee and Blanchard, Philadelphia.)

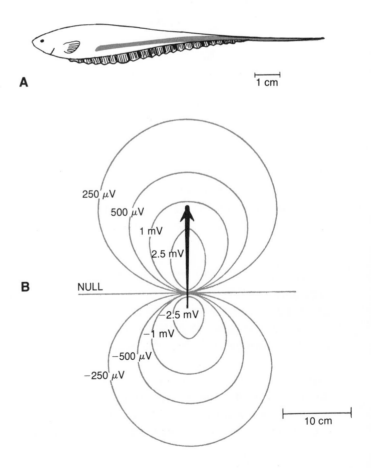

Fig. 8.3-2. **A**. Location of the electric organ in *Eigenmannia virescens*, a weakly electric fish. The *colored area* indicates the site of the organ. (Adapted from Heiligenberg, 1973.) **B**. Approximate equipotential lines of the electrical field of a 19 cm *Eigenmannia virescens*. Electric signals spread out in all directions, as from a physical dipole. The voltages indicated represent the voltages measured in reference to a distant circular electrode surrounding the fish. (Adapted from Hopkins, 1974a.)

types of electroreceptors: *ampullae* which are stimulated by tonic, low frequency signals of less than 50 Hz, and *tuberous receptors* which are stimulated by high frequency waves.

Fish which communicate electrically have two modes of signal generation. All but one of the African mormyrids are "clickers" or pulse species which produce brief pulses at varying rates. Some of the South American gymnotids are called "hummers" or tone species because they emit a continuous, approximately sinusoidal electric tone (fig. 8.3-4). *Eigenmannia* is a typical hummer and emits a tone around 300 Hz. The range of variation among different fish may be as great as two octaves (200–600 Hz), but individual *Eigenmannia* tend not to vary their own pitch by more than 1% unless they are responding to the presence of another fish. When two *Eigenmannia* with nearly identical frequencies meet each other, both simultaneously readjust their output frequency, one to a slightly higher frequency and the other to a slightly lower frequency. This mutual response is referred to as the *jamming avoidance response* (JAR), presumably because it prevents the two fish from confusing each other's signals (Bullock et al., 1972a, b). It is believed that species recognition is an important use of electric communication. The electric sense could be considered analogous to the sense of vision in that signals are transmitted nearly instantaneously. But it is also quite unlike vision since communication distances are very short—no more than 2–3 m—and the signal can pass around physical barriers.

Time to complete the exercise: One 3-hour laboratory period is necessary to record electrical signals and make basic behavioral observations. More time would be needed for a more complete study.

Procedure

The experiments which can be done will depend on the availability of electric fish. There can be a supply problem, depending on your location, the season, and fluctuations in the tropical fish business.

Aquaria
Set up one 5- or 10-gallon aquarium for each available fish. Place a plastic tube with contacts for recording electrodes in each aquarium to provide a place of

refuge for the fish. Electric fish are nocturnal and, in general, spend much of the time in holes or protected areas along the riverbank. Your fish will therefore tend to stay in the plastic tube. Arrange the recording tube so that the experimenter can easily look into the end of the tube. Tape the electrode wires to the side of the aquarium so they do not move about and, if necessary, stabilize the plastic tube so it will not roll. This will assure that changes in signal amplitude are a result of the fish moving about, not the result of movements of the electrodes. Arrange the room lighting so that it is sufficient to view the fish, but not too bright. Many laboratory experiments on electric fish have been done at night, but this will not be necessary unless you plan an extended study of electric fish behavior.

Electrical setup
Connect the electrode leads from the recording tank to the input of your preamplifier. Place a ground electrode at one side of the tank and connect its lead wire to a ground terminal on the preamplifier. Connect the preamplifier output to the input of your

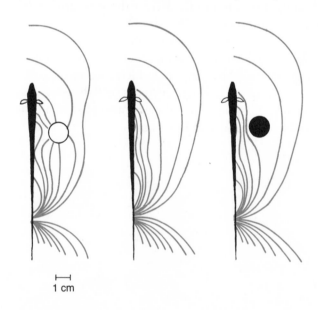

1 cm

Fig. 8.3-3. Distortions of the electric field (*lines of equal potential*) by objects differing in conductivity from the surrounding water. The *center* diagram shows an undistorted field with no objects near the fish; *at left*, an aluminum rod has been moved near the fish; *at right*, a Plexiglas rod has been moved near the fish. Aluminum is a good conductor, and Plexiglas is a good insulator. They distort the electrical field differently. (Adapted from Heiligenberg, 1973.)

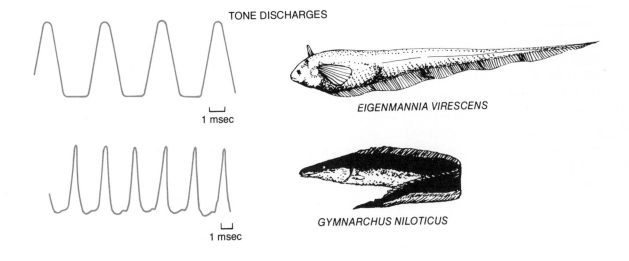

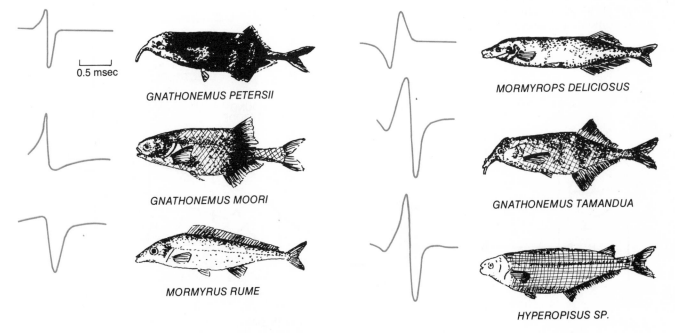

Fig. 8.3-4. Electric organ discharges of tone-producing and pulse-producing electric fish. All, except *Eigenmannia virescens*, are mormyrids of African origin. An upward deflection of the recording trace indicates a positive-going signal. The positive recording electrode was located near the head and the negative electrode near the tail. (Adapted from Hopkins, 1974a.)

oscilloscope. Split the output of the preamplifier by running a second set of leads in parallel to an audio amplifier and loudspeaker. You will thus be able to simultaneously see and hear the output from the electric fish. Connect a set of stimulating electrodes to the output of an audio frequency generator (for tones) or an electronic stimulator (for pulses). These electrodes should dangle in the water at one end of the tank and should be widely separated from one another. This setup will allow you to record the output of the electric fish and to stimulate it with electric tones or pulses (fig. 8.3-5).

The settings on your equipment will vary according to the species of fish used and the geometry of the recording arrangement. Try the following initial settings on your equipment, but be prepared to readjust if necessary.

Preamplifier. Input in differential mode if possible; gain of 100–1,000×; band-pass filters (if available) set at about 10 Hz (low frequency filter) and 10 kHz (high frequency filter).

Oscilloscope. Time base at 5 msec/div for humming species, 0.5 sec/div for clicking species; vertical sensitivity at 50 mV to 0.5 V/div; trigger set on automatic or free run. (This may be reset to internal triggering later to trigger the input.)

Calibration. Adjust the preamplifier and oscilloscope vertical gain to give a total system gain of approximately 1.0 mV/div. Check with the preamplifier calibrator if available.

Audio Amplifier. Gain sufficient to make the output from the fish audible but not offensive to those around you.

Audio Frequency or Pulse Generator. *Off.* Set the amplitude control to its lowest setting even though the instrument is off.

Fig. 8.3-5. Recording and stimulating setup. The fish hides in the tube with attached recording electrodes. The output of the preamplifier is split to drive the oscilloscope display, the audio amplifier, and possibly a tape recorder. The audio amplifier is essential for a full appreciation of the signal pattern generated by the fish. If a tone-producing fish is used, an audio frequency generator would be preferable for stimulating, rather than the pulse generator (electronic stimulator) shown in this diagram.

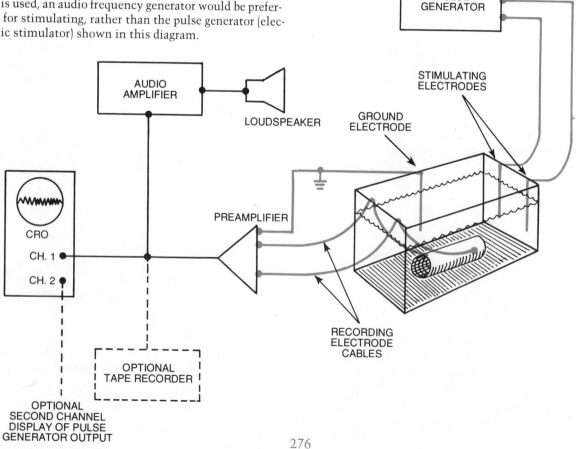

276

Recording Procedure

Turn on your recording equipment. Adjust the oscilloscope vertical gain control until a repetitive waveform appears on the screen. Is your fish a hummer or a clicker? If the fish is a hummer, there could be confusion with 60 Hz. However, this can be readily checked by measuring the period (p) or duration of one cycle. Measure the time between successive peaks and calculate the frequency. For example, if the duration is 5 msec = 0.005 sec, then the frequency = 200 Hz since $F = \dfrac{1}{p} = \dfrac{1}{0.005} = 200$, where p is the period in seconds.

Can you detect variations in the frequency of discharge on the oscilloscope screen or loudspeaker? What is the fish doing while you are recording? Note that the amplitude of the recorded discharge varies as the fish moves. Why? Spend some time trying to correlate the behavior of the fish with its electric organ discharge. This can be done with the aid of a laboratory partner, or just as conveniently by listening to the loudspeaker while you observe the fish.

Experiments

At this point, decide what experiments to do in the time remaining. Try to limit your goals to a set of questions which can be answered with the available time and equipment. The following set of suggestions is intended to guide you, but do not feel compelled to do every exercise proposed or to necessarily follow the order of the experiments suggested. Pick a single species when attempting quantitative measurements.

1. Accurately describe all of the temporal and electrical characteristics of the emitted tone or pulse. For example, measure the peak-to-peak duration of a tone or the amplitude of a pulse.
2. Try to correlate the resting discharge with observable facets of behavior. Resist the temptation to prod and poke the fish or apply other kinds of harsh treatment. What happens when a *small* amount of live food is placed in the aquarium? Food is of biological importance to the fish, particularly to a hungry fish. What is the role of the electric organ discharge in feeding?
3. Experiment with the audio generator. Use the audio generator to apply pure tones of different frequencies to the water in the aquarium. Begin stimulating at the lowest amplitude setting and gradually increase the amplitude until the tone is barely discernible in the recording trace on the oscilloscope. You may want to split the output of the audio generator and display the stimulus waveform on the second channel of the oscilloscope (fig. 8.3-5). This will help to distinguish the stimulus from the electric organ discharge. Can you detect the jamming avoidance response? If the species is a clicker, use a pulse generator (electronic stimulator) to test the effects of single clicks and DC voltages on electric organ discharge and fish behavior.

If the stimulus waveform is visible on the recording trace, you can be reasonably sure that it is detectable by the fish. Since the fish is located in the tube with the recording electrodes, your recording trace is a fair approximation of the intensity of the stimulus as detected by the electroreceptors of the fish. Use low intensities to stimulate. If the stimulus amplitude were increased to match the amplitude of the electric organ discharge on the recording trace, the field strength of the stimulus at the fish would be approximately equal to the field strength of the electric organ discharge as detected by the fish's own electroreceptors.
4. Determine the characteristic resting discharge of the various species at hand. Examine the range of variation among several individuals of the same species. Does the frequency vary? What are the basic differences in the discharge pattern of hummers and clickers?
5. What does the fish do in dim light, e.g., 15-watt red light bulb?

Additional experiments
(at the instructor's option)
It may be valuable to use a polygraph if one is available to make a permanent record of the electric organ discharges of clicking species. If so, connect the output of the preamplifier to the polygraph instead of to the oscilloscope. You can also make a tape recording of the electric organ discharge by connecting the output of the preamplifier to a tape recorder. The tape recording of the fish can then be played back to the same fish, or another fish of the same species or a different species by connecting the tape recorder speaker output to the stimulating electrodes. Con-

sult the tape recorder manual to make sure that this will not damage the recorder by excessive power drain.

Pitfalls and Suggestions

1. Treat the fish gently. The surroundings they are in are already highly unnatural, and more extreme treatment would be unlikely to produce behaviorally meaningful results.
2. Take care not to damage the instruments used for stimulation.

Do not touch the stimulating electrodes together.

3. Use very low voltages in stimulating. You or your instructor may want to place a low amperage fuse in series with one of the stimulating leads to prevent damage to the output transistors of your equipment. Use a 0.1 ampere fuse. Alternately, the output may be protected by placing a 100 kohm resistor in series with each of the stimulating electrodes.
4. Be sure you understand what is being recorded. Your equipment is set up to record potential differences (voltages), not current (amperes).
5. When you finish be sure the aquarium is completely covered so the fish cannot jump out.

Materials

Materials needed at each station

Aquarium, 1/fish (5- or 10-gallon size), *completely covered by a plastic top*

Plastic tube, 1/aquarium (A 20 cm length of thick-walled opaque plastic tubing 7–10 cm in diameter serves as a hiding place for the fish. Thick-walled tubing such as that used for plumbing [PVC, CPVC, or ABS] is suggested to provide sufficient weight to resist being moved by water currents.)

Plastic tube with recording contacts 1/station (Drill a hole 3/16 inch in diameter near each end of one of the plastic tubes just described. The holes should be on opposite sides and no further apart than the length of the fish. Insert a brass machine screw [or cadmium-plated steel screw, size 10–24 or 10–32] into each of the holes. The heads of the screws should be on the *inside* of the tube. Fasten each screw securely in place with a nut. Solder one side of a 100 kohm resistor to the protruding screw threads and the other end to the core of a 1 m shielded cable. Securely fasten the cable to the tube with several wrappings of vinyl electrical tape. Thickly coat the screw threads on the outside of the tube and the resistor and its leads with silicone sealer [Dow-Corning or General Electric, "silicone glue and seal" silicone seal, "silicone bathtub caulk," or "silicone aquarium sealer"]. The silicone coating will prevent short-circuiting the resistor and prevent a stimulator lead from accidentally touching the recording lead above the protective current limiting resistor. Banana plugs, pin plugs, or other suitable connectors should be provided for the other ends of the two cables for connection to the preamplifier input. Connectors should also be provided for grounding the shielding of both leads.

Stimulating electrodes, 1 pair (Obtain two 3 m lengths of no. 18 AWG stranded hookup wire with rubber or thermoplastic insulation. Attach a banana or pin plug to the end of each wire. The other end of each wire need only be immersed in the water to serve as a stimulating electrode. Alternatively, another pair of recording electrodes unattached to a plastic tube can be used as stimulating electrodes through 100 kohm resistors. The use of resistors is desirable to limit current flow should the stimulator output be short-circuited.)

Ground electrode (insulated except at the end)

Preamplifier

Oscilloscope (dual beam if available)

Audio amplifier and loudspeaker

Electronic pulse stimulator or audio frequency generator

Tape recorder and recording tape (optional)

Gooseneck lamp with 15–25-watt red light bulb

Materials available in the laboratory

Extra recording, stimulating, and ground electrodes

Connecting leads appropriate to the equipment at hand (preamplifiers, oscilloscopes, audio amplifiers and loudspeakers, audio frequency generators, electronic stimulators, tape recorder)

Oscilloscope camera and film

Plasticine or modeling clay

Masking tape

Live fish food (large brine shrimp, small worms, small guppies, daphnia, small tadpoles)

Animals

Electric fish (Try to obtain at least 1 fish/station and two species of fish—preferably a hummer and a clicker for the laboratory as a whole.) The availability of electric fish varies. At present, no regular suppliers of biological material list electric fish in their catalogs. Local retail aquarium stores often have these fish, but usually the operators are unaware of their electrical properties. Do not ask for "electric fish" because you are likely to be told that none is available. Instead, explain that you are interested in mormyrid or gymnotid fish which have common names like "glass knife, green knife, black knife, or banded knife fish," or "elephant noses, round noses, black ghosts, or baby whales." Be prepared to recognize the fish yourself. Such fish have the general knifelike shape of *Eigenmannia* (fig. 8.3-2) with a single, unpaired ventral fin, or they may look like those illustrated in figure 8.3-4, often having the "elephant nose" of many of the fish in the genus *Gnathonemus*. You may be told that these are *not* electric fish, when in fact they are weakly electric fish. The help of an enthusiastic amateur interested in tropical fish can be invaluable in locating sources. Try to obtain the names and addresses of wholesale suppliers who might have or be able to obtain such fish. In general, the supply problem is improving, but it remains variable. There may also be seasonal factors involved in supply. We have found that the glass knife fish (*Eigenmannia virescens*), black knives, elephant noses, and baby whales are the most common. It is best to keep the fish separated in individual aquaria, each with a fitted glass or plastic top. Some species are said to fight when put together. The aquaria should be provided with efficient filters and well-aerated water. Temperatures of 23°–28° C are appropriate for most species, with 25°–27° C the preferred range. The temperature should be more carefully controlled if a more quantitative study is planned, since the electric discharge frequency varies with temperature. Provide a day-night cycle; these fish are more active at night and should not be kept in constant light. It is very important to use aged and chlorine-free fresh water. To avoid temperature

shock after purchase, it is best to put the fish in a sealed plastic bag with some water from the store container. Float the bag in the new aquarium until the temperature has equilibrated. Over a period of 30 minutes or so, gradually mix some of the aged water into the plastic bag, so that the fish are acclimated by stages. The fish feed better at night, although night feeding is unnecessary with most species. Some species like *Eigenmannia* will take frozen brine shrimp readily, but it is better to feed live food if available. Feed brine shrimp, *Daphnia magna*, small worms, such as *Tubifex*, guppies ("feeder guppies"), or small goldfish. A mixed diet is advisable if the fish are to be kept for a long time. They do not eat processed food readily. If problems are encountered, consult your local aquarium store operator or a book on aquarium management (e.g., S. H. Spotte, 1970. *Fish and Invertebrate Culture*. Wiley-Interscience, New York).

Notes for the Instructor

1. If you can find a source for the fish, the exercise itself is straightforward. The supply problem is discussed in the previous section.
2. Be sure to test the operation of the audio frequency generator, stimulator, and tape recorder before class. You may wish to provide a fuse in series with one of the stimulating electrodes to protect the stimulator and audio frequency generator outputs. Fuse values of 0.1–0.25 amperes are appropriate.
3. The fish may jump out at night. Cover all holes in the glass or plastic top.
4. Your students may be interested to know that many species of fish not mentioned in the "Introduction" are able to sense electric currents. Stunning fish like *Torpedo* also have electroreceptors, as do catfish, paddlefish (*Polydon*), and probably all of the elasmobranchs, such as the sharks. Receptors in marine fishes are particularly sensitive. Behavioral tests indicate a lower limit of sensitivity around 0.01 μV/cm (or 1 V/1,000 km). This is approximately the size of the voltages which would be generated by a fish swimming through the earth's magnetic field, and suggests that some marine fish may use geomagnetic cues.
5. The Africa mormyrids like *Gnathonemus* produce very brief pulse discharges of less than 0.5 msec

duration. To achieve the close coupling of electric organ cells necessary to produce such short pulses, the mormyrids employ electrotonic coupling between the interneurons of the medulla and spinal cord which coordinate the discharge. (See M. V. L. Bennett, ed., 1974. *Synaptic Transmission and Neuronal Interaction*. Raven Press, New York, pp. 153–78.)

6. Many electric fish will actively swim about in dim light. Knife fish swimming movements are most intriguing.

7. Chlorine can be eliminated by adding 1 drop of hypo, as made up for photographic use, to each 10 gal of aquarium water.

Selected References

Bennett, M. V. L. 1971a. Electric organs. In *Fish physiology*, vol. 5, ed. W. S. Hoar and D. J. Randall. Academic Press, New York, pp. 347–491.

———. 1971b. Electroreceptors. In *Fish physiology*, vol. 5, ed. W. S. Hoar and D. J. Randall. Academic Press, New York, pp. 493–574.

Fessard, A., ed. 1974. *Electroreceptors and other specialized receptors in lower vertebrates. Handbook of sensory physiology*, vol. 3, part 3. Springer-Verlag, New York.

Grundfest, H. 1960. Electric fish. *Sci. Am.* 203: 115–24.

Hopkins, C. D. 1974a. Electric communication in fish. *Am. Sci.* 62: 426–37.

RESEARCH REPORTS

Bell, C. C.; Myers, J. P.; and Russell, C. J. 1974. Electric organ discharge patterns during dominance-related behavioral displays in *Gnathonemus petersii. J. Comp. Physiol.* 92: 201–28.

Bullock, T. H. 1969. Species differences in effect of electroreceptor input on electric organ pacemakers and other aspects of behavior in electric fish. *Brain Behav. Evol.* 2: 85–118.

Bullock, T. H.; Hamstra, R. H., Jr.; and Scheich, H. 1972a. The jamming-avoidance response of high frequency electric fish. I. General features. *J. Comp. Physiol.* 77: 1–22.

———. 1972b. The jamming-avoidance response of high-frequency electric fish. II. Quantitative aspects. *J. Comp. Physiol.* 77: 23–48.

Heilingenberg, W. 1973. Electrolocation of objects in the electric fish, *Eigenmannia (Rhamphichthyidae, Gymnotoidei). J. Comp. Physiol.* 87: 137–64.

Hopkins, C. E. 1974b. Electric communication: Functions in the social behavior of *Eigenmannia virescens. Behav.* 50: 370–405.

Kramer, B. 1974. Electric organ discharge interaction during interspecific agonistic behavior in freely swimming mormyrid fish. *J. Comp. Physiol.* 93: 203–35.

Lissmann, H. W. 1958. On the function and evolution of electric organs in fish. *J. Exp. Biol.* 35: 156–91.

Scheich, H.; Bullock, T. H.; and Hamstra, R. H., Jr. 1973. Coding properties of two classes of afferent nerve fibers: High frequency electroreceptors in the electric fish, *Eigenmannia. J. Neurophysiol.* 36: 39–60.

Westby, G. W. M. 1974. Assessment of the signal value of certain discharge patterns in the electric fish, *Gymnotus carapo*, by means of playback. *J. Comp. Physiol.* 92: 327–41.

8.4 Feeding Behavior
Taste Reception in Flies

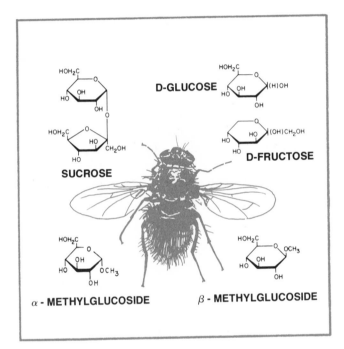

D-GLUCOSE

HOH₂C

SUCROSE

D-FRUCTOSE

α - METHYLGLUCOSIDE

β - METHYLGLUCOSIDE

Introduction

Rationale

Insects have been useful in the study of the chemical senses. Receptors that control the feeding behavior of the fly have been especially useful. The fly tastes with its feet by walking on food! Its taste receptors are contained within hollow hairs which cover the feet (tarsi), the labellum of the proboscis, and, to a lesser degree, other body parts (fig. 8.4-1). If the taste of a food substance is acceptable, the proboscis is extended for feeding. If the chemicals are undetectable, or repellent, the proboscis is not extended. This system has attracted the interest of neurobiologists because of the ease of doing both behavioral and electrophysiological experiments on a relatively simple system. Stimulation of a single hair, and indeed of one neuron in that hair, can elicit a complete behavioral response. Sugars or water initiate drinking; salts terminate or prevent drinking.

Each taste hair is innervated by three to four receptor cells which have dendrites extending to the open tip of the hair where they are exposed to the environment (fig. 8.4-2). At the base of each hair there is a mechanoreceptor which responds when the hair is moved slightly. The classical idea that each hair contains a sugar, water, and salt receptor (three different types of taste neurons) has been supplemented by more recent findings that (*a*) other chemicals in addition to water, salts, and sugars are effective; for example, amino acids, particularly phenylalanine (*b*) there is a fourth taste receptor with still undetermined taste requirements (perhaps fatty acids and inorganic anions) (*c*) there is variation in the physiological properties (and perhaps in behavioral significance) among various receptors and hairs. Nonetheless, it is still generally accepted that behavioral rejection is mediated by increased salt-receptor activity, whereas acceptance is mediated by increased activity in the water or sugar receptors.

The *acceptance* threshold for a given substance is the concentration strong enough to cause proboscis extension in 50% of the tested flies. The *rejection* threshold for unacceptable substances is not so simply defined. For example, the rejection threshold for a chemical can be measured by (a) mixing it in increasing concentrations with 0.1 M sucrose until the proboscis is not extended, or (b) directly stimulating the labellum with 0.1 M sucrose and then touching the tarsi with a solution containing the chemical to cause proboscis withdrawal. Such methods are used to surmount the ambiguity present when a fly fails to extend its proboscis to a weak solution of a chemical. One cannot tell whether the fly is unresponsive because the solution does not stimulate or because the chemical is aversive.

In this experiment we will attempt to characterize receptor mechanisms and whole organism behavior by using the proboscis extension response. Feeding responses are controlled by both sensory input and the state of the central nervous system. For example, a thirsty fly may extend its proboscis to drink water even if the dissolved solute is moderately aversive. A well-fed fly will not drink the 0.5 M sucrose that a starved fly would avidly imbibe.

Time to complete the exercise: One period to prepare the flies and to make an initial survey; another period to test the flies quantitatively.

Procedure

Preparation of flies
All flies should be food deprived for 24–48 hours. Chill at least 30 flies by placing them in the refrigerator at 4° C for 10 minutes. Fasten each fly to a wooden applicator stick by putting a drop of melted sealing wax onto the tip of the applicator stick, reheating slightly, and touching the sticky wax to the

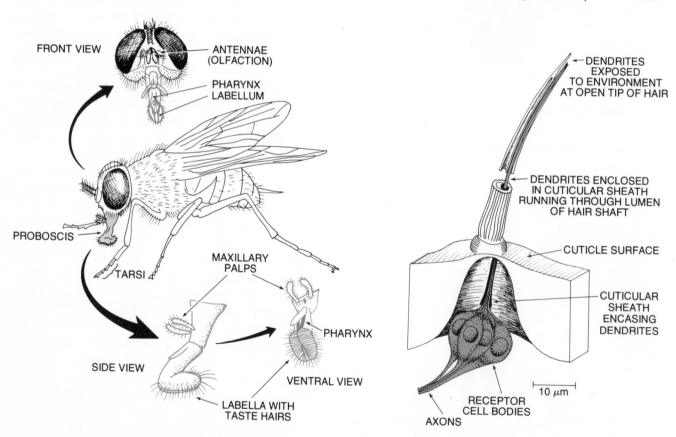

Fig. 8.4-1. Anatomy of the head and proboscis of the housefly. The proboscis is shown in the extended (feeding) position. Taste hairs also occur on the tarsi (feet).

Fig. 8.4-2. Taste hair from the labellum of a blowfly. Each taste hair is innervated by three to five taste receptor cells which have dendrites extending to the open tip of the hair.

dorsal part of the fly's wings and thorax. If only the wings are glued and immobilized, the body will probably not have been heated drastically. Tape the applicator sticks to a holder (a block of wood will do), and number the flies. Keep the flies in a feet-down orientation. Discard any damaged insects in a jar of 95% ethanol.

The feeding responses of newly mounted flies may be erratic so allow at least 1 hour between mounting and testing. (Testing 1 or 2 days after mounting is better, in which case the flies should be fed after mounting by dipping each fly's tarsi into 0.1 M sucrose and allowing it to drink until satiated. Place the flies in a refrigerator or cold room at 4°–10° C until use.)

Preparation for testing

Make up a series of sucrose solutions in one-third log molar steps (i.e., 0.001 M sucrose, 0.002 M, 0.005 M, 0.01 M, . . . 1.0 M). Start with a 1.0 M stock solution and serially dilute it. Label all solution containers. Make up a similar series of solutions of the sugars maltose and fructose from 1.0 M stock solutions. Finally, make up the following concentrations of salts using 1.0 M stock solutions: 0.1 M NaCl, 0.2 M NaCl, 0.5 M NaCl, 0.02 M $CaCl_2$, and 0.05 M $CaCl_2$.

Punch out 100 paper discs from filter paper by using a standard paper punch. The routine procedure for taste stimulation will be to saturate a disc with a test solution and present the disc to the fly's legs. Do not leave a large drop of fluid on the disc. The fly will generally take the disc if allowed to, and will hold on to it indefinitely, but may or may not lower the proboscis and drink. Use the following scale for scoring responses:
1. Proboscis is lowered into the test solution.
2. Proboscis is lowered partially.
3. Paper is retained, but proboscis is not lowered.
4. Paper is rejected.

If the fly responds at level 1, the paper discs should be immediately taken from the fly before it has a chance to imbibe much of the fluid. Flies which respond at levels 2 or 3 should have the discs taken away after 10 seconds. After removal of the disc, a fly's tarsi should be rinsed with distilled water. A good way to do this is to give them a fresh disc thoroughly saturated with distilled water. From 3 to 5 minutes should pass before the next presentation.

Proboscis responses to odor

Allow the mounted flies 10–15 minutes to revive if they have been in a refrigerator or cold room. Test each of 5 flies in turn with distilled water, 1.0 M sucrose, and 1.0 M NaCl brought to within about 3 mm of the front tarsi. Do not touch the fly with the paper disc. Record any positive responses. Now, allow each fly to drink as much distilled water as it will take. After all flies are satiated with water, re-test for olfactory responses.

Proboscis responses to tarsal taste stimulation

Now test each of the 5 flies just used (response to odor) with the test substances, but allow the tarsi to contact and hold the discs for 10 seconds. Score the responses.

Further controls

Determine whether mechanical contact is an essential part of contact chemoreception by the tarsi. Test a dry filter paper. Test the dry filter paper plus the odor of 1.0 M sucrose. Now, what can you conclude about the sensory determinants of proboscis extension?

Testing the spatial requirements for a response

Is proboscis extension elicited by stimulating the labellum in the absence of tarsal stimulation? Use several previously untested flies to test the proposition that proboscis extension can be elicited by stimulating a single tarsal hair. Use 2.0 M sucrose for testing and a dissecting microscope to see the tarsal hairs. A small droplet can be applied with an insect pin or sewing needle.

Rejection responses

As stated in the "Introduction," rejection could be defined as the failure to extend the proboscis when an aversive chemical has been added to the preferred solution, e.g., 0.1 M sucrose. However, you should attempt to demonstrate active proboscis retraction by stimulating the tarsi with the aversive chemical.

Touch a drop of water to the labellum of a food- and water-deprived fly to elicit proboscis extension. After extension, touch the tarsi with 0.5 M NaCl. Repeat the test several times. You may wish to use this method with other possibly aversive chemicals in tests of your own design. For example, inorganic acids might be rejected, but what about amino acids which are constituents of natural foods and generally taste sweet to humans? Try 0.05 M phenylalanine.

Thresholds

Use 6–10 water-satiated flies to determine the acceptance threshold (50% response) for sucrose. Start with the weakest concentration and work upward through increasingly concentrated solutions. Be sure to wash each fly's tarsi after testing. Why not let them drink the sugar? Also, determine the acceptance thresholds for maltose and fructose (start with 0.001 M).

Now, determine the acceptance thresholds for the sugars alpha- and beta-methylglucoside. These two sugars are isomers whose methylation prevents *mutarotation* (changing from one isomer to the other by bond rotation in solution). With these two isomers you can test the relative effectiveness of two sugars whose chemical composition is identical, but whose stereochemistry is slightly different.

Feedback control of feeding
(at the instructor's option)
Feeding stops when the fly's gut becomes distended. Stretch receptors in the foregut sense the distention and relay the information to the central nervous system where the input from the tarsal receptors is inhibited. Inhibition of the tarsal feeding reflex normally terminates feeding. When the recurrent nerve which contains the axons of foregut stretch receptors is experimentally cut, flies become hyperphagic (excess eating). They continue to imbibe sugar solutions because there is no stretch receptor input to initiate inhibition.

As a symptom, hyperphagia can also be produced by eliminating the tarsal input and feeding the flies by applying the sugar solution directly to the labellum. Because the gut stretch receptors only inhibit tarsal and not labellar sensory input to the brain, the fly continues to feed. Why does this not happen to the fly in nature?

You can demonstrate hyperphagia in the following way.

1. Mount 10 fresh flies using Tackiwax instead of sealing wax. Satiate them with distilled water.
2. Use fine forceps to lift and embed the legs of 5 flies in the Tackiwax. No leg should be left in a position

where it can contact a sucrose solution applied directly to the proboscis.
3. Feed each of the control flies by dipping their tarsi into a petri dish filled with 1.0 M sucrose. Allow each fly to imbibe as much of the solution as it will. Use a stopwatch to time the total feeding time of each fly; then repeat the series 5 times, allowing each fly 5 more chances to feed. Measure these feeding times as well, but ignore any partial extensions of the proboscis which do not touch the solution.
4. Feed the flies whose legs have been immobilized in the Tackiwax. Touch the proboscis of each fly to the surface of the 1.0 M sucrose solution. Time the feeding period of each fly, allowing each fly at least 6 chances to feed.
5. Compare the total feeding times of the two sets of flies. Compare the number of trials before each group stopped feeding. Consider the results of this experiment and illustrate with a diagram the feedback loop involved.

Are the flies drinking to obtain a fixed amount of sensory stimulation?
Mount 15 flies. Satiate on water. Test 5 flies at 0.01 M sucrose, 5 at 0.1 M, and 5 at 1.0 M. In each case measure the drinking time. Is it a direct or inverse function of concentration? Interpret. If you have completed the previos section, you can use that data for 1.0 M sucrose.

Pitfalls and Suggestions

1. Mount the flies carefully and discard any damaged ones.
2. Kill all flies at the end of the experiment by immersion in a beaker of 95% ethanol.

Materials

Materials needed at each station
50 applicator sticks (alternative: large pins and styrofoam blocks)
Sealing wax (Recommendation: Crown Sticky-Wax, S. S. White Co., Philadelphia)
Bunsen burner or soldering iron for melting wax
2 wooden blocks for holding mounted flies (about 2 × 4 × 12 inches)
Stopwatch
20 petri dishes

30 test tubes for serial dilutions
Dissecting microscope
Fine forceps (furnished by students)

Materials available in the laboratory
Extra applicator sticks, sealing wax, and petri dishes
Tackiwax (Cenco) (especially valuable when the legs must be pushed into the wax)
Alcohol-filled killing jar
Masking tape
Refrigerator or cold room at 4°–10° C
Cardboard boxes suitable for holding mounted flies taped to wooden blocks
Large plastic bags or polyethylene film
Pipettes, serological, 1 ml and 10 ml
Paper punch capable of producing 1/4 inch (7 mm) paper discs
Filter paper, Whatman no. 1 or equivalent
Solutions:
 Distilled water
 2.0 M sucrose
 1.0 M sucrose
 1.0 M maltose
 1.0 M D-fructose
 1.0 M NaCl
 1.0 M $CaCl_2$
 0.1 M α-methylglucoside (methyl-α-D-gluco-pyranoside)
 0.1 M β-methylglucoside (methyl-β-D-gluco-pyranoside)
 95% ethanol for killing flies
 0.1 M phenylalanine

Animals
Blowflies, *Phormia regina* (black blowfly), or other species such as *Sarcophaga*, *Calliphora*, or *Lucilia*. Houseflies can also be used, but blowflies are suggested. (Obtain 40 pupae or larvae/station/laboratory period. They can be obtained from entomology departments, researchers, and several biological supply houses, such as Carolina Biological Supply Co.) Order pupae which have just pupated. Place them on a thin layer of slightly moistened wood shavings in an enamelled pan (24 × 30 cm). Cover with a similar layer of wood shavings and moisten slightly. Do not let the shavings dry out. The pan should be placed in a fly cage (40 × 40 × 60 cm) screened on four sides and one end. Tacked around the perimeter of the other

end of the cage should be a cloth which is long enough to twist and tie securely with a string. Later the string can be loosened and a hand inserted to remove flies. Pupae kept at 24° C will hatch in about 10 days, at 28° C in about 7 days. As the day of emergence approaches, the eye color turns from white to pink to red. Place a 60 mm petri dish containing dry table sugar in the cage along with a jar of water inverted on two pieces of filter paper in a 100 mm petri dish. This food and water source is essential for the flies as soon as they emerge. Since the pupae do not usually emerge all at once, this arrangement should supply adult flies for 2 weeks at room temperature. If the adults need to be kept longer, store them at 4° C in a container covered with a plastic bag to prevent desiccation. A given fly will survive for at least 2 weeks when cooled.

Notes for the Instructor

1. Timing of the emergence of the flies is critical. Arrange to have the flies emerge 3–4 days prior to the experiment so the students do not have to test newly emerged flies. Deprive the flies of food (but not water) for 48 hours maximum at room temperature prior to testing feeding responses.
2. There is a significant problem if you obtain fly larvae rather than pupae. Larvae about to pupate will crawl and force their way out of many different kinds of containers.
3. You may wish to provide some other kinds of stimulating substances, such as amino acids and fatty acids. Tests of the sensory basis underlying insect repellents would be an interesting project. Tests of artificial sweeteners like saccharin or cyclamate would also be instructive.

Selected References

Information on the molecular basis of chemoreception continues to unfold from research on lower organisms. Particularly promising is the genetic study of chemoreception (Adler, 1969; Isono and Kikuchi, 1974). Recent biochemical evidence has resurrected the hypothesis that enzymes may participate in the transduction of chemical energy—from sugar molecules to a biological response (Adler and Epstein, 1974; Amakawa et al., 1975).

Adler, J. 1969. Chemoreceptors in bacteria. *Science* 166: 1588–97.

Dethier, V. G. 1969. Feeding behavior of the blowfly. In *Advances in the study of behavior*, vol. 2, ed. D. S. Lehrman; R. A. Hinde; and E. Shaw. Academic Press, New York, pp. 111–266.

———. 1976. *The hungry fly*. Harvard University Press, Cambridge.

Gelperin, A. 1971. Regulation of feeding. *Annu. Rev. Entomol.* 16: 365–78.

Oakley, B., and Benjamin, R. M. 1966. Neural mechanisms of taste. *Physiol. Rev.* 46: 173–211.

RESEARCH REPORTS

Adler, J., and Epstein, W. 1974. Phosphotransferase-system enzymes as chemoreceptors for certain sugars in *Escherichia coli* chemotaxis. *Proc. Nat. Acad. Sci. U.S.A.* 71: 2895–99.

Amakawa, T.; Kijima, H.; and Morita, H. 1975. Insoluble α-glucosidase: Possible pyranose site of the sugar receptor of the labellar of the blowfly, *Phormia regina*. *J. Insect Physiol.* 21: 1419–25.

Dethier, V. G., and Gelperin, A. 1967. Hyperphagia in the blowfly. *J. Exp. Biol.* 47: 191–200.

Dethier, V. G., and Hanson, F. E. 1968. Electrophysiological responses of the chemoreceptors of the blowfly to sodium salts of fatty acids. *Proc. Nat. Acad. Sci.* 60: 1296–1303.

Frings, H., and O'Neal, B. R. 1946. The loci and thresholds of contact chemoreceptors in females of the horsefly *Tabanus sulcifrans* Macq. *J. Exp. Zool.* 103: 61–79.

Getting, P. A. 1971. The sensory control of motor output in fly proboscis extension. *Z. vergl. Physiol.* 74: 103–20.

Isono, K., and Kikuchi, T. 1974. Autosomal recessive mutation in sugar response of *Drosophila*. *Nature* 248: 243–44.

Minnich, D. E. 1921. An experimental study of the tarsal chemoreceptors of two nymphalid butterflies. *J. Exp. Biol.* 33: 173–203.

Shiraishi, A., and Kuwabara, M. 1970. The effects of amino acids on the labellar hair chemosensory cells of the fly. *J. Gen. Physiol.* 56: 768–82.

8.5 Conditioned Taste Aversion in the Rat
One-Trial Learning of LiCl Avoidance

Introduction

Rationale

The study of homeostatic regulation through behavioral adjustments has a long tradition in physiology. The topic of interest here is the survival of animals in a world in which some potential food is nutritious and some is toxic.

Most herbivores and omnivores are equipped through evolution with unlearned taste aversions for alkaloids (bitter chemicals), and preferences both for sugars (sweet chemicals) and for Na^+. Alkaloids are commonly toxic. Sugars signify carbohydrate sources of calories. Supplementary Na^+ must be ingested by animals which eat plants because plants are typically rich in K^+, but poor in Na^+.

Plant and animal interactions are characterized sometimes by mutual benefits and sometimes by antagonistic outcomes. The sweetness of fruits encourages herbivority and dispersion of those seeds which are adapted to pass undamaged through animal gastrointestinal tracts. As pharmacologists know, there is also an exceedingly long list of toxic chemicals synthesized by plants. The toxicity of these "secondary or defensive compounds" discourages predation by herbivores (Freeland and Janzen, 1974). Animals, in turn, defend themselves by detoxifying the chemicals or by avoiding the source through a learning process called *conditioned aversion*. Generally, mammals will initially eat only small amounts of novel foods. If sickness results, the animal will not eat that food again even many days later. Such conditioned aversion is a potent example of *one-trial learning* in which the taste of a substance is associated with sickness. It is also remarkable that conditioned aversion can be established even when the sickness follows the taste experience by as much as 6 hours (Garcia et al., 1974).

Considering the ubiquity, potency, and evolutionary significance of conditioned aversion, there is a surprising paucity of information about its physiological basis. There is a growing list of diverse central taste pathways which radiate to areas that may be important in conditioned aversion (Norgren, 1976).

In the laboratory conditioned aversion can be established by almost any procedure that produces a sick animal: x-radiation, injection of cytotoxic chemicals, ingestion of poisons, etc. In this experiment we will utilize a more natural procedure. Rats will drink the pleasant tasting but toxic chemical lithium chloride. The tastes of LiCl and NaCl are almost indistinguisable to the rat. Moderate concentrations of either NaCl or LiCl, such as 0.1–0.2 M, are readily drunk in preference to water. LiCl ingestion makes rats sick. It is not clear which of the several symptoms of lithium poisoning result in the conditioned aversion phenomenon. A change in the state of the central nervous system must occur. Lithium probably creates harmful effects through substitution and interference with sodium metabolism.

For a few years LiCl was used as a substitute for NaCl in humans—until fatalities began to occur. It is fortunate that clinical trials with lithium were not banned at this point because lithium salts have since gained wide acceptance as an effective treatment of the manic phase of manic-depressive psychosis. The theraputic dosage for humans is approximately 1.5 times that required to produce learned aversion in rats (in terms of mg/kg body weight). Patients sometimes report nausea and gastrointestinal upset.

Time to complete the exercise: The minimum time is one laboratory period to expose (treat), and one period to test the rats. As these will be short periods, the students may be asked to establish the water deprivation routine and to measure the water intake of the rats daily throughout the experiment.

Procedure

General comments

We will observe the phenomenon of conditioned aversion to LiCl and test whether this aversion generalizes to other monovalent chloride salts or to saccharin. The degree of generalization is an operational measure of taste similarity to LiCl. A water deprivation schedule will be established prior to the first laboratory. In the first laboratory period you will expose the rats to LiCl, and in a second period measure the effects of conditioned aversion upon fluid intake.

Schedule

The instructional staff will assign the rats for which you will be responsible.

Water Deprivation. (This segment may be carried out by the instructional staff.) Ninety-five hours before the first laboratory meeting, segregate rats in individual cages and deprive them of water. Twenty-three and a half hours later give each rat a water bottle for 30 minutes. Repeat the same 30-minute access period to water for the next 3 days.

On the day preceding the laboratory period determine water consumption by weighing the bottle before and after drinking.

The water deprivation schedule causes rats to drink reliably *during* the laboratory period. In 4 days the rats become accustomed to obtaining their water during the 30-minute period each day. Twenty-three and a half hours is sufficient deprivation to ensure that normal rats will drink, but not so intense as to cause them to drink the aversive taste solutions later.

Activities during the first laboratory period. Label each rat cage with a number. Put the water bottle on the cage and observe the drinking rat for 10 or 15 seconds. Then replace the water in the bottle with the appropriate exposure chemical (table 8.5-1). The chemical bottle should be weighed and placed on the cage for 30 minutes. Then reweigh the bottle and calculate the fluid intake. The major sign of LiCl sickness is that the rat will lie down and remain still on the cage floor.

Rest day. Give all rats at least 1 day of 23.5 hours water deprivation and then 30 minutes water without LiCl. Measure fluid intake for each rat.

Test day. The tests will all be of the same form, namely, measuring the intake of a test chemical in a 30-minute period. Table 8.5-1 presents a suggested list of exposure and test conditions in order of priority. Use no more than 75 ml of chemical solution per rat.

Analysis of the results

Using data from the entire class compare the fluid ingestion under the various conditions tested. Was water intake reduced by the treatment? Arrange the test chemicals in order of similarity to LiCl.

Additional suggested exercises

(at the instructor's option)
1. Test the strength of conditioned aversion as a function of:
   a. repeated trials with NaCl over days (table 8.5-1, experiment 3);
   b. the concentration of LiCl ingested.
2. Make tests for generalization of LiCl aversion to other salts, e.g., NH_4Cl, $CaCl_2$, and Na_2SO_4.
3. Compare the potency of conditioned aversion to a

taste solution (0.01 M saccharin in 0.12 M LiCl) with that to an olfactory solution (0.0001 M ethylaceto-acetate in 0.12 M LiCl). What should the test solutions be here?

Pitfalls and Suggestions

1. Each student should develop a chart showing responsibilities for the duration of the experiment.
2. It is important to make all measures of fluid intake at the *same time* each day. In this way all rats will have the same level of thirst and be in the same phase of their circadian activity cycle.
3. Treat the class data with proper consideration to variability. Are the effects statistically significant?
4. Do you think that generalization of conditioned aversion is a better measure of taste similarity than total volume intake of two chemicals ingested by an inexperienced rat over a 24 hour period?

Materials

Materials needed at each station
Triple-beam balance for weighing the bottles to measure fluid ingestion
Paper towels
1,000-ml volumetric flask
Extra water bottle
100-ml graduated cylinder
Bottles for solutions

Materials available in the laboratory
1 cage/rat (Each cage should have a clip to hold the water or test-solution bottle.)
Solutions:
(100 ml of each of the following chemicals/single exposure/rat)
0.24 M LiCl; 0.12 M LiCl, NaCl, KCl; and
0.02 M saccharin (acidic form, not the sodium salt [add 50 ml of 0.24 M LiCl to 50 ml of 0.02 M saccharin to produce a mixture of 0.12 M LiCl + 0.01 M saccharin])

Animals
8 rats/station (150–200 g females) House the rats in individual cages. Food should be continuously present. Water deprive according to the schedule indicated.

Notes for the Instructor

1. The logistics of numbers of animals and experiments will depend upon space, time, and student access to facilities. Eight to ten rats per condition would provide a solid basis for statistical treatment.
2. It may be simpler for the instructional staff rather than the students to establish the water deprivation schedule and to measure fluid intake on the days when the class does not meet.
3. Water will leak out of a bottle just inverted on a rat's cage until a vacuum is established. This error in weighing can be eliminated if the bottle is inverted and clipped to a wooden block before weighing. Subtract the weight of the block to get the weight of the inverted bottle.
4. H saccharin is a better choice than the sodium salt of saccharin. With the sodium salt there may be aversion generalization to the Na of the saccharin.
5. The first day requires minimal time of actual student work. Urge students to use the extra time to consider the logic of the experiments and develop a written flowchart.
6. Use table 8.5-1 for assigning experiments and rats to each student.
7. It is important to stress that behavioral analysis is a significant part of physiology. Behavior cannot be explained until it is itself characterized.
8. These same rats can be used for further experiments, namely, 7.2, 7.5, 7.7, 7.8, and 7.9.

TABLE 8.5-1
Conditioned Aversion Treatments and Tests

Experiment number	Exposure (Day 5) 30 minutes of	Test (Day 7) 30 minutes of
1.	0.12 M LiCl	0.12 M LiCl
2.	0.12 M LiCl	H_2O
3.	0.12 M LiCl	0.12 M NaCl
4.	0.12 M LiCl	0.02 M saccharin
5.	0.12 M LiCl	0.12 M KCl
6.	0.12 M NaCl	0.12 M NaCl
7.	0.01 M saccharin + 0.12 M LiCl as a mixture	0.01 M saccharin

Selected References

Freeland, W. J., and Janzen, D. H. 1974. Strategies in herbivory by mammals: The role of plant secondary compounds. *Am. Naturalist* 108: 269–89.

Garcia, J.; Hankins, W. G.; and Rusiniak, K. W. 1974. Behavioral regulation of the milieu interne in man and rat. *Science* 185: 824–31.

Nachman, M., and Cole, L. P. 1971. Role of taste in specific hungers. In *Handbook of sensory physiology, vol. 4, Chemical senses 2, Taste*, ed. L. M. Beidler. Springer-Verlag, New York, pp. 337–62.

RESEARCH REPORTS

Mackay, B. 1974. Conditioned food aversion produced by toxicosis in Atlantic cod. *Behav. Biol.* 12: 347–55.

Nachman, M. 1963. Learned aversion to the taste of lithium chloride and generalization to other salts. *J. Comp. Physiol. Psychol.* 56: 343–49.

Nachman, M., and Ashe, J. H. 1973. Learned taste aversions in rats as a function of dosage, concentration, and route of administration of LiCl. *Physiol. Behav.* 10: 73–78.

Norgren, R. 1976. Taste pathways to hypothalamus and amygdala. *J. Comp. Neurol.* 166: 17–30.

8.6 Sexual Behavior
Responses of Cockroaches to Pheromones

Line illustration is adapted from Barth, 1970.

Introduction

Rationale

To most people, even to some biological scientists, communication among animals means communication by visual cues, sound, and touch. The fact is that much of the animal kingdom relies heavily on chemoreception. Ants, for example, recognize each other, follow trails, locate food, and send alarm signals via chemical signals. Karlson and Lüscher (1959) coined the term *pheromone* to describe chemical messengers which are "secreted to the outside of an individual and are received by a second individual of the same species in which they release a specific reaction, for example, a definite behavior or developmental process." Pheromones have been intensively studied both in insects (since they might be useful in programs of biological control of insect pests) and in various mammals. Many pheromones that assist in the regulation of social interactions and sexual behavior are now known. Pheromones have also been effectively used as tools in research on olfactory transduction (Schneider, 1969).

Cockroaches of the genus *Periplaneta* use sex attractants to initiate the courtship behavior which leads to mating. The initial step in courtship behavior is the reception of a female-produced sex attractant by the specific receptors on the antennae of the male. This initial event leads to rapid antennal movements and oriented locomotion by the male. After the male locates the female, a stereotyped sequence of male-female interactions occurs which may or may not lead to successful mating (fig. 8.6-1).

In many insects the chemical structure of the sex attractant is known (see Jacobson, 1972), but this is not the situation in the American cockroach *Periplaneta*. Following a protracted series of unsuccessful attempts to isolate and chemically identify the

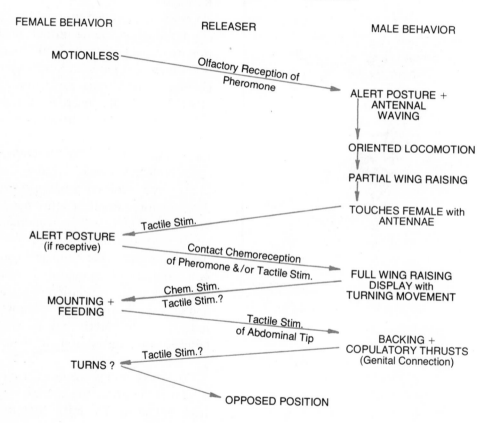

MATING BEHAVIOR OF *PERIPLANETA AMERICANA*

FEMALE BEHAVIOR   RELEASER   MALE BEHAVIOR

MOTIONLESS

Olfactory Reception of Pheromone

ALERT POSTURE + ANTENNAL WAVING

ORIENTED LOCOMOTION

PARTIAL WING RAISING

TOUCHES FEMALE with ANTENNAE

ALERT POSTURE (if receptive)

Tactile Stim.

Contact Chemoreception of Pheromone &/or Tactile Stim.

FULL WING RAISING DISPLAY with TURNING MOVEMENT

MOUNTING + FEEDING

Chem. Stim.
Tactile Stim.?

Tactile Stim. of Abdominal Tip

BACKING + COPULATORY THRUSTS (Genital Connection)

TURNS ?

Tactile Stim.?

OPPOSED POSITION

Fig. 8.6-1. A summary of the mating behavior of *Periplaneta americana* indicating the probable releasers for each step in the sequence (Barth, 1970). This is a typical ethological diagram (ethogram) which presumes that each response produces stimuli which initiate the next response in the sequence.

292

sex attractant, it now seems likely that at least two (possibly synergistic) compounds are involved in *P. americana* sex attraction.

In *Periplaneta* and other insects, the antennae bear two major types of hairlike sensilla: thick-walled hairs which serve as contact chemoreceptors (taste hairs), and thin-walled hairs which are olfactory receptors (fig. 8.6-2).

Sex-attractant reception is of paramount importance in the antennae of male *Periplaneta americana*. The antennae of adult males have nearly twice as many olfactory sense organs as those of adult females (3.9×10^4 vs. 2.2×10^4). Both male and female larvae of the terminal instar, which precedes the adult stage, have about 1.7×10^4 olfactory sensilla, indicating that the male develops additional receptors when it molts to the adult stage. Electrophysiological results indicate that the adult male antenna has sex-attractant receptors which are highly sensitive to the female-produced pheromone, whereas the larval and female antennae have receptors primarily responsive to other odors, such as food odors (Schafer, 1977).

Time to complete the exercise: One to two hours during the normal laboratory period are required for histological examination of the antennae and planning of the behavioral experiments. Two to four hours in the evening are required to perform the behavioral experiments. The behavioral experiments *must* be done in the evening between 8:00 P.M. and 1:00 A.M., or they will not be successful. Several evenings would be required for a more extensive study. The instructor should either provide filter papers which have been exposed to females or arrange for the students to expose such papers at least a week before the behavioral experiments.

Procedure

Sexing cockroaches
Obtain several specimens of *Periplaneta americana*. If other species are available, obtain several examples of each species for comparative examination. Place your cockroaches in several containers whose vertical walls have been smeared with petroleum jelly (Vaseline). An 8–10 cm band of petroleum jelly around the upper surface of the container walls is sufficient to prevent escape.

A
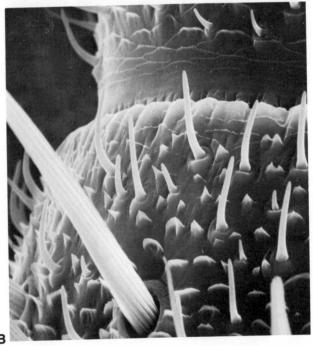
B

Fig. 8.6-2. Antennal sense organs of *Periplaneta americana*. **A.** One antennal segment containing thick-walled contact chemoreceptors (the large hairs or bristles) and thin-walled olfactory sense organs (the small hairs), magnified 240×. **B.** View of thin-walled olfactory hairs and one thick-walled chemoreceptor. Olfactory hairs such as these are usually innervated by two sensory neurons, magnified 600×. (Scanning electron micrographs from Schafer and Sanchez, 1973 and 1976.)

Examine the posterior portion of the abdomen of one *P. americana* and refer to figure 8.6-3A. Both males and females have a pair of *anal cerci* protruding from the tip of the abdomen. These are sensory organs which are sensitive to vibrational stimuli such as air movements (including sound) and vibrations of the substrate. Males also have a pair of *styli* which are smaller and located more medially than the cerci. *Females lack styli*. The presence or absence of styli is the easiest way to tell male from female. Note other evidence of sexual dimorphism: females have a large, vertical slit at the tip of the abdomen from which an egg case (*ootheca*) may be protruding, male cerci are longer than female cerci, and in general the female body is wider than that of the male.

Examine other species which may be available and compare them with *Periplaneta americana*. In other species within the genus *Periplaneta*, the anal styli are harder to see than in *Periplaneta americana*. In some species, like *Leucophaea maderae*, the styli are difficult to see, but the presence of styli is still the most reliable criterion for distinguishing between male and female.

Examination of the antennal sensilla of <u>Periplaneta americana</u>

Obtain a male *Periplaneta americana*. If a newly molted insect is available, choose it for examination because the sensilla will be much easier to discern on its unpigmented antennae. Newly molted insects can be recognized by their striking white color.

Cut one of the antennae off at the base and return the insect to its container. Place the excised antenna on a microscope slide and cover it with a few drops of mineral oil and a rectangular coverslip.

Do not get mineral oil on the microscope stage or objective lenses.

Choose the longest coverslip available (e.g., 24 × 50 mm). Take care to ensure that no air bubbles adhere to the antenna under the coverslip because they will make viewing the sensilla difficult.

Examine the preparation with a compound microscope. Identify the long, thick-walled hairs. Gently depress the coverslip with a dissecting needle and watch for movement of the thick-walled hairs. They

have flexible articulations at their bases which allow the hairs to bend freely when the antenna brushes a surface. Hair movement is detected by the dendrite of a single mechanoreceptor cell attached to the base of the hair. These same sensilla also contain chemoreceptors analogous to vertebrate taste receptors. The tip of each hair is porous and the dendrites of three to four taste-receptor cells in the lumen of the hair are thus exposed to the external environment. These sensilla are classified as *contact chemoreceptor* organs since they are stimulated by fluid contact with stimulatory substances.

Attempt to identify the thin-walled olfactory sensilla. They are much smaller than the thick-walled hairs and are more difficult to see. It may be easier to identify the olfactory sensilla at the tip of the antenna where the cuticle is thinner and more translucent. Each olfactory hair is innervated by two odor-sensitive receptors. Can you discern any differences in the distribution of olfactory sensilla on male versus female antennae, particularly near the bases of the antennae? Sensilla responsive to pheromones are not morphologically distinguishable from other odor receptors.

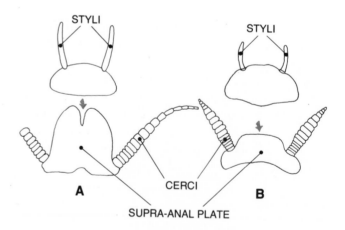

Fig. 8.6-3. Male cerci and styli on the tip of the abdomen of *Periplaneta americana* and *Periplaneta brunnea*. Females (*not shown*) lack styli and in general have shorter, stubbier cerci. **A**. Male *Periplaneta americana*. The styli are very long and slender. The male supra-anal plate (*arrow*) is deeply notched. **B**. Male *Periplaneta brunnea*. The styli are shorter and not as long as the space between their bases. The male supra-anal plate (*arrow*) is truncate or only slightly notched.

Procedure

Collection of attractant on filter papers

The easiest method of collecting attractant is simply to expose pieces of filter paper to isolated females. Either your instructor will supply you with already exposed filter papers, or you will have to expose them yourself, using the procedure that follows.

The following procedure must be initiated at least one week before the exposed filter papers are used in the behavioral experiments. In a week's time the papers will have absorbed a sufficient amount of pheromone. It is advantageous to expose the papers for a longer period if more time is available.

To collect the female-produced sex attractant, place 10 to 15 females in a container with some air holes punched in the lid. The animals should be supplied with a few pieces of lab chow or dry dog food and a piece of apple for moisture. Replace the apple when necessary. Also provide a toilet-paper tube for the roaches to hide in. Obtain a small polyethylene bottle with a wide mouth and punch the bottle full of small holes with a paper punch or sharp instrument. Place a piece of folded filter paper (Whatman no. 1) within the ventilated bottle and put the bottle into the cockroach container. You ought to standardize the size of the filter paper and the length of time it is exposed to a given number of female cockroaches. Include some young virgin females (2–4 weeks old) since older mated females cease pheromone production. Virgins can be obtained by segregating newly molted females from males. Expose filter papers to male adults and/or larvae for use as controls. *The collection containers should be separated from each other and in a different room than the behavioral testing area.*

Alternate method for obtaining cockroach sex attractant
(optional)

Some students may want to attempt a chemical extraction of the sex attractant. A very powerful attractant can be extracted from feces produced by female *Periplaneta americana* in a period of 2–3

weeks before the start of your behavioral experiments. You should also collect the feces of male and/or larvae to make control extracts. Keep the male, female, and larval containers separated (in different rooms if at all possible, and away from your behavioral testing room). Prepare fecal extracts according to the following protocol.

Extraction (Amounts may be scaled down as needed.)
1. Grind 1.0 g feces in 10 ml dichloromethane-methanol (3:1) in a fresh mortar with a pinch of clean sand.
2. Filter into a fresh mortar through Whatman no. 1 filter paper.
3. Grind residue in first mortar with 10 ml dichloromethane-methanol and pour into filter.
4. Repeat step 3.
5. Rinse filter with 10 ml dichloromethane-methanol.
6. Repeat step 5.

Concentration of extract
1. Add enough boiling stones to cover the fluid in the mortar. Cargille 4–12-mesh silica stones are ideal.
2. Evaporate to dryness *in vacuo* at room temperature.

Take care not to boil the fluid in the vacuum chamber. Bleed the air from the chamber slowly, carefully watching the mortar for signs of boiling. Use a cold trap filled with dry ice in the vacuum line to catch the dichloromethane-methanol before it enters the vacuum pump.

Recovery of extract
1. Grind the residue, including the boiling stones, in 20 ml purified *n*-hexane. Work quickly at room temperature.
2. Filter into a flask through Whatman no. 1 filter paper.
3. Wash the mortar with 10 ml *n*-hexane and pour into the filter.
4. Repeat step 3.
5. Wash the filter with 10 ml *n*-hexane.
6. Repeat step 5.
7. Store the extract in a tightly capped container kept inside of a larger, capped container in a refrigerator.

Application to filter paper
An extract of 0.1 ml applied to a 4 cm² piece of filter paper is more than sufficient for behavioral testing. Apply the extract to the filter paper *in a fume hood*.

Use of individual cockroaches as odor sources
(optional)
A third source of pheromone is live or freshly killed insects. For example, a live female can be presented to a group of males which have been isolated from females for a week and the results observed. The female could simply be dropped into the testing arena, or presented inside of a perforated container. If live animals are to be used, be sure to have several females available because some, particularly those which have egg cases protruding from the abdomen or which have recently mated, may not be producing pheromone. Males or larvae can be presented as controls.

Preparation of the behavioral testing area
The room in which behavioral testing is done should be provided with blinds for darkening the windows. The blinds should be kept shut at all times, but some light must be allowed to leak in during the daytime so that the cockroaches are able to establish a normal diurnal rhythm in phase with the natural day-night cycle. The room should be provided with a number of desk lamps with 7.5-watt red bulbs for illuminating the behavioral arenas at night. Keep the red light low by placing the lamps far enough above the arenas so that the light intensity is just sufficient for viewing the cockroaches after your eyes are adapted to the dark. Leave the red lights on during the day and night.

Behavioral observations must be made at night, between 8:00 P.M. and 1:00 A.M. Do not attempt to artificially reverse the day-night cycle by using a light on a timer. You risk failure of the experiment.

A suitable behavioral arena is illustrated in figure 8.6-4. A standard 10-gallon aquarium with a fitted top is ideal. The floor, back, and three sides of the aquarium should be covered on the outside with white paper to provide a suitable background for viewing the cockroaches. The papers can be ruled with a marking pencil in equal-sized rectangles (4 per side) for quantitation of activity. The front and fitted top of the aquarium should not be covered with paper, but should be ruled on the outside with a marking pen in equal-sized rectangles. Place a rubber stopper in the round hole in the center of the fitted top. Prepare the appropriate number of aquaria for the experiments you intend to perform.

In general, the experiments will proceed as follows.
1. Place 5 male adults or larvae in each behavioral arena.
2. Place several pieces of lab chow or dry dog food and a water source in each container. A fresh piece of apple or other fruit may be provided. *Do not* place any cardboard tubes or other hiding places in the arena because this will hinder observation of the initial stages of response to the pheromone.
3. All animals will be placed in their arenas at the same time and left for 3–7 days before testing is attempted. Increasing the length of time that the animals are separated from females should increase the behavioral response.
4. The test for attractiveness will be performed *at night* between 8:00 P.M. and 1:00 A.M. In testing, a small piece of filter paper containing attractant or other substance is pinned to the bottom of a cork or rubber stopper and placed in the hole in the fitted top of the behavioral arena. Observations are then made.

There are some precautions to take.

1. Keep *female* cockroaches out of the testing room.
2. Keep collection containers separated.
3. Keep active filter papers separated. Prior to testing, filter papers may be pinned to the corks or rubber stoppers and the stoppers fitted into baby food jars or specimen bottles to prevent loss of activity and cross contamination. Take care while handling the filter papers in order to prevent cross contamination.

Take extreme care to prevent cross contamination if liquid extracts are used. Use a fume hood during loading. Load control filter papers before opening female extract containers.

4. If you run tests on more than one evening, try to start your observations at the same clock time.

5. Begin observations after your eyes are fully dark adapted.

6. Always present control filter papers to the test animals before presenting filter papers known or suspected to contain attractant.

Experiments

You are asked to design your own experiments. At least two kinds of information can be derived from your tests. A detailed ethological description of sexual behavior can be produced that is limited only by your eyesight and observational powers. It is also possible to quantify behavior to some extent. For example, you might try to determine the increase in activity induced by a given dose of sex attractant. This might be done by counting the number of times a single insect crosses a ruled line or corner of the behavioral arena within a given time period after presentation of the pheromone source. Such an experiment could be performed by marking a single individual with a dab of white paint or typewriter correction fluid.

For those familiar with photography and possessing the proper equipment, it might be advantageous to try to analyze sexual interactions with a camera. Fortunately, the flash of an automatic strobe usually does not seem to bother the cockroaches as long as the flash duration is short and the frequency of flashing is not too great.

Here are some questions you might consider in designing your experiments. Questions 1–8 are probably the most important.

1. What characterizes the male response to the sex attractant alone?

2. What characterizes the male response to a live, pheromone-producing female?

3. How stereotyped are the responses? Is there a qualitative difference between responses to the sex-attractant extract and responses elicited by the presence of an attractive female?

4. What is the effect of the presence of several males on the male response? What would happen if there were only one male present in the behavioral arena? What would happen if a single male adult was placed in the behavioral arena with several larvae?

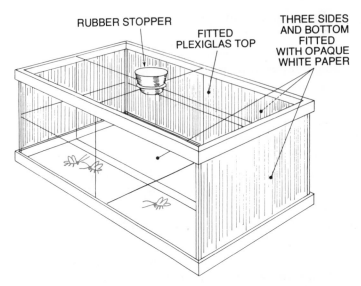

RUBBER STOPPER

FITTED PLEXIGLAS TOP

THREE SIDES AND BOTTOM FITTED WITH OPAQUE WHITE PAPER

Fig. 8.6-4. Behavioral arena. The behavioral arena consists of a 10-gallon aquarium with a fitted top cut from 1/4-inch Plexiglas. A hole is drilled in the top to admit a cork or rubber stopper with the pheromone source (a piece of filter paper) attached. The back, three sides, and bottom are covered on the *outside* with opaque white paper, and each surface is ruled into 4 equal rectangles by the 2 crossed lines.

5. Does the pheromone elicit pseudofemale or homosexual behavior in males?

6. Do the animals habituate to the presence of the pheromone?

7. Is the behavior observed completely sexual in nature, or does it contain elements of other behaviors? How can you tell the difference? What is the role of activity?

8. Does the attractant of *Periplaneta americana* elicit sexual behavior in males of other species within the genus *Periplaneta* (*P. brunnea* or *P. australasiae*, for example)? Does the attractant of *Periplaneta americana* elicit sexual behavior in males of other species outside of its own genus? For example, what is the response of males of *Blatta orientalis*, which is closely related to *Periplaneta americana*? What is the response of *Leucophaea maderae*, which is phylogenetically distant from *Periplaneta americana*?

9. What are the effects of pheromone concentration, the length of time the insects have been isolated from females, and the number of times the insects have been previously exposed to the pheromone on successive nights?

Pitfalls and Suggestions

1. Take every care to prevent cross contamination of containers, filter papers, food, food cups, etc. Remember that you are using your hands to manipulate pheromone sources and the hands can pick up pheromones.

2. When presenting the pheromone to the insects, minimize the possible effects of your presence.

a. Use very dim red light for observations. A red 7.5-watt bulb for each aquarium is more than sufficient.

b. Make no quick movements while making observations.

c. Do not jar the behavioral arena or its supporting table during the course of observations. Take great care in placing the cork or rubber stopper with the filter paper in the fitted top of the arena. Boisterous activity is not conducive to normal behavior.

3. Do not leave the pheromone source in the behavioral arena too long, as this will exhaust the animals and greatly increase the possibility of habituation.

4. Avoid contaminating the air in the test room if possible.

5. It is probably sufficient to have only two control odors, such as distilled water and male-exposed filter papers or extract. Do not spend an excessive amount of time on an elaborate series of controls.

Materials

Materials needed for histological examination of antennae

10–15 microscope slides
10–15 cover glasses (rectangular, 22 × 40 mm or 24 × 50 mm)
Compound microscope
50–100 ml mineral oil

Materials needed for attractant collection on filter papers

Filter paper (Whatman no. 1)
Paper punch (1-hole, hand type for perforating polyethylene bottle)
Widemouthed polyethylene bottles (2–4 oz, snap-cap type preferable)
Insect containers (One-quart canning jars [Mason jars] with wire screens inserted in the lids are ideal.)

Materials needed for attractant extraction (optional)

Insect containers (noted in previous section)
Mortars and pestles
400 ml dichloromethane-methanol (3:1) (made by adding 300 ml dichloromethane [methylene chloride] to 100 ml methanol)
500 ml *n*-hexane (Pentane may be substituted.)
10–12 small storage vials with secure, lined tops (20–30 ml capacity)
Filter paper (Whatman no. 1)
Funnels
Boiling stones (Cargille 4–12-mesh silica are best.)
Vacuum pump or vacuum line
Vacuum jar
Vacuum line moisture trap (Macro trap)
Dry ice for trap

Materials for behavioral testing

Desk lamps with 7.5-watt red bulbs (1/behavioral arena)
Behavioral arenas (10-gallon aquaria or equivalent)
Fitted tops for behavioral arenas (These can be cut from 1/4 inch thick Plexiglas or wood, although Plexiglas is much preferred; cut a 44 mm diameter hole [1-1/4 inch] in the center of each top.)
Cork or rubber stoppers (A no. 9 rubber stopper or no. 22 cork stopper will fit the 44 mm hole in the fitted top.)
Specimen bottles or baby food jars which will accommodate stoppers
White paper or posterboard for arenas
White typewriter opaquing fluid for marking cockroaches
Pins
Lab chow or dry dog food, supplemented by apples
New sponge (cut up to serve as water source)

Animals

Periplaneta americana (Obtain 5 larvae, 10 adult males, and 10 adult females/station.) *Periplaneta americana* can be obtained from Carolina Biological Supply. This is a very popular experimental species which can often be obtained from entomology departments or laboratories doing research on insects. *Periplaneta brunnea* is often available and can be used as a substitute or in combination with *Periplaneta americana* in a comparative study. The two species are quite similar. Figure 8.6-3 will aid you in telling them apart. Other species can also be obtained for comparative studies. Place the roaches in a plastic wastebasket with the upper walls smeared with petroleum jelly (Vaseline) to prevent escape. Provide some vertically standing pieces of cardboard for the cockroaches to climb upon. A sponge wetted with water every few days will supply sufficient water. Feed them laboratory chow or dry dog food. Dry food can be periodically supplemented with apples or other fresh fruit to improve the insects' health. This is probably a good practice to observe with this particular experiment since healthy insects produce more pheromone and display stronger behavioral responses.

Notes for the Instructor

1. Enforce care in handling materials which have been in contact with female cockroaches. Such materials can easily lead to cross contamination or unwanted activation of males.
2. Make sure that the insects chosen by the students are of the proper sex. Females are sometimes accidentally included with males in the testing setup.
3. Make sure that active, undamaged insects are chosen. A lack of antennae or legs can have severe behavioral consequences.
4. Be sure that white backgrounds are used in the testing arenas. *Periplaneta* behavior is almost impossible to observe against a nonwhite background under red light. The testing room should be darkened.
5. Do not be surprised at the large amount of variability in the responses among different males and between different groups.
6. Do not attempt to reverse the photoperiod with a timed light. Observations cannot be made in the daytime.
7. *Periplaneta brunnea* can be substituted for *P. americana*, but in general does not respond quite as well as *P. americana*.
8. Monitor the students' experimental designs. The number of available cockroaches and aquaria will limit the number of tests.

Selected References

Birch, M. C., ed. 1974. *Pheromones*. North Holland, Amsterdam, and Elsevier Press, New York.
Jacobson, M. 1972. *Insect sex pheromones*. Academic Press, New York.
Karlson, P., and Butenandt, A. 1959. Pheromones. *Annu. Rev. Entomol.* 4: 39–58.
Schneider, D. 1969. Insect olfaction: Deciphering system for chemical messages. Science 163: 1031–37.
Shorey, H. H. 1976. *Animal communication by pheromones*. Academic Press, New York.

RESEARCH REPORTS
Barth, R. H., Jr. 1970. The mating behavior of *Periplaneta americana* (Linnaeus) and *Blatta orientalis* Linnaeus (Blattaria, Blattinae), with notes on 3 additional species of *Periplaneta* and interspecific action of sex pheromones. *Z. Tierpsychol.* 27: 722–47.
Roth, L. M., and Barth, R. H., Jr. 1967. The sense organs employed by cockroaches in mating behavior. *Behav.* 28: 58–94.
Roth, L. M., and Willis, E. R. 1952. A study of cockroach behavior. *Am. Midland Naturalist* 47: 66–129.
Rust, M. K.; Burk, T.; and Bell, W. J. 1976. Pheromone stimulated locomotory and orientation responses in the American cockroach. *Anim. Behav.* 24: 52–67.
Schafer, R. 1977. The nature and development of sex attractant specificity in cockroaches of the genus *Periplaneta*. IV. Electrophysiological study of attractant specificity. *J. Exp. Zool.* 199: 189–207.
Schafer, R., and Sanchez, T. V. 1973. Antennal sensory system of the cockroach, *Periplaneta americana*: Postembryonic development and morphology of the sense organs. *J. Comp. Neurol.* 149: 335–54.
Schafer, R., and Sanchez, T. V. 1976. The nature and development of sex attractant specificity in cockroaches of the genus *Periplaneta*. I. Sexual dimorphism in the distribution of antennal sense organs in five species. *J. Morphol.* 149: 139–58.

8.7 Sensitive Plant
Nastic Responses and Conducted Action Potentials in _Mimosa pudica_

Introduction

Rationale

Bacteria, protozoa, plants, and animals often share similar adaptive mechanisms. Photoreactivity, for example, is a common thread running through all phylogenetic levels. Sensitivity to mechanical stimuli is also widespread. While all plants are mechanically sensitive in that their growth patterns are deeply influenced by physical contacts with wind, water, gravity, and other forces and objects in the environment, only a few plants are capable of rapid movement when stimulated. This ability is associated with carnivorous (e.g., Venus' flytrap) or protective (e.g., _Mimosa_) adaptations.

Mimosa pudica is a member of the pea family, Leguminosae. Many members of this family are equipped with organs called _pulvini_ at the bases of

the leaflets, leaves, and petioles. The pulvini contain osmotically active effector cells which cause folding of the leaflet pairs and drooping of the petiole. _Mimosa pudica_, which folds its leaflets in the dark or when disturbed (fig. 8.7-1), is appropriately named: _Mimosa_ is from the Greek for mimic, and _pudica_ from Latin for modest or bashful. The plant hides its leaves when disturbed. Because the movements of _Mimosa pudica_ leaves and stems are independent of the direction of the mechanical stimulus, they have been termed _nastic responses_. This term distinguishes such movements from _tropic responses_ which proceed in a direction determined by the direction of the stimulus. Folding of leaflets in response to mechanical disturbance is termed _seismonasty_.

The rapid nastic response of _Mimosa pudica_ is mediated through interconnected pathways of excitable cells in the leaves, petioles, and stems (fig. 8.7-2). A given pathway is comprised of a series of cells arranged end to end with low resistance pathways between them. The conductile pathways carry propagated action potentials, and are thus analogous to nerve fibers in animals although conduction in plant cells is generally much slower.

In the pulvini at the base of leaflets, leaves, and petioles are a class of effector cells whose turgor pressure holds these structures unfurled and erect (fig. 8.7-1). A disturbance, such as brushing the hand against a leaf, is sufficient to excite conductile cells in the leaves. Excitation is conducted to the pulvinar effector cells, triggering in succession a massive efflux of potassium, a rapid outflow of water, and a drop in turgor pressure. The leaflets fold and the petioles droop. This nastic response is aided by another class of cells arranged as antagonists, which gain potassium and water to increase turgor pressure.

We will explore two aspects of the rapid nastic response. First, mechanical stimulation will be used to examine the nature of the response and its determining factors. Second, you will record conducted potentials from the petioles, stems, and leaves.

Time to complete the exercise: One 3-hour laboratory period. A second session or a longer laboratory period would be useful since the plant requires 10–15 minutes to recover between stimulations.

Procedure

Mimosa pudica is literally a *very* sensitive plant. *Be careful throughout the experiment not to accidentally bump the plant or jar its table.* Moreover, each time the plant is stimulated it will take 10–15 minutes to recover. Therefore, for each test that follows stimulate fresh portions of the leaf or new leaves. Some patience will be required since even in fully recovered and responsive leaflets there may be a

delay of several seconds between stimulus and response, depending on the manner of stimulation and other factors. Examine figure 8.7-1 to learn the meaning of the terms leaf, leaflets, petiole, and stem before proceeding further.

Exploring Mimosa's behavior

Gently touch one of the leaflets at a leaf tip with a thin glass rod or a Pasteur pipette. Can you make only those leaflets in the vicinity of the touch fold? Note that a sufficient stimulus at the tip of the leaf will initiate a wave of leaflet folding toward the base of the leaf.

Pinching stimuli. Use a pair of forceps with rubber-guarded jaws to stimulate by pinching. First, pinch the leaf near its tip.

> **Pinch no harder than necessary to produce a response.**

Can waves of leaflet folding be readily elicited by pinching? In spite of the difficulty in giving a consistent pinch with hand-held forceps, can you get some idea of the force required to get a conducted wave of leaf folding? How much consistency of response is there from leaf to leaf?

Notice that often a wave of leaflet folding will proceed to the base of the leaf, but will not elicit drooping of the petiole. What is the result of eliciting a wave of leaflet folding in a second leaf on the same petiole after the leaflets of the first leaf have folded? We can describe the result of this experiment as a form of *facilitation*.

Pinch a leaflet near the base of a leaf. Does outward (centrifugal) propagation of leaflet folding occur? Does propagation occur in both directions when a leaflet between the leaf tip and base is pinched? Does centrifugal propagation into the leaves occur when the petiole is pinched? Finally, pinch one of the petioles or stems near the base of the plant. Watch for a few minutes.

Brushing stimuli. Pinching is a somewhat unnatural stimulus. Try to elicit the same kinds of responses by brushing a fine glass rod or Pasteur pipette along the axis of one of the leaves. Does sensitivity vary according to the extent or direction of the brushing movement? Does recovery take more or less time than when the leaf was pinched?

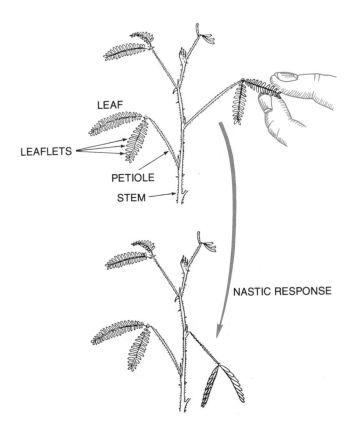

Fig. 8.7-1. The nastic response of *Mimosa pudica*. A touch to the leaf results in folding of the paired leaflets and drooping of the petiole. The effector organs (pulvini) at the bases of leaflets and petioles are not visible.

Damaging stimuli. Use a pair of clean, sharp surgical scissors to cut 2–3 mm off the tip of a distal leaflet. Do this very carefully to prevent jostling and inducing leaflet folding through mechanical stimulation. Watch carefully, allowing ample time to observe the effects of the damage. Does damage always elicit a wave of leaflet folding? In what respects are the movements after damage different from those after brushing or pinching stimuli? Finally, ask yourself if you can clearly distinguish in this experiment between hormonal or electrical propagation of the responses along the leaf and petiole.

Further behavioral experiments
Here are some suggestions for other experiments using simple observational techniques.

1. Measure the conduction velocity in leaves and petioles. Use cutting as a stimulus, stopwatches for measuring, and the pulvinar responses of leaflet and petiole bases as time marks. Is conduction velocity constant along a leaf? Compare centripetal (inward) with centrifugal (outward) conduction velocities.
2. Examine the facilitation of the drooping response of the petiole when two or four leaves which branch from the same point are stimulated in succession.
3. Examine the effect of continuous wind on responsiveness. Does the plant become more or less responsive after a fan has *gently* blown on it for 20–30 minutes? Use brushing stimuli to test.
4. Examine the effects of various levels of illumination on nastic responses. (There are both slow and rapid nastic responses; you have been observing rapid responses.) What happens to the plant after 5, 10, 20, and 30 minutes in the dark?

Recording Procedure

Conducted electrical potentials can be measured by inserting fine wire electrodes into a petiole, stem, or leaf. Since they are much slower than nerve action potentials, these potentials can be recorded equally well on a polygraph or oscilloscope. Wire electrodes in the stems will also pick up the electrical spikes produced by rapid ionic fluxes in the pulvini and by mechanical movement of a stem when it droops.

Recording setup
To keep the leads short, mount the preamplifier near the *Mimosa* plant at the same height as the stems from which you intend to record. Connect the output of the preamplifier to the input of an oscilloscope or a physiological polygraph (fig. 8.7-3). Turn on your equipment and use the following initial settings.

Preamplifier. Input in differential mode if possible; gain of $10\times$; band-pass filters (if available) set at about 0.1 Hz (low frequency filter) and 1 kHz (high frequency filter).
Oscilloscope or Polygraph. Time base or paper speed at 1 sec/div or 1 cm/sec; sensitivity at 50 mV/div or 50 mV/cm; trigger set on automatic or free run.
Calibration. Adjust the preamplifier and oscilloscope or polygraph gain to give a total system gain of approximately 5 mV/div or 5 mV/cm. Check with the preamplifier calibrator if available.

Push a metal rod into the soil and connect the rod to a grounding point on the preamplifier input. Use heavy surgical scissors or good quality shears to cut two 20 cm lengths of fine stainless steel wire. Cut through the wire at a 45-degree angle to produce a sharp point. Avoid bending the wires; once they bend, they stay bent. Attach each wire to one of the inputs on the preamplifier.

Choose a healthy looking and accessible pair of leaves on the *Mimosa* plant. Grip one of the electrode wires between the jaws of a smooth-surfaced pair of forceps about 3–5 mm from the cut end of the wire. Carefully insert the tip of this wire through the stem, several centimeters below the branch point of the petiole from which you intend to record (fig. 8.7-3). Use the same technique to insert the second recording electrode into the petiole about midway between the base of the leaf and the base of the petiole. Insert both electrodes at angles which do not put too much mechanical stress on the stem or the petiole.

Recording propagated potentials
Allow 10–15 minutes for the plant to recover. Meanwhile, make sure all adjustments and connections are complete and calibrate the system gain. When the leaflets unfold, you may begin. Turn on your preamplifier and recheck everything before stimulating.

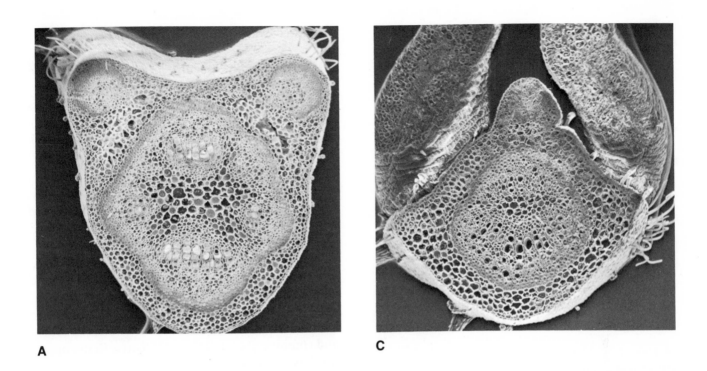

A   C

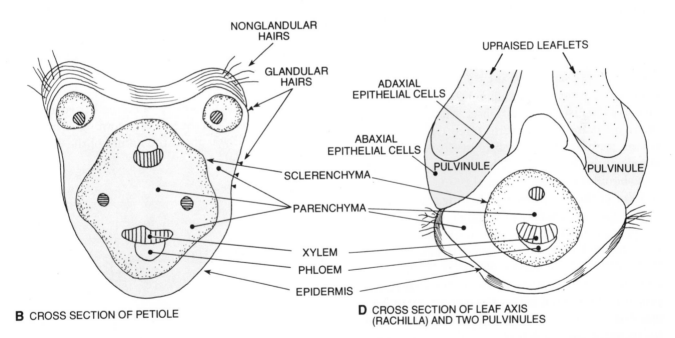

B CROSS SECTION OF PETIOLE

D CROSS SECTION OF LEAF AXIS
(RACHILLA) AND TWO PULVINULES

Fig. 8.7-2. Cross sections of a petiole (*A* and *B* 42×) and leaf axis (*C* and *D* 60×) of the sensitive plant *Mimosa pudica*. The conducted potentials which course through the stemlike tissue probably travel in the phloem and the protoxylem (differentiating xylem). The cells in these regions have resting membrane potentials of about −160 mV, whereas cells in other regions (e.g., parenchyma) have resting potentials around −50 mV. The leaf-

lets fold upward upon stimulation because turgor pressure rapidly increases in the abaxial epithelial cells of the pulvinules while it decreases in the adaxial cells. This is accomplished by the active movement of potassium ions (followed by the osmotic flow of water) from the adaxial cells to the abaxial cells. (Scanning electron micrographs courtesy of P. Dayanandan.)

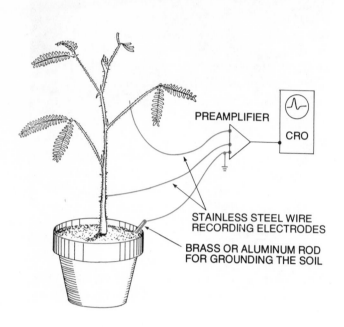

Fig. 8.7-3. Recording arrangement. Stainless steel wires are inserted through the stem and petiole for recording the passage of conducted potentials.

For initial observations use the cutting method of stimulation by carefully snipping 2–3 mm off the tip of one of the distal leaflets. Observe both the activity of the plant and the recording trace. One person should watch the plant, describing its responses aloud, while the other watches the recording trace. You should see a large potential change 1 second or more after the wave of leaflet folding reaches the base of the leaf. This is a propagated potential in the petiole passing the first recording electrode. You may also pick up a spikelike potential as the pulvinus at the base of the petiole reacts (fig. 8.7-4). In addition, you may see a third potential change as a propagated potential passes the second recording electrode in the stem. You will have to allow time for recovery after each response.

After obtaining responses and noting their general form using the previous recording arrangement, shift the recording electrode in the stem to the middle of a leaf. Now, you can record the passage of potentials in the leaf and in the petiole. This arrangement is particularly useful for studying the time courses of facilitory effects and recovery.

Suggested experiments with electrical conduction

1. Characterize the magnitude, waveform, and time relationships of the recorded potential changes. Are the potentials all-or-none, or graded? The potentials recorded with your gross electrodes are, like the compound action potential of a nerve, the summed potentials of many cells.
2. Measure conduction velocity in the petiole electrically. Move the two recording electrodes to a new part of the plant, this time placing both electrodes in a petiole—one near the base of the petiole and one at the distal end of the petiole. Stimulate by snipping distal leaflets as before. Record the time interval between the peaks of the rapid upward and downward deflections of the trace produced as the conducted potential passes the first and second electrodes. Measure the distance between the two electrodes and compute the conduction velocity. Remember, mm/msec ≡ m/sec.
3. Examine the effects of temperature and illumination on conduction. This problem requires some thought to separate the effects of light and heat.
4. Examine the effects of electrical stimulation using an electronic stimulator and another set of wire stimulating electrodes. For example, you might attempt to block the conducted potentials by using DC current to hyperpolarize a region between the site of stimulus and the site of recording. What would this tell you about the nature of the conducted potential?

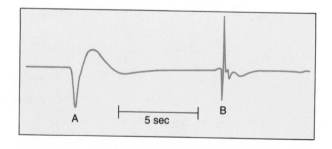

Fig. 8.7-4. Potentials recorded with the arrangement shown in figure 8.7-3. At **A**, the conducted potential passes the recording electrode in the petiole. The rapid potential change at **B** is associated with the response of the pulvinus at the base of the petiole. The waveforms of both potential changes have been distorted by AC recording. The propagated potential would appear as a fully monophasic wave in DC recording.

Pitfalls and Suggestions

1. You should meet no special difficulties other than waiting for a response to occur and waiting for the plant to recover between stimulations. Use this time to think about the design of your experiments. If you do not wait long enough you will get only partial responses.
2. Be sure to check your recording setup carefully before stimulating the plant (e.g., is the preamplifier on?).
3. Be careful around other experimenters. Disturbing a plant wastes time and could ruin an experiment.

Materials

Materials needed at each station
Oscilloscope or polygraph (A polygraph is preferable since it produces a continuous, permanent record.)
Preamplifier (Alternatively, one can plug the electrode wires directly into the input of an oscilloscope or polygraph. The advantages of using a preamplifier are that the electrode wires may be kept quite short, minimizing 60 Hz interference, and the preamplifier band-pass filters may be used.)
Cables and connectors (1 set)
Electrode wire (The wire must be stiff enough to penetrate the *Mimosa* stems. Tungsten wire of about 40 gauge is good, as is stainless steel kymograph pen cleaning wire, e.g., Harvard Ink Cleaning Wire, no. 808. Silver and copper wire are much less suitable because they are too limp. Be sure to remove the insulation present on some wires or the electrodes will not work.)
Metal rod and clip lead for ground connection to the soil
Fine glass rods or Pasteur pipettes
Forceps with rubber-protected jaws or fine rubber tubing slipped over the jaws
Surgical scissors, fine and of good quality
Flat-jawed forceps for gripping electrode wire
Small metric ruler

Materials available in the laboratory
Oscilloscope camera and film
Electronic stimulators
Small fan and rheostat to control its speed
Stopwatches
Dissecting microscope
Extra electrode wire
Heavy surgical scissors or good quality shears for cutting electrode wire (Most wire-cutting pliers will not cut the wire without bending it.)
Desk lamps for strong illumination
Cardboard boxes for light shades
Ringstands

Plants
Mimosa pudica (Have 2–10 plants available/station.) Occasionally, *Mimosa pudica* plants may be found in plant specialty stores or obtained from a hobbyist. Otherwise they will have to be started from seed at least 2, and preferably 4, months in advance. Young plants will produce two leaves per petiole (fig. 8.7-1) and older plants will produce four. Seeds may be obtained locally on occasion (ask for "sensitive plants") but it is usually easier to order them directly from a supplier (e.g., Carolina Biological Supply, no. LB 600). Lightly nick the seeds with sandpaper before planting. Place several seeds atop damp potting soil in a small flowerpot. Cover the seeds with a very thin layer of soil, sprinkle with water, and place the pot in a covered container until the seeds sprout (1 to 2 weeks at room temperature). Keep the seedlings out of direct sunlight until they have reached a height of about 5 cm. At this point, place them in strong light. The use of a 40-watt fluorescent grow lamp on a timer is strongly suggested. Place the lamp 30–50 cm above the plants and supply them with 16 hours of light per day. Keep the soil moist with frequent, but not excessive, watering. Consult a local plant supplier or botanist if problems are encountered.

Notes for the Instructor

1. Ask students to treat the plants with reverence. If they approach the exercise too casually, much time will be wasted with accidental stimulations and false starts. A drooped petiole may require 10–30 minutes recovery time. Leaflets should be at least 75% unfolded before retest. Obviously, if more plants are available, more experiments can be run in a given time period.
2. Several sets of electrodes can be connected to the same preamplifier through an EKG lead selector or similar switching device.

3. A sensitive force transducer may be used to record the mechanical activity of the plant (petiole drooping) while simultaneously recording the electrical activity.

Selected References

Bose, J. C. 1906. *Plant response as a means of physiological investigation*. Longmans, Green, and Co., London.

Bunning, E. 1959. Die seismonastschen Reaktionen. In *Handbuch der Pflanzenphysiologie [Encyclopedia of plant physiology]*, vol. 17 (1), ed. W. Ruhland. Springer-Verlag, Berlin, pp. 184–238.

Higinbotham, N. 1973. Electropotentials of plant cells. *Annu. Rev. Plant Physiol.* 24: 25–46.

Sibaoka, T. 1969. Physiology of rapid movements in higher plants. *Annu. Rev. Plant Physiol.* 20: 165–84.

Umrath, K. 1959a. Der Erregungvorgang. In *Handbuch der Pflanzenphysiologie [Encyclopedia of plant physiology]*, vol. 17 (1), ed. W. Ruhland. Springer-Verlag, Berlin, pp. 24–110.

———. 1959b. Mögliche Mechanismen von Krümmungsbewegungen. In *Handbuch der Pflanzenphysiologie [Encyclopedia of plant physiology]*, vol. 17 (1), ed. W. Ruhland. Springer-Verlag, Berlin, pp. 111–18.

RESEARCH REPORTS

Fondeville, J. C.; Schneider, M. J.; Borthwick, H. A.; and Hendricks, S. B. 1967. Photocontrol of *Mimosa pudica* leaf movement. *Planta* 75: 228–38.

Satter, R. L., and Galston, A. W. 1971. Potassium flux: A common feature of *Albizzia* leaflet movement controlled by phytochrome or endogenous rhythm. *Science* 174: 518–20.

Sibaoka, T. 1962. Excitable cells in *Mimosa*. *Science* 137: 226.

Toriyama, H., and Jaffe, M. J. 1972. Migration of calcium and its role in the regulation of seismonasty in the motor cell of *Mimosa pudica* L. *Plant Physiol.* 49: 72–81.

Weintraub, M. 1952. Leaf movements in *Mimosa pudica* L. *New Phytol.* 50: 357–82.

9

Surgery and Stereotaxic Techniques

9.1 Surgical Instruments and Micromanipulators

Instruments

High quality instruments are important. Scissors which fail to cut at the tips, or forceps with a fishhook point can frustrate the experimenter and ruin the preparation. Be selective in the purchase of your instruments because there is great variation in quality. Crudely constructed no. 5 watchmaker's forceps, for example, are insufficient to remove the delicate membranes covering the surface of the pulsating rat medulla oblongata. Be demanding in the care of your surgical instruments. Nonstainless steel parts may rust. Protect the fine points of forceps and scissors with a sleeve of polyethylene tubing. If fine forceps are damaged during use, carefully hone them to a new point with the finest stone available. A dissecting microscope is necessary for proper honing; you will be amazed at the ease with which the metal is rubbed from the extreme tip. Contamination of instruments with formalin or other fixatives may cause them to damage live tissue later, even after thorough rinsing.

The most commonly used instruments are shown in figure 9.1-1. The caption identifies the most useful. Learn their correct names.

In many instances, operations in the vicinity of major blood vessels or blood sinuses are best done by so-called blunt dissection. Use blunt-tipped forceps (fig. 9.1-1*D, E*) or fire-polished glass probes to separate and move muscles without cutting by scalpel or scissors. During tracheal cannulation a carotid artery can be easily ruptured by probing blindly with a pointed or sharp instrument. Scalpels have their place; but with small animals whose connective tissue is delicate, blunt dissection is often preferable.

Using a micromanipulator

The controls. Most micromanipulators are expensive rack and pinion devices much like the focusing and stage controls of a compound microscope. Two

examples are shown in figure 9.1-2. They are most frequently used to position an electrode on or in excitable tissue. Typically, the movements available include X, Y, and Z directions with coarse and fine controls on the Z axis. Some manipulators have provisions for moving two electrodes independently. Familiarize yourself with the manipulators which you will use by examining each of the controls and the way in which the electrode assembly clamps onto the manipulator. Note that advancement along the Z axis is accomplished by the positive motion of a screw, whereas the return may be made by a spring. Examine the extent of excursion of the controls, particularly of the fine Z control. It is normally kept near the upper part of its range so that you will not reach the lower limit of the excursion at a crucial moment in the experiment. The other controls should be set in the middle of their ranges.

A micromanipulator's purpose is to control electrode movement precisely. That purpose, however, is completely defeated by a heavy-handed operator who whips the controls and vibrates the instrument. To appreciate how easily the electrode tip is jarred

Fig. 9.1-1. Surgical instruments. *Boldface*, those most useful for student kits. **A.** no. 3 scalpel handle; **B.** no. 15 scalpel blade; **C.** dissecting needle (probe); **D.** large forceps; **E.** curved mosquito forceps; **F.** no. 5 watchmaker's (jeweler's) forceps; **G.** one-half curved cutting edge surgical needle; **H.** ear punch; **I.** large scissors; **J.** iris scissors; **K.** hemostat; **L.** 2-oz rubber aspiration bulb for rat; **M.** ruler; **N.** rubber tube for rat artificial respiration.

Fig. 9.1-2. Two types of micromanipulators with separate magnetic stand on the *left* and built-in magnet on the *right*.

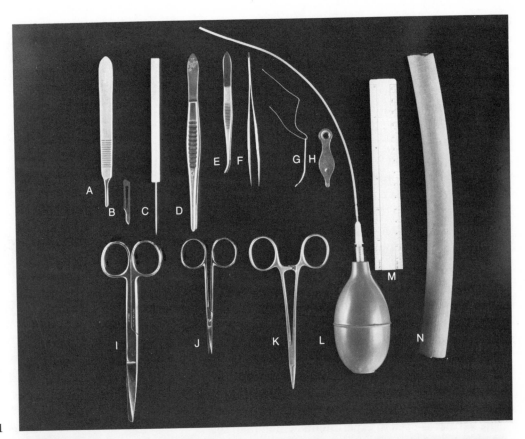

Fig. 9.1-1

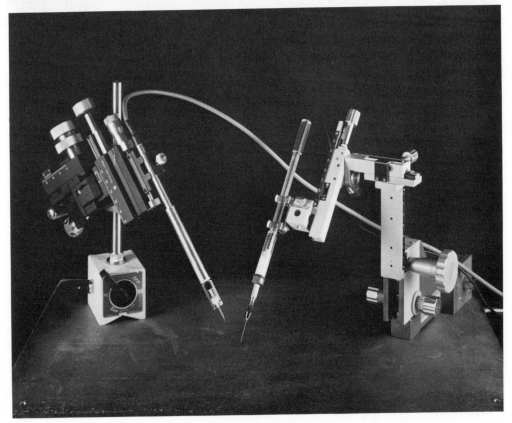

Fig. 9.1-2

by an indifferent technique, insert an electrode carrier which holds a fine insect pin (an insect pin in a pencil will do). Now use a dissecting microscope and lower the tip of the pin into position just above a letter on a printed page. Adjust the microscope to the highest magnification and use all controls in turn (X, Y, Z, and fine Z). Note especially the movements with the coarse and fine Z. See how easy it is to rest too much weight of the hand on the manipulator and thereby wobble the needle tip. Work at developing a comfortable arm position and a light finger touch so that the fine Z control moves the needle smoothly in and out. This will improve your success in recording and stereotaxic experiments.

The vernier. The vernier scale is a crucial part of high quality micromanipulators. Become proficient in reading it. Refer to figure 9.1-3 and note the large scale and the vernier below. The vernier is a device which will subdivide the smallest unit on the major (right) scale into tenths. Note that only the fifth line of the vernier scale is precisely aligned with a line of the major scale. This indicates a reading of 20.5.

The vernier is used in experiments which map the motor cortex (7.2), gracile and cuneate nuclei (7.5), frog optic tectum (7.6), and olfactory mucosa (6.3), and in stereotaxic localization where it is essential to systematically move the electrode a predetermined direction and distance (7.7, 7.8, 7.9).

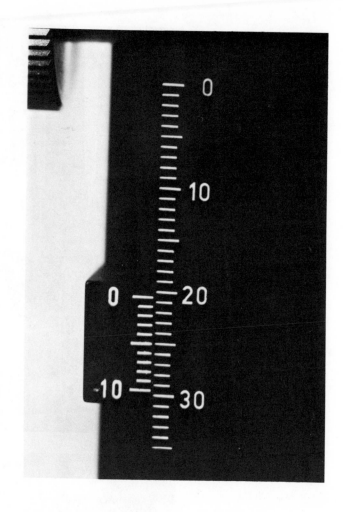

Fig. 9.1-3. A vernier scale on a micromanipulator.

9.2 Pithing the Frog

The most widely used method of immobilizing frogs is the technique of *pithing*. Destruction of the *brain* alone is *single pithing*, and destruction of *both brain and spinal cord* is *double pithing*. Provided it is done rapidly and firmly, pithing is just as humane as injecting an anesthetic.

Single pithing

Hold the frog in one hand, placing the index finger across the head, the thumb on the upper back, and the remaining three fingers under the belly of the frog. Grip firmly, but do not damage the animal with excessive squeezing. Locate the large, flat tympanic membranes on either side of the head posterior to the eyes. Draw an imaginary line across the frog's back, connecting the posterior edges of the tympanic membranes. The foramen magnum (hole in the base of the skull) lies directly under this line where it crosses the midline (fig. 9.2-1).

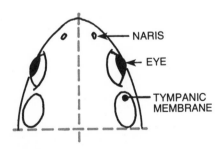

Fig. 9.2-1. Location of the foramen magnum in the frog. Two imaginary lines (*colored*) drawn along the midline and across the back at the level of the posterior edges of the tympanic membranes intersect at the foramen magnum. Insert the pithing needle at the intersection.

Hold a pithing needle as you would grip a pencil. Depress the frog's head to produce an angle at the base of the skull. Relocate the area of the foramen magnum and quickly press the tip of the pithing needle downward through the skin at the midline, then forward through the foramen magnum and into the skull. Sweep the needle several times from side to side and up and down within the skull to destroy the brain.

Humaneness requires that you pith quickly, firmly, and thoroughly.

Withdraw the needle after completely destroying the brain. Place the frog on the table and gently touch both eyes with the tip of the pithing needle. A blink (corneal reflex) indicates that the brain has not been fully destroyed. If the corneal reflex is elicited on either side, immediately reinsert the pithing needle and finish destroying the brain. After no corneal reflex is apparent, place the frog in a pan while the rest of the nervous system recovers from the trauma of brain pithing. After 3–5 minutes again check both eyes for the corneal reflex. If no corneal reflex is present, proceed with your experiment.

Double pithing

Since single pithing destroys only the brain, the spinal cord and most spinal reflexes are left intact. Therefore, do not be surprised to see a single-pithed frog move. Pinch the toes of a single-pithed frog with forceps and observe the withdrawal reflex (see experiment 7.3). When spinal reflexes would interfere with an experimental procedure, it is common practice to *double pith* the frog by destroying both brain and spinal cord.

If the frog is to be double pithed, first destroy the brain, then, *without pulling the pithing needle out completely*, gradually withdraw the needle until its tip is at the foramen magnum. First elevate the needle handle, feeling for the spinal canal underneath, then pass the needle tip posteriorward into the canal. The needle will meet some resistance, but force it into the spinal canal until the frog's hindlegs hyperextend forcefully. This is the critical sign; probe again for the spinal canal if the legs fail to extend. At this point, you have destroyed the spinal cord completely. Hyperextension occurs because when all the muscles are stimulated by destruction of their motor neurons, the extensors overcome the weaker flexors. Lay the frog in a pan for 3–5 minutes, then test for the withdrawal reflex by pinching the largest toe of one hind foot with stout forceps. If withdrawal is elicited, repeat the operation. If not, proceed with the experiment.

Note for the Instructor

Immersion of the frog in 10% ethanol for a few minutes prior to pithing is used in some teaching laboratories. The object of preanesthesia with ethanol is to ensure humane treatment of the frog; pithing may be done more carefully and apparently without pain to the frog. This technique, however, is unsuited to many of the experiments in this manual where the skin, cutaneous receptors and reflexes, or delicate excitable tissues are studied, e.g., experiments 4.1, 5.4, 6.3, 6.5, 7.3.

9.3 Small Mammal Surgery

Introduction

This section provides general methods of animal treatment and surgery to be applied in the six physiological experiments which use rats or gerbils. The guidelines for research on mammals in the United States are clear in their specifications (*Guide for the Care and Use of Laboratory Animals*, Department of Health, Education, and Welfare, publication no. (NIH) 72–73. Available from the Superintendent of Documents, U.S. Government, Washington, D.C.). Experimental animals must not be subjected to unnecessary stress or discomfort.

A novice may conclude that an anesthetized animal that moves at all with toe pinch or scraping of the cranial periosteum must be feeling discomfort. Actually some defensive reflexes persist under proper surgical levels of anesthesia. The animal is completely unconscious and additional anesthetic may jeopardize the chance for recovery in a *chronic* operation. In teaching laboratories, mammals are most likely to be neglected in the hours and days that *follow* a "successful" chronic operation. Attention to proper postoperative treatment (adequate but not *excessive* heat, water, clean cages, etc.) is an important responsibility during chronic experiments. (In an *acute* experiment the animal is not allowed to recover from the anesthetic, but is sacrificed—generally with an overdose of anesthetic.)

General Surgical Procedures for Rats and Gerbils

Handling rodents
Some persons are mildly allergic to rodents. Do do not rub or wipe your eyes after handling rodents. If your eyes nevertheless become irritated, wash your hands and let your partner carry out the handling and anesthetization procedures.

Rats and gerbils are relatively docile. You will, however, need a lab coat or cloth towel when you handle rats because many will defecate after they are picked up. It is prudent to assume your rat will be no exception.

Rarely is anyone bitten by a well-fed young laboratory rat. There is slight chance of being bitten if you avoid poking a finger into a hungry rat's cage, and if you do not suddenly grab and squeeze a rat tightly over the back (hawk's claw approach). There are three ways to pick up a rat: (1) by the *base* of the tail, (2) from above, around the ribs, or (3) from below, under the stomach. If you are inexperienced, you will find it easiest to pick the rat up by the base of the tail. Lift the rat straight up out of the cage without pulling it across the wire grid floor. Do not dangle the rat in the air, but support it on your arm held against your body and cover the rat with the flat of the hand which was holding the tail. Rats are calmed by support underfoot. Inasmuch as you will be handling rats in the future, each partner ought to handle the rat at least once.

Induction of anesthesia in rodents
Survival of the rat or gerbil depends upon accurate computation of the anesthetic dose. First weigh the rat to the nearest 0.5 g. Then calculate the required dosage of anesthetic and inject it as outlined below.

Ketamine. The recommended procedure for giving an intramuscular (i.m.) injection of ketamine is to roll the animal in a cotton towel with the hindpaws just accessible. (Gerbils should be picked up by the base of the tail and placed on a tabletop. While holding the tail, quickly cover the gerbil with a towel. Owing to their quickness, it may take several tries to immobilize the gerbil in a folded towel with only the hindpaws exposed. Try not to overly excite the animal; as one person holds, the other should inject.)

To give the ketamine injection, extend one hindleg and insert the needle into the largest muscle mass, e.g., the calf muscle. The acidity of ketamine will sting the animal so be prepared to inject the solution rapidly; withdraw the needle; and replace the animal in its cage.

Example of anesthetic dosage computation for ketamine (Vetalar; Parke-Davis): Assume (1) that the rat weighs 195 g; (2) that the recommended dosage is 200 milligrams per kilogram of body weight, injected intramuscularly (200 mg/kg bw, i.m.); and (3) that the anesthetic solution has a concentration of 100 mg/cc. Then, the required number of mg is

$\frac{195}{1000} \times 200 = 39$ mg. This is contained in about

0.4 cc of a 100 mg/cc solution of ketamine

$[\frac{39}{100} \times 1$ cc $= 0.39]$. Obtain a 1-cc disposable

hypodermic syringe with a 0.75-inch 23–25-gauge needle. Initially load the syringe with a little more than 0.4 cc from the vial. Set the vial down. Then, with the tip of the syringe upward, pull back on the plunger. Tap the barrel until all air bubbles have risen to the top. Now push the plunger slowly upward, driving out the air and excess anesthetic until the top of the plunger is even with the 0.4 cc line.

If you understand this example, compute the correct ketamine dosage for your rat. (The dosage for the gerbil is 340 mg/kg bw, i.m.)

Sodium pentobarbital. Although it is not necessary, you will probably feel more at ease wearing gloves when intraperitoneally (i.p.) injecting a rat with a dosage of 50 mg/kg bw. One person should use one hand to hold the rat around the back, using the thumb and forefinger to cross the rat's forelegs and the other hand to grasp the hindlegs. Do not squeeze the thorax tightly. The other student should immediately insert the 0.75-inch needle deeply into the abdomen with a quick jab perpendicular to, and a little to one side of, the middle of the abdomen. Do not twist or probe with the needle. *Do not inject yet.* First pull back gently on the plunger. If you draw back blood or urine, remove the needle, empty it, and try again with fresh anesthetic. Otherwise, inject the anesthetic and promptly return the rat to a clean, sawdust-free cage. If you are working alone,

wrap the rat in a cloth towel or diaper to immobilize it for the injection.

Depth of anesthesia

After a ketamine injection, the animal will lose consciousness quickly, but because of the slow decline of somatosensory reflexes it may take 30 or more minutes before major surgery can be initiated. The level of anesthesia will generally continue to deepen for at least 1 hour. Oral reflexes including coughing, swallowing, tongue movements, and salivation tend to remain. Sodium pentobarbital takes full effect in about 20 minutes. Continue to review the instructions while you wait. Once the animal is quiet and prostrate you may shave the surgical area with animal hair clippers. The appropriate areas to shave for the various experiments are: top of the head (experiments 7.7, 7.8, 7.9); back of the head and front and back of the neck (7.5); top of the head and left side of the head beginning behind the left eye (7.2); front of the neck extending laterally (6.6). If an animal under ketamine continues to actively respond to the tightened headholder 30 minutes after anesthetic injection, or displays vigorous movements during the initial phases of surgery, consult your instructor. A rat under surgical levels of pentobarbital anesthesia should show only moderate reflexive jerking when the hind foot or tail is pinched. If there is major squeaking 20 minutes after the pentobarbital injection, give a supplementary dose equal to 25% of the original dose. Wait 15 minutes more. An additional supplementary dose should not be necessary. Check with the laboratory instructor if in doubt.

Problems in anesthesia

One person should have primary responsibility for continuously monitoring the animal's condition. Monitor *breathing, depth of anesthesia,* and *temperature* (legs and paws should not be cold).

Symptoms

Labored or irregular breathing. There may be mucus in the mouth and throat of your laboratory animal. Obtain a large (2 oz) rubber squeeze bulb and tube. (The 25 cm length of polyethylene [PE] 190 tubing is attached to the bulb via a cutoff 1 cc disposable syringe barrel and an 18-gauge blunted hypodermic needle, as shown in figure 9.1-1L.) The end of the PE tubing must not have a sharp point. If the rat appears to be straining, gasping, or audibly wheezing and these symptoms seem to be getting worse, then aspirate the mucus from the region at the back of the tongue. Avoid repeated aspiration because the irritation will stimulate more mucous secretion. Ordinarily 0–4 aspirations during the laboratory period should be sufficient.

Breathing failure. Generally, breathing failure is preceded by irregular or very shallow breathing. Shallow, weak breathing is often indicative of anesthetic overdose, in which case it may not be easy to sustain breathing. Warm the animal and be prepared to assist breathing from time to time.

Trachea not cannulated—If the trachea is not cannulated use the rubber breathing tube shown in figure 9.1-1N. Place it over the nose of the animal and gently breathe into it. (You may wish to label the ends of the breathing tube "rat," and "human.") Breathe only hard enough to obtain moderate chest movements. Five to fifteen breaths will usually restart respiration. Pause 10 seconds to see whether it will breathe unassisted. Place the index finger over the chest to monitor heartbeat. If it slows dramatically, start artificial respiration again.

Trachea cannulated—If the breathing stops and the trachea is cannulated, use the aspirator bulb (fig. 9.1-1L) and place a clean end of its PE 190 tubing against the opening of the tracheal cannula. Pump hard enough to cause the chest to move. Rarely, one may have to clear out the tip of the rat's cannula with the bulb and PE 60 tubing (see page 316).

Cold feet and legs. Move a 60-watt desk lamp close to the animal. To avoid 60 Hz interference during electrophysiological recording, use a bottle or beaker filled with hot water.

Animal moves legs about, or twitches during surgery. The animal may be lightly anesthetized. Check with the instructor.

Headholders

It is usually helpful to hold the animal with a headholder for precise positioning. The headholder in figure 9.3-1 causes no trauma, is easy to attach, and holds the head rigidly with minimal interference for most kinds of operations and sensory stimu-

lation. The straight configuration (fig. 9.3-1A) is used for experiments 6.6 and 7.2, and the right-angle configuration (fig. 9.3-1B) for experiments 7.5, 7.7, 7.8, and 7.9. Your stereotaxic apparatus may have its own headholder. If you are performing a chronic experiment, do not put the animal in the headholder at this time, but read the instructions in the next paragraph so that you will be prepared to carry them out later.

The illustrated headholder requires that you slide the bar with two holes in it into the animal's mouth. First, loosen the wing nut and shift the solid bar to the side. Part the animal's cheeks and push the two-holed bar inward along the roof of the mouth. Avoid pinching or trapping the tongue in the back of the mouth. The ridges along the margins of the bar should slide around the outside of the upper molars which will rest on the milled plate. Push the bar in until the upper incisors drop in the hole (large hole for rats, small hole for gerbils). Without releasing your grip, swing the solid bar over the nose and tighten the wing nut snugly.

If you are doing a chronic operation, turn to page 317. Otherwise, continue with the next section.

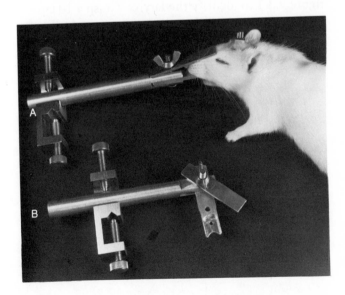

Fig. 9.3-1. Simple headholder for rat or gerbil in two configurations. **A.** Straight; allows rolling head to left or right. The rat has a chronically implanted electrode. **B.** Right-angle; permits pitching the nose down or up.

Acute Operations

Place the animal in the headholder (fig. 9.3-1). Turn the animal ventral side up and clamp the headholder to a stand. Provide adequate support for the animal's body. It is advantageous in acute experiments to insert a tracheal cannula to facilitate normal breathing and to couple to a mechanical respirator when it is used.

Tracheal cannulation

Select a tracheal cannula. The cannula consists of a 2–3 cm piece of PE tubing appropriate for the diameter of the animal's trachea (PE 200 for a 200 g rat; PE 60 for a 60 g gerbil). The rat cannula should be *slightly* flared at one end by passing the tip of the PE tubing briefly through a Bunsen burner flame. The flange of the tubing will make it easier to tie the cannula securely in the trachea. Shave the ventral surface of the neck and make a 2.5 cm midline incision through, but no deeper than, the skin. Use blunt dissection (avoid sharp scissors, forceps, and scalpels) to push the salivary glands laterally to expose the longitudinally oriented band of muscles exactly on the midline. Tearing slightly, push these muscles to the same side as the salivary glands to expose the trachea underneath. Free about 1 cm of the trachea from the connective tissue along the sides. Refer to figure 9.3-2 to identify the larynx. Grasp a 10 cm piece of heavy black thread or no. 1 surgical silk near one end with blunt, preferably curved, forceps and pass the thread under the trachea about five to six

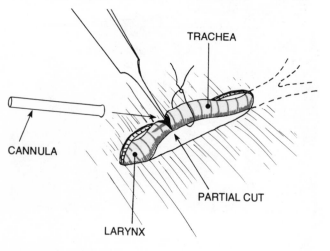

Fig. 9.3-2. Insertion of a flared tracheal cannula made of polyethylene tubing.

cartilaginous segments below the larynx until the short end can be grasped with another pair of forceps and pulled upward. Tie a loose knot as shown in figure 9.3-2. Make a transverse (crosswise) incision with a scalpel about two thirds of the way through the trachea at a level two to three segments below the larynx (colored area).

CAUTION: Do not cut completely through the trachea. Avoid major vessels.

Make a short longitudinal cut in the upper portion of the trachea as shown by the colored line in figure 9.3-2. Use no. 5 watchmaker's forceps to hold the trachea caudal to the cut and insert the cannula tip two to three segments past the thread. Tighten the thread around the trachea and cannula and tie a triple knot. Moderate bleeding sometimes occurs when the trachea is cut, so be ready with the cannula and the watchmaker's forceps *before* cutting the trachea. Use a large (2 oz) rubber squeeze bulb attached via a cutoff 1 cc disposable syringe barrel and blunted 21-gauge hypodermic needle connected to a 15 cm length of PE 60 tubing to aspirate blood and fluid from the rat's cannula. (Alternatively, a 10 cc disposable syringe may be used in lieu of a rubber bulb.) The gerbil's cannula can be cleaned by temporary insertion of an absorbent cotton thread. Recheck for fluid in the cannula after 5 minutes. The rat's incision, but not the gerbil's, should be sutured with two stitches of a 15 cm length black thread. Use a surgical needle and refer to figure 9.3-3. Most of the thread should trail behind the needle. The mattress stitch and square knot promote excellent healing if you have a need to do chronic operations which include skin closure. It would be good experience to use this stitch now as you close the neck incision. To do so, pass a single thread through both skin flaps in one direction, then pass it back through the skin about 3 mm away (arrow). Close the incision and tie the suture with a square knot. Space sutures about 5 mm apart. All knots should be tight and firm, but not too snug against the skin. (Were this a chronic operation, some swelling of tissues could be expected. Tighter sutures could cause discomfort to the rat and scratching at an incision. Chronic tracheal cannulation is not to be carried out with rodents; most would fail to survive.)

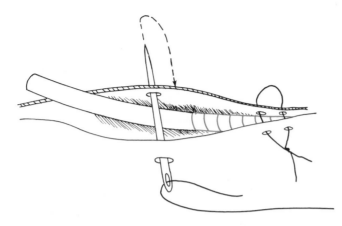

Fig. 9.3-3. Two interrupted mattress stitches being used to close the skin incision around a tracheal cannula. Square knots should be tied on the side of the incision.

After cannulation, return to experiment 6.6, 7.2, or 7.5.

Chronic Operations

Operations in which the animal is expected to recover from the anesthesia are termed *chronic*. As previously noted, a tracheal cannula is not used in chronic operations on rats. To prevent corneal drying with ketamine, apply a slight amount of mineral oil to each eye.

Atropine
Salivation can be reduced with an intraperitoneal dose of 10 mg/kg body weight of atropine sulfate given 15 minutes before the animal is anesthetized. Atropine helps to prevent respiratory failure—the major cause of death in chronic operations which were seemingly successful. Rats are very resistant to atropine; consequently the dose must be high. It is not necessary to use atropine with ketamine anesthesia.

Antibiotics
Rodents suffer fewer infections from operative procedures than carnivores or primates but antibiotics may be of value. Inject 70,000 units/kg body weight of *Bicillin* (a combination of two types of penicillin which acts for a few days) into the gastrocnemius muscle of one of the hindlegs. Massage the muscle gently to spread the antibiotic.

"Semisterile" procedure
Wash your hands with soap after the animal has been anesthetized and shaved. Slightly moisten a piece of cotton with 70% ethanol or an antiseptic solution and wipe off the shaved skin and the pinna of each ear. Wipe or rinse all surgical instruments with 70% ethanol and lay them on a clean paper towel. The needle and thread should be saturated with 70% ethanol and allowed to dry before use.

Identification of the animal
A system of positive identification for each animal is necessary. Mark *all* animals. Unmarked animals are easily confused with normal controls or newly introduced animals. Use an ear punch (fig. 9.1-1*H*) to mark the animals (dyes tend to come off or smear). The marking system in table 9.3-1 will provide positive identification of 15 animals. As soon as the animal is anesthetized make holes in the pinnae appropriate for the animal number assigned by the instructor. If you space the holes too close together, the cells in the narrow tissue bridge will die. Leave a bridge of at least one-hole diameter (2 mm) between adjacent holes and along the edge of the pinna. Punch holes along the top and thin edge of the pinna, avoiding the fleshy edge.

Suggestions concerning recovery from the chronic operation are located on page 323.

TABLE 9.3-1
Ear-Punch System for Coding Animals

Animal No.	No. of Holes	
	Left	Right
1	-	1
2	-	2
3	-	3
4	1	-
5	2	-
6	3	-
7	1	1
8	1	2
9	1	3
10	2	1
11	3	1
12	2	2
13	2	3
14	3	2
15	3	3

Read section 9.4.

9.4 Stereotaxic Procedures

Theory of the Stereotaxic Method

The stereotaxic method is used to accurately place an electrode tip in a neural structure hidden deeply within the brain. Conceptually the method is straightforward. One must have an external landmark or reference point on the animal from which the electrode tip is moved X mm back, Y mm to one side, and Z mm down to the desired neural structure. The actual coordinates of a specific brain structure are obtained from a stereotaxic atlas containing diagrams of the brain in cross section. The experimenter finds the cross section which includes the target structure, determines how many millimeters in front or behind the reference point it is, and then on that cross-sectional diagram measures the distance to the side and down. Several stereotaxic atlases of the rat brain have been constructed. Most use a reference line—the interaural line—determined by ear bars which rigidly anchor the head. In this manual we will use the *bregma* as a reference point, rather than the interaural line. The bregma is the point of intersection of the coronal and sagittal sutures on the dorsal surface of the skull (fig. 9.4-1A).

When the intersection of the sutures lies off the midline (fig. 9.4-1B), it is better to extrapolate a straight line and set the *true bregma* as shown. The skull will be leveled (bregma and lambda at the same Z coordinate). In the rat stereotaxic atlas by König and Klippel (1963), the skull is approximately level and the bregma lies at their anterior coordinate of 7,300 μm. This information, in conjunction with the bregma as a reference point, provides sufficient knowledge to use the König and Klippel atlas to locate any desired structure. The main concern in stereotaxic procedures is choosing a reference point whose distance from internal brain structures is as invariant as possible. The bregma seems to be at least as accurate as other reference points which have been used. In the rostro-caudal axis the error can be kept within 0.5 mm—with a smaller error in the other dimensions. Beneath the bregma and lying along the midline is the midsagittal sinus which marks the division between the left and right cerebral hemispheres. The brain lies approximately 1 mm below the skull surface. Make an effort to examine a stereotaxic atlas.

The stereotaxic apparatus (fig. 9.4-2) consists of a micromanipulator and holding frame. Depending upon the particular instrument, you may find ear bars necessary to hold the head rigidly, even though the ear bars will not be used to determine stereotaxic coordinates. Alternatively, your equipment may consist of a micromanipulator and base plate (fig. 9.1-2) and a headholder without ear bars, similar to that shown in figure 9.3-1.

If ear bars are used, the following practical directions may be of some assistance. For practice, obtain a rat skull and center it in the stereotaxic frame by shifting and locking the ear bars. Level the skull.

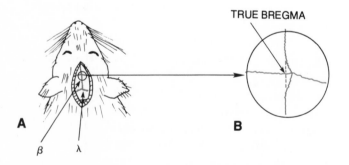

Fig. 9.4-1. Drawing of a rat's head with exposed dorsal surface of the skull (**A**) and expanded drawing (**B**) of the intersection of the coronal and sagittal sutures. β. bregma; λ. lambda.

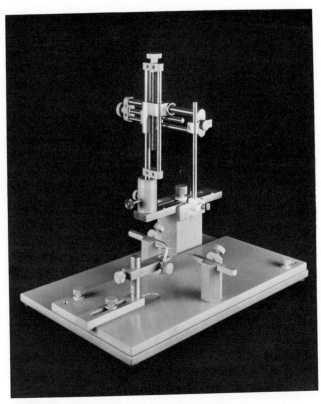

Fig. 9.4-2. Stereotaxic instrument with ear bars and an adjustable incisor bar.

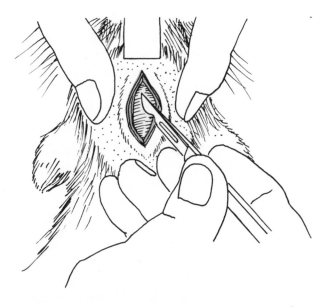

Fig. 9.4-3. Making the initial incision and scraping the periosteum. (Adapted from Skinner, 1971.)

Loosen the left ear bar and remove the skull to a safe place. Examine the right ear of an anesthetized rat until you can see the ear canal. Hook the incisors over the incisor bar, and push the rat's head until the locked right ear bar fits into place. Tip the head as required. Maintain pressure on the head against the right ear bar and slide the left bar into place. If difficulty is encountered in getting the tip of the ear bar into the external auditory meatus (ear canal), then shift the pinna and head skin. When you think you have succeeded, gently push in the left ear bar and look for eye reflexes as the tympanic membranes are stretched. (Sharp ear bars will generally rupture the tympanic membranes, but they will regenerate in a few days.) Lock the left bar in place. If the ear bars are in the proper position, the head should neither wiggle nor be tilted to one side. Support the body adequately. (Call upon your instructor if you need some assistance with this process.)

The Stereotaxic Operation

Attach the headholder to the base plate, and level the top of the rat's head by eye, left and right, forward and back.

Make a 2.5 cm incision in the scalp along the midline with a scalpel (fig. 9.4-3). Stretch the scalp skin slightly with thumb and index finger so that you have resistance to cut against. This is one instance where you may be more firm than gentle. With a hard skull below and no major blood vessels, you cannot damage the brain or the circulation. A no. 15 blade is ideal; number 10 is usable. Since the periosteum is well innervated, you can expect some moderate reflexive jumping. The animal is nevertheless unconscious and feels nothing. Scrape the periosteum toward the sides, and clean and dry the skull with cotton to reveal the suture lines on the top. Identify the sagittal (midline) and coronal sutures and their intersection, the bregma. They are most visible when the surface moisture on the skull has evaporated to dryness. Refer to figure 9.4-1. If during the stereotaxic procedure the rat develops spasmodic or labored breathing not attributable to light anesthesia, then clean out the mucus from the throat using a 2 oz rubber bulb and attached 25 cm length of PE 190 tubing as described in section 9.3 (see pages 314–15). You will have to remove the rat from the headholder.

Special instructions for chronic implantation experiments (unnecessary for lesion experiments) are as follows. Good adhesion of the cement to the skull requires a large, clean, dry skull surface. Scrape far enough laterally to reach beyond the lateral ridge which can be felt as a right-angle demarcation between the top and sides of the skull. Press on the wound margin if it continues to bleed and, if necessary, use gauze or tightly twisted cotton packed against the tissue to stop the bleeding. Further lateral scraping and cleaning of the skull will also help. Avoid using loose and fluffy cotton because it may dry and adhere to the skin. With the scalpel handle rub the bone where it oozes in order to help seal the porous areas of the skull. Dry the surface with puffs from a 2 oz rubber bulb.

Placing the Electrode

General procedures

Attach the stereotaxic micromanipulator to the base plate. Familiarize yourself with its controls, including use of the vernier (refer, if necessary, to section 9.1, page 308).

Instruments and supplies for chronically implanted electrodes are shown in figure 9.4-4. The electrodes are constructed by soldering two twisted stainless steel wires into connectors (Amphenol male Relia-Tac) which are pressed into a block cut from a plastic contact strip. Consult page 337 for full construction details.

Attach the electrode (figs. 9.4-4F and 9.4-5) to the manipulator electrode holder and position it above the bregma with the coarse Z control. The electrode should move up and down perpendicular to the plane of the skull surface. View the electrode from left or right and from front or back, and, if necessary, carefully bend it to make it absolutely vertical. *Take time to make the electrode vertical* (perpendicular to the skull and parallel to the manipulator's Z axis).

Determine the D-V position (dorsoventral = vertical = Z axis) of the bregma by carefully lowering the electrode until it *just* touches the skull surface at the bregma. Read and record the vertical drive vernier scale on the electrode carrier (e.g., 21.3 mm). Raise the electrode a few millimeters and measure the D-V position of the lambda. The two values should agree within 0.1 mm. If they do not, raise or move the electrode to one side so that the head can

be repositioned without hitting the electrode. Level the skull (make the D-V of bregma minus lambda = 0.1 mm or less), then tighten the appropriate clamp firmly to prevent the head from moving when holes are later drilled in the skull.

Make certain the head will not move.

At this point it might be useful to calculate, as an example, stereotaxic coordinates for making bilateral lesions in the thalamic taste nucleus of the sensory thalamus. This structure is located 3.9 mm posterior to the bregma, 1.3 mm lateral to the midline, and 6.7 mm below the upper surface of the skull at the site of electrode insertion. For this you must first set the electrode at the bregma and measure its coordinates. Here are some arbitrary manipulator settings for the bregma:

Bregma
A-P (anteroposterior)   = 51.7
M-L (mediolateral)   = 37.3

Lesion Settings
51.7 − 3.9 = 47.8 A-P
37.3 + 1.3 = 38.6 (left)
37.3 − 1.3 = 36.0 (right)

Thus, one hole would be drilled in the skull at coordinates A-P = 47.8 and M-L = 38.6, and the electrode lowered 6.7 mm from the skull surface (the surface measurement needs to be recorded before the hole is drilled). A sharp scalpel tip can be used to nick the skull where the holes must be drilled. A second hole would be made on the other side of the midline at A-P = 47.8 and M-L = 36.0.

Follow the instructions below to correctly calculate the stereotaxic coordinates from table 9.4-1 and to position the electrode. Double-check.

Place the electrode on the bregma and obtain values for all three coordinates (A-P, M-L, and D-V). Coordinates for the chronic lesion and implant experiments are found in table 9.4-1. Place the tip of the electrode at the appropriate skull location for your experiment by calculating the A-P and M-L (left

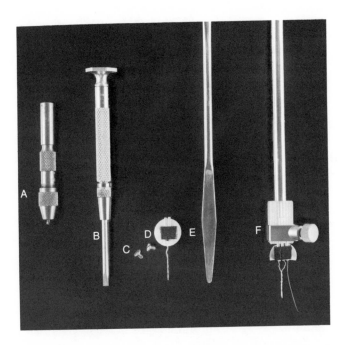

Fig. 9.4-4. Some specialized instruments and supplies used in chronic implantation procedures. **A**. pin vise with no. 52 drill protruding; **B**. jeweler's screwdriver, used by placing the index finger over the top which spins; **C**. two no. 72 fillister-head stainless steel machine screws; **D**. bipolar electrode implant assembly with two twisted stainless steel wires; **E**. large spatula for application of cement; **F**. bipolar electrode and ground wire assembly clamped to an electrode holder.

side) settings for the micromanipulator and moving the electrode to that point. Lower the electrode until it *just* touches the skull and record the D-V setting. Raise the electrode slightly and mark that skull point with a probe or scalpel-blade point. *Check the calculation again* for the micromanipulator settings or you may place the electrode in the *wrong* part of the brain. For experiment 7.7 place a mark on the corresponding site on the right side of the skull (for bilateral lesions). Move the electrode out of the way and drill through the skull with a no. 52 drill bit (0.063 inches, 1.6 mm) protruding 1.25 mm, from a pin vise. It will barely drill through the skull (fig. 9.4-6). The drill begins to bind or grab when it is nearly through the skull bone. Ease off the downward pressure at this point, but continue to turn the bit. Absorb blood, if any, with cotton. Now, if you are carrying out the lesion experiment (7.7), turn to page 248. If you are carrying out the implant experiments (7.8 or 7.9), continue reading.

Implantation preliminaries

In order to ensure that the cap of dental cement does not loosen from the skull it will be necessary to insert two no. 72, 1/8-inch stainless steel fillister head screws. Use the pin-vise drill and the no. 52 drill bit to make a hole on each side of the skull far lateral to the electrode hole. (See the screw positions in figure 9.4-5, but shift the positions if the large screw heads will not give the plastic block clearance as it is lowered near the skull.) Stay well away from bone suture lines and the electrode hole. Use a jeweler's screwdriver (fig. 9.4-4*B*) to insert the screws (fig. 9.4-4*C*) about 1.5 mm into the skull. Finally, puncture the dura mater with the sharp point of a sterile hypodermic needle in the hole where the electrode is to be lowered.

Poise the electrode at the top of the electrode hole, ready to enter the brain. (In experiment 7.9 there will be a third wire [uninsulated ground wire] which should be carefully wrapped around the nearest

TABLE 9.4-1
Stereotaxic Coordinates

Experiment	Brain Region	Coordinates			
		A-P	M-L	D-V	
7.7	Rostral pole of the ventromedial nucleus of hypothalamus (VMH)	−2.0	±0.6	9.4	Bilateral
7.8	Septal nuclei	+0.1	0.8	6.0	Unilateral
7.8	Lateral hypothalamic area (LHA)	−3.3	1.3	8.9	Unilateral
7.9	Dorsal hippocampus	−4.0	3.0	4.2	Unilateral

N.B. Bregma and lambda are in the horizontal plane (skull level). A-P values, in mm posterior to bregma; D-V values, in mm beneath skull surface at site of electrode entry. Based on the König and Klippel stereotaxic atlas of the rat brain.

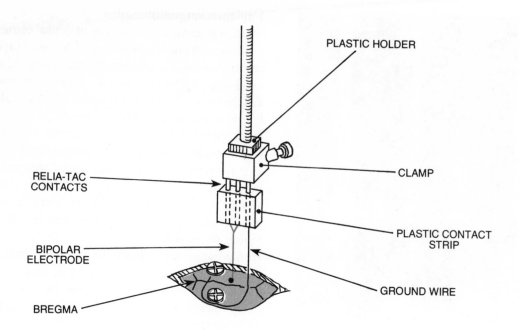

PLASTIC HOLDER

CLAMP

RELIA-TAC
CONTACTS

PLASTIC CONTACT
STRIP

BIPOLAR
ELECTRODE

GROUND WIRE

BREGMA

Fig. 9.4-5. Electrode assembly for experiment 7.9 consisting of a twisted bipolar wire electrode, ground wire, plastic contact block, and three male contacts which can be held in the micromanipulator. Experiment 7.8 requires only two male contacts and no ground wire. Stainless steel screws are shown in place in the top of the skull with the ground wire close to one of the screws.

machine screw [fig. 9.4-5]. Make a note in your data book which indicates whether the ground pin is the most anterior or posterior of the three pins in the plastic block. If you bump the other electrodes in this process of wrapping the ground wire around the screw, you will have to realign the electrodes vertically and reposition them on the bregma to check the coordinates. Be careful.) If there is any uncertainty about the accuracy of the position of the electrode or the micromanipulator, you should move the electrode back to the bregma to see if the original bregma coordinates are the same. Now, slowly lower the electrode through the electrode hole to the proper depth in the brain.

Cementing the electrode in position
A few minutes after mixing, dental cement will harden enough to make it difficult to shape or remove. It will take longer to bond the electrode wire firmly. Consequently, mold the cement into place as soon as you put it on. Retract the skin slightly so that the cement contacts the skull or the adjacent tissue, but does not overlap onto the hairy portion of the skin. Cement that rides over the top of the skin

and glues it down will be a source of infection and discomfort as the skin heals. Pull the skin away and mold or trim the cement so that it has no sharp edges. A photograph of a completed implantation is shown in figure 9.3-1.

Thoroughly dry the skull and surrounding tissue. Mix a small amount of dental cement with its solvent to a liquid consistency in a glass petri dish. Apply the cement around the electrode and the machine screws with a spatula.

Do not touch or move the electrode.

A smaller spatula made by flattening one end of a large paper clip or made from a disposable 1 cc syringe barrel and an 18-gauge needle is useful for more precise work. First, apply the cement in a *thin* layer as high as the top of the screws. When the cement seems hard and the electrode wire is clearly locked in place, carefully release the electrode assembly from the micromanipulator. Gently push the plastic block so that it moves down to a lower position with the pins vertical. Add enough cement to

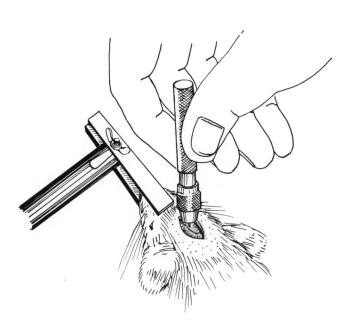

Fig. 9.4-6. Drilling a hole in the skull at a stereotaxically determined locus. Use the same drill bit for the electrode and screw holes. (Adapted from Skinner, 1971.)

cover three fourths of the block, but do not build up a narrow high tower. If a small amount of cement gets on the top of the plastic block or on the gold contacts, clean it off *immediately* before it hardens.

Recovery from chronic surgery

After the operation remove the animal from the headholder. Make sure the pinnae are punched for identification. Watch and listen to the breathing to see that it is quiet and regular. It may be necessary to clear away the accumulating mucus in the throat. Be prepared to aspirate the mucus with the rubber bulb and PE tubing if breathing difficulty ensues.

Place the anesthetized rat in a clean, dry, empty cage. A plastic cage is ideal because it can be cleaned and prepared in advance. Do not add paper, food, or sawdust until the animal is totally awake and has ceased thrashing about. Keep the rat warm with a 60-watt table lamp placed no closer than 40 cm from the rat. The rats may die if they are overheated.

Consult your instructor to clarify responsibility for further care of the rat.

Clean up all instruments and the stereotaxic apparatus. Throw dried pieces of dental cement into the wastebasket, not into the sink.

About 1 week will be required for postoperative recovery.

Pitfalls and Suggestions

1. Be constantly alert for respiratory difficulties.
2. Make the measurements for the electrode position accurately.
3. Be certain the animal's head is held securely so it does not move during operative procedures, particularly during drilling.
4. Do not put too much cement on the skull in initially fixing the electrode in position during an implantation experiment.

Return to the appropriate experiment (7.7, 7.8, or 7.9) and note the remaining features of the experiment.

Notes for the Instructor

1. See chapter 10 for sources of equipment and supplies and construction details for the headholder and implant devices. A steel plate with the headholder on one magnetic stand and a micromanipulator on another magnetic stand makes a suitable and inexpensive stereotaxic instrument, providing that the system is well clamped and rigid. In this case, orient the micromanipulator axes to match the X, Y, and Z axes of the rat head so the micromanipulator verniers may be used to position the electrodes accurately. A single magnetic stand is feasible. Use heavy-duty clamps.
2. Students need to be reminded to punch identification holes in the rat's ears. Keep a record of the names of the students assigned to each animal and have the students tape their names to the temporary and permanent cages. The *position* of the holes on an ear can be used for coding additional rats, but you run the risk of confusing the students.
3. It is very helpful to have a rat skull available for the students to examine. If a brightly colored tag is attached, the skull may be more visible and less likely to be accidentally crushed.

4. Before operations, the rats may be housed in groups of two to eight. After chronic operations, cage them *singly*. In open wire-mesh cages, some rats will tear off their implants. Plastic cages are preferable.

5. Food deprivation is not necessary before an operation to prevent fatal regurgitation. However, it is recommended as a way to minimize variation in the effectiveness of sodium pentobarbital.

6. There are six experiments with rodents (6.6, 7.2, 7.5, 7.7, 7.8, and 7.9). We recommend using ketamine for all, except 7.5, where occasional movements of the rat interfere with microelectrode recording. Ketamine in our experience has several advantages over sodium pentobarbital: there is an excellent recovery rate in the chronic experiments (7.7, 7.8, 7.9), without nursing care during the period immediately following the laboratory; the death rate during acute surgery, particularly of gerbils, appears to be reduced; and responses from motor cortex stimulation are improved (experiment 7.2). Supplementary doses of ketamine are generally not warranted; however, if there were only a partial injection or injection into poorly vascularized tissue, then a dose of 25% of the original would be appropriate. Under ketamine a rapid heart beat, oral reflexes, corneal blink reflexes, and foot withdrawal reflexes remain. Therefore, it is more difficult to judge the depth of anesthesia. Ketamine may be expensive. Sodium pentobarbital is an acceptable alternative, but it will necessitate periodic postoperative aspiration of saliva until chronically operated rats have regained oral reflexes (2–6 hours).

Selected References

STEREOTAXIC ATLASES
Emmers, R., and Akert, K. 1963. *A stereotaxic atlas of the brain of the squirrel monkey (Saimiri sciureus).* University of Wisconsin Press, Madison.

Kemali, M., and Braitenberg, V. 1969. *Atlas of the frog's brain.* Springer-Verlag, New York.

König, J. F. R., and Klippel, R. A. 1963. *The rat brain: A stereotaxic atlas of the forebrain and lower parts of the brain stem.* Willams and Wilkins, Baltimore.

Zeman, W., and Innes, J. R. 1963. *Craigie's neuroanatomy of the rat.* Academic Press, New York.

A bibliography of stereotaxic atlases may be found in:
Heimer, L., and Lohman, A. H. M. 1975. Anatomical methods for tracing connections in the central nervous system. In *Handbook of psychobiology*, ed. M. Gazzaniga and C. Blakemore. Academic Press, New York, pp. 73–106.

10   Laboratory Organization

This chapter is provided to assist the teaching staff in setting up a neurobiology laboratory. The information in the tables and figures in this chapter will allow your business office and technical and animal care staff to procure and construct apparatus according to your needs for the course. If you are initiating a new laboratory, read "To the Instructor" in the Introduction (page ix) before continuing with chapter 10.

Tables

10.1 Setting Up the Laboratory

Establishing a Laboratory

Space considerations

For each station, a movable, but sturdy, 1×2 m table is ideal for supporting and arranging electrophysiological or behavioral equipment. The availability of two (adjacent) rooms is desirable so that experiments which require a darkened room can be conducted simultaneously with other experiments which do not require such a room. Moreover, one room can be arranged as an electrophysiological area and the other as a behavioral, anatomical, or "wet" laboratory. Each room should have air, gas, and water lines, and electrical outlets along the wall at least every three feet. A workbench area should be set up for simple repairs, glass blowing, etc. Whatever your circumstances, try to obtain an area where equipment may remain set up from week to week. This simple arrangement will save both you and your students considerable time.

Animal space is best arranged in an area separate from the experimental area.

Sources and funding

Equipment and supplies can be acquired from departmental and other institutional sources, National Science Foundation (NSF) instructional equipment grants, National Institutes of Health (NIH) training grants, private sources, etc. (see table 10.2-1 for costly equipment items). Some companies occasionally allow educational discounts (e.g., Tektronix), offer reconditioned equipment, or make their surplus equipment available to educational institutions (e.g., IBM). The federal government through the General Services Administration (GSA) offers surplus government equipment to grant-holding institutions. For example, a holder of an NSF Instructional Equipment Grant is entitled to supplement efforts at course improvement through the acquisition of surplus federal equipment. The GSA issues excess property catalogs through its regional offices. State governments also have surplus property programs with central warehouses often located in the state capital or other major cities. Unfortunately, the quality and usefulness of surplus equipment varies greatly. The value of surplus electronic equipment, in particular, depends on access to a technician who is willing and able to make necessary repairs. Consult your institution's property officer for details of local and federal sources.

Managing the Laboratory

Scheduling

The first priority is scheduling experiments which complement the lectures. We have found it useful to do two experiments concurrently. A shortage of electrophysiological equipment is usually the limiting factor. You can, however, have half of the class perform an electrophysiological experiment while the other half dissects the sheep brain or does an observational or behavioral experiment. Students then exchange places the following week. More than two exercises *can* be run at one time, but this is usually quite taxing unless you have considerable experience with each of the specific experiments. We have tried to make the experiments as independent of one another as possible to accommodate various scheduling arrangements. Of course, some experiments should follow one another because there is a natural progression and a transfer of experience (e.g., from experiment 7.2 or 7.7 to experiment 7.8 or 7.9).

Budget

Annual supply and animal costs in our courses have varied from \$30 to \$80 per student per semester, depending on the number of experiments run, the variety of animals used, and the number of credit hours offered. It is valuable to have 4–10 hours per week of part-time assistance in making solutions, washing glassware, etc. Basic supplies should be inventoried at the end of the semester and replenished. Enlist student help by posting a "needs" sheet on the laboratory wall and encouraging the students to write down items in short supply.

Animal needs
After arranging the schedule, check off the animal needs with the aid of table 10.6-1. This table also summarizes the relative level of difficulty of experiments as an aid to sequencing.

Basic laboratory supply needs
Collect the basic supplies listed in section 10.5. Arrange supplies alphabetically in a labeled cabinet for easy access by students and staff.

Specific supply needs for each experiment
After completion of an experiment, collect all the special items that were necessary for the experiment and put the collection into a labeled box or large plastic dishpan. Store it safely away for use next year.

Chemicals
Make a collection of chemicals (refer to section 10.5). All anesthetics, neuroactive agents, and controlled substances ("narcotics") should be stored in a locked cabinet or locked refrigerator. In the United States, controlled substances must be obtained under permit. If your institution lacks registration, you may apply to the United States Department of Justice, Drug Enforcement Administration, P. O. Box 28083, Central Station, Washington, D.C. 20005.

Electronic equipment
While balances, some types of microscopes, or even a set of student polygraphs may be available, you will probably have to buy or borrow some electronic and other equipment to set up a laboratory. Section 10.2 outlines major equipment items for a complete electrophysiological station.

10.2 Electronic and Other Major Equipment

Major Electrophysiological Equipment

Equipment for one setup

Table 10.2-1 lists a range of electronic and stereotaxic equipment which would suffice for even the most technical exercises in this manual. Obviously, few departments could afford to buy many such setups at one time. When acquiring equipment over several years, first select those items which are heavily used (see page 330). We routinely use "obsolete" vacuum tube equipment which works quite well. For example, we have effectively used all of the following Tektronix vacuum tube or hybrid oscilloscopes (with appropriate plug-in units where needed): 502A, 535A, 536, 546, 551, 555, 556, 561A, 564B, and 565. Many other Tektronix models and oscilloscopes of other manufacturers (e.g., Hewlett-Packard, Dumont) would work well. The Heath Impscope is unsuited to the experiments in this manual.

If you are fortunate enough to purchase new oscilloscopes, inquire about factory installation of BNC output terminals on the rear of the chassis and modification of vertical amplifiers to allow picking off the signal from them to drive audio amplifiers or other ancillary equipment such as tape recorders. When vertical amplifiers are purchased, choose high gain differential units with band-pass filters for the recording channel. Less sophisticated vertical amplifiers are suitable for the other channel (hence the choice of vertical amplifiers listed in table 10.2-1).

The listing of equipment in tables 10.2-1 through 10.2-4 does not constitute our endorsement of specific brands; many other companies produce comparable units. Information on specific items of equipment can be obtained by consulting the National Science Foundation's booklet, *A Consumers Guide to Instructional Scientific Equipment* (available gratis from the NSF Publications Office,

Washington, D.C. 20550). It contains an alphabetical listing of 2,000 selected items of equipment in use at 120 undergraduate institutions and the name, address, and telephone number of at least one science faculty member familiar with the use of each item.

The use of an AC preamplifier is advised for most experiments in order to avoid problems with DC electrode potentials and baseline shifts. An inexpensive, unity-gain DC amplifier such as that listed in table 10.2-1 is suggested for intracellular recording (experiment 4.5) and where DC or near DC potentials are recorded (e.g., experiments 6.1 and 6.3).

The audio amplifier and speaker need not be expensive. Audio amplifier gain may be increased by adding an inexpensive preamplifier of the kind used to convert stereo amplifiers originally designed for crystal cartridges to the use of magnetic cartridges (e.g., Lafayette no. 99-02198 or Radio Shack no. 42-2930 phono stereo preamplifier).

For stability and ease of positioning, we prefer to use micromanipulators mounted on magnetic stands which hold to a steel base plate.

Polygraph

Table 10.2-2 lists a polygraph system suitable for use in the neurobiology teaching laboratory. The Narco Physiograph is used as an example, but many other manufacturers produce comparable units. If the polygraph is to be shared with other courses, such as animal or human physiology, you may need to get additional materials and plug-in units which would not normally be used in a neurobiology laboratory (e.g., impedance pneumograph coupler). A cassette tape recorder of the type listed is useful; the instructor can use commercially produced tapes and develop a library of successful experiments for use in laboratory or lecture. Connecting cables are supplied with the different plug-in units or transducers, but it is wise to buy extra cables. Adapters (e.g., Pomona

TABLE 10.2-1
Equipment at a Complete Electrophysiological Station

Oscilloscope System	Display unit (Tektronix type 5111, single-beam storage oscilloscope)
	Vertical amplifier (Tektronix type 5A21N, differential, high gain)
	Vertical amplifier (Tektronix type 5A15N)
	Time base (Tektronix type 5B10N, single-sweep time base/amplifier)
Polygraph System	See table 10.2-2
Preamplifiers	AC preamplifier (Grass P15)
	DC preamplifier (WPI model VF-1 voltage follower, with model EH-3S micro-electrode holder)
Stimulator	Stimulator (Grass SD9, with delay and stimulus isolation)
Audio Monitor	Audio amplifier (Heath AA-18 audio monitor kit)
	Loudspeaker (Radio Shack no. 40-1229 indoor/outdoor speaker)
Manipulators	Micromanipulator (Narishige model MM-3, right hand)
	Two magnetic bases, for micromanipulator and headholder (Enco model 300; or Enco magnet assembly no. 3002 with parts 3003, 3004, and 3005, including 4 or 5 clamps [e.g., Harvard no. 207] and 4 steel, brass, or aluminum rods 16 × 1.3 cm)
	Stereotaxic apparatus (David Kopf no. 400 Student Rat Stereotaxic Instrument with no. 420 headholder and no. 460 manipulator base or, alternatively, 2 heavy clamps, 2 magnetic stands, 1 micromanipulator, and 1 headholder as in fig. 10.3-4)
Camera	Oscilloscope camera (Tektronix type C-5A, Polaroid camera) (1 or 2 needed in lab)
Microscope	Dissecting microscope with boom arm (American Optical no. 53)
	Illuminator (American Optical Starlite)
Ancillary Equipment	Steel base plate
	Faraday cage with blackout cover
	Headholder
	Millivolt calibration box
	(see pages 339–40 for construction details)

N.B. Specific commercial examples used for illustrative purposes only.

TABLE 10.2-2
Polygraph System

Main Frame
Narco desk model Physiograph, model DMP-4B, rectilinear

Amplifiers and Plug-in Units
1 Time and event channel, no. 703-0042
4 Recording channels, rectilinear, type 7070 (1 required for each recording channel)
1 High gain coupler, type 7171
2 Transducer couplers, type 7173
1 DC-AC coupler, type 7170
1 Stimulator, type S1-10

Transducers and Accessories
1 Myograph A (mechanoelectric transducer), no. 705-0001
1 Myograph B, no. 705-0002
2 Myograph tension adjusters, no. 712-0042
2 Transducer stands, no. 712-0032
6 EEG disc electrodes, no. 710-0018
1 Set plate electrodes, no. 710-0007
3 pair pin electrodes, no. 705-0016
1 Sleeve electrode, no. 710-0005
Roll recording paper, no. 713-0005

Additional Equipment for Expanding the Role of the Polygraph in the Neurobiology Laboratory
Tape recorder and playback unit, Physiotape, CDR-411
High frequency display, storage, and playback unit, Narco trace System, 709-1800
GSR coupler, type 7175; impedance pneumograph coupler, type 7212; temperature coupler, type 7174; pressure transducer, type P-1000A; beeper no. 712-0015; ECG lead selector switch, no. 712-0029

N.B. Narco Physiograph with four recording channels as a specific example.

TABLE 10.2-3
Usage of Major Equipment at an Electrophysiological Station: Listed by Experiment

Short titles of exercises	Exercise	Oscilloscope	AC Preamplifier	DC Preamplifier	Stimulator (and SIU)	Audio Monitor	Microscope	Micromanipulator	Stereotaxic Apparatus	Oscilloscope Camera	Polygraph and Accessories	Other Equipment
Oscilloscope	2.3	X										Audio frequency generator (Opt)
Stimulator	2.5	X			X							
Preamplifier	2.6	X	X	Opt	Opt							
Audio	2.7	X	X		X	X						
Electrodes	2.8	X	X		X							Nerve chamber
Camera	2.9	X								X		
Polygraph	2.10										X	
Sodium transport	4.1	X										Active transport device
Cmpd. A.P.	4.2	X	X		X		D			X		Nerve chamber
Cmpd. A.P. and units	4.3	X	X		X		D C			X		Nerve chamber
Giant fibers	4.4	X	X		X		D C			X		Nerve chamber
Membrane potential	4.5	X		X			DB C	X				Micro-pipette holder
Volume conduction	4.6	X	X		X		D	X		X		Special nerve chamber
Coelenterate nerve net	5.1				X		D					
Neuromuscular synapse	5.2	X	X		X		D			X		Nerve chamber, dual-trace CRO
Cardiac muscle	5.3				X						X	
Blood flow	5.4				X		C (or) D					
Chromatophores	5.5						D C					
Visual reception (ERG)	6.1	X	Alt	X				Opt		X	Alt	Photocell
Mechanoreception	6.2	X	X		Opt	X	D	Opt		X		Small loud-speaker (Opt)

TABLE 10.2-3 (continued)
Usage of Major Equipment at an Electrophysiological Station: Listed by Experiment

Short titles of exercises	Exercise	Oscilloscope	AC Preamplifier	DC Preamplifier	Stimulator (and SIU)	Audio Monitor	Microscope	Micromanipulator	Stereotaxic Apparatus	Oscilloscope Camera	Polygraph and Accessories	Other Equipment
Olfactory reception (EOG)	6.3	Alt	Alt	X			DB	X		Alt	X	
Muscle spindle	6.4	X	X			X	D	X		X		
Cutaneous receptive fields	6.5	X	X			X	D Opt	X		X		
Auditory reception	6.6	X	X			X	DB	X		X	X	Headphones, small loudspeaker, audio frequency generator, headholder
Nerve cord	7.1	X	X		X	X	D C	X		X		
Motor cortex	7.2				X		DB	X	Alt			Headholder
Spinal reflexes	7.3				X							
Stretch reflex	7.4	X	X		X					X	Alt	Special percussion hammer and battery holder
Somatosensory representation	7.5	X	X			X	DB	X	Alt	X		Headholder
Optic tectum	7.6	X	X			X	DB	X		X		Plastic dome (Opt)
Hypothalamic lesions	7.7							Alt	X			Lesioning device
Chronic brain stimulation	7.8	X			X			Alt	X			Test arena or Skinner box
Chronic brain recording	7.9	X	X					Alt	X	Alt	Alt	Test arena or Skinner box

TABLE 10.2-3 (continued)
Usage of Major Equipment at an Electrophysiological Station: Listed by Experiment

Short titles of exercises	Exercise	Oscilloscope	AC Preamplifier	DC Preamplifier	Stimulator (and SIU)	Audio Monitor	Microscope	Micromanipulator	Stereotaxic Apparatus	Oscilloscope Camera	Polygraph and Accessories	Other Equipment
Locomotion	8.1						D					Behavioral arenas
Insect flight	8.2						D					Strobe lamp, fan, auto-transformer
Electrolocation	8.3	X	X		Alt	X				X		Aquaria, tubes w/ electrodes, audio frequency generator, tape recorder (Opt)
Feeding behavior	8.4						D					
Conditioned taste aversion	8.5											
Sexual behavior	8.6						C					Behavioral arenas
Sensitive plant behavior	8.7	Alt	X	Alt	Opt		D			Alt	X	Fan and auto-transformer (Opt)

X Needed (Cameras and occasionally microscopes needed
     in laboratory but not in each station.)
Alt Alternate equipment
     (preferred equipment marked X)
Opt Optional
D Dissecting microscope
DB Dissecting microscope
     with boom arm
C Compound microscope

nos. 1795 and 3837) can be used to interface Narco polygraphs with preamplifiers made by other manufacturers.

Narco Bio-Systems has introduced an oscillographic display device called the Narco trace System. It can record, display, and store high frequency signals. It is analogous to a storage oscilloscope. It is also capable of then feeding the signal into a standard polygraph at reduced speed to produce a paper record of the stored trace.

Usage of equipment

Table 10.2-3 summarizes the major equipment used at an electrophysiological station. This table should be consulted when ordering equipment and organizing the semester's needs.

Additional Electrophysiological Equipment

A selection of additional equipment is suggested in table 10.2-4. Some items are of general usefulness; others may be used for only one or two experiments. A multimeter or volt-ohm meter (VOM) is valuable for trouble-shooting cables and batteries.

Cables, connectors, and adapters

We suggest the use of standardized interconnecting cables fitted with BNC plugs to simplify the operation of the laboratory. Order new equipment with BNC connectors. A wide range of adapters is available to convert older equipment to the use of BNC-terminal cables. The cost of adapters is certainly worth the savings in staff and student time. The Pomona Electronics catalog lists the widest variety of connectors and adapters. Some equipment, for example, the small, lightweight nerve chamber in figure 10.3-1, is not readily converted to BNC connections. Nevertheless, the minimization of special cables will lead to a more efficiently administered and maintained laboratory. At a given electrophysiological station it is valuable to have (*a*) six coaxial cables (BNC plug to BNC plug) two of 0.5 m length, two of 1 m length, and two of 1.5 m length (fig. 2.2-4*A*); (*b*) six unshielded leads (banana plug to banana plug) four of 0.5 m length and two of 1 m length (fig. 2.2-6*A*) over which alligator clips may be placed to make clip leads (fig. 2.2-7); and (*c*) three BNC T-connectors (fig. 2.2-4*B*).

Other electrical materials which should be available in the laboratory include extra cables, hookup wire, pin plugs, banana plugs, and an assortment of alligator, minigator, and microgator clips, some on 0.25 m leads. Figures 2.2-5 and 2.2-8 show some other adapters and connectors which may be of value for specific equipment.

TABLE 10.2-4
Additional Electrical and Electrophysiological Equipment

Active transport device (1/station; construct as suggested in exercise 4.1)

Audio frequency generator (e.g., Heath/Schlumberger SG-18A or SG-1271 generator; 1/station needed for experiment 6.6, optional for exercises 2.3, 7.2, and 8.3)

Electrode holders
Monopolar (construct 2/station according to fig. 10.3-2)
Bipolar recording (construct 1/station according to fig. 10.3-2)
Bipolar stimulating (construct according to fig. 10.3-2 or Harvard no. 304 hand electrodes; 1/station)

Electronic calculator (inexpensive model)

Headphones (widely available in audio equipment and electronic stores; 1/station; for use in experiments 6.2, 6.4–6.6, 7.1, 7.5, and 7.6 to detect faint activity without interference from lab noises)

Lesioning device (1–2/lab; construct as suggested in exercise 7.7 or purchase a commercial lesion maker, e.g., Grass model DCLM5)

Micropipette puller (1/lab, e.g., David Kopf no. 700C, or purchase premade micropipettes)

Multimeter (e.g., Heath/Schlumberger SM-666 FET multimeter)

Nerve chamber (construct according to fig. 10.3-1 or use Harvard no. 328 nerve conduction chamber or its equivalent, which should be improved by adding 4 to 6 more electrodes (1/station; for exercises 2.8, 4.2–4.4, and 5.2)

Volume conduction chamber (1/station; construct as suggested in exercise 4.6)

AC power outlet boxes with switch (6 outlets, circuit breaker or fuse; 1/station)

Stroboscopic lamp (e.g., Grass PS22 or PS33 photic stimulator [research and clinical use] or commercial strobe lamp for exercise 8.2)

Tape recorder (with playback function; widely available both from physiological instrument suppliers and audio stores; optional for exercise 8.3 and useful elsewhere; 1/lab)

Temperature meter (e.g., YSI Tele-thermometer model 43TD; 1/lab)

Volt-ohm meter (e.g., RCA WV-547A [inexpensive], Simpson model 260 VOM [rugged], or Simpson model 255 VOM/temperature tester [combines two functions]; 1/lab)

10.3   Electrode and Equipment Construction

Chloriding Silver Electrodes

Gently burnish a silver wire electrode with emery cloth or very fine (320–400 grade) sandpaper. Connect the positive terminal of a 1.5-volt battery to the silver electrode wire you wish to chloride, and the negative terminal to a 5 kohm resistor which is connected to the reference electrode (generally a silver wire). Place both wires in a solution of 0.2 M NaCl and allow current to pass for 15–30 minutes. The silver wire connected to the positive terminal should turn gray. Since the coating is somewhat photosensitive, store the chlorided electrodes in the dark in 0.2 M NaCl. Chlorided electrodes should be electrically interconnected (shorted together) to ensure that their potentials come to an equilibrium, eliminating any slight potential differences between them. Equilibration will occur if they are simply left in place in the chloriding device (see "Construction details" that follows). The chlorided wires should remain in the solution for at least 2–5 minutes before use.

Rationale for chloriding

Physically, chloriding a silver electrode greatly increases the surface area of the electrode, thus reducing its resistance. Chloriding also has an important chemical effect. A plain silver wire used as a positive electrode attracts negative ions. The halo of negative ions which develops repels further movement (current) of negative ions. Even weak electrical voltages produce such *polarization*. Polarization of metal electrodes is most annoying during DC recording because it induces a slow drift in the recording baseline as the effective resistance of the electrode changes. With *nonpolarizable* electrodes the metal wire is coated with a salt of the metal, for example, silver coated with silver chloride. Then if the electrode is made positive, silver ions are readily re-

leased into the salt coating to unite with approaching chloride ions. If the electrode is made negative, silver ions of the salt plate out on the electrode while free chloride ions migrate into the solution. Either way there is no build up of a charge. Such *reversible* electrodes prevent the development of a changing potential difference across the electrode. One of the most stable reversible electrodes is the *calomel electrode* which uses mercury and its chloride salts. The silver/silver chloride electrode is much easier to make and nearly as stable.

Construction details for chloriding electrodes

Make a 9 cm diameter circle from 1/4-inch plywood. In pencil draw two concentric circles 3.0 cm and 5.5 cm in diameter on the plywood. Mark 8 evenly spaced points on the large circle and 4 on the small circle. At each point drive a 4.0 cm finishing nail through the wood, leaving 0.5 cm of the head exposed. Solder a minigator clip to each of the 12 nail points so that the jaws extend down when the plywood is used as a cover for a 400 ml beaker of 8 cm diameter. Solder one end of a 5 kohm resistor to one nail head on the large circle. This will be the connection point for the negative lead from the battery. Solder a single length of hookup wire to the 11 other nail heads to interconnect them. An alligator lead from the positive terminal of a 1.5 V D cell in a battery clip will be connected to the hookup wire.

Fill the 400 ml beaker with 0.2 M NaCl to a level which will cover at least 1 cm of the silver wires which have been placed in one or more of the 11 minigator clips. Salt will rust the clips' springs.

Construction of a Nerve Chamber

(*Experiments 2.8, 4.2, 4.3, 4.4, 5.2*)
The exact dimensions of the nerve chamber shown in figure 10.3-1 are not crucial, except that a 2 mm

separation between adjacent electrodes is recommended. (The Harvard Apparatus Co. no. 328 nerve conduction chamber is improved considerably by adding four to six more electrodes.)

The nerve chamber in figure 10.3-1 is fashioned out of a 115 × 25 × 40 mm acrylic plastic block and a 135 × 75 × 6 mm acrylic plate notched to fit around the block. The chamber rests on the base of the block and on two plastic legs (15 × 10 × 34 mm) glued to corners X and Y of the plate. The top margins around the (stippled) well should be smooth and not lower than the surrounding plastic plate. A pair of microscope slides may be used to cover the nerve chamber. A trace of petroleum jelly provides an airtight seal to keep the humidity close to 100%. Tilt the left end of the block 5° up and mill out to a depth 30 mm below the highest point. This will produce a slope in the bottom of the well which will facilitate transfer of solutions with a medicine dropper. Drill a

2 mm hole in each end. Turn the block on its side and, 10 mm below the top edge, drill 16 holes in the positions indicated which are just large enough to accommodate the electrode wire. Solder one end of a 6 cm piece of hookup wire to each of seven 3 cm long electrode wires. Repeat, using a different color hookup wire, soldering a 5 cm piece to each of nine electrode wires. There should be *no* solder on the portion of the electrode *within* the chamber because bimetallic potentials may result. Insert the straightened electrode wires into and through the predrilled holes just far enough to allow the ends to be crimped over where they protrude from the opposite side of the block. The two different colors of hookup wire should be placed to correspond to the first and second row of pin jacks, respectively. Use acrylic solvent (dichloromethylene) to attach the drilled and notched plate to the block and the two legs to the plate. Cover both ends of each electrode

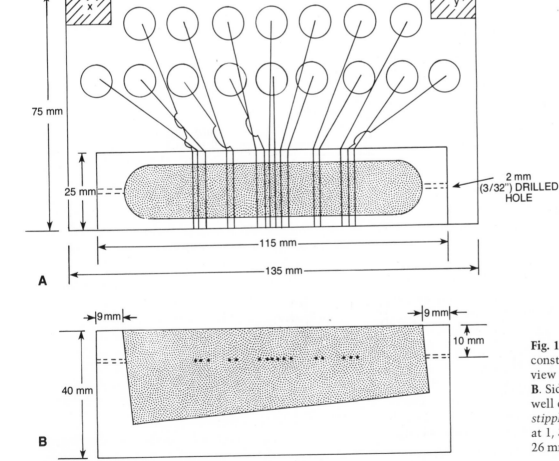

Fig. 10.3-1. Nerve chamber construction diagram. **A.** Top view of entire chamber. **B.** Side view of block and well only. Well area, *stippled*. Electrode holes at 1, 3, 5, 13, 15, 22, 24, and 26 mm to each side of center.

wire on the outside of the block with epoxy cement. An additional strip of plastic shim at the solder joint may be added to make the electrode wires more rigid. Trim the hookup wires to the correct length and solder to the appropriate pin jacks inserted in the top plate.

Materials needed for construction of nerve chamber

1 clear acrylic plastic block (115 × 25 × 40 mm) (trade names: Lucite, Plexiglas, Acrylite, Perspex)

1 clear acrylic plastic plate (135 × 75 × 6 mm)

50 cm 24-gauge (0.5 mm) platinum, palladium, or iridium wire (preferred because it will not oxidize readily and is less easily bent) or 20-gauge (0.75 mm) silver wire

16 all-metal pin jacks

2 pieces of acrylic plastic for legs (15 × 10 × 34 mm)

2 50-cm pieces of 22-gauge hookup wire (plastic covered, stranded). The two pieces should be different colors.

Mono- and Bipolar Electrode Holder

(*Experiments, monopolar: 4.6, 6.1, 6.2, 6.3, 6.6, 7.2, 7.5, 7.6; bipolar: 4.6, 5.3, 6.4, 6.5, 7.1*)

Figure 10.3-2 provides drawings for the construction of an inexpensive and versatile electrode holder and bipolar adapter. The press-fitted pin-vise handle can be removed from the commercial pin vise by placing the pin vise upright so that its flange catches on the edges of a metal vise open 5 mm. Seize the lower part of the handle at right angles with heavy pliers or locking pliers and tap the pliers downward with a hammer. The pin vise fitted to a 12–24 bolt extension can be screwed snugly into the plastic tubing.

An additional pin vise and bolt can be screwed into the partially tapped hole in the plastic block which will slide over the plastic tubing. The separation of the electrodes (one in each pin vise) can be adjusted by bending the electrode wires appropriately. The coaxial cable can be passed through the

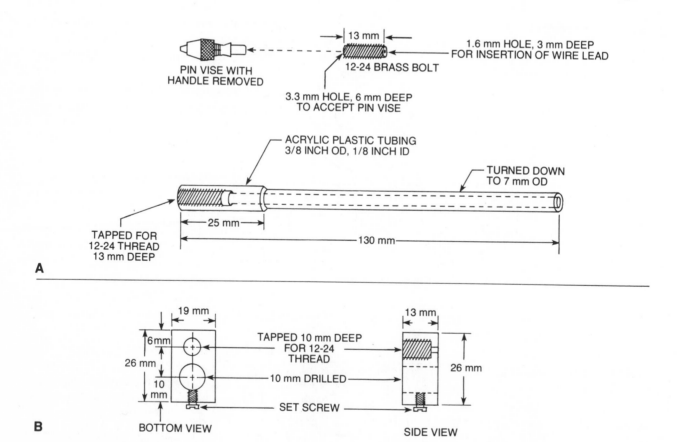

Fig. 10.3-2. A. Monopolar electrode holder. **B**. Bipolar electrode holder adapter.

tube and the central conductor soldered to the brass bolt. The shielding must not touch the bolt.

Materials needed for construction of each monopolar electrode holder

1 1-inch 12–24 brass bolt
1 pin vise (Jensen Tools and Alloys, 4117 N 44th St. Phoenix, AZ 85018. Cat. no. 31B350)
13 cm acrylic plastic tubing 3/8-inch O.D., 1/8-inch I.D. (trade names: Acrylite, Lucite, Plexiglas, Perspex)
1.5 m Belden RG174/U coaxial cable
1 BNC plug (Amphenol 36775)

Materials needed for construction of each bipolar adapter

1 13 × 19 × 26 mm acrylic plastic block
1.5 m Belden RG174/U coaxial cable
1 BNC plug (Amphenol 36775)
1 set screw (e.g., 6-32, 1/4 inch)
1 pin vise
1 1-inch 12–24 brass bolt

Chronic Implant Assembly

(See figs. 9.4-4 and 9.4-5 for examples.)

Construction of electrode assembly

Take two lengths of electrode wire, each about 80 cm long. Clamp one end of each wire into a pin vise which is inserted into the chuck of a drill press. Clamp the remaining free ends into another pin vise held with one hand while the drill press turns at a slow speed. When the wires are well twisted together, stop the motor and release your grip on the lower pin vise. This results in evenly twisted wires for bipolar electrodes. If they do not have at least 3 turns per cm, restart the drill press and twist further.

With wire cutters or sharp wire strippers, cut off 17 mm lengths of the twisted electrode wire. At one end, scrape off 3 mm of the Teflon and underlying enamel insulation from each wire. To do this neatly, use a dissecting microscope and a no. 15 scalpel blade. Hold a male Relia-Tac contact by the tip with a minigator clip, so that the solder well is upright. Heat the well until solder flows into it and then place one de-insulated prong of the bipolar electrode into the *center* of the well. Similarly, solder the other prong to another male Relia-Tac contact.

Clip or saw off from the narrow plastic or nylon contact strip (Amphenol 221-2653) a short block which contains three intact holes. Before you cut off the block, note the direction of the arrows on the strip, which indicate the direction to insert the male Relia-Tac. Now carefully seat the two contacts into adjacent holes with needle-nose pliers. (For experiment 7.9 it will be necessary to add a third lead, an uninsulated ground wire about 4 cm long. This ground wire should be soldered into a male Relia-Tac contact which is then inserted into the third hole of the block. The wire should be fine enough to be wrapped around a small screw, but not so fine that it readily breaks off when wiggled back and forth. A good source of wire is one of the 30 gauge strands from 22 gauge stranded hookup wire, e.g., Belden no. 8503. A small notch in the block next to the ground pin will assist those students who fail to record in their protocol the position of the ground pin on the implanted assembly.)

Measuring from the bottom of the block, trim the *insulated* electrode wires to the following length: experiment 7.8, septal area, 10 mm, lateral hypothalamic area, 13 mm; experiment 7.9, hippocampus, 8 mm. One of the two insulated electrode wires in each assembly should now be trimmed so that it is exactly 0.5 mm shorter than the other. To make a smooth cut, it is necessary to use a sharp sturdy scalpel blade on a microscope slide or other firm surface. Most wire cutters tend to fan out the metal where it is cut. It is imperative that trimming of the electrode tip be done under a dissecting microscope to avoid damage to the insulation or electrode tips. (With adequate laboratory time, students may construct an electrode assembly during the actual implantation procedure. See G. P. Frommer, 1970. *Physiol. and Behav.* 5: 1501–2.)

Construction of leads for chronic stimulation and recording

To make the connector lead which inserts into the implanted electrode assembly for stimulation (experiment 7.8), one can use two 1.5 m lengths of size 26 stranded, plastic insulated hookup wire, e.g., Belden no. 8505. Solder a female Relia-Tac contact to the end of each wire. Cut off a three hole block of the wide plastic contact strip (Amphenol 221-2553) and insert the female Relia-Tac contacts into adjacent holes in the direction of the arrows on the strip. The plastic block should be filed down until it is flush with the female contacts inside. This will ensure a firm grip to the male contacts. Use a cap of acrylic dental cement to make the lead wires and block into a rigid unit. The other end of the wires may be connected appropriately to the stimulating apparatus (see fig. 7.8-2). A suitable recording lead is described next. Obtain two lengths of Microdot cable. Microdot cable is designed to have low noise properties, even when slightly moving. Slip 2 cm of shielding from each wire to one side, twist the shielding of the two wires together, and solder to a short wire which will fit into the female Relia-Tac contact. Solder a female Relia-Tac contact to the shield lead and one contact to each of the two core conductors. Insert the three Relia-Tac contacts into a three hole block of the plastic contact strip in the direction of the arrows on the strip. As indicated above file the block flush with the contacts, and cap with dental cement, leaving a small piece of the shielding exposed to indicate which contact is the ground contact. A BNC plug can be placed on the other end of each of the Microdot cables.

Materials

Soldering iron (fine point)
Fine solder (rosin core)
Minigator clip
2 pin vises (Jensen Tools and Alloys, no. 31B350)
Needle-nose pliers
Metal vise for clamping block
4-inch contact strips (Amphenol narrow, 221-2653; wide, 221-2553, with 0.075-inch spacing of holes)
Relia-Tac contacts (Amphenol male, 220-P02; female, 220-S02)
Electrode wire (0.008-inch stainless, Teflon coated; Medwire Corp. cat. no. 316558T)
Drill press
Wire cutters or sharp wire strippers
Scalpel with sturdy no. 15 blade
Acrylic dental cement
Male BNC connectors
Microdot cable (Microdot no. 250-3804)
No. 26 hookup wire
Flat metal file

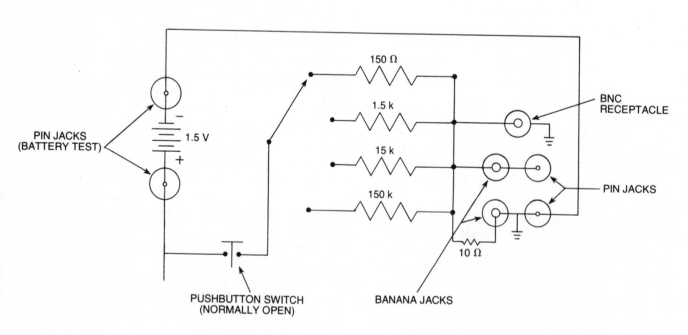

Fig. 10.3-3. Millivolt calibration circuit. The pin jack and banana jack output terminals are optional. The center-to-center distance of the banana jacks should be 1.9 cm to accommodate a double banana plug.

Calibration Circuit

(*Useful in exercise 4.5 and others*)
The circuit in figure 10.3-3 allows the student to calibrate equipment and electrodes with voltages from 0.1 to 100 mV. The chassis is grounded.

Materials needed for calibration circuit

1 1.5-V alkaline AA battery
1 each of 10Ω, 150Ω, 1.5Ω, 15kΩ, and 150kΩ
 0.5-watt carbon resistors (5%)
2 insulated banana jacks
4 insulated pin jacks
1 BNC female receptacle
1 battery holder
1 normally open, momentary contact push-button
 switch
1 rotary switch, single pole, at least 4 positions
1 knob with pointer
1 aluminum two-piece minibox (e.g., Bud
 CU-2106A)
4 rubber feet with attachment screws

Rat and Gerbil Headholder

(*Experiments 6.6, 7.2, 7.5, 7.7, 7.8, 7.9*)
The headholder in figure 10.3-4 can be used in conjunction with a micromanipulator to make stereotaxic electrode placements. In such cases the snout and mouth bars would be attached at right angles to the support rod to facilitate leveling the skull by head rotation (see fig. 9.3-1B). Both the headholder and the micromanipulator must be firmly clamped to a rigid stand, e.g., Enco magnetic stand. The 10–24 screw in the support rod may be cut off to a convenient length.

Commercial stereotaxic instruments generally do not permit optimal head orientation in experiments 6.6 and 7.2. If a commercial instrument is to be used for stereotaxic lesions in experiment 7.7, it may be shared by having students at a second station first expose and prepare the top of the skull using the headholder diagramed in figure 10.3-4. Then the rat may be transferred to the commercial instrument for electrode placement.

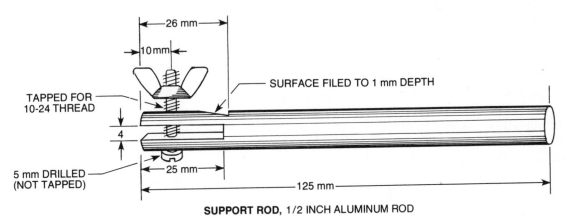

SUPPORT ROD, 1/2 INCH ALUMINUM ROD

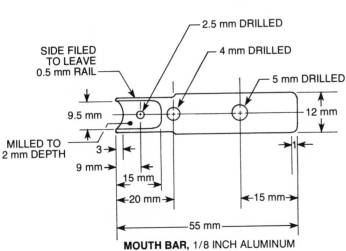

MOUTH BAR, 1/8 INCH ALUMINUM

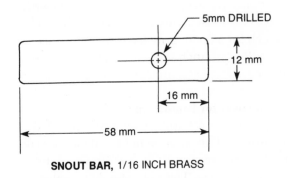

SNOUT BAR, 1/16 INCH BRASS

Fig. 10.3-4. Construction details for rat and gerbil headholder. See figure 9.3-1 for photograph.

Construction of Faraday Cage and Other Items at an Electrophysiological Station

This section considers those items in table 10.2-1 which require some construction.

Faraday cage

A Faraday cage can be constructed as a 93 cm cube with only three sides and a top which are hinged for folding. The front is open. One satisfactory arrangement is to obtain 1/4-inch mesh galvanized screen (hardware cloth) and trim it with a 6 cm wide metal strip folded in the middle to form a frame around each 93 cm square sheet of screening. The four framed sheets can be laid out in an L configuration and connected with three piano hinges which are riveted through the hinge, metal strip, and screen. Properly constructed, the four sheets will fold together for neat storage or unfold into three sides and a top for use. The top should be hinged to one side sheet and should have two clips which grasp the upper framing of the other side, and one which grasps the rear sheet. A 96 cm square pan with 3 cm upturned sides, fashioned from 18-gauge galvanized steel should be used as a bottom into which the screening cage will be placed. (Although the 1/2-inch grounded steel plate to be placed in the pan would suffice for shielding, the open-bottomed screening without the pan could easily be shifted over the corner of a table and fall.) Clips may be used for rigidity on the front portion of the sides of the screening to connect with the upturned flange of the bottom pan.

The considerations in this or any other Faraday cage design are that the cage should: (1) fold for convenient storage; (2) be rapidly and easily set up without an excess of loose hardware; (3) be stable; (4) be large enough for a boom arm dissecting microscope, yet fit on a 36 × 36-inch tabletop; and (5) have all parts in good electrical contact with each other.

Black cloth cover for Faraday cage

Visual experiments 6.1 and 7.6 require controlled light conditions. This is conveniently done by making a black cloth cover with no bottom which fits over the Faraday cage. The front should be a flap sewn only at the top so that it may be lifted up or down. Many, if not most fabrics are quite translucent; check this before the cloth is purchased. The cloth should not allow any light to leak in. A small side flap may be cut for admittance of an adapting or test light beam.

Steel base plate

Each electrophysiological station should have a 16 × 24 × 1/2-inch steel base plate. (Have the supplier neatly cut the plates to the final size.) These dimensions will give adequate working surface while permitting the stand of a boom arm dissecting microscope to fit into the Faraday cage behind the steel plate. The steel base plate should be given a thin coat of paint to prevent rust. A thick coat of paint would reduce the effective pull of the magnetic stands. A 15 cm piece of heavy-walled, rubber vacuum tubing should be placed under each corner of the plate. Lay these out in the floor of the Faraday cage pan in a clockwise sequence, positioning each successive tube 90° clockwise to the previous one. When the tubing is correctly placed, the plate will be isolated from most jarring vibrations, and roll neither left or right nor front or back. Thus upraised, it is also easier to grasp and move as required. Drill a 4 mm hole through the plate in two diagonally opposite corners. This will accommodate a banana plug to ground the plate.

10.4 Suppliers

Animals and Animal Maintenance

(*See also p. 349.*)

Aquarium Systems, Inc.
33208 Lakeland Blvd.
Eastlake, OH 44094
(*artificial sea water and systems*)

Bay Biological Supply Ltd.
Box 71
Port Credit Ont., Canada
(*animals*)

Carolina Biological Supply Co.
Burlington, NC 27215
(*animals and other products*)

Charles River Breeding
    Laboratories, Inc.
251 Ballardvale St.
North Wilmington, MA 01067
(*rats*)

Connecticut Valley Biological
    Supply Co.
Valley Rd.
Southampton, MA 01073
(*animals*)

Gulf Specimen Co.
P.O. Box 237
Panacea, FL 32346
(*aquatic animals*)

Holtzman Co.
421 Holtzman Rd.
Madison, WI 53713
(*rats*)

Marine Biological Laboratory
Supply Dept.
Woods Hole, MA 02543
(*aquatic animals*)

Mogul-Ed Corp.
P.O. Box 482
Oshkosh, WI 54901
(*animals*)

Northeast Marine Specimens Co.
P.O. Box 1
Woods Hole, MA 02543
(*aquatic animals*)

Pacific Bio-Marine Supply Co.
P.O. Box 536
Venice, CA 90291
(*aquatic animals*)

Rana Laboratories
Box 3103
Brownsville, TX 78520
(*frogs*)

Ross Laboratories
625 Cleveland Ave.
Columbus, OH 43216
(*animal care products*)

Sprague-Dawley, Inc.
P.O. Box 4220
Seminole Highway, Rt. 2
Madison, WI 53711
(*rats*)

Biological Supplies

Ann Arbor Biological Center
6780 Jackson Rd.
Ann Arbor, MI 48103

Clay-Adams, Inc.
299 Webro Rd.
Parsippany, NJ 07054

Nasco-Steinhilber
Fort Atkinson, WI 53538

Turtox Products
General Biological Supply House
8200 S. Hoyne Ave.
Chicago, IL 60620

Ward's Natural Science
  Establishment
P.O. Box 1712
Rochester, NY 14603

Chemicals and Drugs

Abbott Laboratories
14th St. and Sheridan Rd.
North Chicago, IL 60064

1-312-937-6100

J. T. Baker Chemical Co.
222 Red School Lane
Phillipsburg, NJ 08865

Bristol Laboratories
Veterinary Products
P.O. Box 657
Syracuse, NY 13201

Burroughs Wellcome and Co.
3030 Cornwallis Rd.
Research Triangle Park, NC 27709

Calbiochem
10933 N. Torrey Pines Rd.
La Jolla, CA 92037

CIBA Pharmaceutical Co.
556 Morris Ave.
Summit, NJ 07901

Diamond Laboratories
Des Moines, IA 50300

Eastman Kodak Co.
Eastman Organic Chemicals
343 State St.
Rochester, NY 14650

ICN Pharmaceuticals, Inc.
Life Sciences Group
26201 Miles Rd.
Cleveland, OH 44128

Lederle Laboratories
Pearl River, NY 10965

Eli Lilly and Co.
307 E. McCarty
P.O. Box 618
Indianapolis, IN 46206

Mallinckrodt Chemical Works
P.O. Box 5439
St. Louis, MO 63160

Merck, Sharp and Dohme
West Point, PA 19486

Nutritional Biochemicals Corp.
Research Biochemicals
26201 Miles Rd.
Cleveland, OH 44128

Parke, Davis & Co.
P.O. Box 476 G.P.O.
Detroit, MI 48232

Schering Corp.
Galloping Hill Rd.
Kenilworth, NJ 07033

Schwarz/Mann Biochemicals
Orangeburg, NY 10962

Sigma Chemical Co.
P.O. Box 14508
St. Louis, MO 63178

Squibb and Sons
Lawrenceville-Princeton Rd.
Princeton, NJ 08540

Wyeth Laboratories
P.O. Box 8299
Philadelphia, PA 19101

Dental Supplies

Acralite Products
Kerr Manufacturing Co.
28200 Wick Rd.
Romulus, MI 48174

L. S. Caulk Co.
P.O. Box 359
Millford, DE 19963

W. Getz Products
Teledyne Dental
1550 Greenleaf Ave.
Elk Grove Village, IL 60007

S. S. White Dental Products
Division of Pennwalt Corp.
3 Parkway
Philadelphia, PA 19102

Dissecting and Surgical Supplies

American Hospital Supply
(major cities throughout the U.S.)

Circon MicroSurgical
Circon Corp.
749 Ward Dr.
Santa Barbara, CA 93111

Ethicon, Inc.
Somerville, NJ 08876
(*suture material*)

Parkell Products, Inc.
155 Schmitt Blvd.
Farmingdale, NY 11735

Plastic Products, Inc.
P.O. Box 1204T
Roanoke, VA 24006
(*canullae*)

Roboz Surgical Instrument
  Co., Inc.
810 18th St. N.W.
Washington, D.C. 20006

Techni-tool, Inc.
5 Apollo Rd.
Plymouth Meeting, PA 19462

George Tiemann and Co.
21–28 45th Rd.
Long Island City, NY 11101

Electrophysiological and Behavioral Equipment

A-M Systems, Inc.
P. O. Box 7332
Toledo, OH 43615

Annex Instruments
P.O. Box 15044
Santa Ana, CA 92705

BRS/LVE
Division of TECH SERV, Inc.
5301 Holland Dr.
Beltsville, MD 20705

Bio-medical Electronics, Inc.
Subsidiary of ILC Industries, Inc.
350 Pear St.
Dover, DE 19901

Dagan Corp.
2010 Minnehaha Ave.
Minneapolis, MN 54404

Electronics for Life Sciences, Inc.
P.O. Box 697
Rockville, MD 20851

Frederick Haer and Co.
P.O. Box 337
Industry Dr.
Brunswick, ME 04011

Grass Instrument Co.
101 Old Colony Ave.
Quincy, MA 02169

Harvard Apparatus Co., Inc.
150 Dover Rd.
Millis, MA 02054

In Vivo Metric Systems
10709 Venice Blvd.
Los Angeles, CA 90034

Lafayette Instrument Co.
P.O. Box 1279
Sagamore Pky. N.
Lafayette, IN 47902

Life Science Assoc.
1525 Berkeley Ave.
Baldwin, NY 11510

Mentor Corp.
3104 West Lake St.
Minneapolis, MN 55416

Narco Bio-Systems
Box 12511
Houston, TX 77017

Ortec, Inc.
1000 Midland Rd.
Oak Ridge, TN 37830

Phipps and Bird, Inc.
Sixth at Byrd Sts.
P.O. Box 2-V
Richmond, VA 23205

Princeton Applied Research Corp.
P.O. Box 565
Princeton, NJ 08540

Scientific Prototype
   Manufacturing Corp.
615 W. 131 St.
New York, NY 10027

Stoelting Co.
1350 S. Kostner Ave.
Chicago, IL 60623
(including bioelectric)

Transidyne General Corp.
462 S. Wagner Rd.
Ann Arbor, MI 48103

W-P Instruments, Inc.
2600 State St.
Hamden, CT 06517

General Electronics

Allied Electronics
P.O. Box 1544
Fort Worth, TX 76101

American Science Center, Inc.
5700 Northwest Highway
Chicago, IL 60646

Beckman Instruments, Inc.
Schiller Park Operations
3900 N. River Rd.
Schiller Park, IL 69176

Brush Instruments
Division Clevite Corp.
3631 Perkins Ave.
Cleveland, OH 44114

Dumont Oscilloscope Laboratories, Inc.
40 Fairfield Pl.
West Caldwell, NJ 07006

GC Electronics
400 S. Wyman St.
Rockford, IL 61101

Gilson Medical Electronics, Inc.
P.O. Box 27
Middleton, WI 53562

Heath/Schlumberger Instruments
Benton Harbor, MI 49022

Hewlett-Packard
1501 Pace Mill Rd.
Palo Alto, CA 94304

Lafayette Radio Electronics
(in cities throughout the U.S.)

Newark Electronics
500 N. Pulaski Rd.
Chicago, IL 60624

Radio Shack
(in cities throughout the U.S.)

Tektronix, Inc.
P.O. Box 500
Beaverton, OR 97005

Electrical Connectors and Adapters

Amphenol Connector Division
Controls-Operation
Bunker-Ramo Corp.
2801 S. 25th Ave.
Broadview, IL 60153

Hamilton Electronic Sales
1216 W. Clay
Houston, TX 77019
(Amphenol male contacts)

Microdot, Inc.
220 Pasadena Ave.
S. Pasadena, CA 91030
(Microdot cable)

Pomona Electronics
1500 E. Ninth St.
Pomona, CA 91766
(connectors and adapters)

General Scientific Supplies

Aloe Scientific
1831 Olive St.
St. Louis, MO 63103

Central Scientific Co.
2600 S. Kostner St.
Chicago, IL 60623

W. H. Curtin & Co.
(major cities throughout the U.S.)

Edmund Scientific Co.
403 Edscorp Bldg.
Barrington, NJ 08007

Sargent-Welch Scientific Co.
(major cities throughout the U.S.)

Scientific Products (S/P)
(major cities throughout the U.S.)

Stansi Educational Materials Division
Fisher Scientific Co.
1259 N. Wood St.
Chicago, IL 60622

A. H. Thomas Co.
Third and Vine St.
P.O. Box 779
Philadelphia, PA 19105

Van Waters and Rogers Co.
(major cities throughout the U.S.)

Stereotaxic Instruments and Micromanipulators

(See also "Electrophysiological and Behavioral Equipment.")

Baltimore Instruments
4610 Hartfort Rd.
Baltimore, MD 21201

Brinkman Instruments, Inc.
Cantiague Rd.
Westbury, NY 11590

Hacker Instruments, Inc.
Box 646
Fairfield, NJ 07006

David Kopf Instruments
7324 Elmo St.
Tujunga, CA 91042

Labtron Scientific Corp.
855-D Conklin St.
Farmingdale, NY 11735

Syringes and Needles

Hamilton Co.
P.O. Box 17500
Reno, NV 89510

Tools, Hardware, Screws, Pins, Wire, Electrode Materials, Insulating Materials, Tubing

Albany Products Co., Inc.
3046 W. 77th St.
Chicago, IL 60652
(stainless steel screws)

Bio Metal Assoc.
P.O. Box 61
Santa Monica, CA 90406
(stainless steel insect pins)

California Fine Wire Co.
338 S. 4th St.
Grover City, CA 93433
(stainless steel wire)

Cleveland Tungsten, Inc.
10200 Meech Ave.
Cleveland, OH 44105
(electrode materials)

Dremel Co.
Dept. 350
Racine, WI 53406
(Mototool for surgical use in lieu of a dental drill)

Driver-Harris Co.
202 Middlesex St.
Harrison, NJ 07029
(electrode materials)

Enco Co.
4520 W. Fullerton Ave.
Chicago, IL 60639
(magnetic stands)

R. P. Gallien and Son
412 W. 6th St.
Los Angeles, CA 90013
(*stainless steel screws*)

Insl-X Products Corp.
115–117 Woodworth Ave.
Yonkers, NY 10701
(*insulating materials*)

Jensen Tools and Alloys
3630 E. Indian School Rd.
Phoenix, AZ 85018
(*quality tools and pin vises*)

A. D. Mackay, Inc.
198 Broadway
New York, NY 10038
(*tungsten and silver wire*)

Medwire Corp.
121 S. Columbus Ave.
Mt. Vernon, NY 10553
(*electrode wire*)

Small Parts, Inc.
6901 N.E. Third Ave.
Miami, FL 33138

Tube Sales
2211 Tube Way
Los Angeles, CA 90040
(*hypodermic tubing*)

Utica Tool Co., Inc.
Orangeburg, SC 29115
(*quality hand tools*)

Xcelite Tools
(*quality hand tools distributed by electronics and
tool suppliers throughout the U.S.*)

10.5 Basic Laboratory Supplies

A supply of basic laboratory glassware is necessary, including serological pipettes, Pasteur pipettes, and medicine droppers with rubber bulbs. Standard tools, including a soldering iron, a variety of screwdrivers and pliers, hacksaw, and wrenches should be available. Special chemicals used for sensory stimulation or preparation of pheromone extracts in exercises 6.3, 8.4, and 8.6 are listed only in the appropriate "Materials" section of each experiment. Other basic supplies and chemicals are listed here.

Basic Supplies

Adapters (three prong, AC)
Air stones (air breakers for aquaria)
Aluminum foil
Applicator sticks (wooden)
Bags (plastic)
Batteries
Brushes
Bulbs (rubber pipetting)
Bulbs (incandescent; for table lamps and microscopes)
Bunsen burners (fine flame, regular, and air and gas blast burner)
Can opener
Capillary tubing
Caps (jar and bottle)
Chalk
Clamps (right angle, swiveling, buret, pinchcock)
Clay (modeling, e.g., Plasticene)
Clippers (animal)
Cloth (black and white)
Cork borers
Cotton
Coverslips (microslide)
Diamond or carbide-tipped pencils (for breaking capillaries)
Electrode paste

File
Filter paper
Fishhooks (nos. 16, 14, 12, 8)
Flashlight
Glass wool
Gloves (for heat protection and glass breaking)
Gloves (surgical)
Glue (white glue, model cement, ferrule cement as used by fishermen, cyanoacrylate adhesive)
Knives
Labels
Lens paper
Magnifying glasses
Matches
Meter sticks and rulers
Mirror
Paper (white and black posterboard)
Paper punch (1- and 3-hole)
Parafilm
Pencils (pens, markers, crayons)
Petroleum jelly (Vaseline) and silicone stopcock grease
pH indicator paper
Pins (insect nos., 2, 1, 0, 00; regular straight pins)
Power cords (AC)
Power outlets (multiple, AC)
Razor blades
Ringstands, tripods, wire squares with asbestos centers, and support rings
Rubber bands
Rubber stoppers
Rulers (protractor, slide rule)
Sandpaper
Saran Wrap
Screen (hardware cloth)
Slides (glass microslides)
Spatulas
Stapler and staples
Steel wool

Syringes (and needles)
Tacks
Tape (Scotch Magic, double-stick, and masking)
Test tube holders
Thermometers (mercury and electronic)
Thread (cotton, nylon, surgical)
Timers (laboratory and stopwatches)
Tongue depressors
Toothpicks
Tubing (glass)
Tubing (rubber, Tygon, surgical)
Wax (paraffin, dental, Tackiwax)
Weights (for balance and experiments)
Wire, electrode (silver and stainless steel)
Wire, hookup (18-gauge, insulated and uninsulated)

Sodium chloride
Sodium hydroxide
Sodium phosphate (dibasic)
Sodium phosphate (monobasic)
Sodium sulfate
Sucrose
Tris buffer (tris[hydroxymethyl]aminomethane; e.g., Sigma Trizma base and Trizma HCl)
Xylene

Basic Chemicals

Acetic acid
Alcohol, ethyl (absolute, 95%, and 70%)
Ammonium chloride
Boric acid (used only to prepare lobster perfusion fluid)
Buffer, pH7 standard (for calibrating pH meter)
Calcium chloride
Carbolic acid (crystalline phenol; exercise 3.2 only)
Choline chloride (exercise 4.1 only)
Copper sulfate (exercise 3.2 only)
Detergent (Liquinox, for cleaning)
Ether
Ferric chloride (exercise 3.2 only)
Formaldehyde solution (formalin, 37% formaldehyde)
Glucose (dextrose)
Glycerin (glycerol)
Hydrochloric acid
Lithium chloride (exercises 4.1, 8.5 only)
Magnesium chloride
Magnesium sulfate
Methyl salicylate (exercise 5.4 only)
Methylene blue (stain)
Mineral oil
Potassium chloride
Potassium ferrocyanide (exercise 3.2 only)
Potassium phosphate (monobasic)
Potassium phosphate (dibasic)
Saccharin acid (exercise 8.5 only)
Sodium bicarbonate

10.6 Animals

Initial Procedure

To order the correct number of animals at the correct times, you must first establish the sequence of the term's experiments. Consider the following points.

1. Exercise 8.1 is intended to be an initial, one-period exercise for developing observational and analytical skills apart from instrumentation. Most other exercises are satisfactorily completed in two periods. However, postoperative recovery requires a minimum of 1 week before testing in experiments 7.8 and 7.9.

2. Some savings in animals can be achieved by scheduling which permits reuse, e.g., 8.5 before 7.2, 7.7, 7.8 or 7.9; 8.2 or 8.6 before 7.1.

3. Experiment 5.1 requires a completely dark room; 6.1, 8.2, and 8.6 require dim light.

4. Animals may have seasonal variation in availability, e.g., earthworms are available in abundance during the spring and summer.

Determining Animal Supply Needs

Consult table 10.6-1 to find the number of animals required per laboratory station per laboratory period. Multiply this value by the number of laboratory sections, the number of laboratory periods per experiment, and the number of stations to obtain the total animal needs for that exercise (e.g., exercise 6.6 cochlear microphonics: 1.33 gerbils × 2 sections × 2 lab periods × 3 stations = 16 gerbils). The number per station per laboratory period listed in the table does not include the savings which can be obtained by repeating the experiment in other laboratory periods or by reuse in a subsequent exercise. Estimates of these savings are given under the comments. Animals to be used in preparatory sessions

with teaching staff must also be added. We have mentioned suppliers in the exercise when sources seem limited. In addition to utilizing the suppliers listed on page 341 and locally known sources, the instructor will find the publication *Animals for Research* invaluable (National Academy of Science, Washington, D.C. 20418, $4.50, 94 pp., 1975 edition).

Placing Animal Orders

Purchase requisitions (orders) should specify: number of animals, size and/or age, sex, species or strain, catalog number, date wanted, shipping instructions, unit and total costs, as well as providing the supplier with address and a person to contact (address and phone number) upon arrival of the animals at a stated delivery site. Investigate the maximum time delay in trucking from the local airport to you.

Most of the animals are hardy and can be expected to survive in the laboratory with little loss for a few weeks. The convenience of a limited number of shipping dates and the savings associated with placing large orders may outweigh the cost and effort of long-term maintenance. Order the animals to arrive on Tuesday, Wednesday, or Thursday to avoid fatal weekend layovers. Be certain to have conditioned aquarium water, sea water, or other "housing needs" readied several days in advance of arrival.

Sources of information on animal supply, care, and use
(*See also page 341.*)

Lane-Petter, W.; Worden, A. N.; Hill, B. G.; Patterson, J. S.; and Vevers, H. G., eds. 1967. *UFAW handbook, the care and management of laboratory animals*. E. & S. Livingstone, Ltd., London.

Leonard, E. P. 1968. *Fundamentals of small animal surgery*. W. B. Saunders, Philadelphia.

TABLE 10.6-1
Animal Usage

Experiment	Page	Animal	No./station/ lab. period	Comments
*4.1 Sodium Transport	82	Frog	1.5	*Rana pipiens*
*4.2 Compound Action Potential	95	Frog	1.5	
**4.3 Compound Action Potential and Single Units	103	*Limulus polyphemus*	0.33	Lobster or crayfish (Alt)
**4.4 Giant Fibers	110	*Lumbricus terrestris*	3	
***4.5 Membrane Potential	119	Frog	1	
***4.6 Volume Conduction	127	Frog	1	
*5.1 Coelenterate Nerve Net	136	*Renilla kollikeri*	3–4	50% reuse after 24-hr rest
**5.2 Neuromuscular Synapse	145	Frog	1.5	2.5 if experiment on page 144 is performed
**5.3 Cardiac Muscle	153	Turtle	1	+1/10 stations for loss in holding tank
*5.4 Blood Flow	159	Frog	1	+1/4 stations for loss in holding tank
		Goldfish (Opt)	1	
		Xenopus laevis tadpoles (Opt)	1	
		Periplaneta americana (Opt)	1–2	Or other winged cockroach
*5.5 Chromatophores	164	*Palaemonetes vulgaris*	16–20	25% reuse after experiment
		Uca pugilator	2–3	
		Crayfish (Opt)	1–2	
*6.1 Visual Reception (ERG)	173	Frog	1	+1/4 stations for loss in holding tank; some reuse of curarized frogs after experiment
*6.2 Mechanoreception	179	Cockroach	1.25	Any species
**6.3 Olfactory Reception (EOG)	185	Frog	1.25	
***6.4 Proprioception (Muscle Spindle)	191	Frog	1	
**6.5 Cutaneous Receptive Fields	195	Frog	1	+1/4 stations for loss in holding tank
***6.6 Auditory Reception	201	Gerbil	1.33	
*7.1 Nerve Cord	210	Cockroach	2–3	Any species; males preferred
***7.2 Motor Cortex	217	Rat	1.33	150–250 g female
*7.3 Spinal Reflexes	223	Frog	2	
*7.4 Stretch Reflex		Human	1	
***7.5 Somatosensory Representation	237	Rat	1.33	150–250 g females
***7.6 Optic Tectum	245	Frog	1	+1/4 stations
		Goldfish (Opt)	1.5	
*7.7 Hypothalamic Lesions	250	Rat	1.25	200 g females—reuse not recommended; +2–4 unoperated controls/lab section
**7.8 Chronic Brain Stimulation	255	Rat	1.25	150–200 g female
**7.9 Chronic Brain Recording	260	Rat	1.25	150–200 g female

TABLE 10.6-1 (continued)
Animal Usage

Experiment	Page	Animal	No./station/ lab. period	Comments
*8.1 Locomotion	264	Various		See page 264
*8.2 Insect Flight	270	*Periplaneta americana*	5–6	Ask for winged adults; 25–50% reuse after experiment
*8.3 Electrolocation	279	Various fish	1	See page 279
*8.4 Feeding Behavior	285	*Sarcophaga* or *Phormia*	40	*Calliphora* or *Lucilia* (Alts); order larvae which have just stopped feeding
*8.5 Conditioned Taste Aversion	289	Rat	8	150–200 g female; 100% reuse after experiment
**8.6 Sexual Behavior	298	*Periplanata americana*	5 larvae 10 males 10 females	Observations in evening. *P. brunnea* (Alt) 80% reuse after experiment
**8.7 Sensitive Plant	305	*Mimosa pudica*	2–10	Having several plants permits more rapid testing; 80% reuse

Consult *page numbers in italics* for information regarding animal supply and care.

Opt   *Optional*   Level of difficulty   * *Beginning*
Alt   *Alternate*   ** *Intermediate*
                                        *** *Advanced*

Lofts, B., ed. 1976. *Physiology of the amphibia*, vol. 3. Academic Press, New York, 520 pp. (Color change; nervous, visual, auditory systems, etc.)

Melby, E. C., Jr., and Altman, N. H., eds. 1974. *Handbook of animal science*, vol. 1. CRC Press, Cleveland. (Housing, reproduction, surgery, etc.). Vol. 2, 1974. (Diseases, some lab techniques, etc.). Vol. 3, 1976. (Nutrition, physiological data, nervous system drugs, hematology, etc.)

Amphibians: Guidelines for the breeding, care, and management of laboratory animals. 1974. Nat. Acad. Sci., Washington, D.C. 153 pp., $5.25.

Animals for research, 9th ed. 1975. Nat. Acad. Sci., Washington, D.C., 94 pp., $4.50.

Fishes: Guidelines for the breeding, care and management of laboratory animals. 1974. Nat. Acad. Sci., Washington, D.C., 85 pp., $5.00.

Guide for the care and use of laboratory animals. 1973. US DHEW (73-23). Available from: Supt. Docu., U.S. Gov't Printing Office, Washington, D.C., $0.55.

Nutrient requirements of laboratory animals. 1972. Nat. Acad. Sci., Washington, D.C., 122 pp., $4.95.

Rodents: Standards and guidelines for the breeding, care, and management of laboratory animals. 1969. Nat. Acad. Sci., Washington, D.C., 52 pp., $2.95.

10.7 Perfusion Solutions, Drugs, and Neuroactive Agents

Perfusion Solutions

Table 10.7-1 lists a series of perfusion solutions which can be prepared from stock solutions (tables 10.7-2 and 10.7-3) and are suitable for the experiments in this manual. Alternate solutions are listed for use with other animals (e.g., toads which might replace frogs in experiment 7.6) or in research projects (e.g., cockroach Ringer II solution for an extended recording session in experiment 7.1).

Mixing stock solutions
Add together the appropriate number of milliliters of each stock solution except $CaCl_2$. Bring this solution to about 750 ml by adding distilled water. Mix thoroughly. Adjust to the approximate pH value by dropwise addition of 10% HCl or NaOH while stirring. Now add the $CaCl_2$. Bring the total volume up to 1,000 ml. This procedure will eliminate precipitation of insoluble calcium salts.

Final pH adjustment
Adjust the pH of the final solution by dropwise addition of 10% HCl or NaOH. Agitate continuously when adjusting the pH, preferably with a magnetic stirrer. Adjust the pH of the solution at the temperature at which it will be used.

Additional buffering
Sea water or perfusion fluids may be further buffered by the addition of Na_2HPO_4 or Tris (next section). Numbers in parentheses in table 10.7-1 indicate that the buffer present may be substituted by another compound.

Tris buffers and other alternative buffers
Tris buffers (compounds containing tris [hydroxymethyl] aminomethane) are useful because they do not precipitate calcium. Sigma Chemical Company offers different Tris compounds which are described in Sigma Technical Bulletin no. 106B. Tris buffers have three major disadvantages: (1) they are relatively more expensive than phosphate or bicarbonate buffers; (2) some pH electrodes give incorrect readings with Tris present; and (3) Tris buffers have a significant temperature coefficient, i.e., the pH changes with temperature. In addition Tris is known to interfere chemically with some physiological processes (e.g., Wilson et al., 1977). However, the advantage of freedom from calcium precipitation generally outweighs these disadvantages. Consult the Sigma bulletin for specific information. Calbiochem offers a free publication, *A Guide for the Preparation and Use of Buffers in Biological Systems*, which reviews basic buffer concepts and suggests alternative buffers. Zwitterionic buffers, such as HEPES and TES, are now used routinely in biochemical studies and will be used increasingly by neurobiologists.

Sea water
Artificial sea water may be prepared from stock solutions (table 10.7-1) or from commercially prepared salts. We have had good results with "Instant Ocean" (Aquarium Systems, Inc.). The specific gravity of artificial sea water should be about 1.025 at 15° C. Bubble sea water with air for several days before use.

TABLE 10.7-1
Perfusion Solutions

(See page 352 for instructions.)

Solution	1.0 M $NaCl$	0.1 M KCl	0.1 M $CaCl_2$	1.0 M $MgCl_2$	0.1 M Na_2SO_4	0.1 M $NaHCO_3$	1.0 M NaH_2PO_4	0.1 M Na_2HPO_4	0.05 M Tris Buffer	1.0 M Glucose	pH	Amount 1.0 M $NaCl$ per 1,000 ml Solution to Make Isotonic Saline	Additions, Comments, &/ Alternate Solutions @ Concentrations from Table 10.7-3	Adapted from
Artificial pond water	0.50	0.5	4.0			2.0								Dietz and Alvarado, 1970
Artificial sea water	401	97	101	52.6	27.7	25		(100)			8.0-8.2	540	Or use commercial preparation	Pantin, 1948; Welsh et al., 1968
Coelenterates: Sea pansy (*Renilla*)			Use sea water					(100)						
Annelids: Earthworm	135	27	18	0.36	0.44			100		(200)	7.4	143		Pantin, 1948
Leech	115	40	18					(100)	200	10	7.4	137		Pantin, 1948; Nicholls and Baylor, 1968
Poly-chaetes			Use sea water					(100)						
Arthropods Crab (*Cancer*)	441	11	102	26.3	23.3			10		(20)	7.6	520		Robertson, 1931
Lobster (*Homarus*)	452	15	250	4.0				10		(20)	7.4	515	Plus 9 ml H_3BO_3 and 4 ml $MgSO_4$	Hagiwara and Bullock, 1957 (after Cole, 1941)
Cray-fish	206	54	108	2.5	24			(10)		(20)	7.4	237		Van Harreveld, 1936
Cock-roach I	160	50	20					10		(20)	7.5		Use for ex. 7.1	Pantin, 1948

TABLE 10.7-1 (continued)
Perfusion Solutions

Solution	1.0 M NaCl	0.1 M KCl	0.1 M CaCl₂	1.0 M MgCl₂	0.1 M Na₂SO₄	0.1 M NaHCO₃	1.0 M NaH₂PO₄	0.1 M Na₂HPO₄	0.05 M Tris Buffer	1.0 M Glucose	pH	Amount 1.0 M NaCl per 1,000 ml Solution to Make Isotonic Saline	Additions, Comments, Alternate Solutions @ Concentrations from Table 10.7-3	Adapted from
Cock-roach II	117	150	40	1.8		80			(40)		7.5	210	Plus 120 ml sucrose	Schafer, unpublished
Horse-shoe crab (*Limulus*)				Use sea water					(100)					
Mollusks Snail (*Helix*)	119	41	9.0	2.5	2.4	16		35	(70)		8.4	136		Pantin, 1948
Fresh-water Clams or Mussels	20.5	20	11					10	(20)		7.8	25.2	Or use 5% sea water; see Welsh et al. for alternative solution	Motley, 1934; Welsh et al., 1968
Marine Bivalves (e.g., *Mytilus*) and Gastro-pods (e.g., *Aplysia*)				Use sea water					(100)					
Squid				Use sea water					(100)					Keynes, 1951 (after Pantin, 1948)
Fish Fresh-water Fish I	94	19	11					10	(20)		7.2			Young, J. Z., in Pantin, 1948
Fresh-water Fish II	101	35	25		250				(20)		7.2	146	Plus 120 ml KH₂PO₄ and 1.2 ml MgSO₄	Burnstock, 1958
Marine Fish	133	24	11	1.5	9.7	4.3			(20)					

TABLE 10.7-1 (continued)
Perfusion Solutions

Solution	1.0 M NaCl	0.1 M KCl	0.1 M CaCl₂	1.0 M MgCl₂	0.1 M Na₂SO₄	0.1 M NaHCO₃	1.0 M NaH₂PO₄	0.1 M Na₂HPO₄	0.05 M Tris Buffer	1.0 M Glucose	pH	Amount 1.0 M NaCl per 1,000 ml Solution to Make Isotonic Saline	Additions, Comments, @ Alternate Solutions Concentrations from Table 10.7-3	Adapted from
Amphibians and Reptiles														
Frog Ringer I	112	32	27				20	(40)			7.2		For frog experiments	
Frog Ringer II	112	19	11		23.8	100				11.1	7.2	133		Richards, 1936
Toad and Lizard	124	38	11		24	8.5					7.2	133		Campbell et al., 1964
Turtle	116	40	20				20	(40)			7.2	125		
Birds and Mammals														
Bird Ringer	116	23	58	2.1		292					7.4	158		Benzinger and Krebs, 1933
Mammal Ringer	154	56	22			24		(40)			7.4	160	For ex. 6.6, 7.2, 7.5, 7.7, 7.8, 7.9	Richards, 1936
Mammal Ringer-Locke	146	54	22			24					7.2			Richards, 1936
Mammal Ringer-Krebs	118	48	26			250				11.1	7.4		Plus 12 ml KH₂PO₄ and 1.2 ml MgSO₄	Krebs, 1950

TABLE 10.7-2
Preparing Sea Water and Perfusion Solutions

Stock Solution	g/liter of Solution
1.0 M NaCl	58.44
0.1 M KCl	7.46
0.1 M CaCl$_2$ (anhydrous)	11.10
or	
CaCl$_2 \cdot 2$ H$_2$O	14.70
1.0 M MgCl$_2$ (anhydrous)	95.23
or	
MgCl$_2 \cdot 6$ H$_2$O	203.33
0.1 M Na$_2$SO$_4$ (anhydrous)	6.25
or	
Na$_2$SO$_4 \cdot 10$ H$_2$O	14.18
0.1 M NaHCO$_3$	8.40
0.1 M NaH$_2$PO$_4 \cdot$ H$_2$O	13.80
0.1 M Na$_2$HPO$_4$ (anhydrous)	14.20
0.05 M Tris buffer	See Sigma bulletin 106B
1.0 M Glucose (dextrose)	180.16

TABLE 10.7-3
Additional Useful Stock Solutions

Stock Solution	g/liter of Solution
1.0 M MgSO$_4$ (anhydrous)	120.39
or	
MgSO$_4 \cdot 7$ H$_2$O	246.5
0.1 M KH$_2$PO$_4$	13.61
0.1 M K$_2$HPO$_4$	22.82
1.0 M H$_3$BO$_3$	61.83
1.0 M Choline chloride	139.63
1.0 M LiCl	42.39
1.0 M Sucrose	342.3

Drugs, Poisons, Neuroactive Agents, and Injectable Solutions

Table 10.7-4 lists various druglike agents used in this manual. Many are hazardous in some way.

TABLE 10.7-4
Drugs, Poisons, Neuroactive Agents, and Injectable Solutions Used in This Manual

Chemical	Synonyms or Form to Use	Comments
Acetylcholine	Acetylcholine chloride	
Adenosine 3':5'-cyclic phosphate (ex. 5.5 only)	Cyclic AMP, cAMP; or use dibutyryl cAMP	Expensive (sodium salt is cheapest); cell membranes are more permeable to the dibutyryl analog
Atropine	Atropine sulfate	Anticholinergic; made up especially for rats
Bicillin	Benzathine penicillin G (Wyeth)	Antibiotic; long acting; injectable solution supplied as 300,000 units/ml and 600,000 units/ml
Colchicine (ex. 5.5 only)		Do not breathe powder when weighing
Croton oil (ex. 5.4 only)		Poisonous; avoid skin contact (supplied by Sigma)
Curare	d-Tubocurarine hydrochloride	Injectable solution supplied as 3 mg/ml; anticholinergic; binds to cholinergic sites on postsynaptic membrane; supplied by Abbott and others
Decamethonium (ex. 5.2 only)	Decamethonium bromide	Cholinergic blocking agent; depolarizing
2,4-Dinitrophenol (ex. 4.1 only)	DNP	Metabolic inhibitor
Eserine (ex. 5.2, 5.3)	Eserine sulfate, physostigmine	Anticholinesterase
Epinephrine	Adrenaline, (Adrenalin by Parke-Davis)	Injectable solution supplied as 1:1,000 solution; slowly oxidizes to adrenochrome (colored) when solution made up from powder

TABLE 10.7-4 (continued)
Drugs, Poisons, Neuroactive Agents, and Injectable Solutions
Used in This Manual

Chemical	Synonyms or Form to Use	Comments
Histamine (ex. 5.4 only)	Histamine dihydrochloride	
Insecticides (ex. 7.1 only)	Use DDT, malathion, or parathion	Segregate glassware used with these substances
Ketamine	(Vetalar by Parke-Davis)	Oral reflexes maintained
Neostigmine (ex. 5.2 only)	Neostigmine bromide	Anticholinesterase
Nicotine (ex. 5.2, 7.1)	Nicotine sulfate	Also used as insecticide (Black Leaf 40); toxic; avoid skin contact
Norepinephrine	Noradrenaline	May be tried in some exercises as an alternative to epinephrine (e.g., ex. 5.5)
Ouabain (ex. 4.1 only)	G-strophanthin	Specific inhibitor of sodium transport
Sodium pentobarbital	(Nembutal by Abbott)	Injectable solution supplied as 50 mg/ml
Succinylcholine (ex. 5.2 only)	Succinylcholine chloride (Anectine by Burroughs-Wellcome; Sucostrin by Squibb)	Injectable solution supplied as 20, 50, and 100 mg/ml; cholinergic blocking agent; depolarizing
Tetramethylammonium (ex. 5.2 only)	TMA, tetramethyl-ammonium hydroxide	Keep tightly closed; ganglionic stimulator
TMS	MS-222, Tricaine methane-sulfonate, Ethyl-m-amino-benzoate, Metacaine, Tricaine (TMS: "Finquel," Ayerst; formerly "MS-222," Sandoz)	Preferred anesthetic for frogs; inject 1 ml of 1% solution/10 g; anesthetize fish by immersion in 1:2,000 solution; store desiccated in freezer; anesthetic most effective when buffered to pH 7-8. (Ohr, 1976)
Urethane	Ethyl carbamate, urethan	An alternate anesthetic for frogs; inject 1 ml of 10% solution/10 g into dorsal or ventral lymph sac; carcinogen

References

Altman, P. L., and Dittmer, D. S. 1972. *Biology data book*, vol. 1, 2d ed. Fed. Am. Soc. Exp. Biol., Bethesda.

Benzinger, Th., and Krebs, H. A. 1933. Über die Harnsäuresynthese im Vogelorganismus. *Klin. Wochenschr.* 12: 1206–8.

Boyd, H.; Burnstock, G.; Campbell, G.; Jowett, A.; O'Shea, J.; and Wood, M. 1963. The cholinergic blocking action of adrenergic blocking agents in the pharmacological analysis of autonomic innervation. *Br. J. Pharmacol.* 20: 418–35.

Burnstock, G. 1958. Reversible inactivation of nervous activity in a fish gut. *J. Physiol.* 141: 35–45.

Campbell, G.; Burnstock, G.; and Wood, M. 1964. A method for distinguishing between adrenergic and cholinergic excitatory innervation of smooth muscle. *Q. J. Exp. Physiol.* 49: 268–76.

Cavanaugh, G. M., ed. 1964. *Formulae and methods V. of the marine biological laboratory chemical room.* Marine Biol. Laboratory, Woods Hole, Mass.

Chem sources. 1977. Directories Publishing Co., Flemington, N.J.

Cole, W. H. 1941. A perfusing solution for the lobster (*Homarus*) heart and the effects of its constituent ions on the heart. *J. Gen. Physiol.* 25: 1–6.

Dietz, T. H., and Alvarado, R. H. 1970. Osmotic and ionic regulation in *Lumbricus terrestris* L. *Biol. Bull.* 138: 247–61.

Facts and comparisons. 1977. Facts and Comparisons, Inc., 1100 Oran Drive, St. Louis, Mo.

Goodman, L. S., and Gilman, A. 1975. *The pharmacological basis of therapeutics*, 5th ed. Macmillan Co., New York.

Hagiwara, S., and Bullock, T. H. 1957. Intracellular potentials in pacemaker and integrative neurons of the lobster cardiac ganglion. *J. Cell. Comp. Physiol.* 50: 25–48.

Keynes, R. D. 1951. The ionic movements during nervous activity. *J. Physiol.* 114: 119–50.

King, J. M., and Spotte, S. 1974. *Marine aquariums in the research laboratory*. Available from Aquarium Systems Inc., Eastlake, Ohio. (Contains a good discussion of sea water, "Instant Ocean," marine animal care, and a bibliography.)

Krebs, H. 1950. Body size and tissue respiration. *Biochim. Biophys. Acta* 4: 249–89.

Lockwood, A. P. M. 1961. "Ringer" solutions and some notes on the physiological basis of their ionic composition. *Comp. Biochem. Physiol.* 2: 241–89.

Motley, H. L. 1934. Physiological studies concerning the regulation of heartbeat in freshwater mussels. *Physiol. Zool.* 7: 62–84.

Nicholls, J. G., and Baylor, D. A. 1968. Specific modalities and receptive fields of sensory neurons in CNS of the leech. *J. Neurophysiol.* 31: 740–56.

Ohr, E. A. 1976. Tricaine methanesulfonate I: Effects on anesthetic potency. *Comp. Biochem. Physiol.* 54C: 13–17.

Pantin, C. F. A. 1948. *Notes on microscopical technique for zoologists*. Cambridge University Press, Cambridge.

Physicians' desk reference to pharmaceutical specialties and biologicals. 1977. Medical Economics Inc., Division of Litton Publications, Oradell, N.J.

Richards, O., ed. 1936. *Marine biological laboratory, formulae and methods*. Marine Biol. Laboratory, Woods Hole, Mass.

Ringer, S. 1883. A further contribution regarding the influence of the different constituents of the blood on the contraction of the heart. *J. Physiol.* 4: 29–42.

Robertson, J. D. 1939. The inorganic composition of the body fluids of three marine invertebrates. *J. Exp. Biol.* 16: 387–97.

Sober, H. A. 1970. *Handbook of biochemistry. Selected data for molecular biology*, 2d ed. Chemical Rubber Co., Cleveland.

Stecher, P. G. 1976. *The Merck index. An encyclopedia of chemicals and drugs*, 9th ed. Merck and Co., Rahway, N.J.

Van Harreveld, A. 1936. A physiological solution for fresh water crustaceans. *Proc. Soc. Exp. Biol. Med.* 34: 428–32.

Welsh, J. H.; Smith, R. I.; and Kammer, A. E. 1968. *Laboratory exercises in invertebrate physiology*. Burgess Pub. Co., Minneapolis.

Wilson, W. A.; Clark, M. T.; and Pellmar, T. C. 1977. Tris buffer attenuates acetylcholine responses in *Aplysia* neurons. *Science* 196: 440–41.

Index

References to illustrations are printed in boldface type.